אין לך יפה מן הצניעות

תנחומא, כי תשא

Nothing is more beautiful than Modesty!

Tanchuma, Ki Sisah

ספר

עוז והדר לבושה

Modesty
An Adornment for Life

Halachos and Attitudes Concerning Tznius of Dress & Conduct

By

Rabbi Pesach Eliyahu Falk

Gateshead, England

146, Whitehall Road,
Gateshead, NE8 1TP,
England.

Trade Distribution

FELDHEIM PUBLISHERS
200 Airport Executive Park, Nanuet, N.Y. 10954

FELDHEIM PUBLISHERS
POB 35002, Jerusalem, Israel

European Trade Distribution

J. LEHMANN HEBREW BOOKSELLERS
20 Cambridge Terrace, Gateshead, England NE8 1RP

Plates by Frank - Jerusalem
Printed in Eretz Israel

זכרון עולם בהיכל ה׳

לזכרון נשמת אדוני אבי מורי ורבי אוהב תורה ולומדיה
בכל נימי נפשו אוהב צדקה וחסד ומשכיל אל דל
ובאמונתו האיתנה קירב הרבה רחוקים תחת כנפי השכינה

ר׳ אברהם צבי בן ר׳ יעקב יהודה ז״ל

נלב״ע י״ב אייר שנת תשמ״ט לפ״ק ומנ״כ בעיר מנשסתר יצ״ו

ולזכרון נשמת אמי מורתי יחידה בצניעותה בפיקחותה
ובמסירתה לבעלה ולחינוך בניה ובנותיה, רודפת צדקה וחסד

מרת שרה בת ר׳ פסח ע״ה

תנו לה מפרי ידיה ויהללו בשערים מעשיה
נלב״ע כ״ה תשרי שנת תשמ״ח לפ״ק ומנ״כ בעיר מנשסתר יצ״ו

ת. נ. צ. ב. ה.

לזכרון עולם בהיכל ה'

הורי חותני וחותנתי החשובים והיקרים שליט"א

הרה"ח ר' **משה** ב"ר יהודה **שטיינהויז** זצ"ל

נלב"ע בעה"ק בני ברק י"ט אדר תשל"ד לפ"ק

ולרעיתו **ליבא נחמה** בת ר' שרגא פאביש ע"ה

נלב"ע בעה"ק ירושלים ח' תשרי תשי"ב לפ"ק

הרב הגאון מורה"ר ר' **אברהם שמואל בנימין**

ב"ר משה **שפיטצער** זצ"ל

גאב"ד דק"ק המבורג יצ"ו

נלב"ע ט"ו סיון תרצ"ד לפ"ק

ולרעיתו הרבנית **אסתר** בת ר' נתן ע"ה

נלב"ע אסרו חג דסוכות תש"ב לפ"ק

ת. נ. צ. ב. ה.

הסכמת הגאון הגדול מורה״ר ר׳ אברהם פאם שליט״א
זקן ראשי ישיבות ויו״ר מועצת גדולי התורה דארה״ב

אברהם פאם

RABBI ABRAHAM PAM
582 East Seventh Street
Brooklyn, New York, N.Y. 11218

בס״ד, י״ד מרחשון תשנ״ה

הנה ראיתי חלק מהספר החשוב ״עוז והדר לבושה״ על ענייני צניעות וקדושת בנות ישרא׳ מאת הגאון מוהר״ר פסח אליהו פאלק שליט״א, שידוע לי מכבר ע״י ספרו הקודם ״מחזה אליהו״ שבו הראה המחבר כחו הגדול בהוראה ורב חילו לאסוקי שמעתתא אליבא דהלכתא, וכבר קלסוהו גדולי ישרא׳ ועטרוהו בהסכמותיהם.

הספר הנוכחי בבירור גדרי הצניעות והלכותי׳, בנוגע ללבושי הנשים ותכשיטיהן וכדומה, הוא ספר נחוץ מאוד וצורך השעה בזמננו, שהפריצות שוררת ברחובותינו והולכת ומתגברת מיום ליום, ורבו הנסיונות לבנות ישרא׳.

קדושת ישרא׳ היא מעיקרי יסודי היהדות ועומדת ברומו של עולם, והיא תהלתינו ותפארתנו, ובזה נפלינו מאומות העולם. ובכן דבר גדול עשה המחבר שנזקק לענין נשגב זה, לחזק הצניעות והקדושה.

והנני מברכו שיצליח בספרו זה, ויקוים בו מגלגלין זכות ע״י זכאי. ובזכות והי׳ מחניך קדוש יקוים בנו רישא דקרא ״ה׳ אלקיך מתהלך בקרב מחנך להצילך ולתת אויביך לפניך״.

החותם לכבוד התורה וכבוד בית ישרא׳,

אברהם יעקב הכהן פאם

(ההסכמות לפי סדר א. ב.)

הסכמת הגאון הגדול מוהר"ר ר' אהרן משה שכטר שליט"א
ראש ישיבת "ישיבת ר' חיים ברלין" וחבר מועצת גדולי התורה דארה"ב.

Rabbi Aaron M. Schechter **אהרן משה שכטר**

ב"ה, י"ג כסלו תשנ"ה

עלתה בידי להפגש עם הרב הגאון הנעלה הרב פסח אליהו פאלק שליט"א, וטעמתי הטוב טעם של לבו הישר הדואג לטובת הדור, וחכמתו אשר ביראת ה' ראשיתה - והם הם אשר סגלו לו הכח לערוך מערכה של עצה ותושיה לכבודם של הבנות מלכים של דורנו, לעטרם בתפארתם, מעלת יופי הצניעות.

לפנים בישראל היה רוח הצניעות האוירה שבה חיינו, ושמירת גדריה טבעי היתה - אמנם בזמננו נשתנה פני הדברים, והבית זקוק לבדק, ולחכם אומן אשר בטעם עליון מעשהו, ואשר ריח יגיעתו בתורה שורה על דבריו, ומטעים בהם נפש הצניעות אשר בעדה עמל.

והנה בגוף הדברים כבר קיבל הסכמות גדולי ישראל ולא על זה באתי. אבל לקול הקריאה למען כבוד ישראל וקדושתם אי אפשר לעמוד מן הצד - הרי אמרו בעקבתא דמשיחא חוצפא יסגי. והמבין יבין איך כל מכשולי דורנו מושרשים בכח הזלזול שהיא נפשו של החוצפא - והדבר פלא איך שבקשת הזלזול נעשה דרישת החיים של תקופתינו ביודעים ובלא יודעים - תרבות של זלזול ממש - וממנו כמה אופנים של גילוי פנים שלא כהלכה. גילוי פנים בתורה שלא כהלכה, וגילוי פנים בישראל שלא כהליכותיה. וזה גם זה מחריבים הנשמה.

מקום מכשול הוא ליעקב אם ידו האוחזת בעקב עשו מדביקו בדרכי עשו ובטעמו - והחושב דפרטי הדקדוקים בדרכי הצניעות מן הקלות הוא, אינו אלא טועה גס בדבר משנה, כי היא נתינת כח להריסת יסוד קיומה של כלל ישראל בהנסיון הנורא של עקבתא דמשיחא.

וכמה צדק המחבר ביגיעתו לעורר גם הבנות היקרות, גם הנשים ובעליהן להקפיד ושלא לוותר על דרכי הצניעות, שהציע לפניהם מתוך יגיעתו במישור ובצדק. ולתת גדולה בזה ליוצר בראשית שלא עשנו כגויי הארצות ולא שמנו כמשפחות האדמה.

אהרן משה שכטר

הסכמה שקבלתי בשנת תשל"ט מהגאון הגדול הראש ישיבה זצ"ל
על ספרי הראשון שו"ת "מחזה אליהו"

אריה זאב גורביץ
ריש מתיבתא דישיבת "בית יוסף"
בגייטסהעד אנגליא
בעהמ"ח ספר "ראשי שערים"

RABBI L. GURWICZ
Principal
Gateshead Talmudical College
Gateshead

כ"ה תשרי תשל"ט

ידידי היקר הרה"ג חריף ובקי עדיו לגאון ולתפארת כש"ת ר' פסח אליהו פאלק שליט"א מחברי כולל הרבנים פה גייטסהעד, הראה לי את חבורו הטהור תשובות בהלכה למעשה בכמה ענינים מסובכים הנוגעים למעשה בימינו אלה. ואף כי ידעתי כוחו מאז, כי ידיו רב לו לרדת לעומקה של הלכה בחריפות ובקיאות, ולאסוקי שמעתא אליבא דהלכתא, כי עוד זכור אזכרנו מימי חורפו עת שהיה בין חובשי בית המדרש של ישיבתנו הק', כי הצטיין תמיד בברור ההלכה. וזה כמה שנים שהוא מגיד שיעור בשו"ע או"ח לפני תלמידים שבישיבתינו הק', ונתקיים בו אמרם ז"ל הלומד ע"מ לעשות מספיקין בידו ללמוד וללמד לשמור ולעשות.

אמנם כעת בעיוני בחיבורו שמחתי לראות כי ממש כדרך גדולי ההוראה דרכו, כי פורש מצודתו על פני ים התלמוד והפוסקים הראשונים והאחרונים, ומעלה פנינים יקרים הן בהלכה והן בסברא. וכבר ראו גדולי ההוראה שבארץ את ספרו ושבחוהו וחזו לו גדולות. ומה אענה אני עוד אחריהם. רק שתקותי חזקה שיקוים בו אמרם ז"ל (תענית ד') "האי צורבא מרבנן דמי לפרצידא דתותי קלא דכיון דנבט נבט" ופי' רש"י שם "כשמתחיל לבצבץ ולעלות עולה למעלה, כך תלמיד חכם כיון שיצא שמו הולך וגדל למעלה".

ואני תפלה שיה"ר שיפוצו מעינותיו חוצה ויזכה להיות ממורי ומאורי ההוראה בישראל.

הסכמה ממרן הגאון הגדול רבה של עיר גייטסהעד שליט"א.

בצלאל בהרה"ג ר' יו"ט ליפמאן ראקאוו
אב"ד דגייטסהעד

RABBI B. RAKOW
Rav of Gateshead

ב"ה, י"ג לחודש מנחם אב תשנ"ד לפ"ק.

הנה ידידי הרב הגאון מוה"ר פסח אליהו פאלק שליט"א, המפורסם בספרו מחזה אליהו, הראה לי את ספרו החדש שעומד להוציאו לאור, ספר "עוז והדר לבושה" על עניני צניעות ולבושי נשים. שני חלקים, חלק בירור הלכות אלו, וחלק ההשקפה בעניני צניעות.

אחרי עיון בספרו נוכחתי לדעת כי משמיא קא זכי ידידי שליט"א לחבר חיבור נפלא כזה, הן בבירור הלכות שאינן מפורשות כל כך, וכ' ידידי הרחיב ובירר וליבן כיד ה' הטובה עליו את הלכות האלו, והן בעניני השקפה לפי רוח התורה וישראל סבא, אשרי לו. ולענ"ד ספר כזה הוא צורך השעה והזמן, ומאוד נחוץ להפיצו בקרב ישראל.

ובאתי בזה לברך את כבוד המחבר שליט"א, כשם שזכה לחבר ספרו אחרי עמל ויגיעה של כמה שנים, כן יזכה לברך על המוגמר ולהוציאו לאור לזכות את הרבים. ובזכות ריבוי קדושת ישראל, שעל ידו מתרבה כבוד שמים, נזכה לגאולה שלמה בקרוב.

הכותב וחותם לכבוד המחבר ולכבוד העמלים בתורה,

הק' בצלאל ראקאוו

הסכמת הגאון הגדול רבה של קהלת יטב לב דסאטמאר לונדון שליט״א.

חיים מאיר הלוי ואזנר

רב דקהל ״יטב לב״ דסאטמאר, לונדון יצ״ו
ור״מ ודומ״ץ בזכרון מאיר ב״ב

בס״ד, יום ג׳ לס׳ אשר ברכו ה׳ תשנ״ה לפ״ק,

כבוד מעלת ידידי הדגול הרב הגאון המופלג טובא מחבר הספר החשוב ״מחזה אליהו״ מוהר״ר פסח אליהו פאלק שליט״א.

שלום רב לאוהבי תורתיך.

אחרי שאני משתדל להמנע עדיין מלאחוז בשרביט ההסכמות, ובפרט כשלא עלה בידי לעיין כראוי בעבודה רבה ומקיפה שהשקעתם במסכת הצניעות דעוז והדר לבושה, הנוגעת בפנמיות נפשו של טהרת וקדושת ישראל, ומה עוד שאאמו״ר עט״ר שליט״א נתן את הסכמתו לספרו הקודם, וספר זה כבר מעוטר בחבילות הסכמות של גדולי התורה, על כן יקבל נא מעכתה״ר שליט״א את ברכתי ברכת הדיוט בלבד, כי לא אכניס ראשי בין הרים גדולים.

וזאת קלטתי בעוברי מקופיא שמשאת נפשו הטהורה בחיבור זה לרומם ולהעלות כל נדבך ונדבך מכלל ישראל למדריגה יותר גבוה ומנושא בדקדוק ההלכה ושמירת הקדושה והצניעות, ואשרי חלקו אם יזכה לגדור בקעה זו, ויהי׳ חלקי עמכם.

ומכנף הארץ זמירות שמענו, שמעו הטוב ופעלו המבורך לקרב את ישראל לאביהם שבשמים ולהביא לכל הפזרים דבר ה׳ זו הלכה. וחפץ ה׳ יעלה בידו להרחיב גבולי התורה והטהרה בכל תפוצות ישראל מתוך בריות גופא, ולהוסיף פעלים למען ה׳ ותורתו כשאיפת נפשו ונפש ידידו.

המוקירו ומכבדו ומאוה לו ברכות עד בלי די,

חיים מאיר הלוי ואזנר

הסכמת הגאון הגדול ראש ישיבת תורה אור שליט״א
על הקונטרס ״עוז והדר לבושה״ שהוצאתי בשנת תשנ״ג.

הרב חיים פנחס שיינברג
ראש ישיבת ״תורה אור״
ומורה הוראה בקרית מטרסדארף
עה״ק ירושלים תתבב״א

RABBI CHAIM P. SCHEINBERG
Rosh Hayeshiva
Torah Ore
Jerusalem

בס״ד כ״ג תמוז תשנ״ג לפ״ק

הנה הובא לפני הקונטרס החשוב ״עוז והדר לבושה״ על עניני לבוש נשים וצניעות אשר נכתב בטוב טעם ודעת ע״י הרב הגאון מורה״ר ר׳ פסח אליהו פאלק שליט״א בעל ספר שו״ת ״מחזה אליהו״ הידוע ומפורסם בכל רחבי תבל בעבודתו עבודת הקודש, בברור ענינים הלכתיים נחוצים הנצרכים לכל בית ישראל.

חם לבי בקרבי בראותי את העבודה הנפלאה שהושקעה בהכנת הקונטרס הזה, אשר בו דברי חכמה, מוסר והלכה משולבים זה בזה, דבור דבור על אופניו, ברורים ובהירים לכל.

הן אמנם באשר הוא ספר פסקי דינים הנני נמנע מליתן הסכמה לכל הנכתב, כי לזה צריכים לעיין היטב בכל פרט ופרט ואין עתותי בידי לעשות כן, מכל מקום התועלת מקונטרס זה מרובה היא עד מאוד, באשר בדורנו הרחוב הרחוב פרוץ ביותר, ובעוונותינו הרבים גם בקרב מחננו ישנה השפעה מכך.

על כן חשוב עד מאוד לעורר ענין זה, וללמד בנות ישראל דעת, שידעו את הדרך ילכו בה ואת המעשה אשר יעשון. ויהי רצון שיתקבלו דבריו אצל רבבות אלפי ישראל מכל העדות, ושוב יתעוררו נשי ישראל ללבוש בצניעות הראויה להן, ותתרבה הקדושה בקרב מחננו.

והנני חותם בברכה שיהא ה׳ עמו, וכל אשר יעשה יצליח.

חיים פנחס שיינברג

הסכמת מרן הגאון הגדול גאב"ד דקהלת התאחדות החרדים דלונדון שליט"א.

חנוך דוב פדווא

אב"ד דהתאחדות קהלות החרדים
לונדון תע"א

RABBI H. B. PADWA

Principal Rabbinical Authority
Of The Union Of Orth.
Hebr. Congregations
78 Cazenove Road,
London N16 6AA

ב"ה

כ"ט טבת תשנ"ה

ראיתי את הספר "עוז והדר לבושה"
אשר חיבר הרב הגאון ר' אליהו פאלק שליט"א,
והנה דבר טוב עשה ללמד בנות ישראל
דרכי הצניעות.

ותחזקנה ידיו.

חנוך דוב פדווא
RABBI
H. B. PADWA
- 78 -
CAZENOVE ROAD
LONDON, N.16
אב"ד דהתאחדות קהלות החרדים

אב"ד דהתאחדות קהלות
החרדים לונדון תע"א

הסכמה שקבלתי בשנת תשל"ח ממרן הגאון הגדול זצ"ל
על ספרי הראשון שו"ת "מחזה אליהו".

יצחק יעקב ווייס
ראב"ד
לכל מקהלות האשכנזים עיה"ק ירושלים תובב"א
ירושלים רחוב ישעיהו 20

RABBI I.J. WEISS
Rosh Beth Din
Of Jerusalem
RECHOV YESHAYAHU 20, JERUSALEM

בס"ד ירושלים עה"ק ת"ו

הן בא לפני האברך היקר הרה"ג חו"ב מוה"ר פסח אליהו פאלק שליט"א מחברי כולל הרבנים דגייטסהעד יצ"ו ותלמודו בידו, בירורי הלכה למעשה בדרך שו"ת אשר בירר בכמה הלכות העומדות על הפרק הלכה למעשה.

ועיינתי באיזהו מהם וראיתי כי רב חיליה לירד לים התלמוד והפוסקים לאסוקי שמעתתא אליבא דהלכתא. והגם כי מחמת טרדותי לא עלתה בידי לעבור על כל הספר, מ"מ החלק מעיד על הכלל, כי יגע ושנה הרבה ושכולו על אדני השכל הישר והבקיאות הוטבע.

ויזכה לזכות הרבים להוציא הלכה לאמיתו של תורה. וידי תכון עמו להוציא לאור עולם ספרו הנ"ל, ויהנו ממנו שוחרי תורה ויהא להם לתועלת בעזה"י. ונזכה לראות בבנין ציון וירושלים בביאת גואל צדק בבי"א.

ע"ז בעה"ח לכבוד התורה ולומדיה היום יום ג' לסדר ועתה ישראל שמע אל החוקים ואל המשפטים תשל"ח לפ"ק

יצחק יעקב ווייס ראב"ד פעיה"ק

הסכמה שקבלתי ממרן הגאון הגדול זצ"ל בשנת תשל"ט
על ספרי הראשון שו"ת "מחזה אליהו".

משה פיינשטיין
ר"מ תפארת ירושלים
בנוא יארק

RABBI MOSES FEINSTEIN
455 F.D.R. Drive
New York 2 N.Y.

בע"ה

הנה הרב הגאון ר' פסח אליהו פאלק שליט"א אשר הוא מרביץ תורה בעיר גייטסהעד חיבר ספר של שאלות ותשובות ובאורים בשם "מחזה אליהו" בעינייני שו"ע או"ח. ובספרו זה נראה איך שהרב המחבר עמל הרבה בדברי הראשונים והאחרונים ז"ל לאסוקי שמעתתא אליבא דהלכתא.

ודבריו נאמרו בטוב טעם ודעת מאוד, בהבנה נכונה בעיון רב. וגם בירר הרבה ענינים בהרחבה ועי"ז יתברר להמעיין בדבריו כל צדדי הענינים. על כן דבר טוב הוא מה שהוא מוציאו לאור עולם לתועלת הלומדים ובני תורה שיהנו מספר זה. ואף שאין הסכמתי על גוף הדברים דעל זה צריך לעבור על כל דבר ודבר וזה אי אפשר לפני מחמת רוב טרדותי, אבל הסכמתי הוא שהמחבר הוא גדול בתורה, וראוי מאוד להתחשב בדבריו כחכם שהורה.

ואני מברכו שיצליחהו השי"ת בחיבור זה ויזכה לחבר עוד חיבורים ויתבדרו ביני רבנן ותלמידיהון.

ועי"ז באתי עה"ח לכבוד הרה"ג המחבר שליט"א

א' דר"ח אדר תשל"ט.

משה פיינשטיין

הסכמת גיסי הגאון הצדיק מורה"ר ר' מתתיהו חיים סלומון שליט"א
משגיח רוחני דישיבת בית יוסף דגייטסהעד יצ"ו וכעת דבית מדרש גבוה דליקווד יצ"ו, ארה"ב.

בס"ד

יום א' לפרשת כי אותך ראיתי צדיק לפני, שנת תשנ"ו לפ"ק
פה גייטסהעד יצ"ו.

לכבוד גיסי היקר האהוב לי מאוד, מרביץ תורה לעדרים הצמאים לדבר ה' זו הלכה, ה"ה הגאון כמוהר"ר פסח אליהו פאלק שליט"א.

מי אני לבוא אחרי המלך מאן מלכי רבנן גאוני ארץ אדירי התורה אשר העידו על גדלותו בתורה וסמכות פסקיו בהוראה, אשר זכה לאסוקי שמעתתא אליבא דהלכתא. גם הביעו דעתם דעת תורה על גודל נחיצות ספרו החשוב "עוז והדר לבושה" כדי להציל ידידות שארנו משחת, תהום הפריצות השורר ברחובות, אשר באורח זו אהלך טמנו פח לבנות ישראל הכשרות והתמימות. רק דבר אחד אני יכול להגיד בתור גיס קרוב ואוהב, והוא להעיד על טהרת רעיון הספר ויצירתה.

והאמת אגיד כי לא ככל הספרים ספר זה, אשר בדרך כלל רעיון הספר הוא פרי הלימוד והעיון שיגע המחבר בתורה לעצמו, ואח"כ העלה חידושיו ומסקנותיו על מכבש הדפוס. אבל ספר זה רעיון הספר קדמה לכל. כי כאשר ראה גיסי הגאון המחבר שליט"א את עני ישראל מורה מאוד, ואפס עצור ואפס עזוב ואין עוזר לישראל, ובנותיהן טובעות בנהר שוטף של פריצות הרחוב, הבין בדעתו הרחבה כי העומד מן הצד חסיד שוטה יקרא, ולבו הטהור ראה כי עת לעשות לה' הפרו תורתיך, והגיע השעה להעלות על הספר מה שהיה עד עתה מהדברים שבעל פה אי אתה יכול לכותבן. על כן קפץ במסירות נפש ממש, והניח עסקיו, והתגבר על כמה מצבים קשים, וריכז כל כוחו ומוחו לטכס עצה איך להציל בנות ישראל מיון המצולה. ואחז בדרך היחידה שיש לישראל סבא, והוא ע"י דברי תורתינו הקדושה, לברר וללבן הלכות צניעות בכל פרטיה ודקדוקיה, וגם לרבות כונותיה.

כי לא כימים הראשונים ימינו אלה, אשר מאז דרכן של בנות ישראל והנהגותיהן הכשרות יסודו על אמונה פשוטה של אל תטוש תורת אמך. אבל כעת אי אפשר לשכנע בלי להסביר ולהוכיח בחכמה טעמי התורה והליכותיה בפרטי פרטיות - וכל העיון ויגיעה הרבה שהשקיע הגהמ"ח שליט"א בסוגיא זו, הוא פרי רעיון הספר, ובמטרה להציל הכלל. וע' במהר"ל שכתב בכמה מקומות בספרו דרך החיים פרק ו' דאבות דעיקר ס"ד לעסוקי שמעתתא אליבא דהלכתא הוא כאשר לומדים בשביל הכלל, כמו משה רבינו שלמד כל תורתו בשביל שיהי' תורה לכלל ישראל. ועל כן זכה הגהמ"ח שליט"א לכל כך הרבה ס"ד למעלה מדרך הטבע, לחבר חיבור שלם על נושא מסובך כזה בתכלית השלמות, בהיקף עצום ובסדר נפלא להלכה למעשה, ובטוחים אנו בזכות הכלל שלא יצא מכשול מתחת ידו.

וזאת למודעי כי גם חלק ההשקפה הטהורה של הספר הלכה ברורה היא ולא סתם דברי אגדה, כי יסודי הדת שנויין כאן, עם כל חומר דבר ה' זו הלכה.

ואני תפלה שיזכה גיסי הגאון המחבר שליט"א ע"י חיבור נפלא זה להחזיר עטרה ליושנה, ויוסיף ה' תת לו כח להרבות עוד יותר כבוד שמים מתוך מנוחת הנפש שלום ושלוה השקט ובטח.

ממני הכו"ח מתוך אהבה עזה להגהמ"ח שליט"א ולמען יקרת קדושת המצוה להסיר מכשול מישראל.

מתתי' חיים סלומון

הסכמת מרן הגאון הגדול זצ"ל לספרי שו"ת מחזה אליהו.
ובחודש אלול תשנ"ג קבלתי רשות מהגאון זצ"ל להדפיסו כהסכמה גם על ספרי זה.

הרב שלמה זלמן אויערבאך | Rabbi SH. Z. AUERBACH

בעיה"ק ירושלים תובב"א | Jerusalem

ב"ה. יום י"ג מנחם אב תשל"ח

למע"כ הרב הגאון הנעלה והנודע לתהלה מוה"ר פסח אליהו פאלק שליט"א. ראיתי את הקונטרסים החשובים אשר כת"ר קרא אותם בשם "מחזה אליהו"*, מלאתי את רצונו ועיינתי בהם.

והנני להגיד נאמנה שמאוד נהנתי מהם. כי ראיתי שכת"ה נחית היטב לעומק הדברים בעיון רב והולך בנתיבי יושר ואמת בהשכל ודעת. ובכוחו הגדול הוא משתדל ומתאמץ לאסוקי שמעתתא אליבא דהלכתא. וגם הדברים ערוכים יפה בטוב טעם ודעת כיד ה' הטובה עליו. ולכן מובטחני שאוהבי תורה ודאי ישמחו בספרו החשוב, ובשערים המצוינים בהלכה ישבחוהו ויברכוהו על כל הטוב שעשה בזה.

אשר על כן יישר כחו וחילו לאורייתא ונותן התורה יהא בעזרו להוסיף ללון בעמק הלכה מתוך הרחבה ושמחה ויהי' ה' עמו. יפוצו מעינותיו חוצה ורבים יאותו לאורו.

בכל חתומי ברכה,

שלמה זלמן אויערבאך

הסכמת מרן הגאון הגדול שליט״א לספרי שו״ת מחזה אליהו.
ובחודש אדר א׳ תשנ״ז קבלתי בכתב רשות מהגאון שליט״א להדפיסו כהסכמה גם על ספרי זה.

שמואל הלוי ואזנר

רב אב״ד ור״מ

זכרון מאיר, בני-ברק

SHMUEL HALEVI WOSNER

Rabbi of

ZICHRON MEIR, BNEI BRAK

הן היה לפני כתב יד שו״ת ספר ״מחזה אליהו״* אשר חבר הרב הגאון המופלג טובא מוהר״ר פסח אליהו פאלק שליט״א יושב על התורה ומזכה את הרבים בעיר גייטסהעד באנגלאנד. והן תשובות הלכה למעשה נתברר בעומק ומיטב הגיון בברור שיטות הש״ס והפוסקים.

ועיינתי בקצת מהדברים וראיתי כמה רב גוברי׳ של המחבר הרב הגאון לרדת לעומק הדברים וחותר למטרת האמת למצות הדברים עד מקום שידו המוכשרת מגעת. וניכר היטב מתוך הספר שהמחבר החשוב שליט״א יגע הרבה מאוד בתורה יגע ומצא כדי מדתו, וזכה לאסוקי שמעתתא אליבא דהילכתא שהיא המדרגה הכי גדולה בלמוד כמבואר בחז״ל.

ע״כ גם ידי תכון עמו להוציא הדברים לאור עולם לזכות את הרבים. ויזכה ללכת עוד מחיל אל חיל להוציא תעלומה לכבוד ה׳ ולכבוד תורתו הקדושה.

בין המצרים תשל״ח לפ״ק

שמואל הלוי ואזנר
רב ואב״ד זכרון מאיר בני ברק

הסכמת הגאון הגדול ראש ישיבת מיר דניו יורק שליט"א.

הרב שמואל ברנבוים

ראש הישיבה

ישיבת **מיר** ניו יורק

כ' כסלו תשנ"ה

הן הובא לפני עלים לתרופה ספר היקר "עוז והדר לבושה" על עניני צניעות דלבוש, והצצתי בו לפי משאת הפנאי ונוכחתי לדעת שהוא ספר חשוב הנכתב במיטב הגיון, ורוח חכמים נוחה הימנו. והנה יחודו של עם ישראל הוא היותם עם קדוש הדבקים בה' ובתורתו ומובדלים מדרכי האומות וכדכתיב ואבדיל אתכם מן העמים להיות לי. אמנם בדורנו ע"י הרחוב הפרוץ הצליח מעשה שטן לערר ולהחליש ענין נשגב זה דקדושת עם ישראל. וכבר מזמן מורגש הצורך שיקום מי שהוא ללמד לנשי ובנות ישראל בינה, לדעת את הדרך ילכו בו ולהצילם עי"ז מלהיות נגררים אחרי העמים אשר סביבותיהם.

ובכן שמחה גדולה היא לי לראות שעתה התעורר הרב הגאון ר' פסח אליהו פאלק שליט"א מעיר התורה גייטסהעד דאנגליה מח"ס שאלות ותשובות "מחזה אליהו" ויט שכמו לסבול לברר האסור והמותר בדבר הלכה זו, ובחכמה ותבונה שילב בהם דברי אגדה להלהיב לבב הקוראים לנקוט שוב בדרך הצניעות והעדינות המבדלת בנות ישראל מבנות אל נכר.

והנה הסכימו לספרו הראשון גדולי מאורי ישראל, ואני באתי במכתבי זה רק לחזקו ולעודדו בעבודתו הגדולה, ולאחל לו הצלחה מרובה שיפוצו מעינותיו חוצה ורבים ישיב מעון.

הכותב וחותם לכבוד התורה והעומדים על משמרת הדת,

שמואל ברנבוים

Table Of Contents

CHAPTER TWO

CHALLENGES TO TZNIUS

CHAPTER THREE

RAISING CHILDREN TO TZNIUS

CHAPTER FOUR

BRACHOS IN PRESENCE OF ERVAH

CHAPTER FIVE

COVERING HAIR - CROWN OF THE JEWISH WOMAN

CHAPTER SIX

TZNIUS IN DRESS - HALACHOS AND REQUISITES

CHAPTER SEVEN

REFINED CLOTHES, JEWELRY AND COSMETICS

CHAPTER EIGHT

THE ISSUR FOR MEN TO HEAR WOMEN SING

CHAPTER NINE

SAFEGUARDING KEDUSHAS YISROEL

CHAPTER TEN

THE EXCEPTIONAL BENEFITS OF TZNIUS

Detailed Table Of Contents

CHAPTER ONE

TZNIUS, OUR BADGE OF DISTINCTION

CHAPTER TWO

CHALLENGES TO TZNIUS

CHAPTER THREE

RAISING CHILDREN TO TZNIUS

CHAPTER FOUR

BRACHOS IN PRESENCE OF ERVAH

CHAPTER FIVE

COVERING HAIR- CROWN OF THE JEWISH WOMAN

CHAPTER SIX

TZNIUS IN DRESS - HALACHOS AND REQUISITES

CHAPTER SEVEN

REFINED CLOTHES, JEWELRY AND COSMETICS

CHAPTER EIGHT

SINGING IN THE PRESENCE OF MEN

CHAPTER NINE

SAFEGUARDING KEDUSHAS YISROEL

CHAPTER TEN

EXCEPTIONAL BENEFITS OF TZNIUS

N.B. The second volume of this *sefer* is in *Lashon Hakodesh* and deals exclusively with the *Mekoros* - the sources, of the rulings mentioned in this volume. It is in an advanced state of preparation and will *B'ezer Hashem* be published in the near future. Whenever stated in this volume "see *Mekoros* ......" this refers to clarifications that are offered in the second volume.

Preface

השיר והשבח לחי עולמים

"Song and praise to He who lives eternally". It seems strange that in this verse song precedes praise. Naturally, one would expect praise, which involves appraisal and assessment, to be mentioned prior to song, since only with proper appreciation does a person burst forth into song. However, at the culmination of an extended effort and at the completion of an endeavor which has involved years of toil, worry and anxiety, the joy and elation is spontaneous and needs no introduction. Once this initial song of joy has been sung, the person pours forth praise to *Hashem* for the great gift He has given. Hence "Song and praise to He who lives eternally".

It is comparable to the mother of a newly born infant who is overjoyed with the gift she has received and has no need to assess the advantages the baby brings in its wake. She has struggled for months hoping that *Hashem* will grant her the privilege of reaching this joyful moment. Now that it has finally arrived and she has given birth to a live and healthy baby, she is overjoyed and naturally bursts forth with gratitude to the Almighty.

So too, the author of a *sefer* such as this, has no need to precede his song with words of evaluation, since the Heavenly gift of having completed such a difficult and formidable task, and having the *zechus* to see a finished product that will *b'ezras Hashem* become a further link in the golden chain of *Sifrei*

Kodesh, arouses a spontaneous eruption of great joy and elation. I therefore earnestly and gratefully sing these beautiful words - השיר והשבח לחי עולמים.

מה אשיב לה׳ - How and with what can I repay *Hashem* for giving me the privilege of enabling people to understand and appreciate the *halachos* and *hashkafos* of this vital subject?

It has been obvious throughout the work that an exceptional amount of *siyata d'shmaya* has guided it from the very outset. It is beyond doubt that this was granted because of the immense need of the Jewish public to be counseled and be given clear directives on this all-important subject. This outstanding *siyata d'shmaya* enabled me to overcome the many great difficulties that were involved in producing a *sefer* on this highly emotive subject.

I pray to *Hashem* that this *siyata d'shmaya* continues to accompany the *sefer* on its future travels, so that only that which is truly the *Ratzon Hashem* - the will of *Hashem*, will be learned from its pages. I pray to *Hashem* that those who are privileged to have a very high standard of *tznius* do not use this *sefer* as a textbook to find alternative opinions to those with which they were educated, and *chas v'shalom* become lax in something which is of the greatest importance to their family and community. Every *sefer* on *halacha* is vulnerable to this type of misuse, as the author must mention two opinions whenever *Klal Yisroel* is divided, with some people following one opinion and others a second opinion. Nevertheless, in the case of *tznius,* which is the "pupil of the eye" of *Kedushas Yisroel,* this would be an even greater disaster than elsewhere. It will become apparent to whoever learns the *sefer* that every precaution has been taken to ensure that no misunderstanding arises.

The *sefer* has been written in a style which will hopefully inspire the Jewish woman and girl to appreciate the beauty of Jewish modesty, as *Chazal* say, אין לך יפה מן הצניעות - "There is nothing more appealing and beautiful than modesty" (*Midrash Tanchuma, Ki Sisah,* 31). This perception will *b'ezer Hashem* encourage her to dress with taste and true refinement. If those who use this *sefer* are influenced to put the *halachos* into practice and if the *hashkafos* presented in this *sefer* result in many of the readers viewing *tznius* as a privilege rather than a burden, then the effort, time and heartache expended in writing this *sefer* will have been very well worthwhile. Any improvement in *kedushas Yisroel* is of immense value and is to be considered an enormous accomplishment.

THE NEED NOWADAYS FOR THIS TYPE OF SEFER

It is with a mixture of happiness and sadness that I write this introduction to the second and greatly enlarged edition of this *sefer*.

On the one hand, the very warm reception that the first [5753] booklet edition received is a cause for great happiness. It demonstrated the feeling of many, that a work of this nature was long overdue and that, *b'ezer Hashem*, the correct approach was taken. It is my fervent *tefilla* that this large and comprehensive volume will likewise merit *siyata d'shmaya* to find favor in the eyes of the public and guide them on the *Derech Hashem*.

On the other hand, sadness is indicated by the very fact that a detailed *sefer* had to be written on this subject. In earlier times there was no need for a *sefer* of this type, because the Jewish woman and girl knew instinctively what was expected of her in terms of *tznius* and refinement. Moreover, she received a sound *chinuch* from a home in which true Jewish traditions were handed down from mother to daughter and from one generation to the next. In our times, however, the moral decay at every level of society and the relentless assault of the media on human decency and morality have unfortunately affected the attitude and sentiment of the *Bas Yisroel* leaving her without proper direction. The impact has been so great that many women and girls have lost the natural feeling for real *tznius* and how a Jewish woman should dress - and are seriously confused in a subject that affects the *kedusha* and *tahara* of *Am Yisroel*.

This downward spiral affects even those who have endeavored to avoid being influenced. There are two elementary causes for this. Firstly, in this generation there is a serious spiritual pollution in the air resulting from the permissiveness and the misconduct of the world at large. This contaminates the atmosphere and comes into contact with everyone. It dulls sensitivities and causes infringements into the holy domain of *tznius*. Secondly, regularly seeing the dress of Orthodox women who have been detrimentally influenced by the world around them, detrimentally influences the *t'mimus* and *tahara* with which a girl was brought up. It causes her to gradually accept fashions that contravene the principles of *tznius*.

Furthermore, many girls are brought up nowadays by mothers who are themselves perplexed or misguided in this fundamental aspect of *Yiddishkeit*. They are therefore unable to give their daughters the right *chinuch* and implant within them a love for *tznius* and refinement. To our sorrow, some of these mothers even impart an adverse *chinuch* to their daughters, as they naturally follow the attitudes and examples they see at home.

Despite what has just been stated, the present day *Bas Yisroel* should not feel indicted and censured by this *sefer*. She is probably as worthy as her counterpart of previous generations, as she has to contend with a far greater exposure to bad influences and her *nisyonos* in this field are much more severe than those of previous generations. This conciliation should, however, make her aware of the great need for frequent *chizuk* and *shiurim* on this all-important topic. To fill this urgent need for instruction and *chizuk* this *sefer* has been written. Realizing our vulnerability, the *tefilla* of וטהר לבנו לעבדך באמת - "purify our hearts to serve You genuinely" should always be on our lips, to help ourselves and our children through these difficult times.

WOMEN SHOULD DRESS PLEASANTLY AND TASTEFULLY

Before learning the *halachos* or reading the *hashkafos* presented in this *sefer*, it should be noted that in Torah law, the need for women to dress pleasantly and tastefully is fully recognized and even greatly encouraged. Concerning the duties of a husband to his wife, *Chazal* say, אוהבה כגופו ומכבדה יותר מגופו - "He loves her as much as he loves himself and honors her even more than himself" (*Sanhedrin* 76b and *Yevamos* 62b). The *Rishonim* explain that "honoring her" refers to buying her fine clothes and jewelry. As far as clothing is concerned, her needs take precedence over his, since her need for pleasant and tasteful clothes considerably exceeds his.

A husband buys his wife a new garment or ornament before Yom Tov to enable her to fulfill the *mitzva* of *Simchas Yom Tov* - rejoicing on Yom Tov. He cannot, however, fulfill his personal *mitzva* of *Simchas Yom Tov* by purchasing new clothes for himself (*Orach Chayim* 529:2). This is once again because the need for fine clothes and jewelry and the great pleasure derived from them is intrinsically feminine. The Torah is only too happy to permit a woman to do that which is essential for her fulfillment as it knows that no harm will come to *kedushas Yisroel* as a result of her dressing in such a manner.

Thus, *tznius* does not deny the woman her natural requirements and far be it from *Yiddishkeit* to prevent a woman having one of her innate and instinctive needs fulfilled. However, whilst she has a legitimate need to have a pleasant and regal appearance, there is no necessity for her to dress in a way that attracts the attention of passers-by. While she has a need to appear pretty and graceful to her husband, family, and friends, she should have no urge to exhibit herself for all to admire her.

To our good fortune, modesty and refinement are an intrinsic part of being a Jewish woman or girl. Women have inherited these treasures from the original "mothers of *Klal Yisroel*", each of whom personified special modesty, bashfulness and *eidelkeit*. It is our duty to reawaken these partly dormant qualities once again within ourselves.

THE HALACHOS AND HASHKAFOS ARE FULLY EXPLAINED

Detailed *halachos* and their underlying reasons have been given throughout. As a result of this, the *halachos* in this *sefer* are more extensive than they would have been had only the basic rules been stated without elaboration. However, years of teaching have convinced me, that if *halachos* are not explained in detail and embellished with sound reasoning, the present generation find them difficult to learn and all the more to remember. *Halacha* must be presented in such a way that the student gains an appreciation of the profound wisdom and truth that lie behind each and every *halacha*. This in turn will infuse the student with a love for *halacha* in general and for these *halachos* in particular.

The same applies to the *hashkafos* and attitudes of any subject in *Yiddishkeit* and especially to a subject as sensitive as *tznius* and refined Jewish taste. By having it explained in depth, the woman or girl will *Bezras Hashem* see the beauty in the *Derech Hayashar*. By being shown the effect external influences have on a person, she will realize that most people just ape others and take a liking to a garment only because it is in fashion. This awareness will enable her to part with widely accepted ways of dress and conduct, and instead adopt a far more *eidel* manner of dress and indeed of practice in general.

In time, she will understand both the depth and breadth of the relationship between the public behavior of women and girls and *kedushas Yisroel*. Towards this goal, an attempt has been made to present detailed *halachos*, with *hashkafos* interlaced into the *halachos* wherever appropriate.

It is fitting at this point to mention that extreme care has been taken throughout the *sefer,* to ensure that, while mentioning the shortcomings of certain types of dress, these defects are not explained in too specific terms. Although it is of utmost importance to give the readership a deep and thorough understanding as to why certain modes of dress are unrefined or even *pritzus'dik*, it is obvious that *tznius* itself cannot and must not be sacrificed in the pursuit of this goal. Due to this, some clarifications were omitted, although they would have given women an even better understanding of the harm involved in certain painful misdeeds that are rampant in today's society.

THE HALACHOS HAVE BEEN RESEARCHED WITH GREAT CARE

The *halachos* in this *sefer* have been compiled with the utmost care and no effort has been spared to ensure that all *halachos* are accurate. Only the absolute *halacha* has been stated, whilst stringencies (חומרות) which are not the accepted opinion of most *Poskim* have been omitted (except when stated explicitly that some people dress in a specifically stringent way for extra refinement). Moreover, great pains have been taken to show the sources of every *halacha*. When the source of a *halacha* is short and concise, the source is given in the main text. Whereas, when a *halacha* requires a careful and lengthy analysis, this has been done in the large addendum which comprises the second volume of this *sefer*. These *halachic* expositions will also enable *Talmidei Chachamim* to delve deeply into the life-springs of Torah from which these *halachos* are derived and uncover additional gems that might still remain hidden.

The extensive display of sources will enable a person learning this *sefer* to see that what has been stated as *halacha* is not a matter of "feeling and personal opinion" but is the *dvar Hashem* itself, derived from *Shas* and *Poskim*. The following is a quote from the introduction to the *sefer* "*Chofetz Chayim*" which is most appropriate for this *sefer* too - וידע הקורא שאפילו כל דבר פשוט שנמצא בפנים הראיתי את מקורו בבאר מים חיים למען יבורר לעיני הכל שספר זה לא חברתי על פי מדת חסידות רק על צד הדין. - "The reader should know that I have quoted sources for even the simplest points stated in this *sefer* so that it should be clear to all that the *sefer* has not been written for the very pious. Rather it lays down the basic *halacha* which everyone is expected to keep".

It must, however, be mentioned, that there are a number of serious acts of *pritzus* which *Gedolei HaPoskim* of our times have condemned, but for which one can neither quote an explicit *halacha* nor a particular saying in *Chazal*. Nevertheless, to the person who has learned all the *halachos* and the numerous sayings of *Chazal* about *tznius* distributed throughout this *sefer*, there will be absolutely no doubt that these disorders are strictly forbidden. The *halachos* and sayings of *Chazal* portray their attitude on these matters in such clear terms, that they can be quoted as sources for the rulings and guidelines laid down by the *Gedolei HaPoskim*.

In this context it should be noted that there is likewise no explicit *halacha* or saying in *Chazal* that refers to the grave *issur* of mixed dancing. The *Poskim*, nevertheless, write in very strong terms about the gravity of this *issur*. The *Chofetz Chayim* alludes to this phenomenon in the *Mishna Berura* (*Biur Halacha* 339 s.v. *L'hakel*) with the words: פשוט הוא ומרוב פשיטתו לא ניתן לכותבו - "It is obvious that mixed dancing is *ossur*, and because it is so obvious, *Chazal* saw no need to write explicitly about it". This fundamental truth has been a guideline when writing about some of the maladies that have engulfed our generation.

GUIDELINES CONCERNING THE HALACHOS CITED

Major *halachic* disputes related to the *halachos* of *tznius* have not been decided in this *sefer*. To do so would not be within the projected purpose of the *sefer*, which was written to encourage and strengthen *tznius* and the keeping of basic *halachic* requirements of modesty. In fact, in some points of dispute there are different *minhagim* in different communities, and it is totally out of place to state in a *sefer* of this nature that one way is more correct than the other. Where such disputes or variation of *minhagim* exist, both opinions have been stated, without sides being taken in any way whatsoever. If, in the extensive *Mekoros* arguments have been stated to support one opinion or the other, this is for the benefit of *Talmidei Chachamim* who may wish to investigate the matter more deeply.

When two opinions are cited in the *sefer,* there is no significance in the fact that one opinion is quoted first and should not be taken to indicate that the first mentioned is the main opinion to follow. Actually, when it was felt that people might understand things in this way, the more widely accepted opinion was mentioned second, so it be given equal status to the opinion followed by a lesser number of people.

If a certain case or example has been omitted, this should not be taken to indicate that it is permitted, or conversely, that it is forbidden. A number of items were left out for a variety of reasons. Firstly, if it was felt that confusion could arise, or that mentioning a certain case could affect the clarity of other parts, the case was omitted. Secondly, certain styles, types of cosmetics etc. were omitted because in some places they are accepted even by *nashim tznuos* and once this is the case in those places they are *halachically* permitted (although even there it might still be *midas chassidus* to refrain from using them) whereas in other areas these same styles are not accepted, and for an individual of these areas to start adopting them would diminish the local standard of *tznius,* which is forbidden. Thirdly, certain fashions that have unfortunately started in some places are not mentioned so as not to give publicity to extremely inappropriate modes of dress. It was considered safer to omit such fashions altogether rather than mention them and explain what is wrong with them.

WHAT THIS SEFER IS DESIGNED TO ACHIEVE

This *sefer*, which lays down the *halachos* in a clear and orderly form, will hopefully enable and even encourage our sisters and daughters to return fully to the true Jewish way of dress. A large proportion of the inappropriate ways of dress and conduct that have found their way into our society originates from a lack of awareness of the *halacha*. There is no doubt that outside influences and vanity, although major contributors, are not the only causes for the lack of *tznius* and general refinement that exist nowadays. Rather, it is the ignorance of the *halacha,* due to which certain ways of dress have avoided public criticism, that has contributed powerfully to the prevailing lack of sensitivity.

Shlomo Hamelech says, לדעת חכמה ומוסר - "[A person should learn] so that he gains knowledge and ethics" (*Mishlei* 1:2). The verse puts knowledge before ethics. *Chazal* explain that this is because: אם יש חכמה יש מוסר, ואם אין חכמה אין מוסר - "If there is knowledge the ethics are meaningful, whilst if there is no knowledge the ethics are valueless". The *Chofetz Chayim* (in his introduction to *Mishna Berura* Vol. 3) explains that *chochma* refers to knowledge of the *halacha*, while *mussar* refers to 'inspirational' encouragement. If a person knows the *halacha* then the inspiring ethics he hears fall on receptive ears, and as a result of the encouragement he will gladly apply himself to keep the *halacha* properly and perfectly. However, if a person is ignorant of the *halacha,* nothing will help overcome his ignorance. He will inevitably do many things wrong even though he has been inspired to appreciate the great importance of the subject matter in general. About such an unfortunate situation the *Kuzari* writes, כוונתך רצויה אבל מעשיך אינם רצויים - "Although you have good intentions your deeds are nevertheless incorrect" (*Kuzari*, Chapter 1).

In the considerable feedback I have received from the first edition of the *sefer* [published in 5753], this truth was confirmed over and over again. Many people are desperately looking for guidance. They are delighted to be shown the *emes* and are eternally grateful for being given a clear exposition of the *derech haTorah*. Some women sewed up the slits in their skirts on the very first evening after becoming aware of the offense in wearing a garment with such a blemish. To experience the sincerity of the *Bas Yisroel* is like finding a beautiful unpolished diamond. Given the correct attention, her *neshama* shines forth and sparkles like a brilliant jewel.

FOR WHOM THIS SEFER IS INTENDED

This *sefer* has been written first and foremost for the fully observant woman or girl, who is particular about *kashrus* and many other aspects of *Yiddishkeit*. It is therefore to be hoped that, when she knows the *halachos* of *tznius* in Jewish dress, she will likewise meticulously adhere to this aspect of *Yiddishkeit*. This approach is in line with what we are taught by *Chazal* that אין מזרזין אלא למזורזין - "Encouragement should be targeted at those who are already on the right path" (*Makos* 23a). From these women and girls it will *b'ezer Hashem* spread to wider circles who look towards their fully observant sisters for authentic *Yiddishkeit*. We pray to *Hashem* that all *Yidden* find their way back speedily to the *derech hayashar*.

The *sefer* is intended for men (married) and women (whether married or not). Although the subject discussed is the *halachos* of dress for women and girls, it is nevertheless an essential *sefer* for men as well. If both husband and wife and both father and mother are aware of these *halachos* and their guidelines, far less oversight and misunderstanding will occur. Moreover, part of the blame for the problem that has developed nowadays lies at the doorstep of the men. It is all too often they who want their wives to look overly attractive even in public, and it is often they who buy ostentatious jewelry for their wives to wear even outdoors. It is therefore most important that they too know the Torah viewpoint and the attitudes of *Chazal* on matters pertaining to the dress and public conduct of Jewish women and girls.

This work is also designed and targeted to be used in schools and seminaries where girls are educated to a *Torah'dik* way of life. The material is presented in a way that each article is self-contained. By studying it, the pupils will have a full understanding as to why this way of dress is right and the other way wrong and unfitting for a *Bas Yisroel*. Ideas for instilling a profound feeling for *tznius* at a young age are presented in Chapter Three and a teacher should be able to extract from there suitable material for the girls she is educating.

Since young girls do not yet have the desire for beautification that develops in the upper teen years, nor do adult girls have to contend with hair-covering which comes after marriage, *chizuk* culled from this *sefer* will fall on very fertile ground indeed. Since at the time of learning the girl has no reason to rebel or to justify her wrong-doings, the impression it will make will be deep and decisive. *B'ezer Hashem* this will produce a generation of girls and young women who are aware of their great heritage and understand that *tznius* is of prime importance during all stages of life.

It is my fervent *tefilla* that the aspirations I have for this *sefer* do in fact materialize. Let it be the *Ratzon Hashem* that the day be near when this much neglected subject is revived to its full glory; and that *tznius* in dress and conduct, together with *ahavas haTorah* and *ahavas chesed,* once again become the pivotal points in the *chinuch* of our daughters.

THE HALACHOS SHOULD BE STUDIED SLOWLY

The material contained in this *sefer* is multi-faceted. There are many *halachic* sections that are interspersed with paragraphs that explain in detail what is wrong with forbidden modes of dress and why the recommended ways of dress are very different. On the other hand, the extensive articles about the *hashkafos* of *tznius* also contain many important *halachic* references about a broad variety of subjects. As a result of this, it is virtually impossible to read and absorb large sections of this *sefer* in one session. Moreover, throughout the *sefer* many forms of *pritzus* of dress are deplored and criticized in no uncertain terms. If the reader reviews the shortcomings of a large number of items one after the other, she could harbor the feeling of being indoctrinated.

Instead, it is recommended that the *sefer* is read or studied slowly - reading or studying no more than two or three features at a time. In this way the information will be appreciated and will not be found to be too heavy. Since the *sefer* is not to be read within a few days, certain points that have already been mentioned earlier in the *sefer*, might be repeated once again at a later stage when appropriate, to ensure that the significance of the point is noted properly.

ACKNOWLEDGMENTS

I wish to use this opportunity to extend my heartfelt thanks to my wife מרת אסתר שתחי׳. Her constant support and encouragement throughout the writing of this *sefer* gave me the required strength, reassurance and confidence to bring this delicate work to a successful conclusion. Whenever I needed her help she would put aside whatever she was doing, be it in the morning, afternoon, or late at night. She would read and review carefully every sentence, paragraph or complete article that I had written. This she would do again and again until all parts of the article seemed presentable and capable of achieving their goal.

It is no exaggeration to say that her association with the creation of this *sefer* is virtually that of a co-editor. We discussed and considered together the contents of each and every paragraph of the English text of this *sefer*. Only when I felt that she was truly satisfied with the contents and general structure of the material, was it finally passed.

Above all, her noble and regal bearing and her sterling character have been a constant model and yardstick for me. They have given me an acute understanding of the refined conduct and sensitive feelings of the true *Eishes Chayil* and *Bas Melachim*. These are of course essential ingredients required for the writing of this type of *sefer*. The *hashkafos* and feelings for *tznius* that were planted within me by my dear parents זכרונם לברכה have been brought to fruition by the companion in life that *Hashem* has given me.

My *tefilla* to *Hashem Yisborach* is that in His kindness He grant us the great *zechus* that our children and grandchildren grow to become true *Talmidei Chachamim*, *avdei Hashem* and people who sanctify His name in the world. Also, may we be *zocheh* to see this *sefer* make a lasting imprint on the community of *shomrei mitzvos*, and awaken within them a deep love and appreciation for *tznius*, both in dress and conduct. Hopefully, the improvement in *kedushas Yisroel* will give *Hashem Yisborach* such joy that it will result in speeding up the long awaited arrival of *Moshiach Tzidkeinu*.

My parents-in-law, R' Favish and Mrs. Ema Steinhaus of Gateshead are worthy of a very special mention in the context of this *sefer*. Their wonderful *derech hachayim* has been a source of direction to us over the years. Furthermore, the deep distress my mother-in-law, a highly professional dress-maker, felt about some outrageous forms of maternity wear, as well as other forms of insensitivity in dress, left a profound impression on me. It doubtlessly contributed largely to awakening within me the feeling that a *sefer* of this nature was needed and must be written.

Due to the unsatisfactory neckline on many dresses, my mother-in-law would train girls in the art of improving the neckline without negatively affecting the dresses' appearance in any way. She thereby infused feelings for *tznius* into many young ladies. All this is apart from *gemilus chasadim* organizations that she has been heading for many years. In the merit of all these far-reaching deeds, may *Hashem* grant her and my *choshuveh* father-in-law *shlita* many years of *simcha* and *nachas* from their children, grandchildren and great-grandchildren who all unreservedly follow the *Derech Hashem*. May it be the will of *Hashem* that we go together to be *mekabel pnei Moshiach Tzidkeinu* with the rest of *Klal Yisroel* בב״א.

I would also like to put on record the considerable assistance and encouragement extended to me by my eldest son הרב חיים נפתלי מאיר נ״י and his wife מרת שולמית שתחי׳. It is they who in the first place encouraged me to write this *sefer* and it is they who suggested many of the features that required exposition. They saw to the publication of the first edition, and they stood by my side throughout the writing of the second edition so that the complete burden did not fall on my shoulders alone.

Also, they have constantly helped me in other affairs in an outstanding and deeply devoted way. It is true to say that their sterling *kibud av v'eim* has been so exemplary that it has been an inspiration to others. My *bracha* to them is ישלם ה׳ פעלם - May *Hashem* repay them their good deeds. They should be *zocheh* to great *hatzlacha* in the *chinuch* of their dear children, my beloved *eineklech*. They should have an abundance of *nachas* from them and see them grow up into true *Talmidei Chachamim* and *anshei emes*.

It is furthermore my obligation and great pleasure to thank a number of *Talmidei Chachamim* who went through the extensive *mekoros* and *birurei halacha* - sources and *halachic* analysis. Also, I must thank most sincerely a number of very learned and dedicated men and many *nashim chashuvos* of Gateshead and elsewhere who kindly read and re-read the English manuscript of the *sefer*. In this way the *sefer* was read many times during its formative and completed stages. All offered valuable and sound advice and no comment, whether major or very minor, was ignored. All this has doubtlessly embellished the contents and style of the *sefer* considerably and everyone who read through part of the *sefer* and gave constructive advice has a share in the overall influence the *sefer* will hopefully have on the *mevakshei ha'emes* - seekers of Truth - who willingly do the bidding of *Hashem* but need enlightenment.

The many comments and examples I heard from family, local ladies, and those that reached me by letter from elsewhere, enabled me to bring to the reader's attention, in this second edition, many inadequate or ostentatious forms of dress that were previously unknown to me. They furnished me with the information I needed to know about the garments and pointed out the shortcomings that the items have. Once informed, I researched the matter to the best of my ability to check on the importance of mentioning this particular trend.

I pray to *Hashem* that all these worthy people reap the rich reward they deserve for going out of their way and sacrificing many hours to scrutinize the manuscript and help in the creation of the *sefer*. Without exception they did all this in order to be *mezakeh es harabim*. As they have an acute feeling for *tznius* and *kedushas Yisroel* I wholeheartedly wish them to be *zocheh* to instill these sensitivities into their own children and grandchildren, and may their offspring be a credit to them, their families and to the rest of *Klal Yisroel*.

Once again I would like to thank *Hashem* for giving me the *zechus* to write this *sefer* and for everything He has given me and done for me מעודי ועד היום הזה - from my earliest youth to this very day. I am particularly grateful to *Hashem* for having directed me to settle in Gateshead. This unique Jewish oasis contains great *Talmidei Chachamim* and *Y'rei Hashem* who hold the fort and battle against the penetration of the secular world.

It is also blessed with *mosdos haTorah*, which are springs from which Torah and *yirah* gush forth developing whole generations of *bnei Torah* and *Bnos Yisroel* who dedicate their lives to the service of *Hashem*. Above all, this town is blessed with having a true *Mara d'Asrah*, HaGaon HaRav Betzalel Rakow *shlita*. His word is law to the members of the *kehilla* and it is largely due to the Rav *shlita* that Gateshead has maintained its level of *tahara* and its high concentration of Torah study. May *Hashem* grant him many years of good health and enable him to continue leading the *kehilla* in such an outstanding way.

ויהיו נא אמרינו לרצון לפני אדון כל

Rabbi Pesach Eliyahu Falk

Gateshead

Rosh Chodesh Teves 5758.

עוז והדר לבושה

Chapter One

TZNIUS - OUR BADGE OF DISTINCTION

A. TZNIUS IN DRESS ALLUDES TO INNER NOBILITY

1. GARMENTS THAT BLEND DIGNITY AND PLEASANTNESS: In the concluding verses of *Mishlei,* Shlomo Hamelech describes the qualities of an *Eishes Chayil* in poetic terms. Concerning her clothes he uses the words עוז והדר לבושה - "She dresses in clothes of strength and regality" (*Mishlei* 31:25). *Chazal* say, אין עוז אלא תורה - "strength lies in conforming with the ordinances of the Torah" (*Shir HaShirim Rabba* 2:10). The clothes of the *Eishes Chayil* are described with the noun עוז, as they display her strength and steadfastness, being totally in compliance with the laws of *tznius*. At the same time her garments are הדר - they are dignified and display tasteful refinement. The verse alludes to two diverse interests that this righteous woman combines with absolute harmony. On the one hand her clothes are an embodiment of strength, as they fulfill to perfection the requirements of the Torah. On the other hand, her clothes are aesthetically pleasing and eminently tasteful. With them she brings *simcha* to her husband, close family and friends.

When a *Bas Yisroel* dresses in a manner that is modest and graceful, the purity of her refined being, her good *midos* and her *yiras shomayim* shine through. They give her the very special *chein* with which *Bnos Yisroel* are blessed, as *Chazal* say, אמר ר׳ ישמעאל בנות ישראל יפות הן - "Rabbi Yishmael said, Jewish girls are particularly good looking" (*Nedarim* 66a).

The attention the *Eishes Chayil* pays to her clothes and general appearance, reveals the inner satisfaction she derives from her great mission in life: to enable herself, her husband and her children to realize their full potential לכבוד השם ותורתו - to the honor of *Hashem* and His holy Torah. The inner tranquillity reflected by her happy countenance and noble manner of dress, bear testimony to the fact that she appreciates the great privilege of building a true Jewish home. Hence, the end of the aforementioned verse in *Mishlei*, ותשחק ליום אחרון - "she completes her life with serenity", born out of a sense of satisfaction and accomplishment.

2. GARMENTS THAT REFLECT FORTITUDE AND REFINEMENT: A further message that can be learned from the verse עוז והדר לבושה is of particular relevance to the times in which we live: There can be no doubt that a major contributory factor to the lack of *tznius* in ladies' wear nowadays is the fact that the Jewish woman finds it very difficult to buy suitable clothes. Garments are manufactured by people who seek the absolute opposite of *tznius*, their motto being "the more eye-catching the better" ר״ל. This makes it very difficult for the *Bas Yisroel* to find blouses and dresses that have a suitable style and color, that are not see-through, that are not tight-fitting, and that have Kosher necklines, hemlines etc.

We are however an עם קשה עורף - a people who do not give in. We know that where there is a will there is a way. Furthermore, we know that *Hashem* puts difficulties in our path only so that we can demonstrate our resolve and iron will to keep His Torah and fulfill His *mitzvos* come what may. Therefore, with עוז, persistence, strength and fortitude, the *Bas Yisroel* does not give in. She feels that she cannot capitulate and admit defeat in a matter of such importance. She knows that she must stay firm when basic issues of *Yiddishkeit* are at stake. Consequently, although with respect to her personal desires the sincere Jewish woman or girl is prepared often to forgo and do without, she will not compromise her principles, even if many obstacles stand in her way. She therefore makes every endeavor to find clothes suitable for herself and her daughters. If nothing can be found, she will have clothes made to the refined styles that would suit her and her family's needs.

When a woman is particular about *tznius,* and ensures that her dress is appropriate for a mother or future mother in *Klal Yisroel,* her clothes generate הדר - splendor and prestige. Her aristocratic manner of dress bears witness to the fact that she has consecrated her life to the service of her Creator. Rather than make worldly desires the essence of her life, she uses the means given to her in a proficient and praiseworthy manner for the furtherance of her true role - to set up a home from which Torah and *Yiras Hashem* shall shine forth. Just as the priestly garments of the *Kohen* are described by the Torah as תפארת - magnificent (*Shemos* 28:2), for they demonstrate that the *Kohen* is engaged in a holy and distinguished service, so too, the garments of the true *Bas Yisroel* demonstrate that her days are filled with true values.

Hence, the strength displayed by the effort she has made to find such refined clothes (עוז) reveals her inner royalty and splendor (הדר). Her personality is a harmonious blend of firmness and tenderness. She is an embodiment of good *midos* and strength of character - אשרנו מה טוב חלקנו.

3. PROTECTING THE INNER QUALITIES AND OUTER CHEIN: A *Bas Yisrael* has deep inner qualities (ie. the way she thinks and feels about things) and also possess considerable outer *chein.* Her deep inner qualities originate from the pure *neshama* that is within her. With these qualities she will nurture a family that will be worthy of being considered a further link in the golden chain of *Klal Yisrael.* Her considerable outer *chein* is typical for *Bnos Yisrael,* and is once again closely related to her pure and beautiful *neshama,* as the exterior reflects the interior.

The inner qualities of the Jewish woman are so special and her outer appearance so *b'cheint* that both must be guarded at all times from contamination, misdirection and misuse. Just as a gem must be continuously protected from theft and damage, and to this end must be kept well covered and in a place of safety, so too, the dress of the *Bas Yisroel* and her refined public conduct, protect her and guarantee her purity - see *Mekoros* 3:1.

The first verse in *bircas kohanim* reads יברכך ה' וישמרך - "*Hashem* shall bless you and protect you" (*Bamidbar* 6:24). On this the *Midrash* comments, יברכך בבנים וישמרך בבנות שצריכות שמירה - " '*Hashem* shall bless you': with sons - 'and protect you': with daughters". The *Midrash* goes on to explain why daughters are referred to with the word שמירה - because "daughters must be protected" (*Bamidbar Rabba* 11:5). Guarding and protecting *Bnos Yisroel* is of such paramount importance that Chazal incredibly equate the word שמירה with girls.

יברכך - "He shall bless you" refers only to having sons, not to having sons and daughters, because to have daughters but not the means and the know-how to protect them, is no blessing at all. Since *bircas kohanim* was given to the Jewish people wherever they are, whether in *golus* between the nations of the world or in *Eretz Yisroel* amongst only *Yidden*, it is apparent that the *Bas Yisroel* must be protected at all times and in all places.

Due to the great importance that must be attached to the protection of women and girls, the *yetzer horah* aims at misrepresenting the requirements of *tznius* and *kedushas Yisroel*. His assault has become particularly potent in our own times as the *golus* moves towards its close and the much awaited era of *Moshiach* comes ever nearer. Just as a flame flares up just before it is goes out, so too, *the tumah of arayos* flares up just prior to the coming of *Moshiach* when the *tumah* of *arayos* will finally be wiped off the face of the earth - *Zechariyah* 13:2 (*Chofetz Chayim al HaTorah*, page 178, note 2). It has come to a point that, as a result of continuous sighting of live *pritzus*, billboards and newspapers, senses have become dulled to the extent that to many people the *halachos* of *tznius* seem unjustified and grossly overstated. However, with a new deeper understanding of the main guidelines and underlying *hashkafos* of *tznius*, and by learning to appreciate the immense depth of *Chazal's* understanding, hopefully a renewed willingness and even eagerness will arise to adhere meticulously to all the *halachos* of *tznius*.

4. THREE CATEGORIES OF DRESS THAT ARE NOT TZNIUS'DIK: The first step in understanding the laws of *tznius* is to appreciate that there are three basic modes of *non-tznius'dik* dress - inadequate dress, ostentatious dress and casual improper dress.

(a) Inadequate dress: Inadequate dress is *ossur* because it can cause men to see parts of the female body that must be covered. This in turn is extremely detrimental to *kedushas Yisroel*. A non-Kosher neckline; see-through garment; tight-fitting blouse, dress and skirt; a hemline that is too high; sleeves that are too short and the uncovered hair of a married woman all belong to this category. [See *Bava Kama* 48a: *Bava Basra* 57b: *S'mak mitzva* 57 and *Mishna Berura* 75:7.] See also 6:A below and *Mekoros* 70.

(b) Ostentatious dress: Ostentatious dress attracts undue attention to the woman or girl. Although, she should have a dignified and *b'cheint* appearance, she should not be dressed in a way that is eye-catching and causes men to look at her. For example, *Chazal* say (*Kesubos* 72b) that it is *pritzus* for a woman to spin bright red thread in public, because particles of the bright fiber fall on her face and forehead and people will be attracted to look at her brightly colored face (see *Tosfos,* s.v. *B'toveh* and E.H. 115:4). Loud and ostentatious hair styles, very fancy or overly elegant dresses, bright red and similar bright-colored clothes, excessive amounts of gold and studs on clothes, highly conspicuous jewelry, and a lavish application of cosmetics - all fall under this classification. [See *Brachos* 20a *Rashi* s.v. *Karvaltah; Tanchuma, Vayishlach s.v.* ותצא דינה*; Rabbeinu Yona, Iggeres HaTeshuva* No.78]. See also 7:A below and *Mekoros* 59:1-3.

(c) Casual, improper dress: When writing about wearing *tznius'dik* clothes, the *Mesilas Yesharim* (chapter 23) writes: ללבוש בגדים צנועים דהיינו מכובדים אך לא מפוארים - "To wear *tznius'dik* clothes means to wear clothes that are dignified but not ostentatious". It is clearly spelt out in his words that to wear undignified, improper clothes is a lack of *tznius*. What is the connection between the dignity of a person's clothes and *tznius*?

The overall attribute of *tznius* is based on an awareness of the constant presence of *Hashem* and man's need to be respectful of Him. For this reason, refinement in all one's actions, whether in public or in private, is an intrinsic part of *tznius* and is expected of both men and women [see *Brachos* 62a and *Eruvin* 100b concerning *tznius* even in the bathroom]. Casual improper wear worn when proper dress would be expected (to the exclusion of a ramble) is an antithesis to the awareness of *Hashem*'s presence - See 6:R:5 below.

Furthermore, casual improper dress exhibits a lack of self-esteem and self-respect, whilst *tznius* entails being aware of the importance of the *Bas Yisroel* and ensuring that she is properly protected. In reference to *tznius* the Jewish woman is called a *Bas Melachim* - a princess (כל כבודה בת מלך פנימה - *Tehillim* 45:14). This indicates that *tznius* is born out of a realization of the Jewish woman's royal status. When she knows she is a *Bas Melachim* guarantees she dresses appropriately which in turn prevents her going to places where *pritzus* is rampant.

Moreover, casual dress projects an undisciplined, wayward attitude to life, whilst modesty entails a style of life in which one is careful to fulfill *halacha* and avoid all forms of intermingling. A casual, carefree way of life is ill-suited to someone who must at all times be cautious. For this reason all that is unrefined such as eating and rejoicing in a lighthearted and frivolous manner is a lack of *tznius*, as stated in *Rashi, Succah* 49b s.v. *Devarim.*

Untidy long hair, garments made of heavyweight (stonewash) denim, garments with exposed unsightly seams, blouse tails that hang out (when it is obvious that this type of tail should not be left to hang out), long baggy sweaters, excessively long skirts (see 6:H:6 below), and hosiery that sags down because it is loose on the leg - are all part of this classification. [See *Taanis* 13b and what *Orchos Tzadikim, Sha'ar Haga'ava* s.v. *Ve'zos* says about unrefined dress]. See also 7:C and *Mekoros* 59:4-7.

5. ISSURIM OF INADEQUATE DRESS AND OVERDRESSING:

When a woman or girl dresses inadequately, uncovering parts of her body that should be covered, or when she overdresses and thereby causes men to be attracted to look at her, she transgresses a number of *issurim*:

- Firstly, inadequate dress frequently involves the *issur* of ובחוקותיהם לא תלכו - the prohibition to dress in a way typical of the *umos ha'olam*, (*Yoreh Deah* 178:1) which is an *issur min haTorah,* see *Rambam Hilchos Avoda Zarah* 11:1. This *issur* is transgressed when a person wears a type of garment that is worn by the secular society because it suits their inclination for immodesty and similar ill-founded considerations. See 1:I:1-3 below and *Mekoros* 8 where the nature of this prohibition is explained at length.

- Secondly, in nearly all cases she contravenes the *issur* of ולפני עור לא תתן מכשול - the *issur* to cause others to stumble and do an *aveira* (*Vayikra* 19:14). In this case, by dressing in an inappropriate manner, she causes men to gaze at her and transgress the Torah prohibition of ולא תתורו אחרי לבבכם ואחרי עיניכם (*Bamidbar* 15:39) which means, "Do not allow your heart or eyes stray and entice you" - see *Mekoros* 74:4-10.

- Thirdly, by exposing areas that should be covered, the woman or girl transgresses the obligation of והיה מחניך קדוש - "Your environment shall be holy" (*Devarim* 23:15). This verse has a number of meanings. One of them is that it is *ossur* for a female to reveal parts of her body as this erodes the sanctity of the society (*S'mak, mitzva* 56) - see *Mekoros* 37:1.

- Fourthly, by exposing areas that should be covered she transgresses the *issur* of לא תחמוד - "Do not desire" (*Shemos* 20:14). According to the rules of Torah interpretations this verse can also be read as לא תחמיד - "Do not make others desire" - see *Sefer HaYirah l'Rabbeinu Yona* no. 254 in the name of the *Mechilta.* When a woman exposes her limbs she arouses the desire of those who see her. Dressing in a *pritzus'dik* way is therefore a violation of this *issur* - see *Mekoros* 37:1 and 68:1.

▪ Fifthly, if a married woman goes out in public with her hair uncovered she transgresses an *issur min haTorah*. This is derived from the verse, ופרע את ראש האשה - "the hair of the woman (*sotah*) shall be uncovered" in *Beis Din* (*Bamidbar* 5:18) which implies that until this point her hair had to be covered because she was a married woman (*Kesubos* 72a). From the same chapter we can also learn that to reveal the chest area is an *issur min haTorah*. This is because *Chazal* (*Sotah* 8a) derive from a verse that not only the hair but also the chest area of the *sotah* is uncovered in *Beis Din* - implying that until this point it had to be covered. To cover these areas is therefore considered דת משה - "a scriptural obligation". [See *Kesubos* 72b, *sefer, Toras Hahistaklus and Mekoros* 37:2-3 for further elaborations.]

B. TZNIUS IS FAR MORE THAN THE "ABSENCE OF PRITZUS"

1. TZNIUS IS A MODEST AND REFINED WAY OF LIFE:

(a) An aspect of *tznius* often overlooked nowadays: For a *Bas Yisroel* to be careful not to dress like the general public is far from sufficient. She may not be dressing in a *pritzus*-like way, but her dress might nonetheless be unrefined and below the standard set by the *halachos* of *tznius*. This is because, whilst *pritzus* is a negative and wrong form of dress and behavior, *tznius* is not simply a neutral, *non-pritzus'dik* type of dress and conduct. Rather, *tznius* is a positively *eidel* way of dress and a distinctly refined manner of conduct. Unfortunately many are not aware of this truth and satisfy themselves with the fact that the accusing word "*pritzus*" cannot be thrown against them - see *Mekoros* 3:1.

To our great misfortune, a large proportion of those amongst whom we live practice appalling and outrageous *pritzus* and have eliminated decency and a sense of shame from their code of conduct. As a result of this relentless exposure to corruption, many of our people, even those who resist imitating those around them, have nevertheless lost the understanding that *tznius* is manifested by positive nobility of character, truly refined behavior and an appreciation for the graceful, dignified and modest forms of dress that so beautifully complement the *Bas Yisroel's* personality.

(b) Kimchis personified the positive aspect of *tznius*: Kimchis merited that her seven sons all served as *Kohanim Gedolim* at some point in her life. When asked by the *Chachamim* what she had done to deserve such children, she answered, לא ראו קורות ביתי שערות ראשי מעולם - "The beams of my house never saw the hairs of my head". On hearing her response, the *Chachamim* said, כל קמחייא קמח, וקמח דקמחית סולת - "The flour of most people is *kemach,* a mixture of coarse and fine flour - whilst the flour of Kimchis is *soles,* fine flour" (*Midrash Tanchuma Acharei* 7, *Vayikra Rabba* 20:11). The *Chachamim* played on the root of her name Kimchis - *kemach,* which means flour. It is, however, unclear, what exactly they were saying in their response to her answer.

It can be explained thus: There are three types of wheat flour סובין, קמח, and סולת. *Subin* is impure flour, in which the bran is still mixed with the flour. By sieving it with a medium sieve these impurities are removed and *kemach* remains. Although *kemach* is free of impurities, it is far from perfect, as it is a mixture of coarse and fine flour. However, if this *kemach* is sieved through a fine sieve, a fine perfect flour known as *soles* is obtained.

The *Chachamim* responded with the following: To most women the predominant meaning of *tznius* is to free oneself of all degrees of *pritzus*. It is a *tahara* process - a purification of the negative desires that exist in the base nature of man. Although they also know about refinement and *eidelkeit,* it is only of secondary importance to them. There are therefore areas, such as in privacy, where they are not particular about it. Kimchis, however, had a far higher perception of *tznius*. To her, *tznius* was much more than the "absence of *pritzus*". It was a positive attribute involving total refinement of character and purity of conduct. It is a form of *kedusha* - a sanctification of her whole being. To her, *tznius* was to be practiced everywhere, even in the privacy of her home where no one is present.

Accordingly, to most people the ultimate *tznius* is to be like *kemach* which is free of all bad matter and impurities. They are like *kemach* which is a mixture of coarse and fine, because they do not fully appreciate the importance of the positive side to *tznius* which is to refine oneself and develop a high degree of finesse and sensitivity. Kimchis was, however, different. Her flour was *soles*. She knew that after all impurities had been removed there is still a high level of positive *tznius* to develop. She therefore "distilled" her character and refined her personality until she was comparable to the finest of flours - *soles*. This is the legacy *Chazal* intended to impart to for us by recording the final part of the conversation between the *Chachamin* and Kimchis.

2. TZNIUS IS LATENT WITHIN EVERY BAS YISROEL: *Tznius* is an inherent and integral part of being a woman. *Chazal* say, הקב״ה ברא את האשה מן הצלע ממקום צנוע כדי שתהיה צנועה - "*Hashem* created woman from an internal rib because a woman's place is the interior, not amongst the public" (*Midrash Tanchuma, Vayeishev* 6). Similarly, *Chazal* say that at the time of creation *Hashem* instructed every limb of the woman to be modest (*Breishis Rabba* 18:3). In the case of the *umos ha'olam,* this inherent tendency has been severely suppressed if not overturned by the ongoing pursuit of pleasures which relate better to *pritzus* than to *tznius* (see *Responsa Maharam Mintz* No. 102). However, in *Bnos Yisroel* the qualities of *tznius* have certainly not been crushed and they are latently there. It should be a source of great encouragement for a *Bas Yisroel* to know that "it is all there" and need only be allowed to surface once again.

An insight into how innate and native *tznius* is to the very being of a woman can be learned from the following *Ma'amar Chazal*. In *Sefer Melachim* we learn that the Queen of Sheba heard of the incredible wisdom of Shlomo Hamelech and decided to go and see for herself if he really was so brilliant. She tested him by asking him riddles - see *Melachim* 1:10:1. In *Midrash Shochar Tov, Mishlei* 1, one of the riddles is recorded and is as follows: The queen brought male and female children before Shlomo Hamelech. They were all dressed the same, were all the same height and all had the same facial appearance. She asked Shlomo to tell her which of the children were male and which were female.

Shlomo Hamelech instructed a servant to place a bowl of nuts and roast kernels before the children and allow them to help themselves to a handsome helping. All the males lifted the corner of their robe forming a type of large pocket which they filled with nuts. The females, however, did not do the so, because of their innate feeling for modesty as lifting the corner of their robe would reveal part of their legs. Instead, they took out a kerchief [which holds less than the pocket made from a corner of a robe] and filled it with nuts. In this way Shlomo Hamelech could tell exactly who was male and who was female without erring. The Queen of Sheba was greatly impressed.

It is apparent from the story that not a single girl lifted the corner of her robe to hold the nuts. This proves that modesty and the need to be covered is very deep and absolute. *Tznius* is engraved in the very character of a girl and has a natural place in her thought processes. The Jewish girl need therefore not acquire *tznius* - she should just keep away from negative influences and a deep seated feeling for modesty and *tznius* will emerge. This feeling can then be positively developed to a greater and greater sensitivity

3. SENSITIVITIES FOR TZNIUS CAN BE AWAKENED: As stated, *tznius* is deeply etched into the soul of a *Bas Yisroel*, and is constantly waiting to be reawakened. The sooner and the more absolutely the woman or girl removes bad influences - including fashion magazines and similar distinctly non-Jewish literature from her home - the more speedily the natural feeling for *tznius* will return to her. With the removal of the negative influence of *tumah* and non-Jewish ideas of dress, her own innate feeling for *tahara* will surface and be revived to the extent that she will gladly and naturally dress and adorn herself in a noble, tasteful and refined manner - see *Mekoros* 2:2.

Just as a first step in restoring a sick person to good health is to ensure that they reside where the air and water are pure, since otherwise they are being continuously contaminated, so too, restoring one's mind and spirit back to "good health" requires that they should not be persistently infected and sullied by the negative import of fashion magazines and the like, which stand for everything that *tznius* utterly disapproves of and holds in contempt.

4. APPROPRIATE DRESS REFINES THE PERSON'S CHARACTER: When the woman with a newfound feeling for *tznius* and *tahara* dresses in appropriate garments, this in turn consolidates the gains she has made thus far and engenders within her an even deeper and more profound feeling for *tznius* than she had felt until now. As time goes on and her dress and conduct improve even further, they will continue to develop within her an even deeper and richer feeling for this cherished trait.

We are taught that חיצוניות מעוררת את הפנימיות - "the physical actions of a person affect his way of thinking, his feeling and his whole inner being" - (*Sefer HaChinuch, Mitzva* 16). Therefore, dressing and behaving in a refined way has the effect of refining her and developing within her greater and deeper feelings for all that *Yiddishkeit* stands for. [Concerning the worry some people have that dressing with greater refinement than one actually feels at present might border on hypocrisy - see 1:L:8 below].

As a woman's sensitivities improve, she will appreciate that a dress or outfit which appeared to be perfectly Kosher (being sufficiently long, having a perfect neckline and adequate sleeves) is in fact inappropriate for the noble character of Jewish woman and girl. Although the measurements are in order, it is coarse, overly loud or ostentatious in color, style, trimmings, buttons, belt, accessories or otherwise. It is therefore only suitable for those who were not given the nobility and *eidelkeit* inborn in *Bnos Yisroel*.

Just as a stain on a piece of clothing that is not noticed in a dimly lit room becomes very evident and obvious once the room is well illuminated, so too, a lack of refinement that is dismissed as unimportant as long as *tznius* is just a vague idea with little significance, becomes an problem once the person becomes more *tznua* and develops a keener feeling for *kedushas Yisroel*.

Although at the outset this woman or girl had little feeling for true *tznius* of dress and conduct, nevertheless, as a result of removing negative influences and practicing *tznius*, a feeling for *tznius* is awakened within her that becomes progressively deeper and deeper. It becomes apparent to her that this trait is the royal stamp of the Jewish female and that the more perfect her *tznius*, the more brightly will shine all her other fine qualities, as *tznius* brings to the surface the inner regality of the Jewish woman.

This process is described by *Chazal* with the words אדם מקדש עצמו מעט מקדשין אותו הרבה - "If a person sanctifies himself in a moderate measure he is assisted from Heaven to attain a much richer and more profound measure of sanctification" (*Toras Kohanim,* end of *Shemini)*. Conducting oneself in a sublime and virtuous manner, engenders a further and deeper urge to live with this type of conduct. See 1:I:11 for further points on this subject.

5. A TZNUA IS INDUSTRIOUS BUT NOT OVERLY ASSERTIVE:

(a) She is modest in spite of her great achievements: As stated, *tznius* extends far beyond dress. It is a trait that shapes the complete character, behavior and way of thinking of the Jewish woman. Instead of seeking recognition and being assertive or aggressive, she remains unpretentious and modest. This is so even when she has great achievements to her credit.

It is heartwarming to read about the achievements and the refinement of Sarah Schneirer *o.h.* The following is a quote from the book "Daughters of Destiny" (p. 200): "The cornerstone of the *Beis Yaacov* Seminary building in Krakow was to be laid. The leaders of world Jewry were there, important personalities of the Torah world and the communal world, writers, thinkers and a great crowd of ordinary people - all gathered together to participate in this event. It was a real celebration - with music, a band playing and speakers being called upon to address the crowd. Amidst this celebration and gaiety, where was Sarah Schneirer, the founder and inspiration of all this? She was standing at the far end of the crowd, together with the women, her friends and neighbors, shedding tears and whispering a prayer".

(b) Although non-assertive, her opinion is sought and respected: It must be made clear, that although all forms of aggressive behavior are unfitting for a Jewish daughter, this does not mean that she must always keep quiet and never voice her opinion. On the contrary, *Chazal* say (*Niddah* 45b) that a woman has בינה יתירה - greater intuition than a man in discerning right from wrong. The Torah actually relates two cases concerning our *Avos* in which outstanding female intuition is displayed. Avraham and Sarah had a disagreement with regard to Yishmael, whilst Yitzchak and Rivka had a disagreement concerning Eisav. On both occasions the wives were right (*Breishis* 21:12 and 27:13), being women of an exceptional high caliber.

In the Torah way of life, a wife's opinion is considered most carefully. It is indeed part of the beautiful partnership between husband and wife that she respectfully presents an alternative point of view for her husband to contemplate, knowing that the final decision will be made only after both outlooks have been examined carefully. See 10:C:7 below for a letter by the great Gaon Rabbi Akiva Eiger *zt'l* written after the death of his Rebbetzen *o.h.*, in which he describes in profound emotional terms the wonderful bond that existed between them, the deep regard he had for her and how he would discuss with her until late into the night problems he had related to issues of *Yiras Shomayim* and *Avodas Hashem* - see *Mekoros* 3:4-5.

(c) Her modesty is apparent when her opinion is agreed to: Even when she is right and her opinion has been accepted, a Jewish woman remains refined and does not take the central role. Moreover, she is particularly careful not to undermine the authority of her husband. Dovid Hamelech compares Jewish daughters to the corner bricks of a wall - בנותינו כזוויות (*Tehillim* 144:12). The *Malbim* explains: When a wall is built the two corners are built first. A string is then drawn from one corner to the other, to ensure that the central bricks are set at the right height. Their position is measured from the corner bricks which literally "set the tone". These corner bricks, however, always shun the limelight and remain at the sides and at the corners even though they fulfilled such an important role. This is *tznius'dik* behavior at its best. Fortunate is the daughter who sees this at home.

(d) Due to her modesty she remains inconspicuous: *Devorah HaNeviah* is a prime example of a woman who performed great deeds but in order to remain safely out of the public eye directed all the credit to her husband. She is referred to in the verse as דבורה הנביאה אשת לפידות -

"Devorah the prophetess, wife of Lapidos" (*Shoftim* 4:4). *Chazal* explain that her husband was unlearned and was not in a position to earn a prestigious place in *Olam Habah* for himself, as the *or haTorah*, the light of Torah, was missing. To rectify this, Devorah undertook to make extra thick wicks for the *menorah* that would produce large, bright and beautiful lights. When they were ready, her husband transported them to the *mishkan* in *Shilo*. Hence, he was called *Lapidos* - a fire torch (although his real name was Barak), because he brought torch-like wicks to the *mishkan*. Lapidos, who brought extra light to the world with these holy wicks, earned through them a rewarding place in *Olam Habah (Yalkut Shimoni, Shoftim 42)*.

Chazal conclude with the following words, מי זיכה לו ללפידות שיהא חלקו עם הכשרים ויבא לעולם הבא הוי אומר דבורה אשתו, עליה נאמר חכמת נשים בנתה ביתה - "Who enabled Lapidos to become worthy and earn *Olam Habah* - it was his wife Devorah. About Devorah it says, 'The wisdom of a woman built her home'" (*Mishlei* 14:1). In return for doing everything herself - and then giving the credit away to her husband so as to remain totally inconspicuous - *Hashem* chose her for the exalted office of *Neviah*. Such a prestigious office would have made any average woman haughty and conceited. Not so Devorah, who had already proven her sterling *midos* and true humility - see *Mekoros* 3:6.

(e) Her modesty earns her the admiration of her family: The respect a refined woman and her husband show each other leaves a deep impression on their children. The children grow up admiring their parents and wishing to emulate all they see at home. Moreover, in the warm atmosphere of such a home, the *mitzva* of *kibud av v'eim* finds very responsive ears. The bond becomes so great that even when married the children continue to seek and treasure the opinion of their parents, because they have learned to appreciate the integrity and attitudes of their parents - see *Mekoros* 65:5.

6. LAUGHING AND TALKING IN A REFINED MANNER:

(a) Refined and coarse ways of laughing: Hearing a comical statement or seeing a comical sight naturally causes laughter. Such a reaction is to be expected of anyone, even from an *eidel* and intelligent person provided the laughter is cultured and the person's refined posture is retained. This is because *halachically* and *midos*-wise there is nothing wrong with a moderate, cultured form of laughter. Although *Chazal* say (*Brachos* 31a) אסור לאדם שימלא פיו שחוק בעוה"ז - "A person must not fill his mouth with laughter in this world [before the coming of *Moshiach*]", this does not mean that he should not laugh at all. See *Tana d'Bei Eliyahu Rabba,* Chap. 13, where *Chazal* say ישמור אדם את עצמו שלא ירבה לשחוק - "A person must guard himself not to constantly laugh". See also *Rambam Hilchos Deios* 2:7 where this is spelt out clearly. See also *Einayim Lamishpot, Brachos* 31a.

There are, however, immodest forms of laughter, in which the person bursts into raucous laughter or screams loudly with laughter. Such behavior - and even lesser forms of outright laughter - is unfitting for a refined and cultured person and even degrades him in the eyes of others. This type of laughter is particularly unfitting for women and girls since, apart from the external unpleasantness of such behavior, it is associated with a loss of self control due to which the person screams. This is in variance with *tznius* - which requires constant vigilance and care. It also reflects a coarseness of character since a refined person does not behave in such a manner.

Chazal say, בשלשה דברים אדם ניכר, בכוסו ובכיסו ובכעסו, ואמרי לה אף בשחקו - "The character of a person can be detected in three ways: by the way he behaves when drunk, by the manner in which he gives *tzedaka*, and by how he reacts when angered. Some say, also by the way he laughs". (*Eruvin* 65b). The wisdom and perception of our holy *Chazal* is breathtaking!

(b) Lightheaded entertainment of the general world: *Chazal* say that when Naomi informed Ruth about the consequences of becoming a Jewess, she said to her, אין דרכן של בנות ישראל לילך לבתי תיאטראות ולבתי קרקסיאות של גוים - "It is not the way of Jewish girls to attend non-Jewish theaters and circuses" (*Ruth Rabba* 2:22). The laughter and light-headedness which prevail in these places is harmful for a Jewish person and particularly for a *Bas Yisroel* whose sensitivities and deep feelings of *tznius* can easily be contaminated. The *neshama* of a *Bas Yisroel* is so precious and delicate that such experiences cannot leave it unscathed.

It should be noted that *Chazal* do not say, "*Bnos Yisroel* should not attend places of non-Jewish merriment". Instead they say, "It is not the way of *Bnos Yisroel* to attend ......", meaning it is out of character for Jewish girls to go to such places. They are naturally composed and refined at all times and it is therefore out of style for them to join coarse and loud forms of entertainment even if they do not involve any immorality.

(c) Healthy and unhealthy uses of humor: *Chazal* say, דרך בנות ישראל לא פרוצות בשחוק - "Jewish girls are not used to jesting," meaning that they do not usually jest and joke; thereby attracting attention of females and males alike (*Midrash Tanchuma*, *Nossoh* 2). When humor and jesting are used incorrectly they are the cause of considerable immodesty. It is characteristic for a humorous person to attract an audience, and if a woman's or girl's sense of humor attracts men, she is misusing a heavenly gift in a most unfortunate way to the detriment of herself and those who associate with her.

However, humor applied in a fitting and healthy measure and in an appropriate setting, is wonderful. So much so, that Rabba would start his Talmudical discourses with a humorous statement to arouse the attention of his disciples - *Shabbos* 30b.

Also, a measure of humor and jesting when apt and fitting can help enormously to lift people's spirits and clear a stifled atmosphere. See *Midrash Koheles* (3:4:4) where *Chazal* say, עת לבכות בשעת אבל, ועת לשחוק אחר האבל - "It is time to cry during the mourning period and time to laugh once the mourning period is over". What do *Chazal* mean with this? When mourning is over is a person expected to jump with joy? There is however a valuable recommendation in these holy words of *Chazal*. Once the twelve months of mourning are over, the person must get back onto an even keel once again. It is therefore recommended that he goes to a *chasuna* or similar source of *simcha*. Laughter and happiness are great healers and will quickly help the person find his correct balance once again.

(d) Talking calmly in public: Shouting and talking loudly whether in the street or anywhere in public is another aspect of uncultivated and coarse behavior. *Tznius* entails a quiet, cultured and refined demeanor and these do not exist when a person shouts or talks in such a manner. *Chazal* say, דרך בנות ישראל לא קולניות (*Tanchuma*, *Nossoh* 2). This is explained by the *Eitz Yosef* to mean that *Bnos Yisroel* do not raise their voices when in public - the root of the word קולניות being קול. Here again, *Chazal* do not say "*Bnos Yisroel* should not...", but simply, "It is not the way of *Bnos Yisroel* .....", indicating that it is instinctive in the make-up of a woman and girl to be modest and refined rather than boisterous and rowdy.

It is so fundamental for a female to be quiet spoken, that *Hashem* created women with a quieter voice than men. Should a woman have a bellicose masculine-like voice it is viewed as a defect in her general make-up. This goes so far that *Chazal* say, קול עבה באשה הרי זה מום - "If a woman has a heavy masculine voice it is a blemish" (*Kesubos* 75a).

When traveling on public transport one sometimes hears *frum* teenage girls talking at the top of their voices as if they own the vehicle and as if no one else was present. This is of course distressing behavior and demonstrates just how far the boisterous, noisy environment and the loud, jazzy music listened to by many of these girls affects them. This music coarsens those who listen to it, to the point that they become uncivilized and even ill-mannered. Regrettably, worlds separate these girls from the praise כי קולך ערב - "Your voice is sweet" given to *Bnos Yisroel* in *Shir Hashirim* (2:14) - see *Kesubos* 75a that this refers to singing and to speaking softly.

When Shlomo Hamelech describes the way of an *Eishes Chayil* he says פיה פתחה בחכמה - "She opens her mouth with intelligence" (*Mishlei* 31:26). With this he means that she speaks intelligently with calm and serenity, as he says in *Koheles* דברי חכמים בנחת נשמעים - "Intelligent people express themselves calmly" (*Koheles* 9:17).

7. TZNIUS IN THE CHOICE OF WORDS:

(a) The Torah teaches us to be careful with our choice of words: The choice of words used in everyday speech should be *eidel,* and words used by the world at large to describe immoral concepts must be avoided so that they do not pass our lips at all. This is learnt (*Pesachim* 3a) from the fact that the Torah is particular to choose only untainted words. When Noach was commanded to take two of each type of non-clean animal into the ark, *Hashem* used the five words בהמה אשר לא טהורה - "the animal that is not clean" (*Breishis* 7:2) rather than the two words בהמה טמאה - "the defiled animal". Since it was possible to use a more refined term, *Hashem* did so. Similarly, *Chazal* always choose as pure a language as possible - see *Sanhedrin* (68b) where the *Mishna* says, דברו חכמים בלשון נקיה - "The words used by sages are as undefiled and as impeccable as possible".

(b) Purity of speech is of maximum importance: It may seem to some that to guard one's tongue and use the cleanest language possible would be an ideal way of life and fit for a world with high morals, whereas, in our day and age, when immorality and corruption gather momentum all the time, it is inappropriate to stress such a seemingly trivial matter. This is however far from correct. *Hashem* especially revealed the requirement of clean language just before the flood - at a time when the world was utterly corrupt - to teach us that instead of ignoring purity of speech at such a time, it was in fact one of the most important things to strengthen. Downward trends always start with leniencies in things which people considered as trivial or of secondary importance. Therefore, our own *tznius* depends on us having a לשון נקיה - a clean and pure tongue, and in our times, more than ever, keeping our speech clean and refined must be a top priority.

(c) Purity of soul is closely related to purity of speech: Speech is the supreme quality of humans over other creatures - see *Targum Unkelus,*

Breishis 2:7. Speech is so significant, that the character of a person is considerably affected by the way he speaks. The root of the word דיבור is דבר - 'a being' or 'an entity'. The connotation of this is that speech is intrinsically associated with the inner self of man, and has a great influence on forming his personality. Hence his very essence is interrelated with his speech. When *Chazal* say that the *geula* from *Mitzrayim* was effected by לא שינו את לשונם - "they did not change their speech", *Chazal* referred both to the Hebrew language itself and to the kind of words they used, because the vocabulary a person uses has a far-reaching effect on his personality and general makeup (*Bnei Yisaschar*, *Nissan* 4:10).

(d) Due to purity of speech we merited coming out of Mitzrayim: On the verse בצאת ישראל ממצרים בית יעקב מעם לועז וכו' (*Tehillim* 114:2) - "When *Yidden* came out of *Mitzrayim*, *Beis Yaacov* from a people of a foreign tongue etc.", the *Chasam Sofer* comments that *Beis Yaacov* refers to women. The verse implies that the merit of the women in *Mitzrayim* lay in the way they guarded their tongue and retained their purity of speech. Although they were in *Mitzrayim*, a place of considerable immorality, they were careful only to speak with a refined and pure tongue. See 3:G below about the immense importance of clean speech regarding children.

(e) *Hashem* loves those who practice purity of speech: Purity and *chein* of speech bring about an endearment between *Hashem* and the person. The verse says in *Tehillim* (45:3), הוצק חן בשפתותיך על כן ברכך אלוקים לעולם - "*Chein* pours from your lips; therefore *Hashem* blesses you forever". It costs nothing to be on *Hashem*'s mailing-list of *brachos*. It is just a matter of taking care to use the gift of speech wisely and correctly. פיה פתחה בחכמה ותורת חסד על לשונה - "She opened her mouth intelligently and teachings of kindness were on her tongue" (*Mishlei* 31:26).

8. TZNIUS INVOLVES NOT DISCLOSING PERSONAL MATTERS:

(a) Keeping secrets is part of the trait of *tznius*: The word *tznius* means to "hide and conceal" that which should be kept private. Part of the trait of *tznius* is to keep secrets and not reveal private affairs. To disclose someone else's secrets is tantamount to rendering that person "bare and unprotected" and is nothing short of *pritzus*. *Sefer Chassidim* by *Rabbeinu Yehuda HaChassid* (No. 350) enumerates seven qualities that are involved in true *tznius*. The seventh quality is כסות הסוד - "keeping and concealing a secret". Similarly, the *Chofetz Chayim* writes in *Hilchos Rechilus* 8:5 "A person is obliged to keep confidential a secret his friend has told him even if no *rechilus* is involved in relating it. This is because it may be damaging to that person if his secret is revealed. Secondly, one is being disloyal in disregarding the condition under which the secret was told. Thirdly, there is a total lack of *tznius* in making public another person's secrets".

To our deep regret this is another aspect of present day *pritzus*. People tell friends and associates the most private and personal matters about their husbands, wives, parents and parents-in-law - matters which they have no right to reveal. There is no excuse for this and it is a lack of the most elementary levels of *tznius*. This has become so frequent an occurrence nowadays that it must be taken as a symptom of a serious breakdown and even abnegation of בושה - bashfulness. The extreme seriousness of a disintegration of the attribute of בושה is evident from the saying of *Chazal*, "Where there is no shame there is no *Yiras Shomayim*" (*Nedarim* 20a).

(b) A person should not reveal even his own secrets: The need for *tznius* and privacy applies also to one's own secrets and private affairs not just those of other people. The *Gemara* (*Megilla* 13b) says that Esther did not reveal her identity - אין אסתר מגדת את עמה, "Esther would not disclose who her people were" (*Esther* 2:20) - because she was a *tznua*.

It should be placed on record that in pre-war years, when a husband had no option but to say that his wife was unable to attend a certain function due to pregnancy he would say, "*Sie ist in andere umshtender*" - "She is in special circumstances" - so as not to mention personal affairs beyond the minimum social requirement. This was Jewish conduct at its best and such refinement of behavior is fitting for the descendants of the *Avos* and *Imahos*.

(c) Educating children to keep secrets: If a mother tells her children that they will be having a baby shortly *b'ezras Hashem*, she has a golden opportunity to educate them to the *tznius* mentioned. She should tell her children that she is telling them the good news so that they can look forward to a *simcha*, *b'ezras Hashem*. At the same time she should add that this is the business of no-one outside their family. They should therefore not talk about it in school nor tell even their closest friends until after the birth. In this way, the children will grow up knowing that a person must be discreet and not divulge secrets that he is told. [Note: Some have the custom not to tell young children anything about an expected *simcha* until the birth has actually taken place. Also, even those who do tell must know that children of six and under are usually unable to keep a secret. Such young children should therefore not be told things that are not to be spoken about].

With such a *chinuch*, a girl will know that there are things, such as physical changes when growing up, that a mother explains to her daughter which must not be discussed at all - not even with her closest friends.

(d) Children educated to keep secrets do not become secretive: It should be noted that educating children not to reveal secrets does not mean the children are being brought up to be secretive and not talk freely about things that are not secret. In fact Esther, who is pointed out by *Chazal* as being a *tznua* and a person who kept secrets (as mentioned above), is the very person about whom *Chazal* say, כל האומר דבר בשם אומרו מביא גאולה לעולם - "Whoever attributes words of wisdom to the one who actually said them - rather than take the credit themselves - brings *geula* to the world" (*Pirkei Avos* 6:6). This is learnt from the fact that Esther disclosed to Achashveirosh the plot of Bigson and Seresh in Mordechei's name, and did not suppress the true source of the information (*Esther* 2:22). This in turn brought about the salvation of *Klal Yisroel*, as we know. From here we see that Esther spoke freely when it was right to speak. She even revealed things that others might not have revealed. However, when something was not to be revealed, she was a master of self-control in speech and did not reveal it.

9. TZNIUS ENTAILS NOT PRYING INTO PEOPLE'S AFFAIRS:

(a) The Issur to intrude into another person's privacy: Just as it is wrong to relate personal matters to those who have no need to know them, so too it is obviously wrong to try to find out this type of information about others. To do so is tantamount to intruding into another person's private domain to which one has no right of entry. This is once again a severe departure from *tznius*. It is irrelevant whether one is looking for faults in the other person, or one is just inquisitive to know their personal affairs.

Friends speculating that a *yeshiva bachur* or a seminary girl has probably gone away on a *shidduch* and surmise whom they are meeting, is severe misconduct and gross *pritzus*. It can also be immensely harmful and hurtful to the people involved. Great misery has been caused by this misbehavior which should be roundly condemned by whoever is in a position to do so.

(b) Yidden took great precautions to prevent forms of intrusion: Bilam the *rashah*, who certainly had no desire to see good in *Klal Yisroel*, was overwhelmed when he saw the way Jewish tents were erected. The entrance of one tent did not face the entrance of the neighboring one, so that people could not see inside one another's tents. They knew that it is a human weakness to be inquisitive and even intrusive. They therefore took the necessary precautions and set up their tents in a way that neither family could in a moment of weakness pry on the other, or even see the others private doings by mistake. In response to this beautiful act of *tznius*, Bilam proclaimed מה טובו אוהליך יעקב משכנותיך ישראל - "How exemplary are your tents, Yaacov; your abodes, Yisroel" (*Bamidbar* 24:5).

It is understood that we too are to set up our homes on these lines. If necessary, one should ensure that the curtains are drawn or the blinds let down in the evening, so that people living across the street or in apartments that overlook one's own, cannot watch all that goes on in one's house.

(c) It is part of *tznius* to positively protect the privacy of others: Not only is it against *tznius* to reveal other people's secrets, it is also part of this cherished *midah* to do whatever one can to positively protect another person's secrets and thereby safeguard their privacy and dignity. *Chazal* (*Bava Basra* 123a) say that Rachel did an act of *tznius* when she transferred the "items of identity" (the *simanim* that Yaacov had given her at the time of their betrothal) to her sister Leah, just before Leah's wedding. Rachel did so to protect Leah and ensure that she would not suffer the embarrassment of being identified as Leah on the night of her wedding.

This was considered an act of *tznius* on the part of Rachel apart from being an act of *chesed* - because *tznius* means "to cover that which is private and personal". It is irrelevant what type of private matter it is, and whether the person covers up his own confidentiality or that of someone else. Accordingly, when, at great personal sacrifice, Rachel took steps to ensure that Leah's secret would not be found out, she was practicing *tznius*, as she was safeguarding her sister's honor and dignity. It behooves us to emulate the traits of our forbearers and safeguard the personal affairs of others just as we safeguard our own.

C. WHAT TORAH DOES FOR MEN, TZNIUS DOES FOR WOMEN

1. TZNIUS IS AN ANTIDOTE TO THE YETZER HORAH: Apart from *tznius* being an outstanding *mitzva* in its own right, it serves a second function upon which much of a woman's *Yiddishkeit* may depend. This is that *tznius* is an "antidote" to the *yetzer horah* for women in much the same way as Torah learning is an antidote to the *yetzer horah* for men. *Chazal* say, בראתי יצר הרע בראתי לו תורה תבלין - "I created the *yetzer horah* (to entice man to sin) and I have created Torah as an antidote to it" - (literally, as a spice to it, see No. 4 below) - see *Kiddushin* (30b). Man is therefore capable of overcoming his *yetzer horah* in whichever area it may attack him, and is consequently held responsible for his sins.

Like everyone else, a woman may at times desire to do things that the Torah has forbidden. For example, she might want to relate an incident which involves *lashon horah*. She may be sorely tempted to eat something which does not have a reliable *hechsher*. She might not be bothered to perform a time-consuming *mitzva* correctly, such as inspecting vegetables properly for insects. Similarly, she might find it hard to say the words of a *bracha* properly and with clear pronunciation, especially when it comes to *Al Hamichyah* and *Bircas Hamazon*. In addition, a woman, whose function is to establish and manage a home and family, does not have Torah learning to counteract her *yetzer horah*. If so, from where should she draw the strength to withstand such natural desires and overcome such weakness?

The answer to this is that women have their own form of "inoculation" against "*nisyonos*" which is the equivalent of Torah learning. This is the wonderful trait of *tznius*, which when kept properly, is all encompassing. It gives so much *kedusha* and strength to the woman that she is capable of outwitting the *yetzer horah* and withstanding its relentless pressure. See 1:E:1 for an in-depth explanation as to how *tznius* functions as a powerful weapon against the *yetzer horah*.

When the *Vilna Gaon* set out on a journey (that he hoped would take him to *Eretz Yisroel)*, he sent a letter of *chizuk* to his family, known as the *Igeres HaGra*. In it he warned them about the need to avoid anger, arguments, jealousy and similar bad *midos*. In particular, he stressed the gravity of the sin of *lashon horah* and other speech-related *aveiros*. Towards the end of the letter, he addresses his mother with the following words: אהובתי אמי, ידעתי שאינך צריכה למוסר שלי, כי ידעתי כי צנועה את - "My dear mother, I know that you do not require my *mussar*, for I am aware that you are a *tznua*". Although the *mussar* given in the letter concerned all types of negative traits, he was nevertheless convinced that his mother, who was an outstanding *tznua*, was above all negative traits and did not require *chizuk* from him to overcome anger, *lashon horah* and the like. He was convinced, that just as being steeped in Torah enables a man to combat his "lower self", so too, being steeped in *tznius* enables a woman to be victorious in the same way. He therefore knew that his mother, who was an exceptional *tznua*, would surely overcome whatever test she would encounter. (Harav Hagaon R' Don Segal *Shlita* quoted in the *sefer, Mi Yirpeh Lach* , page 175).

In some versions of the *Vilna Gaon*'s letter, the above mentioned concept is spelt out explicitly. In a version found in *Aram Tzova* (5626), printed in Shanghai during the Second World War and subsequently reprinted in the *sefer, Cheshbono Shel Olam* (*Bnei Brak* 5723), the following words appear: ותבלין שלו לזכרים עסק התורה ולנקבות הצניעות - "The *yetzer horah* is neutralized in the case of men by being engrossed in Torah study and in the case of women by adhering to *tznius*". (See *Gaon Chassid MiVilna*, chapter 15 note 21 and 1:C:4 and 2:F:1-2 below).

2. TZNIUS COUNTERS A POWERFUL INTERNAL FOE: As explained, *tznius* is a countermeasure to the attempts of the *yetzer horah*. This explains why, subsequent to the sin of Adam and Chava, mankind suddenly felt a need to be clothed (*Breishis* 3:7). Similarly, it is stated in the *Gemara* (*Eruvin* 100b) that the *mitzva* of כיסוי שערות, the obligation for married women to cover their hair - and the obligations of *tznius* in general - were given in direct response to the sin of Adam and Chava. The deeper meaning of this is that, as a consequence of the first sin committed by mankind, the *yetzer horah,* which had previously been man's external enemy, now became an internal foe, interwoven into his emotions and feelings. With this, the passion for sin become far more formidable than it had previously been. To help withstand and overcome this greatly strengthened *yetzer horah*, *Hashem Yisborach* gave mankind an urge to be clothed and practice *tznius* in both dress and conduct - see 5:D:2(h) below for further elaboration.

Women in particular, who do not have the *mitzva* of learning Torah, were given the special *mitzva* of covering their hair in public - a *mitzva* which symbolizes the *tznius* of the Jewish woman. This constant religious mode of dress, and the *tznius* it represents, becomes a power-pack which gives women a firm attachment to *kedusha* and *emes* - which in turn enables them to unmask and expel the *yetzer horah* before he has a chance to do harm.

3. TO BE A TZNUA IS A WOMAN'S ULTIMATE DISTINCTION: The greatest spiritual height a woman can reach, is perfection in matters of *tznius.* This can be seen from the fact that the *Imahos,* although in possession of many outstanding qualities, were immortalized and enshrined by a name that stands for perfect *tznius.* They were given the name *levona,* as the verse says אל גבעת הלבונה - "The *Shechina* visited a hill of frankincense - ie. the

Imahos" (*Shir HaShirim* 4:6). The *Midrash* (*Bamidbar Rabba* 9:13) says, "This name was allotted to the *Imahos* because with their good deeds they were comparable to this delicate and aromatic spice. Moreover, the literal translation of the word *levono* is 'white', and the lifestyle of the *Imahos* exemplified whiteness and purity". A *sotah,* a woman suspected of immorality, brings a sacrifice without the usual *levona* - see *Rashi, Bamidbar* 5:15 because *levona* stands for whiteness and purity, whilst the sotah appears to have behaved in a dark and impure manner.

The name of a person personifies his main qualities. Hence, since the *imahos* were named *levona,* we see that the trait of *tznius* was highlighted in them above all their other qualities. This induced the *Maharal MiPrague zt'l* to write the following (*Gevuros Hashem,* chapter 60): הרי שנשתבחו האמהות בפרט בצניעות, כי עיקר שבח האשה ומדריגתה העליונה היא הצניעות - "We see that the *Imahos* were praised and credited primarily for their *tznius* because **the ultimate distinction of a woman and her supreme greatness is her perfection in *tznius*"**. Such a statement, by as great an authority as the *Maharal,* is a remarkable statement indeed!

In line with the thoughts just expressed, it is fitting to quote the following excerpt from a speech given in *Kislev* 5754 by Harav Hagaon R' Elya Svei *shlita, Rosh Yeshiva* of Philadelphia, New York,:-

"The modern world around us has become entrenched in immorality and preoccupation with the basest instincts. This is painfully obvious when we look around ourselves. Should we, then, look to modern society to determine our values when it comes to men's and women's roles?" The *Rosh Yeshiva* bemoaned the lack of *tznius* in the modern civilization, where there is an almost total breakdown of the traditional separation between boys and girls and between men and women.

"*Tznius* must be the foundation of the Jewish home," the *Rosh Yeshiva* stressed. **"The essence of womanhood is *tznius*, and this trait is woman's anti-toxin to the *yetzer horah.***

"The Torah entrusts its greatest duty to women - the task of 'repairing the world' by building future generations and with this preserving the eternal purity of the Jewish people. Moreover, Jewish women are entrusted with the kindling of the Shabbos lights to symbolize their role in elevating the soul of mankind. They are also given the *mitzva* of separating *challah* - a *mitzva* that demonstrates faith and trust in G-d given as an antidote to, and directly after, the sin of the *meraglim* who lacked such trust.

"There was a time when Jewish mothers would shed tears in prayer for the spiritual growth of their children," continued Harav Svei "Today this is but a distant image fading from our midst".

4. TORAH LEARNING AND TZNIUS HAVE MUCH IN COMMON: The learning of Torah and the adherence to *tznius*, have much in common. They are both constant, ongoing *mitzvos* which are observed in accordance with the person's appreciation of them. Just as there should be no boundary to a man's devotion to Torah, likewise there should be no end to striving towards more *eidelkeit* and *tznius,* at both an external and internal level. The more these two great pillars of *Yiddishkeit* are cherished, the better they are kept. These efforts are well rewarded; they imbue the person with *kedusha* to enjoy Torah, *tefilla*, *mitzvos* and good *midos*, and serve as a most effective antidote to the inroads the *yetzer horah* is constantly trying to make.

Just as Torah learning starts with difficulty and perseverance, but this gradually gives way to love and attachment, so too, *tznius* entails at the start sacrifice and determination - such as not wearing a bright red coat one very much likes, or wearing a dress of the required length while the fashion has changed and everyone is wearing short clothes - but results in a deep appreciation and affinity for all that *kedusha* and *tahara* stand for.

Just as the *yetzer horah* does everything within its power to interrupt a person learning, or make him abandon Torah learning altogether, so too, the *yetzer horah* tries its best to deter a woman from *tznius*. His greatest accomplishment would be to make her abandon *tznius* in dress altogether. The *yetzer horah* knows that Torah learning is the fuel which ignites and drives the man's *neshama*. He therefore tries desperately to disrupt it and thereby prevent the person absorbing this life-giving substance into his being. Similarly, he is aware that *tznius* infuses *tahara* deeply into the woman's being. He therefore does everything in his power to hinder the woman from true adherence to its *halachos* - see 2:F:1-2 below.

Torah learning does not eradicate the person's natural inclinations (i.e. his passions and desires) but rather redirects them to serve in the fulfillment of *Hashem's* will. This is what *Chazal* mean by saying, בראתי יצר הרע בראתי לו תורה תבלין - "I created the *yetzer horah* and the Torah as a spice (an antidote) to it" (*Kiddushin* 30b), which in turn means that the Torah flavors and makes good what would otherwise be considered unfit (*Chofetz Chayim*). For example, the urge to befriend people is directed towards general *ahavas Yisroel* (loving *Yidden*), the streak of hatred is directed towards *sinas horah* (hating evil), the drive to spend money is used to give *tzedaka* and the urge to be miserly is used when considering buying unnecessary luxuries.

Similarly, *tznius*, being the counterpart of Torah learning, enables a woman to use her natural inclinations for the service of *Hashem*. For example, she beautifies herself at home to bring happiness to her husband and close family, rather than to find acclaim in the outside world; she speaks encouraging and heartwarming words (תורת חסד על לשונה), rather than gossip; and she makes it her business to find out if her friend is coping or is in need of help, rather than inquisitively mixing into other people's affairs.

In short, Torah learning and *tznius* are both the central axis upon which one's life turns. Their presence gives forth life, whilst their absence spells destruction. Fortunate is the person who cleaves to the tree of life!

5. IF ATTACHED TO SOURCE, WATER RISES UPWARDS - PARABLE: It follows, that whilst the body naturally pulls the person down to engage in all forms of worldly pleasures and desires, Torah learning and *tznius* call the *neshama* from on high to dominate the person's life and raise the aspirations and the entire body to the supreme service of *Hashem*.

Our *Avos* found their 'partners in life' at a באר - a well (*Breishis* 24:11, 29:1). The Torah is likewise called a *be'er*, באר חפרוה שרים - "A well dug by princes" (*Bamidbar* 21:18). There is something very unusual - and even intriguing - about the waters of a well. Water naturally runs downwards and descends to the lowest point possible. The water of a well, however, rises upwards, which is apparently totally against its nature. This, however, happens because of a special property of water: when attached to its source it rises upwards (as it tries to meet the level of its source). Therefore, the water in a well, which comes from surrounding hills and waters that have been absorbed in the surrounding grounds, rises upwards to meet the level of the waters to which it is attached. Hence, we have a remarkable phenomenon: being 'attached to the source' changes the complete course of events. It causes water to rise upwards and overcome its natural inclination to run downwards.

The same applies to a person who is truly attached to his source. Even though his bodily predisposition and bend would naturally pull him down and cause him to sink into a world of temptation and pleasure, nevertheless, when he is firmly attached to his *neshama,* this trend is reversed and his whole being strives upwards to purity, Torah and *mitzvos*. This 'attachment to the real source' exists when a man is devoted to Torah learning and when a woman fully embraces *tznius* and *chesed*.

Our *Avos* looked for their wives by a well. With this symbolized that they sought a wife, who, like the water of a well, is attached to her *neshama* by an all encompassing trait of *tznius* and wonderful devotion to *chesed*. The *Avos* knew that this attachment sanctifies the woman's whole being and ensures that she is worthy of becoming one of the forebearers of *Klal Yisroel*.

6. "A WOMAN SHOULD WORK ON HER TZNIUS" - CHAZON ISH: It is appropriate in this context to quote from the life story of Rebbetzen Karelitz *o.h.* the mother of Hagaon Harav Nissim Karelitz *shlita* ('Silence is Thy Praise' p.106):

"How much the *Chazon Ish* valued the modesty of a Jewish woman was perhaps best evident in the response he once gave when asked, 'What can a young lady do to match the merit of a young man's learning?'

'Let her work on her *tznius*!' he answered.

"The *Chazon Ish* considered the modesty of the Jewish woman a virtue so vitally important, that the effort in seeking to achieve this goal is a counterpart to the day-and-night Torah study and toil of a man. Simply put, the home needs Torah, and Torah needs a home characterized by virtue".

This statement underscores that which was explained above: *Tznius* involves much more than not wearing garments that are forbidden because of *pritzus*. It is a main artery, giving life to a heart that is to be filled with love and respect for Torah and *mitzvos* - see 7:D:4 below.

The very point made by the Chazon Ish, that true *tznius* requires a very positive effort on the part of the person, while to be inactive and just "not pursue *pritzus*" is wholly inadequate, is spelled out in no uncertain terms in the words of one of the *Rishonim*. Rabbeinu Menachem HaMeiri writes the following in the *Beis Habechira*, *Bava Basra* (57:) מדת הצניעות משובחת עד למאוד .... לא סוף דבר שלא לחזור אחר קלות ראש אלא אף להשתדל הרבה על הצניעות. This means: "The trait of *tznius* is exceptionally praiseworthy........ It does not just entail refraining from frivolous light-headedness; rather it involves a very conscious on-going effort to develop a high standard of *tznius* within oneself."

D. THE AFFINITY OF TZNIUS AND HUMILITY

1. TZNIUS HAS TWO MEANINGS: PURITY AND HUMILITY: The word צנוע, which literally means "hidden", is used to describe two attributes that are seemingly totally different from one another. On the one hand it is used for refinement of dress or conduct, the opposite of which is פריצות, inadequate dress or immoral conduct. On the other hand it is used for the trait of unpretentiousness and humility (ענוה), the opposite of which is גאוה, haughtiness and pride. The same occurs in the English language where the word "modesty" is used by people for both these traits which appear to be unconnected and two very different attributes. Although in both cases something is being "hidden" - in the former case the physical body and in the latter case the qualities and deeds of the person, which are hidden and withheld from the public eye - there is nevertheless apparently no true association between these two attributes. This, however, cannot be the case as they share one and the same name. Hence the question - what is their inner connection?

2. PRIDE - THE ANTITHESIS OF TZNIUS: The answer to the above is that to practice '*tznius* in dress' without possessing the character trait of humility is a totally incomplete *tznius* and of very little value. Without humility and refinement to underpin it, the *tznius* is in jeopardy from the start and in constant danger of being overturned. If a woman or girl is proud and seeks recognition, then even if she tries to dress quietly - as she is aware that a *Bas Yisroel* should dress with *tznius* - her urge for recognition will inevitably lead her to use excessive makeup, jewelry and the like to ensure that she is considered beautiful - see *Mekoros* 3:2.

Pride is a very slippery path. It is impossible to know how far a proud person will slip and how far it will take him off the *derech hayashar*. If at some point a girl who yearns for compliments has to live amongst people who look down at a girl dressed *b'tznius*, she will quickly succumb to the *nisayon* and shed or at least substantially modify her traditional Jewish mode of dress.

Therefore, those who educate girls in high schools and correctly insist on their dressing *b'tznius*, must at the same time develop in their pupils an appreciation for modesty and genuine refinement. Only in this way can the teacher be confident that the values she teaches her pupils will last a lifetime. The same, of course, applies to the basic *chinuch* given at home. From the earliest possible age, parents should implant modesty and unpretentious behavior in their children. For this reason it is particularly important that they rebuke children when they are domineering with their friends.

If a girl's pride is not stemmed in time, the often subconscious craving for admiration could grow to such proportions that her feelings for '*tznius*' will be greatly eroded. A girl's urge to be considered "modern" and "with it" and to be admired as being stylish and "chic", can drive her to wear totally inappropriate clothes that happen to be in the height of fashion. Since she craves for compliments and admiration, she will do anything that guarantees these returns.

Yeshaya HaNavi, in his harsh rebuke to the Jewish women of his time concerning their failings on matters of *tznius* (*Yeshaya* 3:16), starts with the words: ויאמר ה׳ יען גבהו בנות ציון ותלכנה נטויות גרון - "*Hashem Yisborach* said He is angered because the Daughters of Tzion are haughty and walk with their heads held high" (*Shabbos* 62b). Only after this admonishment does he mention that they paint their eyes excessively and engage in similar practices. Evidently, it was the feeling of importance and the pursuit of esteem that brought about their serious abandonment of *tznius* - see *Mekoros* 2:1.

3. THE URGE TO IMPRESS CAN LEAD TO IMPUDENCE: This often subconscious craving for admiration or the urge to be "looked up to" can eventually lead a person "to be daring" and do things which he would otherwise never have done. This is a well known phenomenon in classroom misbehavior. This is usually the force behind the drive in adolescent years to dress inappropriately or differently from everyone around. When this happens, pride has brought on חוצפה - impudence. The shameful dress of some girls e.g. walking around with patterned tights, with brightly-colored clothes and similar garb, stems from a craving to be noticed and impress.

In reality, shame and the need to cover oneself properly are feelings deeply rooted in human nature and particularly in the nature of *Yidden*. This trait is in fact present even in the animal kingdom. *R' Yochanan* says, אילמלא לא ניתנה תורה היינו למדין צניעות מחתול - "If the Torah had not been given we would have learned basic modesty and the need to cover ourselves from the cat," because cats are discreet when carrying out their bodily requirements (*Eruvin* 100b and see 2:H:4(a) below). In spite of this deep rooted nature, the desire for admiration overrides this urge and pushes the person to do things which, if not for their present blindness, would have been out of the question for them to do. Have *Chazal* not taught us that הקנאה

התאוה והכבוד מוציאין את האדם מן העולם - "Jealousy, lust and pride make a person an outcast from society!" (*Prikei Avos* 4:28).

An added twist to this transgression is the fact that once a garment has been worn by quite a few people, others who are not impudent will follow their example. Due to the wrongdoings of the *prutzos*, it will no longer be impossible to wear the garment - in spite of its shortcomings. There is a well known saying of *Chazal* concerning a person who erroneously thinks something is permitted because others do it. As someone is about to take a short cut through a field, the owner of the field shouts to him ליסטים כמותך כבשוה - "This field is private property! The path you see through the field was made by trespassers like yourself and must not be taken as a proof that I have allowed people to cross it!" (*Eruvin* 53b). The same is with immodest clothes - the offenders are חוטא ומחטיא את אחרים - "sinners who also cause others to sin". Little do these individuals realize what a heavy responsibility they carry on their shoulders! - see *Mekoros* 2:1 and 1:3.

4. HUMILITY - CONDUCIVE TO TZNIUS: As mentioned, being unpretentious and shunning the limelight are absolute prerequisites for *tznius*. They are so interdependent that they share the same Hebrew word, *tznius*. When a woman has humility (ענוה), she is naturally bashful (בושה) about everything related to her personal needs and physical requirements. Humility and bashfulness together bring about a deep feeling for *tznius*, because *tznius* is a perfect blend of humility and need for privacy. In short: pride (גאוה) and impertinence (חוצפה) lead to the worst forms of *pritzus*, whilst, modesty (ענוה) and bashfulness (בושה) lead to *tznius* in its finest and most *eidel* form.

In the book 'Eishes Chayil' (a biography of an outstanding *tznua* - see 1:O:2 below), Rebbetzen Elisheva Shechter's *o.h.* humility is highlighted. "Elisheva never displayed her vast knowledge. Whenever the words of the *Rambam*, the *Chovas Halevavos* or the *Mesilas Yesharim* were quoted at the Shabbos table or at a family gathering, she would listen quietly and closely as if the words were new to her. She never hinted that she was fully acquainted with what was being quoted. Only when someone erred in the quotation, or did not explain the meaning precisely, one could hear her murmur, as if she was repeating the correct version to herself. Only then did one get a quick glimpse of how much was deeply and carefully hidden inside her" (page 41).

Chazal teach us, בושתה של אשה מרובה משל איש - "The sense of embarrassment and shame of women exceeds that of men" (*Kesubos* 67b). In the times of *Chazal* women were so refined that a newly-wed young woman would hide her face during a meal with her in-laws, so as not to be seen eating (*Pesachim* 86b). These were the *Bnos Yisroel* of earlier times. When Jewish girls can sometime be seen nowadays walking along the street and in other public areas chewing gum in a most pronounced and undignified manner, a feeling of shame overcomes us at the deterioration of modesty and lack of refinement and sensitivity that has befallen us. To make matters even worse, in this age of casual dress and conduct, many girls do not even understand what is wrong with it!

5. WOMEN ARE RECIPIENTS OF APPRECIATION AT HOME: Women and girls need recognition and self-esteem just like everyone else. However, under normal circumstances a woman receives this at home, where her husband and grown-up children show her recognition and gratitude for all that she does. They also display their high esteem for her special individual qualities. With this healthy home-based recognition, a woman has no need to seek recognition and esteem elsewhere. Therefore, ideal home conditions enable a woman to happily face the world with her natural appearance, without beautifying herself with an overdose of cosmetics.

Likewise, an unmarried girl is appreciated at home and by her close friends. Here again, if this is done in a healthy measure, she should have no need to make a spectacle of her appearance, or ensure that her qualities be praised by all. This is one of the many interpretations of the verse כל כבודה בת מלך פנימה - (*Tehillim* 45:14); the Jewish daughter is held in high esteem at home and is therefore a *tznua* and an unassuming person outdoors.

6. ATTRACTING ATTENTION BY BEING EXCESSIVELY TZNUA: If a girl or woman wears overly *tznius'dik* clothes to exhibit her *tznius* and let everyone know just how *tznua* she is, she is in fact doing just the opposite of *tznius*. A fundamental feature of *tznius* is to avoid drawing attention to oneself, and this person is using *tznius'dik* clothing to do just the opposite. Moreover, "showing off" is hazardous to *tznius*, as explained earlier. It has the potential of causing the person to abandon *tznius* altogether, as pride and *pritzus* are closely related. Since people have a natural inclination to show off, one must be on guard not to allow *tznius* to manufacture the ammunition with which to destroy itself.

It is therefore wrong for a girl to wear a skirt that is almost down to the ground, to wear overly dull or sullen garments, to walk with overly refined steps and so on. As explained, over-exhibiting *tznius* is itself a lack of *tznius*.

It is wrong to do most of these things even with pure intentions because they after all attract attention which is the antithesis of *tznius*. Although she has no bad intentions, she is nevertheless forsaking the sacred call of *tznius* when she behaves in this manner. It is similarly unrefined for a girl to sway excessively during *davening* as she displays her pious qualities for all to see.

The *Gemara* (*Avoda Zarah* 18a) relates a story about the daughter of *Rebbi Chanina Ben Tradyon,* who was such a refined person that her footsteps were particularly soft and unassertive, reflecting her refinement. She was once in Rome and some of the local nobles saw her. They were most impressed with the way she walked and even commented on it. The young lady overheard their comments and immediately "improved upon" her refined walk, so that everyone would notice just how *tznius'dik* she was. For this misconduct she was severely punished as the *Gemara* relates.

Her failing lay in the fact that, although blessed with a fine sense of *tznius*, she allowed her *yetzer horah* to trip her up and cause her to seek to impress others with her special ways. For a person with an acute sense of *tznius*, this error of judgement was viewed as an incursion into the negative realm of *pritzus* and a serious blunder. [Based on the *Mesilas Yesharim* Chap. 16 who explains that she walked with refined footsteps even before hearing the comment] - see *Mekoros* 3:2.

E. RELATIONSHIP OF TZNIUS WITH BASHFULNESS

1. A HEALTHY MEASURE OF BUSHA LEADS TO TZNIUS:

(a) Bashfulness leads to *tznius* in dress: Bashfulness and shame, in an appropriate and healthy measure, are very Jewish traits. When accompanied with the right *chinuch*, they help a girl become a true *tznua*. Concerning *tznius* of dress, *Chazal* say that the word לבושה is a condensed form of the two words לא בושה - "an item that ensures that the person is not shamed by lack of cover" (*Shabbos* 77b). Therefore, once someone is blessed with the right measure of sensitivity and shame, they will naturally feel the need to cover all that should be covered.

(b) *Busha* leads to righteousness whilst *chutzpa* leads to wickedness: The extreme importance of this cherished trait of shame is expressed by *Chazal* when they say בושת פנים לגן עדן (*Pirkei Avos* 5:20) "the trait of shame prevents a person doing wrong and therefore leads him to *Gan Eden*". In the same vein *Chazal* say, כל המתבייש לא במהרה הוא חוטא - "He who possesses the *midah* of shame will not easily sin" (*Nedarim* 20a). In contrast *Chazal* say עז פנים לגיהנום (*ibid*) - "cheek and impudence cause a person to sin, and hence lead him to *gehinom*".

The following is a quote from the *Chorev* by Hagaon Harav Samson Raphael Hirsch *zt'l*, chapter 67: "Flee from the approach of immorality! There stands the guardian "shame" which *Hashem* Himself has set out for you as the guardian of innocence, of moral purity and of holiness. Do not scare away this faithful guardian. Do not trample it down so that it can no longer raise its warning cry when you approach the sphere of the unholy. Be afraid of the animal in you, fear for your future when you catch yourself able to see and hear certain things without being overcome by shame; and avoid associating with those whose shameless speech makes you feel uncomfortable - they are murderers of shame." These are strong but deeply true words.

(c) Women have a greater sense of shame than men: It has been mentioned in 1:D:4 that women have a greater measure of this cherished trait than men, as *Chazal* say, בושתה של אשה מרובה משל איש - "The sense of shame and embarrassment of women surpasses that of men" (*Kesubos* 67b). For this reason, if money is short, a husband must enable his wife to buy clothes she needs before he purchases the clothes he requires (*Yevamos* 62b).

In this vein it is considered unnatural for a girl or woman to walk the streets appealing for alms (*Kiddushin* 22a) or to look for a property to purchase (*Gittin* 52a *Bava Basra* 108b). Moreover, when a man and a woman come to *Beis Din* at the same time for two independent lawsuits, the woman is attended to before the man, because the situation disturbs the woman more than the man (*Yevamos* 100a and *Rambam, Sanhedrin* 21:6). Also, when a woman has a court case with someone, she should whenever possible avoid going to *Beis Din* herself, since it is shameful for a woman to be publicly involved in a court case. Instead she sends someone else to the *Beis Din* to deputize on her behalf (*Shevuous* 30a).

(d) *Busha* and *tznius* - ammunition against the *yetzer horah*: Since women have a particularly rich measure of this *midah,* they are naturally in possession of a "powerful weapon" with which to combat their *yetzer horah.* With *tznius* of dress and conduct, women safeguard their *busha* - bashfulness and keep it intact. This is one of the reasons why *tznius* is of such critical importance to women - and why *tznius* is a source of strength to women in the same way as Torah learning is a source of strength to men (as explained in 1:C above).

2. SHYNESS IS NOT SYNONYMOUS WITH TZNIUS:

(a) Even a shy girl must be carefully educated to *tznius*: Although shyness in young people in an appropriate measure is desirable, and indicates that the young girl will hopefully grow up to have the refinement expected of a *Bas Yisroel*, shyness is nevertheless not at all the same as *tznius*. A girl can erroneously be thought of as possessing *tznius*, because, when she is in public or among people with whom she is not closely acquainted, she withdraws or is even tongue-tied, and her actions are guarded and inconspicuous. This, however, may simply be shyness based on a feeling of unease or of being overawed by those present, which inhibits her from speaking loudly or pushing herself forward. Her character may, however, may really not be so and she would have reacted very differently had she not felt intimidated.

Therefore, if parents see that their daughter is excessively shy and reserved, they must not take this as an indication that she has a natural understanding for *tznius* and does not require education and encouragement to dress and behave *b'tznius*. She may in fact be more in need of such education than other girls. The shyness could eventually subside and bring with it a sudden desire to be outgoing and sociable in order to break free of the shackles of the shyness altogether. If she has not been shown what refined behavior is, she will not know right from wrong.

(b) *Tznius* will stop a person sinning, whilst shyness might not: One must be warned that shyness which has not been developed into *tznius* and personal refinement, is not a reliable medium to stop a person doing even a very serious sin. The Torah writes that Yehuda did not recognize his previous daughter-in-law Tamar because ויחשבה לזונה כי כסתה פניה - "He thought she was a *zonah* for she had covered her face" (*Breishis* 35:15). The *Ramban* explains that it was the way of a *zonah* to cover part of her face and hair, to hide her identity so that she not be ashamed of all who know her. Her natural feelings of unease would have inhibited her but she finds a way around them by masking some of her main features so that people cannot recognize her.

The Ramban furthermore writes that she covers her face כי בעבור שתעיז פניה ותאמר לו ותחזק בו וכו׳ תכסה קצת הפנים - this means (approximate translation), "Because she is about to be brazen and impudent and approach someone to sin etc., she has a need to overcome her natural timidity and self-consciousness (due to which she is uneasy even before people who do not recognize her). This she does by covering part of her face so that she cannot be seen properly". Having overcome the problem caused by her natural shyness, she is now free to pursue her miserable misdeeds. All this underscores that shyness alone will not prevent sin, and that with a determined *yetzer horah,* ways will be found to overcome the constraints and problems caused by the shyness.

In contrast, *tznius* and true *busha* will stop a person sinning (as mentioned in the sayings of *Chazal* quoted in No. 1 above). Firstly, a *tznua* is ashamed of herself, and her modesty and *eidelkeit* will not allow her to do that which is sinful and degrading. Furthermore, a *tznua* is ashamed of *Hashem*, of Whose presence she is very much aware. See *Mishna Berura* (2:1) who writes, והאדם צריך להתנהג בצניעות ובושה לפני הקב״ה ואפילו כשהוא בלילה ובחדרי חדרים הלא מלא כל הארץ כבודו וכחשיכה כאורה לפניו יתברך - "A person must conduct himself with *tznius* and modesty before *Hashem*. This applies even at night and in a secluded room because *Hashem*'s Presence is everywhere and to Him there is no difference between light and dark".

The *Biur Halacha* 3:1 s.v. *Yehei Tznua,* refers to public places such as *shuls* which have inadequate bathroom facilities. He writes in no uncertain terms, that any conditions which undermine human dignity and are degrading to any respectable person, are a breach of *tznius* and could even be subject to an *issur min haTorah* - see 4:B:1(e). Although this conduct has nothing whatsoever to do with immorality, it is nevertheless considered a severe shortcoming of *tznius,* because the person who is aware of *Hashem*'s Presence is compelled to behave with respectability. Therefore, to destroy this personal dignity, means to destroy one's sensitivity and refinement, and inevitably also one's awareness that *Hashem* is Omnipresent.

3. TZNIUS IS DUE TO FULFILLMENT - IN CONTRAST TO SHYNESS: Excessive shyness is associated with a feeling of insecurity and of being inferior. On the other hand, *tznius* develops on the fertile ground of fulfillment and from appreciating the special role of a Jewish woman. The truly tznius'dik woman knows that wives and mothers are an embodiment of purity in the sanctuary of the Jewish home. She also understands that purity requires protection and must be guarded against all forms of contamination. Hence, with *tznius,* she consolidates and protects her lofty position in the ranks of the Jewish people.

Moreover, she dresses with *tznius* because of her deep-rooted satisfaction due to which she feels no need to show off or to seek additional acclaim. In her uncomplicated and happy state of mind, she dresses and behaves with the natural modesty and finesse that is the hallmark of the Jewish woman.

4. A TZNUA IS EIDEL AND REFINED EVEN WHEN FULLY AT EASE: The true test as to whether a particular person's quiet and refined behavior is genuine *tznius* or not, is how this woman or girl reacts when she is completely at ease in her environment and has no cause to feel shy. If she then behaves loudly, dresses carelessly and lacks refinement, her contrasting behavior in public must be mainly because of shyness, not *tznius*. However, if, due to her modesty and finesse she remains in the background, and is quiet and refined even though she has no reason to be shy, her behavior is evidently due to *tznius* and is most praiseworthy - see *Mekoros* 83:5-6.

Chazal say, כל כלה שהיא צנועה בבית חמיה זוכה ויוצאין ממנה נביאים ומלכים - "A daughter-in-law who is modest when in the house of her in-laws will merit having children who are *Nevi'im* and Kings (i.e. men of the greatest caliber)" - *Sotah* 10b and *Megilla* 10b. A daughter-in-law usually feels very comfortable and well-accepted in the house of her in-laws, as the family goes out of its way to make her welcome and help her feel completely at ease - see *Rashi Yuma* 54a s.v. *B'bayis,* and *Kesubos* 71b s.v. *K'kallah.* On the other hand, at her in-laws, she is in the close proximity of men who are not her blood relatives and could therefore be attracted by her *chein* and appearance. This includes her father-in-law and brothers-in-law to whom she is an *ervah*. She must therefore be on guard to be dressed correctly at all times, and to behave with friendliness but at the same time with modesty, so as not to be overly familiar and close.

A woman who practices *tznius* at her in-laws even though she is fully relaxed there, is truly a *tznua*. *Chazal* say about her that, just as she practices *tznius* to safeguard her father-in-law and brothers-in-law, so, too, she will merit having sons who will be *Nevi'im,* whose duty it is to safeguard *Klal Yisroel* from going astray. This is מדה כנגד מדה - an appropriate and fitting reward for her good deeds. Nowadays, when we have no *Nevi'im*, this would mean having sons who are *Gedolei Yisroel*, who stand guard to maintain the *kedusha* and purity of the Jewish people - *Ben Yehoyada* by the *Ben Ish Chai, Sotah* 10b.

On the Verse (*Tehillim* 45:14) כל כבודה בת מלך פנימה the *Midrash Tanchuma* (*Vayishlach* 6) writes, אם תכבד עצמה בתוך הבית תנשא למי שכתוב

בו ושבצת כתונת שש - "If she displays nobility and dignity inside her home she is worthy of marrying [a *Kohen Gadol*] about whom it is written that he has an inner garment of checker work that is made of fine linen [the *k'sones*]". The *Midrash* is telling us as follows: The ultimate modesty is *tznius* that is practiced at home away from the discerning eye of the world. If a woman is aristocratic in her conduct, and displays royal conduct in the inner chambers of her home, ממשבצות זהב לבושה - she will be worthy of marrying a *Kohen Gadol* who dresses in beautiful inner clothes within the privacy of the Sanctuary and stands as a symbol of modesty and *tahara* in *Klal Yisroel* - see *Mekoros* 83:1-6.

F. ATTITUDE TO TZNIUS - REFLECTED IN DRESS AND CONDUCT

1. A TZNUA TAKES NO CHANCES:

(a) A Tznua is careful with her dress, conduct and personal safety: It is part of the nature of *tznius* not to take any chances. A *tznua* will see to it that her garments are guaranteed to cover her properly at all times. For example, if she knows from experience that when her hair is long it slips out of her *sheitel* or *tiechel*, she will keep her hair short to ensure that this does not inadvertently happen (as stated in 5:D:1 below). She will see to it that her sleeves and skirt are long enough to ensure that, whatever position she is in, her elbows and knees will remain properly covered (as stated in 6:H:3 below). If a garment has a slit, she will sew it up and not be satisfied just with buttoning, because when getting in and out of a car the stretching sometimes undoes the buttons (as stated in 6:J:5 below). Similarly, she will ensure that her dress is properly opaque, and will not risk wearing a borderline garment hoping that the dress will not be see-through (as stated in 6:D below).

A *tznua* will not venture into the yard in night clothes even when no one seems to be in sight, because of the possibility that she is in fact being seen (as stated in 7:E:1 below). When using cosmetics she will take care that she does not beautify herself to the point that could cause men to gaze at her (as stated in 7:K:3 below). In the same vein she will not sing in a place where someone other than her closest family could possibly hear her (as stated in 8:B below). Likewise, she will not go out alone late at night when undesirable people may be around; she will not endanger her purity even though it is far fetched that someone will approach her. These are just a few of many such examples.

(b) Ruth safeguarded herself against all eventualities: This character trait of avoiding all risks is vividly portrayed in the story of Ruth. When Ruth went for the first time to the field to collect fallen stalks, the verse says ותלך ותבא ותלקט בשדה - "She went, she came and she collected in the field" (*Ruth* 2:3). *Rashi* asks the obvious: "she came" means "she came home" once again. Since she will have come home only after having collected why does the verse say "she came" before mentioning that she had collected.

To this *Rashi* writes a remarkable answer in the name of the *Midrash*. Ruth, who was a stranger in the district, wanted to make sure that she would know her way home. She therefore went to the field, noted the landmarks, and then returned almost to Naomi's house, thereby checking that she knew the way back. She then set out once again to the field and started collecting. Ruth was afraid that by the time she finished collecting it might be dark and no one would be around to direct her home. Should this happen she would be stranded in the open overnight.

Later we are told (*Rashi, Ruth* 3:6) that, when she went down late at night to the barn where Boaz slept, she did not follow all Naomi's instructions. Naomi had told her that before leaving the house she should dress in Shabbos clothes. Ruth reasoned that to do so was not *tznius'dik*, as she could be seen dressed in finery at that time of the night and be suspected of being a *zonah*. To avoid giving such an impression she took her Shabbos clothes with her and changed only when she arrived at the barn.

Ruth took no chances and ran a "no risks policy". When she had to go out very late at night to the barn, she took precautions just in case people would be around at that late hour and they would form a bad impression of her. She therefore did not don her Shabbos clothes until she arrived at her destination. On the other hand, when she went to collect fallen stalks she took precautions, just in case people would not be around even at that early part of the night to show her the way home, and she would be left to wander overnight, with its inherent dangers.

The trend that comes through in no uncertain terms is that Ruth took no chances. Although things could work out alright, this was not guaranteed, and she would not do something that could endanger her *tznius*. [See further practical applications of "taking no chances" in 9:I below. More about the *tznius* of Ruth in 1:N:4, 6:Q:4, 9:I:7 and 10:C:3 below].

2. A TRUE BAS YISROEL IS HAPPY TO DRESS WITH TZNIUS: *Tznius* is a very positive attribute, and the manner of dress should reflect that the person gladly and happily dresses in that way. By doing so, she makes a constant *Kiddush Hashem* and educates others to do the same. They learn from her to appreciate the strength and inner beauty of the *Bas Yisroel*.

If a woman or girl does not at present feel a love or a positive attitude towards *tznius*, she should not give up or despair. Just as a taste can be acquired by eating the food, so too, by dressing and conducting oneself in a *tznius'dik* manner, a woman or girl can "acquire a taste" and cultivate a positive attitude towards this delightful *mitzva*. [This is provided she does not harbor a distinct dislike for the *mitzva*, because such an outlook could hamper and block the natural effect] - see *Mekoros* 4:4.

When one speaks to *ba'alei t'shuva* about their experiences, they will invariably impart the information that they learnt to value and cherish Shabbos, not by hearing lengthy lectures about it, but by being invited to spend a Shabbos, or participate in a Shabbos meal, with a *heimishe* family, thereby experiencing the atmosphere and warmth of Shabbos. The reality of *kedushas* Shabbos with its many delights, dispel and banish the argument that Shabbos is a difficult day as certain activities and types of enjoyment are forbidden on it. Those who keep Shabbos, know that the beautiful Shabbos spirit is partially born out of these very abstentions, and that in many homes Shabbos is such a delight that it is looked forward to with anticipation from the beginning of the week. The same is with *tznius*: All that might mistakenly be suggested about the hardships and tribulations it causes, fades into oblivion once one feels the bliss and *kedusha* that emanates from it.

3. 'JUST COVERED' OSSUR AND SHOWS UNHEALTHY ATTITUDE: Skirts and dresses that just cover the knee when the person stands straight are incorrect to wear, for two reasons: Firstly, the *Poskim* have ruled that the garment must extend at least a tefach - 4 inches (10 cm.) below the lowest point of the knee, to guarantee proper cover in all positions, as was mentioned above. Secondly, such a garment does not display an appreciation for *tznius*, as it seems to show that the wearer finds it difficult to do what is right. When a garment is "just Kosher", it is tantamount to saying, "Reluctantly, I'll agree to follow the most minimal line of the *halacha*". The same applies to sleeves that just cover the elbows. This is incorrect both in terms of the letter of the law and the spirit of the law - see 6:F:1 below.

Covering till just past the knees (without the additional four inches) has another great drawback. If women and older girls cover just this far, younger girls will certainly do the same. As all parents know, children seem to "shoot up", and are suddenly found to be one or two centimeters taller than they were when last measured. A growing girl, whose dress just covers her knees may "suddenly", as a result of growing rapidly, be wearing a garment that does not even reach her knees, before one is aware about it.

Many people buy food only with the best *hechsher* and only *glatt* Kosher meat; they fit out their kitchen in such a way that there is total separation between milk and meat, to prevent even the slightest mix-up; they likewise spend a considerable sum of money on Pesach, on first class *tefillin, mezuzos* and *arba minim*. Why should the *mitzva* of והיה מחניך קדוש - "the environment in which *Yidden* live should be holy" (from which the obligation of *tznius* is learnt) - be orphaned or treated as a "second class citizen", when most other *mitzvos* have been given a place of honor in our lives??

G. ADHERING TO DRESS OF LOCAL SHOMREI MITZVOS

1. "ACCEPTED NORMS" MAY DIFFER FROM PLACE TO PLACE: Nowadays, many young men and women study far from their home countries. Moreover, many settle after marriage in countries or *kehillos* other than where they were brought up. Furthermore, nowadays many people travel to *Eretz Yisroel* or other countries for Y*omtov* or sightseeing. A danger to *tznius* results from this increased mobility. This must be pointed out so that people are aware of its inherent pitfalls.

The problem that arises is that ways of dress and accepted norms of cosmetics and jewelry (even of fully-Orthodox women and girls) are often very different from one place to another. If people move to a new place and continue their previous lifestyle, they will inevitably attract attention to themselves by being different from everyone else, even though this style of life was typical for everyone in their original place and did not attract attention. *Eretz Yisroel* in particular suffers from people who overlook this fact and this causes in some circles a lessening of standards of *tznius* and refinement. See *Biur Halacha* 75 s.v. *Michutz*, that the local standard must be kept by everyone, including visitors.

This difference of attitudes between different places can be due to a number of causes:-

(a) Different places have different standards of *tznius*: The feelings for *tznius* may be much stronger and the standard of *tznius* much higher in one place than in another. For example, in some places in *chutz l'aretz* people use cosmetics substantially while in devout circles in *Eretz Yisroel* and also in many other *kehillos* in *chutz l'aretz* generous use of cosmetics is disliked and considered as over-beautification. Therefore, to continue one's previous style of life in the new place is beyond the bounds of *tznius*. Similarly, certain styles of dress may be fine in one place but thought of as inappropriate in another.

(b) 'Currently in fashion' differs from place to place: Local ways of dress differ considerably from one place to another. A certain style could be the height of fashion in one place but almost out of fashion in another place. To wear what is locally in the "height of fashion" has the effect of fostering the unpleasant and harmful practice of "fashion-tracking," while to wear the same thing elsewhere could be quite acceptable. For example, certain colors of hosiery may be fully accepted in one place, as they cover the leg very well and cannot be mistaken for the skin, yet are totally unacceptable in another place, being considered as ultra-modern, showy and unrefined - see 6:M below.

[If a woman or girl were to adopt the principle that she will wear whatever can be proven from *T'nach* or *Shas* that our *Imahos* or other *nashim tznuos* wore, maintaining that such items must be fully *tznius'dik*, she would be making a serious blunder. Times have changed, and that which was fully acceptable in those times, would be strange and even extremely unrefined when worn in present-day society!

For example, Avraham Avinu sent jewelry with Eliezer his servant to be given to the girl who would be chosen to be the wife of Yitzchak. Among the items sent was a nose-ring - see *Breishis* 24:47. Evidently, in those days a nose-ring was a refined and respectable piece of jewelry. Nonetheless, it goes without saying that, if a woman wore such an ornament within our society, she would be considered a *prutza*, as she would be adorning herself with something which is ostentatious and extremely unrefined according to present-day norms. This underscores the point stated: places and times differ very much from one another, and one must not assume that everything which is acceptable in one society is likewise acceptable in another].

(c) A person is conspicuous if dressed distinctly different to others: A certain way of dress may be long established among *Yidden* in one place, whilst in a second place this is not a Jewish way of dress. If a woman wears this form of dress in the second place, she not only appears to be copying others, but she is broadcasting her presence wherever she goes, since people notice someone who is dressed very differently from everyone else.

(d) When a stringent opinion is followed locally but not elsewhere: There are certain areas of *Hilchos Tznius* in which there is a dispute amongst the *Poskim*. For example, some *Poskim* forbid a married woman to wear a *sheitel* whilst others permit it. As is well known, nowadays most of *Klal Yisroel* follow the opinion which permits *sheitels*. There are, however, some communities which follow the stringent opinion and strictly forbid the wearing of a *sheitel* - see 5:D:1. Similarly concerning tights, some maintain that only totally opaque tights are Kosher (the opinion of the Satmar Rav *zt'l*) whilst others permit less than this. As stated in 1:G:1 above, a person is obligated not to differ from the *halachic* stringencies and customs that are practiced by the local people - see *Mekoros* 47- 49.

2. REASONS WHY LOCAL STANDARDS MUST BE KEPT BY ALL: As stated, when someone who lives in a place where a certain mode of dress is allowed, visits an area where it is not allowed, she is *halachically* obliged to dress according to the standards of the local community, and must not wear something which local people consider a lack of *tznius*.

To do so would be incorrect on four counts:-

(a) If not common locally, it attracts attention to her: By dressing in such a way she will be different from everyone else and as such will be noticed wherever she goes. To be overly noticeable is wrong, because a woman or girl should be careful not to attract people's attention to herself. (See *Rabbeinu Yona* in *Iggeres HaTeshuva* No. 58 and *Mekoros* 69).

This holds true when there is no valid reason for this woman or girl to dress differently than everyone else. However, if she dresses differently because of a *halachic* issue in which her family or place of origin are stringent, no *issur* is involved. The local people will usually be aware that there are opinions which are stringent, and when a justified reason for dressing differently to others is well known, the negative effect of doing so is greatly lessened. For example, a woman who has her arm in a sling may certainly go out, even though she will be noticed and will strike attention, because it is understood that she is not seeking the attention and it would be unjustifiable to force her to stay at home. So too, when a difference in dress stems from a *halachic* issue that is involved, it can be disregarded.

(b) If uncommon locally, it could well be considered showy: It is wrong to wear something which is locally considered as showy or unrefined. It is an elementary rule of *tznius* that a person must consider the effect their way of dress will have on others (*Sotah* 22a). If others will feel that dressing in this way is a departure from *kedushas Yisroel*, then to do so is undermining *kedushas Yisroel* and will cause a lessening of *tznius*.

(c) Disregarding feelings of others is a lack of *derech eretz*: It is offensive to the local people to disregard their ways. *Chazal* say, דברים המותרים ואחרים נהגו בהם איסור אי אתה רשאי להתיר לפניהם - "Issues which are *halachically* permitted but there are people who are stringent and forbid them, one may not be lenient and permit them in their presence" (*Pesachim* 50a, *Orach Chayim* 468:3,4) - see 6:S:3(c) below.

(d) Causing others to copy her, lowers local standards: By displaying other ways of dress, she could easily influence some of the local girls and ladies to abandon locally-accepted standards and instead copy her way of dress. If this should happen she will have caused a lessening and even partial disintegration of locally accepted standards of *tznius* - see 6:M:3.

The *Ben Ish Chai* writes the following in his *sefer, Chukei Nashim* (Chap. 17), אמת הדבר כי אשה מותרת ללבוש מלבוש המתאים ויפה לה וכו׳ אבל כל מלבוש שאינו מקובל בין הנשים היהודיות אסור לה ללובשה - "True a woman may wear [even in public] garments that suit her well and enhance her appearance. She must, however, not wear a garment that [local] Jewish women feel should not be worn".

3. APPRECIATING THE IMPORTANCE OF THIS HALACHA: This *halacha* is of enormous importance, since women mistakenly think that if in their home town a competent *Rav* allowed a certain mode of dress or cosmetics, they have a license to follow his ruling anywhere in the world. This is most definitely not the case, and the *Rav* himself would agree that in places where the local custom is to be stringent no one has the right to do otherwise.

Mistakes related to this principle of *tznius* cause many inadvertent acts of *pritzus*. They also hamper efforts that are made to improve adherence to the *halachos* of *tznius*, because people see that there are very Orthodox visitors who simply don't abide by the rulings of the local *Rabbanim*. These visitors do not realize that not only is it presumptuous to go against local Rabbinical opinion, but they are utterly wrong in thinking that they can rely on their *Rav* back home, because his *psak* was not given for other localities.

4. STUDENTS MUST DRESS TO LOCALLY-ACCEPTED STANDARDS: Girls coming from different walks of life to an international educational institution such as a seminary must be told as soon as possible about the way of dress that is acceptable locally, so that they dress accordingly. It is sometimes difficult for them to understand why they should not wear a very long skirt, to take but one example, when they come from a *Torah'dik* background where many girls wear such garments. It must be explained to them that a girl may not dress differently from everyone else even if her dress is perfectly *tznius'dik*, as that itself would be a serious flaw in *tznius'dik* behavior.

The same applies in a reverse situation. If a mode of dress is permitted in a seminary, as it is in accordance with the way the local *shomrei mitzvos* dress, it could nevertheless be *ossur* for a girl to dress in that way when she arrives home. If it is not permitted or is disliked in her home-town, being considered as ultra modern (according to local standards) or simply very different to what everyone else wears, then this girl must not wear it at home, even though it was allowed in the seminary.

5. HOME-TOWN STANDARDS MUST BE KEPT WHEREVER ONE IS: If a woman lives in a place which has a stringency concerning what must be covered, but she has gone temporarily to a place where this stringency is not practiced, she remains duty bound to uphold the accepted *minhag* of her home-town even in the second place. For example, if she comes from a community in which women cover the complete forearm, she must keep this *minhag* even when in a place where women do not cover the complete lower section of the arm. Similarly, if a woman belongs to a community which considers it wrong to wear a *sheitel* - and all therefore wear a *tiechel* - it is *ossur* for her to wear a *sheitel* even if she is at present in a community which allows *sheitels* - (*Biur Halacha* 75:2 s.v. *Michutz*).

This is a *halacha* of major significance for seminary girls who must know that they have no right to be lenient on things that are accepted as stringencies in their home-towns - see 6:G:2 below. [An exception to this is something which is not worn in one's home-town because locally it is not Jewish dress, whilst in another area it is Jewish dress, for example, black completely opaque hosiery. People at home do not refrain from wearing it because of a stringency but because it is non-Jewish wear. Therefore, in a place where it is considered Jewish wear, there is no reason not to wear it].

This *halacha* is in line with a general *halachic* rule: A person remains obligated to keep *minhagim* practiced in his home town even if he has gone for some time to a different environment where this *minhag* is not practiced (*Orach Chayim* 468:4). For example if an *Ashkenazi* is visiting a North African *Sephardi* country over *Pesach*, he may not eat "*kitnius*" (all types of pulses, seeds etc.) although the local *Sephardi Yidden* eat *kitnius* on *Pesach* (the abstention from *kitnius* being only a *minhag* of *Ashkenazim, Orach Chayim* 453:1). Similarly, he may not have a haircut from *Shivah Ossor B'Tamuz*, although generally *Sephardim* refrain from haircutting only in the week of *Tisha B'Av* (M.B. 551:82).

If a woman or girl has moved permanently to a new place, she is not *halachically* duty bound to keep the stringencies and *minhagim* of her original home town. Since she does not intend to live there any longer she is no longer considered a member of that community. Instead, she may follow the local *minhag* even if in some ways it is more lenient - as long as the leniency is *halachically* permitted (*Biur Halacha* 75:2 s.v. *Michutz).*

H. TZNIUS - OBLIGATION IN EVERY TYPE OF COMMUNITY

1. TZNIUS WHEN ONLY FRUM YIDDEN LIVE IN THE AREA: Let no one say that her mode of dress will do no harm because she lives among "*erlicher Yidden*" who surely do not look at women and will not notice the ostentatious garments she wears or the excessive makeup she puts on. This way of thinking is erroneous for many reasons:

(a) Great people have great *nisyonos*: Firstly, the more devout the *Yid*, the greater the assault of the *yetzer horah* on him, as *Chazal* say כל הגדול מחבירו יצרו גדול הימנו - "The greater the person the more intense is his *yetzer horah*" (*Succah* 52a). One can in fact see this phenomenon in the physical world around us. The more delicate an item, the more easily and the more speedily it is spoiled by its environment. A fruit such as a peach is far more sensitive to a "bad neighbor" than the coarse potato. So too, *tzadikim* who lead a pure untainted way of life, are in greater danger of being affected by *pritzus* and inadequate dress than people of a mediocre level of *Yiddishkeit*. (See *sefer, K'reina D'igrsa* 1:331).

Accordingly, the special purity of the local inhabitants must never be taken as a justification for lessening standards in matters of *tznius*, as even devout *Yidden* can slip and transgress the *issur* of ולא תתורו אחרי עיניכם - the *issur* of gazing at women and girls (*Bamidbar* 15:39). Therefore, when the guidelines of *tznius* are disregarded by local women and girls, the environment becomes very detrimental even to the finest people in the society. See 6:D:1(b) below where this point is elaborated upon and see *Mekoros* 4:1-2.

Concerning a *sotah* (a woman brought to the *Beis Hamikdosh* under suspicion of having committed adultery), the Torah writes that a *Kohen* should reveal her hair and parts of her body. In connection with that it mentions twice that the *Kohen* should stand with her לפני השם - "before *Hashem*" (*Bamidbar* 5:16,18). The *Midrash* (*Bamidbar* 9:16) explains that these words are repeated as a warning to the *Kohen* not to be enticed by the undone hair and partially revealed body of the *sotah* and slip into הרהורי עבירה - "forbidden thoughts" (see *Pirush Maharzu, ibid*). The *Kohen* is therefore reminded that he is "before *Hashem*" and this awareness should help him control himself.

This saying of *Chazal* is an insight into the power of the *yetzer horah* to entice any type of person to sin, particularly in matters related to *arayos*. Hagaon Harav Henach Leibowitz *shlita, Rosh Yeshivas Chofetz Chayim* N.Y., in his *sefer, Mussar HaTorah,* observes:- Here stands a woman accused of a terrible *aveirah* and likely soon to die a most terrible death before the *Kohen's* very eyes. Nevertheless, if he does not guard himself he may be attracted by revealed parts of her hair and body and this will cause him to sin. A Kohen - the holiest class of person in *Klal Yisroel,* doing his duty in the holiest of places - the *Beis Hamikdosh,* is not safe and secure from the unremitting attempts of the *yetzer horah*. It is incredible how weak and fragile human beings are as far as *arayos*-related sins are concerned.

The *Gaon* and *Tzaddik* Rav Elya Lopian *zt'l* related the following incident: The *Chofetz Chayim zt'l* was once at a meeting with other *Rabbanim* in the town of Grodna when a young female helper walked passed them dressed in an inadequate way. On noticing this, the *Chofetz Chayim* reacted angrily and said to those near to him, "*Vos maint zie, as mir zenen Malachim?*" - "What does she imagine, that we are angels?" When women realize that men are drawn to look at them and might be affected by inadequacies in their dress, they will appreciate the considerable responsibility they have to dress properly and will listen to the detailed *halachos* of *tznius* laid down by *Chazal* - see *Mekoros* 4:5.

A further incident involving the *Gaon* and *Tzaddik* Rav Elya Lopian *zt'l* was as follows: He was once approached by a *bachur* in the *yeshiva* for permission to attend the wedding of a relative in a different town. Reb Elya asked him if he was sure that there would be no *pritzus* at the wedding. The *bachur* tried to avoid the question (for he knew that there would be *pritzus* there) and said, "But my father, mother and myself will sit at a special table," adding, "*Mir vert dos nisht shuten,*" - "It will not do me any harm". Reb Elya shuddered at this response and said to the *bachur*, "Listen to me! I am over eighty years old and blind in one eye" (after an operation he became very ill and lost the sight of one eye), "and nevertheless when I go along the street, I worry lest I stumble into looking at what I may not look at. And you, a young *bachur* with two healthy eyes, tell me that you are convinced that being at such a wedding will do you no harm!" (*Lev Eliyahu* Vol.1 Page 13).

(b) There is no such thing as "All local *Yidden* are perfect": A second reason why a woman and girl must dress with perfect *tznius* even in a fully Chareidi and elite society, is the fact that there are always weaker elements even amongst the finest people. It is a fallacy to maintain that everyone in a society can be classified as a perfect person and a truly *erlicher Yid*. For example, even in the generation that received the Torah and was under the leadership of Moshe Rabbeinu there were people like Dosson and Avirom and Shlomis Bas Divri amongst the *Yidden*. The *Rambam* actually writes (*Hilchos Issurei Biah* 22:19) that there is no such thing as a *kehilla* in which every person is a *tzaddik*. If this was a true assessment of *Klal Yisroel* in the times of the *Rishonim*, how much more must it be true in our times. It is the Jewish woman's responsibility not to cause anyone to stumble because of her, and in that context she must of course consider *all* elements in our society - see *Mekoros* 4:3.

Preventing sin by dressing and behaving modestly is a central feature in the *avoda* of a woman. She has been given this duty so that she rectifies with it the sin of Chava in which she enticed her husband to sin. To atone for that sin, it is the duty of women to ensure that she does not entice men to gaze at her by means of her appearance or charm. Instead, she dresses and conducts herself with modesty and refinement and does everything in her power to prevent men from sinning (Harav Hagaon R' Don Segal shlita, quoted in the *sefer, Mi Yirpeh Lach*, page 174).

(c) Laxity in *tznius* is very detrimental to the family: Thirdly, it is a disaster for *chinuch* if the mother or older sisters pay little attention to their manner of dress. The next generation may have to live in a very different environment from theirs, and it could be totally ruinous for them to have been brought up without a healthy feeling for *tznius* and modesty. *Chazal* say רחילא בתר רחילא אזלא, כעובדי אמא כך עובדי ברתא - "A lamb follows the sheep; so too the deeds of a daughter resembles those of her mother" (*Kesubos* 63a). Just as a lamb follows the older sheep blindly, trusting that they are certainly going the right way, so too, a daughter follows her mother indiscriminately and copies whatever her mother does.

Teachers attempting to impart the *halachos* and *hashkafos* of *tznius* to their pupils are plagued with the question "If this is so important how is it that my mother is not particular about it?" Unless the mother was brought up in a non-Orthodox environment and can therefore be pardoned for not knowing about the importance of *tznius*, very little can be said to set the young girl's mind at rest. Either the importance of *tznius* or the image of her mother's *Yiddishkeit* will suffer a severe setback. Every step must be taken to ensure that neither happens.

2. TZNIUS WHEN ONLY NOCHRIM LIVE IN THE AREA:

(a) *Tznius* applies even in front of *nochrim*: Even if women or girls happen to be in a place where there are no other *Yidden*, it is still imperative that they dress *b'tznius*. Since there are *nochrim* in this area, it is wrong to dress in a way that causes even the slightest degree of provocation to anyone. Apart from this obvious reason, women and girls should at all times behave with *tznius* for their own refinement. In fact, it will be noticed that the greater the instinctive *tznius*, the more the woman or girl practices full *tznius* even in privacy and certainly in the presence of *nochrim*. In *Parshas Vayeirah* (*Breishis* 18:9) we find that when the visiting angels, who appeared like *nochrim*, inquired of Avraham about the whereabouts of Sarah, he answered הנה באהל - "behold she is in the tent". Sarah Imeinu practiced perfect *tznius* and remained in the background even though her visitors appeared to be gentiles.

(b) Dressing with *tznius* secures a woman's safety: A further reason for *tznius* in dress even in front of *nochrim* is that a woman must guard herself from watchful eyes, especially in the dangerous world in which we now live - see 9:I where many present-day pitfalls are mentioned. The secular daily news is replete with tragedies caused by women not taking due care. Frum Jewish women should not think that they are safe from assault ח"ו. The Torah informs us (*Breishis* 34:1) that even Dinah, a daughter of the highly regarded and illustrious family of Yaakov Avinu, had a terrible experience as a result of over-confidence concerning her safety - see *Mekoros* 12:1-2.

We are taught to develop within ourselves the trait of being דן לכף זכות - judging people meritoriously (*Pirkei Avos* 1:6). This trait is, however, only to be used in the context of *Yidden* known to be Kosher and proper *shomrei mitzvos* (although not necessarily *tzaddikim* - See *Rambam* and *Rabbeinu Yona* on the *Mishna*). Whereas for the world at large the rule is כבדהו וחשדהו - "one must respect the person but not trust him". The source of this principle is a saying of *Chazal* לעולם יהיו כל בני אדם לפניך כליסטים והוה מכבדן כרבן גמליאל - "You should always consider people as possible thieves; however, at the same time give them the greatest respect as if they were *Rabban Gamliel*" (*Kallah Rabosi* 9). Girls must be taught not to trust when there is no solid foundation for trust.

(c) *Tznius* in dress prevents mingling with other societies: Apart from all that has been said, it is an indisputable fact that when a woman is clothed in full *tznius'dik* dress she is substantially sheltered from outside influences, since she will not mix with those who propagate alien and negative attitudes. Similarly, by covering her hair completely and projecting the image of a strictly-Orthodox person, a woman is protected from exposure to the attitudes and perspectives of prevailing cultures.

We are taught by *Chazal* that a major cause for the Jewish people being worthy of the redemption from *Mitzrayim* was the fact that they did not change their traditional clothes (לא שינו את מלבושם). This prevented them from integrating into the culture and lifestyle of the Egyptian society (*Bamidbar Rabba* 13:17 and *Yalkut Balak* 768) and prepared the way for a resurgence of a complete Jewish identity.

The verse says in *Shir HaShirim* (6:11) אל גינת אגוז ירדתי - "I paid a visit to a garden of nuts", referring to *Hashem* visiting *Klal Yisroel*. *Rashi* remarks on this in the name of *Chazal*, מה אגוז זה נופל בטיט ואין מה שבתוכו נמאס, אף ישראל גולין לבין האומות ואין מעשיהן נמאסין - "Just as a nut falls into mud and its interior remains perfectly clean, so too *Klal Yisroel* live amongst other cultures but remain unaffected". The point behind the comparison is as follows: The edible part of the nut remains perfectly clean because it is surrounded by a solid wall - the outer shell which separates it from the mud. So too, *Klal Yisroel* are protected by the clothes they are dressed in - the more solid and total the dress, the more effective a shield it is to prevent the penetration of foreign ideas and ideals.

3. TZNIUS IS OBLIGATED EVEN IN AN IMMORAL ENVIRONMENT:

(a) Being strong in the face of adversity: Some may wish to vindicate the permissiveness in dress that has entered our *kehillos* with the excuse that with so much *pritzus* around women are almost helpless as they are naturally drawn to that mode of life. Women must know that this is no excuse at all. Instead of becoming casual and lax in tune with the permissive world that surrounds them, the *Bas Yisroel* is expected to respond to her environment with extra discipline and restraint. By exercising extra *tahara* and refinement, she safeguards herself from the *tumah* of the world around her.

Strength to withstand these tests can be derived from the very assault of the *yetzer horah,* as will be explained, and what appears to be bleak and disheartening can be used as a source of inspiration and encouragement. The well known maxim by *Chazal,* כל הגדול מחבירו יצרו גדול הימנו - "Those who are greater than others have also a much greater *yetzer horah* than them" (*Succah* 52a) has already been mentioned in H:1(a) above. The *Vilna Gaon* writes that the same applies to *mitzvos.* His words as quoted in *Even Shleimah* 4:11:8. are as follows: כל דבר שהוא יותר גדול, לעומת זה היצר הרע יותר גדול, וצריך ליזהר יותר - "Anything that is of greater importance than other things, will be subject to greater attack by the *yetzer horah.* Greater care must therefore be exercised not to stumble".

Accordingly, from the very intensity of the attacks that are made against *tznius* from outside *Klal Yisroel* and from within, we are afforded an insight into just how lofty, holy and singularly important the laws of *tznius* really are. This realization can help a woman or girl remain strong and withstand the tidal waves that threaten to sweep away her *tznius* and real *Yiddishkeit.*

(b) Precautions Jewish girls took to protect their sanctity: It is recorded in the *Gemara* (*Shabbos* 80a) that women who lived in cities used to cover half their faces with a shawl before leaving the house in spite of the inconvenience that they could see only through one eye. On the other hand, those who lived in villages did not cover their faces before going out. *Rashi* explains the reason for this difference. People in cities were corrupt and permissive, whilst those who lived in villages were much more refined (as is still often the case). Therefore, *Bnos Yisroel* living in cities felt it their duty to shroud and conceal themselves as far as possible and went as far as covering half their faces. However, those living in villages did not deem this necessary.

In our society we certainly should not emulate the covering of half the face as done by those city dwellers, because this would attract attention to the Jewish girls and defeat its purpose - see *Mekoros* 69:3. We, nevertheless, have much to learn from the *nashim k'sheiros* of yesteryear. The lower the general morals of the world, the more cautious and more restrained the *Bas Yisroel* must become concerning her clothes, jewelry and makeup.

(c) The *Bas Yisroel* showed incredible resilience in Mitzrayim: During *golus Mitzrayim* there was a vivid demonstration of the strength *Bnos Yisroel* can muster to resist trends of *pritzus* and maintain their *kedusha* and *tahara*. In a place saturated with *tumah* and *Klal Yisroel* in virtually a defunct state, our mothers kept a remarkable level of *tznius*. They did not even engage in conversation with the local inhabitants, since with their innate feeling they understood (without hearing *shiurim* on the subject!) that familiarity through speech leads to more serious forms of familiarity - see *Rashi, Vayikra* 24:11 and *Mekoros* 80:3. The fact that the *kiyor* in the *Mishkan* was made of the mirrors used by women to beautify themselves, alludes to the sanctity of the Jewish women of that time - see 1:R:7 below.

The *tznius* of these women was so special that *Chazal* say בזכות נשים צדקניות נגאלו אבותינו ממצרים - "In the merit of righteous women the Jewish people were redeemed from Mitzrayim" (*Sotah* 11b, see *Maharsha* that it refers to the trait of *tznius*). With such mothers, *Hashem* saw a future for *Klal Yisroel* in spite of the low spiritual state it was in. If our wives and daughters would only follow in their footsteps, we too, would merit a speedy redemption from this debilitating *golus*. - see *Mekoros* 2:5.

(d) Incredible strength Jewish women displayed in the wilderness: We can furthermore see the steel and strength of Jewish women from the way they stood their ground when they were in the desert and did not follow the erroneous ways of the men. When it came to donating jewelry and gold towards the making of the *eigel* (Golden Calf), they resisted and gave nothing (*Shemos* 32:2-3) even though the men were totally enamored by the idea. On the other hand, when the Jewish people were asked to donate towards the erection of the *Mishkan*, women were excited by the opportunity to do such a wonderful *mitzva* and were the first to donate. See *Rabbeinu Bachya, Shemos* 35:20-21 who highlights the contrast between these two instances. These happenings demonstrate that women are capable of holding their own, provided they have a healthy and correct attitude on the matter.

(e) *Bnos Yisroel* are compared to gems - strong and beautiful: Shlomo Hamelech compares the *Eishes Chayil* to a precious stone. He states ורחוק מפנינים מכרה - "Her value is much greater than that of pearls" (*Mishlei* 31:10). Pearls and gems are both strong and beautiful. So too, the *Bas Yisroel* is strong and faithful to the principles of *Yiddishkeit*. At the same time her refined manner of dress and her *eidel* countenance make her as precious and as beautiful as a gem.

4. A TZNUA IS STRONG WHILE A PRUTZA IS WEAK-WILLED: A woman who is a *tznua* is a strong person. She has the strength of character not to be caught in the shackles of worldly pleasures which deter a person from doing right. Her inner being is attached to all that *Yiddishkeit* stands for and she therefore does not succumb to the hollow and vain enticements of the world at large. She is not blinded into wearing unsuitable garments by the urge to project an elegant image. Instead, she proudly appears in full Jewish dress, thinking to herself that for nothing in the world would she forsake even an iota of that which is her most cherished asset - her *tznius*.

On the other hand, the *prutza* is a weak character. Internally, her *Yiddishkeit* lacks strength and warmth. She is therefore attracted by the emptiness and externalism of the surrounding immoral world, and models her life on it. She is so weak that even the inevitable resentment of the local community cannot stop her slithering along with the ways of the world - see *Mekoros* 2:5.

5. RUTH'S STRENGTH IN CONTRAST TO ORPAH'S WEAKNESS: The following is a free translation [plus slight amendments] of part of a *shiur* that Sarah Schneirer *o.h.*, the guardian and mentor of the Jewish women, wrote to her students. It is recorded in the *sefer, Eim B'Yisroel.* In it, Sarah Schneirer portrays the strength and steadfastness of the *Bas Yisroel* who is committed to Torah and *mitzvos* with her whole being:

An emotional scene takes place at the border of the land of Yehuda. Naomi tries to take leave of her two daughters-in-law who refuse to be separated from her. She begs them to return to their palaces and noble families who are waiting with outstretched arms for their return. Naomi does not want them to come to *Eretz Yisroel* and live as Jewish women with her just because of their deep pity for her. She requests them to return to their homes. She thanks them for their loyalty and tells them to get married as soon as possible so that they regain their happiness. They kiss her and say sobbingly, "No, we shall go with you to your nation". They want to stay with Naomi and her people, even though they know how much is demanded by the Jewish faith and how different it is to the relaxed atmosphere of their father's house.

Naomi explains to them how much she appreciates their love. She is thankful to them, yet she cannot let them go with her as they will not find happiness in her home. She tries to dissuade them three times, as is required when accepting strangers. She does not want them to convert as a result of momentary excitement or the pressure of strong emotions. If they do convert, it should be only after careful and calm consideration. Their tears touch Naomi's heart, but she tests them seriously because she wants to know their true character.

Orpah does not have a strong character. Her father's house attracts her like magic. The brightness of royalty and the glitter of wealth wink to her from Moav and she gives in. She realizes the restrictions and demands the Jewish people are obliged to live with, and while the tears roll down her cheeks, she suddenly sees that she will not be able to bear the life in her mother-in-law's house. After many kisses, Orpah departs and leaves Naomi. That evening she gives in to the basest instincts of mankind and throws all forms of decency overboard. Orpah is a soft-hearted woman. She cries and kisses but she has no real mettle or character.....

ורות דבקה בה - Ruth is a pillar of strength; she "cleaves to her" with all her might (*Ruth* 1:14). She holds onto her mother-in-law and will not change her mind. She tells Naomi that she is fully aware what demands *Yiddishkeit* will make on her. She however states that nothing, but absolutely nothing, will stop her living a real Jewish life. She concludes by saying, "I will not be separated from you except by death". The *emes* in *Yiddishkeit* is far more attractive to her than all the luxuries that await her at home.

Naomi still doubts Ruth's total determination - and once again tries to dissuade her. "Look, your sister has returned to her people and her god, follow her!" thinking that the example will help soften her resolve. However, Ruth is adamant. She has fully understood the great task of a Jewish daughter. She knows that *Yiddishkeit* demands spiritual and moral strength. She knows that all *mitzvos* have one and the same purpose - to purify the person, to inspire *kedusha* into him and to refine his *midos*. With this he is finally ready for life. At the borders of Yehuda, Ruth accepts the holy Torah, just as *Am Yisroel* accepted it at *Har Sinai*.

Some time later, Naomi gives Ruth permission to go to a field and collect ears of corn together with other poor people. No one recognizes the princess in her - until Boaz arrives on the scene. After a short while he sees that Ruth is a special person as he notices her 'beautiful' and modest behavior. Boaz finds out who she is. And so the story unfolds, until we find that Ruth is married to Boaz. She eventually merits to become the mother of the family of Dovid Hamelech. She is the foundation stone of the house from which all our kings come and from which soon will come *Moshiach* our redeemer, *bimheirah b'yameinu*, *Amen*.

ଽ ଓ

With a teacher and *mashpia* such as Sarah Schneirer *o.h.* it is not surprising that 93 *talmidos* of the *Krakow Seminary* went in a state of *simcha* to their *akeidah*, as is well known. She instilled in them a deep love for *Hashem Yisbarach* and His Torah, as can be felt in this *shiur*. She furthermore imbued them with a strength and determination not to depart from the *derech hayashar* come what may. זכותה תעמוד לנו.

6. RUTH'S TZNIUS IN CONTRAST TO ORPAH'S LACK OF TZNIUS: The above essay portrays the "strength of character" that is typical of the *tznua* and the "lack of character" that is commonly found in the *prutza*. As explained, this can be seen in Ruth's conversion to *Yiddishkeit* in spite of the limitations such a life would cause her - and Orpah's departure from such a life because the attraction of temporary pleasures and the glamour of a royal household was too much for her to forgo. These two young ladies were both daughters (or descendants) of Eglon the King of Moav, but were fundamentally different from one another - (See *Ruth Rabba* 2:9 and *Tosfos Nazir* 23b s.v. *Bas)*.

Let us examine the final outcome of this episode:- Ruth has the everlasting merit of being mother to *Malchus Beis Dovid*. The story of her life is read on *Shevuos*, the day we received the Torah, because she is an example to everyone of the strength an individual can muster to accept upon himself the yoke of Torah - even though, in her case, it meant sacrificing the life of a princess. Orpah, on the other hand, suffers the permanent disgrace of being the grandmother of Golias, the mighty warrior of the Philistines, who scoffed at *Klal Yisroel* and their beliefs. He, a descendant of Orpah, was ultimately destroyed - by none other than Dovid, a descendant of Ruth, who, in contrast to her, chose the *Derech Hashem* - *Ruth Rabba* 2:20. Evidently, the reward and benefit of steadfastness and *tznius*, and the punishment and impairment of *pritzus*, are both very far reaching.

I. ITEMS OF "OTHER CULTURES"; "HIGHLY FASHIONABLE" ITEMS

1. THE ISSUR TO EMULATE FOREIGN CULTURES: It is *ossur min haTorah* for a man or woman to conduct themselves in a way that is typical of the culture of the *umos ha'olam*. This is in order that they do not adopt values and a code of conduct that are alien to the Jewish religion. The *issur* is learnt from the verse ובחוקותיהם לא תלכו - "Do not follow foreign cultures" (*Vayikra* 18:3). The *Rambam* writes (*Hilchos Avoda Zarah* 11:1), "A Jew should be different from them and should be distinguished by his clothing and other acts, just as he is different from them in his scholarship and views". Upon the upkeep and maintenance of the sharp contrast between the lifestyle of a Jew and that of foreign cultures, rests the entire existence and future of the Jewish people.

2. THE ISSUR APPLIES TO THREE TYPES OF GARMENTS:

(a) A strange looking garment: It is *ossur* for a man or woman to wear a garment that is strange and unattractive and was primarily made to express a certain culture and lifestyle; for example, badly torn and frayed trousers that represent the "I don't care" way of thinking. The same applies to a strange, unbecoming haircut that is typical of certain cultures. If a Jewish person wears such a garment or sports such a hairstyle, he is identifying himself with the ways of the *nochrim* and is demonstrating that he feels drawn to people who do not represent the *derech ha'emes* - the true and correct way. This in turn, can lead him to imbibe the way of life and general outlook of other nations. (See Y.D. 178:1 *Rema* and see *Mekoros* 5:1).

(b) A garment that projects a feeling of superiority: It is *ossur* for a man or woman to wear an item that is typically worn to project an image of superiority and pride. So too, it is *ossur* to sport a hairstyle which serves that purpose - see *Rambam, Hilchos Avoda Zarah* 11:1; Y.D. 178:1 *Rema*. If there is no good reason for the person to wear this item, then wearing it demonstrates a character trait that exists in some other cultures but is undesirable in Torah Law, and shows a desire not to be restricted by the refinement imposed by the Torah - see *Mekoros* 5:3. If follows, that all ways by which people imitate the incorrect customs of other nations are forbidden.

(c) A garment that is *pritzus'dik*: The *Poskim* write that a garment for females that entices the onlooker to gaze at the wearer is subject to the *issur* of *b'chukoseihem*. Being a *pritzus'dik* garment it belongs to other cultures and is foreign to *Yiddishkeit* - see *Mekoros* 46:7. This is of course in addition to all other *issurim* that are involved in wearing such an item. Since it is typical for many of the *umos ha'olam* to wear such an item of clothing it doubtlessly falls under the *issur* of *b'Chukoseihem*, although this is not mentioned explicitly in *Shulchan Aruch.* (See *Responsa Divrei Chayim* 1:30 and *Mekoros* 5:5).

It follows, that all alluring forms of dress, jewelry, makeup and perfume are doubly forbidden (except when a woman is alone with her husband). Firstly, it is *pritzus* to go around in such a way, and one who does so transgresses the *issurim* of והיה מחניך קדוש - "And your camp shall be holy" - *Devarim* 23:15 (*S'mak, mitzva* 57 who numerates *tznius* as a *mitzva min haTorah* within the context of this *posuk*) and לפני עור - "Not to cause others to sin". Secondly, she transgresses the *issur* of *b'chukoseihem* - the *issur* of dressing in garments that are distinctly designed to fit in with the pursuits of other societies. We are fortunate to have a glorious heritage and it is up to us not to contaminate it with foreign implants.

Chazal say (*Sanhedrin* 37a) that the word בגד (*beged* - garment) can also be read as בוגד (*boged* - traitor). With a garment, a woman can either adorn herself or, *chas veshalom*, turn traitor to her people. See *Yeshaya* 24:16 where this tragic misuse of garments is spelt out in no uncertain terms.

3. THE EXTENT OF THIS ISSUR: A garment subject to the *issur* of *b'chukoseihem* may not be worn even if the Jewish person does so with no negative intention, and wants to wear it only because no other suitable garment could be found - *Responsa Divrei Chayim* 1:30. If no other garment can be obtained this item must be substantially changed, so that it becomes Kosher and fitting to be worn - *Responsa HaMaharik* 88 and *Ksav Sofer* Y.D. 175 s.v. *V'hinei*. See also 6:M:3 and *Mekoros* 5.

Whatever is forbidden because of *b'chukoseihem* remains *ossur* even if with the course of time *Yidden* have incorrectly copied the ways of the *nochrim* and this form of hairstyle or dress has become typical for both *Yidden* and *nochrim*. Therefore, even if many Yidden sport a very long forelocks of hair or considerable amount of hair down the back of the head and neck (see Y.D. 178:1 and *Shach*) it is still considered as 'copying' *nochrim* and displaying an affection for their culture and all that it stands for - (*Responsa Chasam Sofer, Orach Chayim,* 159 end of s.v. *Tavna* and *Responsa Avnei Nezer, Choshen Mishpat,* 103 - see *Mekoros* 5:9). However, if the negative nature of the item has come to an end; for example, the garment no longer represents a proud or attention-seeking person as is the case with a man wearing a red shirt, it is no longer subject to the *issur* of *b'chukoseihem* and may be worn by all (*Darkei Teshuva* 178:16 in name of the *Bach* and R' Yitzchak Elchanan zt'l).

4. REFINED ITEMS THAT ARE MADE AND WORN BY NOCHRIM: As explained, the *issur* of *b'chukoseihem* applies to ways of dress and hairstyles that entail reaching out to foreign cultures. It therefore applies only to that which projects a feeling of superiority, that which lacks *tznius*, and that which was evidently introduced to symbolize the religion or civilization of other societies. However, an item which does not embody one of these three stigmas may be worn.

It is therefore permissible to wear a tasteful Kosher piece of clothing, although it was designed and made by *nochrim* and is widely worn by them. Since the Jewish person wishes to wear the garment only because it is graceful and pleasing to the eye, wearing it does not have the character of moving towards the culture of other nations. Since the garment is perfect from the point of view of color, style and thickness there is no reason why it should not be worn. Hence, it does not fall under the *issur* of *b'chukoseihem* and is permitted. (See *Yoreh Deoh* 178:1 in the name of the *Maharik; Iggros Chazon Ish* 3:152, *Responsa Iggros Moshe* Y.D. 1:81 and see *Mekoros* 5:2, 5:7 and 54:12).

It must, however, be mentioned that although not a *halachic* obligation, there is a special advantage in wearing typical Jewish clothes which demonstrate our difference from other nations and cultures. Our ancestors were redeemed from *Mitzrayim* in the merit of the fact that they did not discard the traditional Jewish garb and the more we follow in their footsteps in these matters the nearer we may be to our own redemption - see 2:H:4 below.

5. HOW A GARMENT IS CLASSIFIED AS "KOSHER AND DECENT": *Chachmei HaTorah* must decide which items are "Kosher" and exempt from the *issur* of *b'chukoseihem* and which on the other hand are associated with feelings of pride, of *pritzus* or represent foreign cultures and fall under the *issur* of *b'chukoseihem* - *Responsa Mahari Shtief* 126.

For example, they have established that for a man to wear European clothes i.e. a short jacket, or for women to wear dresses that are not ankle long, is not *b'chukoseihem*. On the other hand they established that to wear a bright red garment (when that was in fashion by *nochrim* - see *Mekoros* 5:5-8.) or for a man to sport an exceptionally long front lock (a very large *chupik*) is *b'chukoseihem* (*See Shach* Y.D. 178:1; *Machatzis HaShekel* quoted in M.B. 27:15 and letter of *Chazon Ish* mentioned in No. 9 below). Rulings must come from *Chachmei HaTorah,* because assessments made by lay people can be tarnished by what they see incessantly in the streets, and by incorrect modes of dress that have already crept into the Jewish society.

Just as Jewish people may wear a non-Jewish garment that is essentially Kosher, so too they may wear a non-Kosher garment if the way it is worn guarantees that it is *tznius'dik*. For example, see-through blouses are obviously not *tznius'dik* pieces of clothing. They may nevertheless be worn by Jewish women and girls if an under-blouse is worn under them or a sweater over them in a way that nothing can be seen through - see 6:D:3. By wearing the item in this way, the wearer demonstrates that she wants to disassociate herself from the ways of dress of the *umos ha'olam* - (see 6:M:4 and *Responsa Ksav Sofer,* Y.D 175).

6. HARM CAUSED BY WEARING HIGHLY FASHIONABLE CLOTHES: All that has been explained in the previous point holds true from the point of view of *b'chukoseihem*. It must however be stated that it is most undesirable to wear a new highly fashionable garment even when the above-mentioned *issur* is not involved. New fashions that are technically Kosher, but very different to what was worn until now, are eye-catching and hence unrefined. Such clothes attract considerable attention and wearing them is accordingly an infringement on modesty - the insignia of the *Bas Yisroel*. These garments might, however, eventually become suitable. This is once the fashion has become widespread and the garment is no longer unusual and eye-catching. Once this has happened a Jewish woman may wear it, provided the garment is *tznius'dik* - see *Mekoros* 58:1-3.

7. FASHION CONSCIOUSNESS CAN EASILY RESULT IN PRITZUS: Regretfully, many of our daughters feel that they must be amongst the first in town to wear clothes of the latest fashion. This urge is the source of much trouble concerning *tznius*. Wanting to dress in this way can easily generate a serious *nisayon* for them to wear a *non-tznius'dik* item if such an item becomes the subject of the latest fashions. Once a girl or woman is deeply "fashion conscious", she will find it difficult to forego wearing an item that is being advertised everywhere as the latest vogue and style to wear. Instead, she will succumb to the demands of the society she so admires, even though she knows that it is wrong to wear this type of item.

Even if she will remain strong and not wear garments which she knows are not *tznius'dik*, craving to be "with it" and dressing in keeping with the latest fashions is nevertheless liable to eventually lead her astray. It can corrode her sense of *tznius* to the point that she will consider certain items as perfect, not realizing that they are very far from that. This downward trend is a natural development. Clothes that this "fashion conscious" young lady has worn for some time will soon seem to her to be too drab and lusterless to wear and she will have an urge to find herself clothes which have a more modern look than the 'outmoded' clothes worn by others in her *kehilla*. The trap is now set. Since she wears clothes that others do not wear she will no longer be kept in check by the way others dress.

Therefore, if she does not possess an acute and critical eye for *tznius* she will soon fall for modern, fashionable clothes that infringe on *tznius*, with nothing to hinder her wearing them. This in turn could detrimentally affect her own standard of *tznius*, that of her family and eventually that of many others. See 7:A:9 below for further details. Unfortunately, once the taste for looking highly attractive and even glamorous has been acquired, it can prove to be very hard to eradicate. Her feelings for refinement and *eidelkeit* might have been numbed to such an extent that only an enormous amount of input can revive this cherished instinct within her.

8. FASHIONS PRECIPITATE CONTINUOUS BUYING OF CLOTHES: If a girls trend to keep up with the latest fashions is not curbed in time, she will want to buy the latest items all the time. As a result of this, she will need a considerable number of clothes, and will demand far more money from her father than is justifiable. Similarly, when married, she will demand far more clothes from her husband than he is obligated to provide her with. This is inevitable because styles change continuously and this involves virtually everything. Also, what is worn during one season would certainly be unsuitable for this woman or girl by the next one. All this can obviously cause an enormous strain on the father's or husband's resources.

Apart from the strain that can be caused, there is no justification for this type of spending. *Mosros* (מותרות) - spending money on totally unnecessary items is always wrong, as will be explained in 7:A:6 below, and spending money to parade the latest fashions is a prime example of *mosros* - see *Mekoros* 62.

9. NOT DRESSING AS OTHER CHAREIDIM - SIGN OF INSTABILITY: A further negative aspect of wearing clothes that are different from those worn by everyone else lies in the very departure from the usual dress generally worn by other *frum Yidden* of that time and place. It should be natural to want to identify oneself with people of one's own way of life. To depart from this, displays a lack of enthusiasm and joy at being part of the *tzibur hachareidi,* and is an unhealthy sign. The *Chazon Ish* writes in a letter (3:152) the following amongst other things (freely translated):-

"It is fitting for those who have *Yiras Shomayim* to dress and conduct themselves in the most *tznius'dik* way, as is the usual conduct of those who are truly *chareidi*. **Also, for an individual to be different and not wear the clothes worn by other *chareidim*, does not reflect well on his internal stability.** Nevertheless, by wearing clothes worn by the nochrim he is not transgressing the *issur* of *b'chukoseihem,* because that *issur* applies only when the person desires to dress like the *nochrim*, not when he is attracted to the clothes because of their elegant appearance ....". (The original text can be found in *Mekoros* 5:7).

As has already been stated, this refers to the early stages of a new fashion. However, once an item is widely worn by the *frum* community it is no longer "an article of the latest fashion" and the stigma no longer applies. Wearing it would therefore not be considered as pursuing the latest trends and fashions.

10. GEDOLIM ABOUT PITFALLS OF "FASHION CONSCIOUSNESS":

(a) 250 years ago - Statement by Hagaon Harav Yaacov Emden *zt'l.* The great Gaon Rabbi Yaacov Emden *zt'l* (in *Siddur Beis Yaacov, Hilchos Tisha b'Av,* Page 314) had these harsh words to say about our weakness in this area: "They (the general Jewish population) are envious of the *umos ha'olam* and copy all their ways concerning adornment of the body. Jewish men, their wives, their sons and their daughters - all do so. They are particular that their clothes are in keeping with the latest fashions down to the last detail. They are even more particular about these matters than the *umos ha'olam,* the very creators of the fashions.

"Even a Jewish maidservant wears fashionable clothes long before the general population has taken to wearing them. All types of very colorful clothes, whether new or old, will not satisfy their craving to be seen in the best finery and to cause people to turn around and admire their attire". These are the words of a *Gadol Hador* who lived 250 years ago. Regrettably, his words apply today as they did when they were written, since to be in with the fashion is considered by many to be a top priority. See 7:A:8 for further elaboration about this disorder which has long afflicted the Jewish people - see *Mekoros* 58.

(b) Today - Speech by Hagaon Harav Shmuel HaLevi Wosner *shlita*: In a speech to women given in *Bnei Brak,* Hagaon Harav Shmuel HaLevi Wosner *shlita, Gaon Av Beis Din* of *Zichron Meir, Bnei Brak,* had the following to say about the pursuit of excessive fashions in our times:-

"Today we find a strange and painful phenomenon. People want to be *bnei* Torah and modern at the same time. Both husband and wife want to lead a life of Torah. When they marry, the woman, like many other young brides, says, 'I want my husband to be a *Ben Torah*'. However, later on, to our dismay, she readily complies with his desire to be modern.

"The modernity expresses itself in the pursuit of inordinate stylish clothing, short dresses, excessive jewelry and in the wearing of long ostentatious wigs '**which is no different than uncovering the hair**'. A woman's head-covering should be refined and modest. Sadly, due to our sins, to many women and in many homes the wig has become a fashion symbol, both in its length and style. When a woman wears such a highly fashionable wig she certainly does not look like the wife of a *Ben Torah*. In fact some are so stylish that the wearer does not even look like a *chareidi* woman but rather like a movie star, and in some cases as a result of the wig she does not even look Jewish!

"In such a home, the maxim that 'where there is no *yirah* there is no *chachmah*' [due to which the husband cannot truly grow in Torah] is forgotten....... The *Rambam* and *Rabbeinu Bachya* have already written that just as fire and water cannot coexist in the same vessel, so it is impossible to combine Torah and a lack of *tznius* in the same house........."

Hagaon Harav Wosner *shlita* concluded his speech with the following words of encouragement, "Dovid Hamelech, who was one of the seven shepherds, one of the greatest of prophets, one of the greatest *ovdei Hashem* of the Jewish nation and the one who would rise up at midnight to thank *Hashem* for His righteous ordinances - said with *ruach hakodesh,* ועם האמהות אשר אמרת עמם אכבדה - '[If I will merit to be] with the maidservants that you have mentioned, I will be honored' (*Shmuel* 2:6:22). On this verse

Chazal say something remarkable. Dovid said, 'If only that my portion in the World to Come will be with the Jewish mother' (*Bamidbar Rabba* 4:20). Dovid Hamelech, the most exalted of men - the *yedid Hashem* - felt that the Jewish mother represents the loftiest level one could reach, and that she receives the highest possible reward in the World to Come.

"Therefore, Jewish mothers and daughters, preserve the precious treasure which has been given to you - the Torah observant home. Preserve the sanctity of the generations. Guard your property forever. Let there be אין יוצאת ואין צוחה - 'No breach and no outcry in our places' (*Tehillim* 144:14). Be on your guard so that no Jewish child goes astray. In this merit, and in the merit of guarding your priceless possession - the *chareidi* home, the *chareidi* husband, the *chareidi* son and daughter, the *Ben Torah*, the *Bas Yisroel* - may we merit to supply legions of soldiers to *Hashem*, who, with great mercy, will march with you and with us, to greet *Moshiach*, speedily in our times".

11. THE IMMENSE INFLUENCE CLOTHES HAVE ON THE WEARER:

(a) Direct influence of the *tahara* or *tumah* of the garment: The immense positive influence good clothes can have upon their wearer can be seen from the clothes a *Kohen* wears when doing *avoda* in the *Beis Hamikdash*. *Chazal* say, בזמן שבגדיהם עליהם כהונתם עליהם אין בגדיהם עליהם אין כהונתם עליהם - "When the *Kohanim* wear their special clothes they have the proper *kedusha* of *Kehuna*; when they do not wear their clothes they do not have the full *kedusha* of *Kehuna*" (*Zevochim* 17b). Evidently, clothes can affect a person to such a degree that his special sanctity is dependent on them. Interestingly, the clothes of the *Kohen* had to be exactly the right length for him - not too long and not too short. For this reason the verse refers to them with the words ולבש הכהן מדו בד (*Vayikra* 6:3) which comes from the word מדה - "measure" - see *Rashi*.

So also the *Bas Yisroel* who wears clothes of *tznius* that are fitting in style and size, is sanctified by them for her special role in the service of *Hashem*. For this reason, the garb of the modest woman is described with the words ממשבצות זהב לבושה - "They are like the garments that have golden settings" (*Tehillim* 45:14), which refers to the clothes of the *Kohen Gadol*.

In the *selichos* starting with אתה הרואה (said on the fifth day of the *Aseres Yemei Teshuva* according to the version of Western Europe) the following is stated about the Jewish daughter: לובשת ענוה מביאה היראה, למלך שוה ראויה ונאה - "She is dressed in clothes of modesty that generate *Yiras*

Shomayim; she is fit and becoming for a king". The message is clear. Not only do her modest clothes not cause sin as do other clothes, but they positively generate an atmosphere of *Yiras Shomayim* over her and amongst those who are in her close proximity. Moreover, her modest clothes are not unseemly and unbecoming - on the contrary they confer upon her a special *chein* and pleasantness which endear her to those close to her.

In contrast, bad clothes have a detrimental and injurious effect on their wearer. They diffuse an impurity which is transmitted to the person wearing them. The *Chasam Sofer* writes that Yaacov, who always spoke only the truth, would have found it very difficult if not impossible to deviate from the truth and say, אנכי עשו בכרך - "I am Eisav your firstborn" (*Breishis* 27:19). To help him overcome this difficulty Rivka advised him to dress in the clothes of his wicked brother Eisav. She knew that the negative effect of such clothes would enable Yaacov to stand down from his lofty position in the service of *Hashem* and do something which he otherwise would have found almost impossible to do (*Chasam Sofer Al HaTorah, Breishis* 27:36 s.v. *Halo Otzalto*). Such is the all-powerful influence of the *tumah* that can be transmitted by clothes.

In the light of this we can appreciate the negative effect of ostentatious clothes, grossly inflated hairstyles and excessive jewelry with which a girl boasts and brags, and in general, attracts attention to herself. Not only do these clothes bring *tumah* to the world, but, being "articles of *tumah*", they rebound on their wearer and influence her more and more in the negative direction. On the other hand, refined clothes *eidel* ornaments worn with *tznius* and purity of mind, underpin *kedushas Yisroel.* Being "articles of purity" they constantly inject higher degrees of *tahara* into their wearer.

(b) Clothes constantly remind a person of his allegiance: A person is aware at all times of the clothes he wears and is reminded by them of the allegiance that is implied by the clothes he wears. Consequently, when a woman or girl wears refined clothes they continuously remind her that she has undertaken to conduct herself in a way that fully preserves *tznius.* In contrast, when a woman or girl wears *pritzus'dik* clothes, she is constantly reminded that self-beautification is of such paramount importance to her that she is willing to wear anything, even unrefined and *pritzus'dik* clothes, in order to look glamorous and gain admiration for her appearance.

The significance of this issue is closely illustrated by the words of the *Rambam* in *Hilchos Mezuzah* (6:13) where he writes: אמרו חכמים הראשונים כל מי שיש לו תפילין בראשו ובזרועו, וציצית בבגדו, ומזוזה בפתחו, מוחזק הוא שלא

יחטא שהרי יש לו מזכירים רבים - "The early Sages said that whoever has *tefillin* on his head and arm, *tzitzis* on his clothes and a *mezuzah* on his door is guaranteed not to stray, for he has many reminders to keep him on the right path". Just as *tzitzis* remind a man that he is a servant of *Hashem*, so too does the *tznius'dik* dress of a woman serve as her "identification tag" so that she remain constantly aware of her purpose in life. If, on the other hand, her clothes reflect a totally wrong scale of values they have the opposite effect and steer her further and further away from the correct course.

This is an ideal example of that which *Chazal* teach, מצוה גוררת מצוה ועבירה גוררת עבירה - "A *mitzva* brings further *mitzvos* in its wake and an *aveirah* causes further *aveiros* to be done" (*Pirkei Avos* 4:2). A *tznius'dik* outfit brings in its wake further *tznius* whilst a *pritzus'dik* outfit incites the person to wear more such clothes.

J. BUYING AND SELLING CLOTHES

1. THE ISSUR TO SELL FORBIDDEN CLOTHES: It is *ossur min haTorah* to sell an immodest garment to a Jewish woman or girl (unless the garment can be worn under other clothes, e.g. a see-through blouse, and it is to be hoped that she will do so) - see *Mekoros* 74:4-9. To do so involves the *issur* of לפני עור לא תתן מכשול - "Do not cause a fellow-Jew to trip and transgress an *issur*" - (*Vayikra* 19:14). Even if the customer is capable of purchasing this garment in a non-Jewish store elsewhere, an *issur d'Rabanan* of aiding and abetting a person to do an *aveirah* (מסייע ידי עוברי עבירה) still exists - (*Shach* Y.D. 151:6). The same applies to selling immodest *sheitels*.

A grave responsibility therefore lies on those who sell forbidden ladies' and girls' clothing. On the other hand, refusing to sell such items and foregoing the potential profits they could earn constitutes a *kiddush Hashem*, which will be richly rewarded. (See *Responsa Shevet HaLevi* Y.D. 1:62).

2. SHOPKEEPERS SHOULD ENCOURAGE TZNIUS: Ladies who sell skirts, dresses and outfits should dissuade their customers from buying garments that are tight on them. Even if this customer is so affected by all that she sees that she would be quite happy to wear such a garment and might even try to buy it elsewhere, it still remains *ossur* to sell it to her, as explained above. In attempting to dissuade her, one should explain to her that such clothes would effectively spoil her refined appearance, quite apart from not being suitable for her from the *halachic* point of view.

There is reason to be envious of these shopkeepers, since it is in their hands to educate the ladies who come to their shops and ensure that they buy the right types of clothes. Sadly, only a few use this heaven-sent opportunity to improve this eroded area of *shemiras hamitzvos*.

3. SUITABILITY OF A GARMENT MUST BE CAREFULLY CHECKED: Shops selling dresses and outfits should if possible have two mirrors facing each other, so that the person purchasing a garment can see what it looks like on her from all angles. All too often a garment that has an inadequate front neckline is pulled down from the back giving the impression that it is in order, whilst in fact the back part of the neckline thereby becomes exposed. Two mirrors facing each other will prevent this and similar oversights.

It should be mentioned that it is altogether incorrect to wear a dress which is only Kosher around the neck when pulled down at the front or the back. The garment can easily move out of that position and once this happens the neckline will no longer be Kosher.

4. YOUNG GIRLS SHOULD NOT BUY CLOTHES BY THEMSELVES: It is highly recommended that a young daughter be accompanied by her mother when she buys clothes for herself. In this way the mother can show her what styles and colors come into question, how to check whether a material is see-through and how to check that the neckline, hemline and sleeves of a dress or outfit are in order. The mother can impart to her daughter much *chinuch* for life during such visits. On the other hand, a young girl's wish to look pretty will usually render her a poor judge for her own clothes.

When a girl goes shopping by herself and comes home with an outfit, she has already taken a liking to it and thinks it suits her well. Her parents, who see its faults, will find it difficult to persuade her to return it because of its shortcomings. What usually happen is, that now that she has bought it and set her heart on it, her parents allow her to keep it, provided its shortcomings are not too serious. Sometimes they will even capitulate quickly because of all the unpleasantness involved. Hence, they will allow her to wear something they would never have bought for her in the first place. Had the mother and daughter gone shopping together, this problem would never have arisen, and their daughter would have had a refined outfit to wear rather than something that at the best is only marginally suitable.

K. GUIDANCE SHOULD BE SOUGHT

1. SHA'ALOS MUST BE ASKED CONCERNING TZNIUS: Surprisingly, many people who know that they are not proficient in *halacha* - and must ask a *sha'aloh* when a mix-up occurs in the kitchen or when a problem arises on Shabbos - are nevertheless of the opinion that they can *pasken* for their daughters how far a collar may be open, how long a skirt must be, etc. They obviously do not realize that a code of conduct has been laid down in the *Shulchan Aruch* and in the *Sifrei HaPoskim*, and that *sha'alos* must be asked in these matters just as in all other areas of everyday life.

However strong a person's feelings for *tznius* are - or for that matter, for any other part of *Yiddishkeit* such as Shabbos, *kashrus*, *ribis* etc. - he will err and fall short of his duty, or alternatively be overly stringent, if he does not know what the *halacha* requires of him. As long as he is unaware of the laws laid down in the *Shulchan Aruch,* he will inevitably live with numerous errors, because the intricacies and considerations of *Chazal* and the great *halachic* authorities go far beyond the calculations an average person can possibly make. Moreover, even if he is enthusiastic about the issue of *tznius* knowing its ethical background, nevertheless without knowledge of the *halachos* he will mistakenly do wrong (See the preface of this *sefer*). It is therefore of paramount importance to learn the *halachos* of *tznius* in a *shiur* or from a *sefer* - or to inquire from a *Rav* when a question arises.

2. APPRECIATING THE DAAS TORAH OF OUR GREAT POSKIM: Some people harbor the opinion (although often left unspoken) that *Poskim*, who are great and holy men, are certainly "out of touch" with the needs of women, and hence their rulings on these matters need not be accepted. The truth, however, is that the opinions of the *Poskim* are mostly based on exclusive proofs drawn from *Shas*, *Midroshim*, *Rishonim* etc. These are the *dvar Hashem* itself (as all Torah literature is written with Divine inspiration) and *Hashem* Who created humanity certainly knows the needs of women.

That which the *Poskim* cannot prove from an explicit source, is decided upon by a thought-process which has been tuned and refined by tens of thousands of hours of Torah study (and with elderly *Talmidei Chachamim* even hundreds of thousands of hours) which enables them to perceive where the pure truth lies. This process is called דעת תורה - an opinion born out of Torah thought. Their thought-process has not been affected by secular and non-Jewish ways of thinking, because they have never come into contact with them.

On the other hand, those who think that our *Poskim* are "out of touch" have usually learned very little Torah. Their opinion will have been inadvertently developed from the papers and magazines they constantly read, from the comments they hear from the atheist on the radio, and from the latest fashions and misbehavior they see on the streets many times each day. Which of these two groups of people are "in touch" with the *emes*? Let us thank *Hashem* that we have these *Gedolim* who maintain a degree of clarity and sanctity in a world that is so confused and immoral - see *Mekoros* 6:1-3.

3. KEEPING HALACHA METICULOUSLY IMPLANTS YIRAS HASHEM: Not only is knowledge of the *halacha* a prerequisite for doing what is right, but there is much more to it - the *Yiras Shomayim* of a person grows when he keeps *halacha* properly without compromise. For example, when a woman does not brush talc-powder from a dark-colored dress on Shabbos, nor clean a coat that has fallen onto the floor (which are forbidden under the *melacha* of *Melaben,* laundering, - see *Rema* O.C. 302:1), she acquires a healthy measure of *Yiras Shomayim*. Similarly, when a man does not borrow money he urgently needs until he has checked with a *Rav* that the conditions that are being made do not conflict with the *issur* of *ribbis*, he is putting the *halachos* of the Torah above all other considerations. He thereby grows in his devotion to Torah and *mitzvos*.

Likewise, when a woman or girl keeps a Kosher neckline and ensures that her sleeves are as long as they should be, although most of her peers have given in to the hot weather and even ridicule her for being 'so *frum*', she is thereby heightening her dedication and loyalty to all that *Yiddishkeit* stands for. As we know, the first firm step in *Yiddishkeit* is to say נעשה - "we will perform what *Hashem* asks of us", and only after this do we say נשמע - "we will hear, understand and fully appreciate"! (*Shemos* 24:7).

When a *Talmid Chacham* asked the *Chazon Ish* what he could do to ascend to a meaningful level of *Yiras Shomayim*, he gave him the following advice: "Fulfill *mitzvos* to their fullest detail. This is the one and only assured way of reaching the heights to which you aspire. Do not accept from anyone that there is another easier and quicker way to reach such perfection, since there is simply no other way" (see *P'aer Hador,* 3, page 11).

4. NOT FALLING FOR QUOTES THAT CONTRADICT RULINGS: Since *tznius* of dress is a very emotive subject, some people have the tendency to research the issues themselves to see if they can prove that a certain area does not (or does) require cover. These people will at times come up with statements they have found in *Chazal* or in a *Rishon* which seem to contradict a *p'sak* given by an accepted *halachic* authority. People must be warned not to take such proofs at face value, irrespective of how convincing they may seem to be. The research was probably done with an eye on being lenient or stringent, not in order to honestly research the issue and find the *emes*. When that is the case, one must be suspicious of the proof, particularly as a *halachic* authority has said otherwise - see *Mesilas Yesharim,* Ch.6.

Moreover, even if the proof seems sound, this does not necessarily mean that the *halacha* is exclusively proven from it. There are often conflicting opinions in *Chazal*, and the *halacha* could well be at variance with the quote that was found. Apart from this consideration, there are a number of additional reasons why the *halacha* cannot simply be fixed on the basis of a proof that has been found. Some of the far reaching reasons are as follows:-

- The first and most obvious consideration is that without a broad and deep understanding of Torah literature one cannot be sure that there is no flaw in the proof given. Any Torah scholar will bear testimony that on almost every page of *Gemara* there are refutations to proofs that seemed at first sight to be very sound. *Chazal* also make profound analytical distinctions between subject matters that seem to be one and the same.

- Secondly, the *Ramban* in his introduction to *Milchemes Hashem* (beginning of *M'seches Brachos*) warns Torah scholars not to rely exclusively on proofs to decide *halachic* issues. He writes that, without an intuitive feeling for the *emes* culled from the general approach of *Chazal* to this and closely related issues, proof alone is unreliable. Those acquainted with the *Teshuvos* of the *Chasam Sofer* will know that this viewpoint is the very corner stone of the *Chasam Sofer*'s approach to *halacha*.

- Thirdly, considerable *siyata d'shmaya* is required to decide delicate *halachic* matters correctly. For a person to merit such *siyata d'shmaya.* he must be a *tzaddik* in his personal life. Hence, true greatness in *halacha* depends on greatness in *Avodas Hashem*. Due to this, the *Sanhedrin*, the greatest court of justice of the Jewish people, was situated in the courtyard of the *Beis Hamikdash* rather than anywhere else - see *Rashi, Shemos* 21:1. The considerable *Yiras Shomayim* that enveloped those who are in close proximity to the *Beis Hamikdash* guaranteed that their rulings would be completely in line with the *ratzon Hashem*. It is remarkable, that the most universally accepted *sefer* on *halacha* written this century, the *Mishna Berura*, was written by none other than the most admired *tzaddik* and *kadosh* of our era - the *Chofetz Chayim*. Due to his great *tzidkus* he attained the *siyata d'shmaya* required to fix the *halacha* that guides *Klal Yisroel* on a day to day basis.

The *Gemara* (*Eruvin* 13b) discusses the great wisdom of some of the *Tanaim*. It relates that there was a clever *Talmid Chacham* in the town of Yavneh who produced one hundred and fifty proofs from the Torah that a *sheretz* (a short-legged creature such as a weasel) is *tahor* - is a 'ritually clean' animal and may be eaten. The *Rishonim* ask what was the purpose of such mental gymnastics since *sheratzim* are definitely *tomeh* as is written explicitly in the Torah (*Vayikra* 5:2) and, if so, what was the point in bringing proofs that they are permitted when they are definitely *ossur*?

In the introduction to the *sefer, Bigdei Yesha* on *Orach Chayim* (a *sefer* frequently quoted by the *Mishna Berura* and written in the times of the *Noda b'Yehudah*), the author writes as follows: This young *Talmid Chacham* was engaged in a most important mission and spent his time on a worthy quest. He wanted people to know that a person can produce an endless string of proofs to determine that something is permitted, and in spite of all the proofs that seem irrefutable, the truth might be just the opposite and the issue at hand is definitely *ossur*. We are to learn from this that if a person is ignorant of what is written elsewhere in the Torah, lacks the intuitive feeling for the *emes* or lacks *Yiras Shomayim*, his reasoning and his proofs are unreliable and must not be granted *halachic* credit.

L. ENCOURAGING OTHERS TO DO WHAT IS RIGHT

1. MAKING A PERSON AWARE OF AN OVERSIGHT: It is obvious that many transgressions concerning dress are committed totally unintentionally without the woman wanting to dress incorrectly or to cause men to look at her. It is often simply because of ignorance of the *halacha* or a lack of awareness of how the garment appears on her. Since she cannot see all around her own neckline, she is often unaware that part of the neckline is too low. It is therefore extremely important that women inform their friends if they see that their dress is not quite up to standard. This is the most frequent oversight of all because, as stated, the woman cannot see her own neckline properly. Experience has shown that sometimes a woman must be told a few times until she succeeds in getting it correct.

2. THE MITZVA TO HELP OTHERS CORRECT THEIR WAYS: As is well known, it is a *mitzva min haTorah* to help others correct their mistakes (הוכח תוכיח את עמיתך). There can hardly be a more important area in which to fulfill this *mitzva* than in connection with *tznius* and *kedushas Yisroel.* If people would do this, the standards of *tahara* and *kedusha* would improve considerably. It is, of course, very difficult to admonish another person and particularly on this type of issue. However, if one realizes what is at stake and how great a *zechus* it is to help rectify things of such importance, a way can surely be found to communicate the message in an acceptable manner.

In a *hesped* the *Chasam Sofer zt'l* said at the *levaya* of his Rebbetzen (the daughter of R' Akiva Eiger *zt'l*) he explained all the *p'sukim* of the *Eishes Chayil.* He referred each verse to her and showed how she epitomized the qualities mentioned in that verse.

The verse *says,* זממה שדה ותקחהו מפרי כפיה נטעה כרם - "She contemplated buying a field and decided to do so; with the effort of her palm she planted a vineyard" (*Mishlei* 31:16). On this the *Chasam Sofer* said the following: שדה refers to an unplanted plot of ground on which no produce grows (as opposed to שדה זרוע - "a planted field"). A vineyard, in contrast, is an area which has fruit bearing trees. The woman referred to in the verse purchased an unplanted field after carefully considering the matter, and with great personal effort transformed it into a fruit-bearing vineyard. The unplanted field alludes to people who have neither Torah nor *mitzvos* to their credit. The *Eishes Chayil* wondered whether she has the ability to influence these people to improve their ways, but decided that since the stakes are so high she must try. The result was remarkable. There was a considerable change in these people and in a short time they were producing an abundance of good deeds. Hence, through her effort she transformed a bare field into a fruit bearing area.

The *Chasam Sofer* continued by saying that his Rebbetzen was just like the *Eishes Chayil* described. She would notice women who did not have a proper *chinuch* and therefore lacked *tznius.* Due to this, their dress violated basic *halachic* guidelines. He mentioned in particular that they would inadequately cover their legs and hair. His Rebbetzen would take upon herself to impress on these women the importance of *tznius,* and thereby influence them to dress correctly. The result was invariably dramatic, with many changing their mode of life as a direct result of her wonderful guidance. She truly bought a barren field and transformed it into a fruitful vineyard (*Drashos Chasam Sofer* Vol 2, page 772).

When censuring someone for dressing inappropriately, it is important to stress that one is aware that she is not dressing in inadequate clothes intentionally and that it certainly is just an oversight. In fact, it has been seen time and again that this is the truth - the vast majority of wrongdoings concerning dress have no malicious intent or bad origin whatsoever. They are simply a form of ignorance or unawareness caused by the incessant attacks by society and the media on the woman's natural sensitivities. By stressing these points there is hope that the offender's goodwill will be awakened, rather than cause her to react to the reproach negatively or feel offended.

3. A CLOSE FRIEND SHOULD APPROACH HER: It should be noted that a close friend of the offender or a neighbor with whom she has a very good relationship is usually the best person to approach her, since with them she is least likely to react in self-defense. Such a friend or neighbor would also know the most appropriate way of putting the message across. Since the offender is aware that this person is a good friend of hers, she is likely to take it the right way, rather than feel that she is interfering in her personal affairs.

Accordingly, when a problem is noticed that may not be ignored, it is advisable to find out first of all who the offending person's friends are. The problem should then be discreetly discussed with one of them with the aim that she approach the offender and be instrumental in correcting the situation. A number of case histories are known where this was found to be the correct approach, both with adult girls and with married women. Usually it is best if just one friend goes alone so as to keep as low a profile as possible. However, in some very severe cases it will be found that if two friends go together it is easier for both of them to accept the mission. Moreover, when two people come together the visit carries more weight than when just one friend comes alone.

4. A CLOSE FRIEND SHOULD OFFER TO IMPROVE THE ITEM: If the friend is good at sewing, it is an excellent idea for her to immediately offer to rectify the piece of clothing. For example, to offer to tighten the head-wear so that it does not slip back, to sew up the slit, to improve the neckline so that it sits correctly round the neck, to improve the back top closure of a dress so that it does not open as frequently happens, to let down the hemline so that the garment is the right length and so on. In this way the burden of having to rectify the fault is immediately taken off the wearer, and the *yetzer horah* for procrastination is averted. Also, the offender will realize the sincerity of her friend's plea. Not only has her friend risked their friendship because she feels so strongly about the issue, but she has demonstrated her true friendship by kindly offering to help her put the inadequacy right.

If the friend or neighbor is incapable of improving the garment, it would still be advisable for her to recommend to the offender someone who is capable of doing so, either free of charge or for payment. Alternatively, she should tell her where a garment with Kosher specifications can be obtained. Should the problem be a *sheitel* that has an unacceptable style, she should recommend an ideal person for her to go to in order to improve the *sheitel* and give it a more refined style without spoiling its quality and good appearance. The extra effort taken to supply this type of information may be very much appreciated and could make all the difference.

The *Vilna Gaon zt'l* in his commentary on *Mishlei* (12:18) writes that the ideal censure is one in which the offender is offered specific advice on how he can better his ways. This is the meaning of the verse - ולשון חכמים מרפא - "Words of rebuke from a wise person contain recommendations on how to heal the fracture".

5. APPROACHING A MOTHER ABOUT HER DAUGHTER'S DRESS: It is obvious that if a young girl dresses inadequately and the mother is apparently at fault, then the mother should be approached by one of her friends who should explain to her that the *halacha* requires that even a young girl does not walk around dressed in such a way. If the mother is not to blame, as the girl insists on dressing in this way, local *mechanchim* must put much thought into how to approach her in the right way. Here again, friends may prove to be the best medium. As each of us will have experienced many a time, there is a special *siyata d'shmaya* when one attempts to do the right thing, especially in an area as dear to *Hashem* as *kedushas Yisroel*.

6. HOW THE CHOFETZ CHAYIM CENSURED A FATHER: The *Chofetz Chayim* was once in Bialystock and stayed with a relative of his who was a wealthy textile merchant. As the *Chofetz Chayim* was speaking to his relative he noticed that the fourteen year old daughter of his relative was wearing a garment which was obviously far too short. He reacted by telling the father that he would like to speak to him privately, which he subsequently did.

After the *Chofetz Chayim* left the house, the wealthy man called his daughter and told her that the *Chofetz Chayim* had said to him the following: "Reb Chayim, you sell cloth for outfits and dresses. Why are you miserly when it comes to the cloth you make available for your daughter's clothes? If only you would spare her an extra half meter, her garment would be the right length and far more appropriate!" (*Chayov Upeolo Shel haChofetz Chayim,* Chapter 99, page 1012).

There is much to learn from the way the *Chofetz Chayim* dealt with this person. Firstly, he was careful not to embarrass anyone - especially a father in front of his daughter. He therefore called the father into a side room and did not speak to him within earshot of his daughter. Secondly, the psychology the *Chofetz Chayim* used when talking to the father was to assume that he agreed that the garment was too short. Thirdly, he left it to the father to talk to the girl. Once again, he assumed that the girl would be only too willing to dress in a more appropriate manner, and that there was no need to attack her with "big guns". Moreover, in this way he involved the father in his campaign for improved *tznius*. Finally, he demonstrated *tznius* by his very behavior. Since talking to the father would suffice and he could avoid talking to the girl or her mother, he left it at that.

7. IF APPROACHED CORRECTLY PEOPLE USUALLY COMPLY: For those who feel that rebuke in this field must backfire, it could be interesting to read the testimony of an American girl (later Rebbetzen Chava Pincus) who went from the States to Cracow in 1932. She writes the following about her first meeting with Sarah Schneirer *o.h.* (Daughters of Destiny p.194):

"The following incident during that first meeting left an indelible impression. I was dressed in a light, sand-colored silky dress, trimmed past my knees. The neckline, too, I thought was proper; but I soon found out that it did not meet the requirements of Sarah Schneirer. She greeted me warmly, in her deep Galician Yiddish. Although I did not understand every word she said, I truly felt welcome.

"Still smiling, she approached me, took a large pin and pinned up the neckline of my dress, saying something to the effect that in *Beis Yaakov* we insist on one hundred-percent *tznius* and cannot compromise in any way whatsoever. Some of the girls - my new friends and protectors - stood aghast. As for me, oddly enough I felt no resentment or embarrassment. It must have been her unassuming simplicity and obvious sincerity that somehow made her gesture seem both natural and in place. No, I did not feel any embarrassment! I followed her into the room and seated myself at her side to say *Shir HaShirim* for the first time in Cracow."

8. "IT IS HYPOCRITICAL IF I DRESS B'TZNIUS" - ERRONEOUS: Women and girls will sometimes refuse to implement an improvement in their way of dress although they fully understand the importance of wearing refined and *tznius'dik* clothes. On close questioning as to why they resist changing, they answer that they feel it would be hypocritical for them to dress in this way. They are far from refined and it would be a falsehood on their part to dress in a way that projects an image of *eidelkeit*.

These women and girls must be told that although they mean well they are very mistaken. Hypocrisy applies when one's actions are totally insincere and one is assuming a false appearance of virtue. It therefore applies when a person tells others to behave in a certain way, stressing how important it is to do so, but the person himself makes no attempt to behave in that way. It furthermore applies when a person behaves in a certain way just for his "public image" - to make a good impression and create a virtuous image, whilst in private he willingly does just the opposite.

However, when a person conducts himself in a perfect manner because this is the ideal way to behave, and he yearns for the day when his inner person or his private and personal conduct will fit the fine image his public conduct projects, there is absolutely nothing wrong in conducting oneself with impeccable public behavior. Actually, in the case of *tznius'dik* clothes this is especially correct, since to dress inadequately is harmful to society at large. It is therefore totally out of question to conduct oneself in a way harmful to other Jewish people just because one knows that in privacy or in one's inner thoughts and emotions there is still much to be desired.

Concerning the feeling of falsehood, the person should be told that in the ways of the Torah a person is in fact recommended to do things which are above his present standard, in order to improve. Actions mold a person's character, and he may well reach the required standard by conducting himself in this virtuous way. The *Chinuch* (16:1) writes האדם נפעל כפי פעולותיו - "A person's qualities are formed by his actions". For example, by training a child to be tidy, parents put orderliness and regularity into the child's life, and these eventually become second nature to him. Due to this great truth we educate our children to behave perfectly concerning obligations between man and *Hashem* and between man and man. This training, although artificial at the start, makes a deep and indelible impression on the child and will last him a life-time. Similarly, when a woman or girl dresses in an appropriate and *tznius'dik* manner, this proper conduct works its way "from the outside in" and as a result of it, she will become a thoroughly refined and *eidel* person.

M. THE EXCEPTIONAL RESPONSIBILITY OF PARENTS

1. FUTURE ATTITUDES DEPEND ON A SOUND CHINUCH: Parents, and particularly the mother, have a very special obligation to ensure that a girl grows up with a positive attitude towards *tznius* and a healthy appreciation of it - (see Chapter Three concerning the importance of implanting a healthy feeling for *tznius* from a very young age). In *Shir HaShirim* (7:2) Shlomo Hamelech compares the *tznua* to a piece of jewelry shaped by a craftsman, מה יפו פעמיך בנעלים וכו׳ כמו חלים מעשה ידי אמן (see *Rashi* and *Rinah Shel Torah* by the *Netziv zt'l).* Just as a piece of jewelry is shaped with great care and devotion, so too, the *tznius* and inner qualities of the *Bas Yisroel* are a result of years of painstaking nurturing by parents and teachers alike.

Whilst it is beyond the scope of this *sefer* to deal with general *chinuch* problems, a number of important points concerning *chinuch* of *tznius* must nevertheless be mentioned, because many a problem can be prevented with ease, if, from the start, the mother takes the correct approach. We are referring to a mother who lives up to the basic standards of *tznius* herself. Otherwise, the girl will view her mothers censure on these matters as pure hypocrisy and it is likely to have the opposite effect to the one desired.

If difficulties such as resistance or rebellion arise, the advice of a wise *Torah'dik mechanech* should be sought as soon as possible. Broadly speaking, with warmth, encouragement, praise and reward, many a difficulty in *chinuch* can be overcome or even be avoided - see *Mekoros* 7:1.

2. CHINUCH MUST NOT BE LEFT TO SCHOOL OR CHEDER: Children must be trained in *tznius* and good *midos* at home long before they go to school or *cheder*. It is a fallacy to imagine that one can simply leave this and other parts of elementary *chinuch* to the school or *cheder*. There are many points to mention. The following are some of them:-

▪ Allowing the child to grow to the age of five with no *chinuch* at all, or at least not in these important areas, means denying the child the purest type of *chinuch* which is a *chinuch* that precedes an opposite mode of behavior - see 3:C:1 below.

▪ The child forms the impression that this is not a matter of considerable importance to the parents. Otherwise it would not have been possible for the parents to have disregarded the issue all this time.

▪ Such a child will probably not be given a comprehensive *chinuch* from the school or *cheder*, because schools are only geared to complement what the child has already received from home.

▪ Intelligent parents understand their child and his needs better than anyone else. Since *chinuch* should be given according to their child's personal needs (חנוך לנער על פי דרכו - "Educate the child by the means most suited to him" - *Mishlei* 22:6), parents are supremely suited for it and it is wrong to leave it completely to the teacher in school or *cheder*.

▪ The value of being told lovingly by mother or father on a one-to-one basis in the home-setting cannot be matched by a teacher in a classroom situation away from home.

▪ Other parents who are far more careful with the *chinuch* of their child may not want their child to play with and befriend a child that is not given a proper *chinuch* at home. If this were to happen, the parents would be to blame for the fact that the child has difficulty in finding good friends.

3. MOTHERS SHOULD DRESS TASTEFULLY AT ALL TIMES: It is most important that the mother dresses at all times in a respectable, reasonably attractive and tasteful manner. Her clothes should be as colorful as is appropriate, and should always be clean and presentable. If the mother dresses in this way, her daughter will grow up considering *tznius* as an attribute belonging to a mode of dress which she herself would like to emulate once she is an adult.

On the other hand, if the mother does not care about her dress and looks drab and dull (even if only indoors), the daughter will associate *tznius* with a colorless, dreary and boring way of dress to which she does not aspire. If the mother's clothes are not always in good condition and clean, the girl might relate *tznius* to shabby and neglected clothes. Should this happen, it could be most difficult to uproot this mistaken concept and make her understand that *tznius* is in fact totally compatible with a tasteful and aesthetic way of dress.

It must be mentioned that, quite apart from the *chinuch* of the children, it is a woman's obligation towards her husband to always look appealing to him. With this she brings warmth, happiness and contentment to the home. In our times, when husbands are exposed to so much corruption, it has become more important than ever that when he comes home he finds his wife cheerful and dressed in a pleasing way. It is important that even the housecoat she wears is colorful and clean, since that is the garment in which he sees his wife a large part of the time. Unfortunately, some women dress very well when outside the house, but neglect this whole area when at home among just the close family, often wearing a soiled or shabby housecoat and apron. By doing so, they are perpetrating an injustice towards their husbands and are harming the *chinuch* of their children. See 1:R below for an extensive treatment of this subject and see *Mekoros* 2:3-4, 4:2, 7:9-10.

4. FATHER'S RESPONSIBILITY FOR CHINUCH OF DAUGHTERS: Although the role of the mother has been stressed, it would be wrong to give the impression that the father is exempt from the *chinuch* of his daughters concerning clothes and similar matters. In fact the father must always see to it, and if necessary demand, that all *halachos* and accepted standards of *tznius* are kept by his daughters. Just as a father feels a great responsibility to find a good *cheder* or *yeshiva* for his sons and constantly keeps a close watch on their progress - so, and no less so, he must ensure that his daughters are given the very best *chinuch* available. He must constantly watch out for any lapses in standards of *tznius* or general refinement.

This interest should not start when the daughter is a teenager and already somewhat set in her ways. Rather, it should be implemented from as tender an age as possible. The sincerity of the father on these types of issues will make an enormous impression on the pure soul of his young daughter and will stand her in good stead for the rest of her life - see *Mekoros* 7:1-3.

5. FATHERS UNDERRATE EFFECT OF THEIR DAUGHTER'S DRESS: A note of caution must be mentioned concerning the attitude of some fathers towards the way their daughters dress. Fathers are sometimes very poor judges as far as the *tznius* of their daughter's clothes is concerned - and some fathers even ridicule words of reproach that are said to them regarding this matter. This stems from a number of reasons:

▪ Firstly, father often do not realize that others can be affected by his daughter's appearance although he is indifferent to it. In a good *chinuch*, however, a father will take utmost care to ensure that his daughter dresses as is *halachically* required, and will consider the effect she can have on others.

▪ Secondly, fathers often think of their school-age daughter as still a 'young girl' (sometimes caused by a friendly nick-name that she had as a young girl still being used by the father) and do not realize that she is in fact a young lady and old enough for her inadequate dress or lack of refinement to be detrimental to men who see her. Occasionally, they are blinded by their daughter's desire to overdress or sport ostentatious jewelry. Out of their love for their daughter they fail to see the harm it can cause her and others.

▪ Thirdly, the *Sefer Chasidim* by *Rabbeinu Yehuda HaChassid,* Chapter 41 writes that young people have a stronger urge to intermingle than people who are no longer so young. The same is stated by *Rabbeinu Dovid* in the *Taz*, E.H. 115:7. A person who is middle aged is therefore largely out-of-touch with the urges of young people and particularly those that are unmarried. Therefore a fathers opinion will sometimes be based on an invalid yardstick that gives him a wrong reading. Only *Gedolei Yisroel* who are guided by sayings and warnings of *Chazal,* are in possession of the accurate yardstick even when they are of a very senior age.

6. CHINUCH FOR TZNIUS DOES NOT END AT BAS-MITZVA: The parents' obligation to educate their daughter on matters pertaining to modesty and *tznius* does not come to an end once she becomes *Bas-mitzva*. Although as far as training to do *mitzvos* such as *netilas yadayim* and saying brachos before eating is concerned, the obligation to train a child ends once he reaches adulthood (due to which the father says the *bracha* of "*Baruch sheptorani*" during the *Bar-mitzva* period - O.C. 225:2), *tznius* is different.

This is because, whenever training for an issue is naturally required beyond the *Bar-mitzva* or *Bas-mitzva* age, the obligation of *chinuch* extends into the child's adult years. For example, the rule that the obligation of *chinuch* terminates at twelve or thirteen does not apply to such things as *chinuch* for learning Torah, for good *midos*, for *Yiras Shomayim*, for behaving with modesty or for dressing *b'tznius*, since concerning these parts of *Yiddishkeit* it would be wholly inadequate to only train the children during their pre-*Bar-mitzva* or *Bas-mitzva* years (*Kiddushin* 30a. *Shulchan Aruch Harav, Hilchos Talmud Torah* 1:6). In fact, on issues of *tznius*, a girl needs more guidance during her adolescent years than when she was younger, because desires for forms of dress, adornment and makeup which involve degrees of immodesty are far more intense during adolescent years.

Accordingly, both parents are responsible for their daughter's conduct as long as they can influence her. That is often until she steps under the *chupah*.

It is understood that the older the girl, the more thought must be invested into how to approach her on these matters. To our good fortune, the Torah gives us guidance on the most elementary principles of how to approach and to influence women to keep Torah and *mitzvos*. Moshe Rabbeinu was told by *Hashem Yisborach*, כה תאמר לבית יעקב ותגיד לבני ישראל - "Say the following to the Jewish women in a warm and gentle manner, and communicate it to the men of *Klal Yisroel* in a firm and authoritative manner" (*Rashi Shemos* 19:3). From here we see that women must be spoken to with compassion and encouragement rather than in a harsh and demanding manner.

Parents who genuinely feel the importance of *tznius,* will succeed in implanting these convictions into the next generation, because sincerity is "infectious" and highly influential. Dovid Hamelech says in *Tehillim* - אשרי איש ירא את ה׳ במצותיו חפץ מאוד גבור בארץ יהיה זרעו דור ישרים יבורך - "Happy is the man who is a sincere *Y'rei shomayim,* who has a great yearning for *mitzvos*; his children will be people of great spirit, his family will be upright and blessed" (*Tehillim* 112:1,2). The sincerity of the father has a intense effect on his children. His words, spoken from the deep inner feelings of his heart, leave a profound mark on them.

N. PARENTAL PRESSURE TO DRESS INAPPROPRIATELY

1. KIBUD AV DOES NOT OVERRIDE OTHER OBLIGATIONS: Occasionally, a girl is fully prepared to dress in accordance with the *halacha*. However, her parents exert pressure on her to dress or use makeup in a way that would infringe on the requirements of *tznius*. It is self understood that in the first place she should try to convince them that her opinion is correct. The arguments presented in later notes (see 1:Q:2) will hopefully assist her. However, if this does not help, the girl must know that although *Kibud Av V'em* is one of the most important *mitzvos* and one must do everything that is within one's power to fulfill the wishes of one's parents, nevertheless, in matters such as these (and other clear cut *halachos*) the girl must stand her ground and not yield to their desire.

This is because fulfilling a *mitzva* (*min haTorah* or *mid'Rabanan*) is an act of honoring *Hashem*, and it is a principle of *Mitzvas Kibud Av V'eim* that one must not forgo the honor of *Hashem* because of the honor of parents (Y.D. 240:15). This girl must therefore try to convince her parents that she would be most unhappy wearing these clothes, using such makeup, etc. If this does not help, she must still not give in.

However, even under these trying circumstances, she must behave towards her parents as politely as possible [talking calmly and not arguing with them - which is the *issur min haTorah* of לא סותר דבריו - "a son must not contradict or argue with his father" - Y.D. 240:2]. Instead, she should explain to them that although she respects them deeply, in this instance it is not possible for her to comply with their wishes. If opportune, she should give them this or a similar *sefer* as this might help to change their attitude. See 9:C:2(c) for a further example of a *tznius* requirement that clashes with the wishes of a father - see *Mekoros* 8:1.

2. A DAUGHTER MUST SEEK GUIDANCE HOW TO REACT: The issue we are dealing with in this section is of a most sensitive nature. On the one hand, obligations of *tznius* could be at stake, whilst on the other hand the enormously great and important *mitzva* of *kibud av v'eim* might be infringed upon without justification. The area of disagreement might be about something which is just an extra refinement of *tznius* that the daughter would like to implement and to which her mother disagrees. In such a case, the daughter must in fact do what her parents want, since only true obligations or true *issurim* override *mitzvas kibud av v'eim*, not stringencies that are up to the person to do or not to do - see *Responsa Arugas Habosem* O.C. 19. See also 7:D:4 below concerning what is Halacha and must be kept and what is a stringency and is beyond her standard and can be drooped.

It is therefore imperative that the girl first checks with a *Rav* to confirm that she is correct in refusing to wear what her parents want her to wear and that she is behaving correctly in refusing to comply with their wishes. She should listen carefully to his answer, since the *Rav* might add a bit of advice or add a clause to his *p'sak* which changes the picture very substantially.

3. SEEKING A SHIDDUCH - NO JUSTIFICATION TO RELAX TZNIUS: A father looking for a *shidduch* for his daughter, will occasionally encourage her to dress in strikingly beautiful clothes or to beautify herself with lavish jewelry and makeup, so that she will be exceptionally good-looking and attractive. With such advice the father is unknowingly corrupting his daughter, since such dress does great damage to the girl's feeling for *tznius*. While *Chazal* instruct a father to dress his daughter who has reached marriageable age in attractive clothes so that she projects an appealing and lovely image (*Kesubos* 52b), he must not encourage her to beautify herself to the point that her appearance is striking and entices people to gaze at her.

The following is a free translation of the holy words of the *Ohr Hachayim* on the verse, ואל תחלל את בתך להזנותה - "Do not profane your daughter and cause her to be immoral" (*Vayikra* 19:29) where he warns about this serious mistake: **"In this verse the father is warned not to treat his daughter as a discredited person and cause her to show-off her beauty for all to see. She is a *Bas Melachim* - a princess - and requires sheltering. Even if the father is motivated in displaying her beauty by the need to find her a *shidduch*, he must nevertheless not cause her to go out in ostentatious clothes, as this will undermine her purity; it will kindle a fire of immorality within her which in turn can have harmful results. Also, by appearing in public in such dress, she arouses the fire of desire in the eyes of those who see her. Therefore, the father who makes his daughter appear in public overdressed and over-adorned, will be held responsible for bringing corruption to the world, etc."** *Yidden* of every walk of life have the greatest respect for the words of the *Ohr Hachayim*. Hopefully these words of the *Ohr Hachayim* will be treated with no less reverence.

4. TZNIUS IS A "PROFITS ONLY" INVESTMENT: No girl should think that by being a *tznua* and staying out of the limelight her chances of finding a *shidduch* are diminished. The truth is just the opposite. People looking for a suitable girl for their son will consider her *tznius'dik* way of dress and her refined and noble conduct, as proof that she is a girl with special qualities and values, and just the type they are looking for.

The last words in the *Eishes Chayil* read ויהללו בשערים מעשיה - "and her deeds shall be praised in public" (*Mishlei* 31:31). The *Malbim* writes that if a woman's praise is her external beauty, it is wrong for her praise to be discussed or talked about in public. However, when a woman's praise is *Yiras Hashem,* to the point that she is called an אשה יראת ה׳ - "a woman who embodies *Yiras Hashem*", it is appropriate for her praise to be spoken about in public. Such publicity leads to an even greater appreciation of *Yiras Hashem* and makes people aware how great its value is. So also, when a girl is a *tznua,* her essential qualities will be well recognized and will form an important part of her general acclaim and praise.

Ruth behaved in the field with exemplary modesty, so that the harvesters would not be attracted to her and try to befriend her - See *Rashi, Ruth* 2:5. By doing so she was successful in keeping them away. However, her exceptionally modest behavior caught the attention of the *Gadol Hador*, Boaz, who was amazed at her noble character and *eidelkeit*. This in turn led to her *shidduch!*. Distancing herself from men ultimately led her to a wonderful union that was to secure her a foremost place in the history of *Klal Yisroel*. "Keeping out of the limelight" resulted in her becoming the grandmother of Dovid Hamelech and even sitting in a place of honor in his palace - (see 6:Q:4 and 9:J:7 below).

This should be one of our mottos for life: Doing what is right can only lead to greater and greater benefits. Shlomo Hamelech coined a phrase to that effect that we must take with us on our travels through this world, שומר מצוה לא ידע דבר רע - "He who obeys the commandment will know no real harm!" (*Koheles* 8:5) - see 2:K:4 and 9:A:4 below.

O. UNIQUE RESPONSIBILITY OF TEACHERS AND MATRONS

1. THE FAR REACHING EFFECT OF A TEACHER'S WAY OF DRESS:

(a) The great responsibility of a teacher: Teachers and matrons who are responsible for the welfare of young or adolescent girls must be even more careful than others that their dress and general appearance reflect true Jewish modesty. They provide a role model to their pupils and charges as girls look up to them and naturally assume that their way of dress is undoubtedly perfect. Therefore, if they are lax in this all-important area it is tantamount to misleading those who are in their care. On the other hand, if they dress in a truly fitting manner, they instill with this a healthy attitude towards *tznius* in the hearts and minds of their *talmidos*. Teachers should view implanting in the girls a feeling and appreciation for *tznius* as the culmination of all their efforts, since with *tznius* they are bringing to fruition all the *yiddishkeit* they have taught them - see *Mekoros* 9:1, 9:5-6.

(b) There must be no negative influence from the teaching staff: The author of this *sefer* has been involved in incidents when seminary graduates with sound *hashkafos* teach in Orthodox Jewish schools and are eager to impart an understanding for *tznius* and refined dress to their pupils. Their efforts have, however, been frustrated and come to nothing, because the school in which they teach employs a Jewish lady teacher who turns up with a dress that has a slit, a wholly unsatisfactory neckline, a garment of inadequate length and similar shortcomings. Since the headmistress employs a teacher who goes around in such clothes, the pupils conclude that she does not attach much importance to matters of *tznius*. As a result of this, all that is said to the pupils about *tznius* and personal refinement falls onto deaf ears.

If these young teachers do not feel capable of speaking directly to the headmistress or to the offending teacher herself, they should write a modest but firm letter to the headmistress, stating their great concern and misgivings at the fact that the school employs a teacher whose dress projects a distinct lack of *tznius* and that the pupils are obviously aware of this. They are therefore requesting the headmistress to do all that is in her power to correct this matter and ensure that the required improvements are brought about.

(c) A teacher gains great *chizuk* from teaching about *tznius*: One of the most effective ways for a girl to maintain the standard of *tznius*, *Yiras Shomayim* and *ahavas haTorah* she has absorbed at home or in her seminary, is by teaching others and imparting these values and riches to them. By teaching others, and pondering ways of explaining the importance of these issues to them, she personally gains enormously. The effort to give, will serve as a constant source of self *chizuk* which is so vital in the confused times in which we live.

In *seforim* this issue is compared to the Torah principle of, איידי דטריד למפלט לא בלע - "When [meat] is busy exuding [blood] it will not absorb [blood that falls on it]" (*Chullin* 113a). Due to this principle, if blood falls onto a piece of meat which has been salted and is in the process of exuding its own blood, it is not rendered *treife* by the new blood. Since the meat is busy exuding its own blood it will not absorb the new blood that falls on it - Y.D. 70:1. Similarly, a person who is busy imparting Torah truths and passing them on to others, is naturally safeguarded from absorbing the falsehoods and enticements that blow in his direction and threaten to be absorbed into his conscious or sub-conscious mind.

2. HOW A WONDERFUL TEACHER INSTILLED A LOVE FOR TZNIUS: It is gratifying to read a tribute to an excellent teacher in the book entitled *"Eishes Chayil"*, the biography of Rebbetzen Elisheva Shechter *o.h.* She, an outstanding woman, mother and teacher, lived in *Eretz Yisroel* and was the wife of a *Rosh Kollel* in the town of Rechasim. She died in *Tishri* 5750 - 1989 at the young age of thirty. In spite of her young age, she left behind a very rich legacy. We will mention several striking points:

(a) The impression she made on those who saw her: Towards the beginning of the book (page 46) the writer describes her as a young mother: "As Elisheva grew older, her modesty grew in stature. She was an example of true *tznius*; in her appearance and in her actions. She lived with a simplicity that was so internalized that it was natural. She lived with the creed - 'the glory of *Hashem* is in the unrevealed' - (כבוד אלוקים הסתר דבר - *Mishlei* 25:2).

One of her neighbors described her: 'She was the image of the Jewish mother - so modest. Her headscarf - always neatly tied, worn as one wears a crown, with grace and majesty. Her face - pure and noble. She was never conspicuous in her outward appearance and yet she was always outstanding in her simplicity and modesty'.

She herself was a paradigm of Jewish modesty. Her dress was clean, her needs, humble. Her words were always soft and low keyed. All external elements of her dress and personality were quiet and unassuming. She represented the Torah dictum, 'Walk humbly alongside *Hashem*' - הצנע לכת את ה' אלוקיך - *Micha* 6:8)."

(b) The influence she had on her neighbors: The impact she had on her immediate environment is described later in the book (page 101). "Without lecturing or fanfare, she had a major impact, for her regal bearing, combined with her modest simplicity, attracted the curiosity of her non-observant neighbors. They saw that the Torah way of life was paved with serenity and satisfaction - that it was a pleasant way of living.

"Neighbors whose choice of fashions could hardly be described as reflecting a sense of modesty, found themselves slowly changing their dress. One male neighbor who rarely walked around fully clothed began to be more careful of his appearance. His friends asked him for the reason behind his obvious change. He explained, 'I simply can't walk around like that in front of the *Rabbanit*'."

A young Talmudic student came to visit the family during the week of the *shivah* and told the following story (page 99):

"I used to live near your home as a non-Orthodox young boy. Very often I went on the same bus as your daughter. Her unusual fine behavior, the way she carried herself with nobility yet with modest humility and the way she never wasted her time on the bus, impressed me deeply. Even though I was very young, I said to myself: 'if observant people are like that, then there must be something to their way of life'."

Some time later, the young boy became a fully observant young man!

(c) How she inspired her co-teachers: One of the teachers on the staff of the school in which she taught described her in the teacher's room. "How inspiring it was to look at her. She exemplified the principle of 'strength and dignity are her clothing'- (עוז והדר לבושה - *Mishlei* 31:25). She personified the dignity of a woman who was neatly outfitted, while having the strength of character to avoid the mad dash after fashion and never minding 'what people had to say'.

"Her chair is empty - in our room and in our hearts! That growing emptiness should inspire us to try to fill the void she has left. How I wish it were possible for [us to have once again] just a little of the grandeur that filled that corner of our teacher's room" (page 53).

(d) The impact she had on her students: Further on in the book, when describing her as a teacher, the writer records (on page 145) what her pupils would say:

"Next to our teacher, we just couldn't wear hair styles that didn't match our *Beis Yaakov* life style".

"When you stood near her, you felt very uncomfortable wearing clothes in colors or styles that weren't according to *halacha*".

"She didn't always say anything, but we felt ourselves squirming inside if we weren't dressed properly and she happened to notice".

Pupils would furthermore recall: "The teacher never told us, "Don't wear this or that, or don't comb your hair this way. She would just gently suggest, 'I wouldn't wear that'. Very often she would only hint at what she meant and we got her message. Usually we'd see some facial grimace, and a long silent stare and that was enough to understand what she meant!

Whether she spoke or was silent, there was always a reaction. She was sensitive to our failings and left us slightly ashamed and very determined to dress better tomorrow. We knew that she'd notice that too!".

(e) How she planted deep feelings of *tznius* in her students: The book continues to describe the importance she attached to teaching about *tznius*: "Elisheva was constantly aware of the problem of proper and modest dress for a young woman. She asked advice from her husband and mother as how to 'instill this concept' rather than teach it. She knew that it was a feeling that needed internalization in order to achieve its external effect.

She would be heard to say: "How can one instill sensitivity to *tznius*? It must be something that is understood by the heart, not dictated by notes from a teacher. We must get to the root of the problem. Our treatment must be deep, deep into the soul. We mustn't relate to *tznius* as a collection of do's and don'ts. When we treat it in such a petty manner we reduce its value. A girl must be guided so that she can make her own lists of do's and don'ts - one that reflects the Torah values we try to instill in her. It must come from within".

She included this topic in many of her weekly *parshas hashevua* lessons. Short remarks on *tznius* were consistently part of the subject matter of her lessons. Her first class of the year was always devoted to the subject of *tznius* in all of its aspects. In this manner she showed the girls what her real priorities were.

(f) How she taught her pupils not to go to unsuitable places: The all important principle of guarding oneself from contamination she instilled into her pupils during a class trip. A student related the following (page 138):

"We went on a short day trip in the area of Haifa passing a certain place the entire class wanted to see. We begged her to let us detour and tour this particular area. She explained that she had never been there and therefore could not take her students.

"We begged her with all the powers of persuasion we possessed, but to no avail. She didn't get angry or raise her voice. With a simple 'No! And that's that!' she stood her ground. It was against her principles to take her students to visit a place where she had never been or was sure was suitable. She put us off, saying that if any of us really wanted to go, we could ask our mothers or grandmothers to take us.

"As our teacher, I'm sure now that she wanted us to have a good time that day. It must have been very difficult for her not to give in to our pouting and persuading. However, her deep belief that her refusal was justified and logical made her able to withstand our disappointed looks."

(g) How she would react to a rebellious individual: Concerning how to handle an individual who needed disciplining in matters of *tznius*, the following is recorded (on page 149): "A colleague of hers asked Elisheva's opinion on how to approach a particular student who did not dress properly.

"I discussed the problem with the girl and still there is no difference in her appearance" complained the teacher. Elisheva answered her forcefully, 'Keep mentioning the issue. Do not give in or give up! Even if you feel uncomfortable with the idea of reprimanding a girl about the same thing, you must not relent. Be tactful, but obstinate. Refuse to accept the way she dresses. The results are sure to follow. Maybe not immediately but they will come.'

"Elisheva attempted to crown each student with an inner grace and beauty, for she knew that the crown of modesty is the highest reward adorning a Jewish woman, from ages bygone and will be for ages hence". (*Culled from the book 'Eishes Chayil' with kind permission of Feldehim Publishers*).

These very interesting and highly informative paragraphs contain guidance that many teachers will find useful, and chizuk that can encourage many to try even harder when difficulties prevail. They have been recorded at length because of the great value in transmitting guidance and chizuk to our teachers and sisters. This is so important that it justifies every expenditure of effort.

3. THE RESPONSIBILITY OF WIVES OF TALMIDEI CHACHAMIM: Special mention must be made concerning wives of *Rabbanim* and *Talmidei Chachamim*. If they do not dress to the standard the *halacha* requires, they will be held responsible for the apathy and indifference of the rest of the town on issues of *tznius* and general refinement. They should take note of the following *Chazal* - כל פירצה שאין בה מגדולי ישראל אינה פירצה. Freely translated this means, "A breach which involves important people is a serious breach and its power of destruction is far-reaching" (*Breishis Rabba* 26:5).

People assume that whatever these women do has obviously been sanctioned by their husbands. They consequently jump to the conclusion that there must be a *halachic* justification to be lenient in these matters, and that those who preach differently are "*machmirim*" at the expense of the pleasure and happiness of women. They will consider a Rebbetzen's way of dress as conclusive proof that there is nothing wrong in being lax (even though they must be aware of the fact that women sometimes do things which are not to the liking of their husbands, since there is a desire to look glamorous, to follow up-to-date fashions etc., any "proof" that indicates that one may be lenient is accepted as good enough evidence to justify doing so.)

Concerning the garment of a *Talmid Chacham,* we are taught that his robe is long (*Bava Basra* 57b) and that his garments are clean and unstained (*Shabbos* 114a). He is the aristocracy of the Jewish people and his outer garb reflects his inner worth. Being well covered (wearing a full size robe) and neatly dressed (clean and pleasant) ensures that the correct image is projected. *Chazal* say that אשת חבר כחבר - "the wife of a *Talmid Chacham* is comparable to him" (*Shevuos* 30b). She too is an aristocratic individual. It is therefore fitting that, like her husband, her outer garb exhibits the type of person she is. She should therefore wear a garment that comfortably reaches an adequate length, and items that have a refined *Yiddishe* taste. She will then serve the same function as her husband, the *Talmid Chacham,* who teaches Torah and its values to others. With her *eidel* dress and aristocratic bearing she too will teach others the ways of the Torah and that refinement of dress and conduct, is both beautiful and essential - see *Mekoros* 9:3-4.

P. THE SPECIAL RESPONSIBILITY OF HUSBANDS

1. HUSBANDS MUST INSIST ON TZNIUS AND REFINED CLOTHES: The person most directly responsible for ensuring that a woman dresses correctly is her husband. He is probably aware whether her taste, as far as clothes are concerned, is within the parameters of *tznius*, or, as happens all too often nowadays, extends beyond acceptable limits. Most women are blessed with the attribute expressed by *Chazal* with the words איזה אשה כשרה העושה רצון בעלה - "Who is a good wife? - She who fulfills the wishes of her husband" (*Tana D'bei Eliyahu* 9). Therefore, with encouragement from her husband, and an understanding but firm stand on this matter, potential problems can safely be averted. The facts are, however, that unfortunately, even in homes where all other *mitzvos* of the Torah are scrupulously adhered to, this area of *halacha* is often neglected. Both fathers and husbands allow modes of dress that violate *halacha* and דרכי הצניעות - see *Mekoros* 10.

Husbands sometimes relinquish their responsibility for this issue, saying that they have tried time and again to influence their wives to dress in a fully Kosher manner and have had no success. The following incident may contain the answer to these husbands. A number of years ago, Maran Hagaon Harav Elazar Shach *shlita, Rosh Yeshivas Ponevez*, spoke to young men in *Bnei Brak* about *tznius*-related issues. After the *shiur* a young man came up to the

Rosh Yeshiva saying that he had given up trying to influence his wife on these matters because she simply did not accept it from him.

To this the *Rosh Yeshiva shlita* answered, "*Chazal* say it is natural for a woman to do her husband's desire and bidding, and only very few disregard their husband's wishes. Therefore, if you really wanted your wife to dress in a fully Kosher manner with all your heart, she would almost certainly agree to do so. Since she does not comply, it would appear that you are not truly concerned about your wife's mode of dress even though you say you are, and she detects this lack of sincerity in you" - see *Mekoros* 10:3.

2. HE SHOULD EXPRESS DOUBTS HE HAS ABOUT A GARMENT: When a husband knows that his wife is a refined *Bas Yisroel* who is not inclined to seek acclaim and certainly does not want to attract the attention to herself, he is likely to trust his wife's taste unreservedly. He will therefore remain quiet when his wife comes home having bought a dress or coat which seems to him to be rather loud, rather tight or to have some other shortcoming. Since he knows his wife's impeccable character, he will put his feelings down to a lack of understanding on his part about ladies' clothing.

It is important for such a man to know that women usually have a greater appreciation for beauty and elegance and are more attracted to it than men. This liking has nothing to do with projecting their own image and role - it is simply that women possess a greater affinity for beauty than men. Due to this love for elegance and design, they are prone to err in their judgment as to what is calm and refined more than men who can be more objective.

On the verse גם ושתי המלכה עשתה משתה נשים בית המלכות אשר למלך אחשורוש - "Also Queen Vashti made a feast for women in the royal residence of King Achashveirosh" (*Esther* 1:9), the *Midrash* comments: בית המלכות, בית הנשים מבעי ליה, אמר ר' אבין רוצה אשה בבגדים מצויירין ובתים מצויירין מלאכול עגלים מפוטמים - "The women were entertained inside the palace because women enjoy beautiful clothes and an exquisitely decorated building more than they enjoy a feast of delicious foods". Therefore, although the men were entertained outdoors in a marquee (*see Esther* 1:5), the women were brought into the palace itself to be entertained there. We see from this that women have a greater appreciation for beauty than men. This phenomenon is well known. For example, women notice the flowers, the decor and the color scheme at a *chasuna* in quite a different way to men.

Accordingly, if a wife has purchased a *sheitel*, outfit, coat or shoes and the husband thinks that it might be too elegant and classy or excessively colorful, he should mention his reservations to his wife, since there could be some truth in his feelings. If necessary, they should seek advice from a third person who is known to have a healthy sense of both beauty and refinement.

3. CALAMITY OF HUSBANDS DEMANDING UNREFINED CLOTHES: Shamefully, it must be put on record that not only do many husbands not fulfill their duty of ensuring the purity of matters pertaining to their home, but they actively encourage their wives to wear provocative *sheitels*, hats, dresses, outfits and tights, to wear flashy or excessive amounts of finery, to use improper amounts of makeup, perfume etc. Such demands are made all too frequently because of what husbands have seen on the street, read in the newspapers, come across in offices etc. Fueled by personal pride, they want their wives to look no less attractive than the other women they encounter.

All that can be said is - "Woe to our generation that has stooped so low!" The damage to *kedushas Yisroel* caused by these husbands is beyond appraisal, particularly as many wives are not strong enough in their resolve in these matters and will do anything to please their husbands. These husbands, who may well be considered as "*heimishe Yidden*" and may even be prominent members of the *kehilla*, are literally aiding and abetting the spread of *pritzus* in *Klal Yisroel* ר״ל - see 1:Q below.

4. WIVES ARE AT TIMES TO BLAME FOR HUSBAND'S ATTITUDE: Although there is no way to condone the desire and request of husbands that their wives look highly attractive even outside the house, it must nevertheless be stated that wives are sometimes responsible for the fact that their husband has such an attitude. If, without the bidding of her husband, a woman dresses inappropriately and glamorously when in public, she causes her husband to expect her to look glamorous whether at home or outdoors. If she suddenly stops dressing in this manner, her husband may well miss it, claiming that he needs his wife to look very beautiful at all times. Therefore, before a woman takes this wrong step of over-dressing in public, she should beware that she is starting on a one-way journey from which it will be very difficult to return.

5. CHASANIM SHOULD BE BRIEFED ABOUT TZNIUS OF DRESS:

(a) Harm caused by young men having mistaken conceptions: To our discredit, even some quite learned husbands have been caught in the trap of condoning *non-tznius'dik* ways of dress, due to not being well enough informed before marriage what the requirements of *tznius* in women's dress are and what they aim to achieve. Some young husbands have heard that people consider "being modern" and "with the latest fashions" synonymous with "being good-looking" - which is a great falsehood, and the cause for much of the lack of *tznius* that occurs in the *chareidi* community. It is therefore the duty of parents and *Rabbanim* to ensure that a healthy respect and appreciation for *tznius* and all that it stands for is instilled into the minds of their sons and *kehilla* members. In fact, many *Rabbanim* constantly "stand on guard" in order that attitudes do not decline in this all-important matter, and periodically mention *tznius* and its obligations in their speeches.

(b) The positive result of briefing *chasanim* on *tznius* of dress: Since husbands must have a healthy understanding of *tznius*, it would seem appropriate to arrange that whoever learns *halachos* with a *chasan* and prepares him for his *chasuna* should also teach him the basic *halachos* of *tznius*. Moreover, it might be right for parents or *mechanchim* to educate *bachurim* in the basic concepts and importance of *tznius*. Although a detailed *chinuch* about different forms of dress is obviously not for them, nevertheless the general facts that inadequate and ostentatious dress are both wrong and very harmful, should be known by all. Young boys and *bachurim* are educated that it is *ossur* for them to gaze at women and girls. It is therefore perfectly in order to tell them that, due to this very *issur*, females must dress and cover all that is *halachically* required, and that they must not dress in public in a particularly attractive manner, since this entices men to look.

Apart from teaching *chasanim* the *halachos* or making *bachurim* aware of the basic concepts, when a father who knows the *halachos* of *tznius* tells his daughter that her neckline is or is not good or that the color of an outfit is fine or is too loud, he should allow his sons to hear his comments, since this is a perfect setting for the *chinuch* of the sons as well as the daughters.

(c) Women will not reply, "But my husband says it is alright": If this matter could be implemented, girls would not occasionally dress incorrectly and then defend themselves with the invalid excuse "My father allows me to dress in this manner!" Similarly, a woman would not justify her wrong-doings with "I've asked my husband and he says this dress is fine". These types of answers are frequently given, but are usually fallacious and ill-founded. Many fathers and husbands have never studied these *halachos* and therefore have no idea what is and what is not permitted. However, if men were educated to at least appreciate the importance and significance of *tznius* in general and how much it affects *kedushas Yisroel*, they would not take the liberty to voice an opinion before checking it out in *seforim* or asking a competent *Rav*. Ideally, fathers and husbands should know the actual *halachos*, since knowledge of the *halachos* is the greatest safeguard to prevent intrusions being made.

(d) Wives will not suffer the dilemma of being given unfitting gifts: If a husband understands that refinement and modesty are the very life-blood of *tznius*, much unpleasantness and heartache can be averted. For example, when a husband buys his wife earrings on the occasion of her birthday or a *Yom Tov*, it can bring them much happiness, or it can conversely cause them much anguish: If the earrings are *eidel* and fitting for her to wear, she could well be overjoyed with them. Her husband will feel that she appreciates the effort he has put into finding such delightful and fitting jewelry. However, if her husband comes home with long drop-earrings or large ring-earrings, his wife is likely to be in a terrible dilemma. On the one hand she does not want to seem to be ungrateful and unappreciative of the effort her husband has put into buying her this present. On the other hand she cannot possibly wear such earrings as they are very eye-catching and anything but *eidel*.

How should this poor woman extricate herself from the quandary she finds herself in? She will have to broach the subject very carefully, so as not to offend her husband and to avoid hurting his feelings. If only he had been briefed before marriage about the basic requirements of *tznius*, this unnecessary pain and trouble would have been avoided.

Although a young newly married man cannot be expected to know which jewelry is refined and which not, nevertheless, had he been briefed about *tznius* before his wedding, he would know that he cannot trust his own feelings at this stage. Instead, he must seek the advice of his mother, sister etc. whom he knows are *tznuos* and who would advise him correctly.

Q. PRESSURE FROM THE HUSBAND TO DRESS IMMODESTLY

1. THE WIFE'S DILEMMA: As has just been mentioned, one of the most depressing and unfortunate features that has developed from the *pritzus* in current times, is the phenomenon of Orthodox women who are willing to dress in a refined and correct manner whilst their husbands demand of them to dress in the latest fashions. They want them to wear unrefined dresses or a bright red coat, use loud and overly attractive cosmetics, go about heavily perfumed, etc. It is very difficult to suggest to the young lady that she ignore her husband's request, since this can have devastating repercussions on their family life. On the other hand, she must not agree to do something forbidden even if her husband wishes her to do so.

2. SHE MUST RESIST WITH CONVICTION AND PERSUASION: This young lady should try to change her husband's attitude by approaching him on this sensitive matter. If he would agree that she dress in the clothes he desires only behind closed doors, whilst in public she dresses as is fitting, then she would willingly do her husband's bidding. However, if he wants her to wear these clothes even in public, she cannot concede because of the *issurim* involved. The following are a number of suggestions for lines of persuasion that she could try in such a case :-

(a) Explaining that 'being an obligation' she cannot capitulate: Firstly, she should explain to her husband that if the way he wished her to dress had been a matter of taste, she would have acceded to his desire. She fully concedes that it is her duty to dress in a way that pleases her husband even if it is not quite to her taste. However, the issues at hand are in fact *halachos,* which are *issurim* either *min haTorah* or *mid'Rabanan* (as can be seen in the sources quoted). She should say to her husband that he would surely not expect her to buy a delicious cake which is known to contain lard (pig fat and *ossur min haTorah*) or non-Jewish wine (*ossur mid'Rabanan*). Likewise, he should not expect her to flout the laws of *tznius* and dress in a forbidden way. Hopefully this irrefutable approach will meet with her husband's consent.

(b) Explaining what she will gain if she dresses properly: Secondly, she should explain to him that *tznius* is a considerable enrichment of the person. *Tznius* symbolizes both the depth and quality of the person, with continuous practice of *tznius* very much enhancing these qualities. On the other hand, dressing in a coarse or showy manner makes the person cheap and hollow. There can hardly be a more valuable investment for their future lives and the lives of their children than to adopt *tznius* as standard practice in their lives - see 10:A-B below.

(c) Explaining that correct dress will bring respect to both of them: Thirdly, in certain cases it would be appropriate for her to say that if he would allow her to dress in a truly Kosher manner, this would arouse an admiration for both of them. People will appreciate both his and his wife's steadfastness in doing only what is *halachically* right rather than copying the misdeeds of the world around them. Eventually, people might even express to either of them their genuine admiration for her *tznius'dik* way of dress.

Even if her husband does not respond favorably right away, she should nevertheless take heart and not despair. Since she is convinced and earnestly wants to do only what is right, she will surely be successful in the end in winning her husband over to her way of thinking. She has most probably heard of the teaching that דברים היוצאים מן הלב נכנסים אל הלב - "Words said with true sincerity find their way into the heart".

(d) An ideal wife encourages her husband to do the *Ratzon Hashem*: The praise this woman richly deserves has been expressed by Shlomo Hamelech. He says in *Eishes Chayil*, גמלתהו טוב ולא רע כל ימי חייה - "She repays him good but not evil all the days of her life" (*Mishlei* 31:12). Being an appreciative wife, she is grateful for all that her husband does on her behalf and is therefore happy and willing to repay him by supporting him fully in all his endeavors. In particular she tries her very best to comply with all that he wishes of her. Concerning this harmonious family setting, the verse says that she will repay her husband by doing all that is good and advantageous to him - but will not concede to do that which is bad for him and to his detriment". For example, if he wants her to obtain money through false pretenses, she will resist doing so, as she knows that not only is it wrong to do so but that it could ultimately harm him. Hence, the *Eishes Chayil* "repays him good but not evil" - she makes every endeavor to repay him with the good he would like, but will not do for him that which is bad and evil even if he mistakenly desires it and asks it of her.

On the role of a wife as an *ezer k'negdo* (*Breishis* 2:18) *Chazal* say, זכה עוזרתו לא זכה כנגדו - "If he is virtuous she helps him; if he is undeserving she opposes him" (*Yevomos* 63a). The *Chofetz Chayim* used to explain this saying as follows: Every wife is both an *ezer* (a help) and a *k'negdo* (an opponent) as is evident from the verse '*ezer k'negdo*' in which every wife is given both titles. However, a good wife is truthfully an *ezer* - a helpmate to her husband - but occasionally, to achieve this very goal, she must be a *k'negdo* - an opponent. This is when for her husband's sake she must refuse to do something he asks of her. On the other hand, a bad wife is truthfully a *k'negdo* - an opponent to her husband - but occasionally she behaves as an *ezer* - a helpmate to him. This is when she complies positively to a wish of his to do a wrongdoing, to which she should in fact have reacted negatively (*Sichos HaChofetz Chayim* No.19. The same explanation is given by the *Netziv* in *Breishis* 2:18).

It is remarkable that when *Chazal* portray 'a wife who saved her husband' they single out a woman who 'resisted' her husband's wrong desire, and when giving an example of 'a wife who destroyed her husband' they mention a woman who 'supported' her husband's bad designs. The Gemara says (*Sanhedrin* 110a) "What is the meaning of the verse (*Mishlei* 14:1) חכמת נשים בנתה ביתה - 'With the wisdom of women she established her home'? This was the wife of On Ben Peles who resisted and prevented her husband from going along with Korach through to the bitter end. Who is referred to when the verse says ואולת בידה תהרסנה - 'The fool actively destroys'? This is the wife of Korach who encouraged her husband in his feud with Moshe Rabbeinu." Accordingly, the woman, who because of her commitment to tznius, resists dressing the way her husband would have liked, is held in high regard and is one of those about whom the verse says חכמת נשים בנתה ביתה.

3. SHE MUST SEEK ADVICE AND NOT DO IT ALONE: It is critically important to establish beyond doubt that the wife has not erred in her refusal to wear what her husband demands. Their complete *shalom bayis* may be jeopardized if it transpires that the wife has taken a firm stand when she was in fact very wrong in doing so. She must therefore ask a competent *Rav* whether the request of her husband is something she may not accede to, or whether it is not totally *ossur*, and although it would be better if such a garment or piece of jewelry were not worn, under the circumstances it would be correct for her to accede to the demands of her husband. The *Rav* may also have practical experience with *shalom bayis* and know this couple well. In such a case he may be able to advise in a profound and incisive way what she should do.

4. GENERALLY, A WIFE TRIES TO MEET HER HUSBAND'S WISHES: Although, under the trying circumstances described, a woman should not capitulate to the wishes of her husband, this is an exception to the normal rule, since generally a woman makes every effort to meet the wishes of her husband. The beautiful partnership between husband and wife generates the blissful atmosphere that is found in a *Torah'dik* home.

This requires that the husband carry on his shoulders the heavy responsibility for the *chinuch* of the children. He sees to it that they develop into ideal *Yidden*, both in their devotion to Torah and *mitzvos* and in their social conduct with people. In all this his wife stands at his side to assist him in his quest to fulfill his mission. She recommends what she thinks the "captain of the ship" should do under given circumstances. As she is his devoted help-mate and advisor for life, he depends heavily on her opinion and considers what she has to say with utmost care. A deep mutual trust is born out of this ideal arrangement. About it the verse says, בטח בה לב בעלה - "Her husband's heart relies of her" (*Mishlei* 31:11).

Since the husband carries the ultimate responsibility for the family, she treats him with considerable respect, thereby giving him the backing and security he requires - see *Rambam Hilchos Ishus* 15:20. As he is predominantly responsible for the general tendency and direction of the family, she takes guidance from him and makes every effort to see things the way he sees them. One of the *Rishonim*, Rabbeinu Menachem haMeiri writes about a good wife in his introduction to *Eishes Chayil,* לומדת מדות אישה עד שתדומה בת בעלה - "She learns from her husband's attributes to the point that she would pass as her husband's daughter!". This positive attitude enables her to agree with her husband when he stands firm by his opinion even regarding issues about which she had originally thought otherwise.

For a woman to submit as far as possible to the decisions of her husband may seem a sign of weakness - as if she is too feeble to stand up for her own opinion and rights. In truth, it is just the opposite, as such conduct usually results from *midos tovos* and from having a healthy and balanced personality.

Yael, the woman who slew the powerful general Sisra after inviting him into her tent, bringing with this a major victory to the Jewish people, was a woman of the type of high caliber just mentioned. *Chazal* say the following about Yael: וכי מה טיבה של יעל שבאת תשועה גדולה על ידה, אמרו אשה כשרה היתה ועושה רצון בעלה, מכאן אמרו אין לך אשה כשרה בנשים אלא אשה שהיא עושה רצון בעלה - "What special qualities did Yael have that such a major salvation should come through her? Our Sages say that Yael was a virtuous woman who would respond favorably to the wishes and aspirations of her husband. From here we learn that the quality and distinction of the virtuous wife lies in her conformity with the wishes and aspirations of her husband" (*Tana D'bei Eliyahu* 11; *Yalkut Shimoni, Shoftim* 42; *Rema,* E.H. 69:7).

In Yael we have a woman praised by *Chazal* for the way she complied with the ideas and wishes of her husband. At the same time we see that, rather than being a weak-willed person, Yael had the outstanding courage and stamina to kill single-handed the mighty warrior Sisra, the general and commander-in-chief of the Canaanite nation. This is the message *Hashem* wants us to learn. Being a faithful and devoted wife is a display of fortitude and real substance, rather than a lack of personality and firm character.

R. A WIFE'S DRESS SHOULD PLEASE HER HUSBAND

1. THE APPEAL OF A WIFE'S DRESS PROTECTS HER HUSBAND: Apart from the public appearance of a woman, it is of maximum importance that a woman dresses at home in a way that she looks clean, pleasant and appealing at all times. To dress in this way is a necessity, so that the husband does not feel deprived and seek his needs by looking elsewhere. Nowadays it has become an obligation greater than ever before, since the husband is surrounded and constantly influenced by the permissive society in which we live, as has been stated - see *Mekoros* 2:3, 4:2, 7:9-10 and 66:1.

Chazal actually stress the point that even a *Talmid Chacham* needs a wife who is appealing to him even though he is immersed and preoccupied with his Torah studies - (*Shabbos* 25b). The *yetzer horah* pursues everyone and will find a foothold even in the most unexpected circumstances. It is our duty to outwit him by countering his allurement by the correct type of attraction. Furthermore, it is the duty of husband and wife to safeguard each other from harm, and to direct one another to the *Derech Hashem*. The *Gemara* says, כל אדם שאין לו אשה שרוי בלא שמחה בלא ברכה בלא טובה בלא חומה בלא תורה - "Whoever does not have a wife is without joy, blessing, goodness, without a protective wall and without Torah" (*Yevamos* 62b). Listed amongst the many blessings a wife imparts to her husband, is the fact that she is a protective wall around him, shielding and sheltering him from the many harmful enticements of the world at large.

The *Eishes Chayil* is praised with the words נודע בשערים בעלה בשבתו עם זקני ארץ - "Her husband is well known as he sits in counsel with other *Talmidei Chachamim*" (*Mishlei* 31:23). Apparently, this is a praise for the husband, not for her. If so, why does it appear in the verses of *Eishes Chayil*? The answer is that this is a praise and credit to both husband and wife. If not for the quality of his wife, the protection she offers him and the encouragement she gives him, he would not have reached these heights - see *Mekoros* 4.

2. WIVES OF GREAT MEN ARE PARTICULAR ABOUT THEIR DRESS: The *Gemara* (*Taanis* 23b) relates that *Abba Chilkia* once arrived back to his home-town after being away on a journey and his wife came out to meet him. Before leaving the house, she adorned herself with jewelry beyond the level with which she would usually have left the house. The *Gemara* continues that the disciples of *Abba Chilkia* noticed this, and asked their teacher why his wife had done so when it was unusual for her to dress like this out of the house. To this he answered: "She has adorned herself in this way כדי שלא אתן עיני באשה אחרת - so that I do not set my eyes on another woman". With this he implied that it is the responsibility of a wife to appear even in public in a way that ensures the husband's contentment and satisfaction with the appearance of his wife.

On the very same page of *Gemara* we are told what great *tzadikim Abba Chilkia* and his wife were. The *Gemara* relates that whenever there was a drought the *Chachamim* would send a message to *Abba Chilkia* to pray for rain and his prayers were invariably answered. It furthermore relates that once during a serious drought both *Abba Chilkia* and his wife prayed for rain. He stood in one corner of the room and his wife in another corner. As soon as they finished praying, a rain cloud appeared in the sky nearer to the position of his wife, as a sign that her prayer was answered first. The *Gemara* explains that this was because, being at home all day, she would give food to the poor as soon as they asked for it, whilst *Abba Chilkia*, not being at home all day, could not give the poor immediate assistance.

The fact that such great and holy people considered it important for the wife to look appealing to her husband, should serve as an eye-opener to many who dress nicely outside the house but do not bother to look appealing indoors. These great people obviously felt that for a wife to find *chein* in the eyes of her husband at all times underpins *shalom bayis* - marital harmony - and safeguards *kedushas Yisroel*.

[Note: The story just recorded concerning *Abba Chilkia,* must not be dangerously misunderstood. His wife did not appear in public in the special finery and jewelry that some women wear in privacy to find special *chein* and appeal in the eyes of her husband. If she had such adornments (which is unlikely - see below) they were for her husband alone, and she certainly did not appear with them when out amongst the public. What she did wear in public was jewelry and clothing that improved her appearance to the extent that her husband would feel that his wife was appealing to him and had considerable *chein*. Since even this was more than she usually wore in public, his *talmidim* remarked about it in their desire to learn from all that their *Rebbe* did. The *Chofetz Chayim* in his *sefer, Geder Olam*, Chapter 4 page 8 stresses this point and writes: להתקשט לפני בעלה... זה שייך רק בביתה לבד ולא בשוק - "What she might adorn herself with in order to truly appeal to her husband.......should be worn in privacy, not in public".

Chazal mention that Leah Imeinu erred slightly in this matter and when she went towards Yaakov (after the incident with the *dudaim*, the flowers - *Breishis* 30:16), she displayed more finery than was fitting to display in public. In later years this resulted (according to an opinion in *Midrash*) in her daughter Dinah leaving her home overly adorned to watch the dances of the local girls. This had the tragic outcome that she was assaulted and defiled by Shechem who was attracted to her - (see *Breishis* 34:2, *Midrash Breishis* 80:1 and *Chidushei HaRadal* point 2). This incident is recorded in the Torah for all times, so that *Klal Yisroel* learn to be careful with the dress and jewelry their wives and daughters wear outdoors.

Regrettably, husbands who want their wives to look exceptionally beautiful and glamorous are often unaware of the Midrash and the critical line in the *sefer, Geder Olam* just recorded. They think that their wives may display before the world at large all that they like them to wear when they are at home. This is cause for much *pritzus*. [In fact, most Torah-orientated husbands do not seek such glamorous clothes or adornments even at home. On the contrary, due to their appreciation of true values of life, they consider such aspirations as a form of over-indulgence, at least for people like themselves - see 7:K:5 below].

It is a very sad reality, that some young women who as girls dressed modestly and with refinement, seem to lose all sense of "*tznius*" during the first year or two after their marriage, with the fallacious excuse that "I must dress like this for my husband". Even if this were true, it would be strictly for home use only, not so that they adorn themselves in front of others where their appearance "*stecht ois die oigen*" (causes jealousy), invites men to transgress the *issur min haTorah* of "*v'lo sosuru acharei eineichem*" and does untold harm to *kedushas Yisrael!*].

3. THE WIFE'S APPEARANCE IS ESSENTIAL FOR SHALOM BAYIS: The appealing appearance of a wife (in a moderate measure in public and if necessary to a greater measure in the privacy of the home) is not just an antidote to the *yetzer horah* as described, but also a very positive need and part of the wife's input into building a happy and contented home. We find in *Chazal* that *Hashem* beautified Chava before presenting her to Adam by arranging her hair in an attractive manner - (see *Shabbos* 95a and 5:H:4 below). At that time there was no other woman in the world so Adam could not set his eyes on a second person. Nevertheless, *Hashem* saw it a necessity to beautify Chava, since for her to be good-looking and have an appeal was of considerable positive importance.

Chazal say אשה יפה אשרי בעלה מספר ימיו כפולים - "a good-looking wife causes her husband happiness, his days are doubled" (*Yevamos* 63b) because her husband finds his partner delightful and appealing. Moreover, *Chazal* (*Bava Basra* 22a) tell us that *Ezra HaSofer* instituted that peddlers selling perfumes travel frequently through towns so that women could obtain what they required to make themselves appealing to their husbands. Therefore, for a woman to disregard her outer appearance is most incorrect.

Shlomo Hamelech says in the verses of *Eishes Chayil* בטח בה לב בעלה ושלל לא יחסר - "Her husband's heart has full confidence in her, and [due to her fine ways] he lacks no spoil" (*Mishlei* 31:11). It seems that the advantages gained from a good wife are compared to "spoil" which is taken from an enemy during a successful military campaign. However, this verse can be very well understood with what has been explained. When a victorious army takes spoil, they are doubly happy. The vanquished enemy has been weakened by losing the spoil, whilst they, the victors, have been strengthened for any future confrontation, by obtaining the spoil (see *Meshech Chochma*, end of *Lech Lecha* s.v. *Od)*.

The gains a husband has from a good and sensible wife are twofold and are truly to be compared to spoil. Her delightful conduct and her way of dress enable him to "brush aside" the lurking *yetzer horah* who wishes to entice him to sin. At the same time, she provides her husband with contentment, security and a blissful peace of mind. Hence a great סור מרע (prevention of bad) and a considerable עשה טוב (positive good input) are the consequences of a wife's perfect conduct in this matter.

4. JEWELRY EXISTS TO IMPROVE APPEAL AT HOME - MIDRASH: The *Midrash Tanchuma* in *Parshas Vayishlach* (5) discusses a woman wearing a highly attractive ornament in the street on Shabbos. On this the *Midrash* concludes with the following words:- אמרי רבנן, אף בחול אסור לצאת בהן לרשות הרבים, מפני שהעם מסתכלים בה ופגם הוא לאשה, שלא ניתנו תכשיטין אלא כדי שתהא מתקשטת בהן לביתה, שאין נותנין פרצה לפני הכשר, ביותר לפני הגנב - "Our Sages have said that such an item should not be worn in public even on a weekday, because it attracts attention, and it is a defect in a woman if she causes attention is be drawn to her in public. Jewelry was given to mankind so that a woman can look attractive at home, not so that she can parade with it in full glare of the public eye. A person would not leave a breach in a wall unrepaired because someone could exploit it, especially when he knows that a thief is around."

The last remark means: Man has a *yetzer horah* which is like a thief. For a woman to overdress or overly decorate herself with jewelry and cosmetics is like presenting a breach to a thief. Although the *halacha* is somewhat more lenient than is implied by this *Midrash* and a woman may go out with a moderate amount of jewelry, nevertheless, the attitude spelled out in the *Midrash* is of paramount importance: **"Jewelry was presented to mankind so that a woman can look attractive at home"** - not so that she can make herself glamorous in the eyes of the world (See *Responsa Shevet Halevi* 6:33:2). See also 7:H:1 below that perfume is predominantly for home use, and see 7:K:1 concerning cosmetics.

In the topsy-turvy world of today, there are many women who are extremely particular about their outdoor public appearance, but pay very little attention to their looks and appearance at home - the place where their husbands see them regularly, day in day out, morning, noon and night. True, she may and should look pleasing when going out, because *Hashem* gave women *chein* to look graceful at all times, but to forsake her appearance while at home, when she is with her partner for life, is unforgivable.

5. NOT WEARING CLOTHES THAT THE HUSBAND DISLIKES: A husband may on occasion make an unfavorable remark about the new head-wear, dress or outfit, or new shoes that his wife has purchased. She certainly need not run and exchange or discard the new item due to her husband's initial feelings, as they might just be a transitory dislike due to not being accustomed to them, or, as is more likely to be the case, he likes seeing his wife in the attire he is familiar with, and his disapproval is likely to subside once he is accustomed to the new apparel. However, she must take note of his remark and watch out for further signs that the item disturbs him. Should this persist, the item should be changed, because a wife must be dressed in a way that finds appeal and delight in the eyes of her husband.

In the same vein, the housecoat a wife wears should be cheerful and colorful. If the husband persistently shows a dislike to a certain one, or feels that one that was pretty in the past now looks shoddy she should stop wearing it. Sometimes, a husband will not make a major issue of it, but a wife can usually detect how her husband feels even if he does not say it in so many words.

In some places, when the weather is hot, women do not dress in their regular attire for a large part of the day or even the whole day. Instead, they wear a housecoat, some of which are plain and do not have the design or flair of a dress. If the husband is happy with this arrangement then everything is alright, provided the housecoat is Kosher (which is particularly important when there is a visitor in the house or she opens the door to a caller while dressed in it - see 6:K below). However, should she notice that her husband does not like to see her for extended periods of time in such a housecoat and evidently wants her to be properly and appealingly dressed, then she must dress in that manner. As stated, dressing in a way that pleases the husband and having an appealing appearance in his eyes, are of paramount importance. See 7:C:3 that a wife should be dressed tastefully and with obvious care, and how wrong it is if she looks unkempt and drab.

The verse says, כל כבודה בת מלך פנימה, ממשבצות זהב לבושה (*Tehillim* 45:14). This means, "The prestige of the Jewish princess is her privacy - she stays within the confines of her home; she dresses (at home) in delightful clothes". It is interesting to note that this verse, which refers to the modesty of *Bnos Yisroel*, mentions two points: First, the *tznua* is predominantly at home, not in public areas (see *Rambam, Hilchos Ishus* 13:11). Secondly, while at home she dresses delightfully. Although she is a great *tznua*, she nonetheless attaches importance to her appearance in the presence of her husband and close family.

6. TZNIUS IS A FINELY TUNED TOOL: *Tznius* is a very exacting art. In public, *tznius* calls for an apparel that projects refinement and pleasantness, whilst at home, *tznius* calls for special *chein* and when necessary even beautification. This is in fact typical of every *midah* (trait). Different circumstances call for different reactions. To be harsh when one should be kind and forgiving, or to be soft and accepting when one should be strict and unyielding, are both wrong. The same Avraham Avinu who in his great kindness always brought the poor into his house, understood that for the sake of one of his sons (Yitzchak) he must take his other son (Yishmael) and send him out of the house! So too, *tznius* will sometimes call for dressing in a way that is not eye-catching whilst at other times calls for a woman to dress in a way that is very appealing - see 7:B:4 below.

7. THE KIYOR WAS MADE OF MIRRORS BELONGING TO WOMEN: A most significant insight into the importance and holiness that is attached to women ensuring that they look attractive and pleasing to their husbands, can be learnt from the fact that the *kiyor* - the water-holding cistern - was made from the copper mirrors used by women to beautify themselves for their husbands - (see *Rashi, Shemos* 38:8). The *Kohanim* washed their hands and feet at the *kiyor* and were then fit to sacrifice *korbanos* in the *Beis Hamikdash*. It seems quite incredible that the *kiyor* - the vessel which infused the *Kohanim* with *kedusha* in readiness for doing the *Avoda* - should have been made from mirrors used by women to beautify themselves for their husbands, which is usually thought of as an activity that is far removed from *kedusha*.

Hashem, however, obviously views this activity quite differently. Evidently, in His opinion when women enhance their appearance for their husbands (and not to achieve general acclaim), they are engaged in guaranteeing the sanctity of *Klal Yisroel*, as has been explained. It is therefore fitting that the mirrors associated with that pursuit be used to produce another act of sanctity - the *Avoda* in the *Beis Hamikdash* which generated sacredness to the whole of *Klal Yisroel*. (See commentary of HaRav S. R. Hirsch on the verse mentioned, who writes in a similar vein).

Chapter Two

CHALLENGES TO TZNIUS

A. PEER-PRESSURE

1. HARM IN MIXING WITH THE WRONG TYPES OF PEOPLE:

(a) The pressure a girl is under when peers treat her with contempt: One of the most basic and powerful causes for choosing a mode of dress is peer-pressure, as no one wants to be considered a queer, or a misfit in their society. On the contrary, everyone has an innate desire to be accepted and appreciated by peers and friends alike. This impulse can lead a woman or girl to feel a powerful need to change her conduct, her way of talking, mode of dress and even her attitude, so that they are in line with the society to which she now belongs.

Resulting from this urge, if a woman's or girl's newly found friends go around with hair-styles or garments that are excessively showy and were not to her liking at all, it will probably not take long before she accepts these styles and even develop an appreciation for them. It could even happen that she will consider having a similar hair-style herself or wearing clothes that are comparable to theirs, as she no longer sees anything wrong with them. Just as a person can acquire a liking for jazzy music that he personally used to utterly dislike, to the point that he thoroughly enjoys it, so too, feelings for almost any type of dress can be acquired. What is "pleasing to the eye" can become so misdirected, that a woman or girl can develop a liking for a fashion which she herself originally considered coarse and unfit.

In the case of fashions, peer-pressure could cause this to happen even quicker than in other areas, because the assault by friends in this matter can be particularly devastating. If they make fun of her as being a "Frummy", naive or old-fashioned, her resistance could crumble overnight. The maxim of ליצנה אחת דוחה מאה תוכחות - "A single mockery can repulse a hundred convincing arguments" is particularly relevant in this context. [See *Mesilas Yesharim*, Chapter 5 where the damage of mockery is described in detail].

(b) Everyone can be detrimentally affected by peer-pressure: The Torah tells us that Moshe Rabbeinu added the letter 'י onto the name of הושע turning it into יהושע. This was an expression of prayer: י-ה יושיעך מעצת מרגלים - "May *Hashem* save you from the evil intentions of the *meraglim*" (*Bamidbar* 13:16). Moshe Rabbeinu foresaw the sin of the *meraglim* and the resulting danger that Yehoshua would be in. Although Yehoshua was a very close disciple of Moshe Rabbeinu and was saturated with belief and trust in *Hashem Yisborach* that he had learnt and absorbed from his master, he was nevertheless in mortal danger of being influenced by his comrades and partners in mission. This illustrates just how vulnerable a person is to being influenced by associates, even in areas where he is fully convinced that one must think and behave differently. In this vein, *Chazal* say הרחק משכן רע - "Distance yourself from a bad neighbor" (*Pirkei Avos* 1:7).

A further example is the following:- When Avraham instructed Eliezer not to take a wife for Yitzchak from the daughters of Kna'an, he said to him, לא תקח אשה לבני מבנות כנען אשר אנכי יושב בקרבו - "Do not take a wife from the daughters of Kna'an amongst whom I dwell" (*Breishis* 24:3). The *Chasam Sofer* asks why did Avraham mention that he lives amongst the Kna'anim - a fact obviously known to Eliezer and apparently totally irrelevant as far as the instruction is concerned?

To this the *Chasam Sofer* answers that Avraham was implying the following: Had he lived elsewhere he could have taken a girl from Kna'an, because the good influence of Avraham and Yitzchak's home could be relied upon to change the girl to such an extent that she would become a fitting daughter-in-law for Avraham. However, since they live amongst the Kna'anim, this purification will not happen. The girl will continuously meet up with old friends and acquaintances, and this will prevent her integration into the new culture and values of Avraham's house. The influence of such friends is so great that even the overwhelming spirit of Avraham home would overcome the negative influence that is discharged from friends and class-mates alike.

It follows that friends, associates and society in general can have a far reaching effect on a woman's or girl's outlook on *tznius*. Even if she was brought up to like only that which is modest and refined, she could acquire a liking for forms of dress, ornamentation and beautification that are far from modest - as a result of the friendships she has made or the society amongst which she mingles at present. Since these women and girls dress in this way, she may quickly lose sight of what is wrong. The stronger her affection for these people, the more powerful the peer-pressure will be and the quicker she will be brought round to their way of thinking as subconsciously she will associate this form of dress with people she admires.

2. BENEFIT GAINED FROM MIXING WITH RIGHT TYPE OF PEOPLE:

(a) The finer her friends, the finer a person she will become: As stated, the urge to be accepted by one's society is deeply etched into human character and has a far reaching effect on every person. Just as an association with people who do not understand *tznius* leads to the negative results described, so too, when a woman or girl mixes with the right society she gains enormously from the healthy association. Being within a valuable group of people and cultivating some very positive friendships could develop within her a completely new outlook on matters critical to *Yiddishkeit*. If until now she had a weak feeling for *tznius*, her new association with a thoroughly dignified and *tznius'dik* group of women could give her an appreciation and even a liking for refined and modest modes of dress, because the people whom she admires and feels comfortable with dress this way.

Even a man as great as the *Tana* R' Yosi Ben Kisma responded to a person who wanted him to settle in a non-Torah environment with the following words: "If you were to give me all the gold, silver, precious gems and jewels in the world I would only live in a *Torah'dik* environment" (*Pirkei Avos* 6:9). He knew that the prevailing attitudes of the local inhabitants amongst whom he would live would affect his total commitment and love for Torah and *mitzvos*. Therefore, he refused to live where Torah was not fully appreciated and insisted that he could only live in a *makom* Torah. Our great luminaries were acutely aware of how much a person is negatively affected by bad surroundings and how much he depends on positive help from good surroundings.

The message is clear. A woman or girl must make every effort to avoid befriending those who are out of touch with *tznius*. She must ensure that she remains far from their society to avoid being influenced and contaminated by them. Instead, she should strive and make every endeavor to belong to the finest and noblest group of women possible. If she successfully strikes up one or two close friendships with such women, this could prove to be a life-long anchorage for her and her family in the realm of *kedushas Yisroel*.

(b) Observing those who live with impeccable *Yiddishkeit*: Ruth, who became a symbol of *emuna*, *bitachon* and *tznius* to the Jewish people, had an outstanding mentor - Naomi. *Chazal* say that Naomi's name personified her qualities: נעימים מעשיה - "her deeds were delightful and pleasant" (*Ruth Rabba* 2:5). Ruth lived in the company of this very special woman and learnt all that is important in *Yiddishkeit* from her. This did not happen by simply being physically close to her. Rather, *Chazal* say, רות, על שראתה דברי חמותה - "Her name is Ruth (which means seeing) because she observed with a careful and watchful eye the words and deeds of her mother-in-law" (*Ruth Rabba* 2:9). She paid close attention to everything she saw - knowing that by observing the ways of a *Yorei shomayim* and a *tznua* she would learn to deeply appreciate her qualities and then personally adopt them herself. Girls should learn from this that, while being in good company is a healthy setting for growing into a fine *Bas Yisroel*, real heights of *Yiras Shomayim* and *tznius* are attained by observing closely those who are outstanding in their *Yiddishkeit*.

(c) The contentment of those who have chosen the right path: When a woman or girl is determined and persists in living and conducting herself totally according to the guidelines of the Torah she is a deserving recipient for the contented and rich life promised to those who steadfastly cling to the Torah - עץ חיים היא למחזיקים בה ותומכיה מאשר - "Torah is a tree of life to those who cleave to it in spite of difficulties; those who ensure its fulfillment shall be happy and fortunate" (*Mishlei* 3:18). This woman will eventually realize that the choice of friends and society she made twenty-five years ago and the special women she chose to admire and emulate, ultimately gave her the husband she has, the children she has and the home she runs. She would not exchange them for anything in the world. The art is to foresee this happy and intensely satisfying result while still far back at the cross-roads!

B. ISSUR FOR WOMEN AND GIRLS TO SEE IMMORAL CONDUCT

1. SEEING PRITZUS IN STREETS CAUSES A DECLINE OF TZNIUS: There can be no doubt that the deterioration of *tznius* in our times is a direct result of the constant and overwhelming publicity given to immorality in all its manifestations. People are exposed to this misguided way of life when they read the daily newspapers, in which terrible acts of immorality are discussed in the greatest detail, often with the accompaniment of pictures of the people who perpetrated these misdeeds. Moreover, when simply walking along the street, whether in the summer or winter, it is impossible to avoid coming across the most appalling forms of female dress and different forms of immoral conduct. To our dismay it can be said about our generation, ומלאה הארץ זמה - "The world is overrun by immorality" (*Vayikra* 19:29. See *Yevamos* 37b that the word הארץ does not refer only to *Eretz Yisroel*).

Even when a person of the highest morality sees misconduct - and is sincerely disgusted by what meets his eyes - he is nevertheless detrimentally affected. The "power of sight" is so great that an impression is made even though the person knows it is evil and he utterly despises it. In *Devarim* (29:16) *Hashem* warns the Jewish people not to be influenced by the *avoda zarah* they will encounter in *Eretz Yisroel*. In this context *Hashem* says: ותראו את שיקוציהם ואת גלוליהם וכו' - "You shall see their repulsive and revolting idols etc. Beware not to be drawn to serve them etc". It seems strange that people who view an *avoda zarah* as repulsive and revolting should be drawn to it and be in danger of serving it. The Brisker Rav, Maran HaGaon HaRav Yitzchak Zev Soloveitchik *zt'l,* explains that this is quite understandable when knowing the intense power of sight. A person can see something that truly disgusts him and nevertheless be so deeply affected by it that he is eventually drawn towards it.

2. MEN AND WOMEN ARE BOTH AFFECTED BY SEEING PRITZUS: While men are generally aware that it is *ossur* for them to look at immoral sights such as those mentioned, many girls and women mistakenly think that there is nothing wrong in their looking. This could not be further from the truth, as everyone is affected by *pritzus* (immoral conduct) without distinction. In fact the *issur* of ולא תתורו אחרי לבבכם ואחרי עיניכם - "Do not stray after your hearts and after your eyes", is applicable to females just as to males - *Sefer HaChinuch, Mitzva* 387 - see *Mekoros* 12:4.

The following is a quote from a speech by one of the *Gedolei Hador*, Maran Hagaon Harav Shmuel Wosner *shlita*, delivered on the 13 *Adar* 5753 in *Bnei Brak*: "A fatal error is being made. Some people mistakenly believe that only men are forbidden to look at immodest pictures, movies and books. The truth however is that the *issur* of ולא תתורו אחרי לבבכם ואחרי עיניכם - 'Do not stray after your hearts and after your eyes' applies both to men and to women. This *issur* applies at all times. Women do not realize how much damage they bring upon themselves and their families by reading forbidden books and watching forbidden films."

Maran Hagaon Harav Moshe Feinstein *zt'l* writes the same in his *Responsa Iggros Moshe,* E.H. 1:67. He states there that it is *ossur* for girls and women to see serious *pritzus*, such as *pritzus'dik* misconduct of people or *pritzus'dik* pictures in magazines or films. In this *Responsum* he explains that since these arouse impure thoughts which are forbidden for men and women alike there is no place to make a distinction between men and women concerning this issue - see *Mekoros* 12:4-6. Exactly the same is written in a proclamation by the Steipler Gaon *zt'l,* which is reproduced in the *sefer, K'reina D'igrsa* 1:117 and translated into English in 2:C:1 below.

3. A "TREIFE BEACH" IS TREIFE FOR MEN AND WOMEN ALIKE: The widely assumed rule that men may not go to a "*treife* beach" while women may go to such a place, is unfounded and fallacious. Women and girls may not go to beaches which are populated by both men and women, since such beaches are inevitably places of gross immodesty if not outright indecency, and as stated even women may not see indecent conduct. It is remarkable that people generally know that women and girls may not go to mixed bathing and are extremely particular about it (as it is severely *ossur* - *Gittin* 90b). They nevertheless think that to swim at a seaside used by men and women, or to sit on the open beach and see the indecent conduct of immodest people is permissible and beyond reproach. This is a grave error, and urgently requires rectification by *mechanchim* who bring the *dvar Hashem* and pure *halacha* to girls of the next generation.

4. SEEING PRITZUS CAUSES IMMODEST AND IMPURE THOUGHTS: There are women who think that just as they may go swimming with other women and see them in a partially unclad state, so they may see all types of pictures of immodestly-clad women and gaze at such sights in the street. This is a serious misconception; the two issues are not comparable. No harm is caused when a woman sees another woman's body in an acceptable setting. It is however very harmful for a woman to see another woman exposing herself for everyone to see and behaving in a manner that even the *umos ha'olam* know is distinctly *pritzus'dik* - see *Mekoros* 11.

Pritzus is highly contagious, as *tumah* is *metameh* - impurity defiles whoever comes into contact with it. It is part of the general principle that *Chazal* have taught us, עבירה גוררת עבירה - "one sin leads to another" (*Avos* 4:2). No one should think that they are beyond being affected by seeing *pritzus*. We are taught never to overestimate our own steadfastness (אל תאמין בעצמך עד יום מותך - "Do not trust yourself until your last day" meaning, 'you should not be overly confident' - *Avos* 2:4) and never to underestimate the effect of seeing evil. Even Dovid Hamelech, one of the greatest and holiest of all men, beseeched *Hashem,* העבר עיני מראות שוא - "Avert my eyes from seeing futility" (*Tehillim* 119:37).

The *Chazon Ish* was asked by someone whether it was permissible for him to become a partner in a cinema which would definitely not open on Shabbos. The *Chazon Ish* retorted incredulously, "And to tear out all the thirteen principles of faith is of no concern to you?!" It was clear to the *Chazon Ish* that watching immorality devastates not just the person's *kedusha,* but also his basic belief in *Hashem,* in the words of holy Torah, in reward for *mitzvos* and punishment for *aveiros*, and in all other facets of *emuna.* (Hagaon Harav Meir Greineman *shlita* in his *sefer, Dinim v'Hanhagos MiMaran HaChazon Ish,* 9:20).

5. SEEING IS "A FORM OF CONTACT" AND CONTAMINATES: Seeing *tumah* does not just arouse dormant base instincts that are in a person. The harm caused by seeing *pritzus* extends far beyond the boundaries of influence and effect as they are normally understood. To us it seems that if a person sees a *tomei'dik* sight but has absolutely no *yetzer horah* for what he sees, he remains totally unaffected by the sight and is as pure after seeing the sight as beforehand. The truth of the matter is not so. Every person is detrimentally affected by what he sees, even if it is of no interest to him. When seeing *tumah,* one is, in fact, in direct contact with the *tumah* (comparable to touching it) and, as we know, when a *tahor* touches a *tamei*, the *tahor* becomes defiled, even if the touching was totally unintentional. [However, real physical *tumah* is not transferred by sight, because contact by sight is obviously of a more subtle nature.]

Since in Torah terms, seeing is a form of "contact" a person literally absorbs some of the spirit and influence that exudes from the person he looks at - See *Toras Chayim, Eruvin* 13b - see *Mekoros* 11:1.

Chazal say אסור לאדם להסתכל בצלם דמות אדם רשע - "A person should not gaze at the image of a person who is a *rasha*" (*Megilla* 28a). In contrast, the verse says והיו עיניך רואות את מוריך - "Your eyes shall see your teacher" (*Yeshaya* 30:20). Since looking intently causes a person to absorb some of the spirit of the person he is gazing at, he must avoid looking intently at the wicked. In the same vein, he should make a special effort to see the righteous, so that some of their holy spirit be transmitted to him. Since sight is a form of physical contact between people, a person can also "give of himself" and beneficially influence the person he is looking at. Within this context, we know of the immense powers of *ayin hatov* and *ayin horah*.

Based on the power of "taking and giving by sight", Moshe Rabbeinu wanted at least to 'see' *Eretz Yisroel*. With this he could absorb some of its *kedusha* into himself (*Rashi, Devarim* 32:52 s.v. *V'shomoh* and *Kli Yakar Devarim* 3:25) or the reverse, influence *Eretz Yisroel* by giving it some of the great *kedusha* that was within him (*S'forno, Devarim* 32:49 and *Breishis* 48:10). In short, the power of sight is so great that by looking at an entity one can either take substantially from it, or alternatively give it a considerable amount.

Once this great truth has been understood, one begins to grasp the immense influence seeing *pritzus'dik* ways of dress and behavior has on both males and females, and why we must make every effort to avoid them. As explained, not only is the dormant *yetzer horah* of man aroused by such sights, but he literally absorbs into himself part of the *tumah* that emanates from the person who walks around in *pritzus'dik* dress - see *Mekoros* 11:2.

6. EVEN FACING IS "A FORM OF CONTACT" AND CONTAMINATES: The great concept just explained goes a step further. This is that facing a *tamei* sight contaminates a person even if he does not actually look at it (although looking adds considerably to the effect). This incredible truth is written in the following words of the *Alshich Hakadosh*: After leaving the Ark, Noach drank wine, became intoxicated and exposed himself inside his tent. The Torah relates how his two sons Shem and Yefes took a garment and וילכו אחורנית - while walking backwards, approached their father and covered him. The *Alshich Hakadosh* asks: Why did they walk backwards which is very awkward and can easily have caused them to trip? It would have been much simpler to have walked forward with closed eyes.

To this the *Alshich* writes: They did not want their faces to come "face to face" with this *tamei'dik* sight as it would have contaminated them even though their eyes would have been closed and they would have seen nothing. He explains that the face of a person is his *Tzelem Elokim* and when it faces *tumah* it absorbs some of the *tumah*. This in turn affects the person negatively, even though he has not physically looked at the *tumah* - *Toras Moshe* by the *Alshich*, *Noach* 9:23. If we consider these extraordinary words, and then reflect on the extent to which our faces unfortunately have to come into contact with *pritzus*, it is hardly surprising that *tznius* is urgently in need of a *chizuk* in our times! The *Alshich's* holy words should also inspire both men and women to steer clear, if at all possible, of streets where *pritzus* is rampant, even if they intend to be careful not to look intently at the *pritzus* that is there.

The following incident occurred with the great *Ponevez Mashgiach,* Maran HaGaon HaTzadik HaRav Yechezkel Lewenstein *zt'l*. The *Mashgiach* was traveling in a car together with his *talmid*, Harav Hagaon R' Shlomo Brevda *shlita*, when the latter noticed that the *Mashgiach zt'l* had suddenly ducked his head right down, as if afraid that something might hit him. When asked by Harav Brevda *shlita* what was the matter, he responded that their car had stopped in the traffic just outside a cinema. The whole area was floodlit by bright arcade lights of the cinema and the lights shone right into their car. He was ducking to prevent these lights shining on his face.

He added, "We have no idea how much harm is caused to our *ruchnius* by being in contact even just with light that comes from a place designated for immorality!" To avoid this contact, he ducked down - and did not suffice with just closing his eyes, which was easy enough to do (*Kedushas Hachayim,* page 436). Evidently he knew that if a person faces *tumah* he is in contact with it, even if he does not actually look at it, as is stated in the words of the holy *Alshich* mentioned above.

7. GUARDING CHILDREN FROM SEEING IMMORAL SIGHTS: Understanding the points explained above, should bring about an appreciation that both boys and girls must be educated from a tender age that we *Yidden* must surround ourselves only with *tahara*. Whenever possible they must be protected from even the slightest contact with all forms of immorality. After all, was it not the plan of *Hashem Yisborach* that we

Yidden live in *Eretz Yisroel* surrounded only by *shomrei Torah umitzvos*? If, inadvertently, children have been exposed to sights they should not have seen, parents must allow their children to know their disgust and outrage at such conduct - see *Mekoros* 12:1-3.

8. AVOIDING BAD SIGHTS AS FAR AS POSSIBLE: Shortly after the *chareidi moshav Komemiyus* was established, the *Chazon Ish zt'l* commented to the *Rav* of *Komemiyus*, Hagaon Rabbi Binyamin Mendelson *zt'l,* that he was amazed that fifteen families moved with him from K'far Ata, where there was communal life and business opportunities, to *Komemiyus*, which was at that time a barren and desolate place and somewhat insecure.

To this Rabbi Mendelson replied, "*Chazal* say that a person is a *rasha* if he needlessly walks along a street in which immodesty can be seen, even if he intends to keep his eyes closed, because he could have gone a different way where he would not be faced with these *nisyonos* (*Rashbam*, *Bava Basra* 57b). He is a *rasha,* because he is putting himself in a position that, in a moment of weakness, could easily cause him to sin. We are in this situation. Since there is no *pritzus* in *Komemiyus* whilst elsewhere the problem exists in abundance, we felt it our duty to move to *Komemiyus*".

The *Chazon Ish* was overjoyed with the answer. His face lit up with happiness that in our day and age there were people with sufficient *yiras shomayim* and strength of character to behave in this way. (Related by Rabbi Binyamin Mendelson's son Rabbi Menachem Mendel Mendelson *shlita*, the present *Rav* of *Komemiyus. Sefer Kedushas Einayim* 16:33 and *P'aer Hador* 3:306).

During the first few years of its existence, there were no roads in *Komemiyus* and the tracks were full of mud and slime. Due to this, when people went along the street their shoes quickly became caked in mud. Visitors to the *Komemiyus Rav* said to him, "How can you live in a place where your shoes become filthy every time you go along the street?" To this he replied, "We prefer the struggle of muddy shoes in *Komemiyus* than to suffer from 'muddy eyes' as can so easily happen in large towns" (*ibid.*).

9. MAINTAINING PURITY AMIDST ADVERSITY - A GREAT MERIT: The *Navi* (*Malachi* 1:2) says the following about *Hashem*'s special relationship with Yaacov: אהבתי אתכם אמר ה', ואמרתם במה אהבתנו, הלא אח עשו ליעקב נאם ה', ואהב את יעקב ואת עשו שנאתי - "I love you", says *Hashem*. To your response, "Why am I loved - have I not sinned?" *Hashem* answers,

"Eisav is a brother of Yaacov - and Yaacov could easily have been affected by Eisav's way of life. However, Yaacov distanced himself from Eisav and thereby maintained his purity". *Hashem* therefore concludes, "I despise Eisav for choosing an immoral way of life, and in contrast, I love Yaacov, who, in spite of being exposed to a very negative influence, tries hard to live *b'kedusho v'tahara*!" These are the words of the *Navi*. It is up to us to remain deserving of *Hashem Yisborach's* love!

C. DEVASTATION CAUSED BY NEWSPAPERS AND BOOKS

1. MOST NEWSPAPERS HARM BOTH ADULTS AND CHILDREN: Parents must be extremely cautious in the choice of newspaper they bring into the house. Adults and even children read everything, especially material for which the person has a *yetzer horah*. Such papers are lethal for all members of the family, even though the damage is often not apparent for quite some time.

Case histories are known of girls who had a very good start in life, succeeded in their teenage years and developed into fine young women. Eventually, however, they became shallow and superficial, losing their Torah outlook and former refinement. When questioned how this distressing decline occurred, they confessed that the daily papers and magazines which came into their parents' home had a very detrimental effect on them. It took them on a day by day excursion from the purity and refinement absorbed by their *Torah'dik chinuch* into the grime and impurity which exudes from the daily press. Being highly impressionable girls, the effect of this progressive poisonous intake was the extraction and expulsion of most of the values that they had previously absorbed. If we wish to proudly cleave to our heritage and appreciate the beauty and purity of Jewish life, we must have the strength to fulfill the commandment of לא תביא תועבה אל ביתך - "Do not bring an abomination into your home" - *Devarim* 7:26 - see *Mekoros* 7:3.

In a proclamation concerning most secular newspapers, the *Steipler Gaon zt'l* writes as follows (slightly amended to be readable in English):

> *"I am distressed to hear that newspapers and weeklies which report on immorality, idolatry and murder are brought into Orthodox homes - under the misapprehension that reading about immorality only harms men, while females remain unaffected. People therefore allow women*

and girls to read all the news items in these papers. This is totally wrong, because men, women and children are all included in the issur of ולא תתורו אחרי לבבכם ואחרי עיניכם, as the sensual instinct of everyone is aroused when they read about romances or immoral practices. It is therefore strictly ossur to allow such papers into a Jewish house and an even greater issur to read such newspapers and look at the indecent pictures printed in them.

"Apart from arousing the yetzer horah, reading these papers has the effect of causing people to become indifferent to Yiddishkeit, to lose their Yiras Shomayim and to abandon their emuna. Therefore, whoever brings these newspapers into the house will be held responsible for grievously injuring himself and his family. Altogether, who can foresee the serious consequences of allowing such material into one's home.

"It is the responsibility of the Jewish woman, who attends to all the needs of the household, to safeguard herself and members of her household by insisting that such newspapers are not allowed access into the house. If she takes this approach she will merit blessings in this world and riches in the next" (K'reina D'igrsa 1:117).

2. PUBLIC LIBRARIES AND THEIR BOOKS: DANGER TO CHILDREN: Having mentioned newspapers, it is appropriate to mention another most dangerous pastime that can destroy the *chinuch* one is giving at home. This is children taking books out of public lending-libraries by themselves. Nowadays, a large proportion of children's books contain *pritzus* and bad *midos* both in the text and the illustrations. When impressionable youngsters read these books, their purity and refinement can be impaired for life. This occurs too frequently for the danger to be taken lightly - see *Mekoros* 7:4.

Ideally, therefore, parents should direct their children to use only a Jewish library run by refined and responsible people. Alternatively, parents should accompany their children to the public library - to ensure that bad books do not even come into their hands, let alone be taken home to be read in detail. We must be constantly aware that the society in which we live is corrupt, and as parents it is our duty to safeguard our children from outside influences as far as is humanly possible.

School text books must obviously not contain material that is harmful to a child's mind. This applies particularly to books on biology which often contain unfitting text and pictures. Some teachers remove the offending pages but leave the table of contents intact, although it too may be harmful.

Also, there are 'school reading books' which advocate corrupt *midos* (character traits) or describe immoral conduct. Such books should preferably not be used at all, or at least have the offensive passages blotted out.

3. ABSURDITY OF BRINGING "TREIFE STREET" INTO THE HOME: It is sad enough that we live in a *golus* where going out to the street brings us into contact with society at its worst. However, *Baruch Hashem* we have homes and we have the means of keeping alien cultures safely on the other side of the front door. In this way at least our homes are a haven of refuge from the *pritzus* the family is exposed to whenever they venture out. By keeping "the street" out, we can hope that our children will be imbued with the *tahara* of our homes rather than the *tumah* of the streets ח"ו.

There are however some people who foolishly invite "the street" and all its maladies right into their homes, thereby exposing the family constantly to the ideas and ideals of the outside world. Bringing *treife* newspapers and books into the home for everyone to read, is exactly that, since they are saturated with *giluy arayos* and *shefichas damim*. Is it surprising that a teenage girl who has been reading such papers and books, sets her heart on wearing clothes and jewelry that are so provocative that they are incompatible with any standard of *tznius*?

If this is the case with newspapers what should be said about television? Those who bring this monstrous machine into the house sit themselves and their children down to a live and vivid display of *znus*, murder, theft and all the vices of the world. The corrupt state of present day youth bears ample witness to the damaging effect of watching these sights. Hiding the television in the bedroom or strictly allowing only "clean" things to be watched is no justification for harboring such a source of harm in one's home. The Torah's way is to forbid a person to have a faulty weight in his possession lest he swindles with it at a time of weakness (*Vayikra* 19:36). Similarly, a television, which shows the most despicable sights at the flick of a switch, may not be kept in the house lest one capitulates to temptation.

Concerning the qualities of *Yerusholayim,* Dovid Hamelech says, כי חזק בריחי שעריך ברך בניך בקרבך - "For He strengthened the bolts on your gates, He blessed the children that are within you" (*Tehillim* 147:13). He ensured that alien forces and cultures could not penetrate the gates of *Yerusholayim* and then blessed its children with physical and spiritual prosperity. Similarly, by keeping our front door firmly closed to outside influences, the next generation will *bezras Hashem* be blessed in many ways. They will grow up with true unadulterated *Yiddishkeit* and a love for *Hashem* and His Torah.

4. ENSURING THAT PLENTY GOOD LITERATURE IS AVAILABLE: To ensure that negative material is not brought into the house, it is the duty of parents to make certain that interesting, Kosher reading-material is available. This is essential as girls, and to a degree also boys, spend much time reading books. When supplying them with seemingly Kosher secular material that imparts general knowledge about plants, the animal kingdom, seasons, planets etc., it is important to guarantee that they do not innocently digest doses of *tumah* and *kefiroh* in the process - as this can be found even in books that are generally considered Kosher. It is usually the mother who can monitor this matter properly.

For example, if a family has a children's encyclopedia of interesting facts, the mother should "doctor" it before giving it to the children by running a black marker over all places where it is stated that the world is far older than the Torah says it is. If the anatomy of the human body is discussed - and all the more if it is illustrated - those pages should be cut out or at least glued together (preferably cut out, since, in his curiosity, a child may be tempted to unstick the pages). Should a breakfast cereal show a particularly *treife* picture on the outer carton, the mother may decide not to buy that cereal for the time being or, alternatively, to pour its contents into a plastic container so that the outer carton need not be brought to the table.

In contrast, parents should obtain literature which positively imparts to its readers *emuna*, a love for Torah and an appreciation of good character traits. They should bring into the house biographies of *Gedolei Yisroel* and *nashim tzidkanios.* which are available in abundance in our generation, as these infuse Yiras Shomayim into the hearts of their readers. This is just one of the many ways that the *emuna*, *shemiras hamitzvos* and the spirit of *kedusha* that prevails in the Jewish home can be cultivated by the Jewish woman.

5. TWO-WAY VIDEO TELEPHONES - A GRAVE NEW DANGER: Mention must be made of an extreme danger to the *tznius*, *kedusha* and *tahara* of our children and even ourselves. It is lurking around the corner, but at present most people are totally unaware of it.

Recently, telephone companies have been marketing what appears to be just a harmless item of additional luxury. This is a video telephone which enables the people to see one another on a screen that is situated above the phone. People are likely to bring such a video telephone into their home with the best and purest intentions such as to give their elderly parents the great *nachas* of seeing their children and *eineklech* frequently on the screen. Also, different parts of a family can feel much closer when they see one another frequently. The bitter truth of the matter is, however, that by obtaining this item, they will have made a start at bringing a most lethal object into their house, which can wreck the *kedusha* and *tahara* of their home with no more than a couple of phone calls, as will be explained. This section will suggest some of the uses one can expect the two-way video communications to be put to.

The main danger will arise when these systems are more sophisticated and more advanced than they are today. This may still be some years away, but it is just a matter of time till they will be available. Then a large, sharp, colored image will be seen, in contrast with the poor picture that is shown on the screen at present. In fact, with the electronic world changing rapidly, it is impossible to predict the exact form such a two-way video communication facility will have. It is, however, almost certain, that such equipment will become very widespread, considering the wide use of computer modems (which have some of the two-way features). This is compounded by the fact that television companies are already talking about the possibility of using telephone cables to transmit television signals. Once this is possible, it will also be possible to send high quality video pictures. It is therefore of immense importance that people should be forewarned in good time and should not be trapped in a quicksand from which there is almost no escape.

Considering the dangers, people are advised not to let even the present-day video-telephone into their homes, since once two-way video communications is introduced into the Orthodox community, it will inevitably lead to facilities being brought up to date as they become available. It will then be too late to prevent the crippling results that are explained below. Some of the dangers are as follows:

(a) Ability to call up videos from a video bank: At present people can call recorded train and plane timetables, the weather forecast, sport scores and many other things. Once the two-way video-telephone has been widely distributed, not only will these things be available on the screen but one will be able to "dial a video" from a video bank. One will be able to obtain whichever video one desires (either through an operator or by dialing a certain code number) and it will be "piped" through the telephone line onto the screen. Our *Gedolim* have expressed their great concern about the penetration of video machines into people's houses, as they can be used to see immoral videos as well - see 9:H:5 below. Soon a person will be able to dial a video and watch *giluy arayos* or *shefichas domim* without having to suffer the disgrace of entering a video store.

Moreover, now one can "dial the radio" and listen to a radio program. When the above is available one will be able to "dial the television" and watch television programs for minimal cost. Thinking about the potential hazards of such machines, gives a person a deep sense of fear for the *nisyonos* that the next generation will have to live with.

(b) Danger of immoral phone calls with visual accompaniment: When such visual accompaniment becomes a widespread reality, a person will be able to call certain lines and not only hear vulgar speech (*nivul peh*) in its worst form, as is already available and used by weak individuals, but will additionally be able to see it with a live accompaniment, *rachmana litzlan*. Seeing immorality damages the *nefesh* of a person in a much more profound way than when he hears about it, as *Chazal* say, אינו דומה שמיעה לראיה - "Seeing something has a much greater impact than hearing about it" (*Mechilta*, *Yisroh* 19:9). Due to its extreme severity, we say a special confession for it on *Yom Kippur*: על חטא שחטאנו לפניך בשיקור עין - "For the sins we have committed before You by viewing forbidden sights".

Although the danger of any telephone being misused must not be ignored, the new possibility of seeing *toeivah* in the privacy of one's home whenever one wants, is a harrowing and frightful added dimension. Apparently, in some families, telephone abuse has become quite a problem. If we are not careful it will become many times more severe once the *Satan* has both sound and sound at his disposal. If a child falls into this trap, *chas veshalom*, it will be his parents' fault for having brought this dangerous form of communication into the house.

(c) Vulnerable to misuse by engaged couples: In some circles engaged couples do not meet at all. This was the original Jewish way - See *Redak Breishis* 24:65 on the words ותקח הצעיף ותתכס. In other circles they do meet but only infrequently. In still other circles they meet far too frequently, to the detriment of their *kedusha* during the engagement period and the *kedusha* that will prevail in the home they set up together. It is not within the scope of this *sefer* to write what *Gedolei Yisroel* have to say about this problem - see *Mekoros* 65:5.

Until now one knew that at least when the *chasan* and *kallah* were in different towns this over-meeting was curbed. However, with the inroads of the video facility a *chasan* (who lacks guidance and knows no better) will be able to call his *kallah* and see her face-to-face almost at all times, whether in day-time or night-time attire. The *churban* to *kedusha* and *tahara* that will be caused by this aspect alone defies description - see 3:B:2(b). In fact it would seem that the danger of two-way video communication is far greater than that of television and videos put together.

The danger is enormous and we must make sure that this source of *tumah* does not accidentally slip into our homes. Many people made a mistake when television first came out, thinking that it was a wonderful educational tool to teach the family about different countries and interesting scientific facts, and in general a pleasant and interesting way of hearing world news. It then turned into the beast it is fully recognized to be today, devouring people's hearts and souls and destroying their lives. We must not make the same mistake once again.

(d) Peril of malicious calls: There is also a danger of hate callers ringing homes and frightening people with dire warnings and at the same time showing a masked face and possibly even a weapon. With the increase in anti-Semitism in recent years this is becoming a distinct possibility. It takes just one sick mind to persecute a large number of people. Such a call could haunt a person for days if not weeks, *rachmana litzlan*.

(e) Hazard when marketing is done by phone: Many firms market things by calling up people with the hope of gaining their custom. People receive calls from firms dealing in double-glazing, loft-insulation, central heating, carpets, furniture and the like. At present, if a person is not interested in the offer he cuts the caller short by replying, "Thank you for calling but I am not interested". Once these two-way videos are widely circulated, people will be contacted by models rather than the normal saleswomen one meets in a store. Firms will employ them because they will hold the attention of the potential customer. In truth this is a danger not just for children but also for adults.

(f) Menace when inquiring about a product: One can foresee a time when calls to inquire about a product or service will be met by a woman whose job will be to monitor the phone and also to entice people to use the goods or services provided by this firm. This has been done in catalogues for years, but live contact has a totally different attraction and power of influence. There is no reason why big chain stores, vying with one another to win customers, should not jump onto the bandwagon and do the same. They could show a live video demonstration to show how well the product functions. It will be presented with an eye to holding the person's interest.

(g) Short videos while the call is "on hold": Nowadays, if a firm wants its caller to hold for a couple of minutes as they are not ready to speak to him, they play some form of music to keep him occupied. One can envisage the day when instead of music they will "entertain" the caller with a two minute video film that will be designed to encourage him to call the firm again in the future.

(h) "We can switch off the video whenever we want" - gross error: There will of course be those who will say, "But the video has a button and one will be able to switch it off at will". Here again, people claimed the same thing when television first came out, and with that, blemished the *nefesh* of their children forever - see *Mekoros* 4:4. The Vilna Gaon explains the verse חכם ירא וסר מרע, וכסיל מתעבר ובוטח (*Mishlei* 14:16) as follows:- "The wise man is afraid he might fall into sin. He therefore avoids the evil and keeps his distance from it. A fool, however, is confident in his righteousness and convinced he will not stumble. He will even purposefully walks past the evil trusting that it will not entice him". How appropriate these words of wisdom are for many of our present-day situations!

The verse says, אם און בידך הרחיקהו, ואל תשכן באהלך עולה - "If you have means of sin in your hand distance it, do not allow iniquity to dwell in your house!" (*Iyov* 11:14). From this verse, *Chazal* laid down a *halacha* that if a person has a document in his possession with which he could claim money that is no longer owed to him, he is obliged to destroy it. If he retains it in good order he might be overcome by a desire for money and in the future, at a moment of weakness, use it to dishonestly extract money from his original creditor (*Kesubos* 19b, *Choshen Mishpat* 57:1). This teaches us that a person must not rely on the fact that he has a clean record so far.

A similar *halacha* has already been mentioned in 2:B:8 above. The *Rashbam* in *Bava Basra* (57b) writes that a person who needlessly goes through a place where seriously immodest sights can be seen, is a *rasha*, even if he closes his eyes, because in a moment of weakness he could open his eyes and look. The same is in our case; in a moment of diminished self-control a person could flick on the button of the video. *Chazal* knew the tremendous drawing power of the *yetzer horah* and considered bringing oneself close to sin as an act of *rishus*.

A conventional telephone is an essential commodity. It therefore does not fall under the prohibition just mentioned, even though it could in theory be misused. A telephone with video accompaniment is, however, a non-essential item and is therefore subject to the *issur* mentioned, particularly as its dangers are very considerable and of a totally different class to that of a normal telephone.

(i) The exceptional danger to children: An added dimension to this danger is the fact that even if an adult could have relied on himself how can he possibly take responsibility for the actions of his young sons or daughters? To give an example, the following is a quote from an article in the Jewish Observer (May 1994, page 11). "At the *Agudas Yisroel* of America convention I related an incident that I had heard from a high school teacher. A student of hers confessed to being hooked on movies. When the parents were asleep she and her older sisters would slip away to an all night video outlet, rent videos, play them and return them by three or four a.m. before the parents woke up. When I told this story I did not realize how widespread this phenomenon is. Subsequently, I attended meetings of *Roshei Yeshiva* and *mechanchim* to discuss this problem and there testimony was given to numerous similar episodes," *Hashem yerachem*.

(j) An intelligent person foresees danger: Shlomo Hamelech says in *Koheles* (2:14), החכם עיניו בראשו והכסיל בחושך הולך - "The wise person is farsighted and is watchful for potential hazards, whilst the fool proceeds in darkness and sees no need to take precautions". Preventing pitfalls that can grievously injure members of our family must be our top priority. The *Chofetz Chayim* campaigned for the holiness of our mouths. Had he lived in this generation he would surely have warned us incessantly about the need to safeguard the holiness of our eyes which is under such threat nowadays.

(k) The *issur* proclaimed by the *Bedatz* of *Yerusholayim*: The following is the translation of a letter released by the *Bedatz* of *Yerusholayim* on the 17 *Ellul* 5754:-

> *We have heard with trepidation about the impending dangers that will be generated by the telephone with video accompaniment which is almost sure to be launched. It is unnecessary to explain the immense* sakonoh *and the devastating impact this machine can have. Now, to forestall the evil and prevent this dreadful hazard from coming into our homes to smite us spiritually, we announce our Torah-based opinion that it is absolutely forbidden to bring this implement of destruction into our homes as its evil potential is unforeseeable, Hashem yerachem.*
>
> *Whoever truly respects the word of Hashem and worries for the safety of his children will not allow this type of telephone into his home,*

nor his warehouse, nor his shop etc. Anyone who transgresses this prohibition should beware of the retribution given for flouting the words of sages. We pray that a ruach tahara descends on us and that we will merit a year of redemption with the speedy arrival of Moshiach Tzidkeinu.

Written and signed, yearning for a merciful salvation for Klal Yisroel.

RABBI MOSHE ARIEH FREIND, RAVAD
RABBI AVRAHAM DOVID HOROWITZ
RABBI YISROEL MOSHE DUSHINSKY
RABBI BINYAMIN RABINOWITZ
RABBI YISROEL YAACOV FISHER

(l) The *issur* proclaimed by *Gedolei HaTorah* of *Bnei Brak*: The following is the translation of a letter signed by the *Gedolei HaTorah* of *Bnei Brak* about the danger of telephones with any form of video accompaniment:-

We are terrified to hear of the new danger that looms ahead of us which can cause the foundations of Yiddishkeit to crumble together with all boundaries of Tznius and tahara. This is the Video Telephone which will soon be marketed world-wide. We see in this the danger of a spiritual holocaust, rachmana litzlan. Furthermore, if we do not confront this danger in good time the resulting outcome is beyond assessment.

We have therefore decided to prohibit this machine with an all-out ban. It is forbidden to bring it into one's house, factory, office or anywhere else. This prohibition shall have no exceptions whatsoever. He who heeds our words shall be blessed with all his spiritual and physical needs. Hashem in His mercy should assist us in our struggle on His behalf and we should all merit the speedy redemption of our people.

RABBI SHMUEL HALEVI WOSNER
RABBI MICHEL YEHUDA LEFKOVITZ
RABBI AHARON LEIB STEINMAN
RABBI NISSIM KARELITZ

6. ACCESS TO "THE WEB" - GRAVE DANGER TO YOUNGSTERS: All that has been mentioned in connection with the two-way video communication is of secondary significance to a menace of extraordinary proportions that has already taken serious hold in the world. It is considered to be the greatest danger to morality of all times - far greater than that of television and videos - and even the non-Jewish world is deeply apprehensive of the corruption and indecency it is imparting to many of its viewers.

This is the easy accessibility to the vast electronic network known as the "Information Super Highway", the "Internet" or the "World Wide Web". A computer can be fitted with a facility which enables its operator to communicate with other computers anywhere in the world - and receive or send information on any subject that may interest him. Operators can contact each other world-wide for a nominal sum - no more than the cost of a local call. At present there are about a hundred million computers linked together with such programs! A lot of the information that is being sent down these highways is of an illicit nature. The *yetzer horah* uses sophisticated sounding names such as "Information Highways" and "Internet" to gain entry. Once in, he starts destroying the unsteady remains of humanity.

This facility, while on the one hand excellent and indispensable for commerce and professions, is a terrible threat to children, teenagers and young people. With it they can access pictures and films created by the sick minds of those of the lowest moral depravity and view them in the safety of their homes without anyone being aware of it. The viewer can see sights of live immorality that are more terrible and devastating to the *neshama* of the *Yid* than has ever been known. However, since others have already detailed the gruesome particulars of this looming danger (Jewish Observer, Adar 5755 / February 1995 and Ellul 5755 / September 1995), there is no need for the facts to be repeated in this *sefer*.

In the light of this terrible danger, parents who have a computer at home for the children to use, are strongly advised not to have a modem plus a communications program which enables connection to the Internet. They should also not allow their children to play with friends who have a computer that has a modem with a communications program in their homes. A computer without the means to connect to the Internet may not be as efficient and up-to-date as one with such a facility. However, as a result their children's *neshamos* will be saved, and they will be able to grow up with healthy morals. This is a very small and insignificant price to pay to prevent something which is "life-threatening" from entering the house.

If the parents require a home-based computer which must be connectable to the Internet for their profession or business, it must be strictly out-of-bounds for anyone other than the parents. Alternatively, there are Internet Service Providers which do not allow access to certain areas, and programs are available which allow parents to decide which areas can be accessed.

If we consider for a moment that the Torah forbids a man to purposefully gaze at the face of a woman or girl (the *issur* of ולא תתורו אחרי לבבכם ואחרי עיניכם) because this can eventually lead to immorality (See *Rambam Hilchos Teshuva* 4:4) we must tremble with fright at the massive assault the *yetzer horah* has made on the world of today. If gazing at the face of a woman can be so harmful to a healthy *nishmas Yisroel*, can we assess the effect of severe immoral sights on the debilitated remnants of *Klal Yisroel* of today? We are however fully convinced that these tactics are the last powerful flicker of the *yetzer horah* before he has served his purpose with the coming of *Moshiach Tzidkeinu*. We will withstand this test, just as we withstood all other attempts at eroding our *Yiddishkeit*. With the strength of this understanding we will ensure that our homes are fortresses of true uncontaminated *Yiddishkeit* and we will guard our children and youth so that we can proudly go with them towards *Melech HaMoshiach* בב״א.

D. SPIRITUAL POLLUTION CAUSED BY PEOPLE'S MISCONDUCT

1. THE WORLD AT LARGE IS CORRUPT - POLLUTING THE AIR: As we delve into the state of *tznius* of a large segment of *Klal Yisroel* in our day and age, it is apparent that there has been a sharp decline in feeling for *tznius* and refinement over the past three decades. This leaves us with a bitter taste, since it is hard to believe that such a sizable proportion of *N'shei* and *Bnos Yisroel* have lost their natural and innate feeling for *tznius* - the treasure of the *Bas Yisroel*. It is also hard to believe that Jewish women and girls of today are substantially inferior to their mothers and grandmothers, in spite of the fact that *chinuch habanos* has improved over the last few decades with excellent schools and seminaries.

The truth, however, is that today's women and girls are not less valuable than women of previous generations - and are to a great extent not to be blamed for the existing decline. The *nisyonos* (tribulations) of our times are considerably greater than they were in the last generation. The main contributory factor is that our senses and feelings have become dulled as a direct result of the *tumah* which exists in the world today. Hence it is the times that have changed, rather than the women. If there would be a great *chizuk* by *N'shei Yisroel* in matters pertaining to *tznius*, the purity such *chizuk* would generate would help counter the *tumah* that exists in the air. It is with this in mind that the effect of the 'misdeeds of the world' on *Klal Yisroel* are now to be explained - see *Mekoros* 13:1-3.

2. THE "IMMORAL POLLUTION" AFFECTS EVERYONE: It has been stated (in 2:C:3 above) that with a "closed-door policy" the influence of the outside world can be kept out of our homes. This statement is true as far as direct influence is concerned. However, it is not possible to completely seal off one's home and prevent the influence of the outside world from creeping in. We live nowadays in a thoroughly contaminated environment, because corruption and immorality pollute the entire atmosphere. This pollution has a detrimental effect on people's attitudes and on their way of thinking. We see, for example, that the misdeeds of man at the time of the *mabul* influenced even animals and birds, and caused them to behave immorally. The animals lived in an atmosphere contaminated by the wrongdoings of people and this affected them to such a great degree - see *Mekoros* 13.

In this generation, the pursuit of permissiveness is worse than in many previous generations. People read in newspapers and see on television a mode of life whose description must be categorized as *nivul peh* (unclean speech). Consequently, even if we close our doors to the outside world we are still being unceasingly bombarded by an extremely polluted atmosphere.

We can perceive this environmental contamination when we see that a radio switched on anywhere in a house will pick up radio waves and churn out language that no decent person, never mind an *erlicher Yid*, would ever use. Likewise, it produces defiled songs that we would never sing. This demonstrates that the very air is polluted in a most serious manner and that closed doors and windows cannot keep this out completely.

A remarkable incident occurred during the stay of Rabbi Elchanan Wasserman *zt'l* in America to raise funds for his *Yeshiva* in Baranovich, which illustrates the power of spiritual pollution. The following is an excerpt from the book "*Reb Elchanan*", page 337:

Reb Shrage Bloch called himself "*dem Rebben's baal agoloh*" (the Rabbi's wagon driver). One day he came to the Goldin house (where Reb Elchanan stayed) and excitedly announced, "Today I saw a Divine revelation!" He explained, "I was driving Reb Elchanan in my car. He does not look outside his four *amos* and does not know New York. Yet, as we crossed Times Square, his face suddenly contorted as if stung by a bee. He called resentfully to me, 'A stench rises from this place. Where are you taking me? This place reeks of *tumah*.' He did not relax until we left the area.

As we continued our drive he inquired about the nature of the location and why it emitted the repulsive odor. I informed him, "This is where people are inflamed to sin". Reb Elchanan lapsed into a reverie and his face became even more serious. Finally he exclaimed, 'It is beyond me how it is possible to study and teach Torah in a place like this' " - see *Mekoros* 11:1.

Our *Gedolim* have a very fine sense of smell!

3. THE POLLUTION CAN BE COUNTERED BY PURITY OF TZNIUS: The *Beis HaLevi* in *parshas Noach* elaborates on the truth stated, and writes that every *aveirah* a person does spreads *tumah* in the world and causes others also to sin. If a single *aveirah* has such an effect, can we possibly calculate or comprehend the pollution caused by the immorality of millions of people who live in accordance with the ways suggested by the permissive society? The *Beis HaLevi* then writes that in a similar vein every *mitzva* a person does purifies the air and spreads cleanliness and *kedusha* in the world arousing others also to do the *mitzvos*. All this is incorporated in the saying, מצוה גוררת מצוה ועבירה גוררת עבירה - "One *mitzva* leads to another and one *aveirah* leads to another" (*Avos* 4:2). Since *mitzvos* have the potential of purifying the air and affecting everyone, a *chizuk* in *tznius* by many people will have a remarkable decontaminating affect - see *Mekoros* 13:1.

It is noteworthy that the *Mekubal*, Hagaon R' Chayim Yehuda Leib Auerbach *zt'l* of *Yerusholayim* (father of Hagaon Harav Shlomo Zalman Auerbach *zt'l*) wrote in 1932, in his approbation to the *sefer, K'doshim Tihyu* on *tznius*, that already at that time the atmosphere in *Eretz Yisroel* was affected by *pritzus*. He goes on to say that writing a *sefer* and protesting against *pritzus* has the effect of purifying the air. Hence, *shiurim* and *drashos* given to strengthen *tznius* are "air purifiers" and they lay the foundations on which we can hope to achieve great improvements - see *Mekoros* 13:2.

Similarly, advocating and standing up for *tznius* is so powerful that it can ward off negative decrees that would force people into the adverse world of *pritzus*. At the time of the turmoil concerning the frightful decree in *Eretz Yisroel* of *giyus banos,* the conscription of girls into the army - against which *Gedolei Yisroel* fought tooth and nail - a few hundred highly motivated women demonstrated in defiance of the decree outside government buildings with great *mesiras nefesh*. They were clubbed by the merciless police and hosed with powerful jets of water from fire-engines, but they maintained their position and continued to demonstrate.

When the *Chazon Ish* was told about this exceptional demonstration, he responded in a most unexpected manner: "If these women would have shown this degree of *mesiras nefesh* when *pritzus'dik* trends began to make inroads into our community, and if with fortitude and *mesiras nefesh* they would have strengthened the fortress of *tznius* in *Klal Yisroel*, then this decree to force *pritzus* onto our daughters would never have been issued in the first place". The *Chazon Ish* was convinced that true pursuit of *tznius* removes potential dangers concerning this area of *Yiddishkeit* from the Jewish people.

4. NISYONOS THAT SURROUND US CAN BE SELF-INFLICTED: The *Brisker Rav*, Maran Hagaon Harav Yitzchak Zev Soloveitchik *zt'l,* once said, that every decree made by those who wish to uproot Torah observance is caused by *shomrei Torah umitzvos* having slackened in that particular area of *Yiddishkeit*. The attempt to force *yeshiva bachurim* in *Eretz Yisroel* to do military service was caused by *bachurim* not making sufficient effort in their *limud haTorah*. The terrible *gezeirah* of *giyus bonos*, conscription of girls into the army, was caused by Jewish girls lacking *tznius* in dress and conduct. When a decree is made against *shemiras* Shabbos, it is because people are being lax in its upkeep and do not bother to learn the *halachos* of Shabbos thoroughly. This is part of the inner meaning of the saying, פירצה קוראה לגנב - "the breach invites the thief" (*Succah* 26a and *Rashi Devarim* 22:23). Had one not breached the defenses, the enemy would not have been aroused.

Concluded the *Brisker Rav*: If people improve and rid themselves of these shortcomings, the decrees and *gezeiros* will likewise disappear in a short time. Therefore, if *bachurim* strengthen themselves in *limud haTorah*, girls conduct themselves with *tznius*, and people are careful with the *halachos* of Shabbos, the respective *gezeiros* are annulled - see *Mekoros* 3:3.

It follows, that we must be wary about blaming all our shortcomings on the immorality that prevails and the pollution it causes (which is an upsurge of *tumah* before the arrival of *Moshiach* - see *Sotah* 49b and *Chafetz Chayim al HaTorah,* page 179) as explained in No.1 above. It could well be that not all our difficulties result from these circumstances. Rather, some of the more direct problems (such as the difficulty women and girls have in buying dresses and outfits that are *tznius'dik*, which is almost like a *gezeira* against *tznius*) might be a result of a lack of effort and even apathy that exists in *Klal Yisrael* in matters related to *tznius* and personal refinement.

E. BEING LAX BECAUSE MEN ANYWAY SEE PRITZUS

1. 'LACK OF TZNIUS IS NOT SO HARMFUL NOWADAYS' - FALLACY: One of the causes for the trend of being lax in fulfilling the requirements of *tznius* is that subconsciously women and girls reason, "Why should I have to dress in *tznius'dik* clothes to preserve *kedushas Yisroel*? There are, after all, hundreds and even thousands of females walking the streets who are not properly dressed. Men are therefore accustomed to seeing such sights and nothing significant will result from Jewish women like myself not keeping to the *halachic* standard of Kosher clothing". The answer to this is threefold.

2. *REASON ONE* -

- WOMEN NEED TZNIUS FOR THEIR PERSONAL REFINEMENT:

(a) Inadequate dress cheapens her in her own eyes: Although being a danger to *kedushas Yisroel* is a very important aspect of the need to dress in *tznius'dik* clothes, it is certainly not the whole reason for it. Dressing in this way is a natural requirement for the aristocratic and refined person embodied in the *Bas Yisroel*. She feels her worth and importance when she is properly dressed and presentable, whereas if she appears in public in inadequate dress her self-image is detrimentally affected and she is cheapened and denigrated in her own eyes. This, in turn, affects her whole *Yiddishkeit*. This applies even if she is adequately covered but the color or style of her garments is loud or coarse and does not fit the *eidelkeit* and image of a *Bas Yisroel*.

(b) Inadequate dress shatters her natural feelings of modesty: Moreover, *Hashem* planted within a female a strong natural urge to cover herself and dress in a *tznius'dik* way (as has been explained in 1:B:2 above), and it is of paramount importance that this urge is not undermined. This is a personal feeling of modesty and refinement, which is unrelated to others seeing her and being negatively affected by her way of dress. It has already been mentioned that the *Gemara* (*Eruvin* 100b) says that had the Torah not been given we would have learnt the "trait of *tznius*" from a cat, which instinctively behaves with distinct privacy concerning its bodily needs (see *Rashi*, *ibid.*). People are likewise expected to exercise personal refinement in this context - see *Orach Chayim* 3 where a whole chapter in *Shulchan Aruch* deals with these *halachos* of *tznius*. (See 1:D:4 above and 6:R:5 below concerning the role of the *umos ha'olam* in this aspect of *tznius)*.

The *Maharal MiPrague* points out that the *tznius* mankind could have learned from the cat is an instinctive urge not to expose private parts of the body irrespective of whether it affects others or not. It is a need to maintain one's privacy and results from a deep sense of self-respect which exists even in animals. The *Maharal* explains that the trait of *tznius* is so basic in the fabric of the world that it is exists in both humans and animals - (*see Nesivos Olam, Nesiv HaTznius, Chapter One,* s.v. *B'Perek Hamotzi*).

(c) Women must sustain their special urge for privacy: Although the urge for privacy and feeling of embarrassment is characteristic of all humans, it is particularly strong in women, who have been blessed with a far greater instinctive need for *tznius* than men (to safeguard *kedushas Yisroel*) - see 1:B:2 above. *Chazal* actually paraphrased this distinction with the words בושתה של אשה מרובה משל איש - "The feeling of shame is more acute in women than in men" (*Kesubos* 67b) and for this reason they said האשה קודם לאיש לכסות - "If there is only enough money to buy clothes for one person, a woman's clothes have precedence over a man's" (*Mishna*, *Horiyos* 3:6).

In this vein it is noteworthy that the sublime *sefer, Peleh Yoetz* writes (in the section on *tznius*) that it is wrong for a female to say the *bracha* of *Asher Yotzar* aloud to give male members of the family the opportunity to say *amen*. Generally, it is commendable to say a *bracha* aloud, as it helps the person concentrate (M.B. 185:3) and it enables others to answer *amen*, as mentioned in *Sefer Chassidim* section 254. See also *sefer, V'imru Amen,* page 52 No.25, who mentions saying the *bracha* of *Asher Yotzar* aloud. Nevertheless, when a female is in the presence of a male it is unfitting for her to do so, as it undermines her exceptional feelings for privacy.

Therefore, even if it were true that people who surround a Jewish woman could be unaffected by her lack of Kosher dress, it would nevertheless be considered a major departure from correct practice if she would walk around with inadequate dress. This is "if it were true" that men would not be affected by her dress because they see *nochrios* in extremely inadequate dress. The truth however is that her reprehensible conduct will all the same affect others, as will be explained in the following two points.

3. *REASON TWO* -

- PRITZUS BY "ONE WHO KNOWS BETTER" IS VERY HARMFUL: Orthodox Jewish women must realize, that when those who "know better" do not dress properly, there is far greater *pritzus* involved than when this is done by someone who knows no better. Those who "know better" and nevertheless overstep the permitted boundary, appear to have an urge to show themselves off or attract attention, and making such an impression is provocative. On the other hand, when a *nochria* walks around sleevelessly or otherwise inadequately dressed, she knows no better and is more easily ignored (unless her dress or behavior is particularly outrageous). Thus, when a *Bas Yisroel* walks around with a wide open neck or a slit, it is far more detrimental than when a *nochria* dresses in this way.

4. *REASON THREE* -

- PEOPLE ARE DRAWN TO THOSE OF THEIR OWN BACKGROUND: If a Jewish woman or girl dresses inadequately and with that provokes the attention of a Jewish man or youth, the impact on the man or youth is much more powerful than when a non-Jewish female causes a similar provocation. Someone from a person's own background naturally holds much greater appeal to him than someone of a totally different faction and society.

On the verse ותהי אסתר נושאת חן בעיני כל רואיה - "And Esther's appearance appealed to all who saw her" (*Esther* 2:15), the *Gemara* says, מלמד שכל אחד ואחד נדמתה לו כאומתו - "This means that whoever saw her thought that she belonged to his own people and background" (*Megilla* 13a). Since she appealed to everyone and people are not usually charmed by those who are of a totally different background, *Chazal* understood that every individual felt that she belonged to his own people. Similarly, the *Gemara* (*Bava Kama* 92b) quotes a saying from *Ben Sirah*, כל עוף למינו ישכון, ובני אדם בדומה לו - "Every bird dwells with its own variety; so too, people are attracted to their own type". It is therefore natural for the *pritzus* of a Jewish female to be far more provocative and do much more harm to a Jewish male than the *pritzus* of the *umos ha'olam*. For example, even if a man regularly comes across non-Jewish women with very low necklines and is so accustomed to it that it leaves him almost unaffected, nevertheless, should he see a Jewish woman or girl in a similar inadequate attire, it could well cause him to transgress the *issur* of ולא תתורו אחרי עיניכם [see 4:B:1(e)], by looking at her and being attracted by her appearance.

To a degree, the same applies within Jewish society, between those who are *shomrei mitzvos* and those who unfortunately are not. As far as an Orthodox male is concerned, an Orthodox female is of his own society, and he will take note of her long before he will take note of a female who belongs to a different society. Therefore, a deficiency of *tznius* within the *frum* community is the most harmful setting a lack of *tznius* can have. Consequently, the partial justifications voiced by many, that with society being so deficient in *tznius*, a shortcoming in the dress of a *Bas Yisroel* is not so harmful, is in fact an invalid excuse. Besides, those who live in really *frum* vicinities may seldom see *pritzus* of non-*frum* women.

F. "I LIVE FOR MY CHILDREN" - EXCUSE FOR ALL INADEQUACIES

1. DECEPTION OF YETZER HORAH CAUSING MEN NOT TO LEARN: The *yetzer horah* will use every means at his disposal to achieve the goal he has set out to attain. There is no part of *Klal Yisroel* that he does not attempt to mislead, and he will often use the very special qualities of people, or of a community as a whole, to lead them astray and inject *tumah* into an otherwise holy environment.

A well known method of the *yetzer horah* to divert a person from *limud haTorah*, *tefilla* and proper observance of *mitzvos*, is the feeling: "I am putting all my efforts into bringing up my children as best as I possibly can, *B'ezer Hashem* my sons will become *Talmidei Chachamim* and valuable *Yidden*". With this excuse, the father spends all his time in the pursuit of more and more money, instead of doing what *Hashem* expects him to do concerning his own life. He is at peace with himself, as he is after all "doing everything for his children".

Sadly, when these children grow up they are likely to follow in their father's footsteps, wasting their own lives away, while vindicating themselves with the same excuse, "I am doing everything for my children who will hopefully become outstanding *Yidden*". *Chinuch habanim* is of course extremely important, but it is a deception of the *yetzer horah* to make it into "everything" and thereby justify neglecting one's own life and *Avodas Hashem*. In fact, not only is it wrong, but, as explained, each generation grows up and once again neglects itself - everyone is working for the elusive "ultimate children" who seldom materialize (as is said in the name of the Rebbe of Pscische *zt'l)*.

2. DECEPTION OF YETZER HORAH CAUSING NEGLECT OF TZNIUS: In line with what has just been explained, the *yetzer horah* diverts women from their personal duties to *Hashem* and *Klal Yisroel* - which is *tznius* in dress and in general conduct. When mothers send their *b'cheint* little boys to *cheder*, they can be overcome with a deep feeling of complacency as far as their personal life is concerned. They bask in the satisfaction that they are bringing up a family in true Jewish tradition. The more the children develop into "lovely *yiddishe kinderlach*", the more powerful is the *yetzer horah*'s case that they are "giving their lives to their children".

Since living for their children becomes the 'beginning' and the 'end' of everything, these women will sometimes allow themselves the "minor liberty" of dressing in fashionable clothes even though they are only borderline Kosher or not even that. Here again, when the daughters grow up, they will be no different from their mother. They will neglect their own personal obligations with the justification that they are living for their children and doing everything possible to give them a perfect upbringing.

Such a mother will of course not forsake *mitzvos* such as *Bircas Hamazon* and *bikur cholim*. Nevertheless, when it comes to dress, her wish to look attractive and to be "with it", causes her to succumb to her desires, with the excuse that she considers bringing up her children to be her one and only duty. She is reacting much the same as the man described above. He also *davens*, says *Bircas Hamazon* etc. and may even give *tzedaka*. However, he gives in to his drive for more and more money and wastes nearly all his time on this pursuit.

This *tznius* problem afflicts every section of the *yahadus hachareidis* without exception. Even communities that have a very strong feeling and sentiment for *levush Yisroel* and *tznius* are afflicted by the complacency of "I am bringing up my children in the best possible way" or "I am sending my children to the best school available - what more can be expected of me?" As stated, with just such excuses a mother justifies her neglect of the treasure of the Jewish woman - namely true *tznius* and personal refinement. It is particularly painful when one realizes that powerful inroads have in this way been made even into the camp of staunch upholders of our holy tradition.

There are, of course, thousands of mothers who are a pride to *Klal Yisroel* in the way they look after their children and also their own obligations. Nevertheless, this problem is widespread and very deep-rooted. This deception of the *yetzer horah* should whenever possible be highlighted by speakers who give *chizuk* to women. When the *yetzer horah* is unmasked and his devious ways exposed, people are in a much better position to withstand him.

3. DAMAGE CAUSED BY A MOTHER'S UNSATISFACTORY DRESS: A headmistress of a girls' school in the U.K. complained bitterly to the author of this *sefer* that she feels helpless when trying to influence her *talmidos* who come from very *heimishe* homes about aspects of *tznius* of clothing. When the girls are told that their tights are too thin, their necklines are not Kosher, their skirts are too tight or short, or their earrings excessively large - they answer that their own mothers dress in this way! They therefore argue that there must be an opinion which considers this to be within the norms of *tznius* (even when this is not the case at all) and that it is evidently their *minhag* to follow this opinion. When a pupil says this, the teacher is usually at a loss for an answer!

Had the children come from a background of much less *Yiddishkeit*, the teacher could explain to them that their mother never had the opportunity to learn all the *halachos* about this subject, and that it is in fact quite remarkable how much she does know and keep. For this, their mother would have had our greatest admiration. However, when the mother comes from a *chareidi* background and was brought up in surroundings steeped in Torah and Yiras Shomayim, what can one say to such girls? If mothers would only realize the consequences of the "minor liberties" they take, they might reconsider their ways for the benefit of their own children.

The *Navi* Amos writes in the name of *Hashem* that although the Jewish people had transgressed the three cardinal sins, *Hashem* would still have been merciful with them. However, due to an additional fourth sin that they committed, His great anger erupted. The fourth of these serious sins was - "A man goes together with his father to commit an *aveirah*, thereby profaning the holiness of *Hashem*'s Name" - *Amos* 2:2 the *Haftorah* to *parshas Vayeishev*. Harav Mendel Hirsch (son of Harav Samson Raphael Hirsch) explains, that when a father, in whose hand the *chinuch* of his son is entrusted, turns traitor to the *mitzvos* of the Torah and instead of giving his son a *chinuch* does just the opposite and encourages and even accompanies his son on a mission to an *aveirah* - this more than anything else arouses *Hashem*'s extreme anger.

The religious practice of the young generation rests first and foremost on the *chinuch* they receive from their parents. When this is totally overturned and parents lead their children away from *Yiddishkeit* there is reason for anxiety for the future of their family. Similarly, if a mother dresses in a way that encourages her daughter to dress in an inadequate manner, this must be viewed as a serious failing in the duties *Hashem* has entrusted into her hands. Let us not forget: We all need and seek *Hashem*'s mercy. Being His faithful emissaries for the healthy development of the next generation makes a person a suitable candidate for *Hashem*'s bountiful benevolence, granting him a healthy and enriched long life.

G. "EASY YIDDISHKEIT" CAN LEAD TO VANITY

1. NOWADAYS WE HARDLY HAVE NISYONOS TO KEEP MITZVOS: A further contributory factor to the decline in *tznius* of clothes in our times is the relative ease with which we observe Torah and *mitzvos*. Most of us are no longer used to fighting for *Yiddishkeit* and overcoming *nisyonos*. On the contrary, *mehadrin min hamehadrin Yiddishkeit* is available in all large Jewish centers, be it in connection with Kosher foods, *shatnez*-free garments, Jewish schools, *chadarim*, *yeshivos*, seminaries, *shuls*, *shtieblech*, *mikvaos*, etc. Nowadays, we even have *parve* milk and *parve* salami, so that whether we are meaty or milky, or it is in the "Nine Days", nothing is missing! We have instant *shemiras hamitzvos* laid on for us and are no longer used to fighting and struggling for it!

2. THE SATAN TRAPS A PERSON BY HIS CLOTHES - ZOHAR: Since we are not used to overcoming *nisyonos*, the great *yetzer horah* of vanity has a field day. It is so deeply implanted in the nature of man, that it must surge forth when the person is off-guard. This idea is found in an incredible statement of the *Zohar Hakadosh* in the *sedrah* of *Vayeishev* (No. 238).

On the verse, ותתפשהו בבגדו - "She grabbed hold of him by his garment" (*Breishis* 39:12), it says:- מאי אורחיה דיצר הרע, כיון דחמי דלית בר נש קאים לקבליה לאגחא ביה קרבא, מיד ותתפשהו בבגדו ותאמר שכבה עמי, ותתפשהו בבגדו דכד שליט יצר הרע עליה דבר נש אתקין ליה, וקשיט ליה לבושוהי מסלסל בשעריה, ההי"ד ותתפשהו בבגדו לאמר אדביק עמי - "When the *yetzer horah* sees that a person is not going to resist and fight him, he immediately encourages him to beautify himself and pay undue attention to his clothes and hair. The *yetzer horah* knows that with vanity he can win the person over. This is the meaning of ותתפשהו בבגדו - **'The *yetzer horah* grabs him by his garment'** meaning that his method of bringing a spiritual downfall is by homing in on the temptation of clothes. ותאמר שכבה עמי - The *yetzer horah* then says, **'Now that I have caught hold of you, you are mine'**." See 7:A:1 below where the words of the *Mesilas Yesharim* on this subject are quoted. See *Mekoros* 28:10-12.

3. LAZINESS IS HARMFUL TO THE CAUSE OF TZNIUS: Laziness is a further spin-off of the "easy *Yiddishkeit*" climate in which we live. It is a harmful trait that afflicts many of us often causing people to walk around in inadequate dress. Due to it, a girl might not bother to ensure before leaving the house that her hair, her neckline, her arms etc. are in a fitting state to appear in public. Similarly, a married woman may emerge from her house with some of her hair showing through her *sheitel* because she could not be bothered to check her appearance in the mirror before leaving home.

If a woman has bought herself a dress which she hopes is not see-through but this has not been checked out, then laziness may well cause her to "accidentally" appear in public in a totally unacceptable manner of dress. Had she taken the bother to check it out in the sunlight, this mistake would not have occurred.

It is remarkable how the beautiful verses of the *Eishes Chayil* stress again and again just how far an *Eishes Chayil* is from being afflicted by laziness. Evidently, being diligent and industrious are preconditions for living a Kosher life oneself and also for being the asset to the community every person is expected to be.

The verse says בעצלתיים ימך המקרה - this means, "As a result of laziness and not repairing the leak in time, the roof gives way and collapses, causing extensive damage" (*Koheles* 10:18). *Chazal* say that this verse refers to a woman: על ידי שאשה זו מתעצלת מלכסות את עצמה כראוי ימך המקרה - "As a result of a woman not bothering to cover herself in a fitting manner, the roof collapses" (*Vayikra Rabba* 19:4). Her not dressing properly is caused by nothing more than a little laziness, but it can result in serious damage. She may not want to do wrong, but the damage follows automatically, just as a roof will collapse automatically if a leak is not quickly seen to!

4. GREATER DEVOTION TO MITZVOS CAN HELP CONSIDERABLY: It follows from the forthright words of the *Zohar* mentioned above, that if we show the *yetzer horah* that we are not easy prey, he will relax his grip. If we are careful with *kashrus*, for instance by thoroughly checking vegetables that require *bedikah*, using only reliable *hechsherim*, and inspecting clothes that could contain *shatnez*; if we *daven* and say *brachos* properly; if the outstanding *mitzva* of *kibud av v'eim* is in the forefront of our minds - then the *yetzer horah* will reduce his immense efforts to mislead us in every field, and temptations concerning *tznius* will also recede.

As a result of exercising extra care in everyday *Yiddishkeit* (the trait of זהירות), the problem of being lethargic and lazy when matters need to be urgently taken in hand (rather than behaving with זריזות, as mentioned in no.3) will likewise be remedied. *Chazal* say זהירות מביאה לידי זריזות - "Conscientiousness leads to diligence" (*Avoda Zarah* 20b). Accordingly, by exercising a more faithful form of *Yiddishkeit*, a new motivation and even eagerness will emerge, driving the person to live up to the true image of a *shomer Torah u'Mitzvos.*

H. PRIDE AT BEING PART OF THE AM HANIVCHAR

1. SELF-ESTEEM LESSENS URGE TO COPY OTHER SOCIETIES: The most elementary remedy to the problems mentioned above, is to learn the *halachos* and seek *shiurim* and *chizuk*, thereby maintaining a healthy Torah perspective on *tznius*. A further point that can be of great support to prevent a person being influenced, is to feel a deep pride at being a *Bas Yisroel* and a member of the *Am Hanivchar*. Although humility is a great virtue and always to be encouraged, having self-esteem is no contradiction to the trait of humility as long as the person feels he deserves very little credit for qualities which were bestowed upon him. Self-esteem can be enormously helpful in holding one's own, and in not being impressed and influenced by the "happy go lucky" and the "all lusts fulfilled" way of life of the *umos ha'olam* (which all too often ends up in the misery of an unfaithful spouse, a broken marriage or the "*nachas*" from adult children who do not let their parents enter their homes).

Boaz said to Ruth, בתי אל תלכי ללקוט בשדה אחר - "My daughter do not go to glean in another field" (*Ruth* 2:8). The *seforim* write that metaphorically Boaz advised Ruth, that although elsewhere the grass may look greener, this is a misconception and very far from the truth. It is only from the distance that the lives of others may appear to be happier than ours whilst in truth we are the most fortunate of people.

One need not have the wisdom of Shlomo Hamelech to appreciate this truth. Who lives with the true bliss of *shalom bayis* (marital harmony)? Who can sincerely sing the praise-laden verses of the *Eishes Chayil* about their wives? Who has *nachas* from their devoted children and grandchildren? Who has a Shabbos and a *Yomtov*? A *seder* night? A *Succah*? Are their Sundays and festivals any comparison or even a semblance to what we have? Who has the Holy Torah with all its thought-provoking teachings? Who can sing with an inner happiness and true sincerity the words אתה בחרתנו מכל העמים אהבת אותנו ורצית בנו ורוממתנו מכל הלשונות וקדשתנו במצותיך - "You have chosen us from all nations; You have loved us and found good qualities in us; You have raised us above all tongues and sanctified us with Your *mitzvos*" (*tefilla* of *Yomim Tovim*)?

2. IT SHOULD BE UNFITTING TO "APE" THE UNDERPRIVILEGED: The true Jewish daughter is grateful for having a *derech hachayim* that secures her future happiness in every way. She thinks to herself that, just as she would not learn from primitive tribes to walk around half naked, because she is civilized and fundamentally different than them, so too, she has no interest in learning how to dress and conduct her life from those who have no lasting happiness and satisfaction from the way they manage and run their affairs. She has compassion on those who sadly know no better and may wish she could extend a helping hand to enlighten them to the *emes*. However, to take guidance from them, particularly on such an all-important issue, is totally out of the question. She has a wonderful religion and wonderful co-religionists to look up to. She has a tradition that provided guidance long before modern fashions began and will continue to provide guidance at a time when the fashions of today will no longer be remembered.

3. THE BAS YISROEL IS LIKE A ROSE AMONG THORNS: The verse says כשושנה בין החוחים כן רעיתי בין הבנות - "like a rose between thorns so is my beloved one amongst other daughters" (*Shir HaShirim* 2:2). A rose is a beautiful flower with exceptionally delicate and graceful petals. It seems amazing that such a tender and graceful flower survives when it is surrounded by the strong and sharp thorns of the rose bush. They should apparently tear the petals to pieces, giving the flower no chance of survival. Its secret of survival, however, is that the flower always grows either out of or up and above the thorny branches, in such a way that no contact can be made with them. It stands so distinct from the rest of the branches that even a strong wind will not throw the flower against the thorns.

Shlomo Hamelech compares the *Bas Yisroel*, living amongst forces that could do her tender *neshama* so much damage, to a rose that survives amongst thorns. She can survive between the nations of the world with the same strategy as the rose - by being proud of her heritage and rising above negative influences. By holding her head up and keeping as far away from their culture as possible, she remains unscathed, and grows to full maturity as a graceful and *eidel* daughter of *Yisroel* (*Chayei HaMussar* Vol. 3, Page 107, in the name of the great *ba'al mussar*, Harav Avraham Zelmenes *zt'l*).

There can be nothing more rewarding than the feeling that one is a healthy and strong link in a heritage that has existed ever since we stood at *Har Sinai*. We can awaken this gratifying feeling within ourselves by genuinely cleaving to the practices and ways that have been an integral part of *Klal Yisroel* from the earliest times.

4. DRESSING TO HIDE ONE'S "JEWISHNESS" - ERRONEOUS:

(a) Covering nakedness is a basic human requirement: Jewish women and girls should appreciate their good fortune in being taught to dress correctly, even though it is very different from the way others dress at present. The Jewish way of dress, in which the upper sections of the legs are fully covered, to take but one example, directs people to cover nakedness, and is the way all females should dress whether Jewish or not. Therefore, rather than feel that the *halacha* is making demands on them they should understand that it is directing them to basic decency.

In the *Bircas HaShachar* we say a *bracha* on having a belt with which to gird ourselves (אוזר ישראל בגבורה) and on having the means to cover our heads (עוטר ישראל בתפארה). In both these *brachos*, ישראל, the Jewish people, is mentioned - because girding oneself to separate the upper body from the lower body and covering one's head are special requirements of Jewish people that are not shared by other people. However, in the *bracha* on having garments to wear in general, מלביש ערומים, "He dresses the naked", ישראל is not mentioned. This is because every human being should be properly dressed. Since dressing properly is not just a Jewish quality but a human quality, the *bracha* refers to all humanity (M.B. 46:9).

Accordingly, when we dress so that all that is considered nakedness is covered, we are not doing something typically Jewish but something that is typically and essentially human as it is one of the ways in which man differs from animals. Consequently, when we dress correctly, rather than feel embarrassed in front of others who dress inadequately, we should be grateful that we are at least behaving in the way that is fitting for all human beings.

(b) A Jewish person should be distinguishable: For Jewish women and girls to defend an inadequate manner of dress they have adopted, such as a loose neckline or tights that do not cover the leg well, with the excuse that they do so because they find it too unpleasant to be recognized as Jewish women within a non-Jewish society, is incorrect for a number of reasons.

- Firstly, the excuse is a fallacy, as is obvious from the fact that many men of the same society voluntarily wear typical Jewish garb, for example a hat (rather than a *yarmulke* which is less noticeable), a beard, a dark suit, etc. and do not claim that to avoid harassment they have to dress in a way comparable to others. If so why should women be overly self-conscious of their Jewish appearance and insist that they cannot wear Kosher clothing because they will be seen to be different?

▪ Secondly, it is wrong for there to be no apparent distinction between a Jewish person and a non-Jew. Just as we dress at least somewhat differently on Shabbos from the weekdays, because Shabbos is sanctified by its many *halachos* and must not be confused with weekdays (O.C. 262:2), so too, we should dress somewhat differently from the other nations of the world because we are a people sanctified to keep the *mitzvos* of the Torah and must not allow ourselves to blend into the nations of the world. The *Rambam* writes (*Hilchos Avodas Kochavim* 11:1), יהיה הישראל מובדל מהן וידוע במלבושו ובשאר מעשיו כמו שהוא מובדל מהן במדעו ובדיעותיו - "A Jewish person should be different from them and should be recognizable by his clothes and conduct just as he is different in his culture and concepts" - see *Teshuvos Maharik* 88 and *Drashos Chasam Sofer,* vol. 1 page 309.

It is appropriate to mention what an early *Acharon*, the *Mahari Brunna*, *Teshuva* 34 writes about men wearing a *yarmulke*. He writes, אנן דדיירינן בין האומות ואינהו אזלי בגילוי ראש ולא מינכר ביניהון אלא בכיסוי הראש, חשיב השתא [ההולך בגילוי ראש] כעובר על דת יהודית - "Since we live amongst the *umos ha'olam* who go bareheaded, a man is obligated to cover his head. Otherwise there will be no distinction in dress between them, and one transgresses *das Yehudis* [which requires that we be distinguishable from the *umos haolam*]".

Although the overall manner of dress need not be different to the way non-Jews dress (see 1:I:4 above), and even in the times of *Chazal*, Jewish women dressed similarly to the local manner of dress (see *Shabbos* 65a *Rashi* s.v. *Aravios and Medios*) - nevertheless, a Jewish person must be distinguishable in a significant way from his non-Jewish counterparts - (see *Responsa Arugas Habosem* Y.D. 136 and *Responsa Beis Shlomo* 197).

On the verse הן עם לבדד ישכון - "Behold a people dwells independently" (*Bamidbar* 23:9), *Chazal* say the following words, מובדלין הן מן העובדי אלילים בכל דבר, בלבושיהן ובמאכלן ובגופן ובפתחיהן - "They are different from other nations in every way - in their clothes, their food (eating only Kosher food) their bodies (the *mitzva* of *Bris Milah*) and their family life" - (*Yalkut Shimoni*, *Balak* 768). It is interesting to note that the first mentioned is the difference in clothes. Evidently, the independence of the Jewish people is ensured first and foremost by their typical clothes. Accordingly, to positively hide all signs of our Jewishness is far from the correct manner of conduct.

The *Maharal MiPrague* in his *sefer, Netzach Yisrael,* end of chapter 25, writes, וכן המלבושים אשר ישראל נבדלים מהם וכו׳ וגם ההבדל זה פרצו מאוד עד

שרוצים לדמות להם בכל מה שאפשר ואין זה אלא להכביד גלותינו - freely translated he says "The distinction in clothing....However, they have breached this fence badly and do whatever they can to hide their identity and look like others. This causes the *galus* to become more severe *rachmana litzlon*".

(c) Nothing is lost by others realizing that we are *Yidden*: Looking different than the *umos ha'olam* should not be considered as a source of trouble and a contributory factor to the bitter *golus* we are in. On the contrary, in Mitzrayim the attribute of dressing in typical Jewish garb helped in speeding up our redemption, as *Chazal* enumerate שלא שינו את מלבושיהם - "they did not change their traditional Jewish garb" amongst the prime merits which enabled the redemption to take place (see *Pesikta Zutoh, Shemos* 6:6).

In fact, wearing only traditional Jewish garments in Mitzrayim was not *halachically* required, as one may wear the clothes of *nochrim*, provided they are Kosher, as stated above. In the merit of drawing such a profound demarcation line between themselves and others they merited the *geula*. If we similarly ensure that our Jewishness is evident and stop fantasizing that this is the source of all our misery, this will once again help bring our redemption בע"ה with the arrival of *Moshiach* speedily in our times.

5. THE NEED FOR SEGREGATION FROM OTHER CULTURES:

(a) Comparable to the segregation of Shabbos from weekdays: In the *bracha* of *Havdalah* we say about Hashem, "He separates between holy and mundane, between light and dark, between *Yisroel* and other nations, between Shabbos and six working days". The segregation between light (which refers to day), and dark (which refers to night), is total. Night never appears in the middle of the day, nor does the light of day emerge in the middle of the night. So too, the segregation between Shabbos and weekdays must be total, to the point that on Shabbos we do not move items that are used for jobs forbidden on Shabbos (*muktza* - O.C. 308:2 and *Rambam, Hilchos Shabbos* 24:12) nor talk about activities we may not do on Shabbos (*v'daber davar* - O.C. 306:1.) Furthermore, we dress on Shabbos into different clothes than those worn on weekdays (O.C. 262:2). As a result of this far-reaching segregation, the *kedusha* of Shabbos is safe from infiltration and not influenced by the activities of the six working days of the week.

In a similar manner, the segregation of *Am Yisroel* from the culture of the *umos ha'olam* must be total, so that our way of thinking, dressing and general conduct remains unaffected by alternative cultures and customs. Even the *issurim* of *mukza* and *v'daber davar* apply (in a way) to the separation of *Klal Yisroel* from the *umos ha'olam*. *Muktza* applies by not taking into our hands books and newspapers that contain unsuitable material, and *v'daber davar* applies, by not uttering words or using expressions that are unfitting for the pure lifestyle of a Jewish person. We are also not to dress in clothes that represent a life that is foreign to ours. Hence, just as a perfect separation must exist between Shabbos and weekdays (בין יום השביעי לששת ימי המעשה) so too, a perfect separation must exist between *Klal Yisrael* and all other people (בין ישראל לעמים).

(b) Whatever could cause familiarity should be avoided: People are aware that they must be cautious of the 'doubt time' called *bein hashmashos*. For example, to *daven Mincha* during definite daytime because *bein hashmashos* might be too late to daven (M.B. 233:14). Similarly, to refrain from *melachos* late on Friday afternoon because *bein hashmashos* might already be Shabbos and one would be violating Shabbos (O.C. 261:1).

This principle applies also to the separation between "our people and other nations" (בין ישראל לעמים). A person must keep away from that which might expose him to the culture of others, even if this is not certain. For example, if going to a certain place of entertainment, reading a certain book or befriending a certain person could bring him into contact with *arayos*-related matters or inculcate him with non-Jewish ways of thinking, he must keep clear from them. He cannot afford to take such risks - because contacts that are unsuitable and the consequences of the familiarity can be very damaging. [See *Sefer Hamitzvos LaRambam*, *Issurim* 30. that *b'chukoseihem* is a Torah prohibition. One must therefore refrain even when in doubt].

It is remarkable that every Shabbos starts and finishes by keeping the "doubt-periods" of *bein hashmashos* with the full stringency of Shabbos. These 'periods of doubt' surround the inner day of definite Shabbos. Being scrupulous and cautious during "doubt-times" indicates full dedication to the adherence of Shabbos and it is these two outposts which infuse the full *kedusha* into the complete day of Shabbos. So too, by being careful in the doubt-areas of *b'chukoseihem* we demonstrate our total commitment to Torah and *mitzvos* and thereby infuse our lives with *Kedushas Yisroel*.

(c) Wise people understand the great need to prevent familiarity: Before *havdalah* is made on wine, a basic *havdalah* (אתה חוננתנו) is said within the *bracha* אתה חונן recited in *Maariv* of *Motzoei Shabbos*. The *Yerushalmi* explains that it is said in this *bracha* because אם אין דעת הבדלה מנין - the *bracha* of אתה חונן refers to intelligence and "if there is a lack of intelligence there is no understanding for distinction" (*Yerushalmi Brachos*

5:2 and M.B. 294 *Sha'ar Hatzion* 2). The greater the understanding, the more the person perceives the difference between the holy and the mundane.

Accordingly, the wiser and the more intelligent a person is, the more he perceives the difference between *Yidden* and other people, foresees pit-holes and dangers of subtle incursions, and takes due precautions. It is the fool who is overconfident and presumptuous, and sees no danger to himself or his children when they participate in national sports such as large inter-city football matches and car racing, or relax and play with adults and children of other faiths etc - (see *Yalkut Shimoni, Shemos,* verse 1:7 on words *Vatmalei ha'aretz osom; Sefer HaChinuch, Mitzva* 262 and M.B. 307:59).

The wisest of men, our Holy *Chachamim,* understood that intermarriage *r.l.* can be triggered by things which most people would consider as virtually harmless. For example, they forbade *bishul akum* (foods cooked by a *nochri*), *pas akum* (bread baked privately by a *nochri*) and *stam yeinam* (wine touched by a *nochri*) - because an association with the *umos ha'olam* through food and drink can start a subtle entry into their lives and end up in total affiliation *r.l.* Other aspects of their culture must similarly be treated with utmost caution, so that they do not detrimentally affect our lives.

I. ASSESSING IF ONE'S MANNER OF DRESS IS TZNIUS'DIK

1. "WOULD I MIND MEETING A CHOSHEVE PERSON?": In the inner recesses of our hearts most of us know only too well what is a *tznius'dik* way of dress and what is not. The *neshama* of the *Bas Yisroel* yearns for *tznius* and feels an inadequacy when it is absent. A visitor from the United States related the following wonderful way of strengthening our perception:

When she was a teenager her mother would tell her that when she was fully dressed and ready to go out, she should stop for a moment and think to herself how she would feel if when out on the street she would meet Rebbetzen Kaplan (the founder of the *Beis Yaacov* movement in America). If she knew she would feel fine and would even be delighted at the chance encounter with such a *choshuve* person, she could rest assured that she was dressed as a *Bas Yisroel* should be dressed. However, if she knew that she would be embarrassed to meet her and would dearly hope not to be noticed, there was obviously something wrong with the way she was dressed. Either

her dress, her jewelry, her hair style, her neckline, the way she had pushed up her sleeves or something else was not up to the standard it should be.

In other words, we often do not need to be told that what we are doing is incorrect, as we instinctively know that it is so. It is just due to our desire to look pretty that we are temporarily blinded into thinking that it is acceptable. If we arouse within ourselves the trait of בושה - shame, the desire not to be seen as a sinner or as a *prutza* will quickly remove the blindness and we will once again see things in their true and correct light.

2. THIS TYPE OF REFLECTION SAVED YOSEF FROM SIN: When *Yosef Hatzadik* was in the throes of his great *nisayon* with the wife of his master, he managed to emerge unscathed because נראית לו דמות דיוקנו של אביו - "the image of his father appeared to him in a vision" (*Rashi, Breishis* 39:11). The *yetzer horah* tried to convince Yosef that for a number of reasons he should give in to the request of his master's wife, and Yosef became confused whether or not to accede to her wishes (*Rashi ibid)*. However, when he reflected on how he would feel if his holy father *Yaacov Avinu* was watching him at this moment, he immediately saw the *emes*, and refused to be drawn into what would have been a major *aveirah*. Similarly, the *Mashgiach* Rabbi Yecheskel Lewenstien *zt'l* used to say that, when in doubt, a person should think what his Rebbe would have said in such a case.

In a similar vein, a woman or girl should reflect on how she would feel if she were to encounter an esteemed person. If she would quickly close her collar a little more or pull down her sleeves to a more appropriate length, she is evidently aware that her dress is not quite right. By reflecting in this way she will be able to keep herself very much in check.

It must however be added that, due to the confusion that reigns in the world nowadays, there are some women and girls who are so perplexed in matters of *tznius* that they would not be ashamed to meet even the most notable person in the attire they are wearing, although it is quite inadequate.

3. APPRECIATING TZNIUS IS A SAFEGUARD AGAINST MISTAKES: Even women and girls who try to keep the rules of *tznius* are often perplexed due to being influenced by all that they see. If only they were aware of this problem, they would be much less vulnerable. Knowing their confusion, they would treat each new fashion with the utmost suspicion. Only when fully convinced that it is refined, would they decide to wear it.

Also, an awareness of the immense importance of *tznius* is a major defense against errors that can occur due to ignorance. When in doubt whether something is permitted or forbidden, a person will react quite differently when he considers the issue to be extremely important and the consequences of violation to be serious, than when he views the subject as no more than a trivial matter and doing wrong as only a minor infringement. Knowing that a lack of *tznius* involves many *issurim (lifnei Iver, V'hayah machanecha kadosh),* and is a subject that lies at the heart of *kedushas Yisroel*, a woman or girl will wear something only when she is certain that it is perfectly in order for her to wear it.

The *Steipler Gaon zt'l* refers in *Chayei Olam* 2:8 to those who rely on doubtful opinions in questions of possible *chillul* Shabbos. He writes that, if a person would know that if he did an act of *chillul* Shabbos, whether intentionally or inadvertently, he would immediately contract a serious ailment, *rachmana litzlan*, he would be very careful and take no risks. The same is to be said about *tznius*. If a woman would know that an infringement on *tznius* would cause a serious ailment to occur, she would be exceedingly careful to ensure that no error happened. The comparison of our issue to the words of the *Steipler Gaon* is particularly pertinent as the *Gemara* (*Shabbos* 62b) attributes forms of serious ailment to *pritzus* - see *Mekoros* 26:2-3. An awareness such as this can shake a person into thinking carefully before copying the ways of the *umos ha'olam*.

J. PUBLIC RALLIES FOR THE FURTHERANCE OF TZNIUS

1. THE GREAT VALUE OF SUCH GATHERINGS: Calling a rally or public meeting of women and girls for the furtherance of *tznius* is a powerful means of bringing the message home to a large number of people. We are all aware of the enormous impact the *shemiras halashon* rallies have had in *Eretz Yisroel*, drawing crowds of over ten thousand and penetrating deeply into the public's consciousness. The improvement in that field is most impressive. If the *Chofetz Chayim zt'l* were with us today he would doubtlessly be delighted that his efforts have finally made such inroads. There is every reason to believe that if *kinusei nashim* were made for *tznius* a similar impact could be made on the momentous issues of modesty and *kedushas Yisroel*. In fact, a start has already been made in the United States, sponsored by both

Chassidishe and *Litvishe mosdos* of *chinuch* for girls. The attendance and the degree of *hisorerus* have been very encouraging.

The saying of *Chazal* כינוסן של צדיקים הנאה להם והנאה לעולם - "When righteous people gather together it is beneficial both for the participants and for the rest of society" (*Sanhedrin* 71b) applies very much to this type of *kinus nashim*. The participants themselves gain considerable *chizuk* from such a meeting, and very tangible fruits in the field of refinement and *tznius* can be expected from such encouragement. Furthermore, when the participants dress henceforth with greater refinement and project a more *tznius'dik* image, this in turn, sets a standard and example for the rest of the community. Hence such gatherings are truly "beneficial both for the participants and for the rest of society".

Arranging such a rally entails the cooperation of many people. Since some people do not realize what can achieved and might even dissuade others who would have wanted to help, it will therefore be explained below what type of *chizuk* in the keeping of the *halacha* can result from meetings.

2. SPEAKERS CAN GIVE WOMEN A TREMENDOUS CHIZUK: At such gatherings, speakers who are steeped in Torah, Yiras Shomayim and *yiras cheit* can make an impassioned plea to Orthodox women and girls to improve their standards in this holy sphere. One will usually find, that rather than shower their listeners with "fire and brimstone" about the *gehinom* that awaits the transgressor, they elevate the self-esteem of the Jewish woman by pointing out her importance and the great effect she has on *Klal Yisroel*. Her very being is that of an "*ezer k'negdo*", an indispensable help-mate. It is in this capacity that she helps and protects the Jewish people by setting the right tone and projecting *simcha* with *Yiddishkeit,* (See *Rashi, Shemos* 19:3 on the words כה תאמר לבית יעקב).

It is usual for a speaker to portray the central role women play in the development of Jewish life both at home and out in the street. He shows that they can "make it" or, *chas veshalom*, "break it" - it all depends on them. If they act with righteousness and *kedusha,* the whole of the community gains tremendously from them, whilst if they display a carefree frivolous mode of conduct, the whole community, Heaven forbid, suffer a spiritual setback as a result of their conduct.

3. IMPORTANT HALACHIC POINTS CAN BE HIGHLIGHTED:

(a) Dispelling the notion that there is always a "second opinion": At such a rally important but neglected *halachos* related to *tznius* can be highlighted. Moreover, people tend to disbelieve *halachos* that they have not previously heard. It is common for people to think that there must be a dispute about the matter, and although a lecturer in a high school or seminary has taught the girls a *halacha* they are quite convinced that he could just as well have stated a different view and been much more lenient. The falsehood of this oft repeated untruth is the cause of much of the difficulty in influencing people. A speaker of great *halachic* stature, who is regarded as an expert in the field of *halacha* will, however, dispel such misconceptions, in a way that the written text may not be capable of doing.

(b) Refuting the excuse, "But it's the *minhag* to dress in this way": It would be useful to suggest to those assembled that people have a tendency to justify many iniquities, including ways of dress which contravene *halachic* guidelines with the premise that "the *minhag* is to dress in this way" and *minhagim* carry a lot of weight even within the parameters of *halacha*. In connection with this it must be explained that a custom has the *halachic* status of *minhag* only when it was introduced or at least supported by *Gedolei Yisroel*, whilst a mode of conduct that has been started by ordinary people does not have the status of *minhag* (*Yoreh Deoh* 214:1; *Chazon Ish, Orach Chayim* 39:8; *Sdei Chemed, Mareches Mem,* Chap. 38 s.v. *U'mikol makom im haminhag*). About such unauthorized types of *minhagim* the *Poskim* write (in the name of the *Shloh Hakadosh*) that מנהג has the same letters as גהנם as it can lead people astray.

(c) Warning not to mistakenly compare one situation to another: The speaker can furthermore explain to the audience how mistaken assumptions have arisen by people erroneously comparing one situation to another. For example, people think that those who come from a place where a certain leniency is practiced with the consent of a local *Rav*, have the right to continue doing so wherever they happen to be. This is totally incorrect as has already been pointed out (in 1:G above). Similarly, people think that styles of clothes that are worn by Orthodox women in one country may automatically be worn everywhere. Again, this is a fallacious assumption as this may be a form of *pritzus* in the second place where men are not accustomed to see women in such attire and it therefore attracts their attention.

When such ideas are explained by mouth it is often easier and less tedious than to read it in a *sefer*. All these points can be conveyed with great clarity and conviction at a public meeting. It is therefore an outstanding act of *zikuy harabim* (aiding the public spiritually) to organize such an evening.

(d) Addressing only the worst mistakes people make: Occasionally a person will address an audience that knows very little about "*tznius* of dress". These people are liable to have several failings and it is recommended that the speaker does not mention all of them from the start, as this could result in none being accepted. Rather, he should mention the most serious infringement and endeavor to rectify it, avoiding, at present, mention of the secondary issues. For example, if the women wear trousers and also have necklines which are not very low but are not fully Kosher, the main thrust must be to make them aware that wearing trousers is considered major *pritzus* and only eventually should an attempt be made to educate them to the full details of *tznius'dik* dress. Although one may not expressly permit an *issur* (even to improve *Yiddishkeit* in general) a person may avoid mentioning an *issur*, although this could be misconstrued as a form of consent, to enable rebuke concerning a more severe *issur* to make better headway - see *Sotah* 48a *Rashi* s.v. *Levetuli hai.* See also *Mekoros* 44:3-4.

4. RALLIES ARE NEEDED ALTHOUGH SEFORIM ON TZNIUS EXIST: As has been explained, a rally has an important role to play even if *seforim* about *tznius* are available. Some further advantages are as follows:-

- Firstly, the difference between the void and vacuity in the lives of the *umos ha'olam* due to which external beautification is so important to them and, *lehavdil*, the sense of accomplishment and fulfillment that fills the life of a *Yid* cannot be depicted and portrayed in print as effectively as it can by a speaker.

- Secondly, there are at times wrongdoings and shortcomings that occur in one place but do not occur in most other places. When this is the case it is best not to mention it in a *sefer* so as not to give wrong ideas to the weaker elements of most other societies. Moreover, to inform those who do not know that these wrongdoings take place could be a *chillul Hashem* - see *Mekoros* 9:1. Such things may have no place in a *sefer*. However, in a local rally the local iniquities can be spelled out in no uncertain terms.

- Thirdly, there are occasionally points that are distinctly feminine and should only be discussed amongst women. Such points cannot be written in a *sefer* which could come into the hands of men and boys. A lady speaker at a rally can state these things once the *Rabbanim* have spoken and left the auditorium.

- Fourthly, and very importantly, fashions change continuously and new cuts, styles and ideas are produced for every season. Moreover, the industry for techniques that add glamour and attraction to females works ceaselessly. A *sefer* can of course only mention modes of dress, jewelry, and cosmetics that exist at the time of writing, whilst the latest ideas and misdeeds will not be mentioned in it. An annual rally is, however, an excellent opportunity for *Rabbanim* and speakers to warn people about the latest fads and fashions that threaten the unsuspecting and credulous *Bas Yisroel*. If one considers the decline in refinement that has occurred over the last two decades, this reason for organizing rallies must be considered a compelling truth.

5. THE IMPORTANCE OF GIVING CHIZUK TO WOMEN AND GIRLS: The following is a quote from a letter by the venerable *Rosh Yeshiva* of *Ponevez*, Maran Hagaon Harav Elozor Menachem Man Shach *shlita*. It was written on the fourth of *Ellul* 5728. It addresses two important issues: Girls giving *chizuk* to one another after they have left seminary and arranging *shiurim* so that they frequently receive new *chizuk*. The original is printed in *Michtavim U'Maamorim* 3:170.

"Originally, Jewish people had no need for groups and organizations, for Jewish life was generally well organized. Conduct at home was perfect. A word uttered by a father or mother was holy to all members of the household; their opinion was decisive and final in every way. There were no breaches in modesty and the Jewish woman stayed in the sanctuary of her home. Even the streets were alright. All this was tens of years ago.

Nowadays the situation has changed from one extreme to the other. Shocking things happen and the streets have become terribly corrupt. Opinions and views that utterly oppose *Daas* Torah reign supreme, with those who propagate these opinions well organized into parties, thereby wielding considerable influence over all. They are strangers to the spirit of Torah and to authentic Judaism. Having forsaken the ethics of the Torah and *Yiddishkeit* they draw their ideas and aspirations from fractured wells. Slowly but surely their ways have penetrated even into *Chareidi* homes as we see that even in these circles a daughter rebels against her mother. This is just as *Chazal* (*Sotah* 49b) have predicted it would be in the epoch of the *Moshiach*. [The actual statement of *Chazal* is, באחרית הימים בת קמה באמה - "At the end of the *galus* there will so much *chutzpa* in the world that a daughter will rise up against her mother"].

Under these circumstances individuals cannot hold their own. They are unable to maintain a *Torah'dik* way of life against such forceful winds. Therefore, it is the "duty of the hour" to create organizations and *chizuk* groups. Two people together are far stronger than one person alone. Now is the time for G-d fearing people to talk, inspire and encourage one another.

Hence, it is an obligation on all girls who have been educated in the *Beis Yaacov* schools and seminaries to organize themselves into groups. This will enable them to exert a positive influence on one another and call in speakers to address them on important matters. They will also be able to pursue activities that belong to being part of an organization. My blessings are that the grace of *Hashem* rest on all your undertakings for the strengthening of *Yiddishkeit* and furtherance of true Jewish conduct."

6. CHIZUK SHOULD BE FOLLOWED WITH ACTUAL IMPROVEMENT: For people to gain a lasting benefit from a *chizuk* it is important that they put the *chizuk* into practice as soon as possible. After hearing the *halachos* of "*tznius* in dress" and the immense importance that must be attached to the subject, people are still only superficially involved. However, once they have made a meaningful contribution to the cause, they become emotionally involved, as it is human nature to become emotionally attached to something one has worked for and put an effort into - (see *Bava Metziah* 38a, *Rashi,* s.v. *Kav*). Therefore, if after a *shiur*, women take their dress or their daughter's dress and improve its neckline or hemline, they become emotionally associated with the elevated and sublime world of *tznius*, and forge a strong bond with it.

On the other hand, if people do not put the *chizuk* they hear into practice right away, and instead delay it for the time being, not only will they not gain the advantages mentioned, but the procrastination will have the effect of weakening the *chizuk* they may have acquired. People must satisfy their conscience as to why they have not yet reacted. The natural process of justification is to subtly lessen the severity of the matter in their own mind, to the point that they see no urgency to attend to the issue immediately. It follows, that reacting straight away is positively good and brings the wonderful trait of *tznius* close to the person's heart, whilst not reacting right away is distinctly harmful and causes a person to lose sight of the importance of *kedushas Yisroel* - see *Emuna U'Bitachon L'haRamban,* Chap.19.

Accordingly, if a woman wears a snood or beret that slips back, causing the front section of the hair to show, hears in a *shiur* that a married woman should have all her hair covered, she should, if at all possible, correct her snood that very evening. She should either tighten the elasticized band to prevent it slipping back or fix into the inner front rim a band of non-slip material so that the snood or beret is held firmly in position. Should she not be capable of correcting the snood or beret right away, she should wear an alternative type of head-wear such as a *sheitel* or a *tiechel* until her snood has been made Kosher. In either case, she must take the matter in hand right away. As stated, this will make the *chizuk* she has heard a *kinyan olam* - an everlasting part of herself.

As has been mentioned in the preface, it is difficult to describe the great *simcha* a speaker experienced when he was told after a *drasha* on *tznius* that a woman went home from the speech and spent the better part of that night sewing up the slits in her dresses and skirts. See also the moving letter reproduced in 7:M:6 below. We are deeply proud of the way many Jewish women and girls gladly do the *Ratzon Hashem* as soon as they become aware of it. From their reaction it is evident that in most cases just "lack of knowledge" is the cause for inadequate dress. Therefore, as soon as they become aware that a certain form of dress or hair style is wrong, the natural urge to do right that is within the pure well-meaning *Bas Yisroel*, quickly results in substantial changes being made.

7. THE SPEECHES SHOULD BE RECORDED AND DISTRIBUTED:

(a) The great value that can be gained from Torah tapes: When a rally takes place or a *drasha* of *chizuk* is given on issues such as *tznius*, it is of immense value for tapes to be made of the speeches. There are usually parts of a speech which a person has not fully understood or appreciated. By hearing the speech once again every part of it can register properly. Tapes also enable a person to be inspired again and again, whenever he feels the need. Moreover, many people who could not hear the original speech are able to hear it and gain inspiration from it. The positive value that *Klal Yisroel* has gained from Torah tapes is enormous. How much Torah is learned during travel as a result of the vast array of Torah tapes available? These tapes occupy the person's mind with *divrei* Torah for many hours and at the same time prevent him from being contaminated by all that he would otherwise hear on the radio.

Ex-seminary girls who live in places where they are not able to gain the *chizuk* can maintain their standard of commitment by making full use of tapes. With them they can absorb not only the content but also the *ruach* (spirit) with which the *shiurim* were given. This has a much greater impact than they would have gained from reading and re-reading printed versions of the *shiurim*.

(b) Some *kiruv* and *tznius* tapes are not suited to all listeners: Having sung the praises of Torah tapes, a word or two of caution must be mentioned.

There are tapes of speeches given to newcomers to *Yiddishkeit*. These tapes are sometimes not suited to those who are fully committed to Torah and *mitzvos*. The questions raised can sow unnecessary confusion into the innocent mind of the person who was brought up with the correct *hashkofos*. Also, some of the expressions used and some of the references that are made are suited specifically to people who have lived amongst the *umos ha'olam* and know the way they speak and the latest scandals that have occurred. Due to *tznius* these are best not imparted to those who are fortunate enough never to have come into contact with them in the first place.

(c) Tapes should not substitute going to the actual *shiurim*. Although many Torah tapes are wonderful and give enormous *chizuk* they should not be considered as the perfect alternative to going to *shiurim* in the first place where one can both hear and see the Torah personality speaking. Much of the depth of what is being said is learned from the facial expressions and hand-movements of the speaker which are absent in a tape. Also, *kedusha* is transmitted by seeing a *Yerei shomayim* (especially when he is imparting *divrei* Torah) and this cannot be obtained from a tape which is a lifeless object. See *Gemara* (*Eruvin* 13b) where Rabbi Yehuda, known as *Rabbeinu Hakadosh*, says that he became what he was by seeing the back of Rabbi Meir whilst sitting behind him at *shiurim* (the room was so full that his place was behind his *Rebbe*). Rabbi Yehuda continued, that had he merited having a frontal view of Rabbi Meir, he would have become even greater.

We see from this that hearing the words (with all the fire that is put into them) does not impart to the listener that which he gains when seeing the *Rebbe* himself. Accordingly, whilst tapes are a wonderful supplement when a *shiur* or *drasha* cannot be heard live, the greatest value is gained by attending the original *shiur* or *drasha* and both seeing and hearing the Torah thoughts of a *Talmid Chacham*.

K. CHALLENGES OF THE SUMMER ENRICH ONE'S TZNIUS

1. THE CHALLENGE TO TZNIUS: Summer time, with its bright sunshine and warm weather, is a "time of challenge" for the Jewish girl. As the months progress and the summer becomes hotter, her dress will prove whether she upholds the standard of *tznius* required of the Jewish girl. During this time she is likely to have a strong urge to open the top button of her blouse so as to free her neck, and she could be reluctant to insert a pin to ensure that nothing beyond the neck is exposed. Similarly, she might desire to wear a light sweater or T-shirt with a neckline which is too loose or which has sleeves that do not properly cover the elbow. Even if her dress, blouse or T-shirt do have long enough sleeves she impulsively wants to pull them up above the elbow so that she can feel a cool breeze on her arms.

She could have an urge to wear thin tights which do not cover her legs well, with the excuse that anything thicker than this is too warm and causes some discomfort. Often, the urge is because the thinner tights match her summer clothes much better than the thicker ones, and therefore add to her overall appearance. Also due to this second reason she might want to wear skin colored tights that are almost unnoticeable. She might even contemplate wearing a blouse or dress which is somewhat see-through because such garments are cooler and more pleasant to wear than others. Moreover, during the summer months she could be inclined to shorten her skirt because during these months fashions are often shorter and she likes "to be with it".

Since some women and girls take great liberties in the field of *tznius* during the summer months this innocent girl becomes temporarily oblivious of the *issur* of leaving uncovered areas that must be concealed. It sometimes goes so far that she feels that she will be completely "out of tune" if her dress is as Kosher in the summer as it is during the winter months.

2. TEST ENABLES PERSON TO DEMONSTRATE HIS COMMITMENT: When encouraging girls to withstand the "challenges of the summer" it should be explained to them that it is quite natural to have the above mentioned urges, and to find dressing with due *tznius* quite a *nisayon* - a test. They are after all only human beings and comfort and well-being is of paramount importance to everyone. They should not imagine that the many women and girls who live in hot climates, such as those of *Bnei Brak* or

Yerusholayim, and nevertheless dress with perfect *tznius*, are people who are insensitive to heat and have no particular urge for comfort.

This is certainly not the case and these people are as human as everyone else in every way. However, they have been educated to appreciate that real living means upholding one's principles even if it would seem temporarily to have been more agreeable and comfortable to have done otherwise. These fine daughters of *Am Yisroel* understand that difficulties are there to be surmounted and to enable us to prove our total devotion to the *halacha*.

A man comes home after a long day and sits down to learn with his *chavrusa* even though he is tired and would have preferred to go for a walk or to bed. He does so because he knows that to learn Torah every day is an absolute must, as without it the *nishmas Yisroel* is deprived of its source of life and energy. Similarly, a mother is continuously on-duty, educating her children and developing within them good character traits. She tries her best not to display frustration or anger which are harmful to the children, even though she is often put to the test and after a long day is frequently exhausted. Her children are entrusted to her care and their future depends on the education they get from her. She will, therefore, not allow fatigue or strain to cause her to forsake her sacred duty.

So too, if a woman knows that *tznius* is the very being of the *Bas Yisroel* and that it is as important for women to dress *b'tznius* as it is for a man to learn Torah (see 1C above), she will not allow inconvenience to deter her from doing that which is all important - see *Mekoros* 2:7.

3. "PASSING A TEST" DEEPENS A PERSON'S COMMITMENT: Girls should furthermore be given to understand, that just as the summer is a time of challenge concerning *tznius*, so too, it is a time for growth in *tznius* and for their *tznius* to become greatly enriched and deeply consolidated within themselves. This is because when a person has had a *nisayon,* a test, which he has mastered well, he becomes greatly strengthened in his commitment to that ideal as a result of withstanding the test.

When *Hashem* put Avraham Avinu through ten tests He did not do so in order to see whether or not Avraham would withstand the tests, since He knew only too well just how strong a person Avraham Avinu was. Rather, they were "growth injections", to enable latent and potential feelings that were within him and had not yet materialized to become a powerful reality (*Breishis Rabba* 55:2). Correspondingly, when a very good looking woman or girl dresses in perfect *tznius* and takes precautions that admiring eyes do not gaze at her, she thereby develops a deep and strong bond with the cherished trait of *tznius* - see *Mekoros* 2:6-7.

In the same vein, rather than considering summer as a totally negative time as far as *tznius* is concerned, it should be viewed as a time when *tznius* can be intensified, enhanced and greatly reinforced. Summer time is a time of great contrasts. Whilst the world that surrounds us is engaged throughout summer in an ongoing dive into the abyss of the impure, those who wholeheartedly dedicate themselves to the service of *Hashem*, soar upwards in their attachment to Torah, *mitzvos* and *tznius*.

4. TZNIUS IS WITHIN THE EMOTIONAL STAMINA OF EVERYONE:

(a) *Mitzvos* do not cause harm: An additional thought which can give much encouragement is as follows: *Mitzvos* are never beyond the physical and emotional stamina of a person. This principle is referred to in the verse, שומר מצות לא ידע דבר רע - "He who performs *mitzvos* knows no harm" (*Koheles* 8:5). Although discomforts can be experienced when doing the will of *Hashem* (this is called, הפסד מצוה - deprivation experienced when doing a *mitzva* - see *Avos* 2:1), these are of a minor nature and no real harm is caused. Accordingly, the thought that might cross a girl's mind that to dress in a *tznius'dik* fashion in the height of summer "is going to exhaust me" or "is too great an emotional strain, as others who have no understanding for *tznius* will think I am crazy" are imaginary arguments but not factually correct.

(b) *Hashem* asks of man only as much as he can cope with: The verse in *Tehillim* (147:16) refers to *Hashem* as a, נותן שלג כצמר - "The One who sends snow that settles like a blanket of wool". An additional interpretation to these words is given by the *Chidushei Harim* - "*Hashem* sends as much snow as there is wool to warm oneself" - meaning that *Hashem* brings to man only as much as he can cope with. It is the same with *tznius*; even if dressed as is *halachically* required, a woman or girl is assured that she will not find the demands of *tznius* too difficult to cope with - see *Mekoros* 6:4.

(c) *Hashem* controls how the weather affects each person: The great truth just stated goes a step further. Even if a woman or girl is exposed to very hot weather, she will not suffer harm by being dressed *b'tznius*. It will not cause overheating, nor dehydration due to excessive perspiration. Although this may seem against the rules of nature, nature itself is firmly in the hands of *Hashem*. *Chazal*, in their beautiful way, describe the unique and singular power of *Hashem* to guard a person from adverse weather conditions. The verse says, משליך קרחו כפיתים - "He sends His ice according to a person's sustenance" (*Tehillim* 147:17). To this *Rashi* adds in the name of *Chazal* - "a poor man who is short of covers is less affected by the cold than others who have plenty of covers". Similarly, since *mitzvos* cause no harm, those who dress *b'tznius* will not be affected by weather conditions as it would naturally affect others who are more scantily dressed. When looking through the spectacles of Torah and *emuna* we see a different world than the one generally thought to exist! (See *Ohr Hachayim, Shemos* 14:27).

5. TZNIUS IN THE HEIGHT OF SUMMER IS A KIDDUSH *HASHEM*: Girls can furthermore be inspired by the fact that dressing in *tznius'dik* clothes in the height of summer makes a considerable *kiddush Hashem*. People are quick to view the exemplary conduct of others as only superficial, and are quite convinced that the moment a difficulty arises the conduct will be discontinued. With this attitude they remain unimpressed by what they see and take no inspiration from it. However, once they come across a display of true *Yiddishkeit* which is being kept even in adverse conditions, and even when it means projecting an image of not being "with it", they realize that they have come face to face with people who are indeed committed to keeping the *halacha,* come what may. This in turn could have a profound effect on them and encourages them to improve their own *Yiddishkeit*.

The merit and reward for making a *kiddush Hashem* and influencing others to do the *ratzon Hashem* is far beyond our comprehension. The verse in *Tehillim* (20:3) reads, ישלח עזרך מקודש ומציון יסעדך - "He shall send your assistance from Kodesh (lit. holiness) and your support from *Tzion* (lit. a signpost or proof)". On this the *Midrash* comments, מקודש מקידוש השם ומציון מציונן של מצות - "*MiKodesh* - He shall send His assistance because of the *kiddush Hashem* you make with your good deeds. *MiTzion* - He shall send His support because of the *mitzvos* you perform with such perfection that they bear witness to your devotion and support for the fulfillment of *Hashem*'s will".

We learn from here that as a reward for making a *kiddush Hashem* with the good deeds and *mitzvos* we perform, we will enjoy the assistance and support of *Hashem Yisborach* in all our endeavors. Hence, our future health, wealth, *nachas* from our children and general *simcha* in life can be contingent on the *kiddush Hashem* we make by dressing in accordance with the *halacha*, especially at a time when the *halacha* is sadly forsaken by many others. All will agree that the inconvenience experienced by dressing with real *tznius* during the summer months is a small price to pay for a *mitzva* which yields such magnificent dividends!

L. SHABBOS - A TREASURE NOT TO BE MISUSED

1. ON SHABBOS WE LEARN TO APPRECIATE OUR YIDDISHKEIT: Shabbos is one of the greatest treasures *Klal Yisroel* possesses. It is a day of tranquillity and contentment which enables the Jewish person to reflect and strengthen his *emuna* and trust in the Almighty. This in turn elevates the person to a different level of spirituality than he has during the week. For this reason Shabbos is called a יום מנוחה וקדושה - "A restful and elevating day" (*Tefillas Mincha*).

On Shabbos, we see more than ever the great gulf that separates *Am Yisroel* from the *umos ha'olam* and experience the encouraging feeling of our good fortune at belonging to *Am Yisroel*. *Kedusha* and *mitzvos* are intrinsic parts of our purposeful lives whereas almost all other nations lead a fully mundane existence. With a deep appreciation of this, we will not be tempted to take part in the apparent pleasures of other people.

2. SHABBOS IS A SOURCE OF BLESSINGS: Amongst its many qualities, Shabbos is a "source of blessings" for those who keep it properly (in deed and in spirit), as we say in *Lecha Dodi,* כי היא מקור הברכה - "For Shabbos is the wellspring of good fortune". This is the meaning of the words ויברך אלוקים את יום השביעי - "And *Hashem* blessed the seventh day" written at the end of ויכולו - Shabbos was turned into a source of blessing (see *Ohr Hachayim, Breishis* 2:3). It is obviously up to us to ensure that our own conduct and that of our children on this holy day make us deserving candidates for these blessings.

3. WOMEN PREPARE FOR SHABBOS IN A WONDERFUL WAY: Women have a very special bond with Shabbos. They invest an enormous amount of energy and effort into preparing for each and every Shabbos and thereby honoring it. They cook the Shabbos meals, bake the *challos*, prepare the Shabbos clothes for the family, tidy the house, cover the tables with white tablecloths, change their attire in honor of Shabbos, light the Shabbos candles etc. These actions which are done with a devotion and love for

Shabbos, to ensure that it will really be a delightful and special day, naturally make women most deserving recipients of the many blessings that Shabbos has to offer.

4. SHABBOS MUST NOT BE MISHANDLED ONCE IT ARRIVES: It is a great pity if, in spite of all she has done in honor of Shabbos, Shabbos withholds its blessings from her because of the offenses she commits against it, albeit unintentionally. For example, if she wears Shabbos clothes that are unrefined in size, style or color, if she adorns herself with excessive and ostentatious jewelry, if when she goes for a walk it appears to the onlooker that she is showing-off her appearance, her exquisite clothes or her expensive jewelry, if she uses makeup that is forbidden on Shabbos such as rouge and foundation, then Shabbos, which is a day of extra service to *Hashem*, turns into a meaningless and even negative day.

With each of these *issurim* the woman or girl who did so much in preparation for Shabbos causes grievous injury to the holy day of Shabbos and *kedushas Yisroel*. Shabbos was given to help refine our whole being, and in her case the tranquillity and opportunities of Shabbos are being used to do just the opposite.

If she goes to *shul*, as many do on Shabbos morning, in the clothes, jewelry or make-up mentioned, she is adding insult to injury, since it is an offense to come to the Kings palace dressed in a manner the King detests. This is alluded to in the verse, כי אין לבא אל שער המלך בלבוש שק - "For one is not to enter the gates of the kings palace dressed in sackcloth ie. in lowly and unfitting clothes" (*Esther* 4:2). See *Chinuch, Mitzva* 149 that this verse alludes to the palaces of the King of Kings, *Hashem Yisborach*.

Obviously, she does most of these mistakes due to oversight. She bought this beautiful Shabbos dress in honor of Shabbos and did not realize that its neckline or hemline needed extensive change. She wears ostentatious jewelry because she craves to look pretty and does not realize that by wearing this type of jewelry she attracts attention to herself and can cause a passing man to gaze at her (the *issur* of ולא תתורו אחרי עיניכם). She is not aware that almost all forms of cosmetics may not be applied on Shabbos. Although this could well be true, these wrongdoings nevertheless remain *pritzus* or *chillul* Shabbos, and an error in judgment does not leave the person innocent. The person has still done a major *aveirah* and caused extensive damage.

There can be nothing more rewarding than to feel that one is a healthy and strong link in a heritage that has existed ever since we stood at *Har*

Sinai. We can awaken this gratifying feeling within ourselves by cleaving to the practices and ways that have been an integral part of *Klal Yisroel* from the earliest times.

5. DEFENDING KEDUSHAS SHABBOS AND KEDUSHAS YISROEL: Every woman and girl must know that even if others in her own circle trip up on some of the wrongdoings mentioned, this is no license for her to follow suit and profane Shabbos or behave even unintentionally in a way that is injurious to the purity of the Jewish woman. A girl who has Yiras Shomayim will defend *kedushas Yisroel* and *kedushas haShabbos* and ensure that she and, if possible, her close friends disassociate themselves from incorrect behavior. This steadfastness will merit a gradual resurgence of *kedushas* Shabbos and will encourage others to follow her good example.

The tranquillity of Shabbos will then conform with the description given in *Tefillas Mincha* of Shabbos, מנוחה שלמה שאתה רוצה בה - "A perfect rest as You desire it to be". Let us ensure that Shabbos feels a truly welcome guest in our home - not just on *erev* Shabbos but also on Shabbos itself - by the way we treat it once it is with us. Rich physical and spiritual dividends are paid for true *Shemiras* Shabbos and will בע״ה not be long in arriving.

6. THE BRACHA MANY GIVE TO DAUGHTERS ON FRIDAY NIGHT: Since Shabbos is a "source of blessings" it has been chosen as the appropriate time for parents to bless their children (as is practiced in many communities). Fathers and mothers lay their hands on their daughters' heads and bless them with the words ישימך אלוקים כשרה רבקה רחל ולאה - "May *Hashem Yisborach* assign you the blessings of Sarah, Rivka, Rachel and Leah". With this, the parents beseech *Hashem* that their daughter should develop the personal qualities of humility, modesty and refinement which personify the *Bas Yisroel*. Moreover, they request that she find a worthy and valuable partner for life and merit to give birth to and nurture a generation of true servants of *Hashem Yisborach* who will be part of the building-blocks of the future *Klal Yisroel*. Just as the *Imahos* were blessed with these values, so too, their daughter should be found worthy to receive them.

All four *Imahos* were brought up in an environment completely alien to *Yiddishkeit* and nevertheless became wonderful women and great mothers of *Klal Yisroel*. So too, their daughters, even if they are surrounded by an immodest world, should have the strength of character to repulse these negative influences and grow up blessed with the attributes of modesty and refinement, and be worthy of becoming future mothers in *Klal Yisroel*.

M. TEFILLA - A GIFT FROM HEAVEN

1. TEFILLA: CHILDREN BE PROTECTED FROM BAD INFLUENCES: The beautiful practice of blessing one's children (performed by almost everyone at least on *erev Yom Kippur*) discussed in the previous point inspires us to a further observation. This is that parents should always pray to *Hashem* that He protect their children from bad influences and guide them onto the right path. For this reason, mothers use the cherished moments after kindling the Shabbos candles to address a silent *tefilla* to *Hashem Yisborach* that their children grow up to be *y'reim ushleimim* and are not led astray *chas veshalom* by temptations. Such *tefillos* are necessary and appropriate more than ever in our times when dangers are constant and very intense. *Tefilla* is the one medium of salvation that is always available to us. With it we hope for the *siyata d'shmaya* we desperately need - see *Mekoros* 11:2-4.

2. TEFILLA: THAT CHILDREN FOLLOW THE DERECH HAYASHAR: The *Mishna Berura* (47:10) writes, "Parents should always pray for their children that they willingly learn Torah, become *tzadikim* and possess good *midos*. They should concentrate on these requests particularly during ברכת התורה when saying אנחנו וצאצאינו, during אהבה רבה when saying ותן בלבנו להבין ולהשכיל and during ובא לציון when saying the phrase למען לא ניגע לריק ולא נלד לבהלה. In the introduction to the *sefer, Chinuch Yisroel*, the author writes, "I know of an incident where a person came to the *Satmar Rav zt'l* requesting a *bracha* to be successful in the *chinuch* of his children. To this the *Rebbe* responded, 'A better approach would be to get up early in the morning and shed tears on a *Tehillim* and in prayer that you be granted success in the *chinuch* of your children'" - see *Mekoros* 7:8.

3. POWER OF A WOMAN'S TEFILLOS FOR HER CHILDREN: In *Igeres HaTeshuva* (No.79), *Rabbeinu Yona* writes the following: "A woman should take care to *daven* ..... Her main requests at the end of *Shemone Esrei* should be for her sons and daughters. She should pray that they be *yirei Hashem* and that her sons be successful in their Torah learning. This should be her main prayer because the supreme merit of a woman in *Olam Habah* is the fact that her children serve *Hashem*, do His bidding and have Yiras Shomayim. When she leaves this world and the children she leaves behind have Yiras Shomayim in their hearts and are occupied with Torah and *mitzvos*, it will be as if she is still alive and is personally doing all these *mitzvos* and will merit to have a most exalted place in *Olam Habah*."

A man brought his young boy to the *Brisker Rav*, Maran Hagaon Harav Yitzchak Zev Soloveitchik *zt'l*. The father requested a *bracha* that his child grow up to be a true *Talmid Chacham* and *Yorei shomayim*. The *Brisker Rav* responded, "If you learn with your son he will become a true *Talmid Chacham* and if your wife *davens* and implores *Hashem* that her son grow up to be a *Yorei shomayim*, he will become a *Yorei shomayim*" (see *Toldos Yaacov*, page 118). To the *Brisker Rav* the *tefillos* of a mother for the future of her young child were all important. Furthermore, he considered them to have an even greater significance than the *tefillos* of a father. A mother is closer to her young child than the father. Her *tefillos* are therefore said with a greater keenness and greater sincerity. Also, women are more emotional and closer to tears than men. As a result their *tefillos* are more likely to be said with a *lev nishbor* (a broken heart) which are the most loved *tefillos*.

It is likewise recorded that the *Chazon Ish* once remarked concerning those who after generations of detachment from *Yiddishkeit* find their way back, that this is due to their grandmother or great grandmother. He explained that when the first generation turned its back on *Yiddishkeit* their mother was deeply distressed and shed many hot tears. Those hot tears brought later descendants back to the *derech hayashar* (*ibid.*).

In this context, we find that particular mention is made of the mother *davening* for her children, רחל מבכה על בניה מאנה להינחם - "Our mother Rachel cries relentlessly for the redemption of *Klal Yisroel*, she will not be consoled" (*Yirmiyah* 31:14). Also, see *Brachos* (31a) that many *halachos* of *tefilla* are learnt from Channah, as she *davened* for a child. Evidently, Channah had a natural understanding for how a person is to *daven*.

4. THE CHOFETZ CHAYIM RECALLS HIS MOTHER'S TEFILLOS: It is related in the *Chofetz Chayim's* life story that in the year 5684 a son-in-law of the *Chofetz Chayim's* sister found in his mother-in-law's house an old *Tehillim* that had belonged to the *Chofetz Chayim's* mother. He brought it to the *Chofetz Chayim*. When the *Chofetz Chayim* saw the *Tehillim* he took it into his hands and kissed it lovingly. With tears in his eyes he said to those present, "You cannot imagine how many tears my mother *o.h.* poured over this *sefer Tehillim*. Day in, day out before daybreak my mother would pour out her *tefillos,* and pray to *Hashem* that her son grows up to be an upright and good *Yid*' (*Chayov U'Pealoh Shel HaChofetz Chayim*, page 26).

N. BIOGRAPHIES WITH PICTURES HARMFUL TO TZNIUS

1. "NON-KOSHER" PHOTOGRAPHS OF CHOSHEVE WOMEN: Some of the excellent biographies of Gedolim and of great women that are published nowadays contain pre-war photographs of female personalities who are in an inadequate state of dress. They have sleeves rolled up over the elbow, a knee not properly covered, a blouse with more than the neck showing and similar problems. The reproduction and mass dissemination of these pictures is a considerable stumbling block to all who read these books.

For men this is certainly harmful, as a man must not see an inadequately dressed female even just in passing. For women and girls these books are likewise very detrimental as they appear to contain "live evidence" that in pre-war years the general *frum* public and even *chosheve* people were not careful with aspects of dress that are considered nowadays to be essential. Since it is *halachically* wrong to appear amongst men with these inadequacies, publicizing these photographs is an unintentional attack at the very heart of *tznius* and a major disservice to *Klal Yisrael*.

2. FAMILY PHOTOS WITH INADEQUATELY DRESSED RELATIVES: Similarly, there are biographies of *Gedolim* in which large family pictures appear. Occasionally a female relative appears on these pictures wearing a tight-fitting skirt or standing in an *untznius'dik* manner. Here again, issue must be taken at publishing such pictures and for giving the impression that the *Gadol* consented to the young lady dressing or standing in such a way, while that was surely not the case. Books that are potentially excellent reading material for girls, as they impart sound *hashkafos* and would contribute much to *chinuch* for authentic *Yiddishkeit,* are turned into harmful material as a result of these pictures.

3. HOW THE "NON-KOSHER" PICTURES CAME ABOUT: Concerning the basic question as to how these *chosheve* women went around in an inadequate manner of dress, the answer in most cases is probably quite simple; when the picture was taken the woman was almost certainly in a private garden and totally out of the eye of the public. Her friend took the photo there in the garden and neither of them ever imagined that this picture would be published in a book to be seen by hundreds if not thousands of people. Since she was in a secluded area, she was not so careful to ensure that all was fully covered. The desired practice of dressing with full *tznius* even in private, is predominantly for a *tefach,* whilst the amount uncovered in these pictures is invariably less than a *tefach* - see 6:Q:1(c) below. Publishing these pictures is therefore *lashon horah* (slander) and even *motzi shem ra* (untrue slander) on these *chosheve* women, since they give the impression that these women were careless in matters of *tznius* and this need not be true at all.

That is as far as real Torah homes are concerned where *halacha* was kept to its fine details. It must, however, be conceded that during pre-war years the dress of the ordinary *frum* Jewish woman was wanting in many types of communities and there was a considerable lack of knowledge concerning the *halachos* of *tznius* in dress. In general, in those post-*haskala* years many areas of *halacha* were in need of serious improvement (such as the details of the laws of Shabbos, *shatnez, yichud, ribbis, bedikas tolaim, shemiras halashon* - due to which the *Chofetz Chayim* wrote many articles) and the leaders of *Klal Yisrael* had to awaken the people to the most pressing issues first, such as the *issur* of *lashon horah* which is the cause of strife within the family, within the community and between one community and the other. Since *pritzus* of dress of the *umos haolom* was far less a problem in those times than it is nowadays, there simply was not the urgent need to address the issue of '*tznius* of dress' that exists nowadays. Many people therefore erred in this subject, just as they erred in many other areas.

Hopefully, as a result of this and similar protests, publishing houses who reproduce photographs, will in the future either omit inappropriate pictures altogether or "doctor" the pictures beforehand, thereby ensuring that harmful parts of the pictures are not reproduced.

Chapter Three

RAISING CHILDREN TO TZNIUS

A. CHINUCH FORMS STRONG BOND TO YIDDISHKEIT

In the following notes some basic guidelines are provided for bringing up children with a healthy sense of *tznius*. Many points concerning *chinuch* have been mentioned in other articles of this *sefer*. There is nevertheless a need for a basic discussion on the significance of *chinuch* for this all-important area of *Yiddishkeit*.

1. IT WILL BE NATURAL FOR HER TO DRESS WITH TZNIUS: Given the right *chinuch*, it should *b'ezer Hashem* become as natural for a girl to dress in a *tznius'dik* fashion as it is for her to look after her basic needs such as dressing in a pleasing manner, combing her hair, polishing her shoes and generally looking respectable. She will view *tznius* as a cherished part of womanhood rather than something restrictive and she will understand that this is something we *Yidden* are very proud of. After a start in life with the correct attitude, the girl will hopefully grow into an adult with a full awareness and appreciation of the importance of modesty in conduct and dress.

When Boaz noticed the modest conduct of Ruth and inquired about her identity from the leading harvester who stood right by him, he asked, למי הנערה הזאת (*Ruth* 2:5). He did not ask, מי הנערה הזאת, "Who is this girl?" but למי הנערה הזאת, "To whom does this girl belong?" He inquired about her family because it interested him to know which family raises a daughter to conduct herself with such exemplary modesty. It was quite obvious to Boaz that such *tznius* must be the result of considerable parental input as it does not usually develop of its own accord (*Simchas Haregel by the great Gaon Chida zt'l*).

2. SHE WILL BE FORTIFIED TO FACE THE WORLD: As a result of being given the right *chinuch* at home from a tender age, she will not be thrown off-balance when in the course of time she ventures out into the world and sees that many Jewish women do not dress in line with the *chinuch* she was given. She will understand that due to external influences they have forsaken one of *Klal Yisroel's* finest attributes. Seeing others lax in a subject that she understands to be so important, will encourage her to be doubly scrupulous, for her own sake and for that of others. She has seen just how easily people can be affected by the suggestions of the permissive society in which we live.

The verse says in *Eishes Chayil*, לא תירא לביתה משלג כי כל ביתה לבוש שנים - "She does not worry when her family is exposed to snow, for her entire household is dressed in scarlet wool" (*Mishlei* 31:21). Whilst the *Eishes Chayil* warms her own house, she cannot warm the cold and frosty outer world. Due to this, when her children go out they could apparently suffer frost-bite and sickness. The *Eishes Chayil*, however, need not worry as she has dressed her family warmly and they are well protected from the snow and ice. Metaphorically, the verse conveys the following:

Whilst the *Eishes Chayil* warms her home thoroughly with a spirit of *Yiddishkeit*, she cannot change the frosty indifference of the world at large, with which her children will inevitably have contact. She need, however, not be overly concerned, as she has enthused her children with a love and fervor for our sacred heritage. This will not be cooled by the apathetic and indifferent attitude of those who have no understanding for *Yiddishkeit*. The *chinuch* she has given her children has dressed them in protective clothing that ensures they remain warm and comfortable even when exposed to the hostile world.

B. UTILIZING SITUATIONS TO IMPRESS THE CHILD

Parents should always watch out for ideal situations when they can transmit the correct *hashkofos* and attitudes to their young children. The following are a number of examples.

1. EDUCATING HER TO ADMIRE TZNIUS AND DISLIKE PRITZUS: Parents must teach their children to consider *tznius* a delightful and admirable way of dress, and *pritzus* as something deplorable and shameful. If a child senses that her parents view a girl wearing a Kosher and tasteful dress as a pleasant and graceful sight, when she grows up she will be only too happy to follow in the footsteps of those who dress in such a way. However, if she does not get the impression that *tznius* is delightful and *pritzus* degrading and shameful, but rather thinks that the former is merely "good conduct" and the latter just a "wrongdoing" she will not develop a love and admiration for *tznius*. Much thought and effort goes into a good *chinuch*, and *tznius* is certainly deserving of a place of prominence within these efforts.

When a girl stresses time and time again how beautiful this or that person is she is evidently attaching great importance to external beauty. So that she retains a balanced view, her parents should explain to her that very good looks are certainly a welcome addition. However, external beauty by itself is of little value. Moreover, very often, others who are not so strikingly beautiful are more valuable people than those who possess exceptional good looks. True, the Torah mentions many times that our *Imahos* were very beautiful. This must, however, be understood in the context of the Torah's viewpoint of welcome beauty. This is that when a woman's *midos* and personal desires are close to perfect, a very special beauty that emanates from her great *p'nimius* (inner person) is strongly evident on her outer appearance.

The reason for this is that usually there is a conflict between the person's inner *neshama* on the one hand, and his emotions and outer body on the other hand, with the person struggling throughout his life to maintain some sort of harmony. When this is the case, the body does not reflect the inner beauty of the person. However, when there is no conflict whatsoever between the inner and outer person, and on the contrary they are in perfect harmony and even complement one another, the glow of the heavenly *neshama* radiates its light through to the exterior of the body and a special beauty and great *chein* is apparent on the person's countenance and whole bearing. (*Rabbeinu Tzadok HaKohen* in *Kedushas Yisroel,* pages 49-50) - see 7:K:11 below. It is in this context that the Torah stresses the beauty of the *Imahos* - their appearance bore witness to the quality of their whole being.

When the clothes that are worn are in perfect harmony with the needs of the *neshama*, a *chein* is not only apparent on the physical person but also on the clothes - hence the *bigdei kehuna* that are described as לכבוד ולתפארת - "garments which bring honor and splendor to their wearer" (*Shemos* 28:2 and 28:40).

Similarly, *Yerusholayim shel Matah* (the *Yerusholayim* that is in this world) has a counterpart and "*neshama*" - this is *Yerusholayim shel Ma'alah* (The Heavenly *Yerusholayim*). When *Yerusholayim shel Matah* corresponds perfectly to its higher partner it is an incredibly beautiful city, כלילת יופי - "the epitome of beauty" (*Eichah* 2:15), because when total harmony exists, the *ruchnius* of the upper *Yerusholayim* radiates through the bricks and mortar with which the lower city of *Yerusholayim* is built.

Yerusholayim was such an incredibly beautiful city that when a visitor came through the gates of the city he had to stop. He was awe-struck by the majesty and outstanding beauty that met his eyes. This is the interpretation given by the *Ibn Ezra* to the verse, עומדות היו רגלינו בשעריך ירושלים - "Our feet were rooted at the gateways of *Yerusholayim*" (*Tehillim* 122:2).

2. HIGHLIGHTING NASHIM TZIDKANIOS FROM THE SEDRAH: The Shabbos table is an ideal opportunity to instill a love for *tznius* in the pure and tender hearts of young children. The great *nashim tzidkanios* mentioned in the Torah could be discussed and their outstanding trait of modesty highlighted. The purity of their way of life and the wonderful children they had as a result of it should be underscored. Lessons culled from the lives of our great *Imahos* will inspire not just young children but also teenagers and adults alike.

The following are examples. Many of them are suited to young children. Some are, however, too remote for young children and are only for teenagers and adults:-

(a) Sarah Imeinu:

▪ Sarah Imeinu is portrayed in the Torah as an outstanding *tznua*. Firstly, she showed exceptional *tznius* and refinement by staying in the seclusion of her tent when three male guests were being entertained by her husband next to her tent . She felt it wrong to appear before these men since her husband was with them and her presence was not needed - see 1:H:2(a) above - see *Mekoros* 60:15.

▪ We have a further insight into Avraham and Sarah's incredible modesty from the following: Although Sarah was exceptionally beautiful (see *Megilla* 15a that she was one of the four most beautiful women ever to have lived) she and her husband were so modest and unpretentious that neither of them were aware of her exquisite beauty (*Responsa Noda BeYehuda* O.C. 1:24). Due to this, both Avraham and Sarah traveled down to *Mitzrayim* totally unaware that she would be in grave danger once they reached *Mitzrayim* because of her exceptional beauty. However, as they crossed a bridge Avraham Avinu suddenly became aware of this, since he saw a reflection of her on the water surface and realized how beautiful she was (see *Rashi Breishis* 12:11). Only then did they decide to take the precautions described in the Torah.

(b) Rivka Imeinu:

▪ Rivka Imeinu was likewise an outstandingly modest person. This is evident from the fact that Yitzchak Avinu found in Rivka all that he had experienced when his great mother Sarah was alive, as Rashi says on the words ויביאה האהלה שרה אמו (*Breishis* 24:67) ויביאה האהלה והרי היא שרה אמו - "Yitzchak brought her into the tent and behold she was Sarah his mother". Having such a wife, was to him as if his mother had "come back to life" once again. Hence the words of Rashi, והרי היא שרה אמו - "Behold she was Sarah his mother". Sarah was an outstanding *tzadekes* and due to that, signs of *Hashem*'s appreciation of her were evident in her tent. Since Rivka earned the same honor, she was evidently of the same or at least very similar caliber. See also *Breishis Rabba* 60:16.

Although Sarah died at the age of 127 whilst Rivka was a mere three years old at the time of her marriage, it was nevertheless possible for Rivka to reinstate the exalted manifestations precipitated by Sarah Imeinu. Hence, we see the power of Yiras Shomayim, *chesed* and *tznius*. They enable a girl of a tender age to attain the status of a woman of great worth.

▪ Yitzchak was a fully grown 37 year old man who had already risen to the dizzying heights of laying himself down to be sacrificed. He nevertheless missed his mother sorely and although it was three years since her passing he remained unconsoled. When he married Rivka he was finally consoled as the Torah says, וינחם יצחק אחרי אמו (*Breishis* 24:67). We see from this whole episode the indispensable role of a mother and wife in *Klal Yisroel*. First, a mother nurtures her son and ensconces him in a home replete with *kedusha* and goodness. Then a wife takes over and builds him a home that will ensure his further development as a person of great value and esteem.

Although Avraham and Yitzchak were outstanding *tzadikim*, nevertheless, the tent in which they lived did not merit having a "light that burned from *erev* Shabbos to *erev* Shabbos", did not experience the "blessing in the dough" and the "Heavenly cloud that hovered over the tent" was not present (as stated in *Breishis Rabba* 60:16). Only Sarah and then Rivka merited having them. We see from here that for a home to have a true elevated atmosphere, and for the presence of the *Shechina* to be felt within it, there must be a mother or a wife in the home.

▪ When Rivka first saw Yitzchak, the verse says, ותפול מעל הגמל - "She fell off the camel" (*Breishis* 24:64). This means that as soon as she spotted him she immediately slipped off the camel. The *R'dak* explains (in his commentary on the *Torah*) that on hearing that he was Yitzchak she "dived for cover". Due to her modesty and bashfulness, she hid herself from her *chasan* rather than appear immediately before him face to face - see *Mekoros* 65:8.

A further reason for slipping immediately off the camel is given by the *Rashbam*. She had been riding on the camel's back with her legs apart in order to procure a proper grip on the animal's back and ensure her safety. Now that she saw Yitzchak coming towards her, she felt it would be distinctly unrefined for her to remain in that position - see 9:J:8(b) below. She therefore slipped off the camel as quickly as possible.

▪ The actual marriage of Yitzchak and Rivka is described by the Torah in a few words ותהיא לו לאשה ויאהבה - "He took her as a wife and he loved her" (*Breishis* 24:67). In these short words the Torah informs us that Jewish modesty requires that the emotional bond between husband and wife develops after marriage not before it. Before marriage the relationship between *chasan* and *kallah* is only that they have found *chein* in one another's eyes and are confident that they will be able to form a happy union and together build a home לכבוד ה' ותורתו - to the honor of *Hashem* and His Torah. This is how it was possible that Rivka, who had never met Yitzchak, but understood from Eliezer what type of person Yitzchak was, readily agreed to be married to him. (See commentary of HaRav Samson Raphael Hirsch zt'l on the above verse).

(c) Rachel Imeinu and Leah Imeinu:

▪ Concerning the two *Imahos* Rachel and Leah - their incredible modesty speaks for itself. They lived for seven years in very close proximity to Yaacov Avinu, and there was nevertheless absolutely no contact between them. As a result of this, Yaacov Avinu remained so unfamiliar with these two young ladies that it was possible for Lavan to trick him on his wedding day and present him with the wrong girl. This was even though they looked totally different to one another. [If only, present day *chasanim* and *kallos* would learn a chapter of "authentic Jewish conduct" from the stories concerning marriage related in our holy Torah] - see *sefer*, *Ben Yehoyada* by the Gaon and Tzaddik Harav Yosef Chayim from Baghdad, *Megilla* 13b s.v. *U'mai tzniusoh. See also Mekoros* 83:3.

▪ When Yaacov met Eisav he was asked by Eisav, "Who are these women and these children?" wondering whether they were his wives and children or just maidservants and their offspring. Yaacov answered, "They are my children - the children that *Hashem* has granted His servant" (*Breishis* 33:5). It seems strange that although Eisav asked about both the women and the children, he only answered about the children and did not utter a word about the women. The Ramban addresses this question and writes that due to modesty, Yaacov Avinu did not find it fitting to introduce his wives to a male. He therefore simply ignored that part of the question and answered only about the children, stating that they were his children that had been granted to him by *Hashem*.

(d) All four Imahos:

▪ Devorah *HaNeviah* sang her famous *shira* - her song of praise to *Hashem* after Yael killed Sisra and the Kna'anite army was defeated . In the *shirah* she used the term, מנשים באוהל תבורך - "She (Yael) should be blessed by the women of the tent" (*Shoftim* 5:24). *Rashi* explains that, "the women of the tent" are our *Imahos*. They are referred to with this title because concerning each one of them the Torah mentions her *tznius* in connection with her tent - *see Breishis* 18:9, 24:67 and 31:33. Each one of our *Imahos* was a personification of modesty which is symbolized by the sanctuary of a tent.

A tent is usually just a temporary abode, whilst a house is a permanent dwelling place. Our *Imahos* looked at life in this world as just temporary in which a person prepares himself for a blissful future in *Olam Habah*. They therefore paid their full attention to all that was important and substantial and were not enticed by the transitory pleasures of this world. In this way, good *hashkafos* have a direct bearing on the *tznius* of the person.

In this vein the verse says, מה טובו אוהליך יעקב משכנותיך ישראל - "How precious are your tents (homes) Yaacov, your sanctuaries (*Batei Midrash*) Yisroel" (*Bamidbar* 24:5) - when people understand that their homes in this world are just tents, they are inspired to pursue real values, and *Batei Midrash* are fully occupied by men learning Torah - encouraged to do so by wives who appreciate the greatness of Torah learning. Hence, אוהליך יעקב leads to משכנותיך ישראל.

3. MOTHERS SHOULD EXPLAIN WHY ITEMS ARE NOT SUITABLE: When a mother goes shopping with her young daughter, she could point out to her dresses and outfits made of pretty materials that would have suited her well. She should then show her why they are nevertheless totally unsuitable. For example, the neckline is too loose to be Kosher; the hem is not the refined type suitable for *Yidden*; the sleeves are too wide and will ride up to reveal the upper arm; there is far too much glitter on the dress as an excessive amount of colored glass beads and sequins have been sewn onto it; the style of the dress is generally unrefined, and so on. In this way the daughter will know what is a Kosher dress and what is not. She will also see how her mother decisively rejects these dresses and does not ponder whether or not to buy them.

4. TELLING HER HOW BECOMING HER TZNIUS'DIK DRESS IS: When a girl appears for the first time dressed in a new dress or outfit her mother has bought her, the father should comment on what a nice garment it is, how well it fits her. Finally and most importantly, the father should express his delight at how *tznius'dik* it is. These heart-warming comments will leave their mark on her tender *neshama* and she will look forward to having more such valued clothes in the future.

Even if the girl is clearly aware how well the clothes suit her and how refined she looks in them, it is still very heart-warming and encouraging when this is confirmed to her by others. *Chazal* say, יודעין היו מלאכי השרת שרה אמנו היכן היתה, אלא להודיע שצנועה היתה כדי לחבבה על בעלה - loosely translated, "The visitors asked Avraham, 'Where is Sarah your wife?' although, being *Malachim* - angels, they knew very well where she was. They nevertheless asked about her whereabouts, because they knew that the surprise they would show at her not being present would confirm to Avraham just how *tznua* she was. This in turn would make Avraham even more appreciative of her" (*Bava Metziah* 87a; *Rashi Breishis* 18:9). Although Avraham surely knew that Sarah was a *tznua,* since they both practiced outstanding *tznius* all the time, nevertheless, to hear this from others would make him even more aware of her *tznius* (Harav Hagaon Yerucham Levovitz *zt'l* from Mir). So too, when parents tell their daughter how perfect and how refined her new dress or outfit is, this is a considerable encouragement to her, even if she is already fully aware of these facts.

5. INSTILLING FEELINGS FOR TZNIUS DURING SEWING LESSONS: When girls are taught sewing in a school or seminary, every effort should be made to find teachers who have Yiras Shomayim and a deep sense of *tznius*. Together with the art of sewing, such teachers could transmit to their pupils what is and what is not "*Yiddishe chein*" and how the Jewish way of design aims at both covering and disguising areas of the body. The teacher should point out how diametrically opposed the Jewish viewpoint of female dress is from that of the *umos ha'olam*. With such a training the girls will be fortified for life, and the importance of *tznius* will be etched deeply into their intellect and subconscious mind. (See 6:E:6 below, concerning the importance of training girls nowadays in the art of sewing and dressmaking.)

This complies with one of the fundamentals of *chinuch*. The best form of defense and protection is to ensure that the person resolves to do what is right long before the problem has arisen and long before passions pull him in the wrong direction. In this way the person will have seen the *emes* to its full extent before the *sheker* has had a chance to present itself.

For a Jewish school etc. to employ a youthful non-Jewish or irreligious sewing teacher could be harmful for the girls since a sewing teacher will inevitably speak about her attitudes and tastes, and what she considers should be the aspirations of a girl, as far as dress is concerned. As we know, these will be utterly devoid of *tznius* and refinement. Furthermore, such people usually have an aversion and antipathy to modesty in dress and behavior. If she is a good teacher and the girls "take" to her teachings the damage caused by her attitude can be quite considerable.

C. DEVELOPING TZNIUS FROM A VERY YOUNG AGE

1. ENSURING THAT GOOD INFLUENCES PRECEDE THE BAD ONES: As was mentioned above, a major feature of good *chinuch* is to establish a correct mode of conduct before an incorrect one has a chance to take hold. This principle is particularly relevant when it comes to *tznius* of clothes. If one allows a young girl to develop a liking for excessively pretty and exquisite clothes she will miss them when at the age of six or seven her mother buys her neat and pleasing clothes that are simpler than those she has been wearing till then. This subtle tug on the strings of her heart which longs for the really superb clothes she has been wearing hitherto, may result in the child never really appreciating the beauty of *tznius*. (See similar case in M.B. 343:3).

2. EARLY IMPRESSIONS ARE ALL IMPORTANT: *Chazal*, in their immense wisdom and insight, compare *chinuch* to writing. They say, הלומד ילד למה הוא דומה לדיו כתובה על נייר חדש - "Learning young (leaves an impression like that of) durable ink written on paper that has never previously been written upon" (*Pirkei Avos* 4:25). They compare *chinuch* to writing because the parent writes a directive for life on the heart of the child. When one writes on paper from which previous writing has been erased, the new letters are not perfect. The impression left on the paper from the first script causes the new writing to be indistinct and sometimes even blurred to a degree. So it is with *chinuch*. The lingering impression left by negative habits that were practiced by the child for a number of years, might diminish or even obscure the deep impression which the *chinuch* could have made. Sometimes, the hang-over from early impressions may be so severe that it causes a resentment of Kosher ways of dress and prevents the implementation of correct habits - see *Mekoros* 4:4.

The verse says about the *Eishes Chayil,* צופיה הליכות ביתה - "she keeps a watchful eye on the ways of her family" (*Mishlei* 31:27). *Rashi* explains that this refers to educating her family to the qualities of truth and *tznius*. The deeper meaning of this is as follows: The word צופה (to look) is different from the more commonly used word רואה (to see). *Tzofeh* is used for a "searching look into the future" as is found in the *tefilla* of *Rosh Hashana,* צופה ומביט עד סוף כל הדורות - "He looks searchingly to the end of all generations". The mother, who is a woman of valor, knows that developing the traits of truth and *tznius* in the heart of a child is a slow and gradual process. It is like erecting a building which needs careful planning and the laying of pipes and cables from the very start.

So too, with *tznius* - long before the child becomes a young lady, the mother must have firm ideas concerning *tznius* and the refined person she would like her daughter to grow up to be. Moreover, as early as possible she should infuse ideals of *emes* and *tznius* into her child's heart and carefully nurture these qualities throughout the child's growing years.

3. CHOFETZ CHAYIM ZT'L ON CHINUCH OF TZNIUS: The following is a translation of the deeply sincere and emotional words of the *Chofetz Chayim* in *Geder Olam* Chapter 8.

"Since a lack of *tznius* leads to poverty and other misfortunes, every man and woman must guard their conduct to ensure that it complies with ways of *tznius*. They must also encourage their daughters to this end, so that from their early childhood they will be accustomed not to go in ways of *pritzus*. For example, due to our sins, in some places people think it permissible for young girls to wear sleeveless blouses and dresses. Woe, woe to us ! How many serious sins are involved in such a way of dress etc. How many invalid *brachos* are caused by such garments .....

"In contrast, if the parents train their daughters from a tender age to dress in ways of *tznius* they will remain with this practice also when they are adults, and will merit having fine and virtuous children, as can be seen from the many quotes from *Chazal* that we have mentioned."

In all matters of everyday *halacha* the *Chofetz Chayim* is our *Rebbe* and mentor, as his rulings in the *Mishna Berura* are universally accepted. His opinions on matters of *tznius* must therefore be treated with the same reverence and be fully adhered to.

4. TRAINING A GIRL NOT TO CAUSE OTHERS TO BE ENVIOUS: If a child has been given a particularly pretty piece of jewelry which would probably arouse the envy of her friends, her parents should not allow her to wear it in school. Quite apart from the obvious danger of making her boastful, she must be taught not to do things in front of others which arouse their envy.

A person must be sensitive to the feelings of others and not cause them to desire something which they are not able to obtain. The verse says, לא

לא תחסום שור בדישו - "Do not muzzle an ox while it threshes" (*Devarim* 25:4) as it hurts the ox to see food that it is unable to eat. From here we see that to arouse a desire for something that will not be obtainable is an act of cruelty - (see *Noam HaMitzvos* 596).

It is similarly incorrect for a girl in a school or seminary to wear an extremely beautiful item, such as an exceptionally pretty brooch or necklace, if it is far beyond the standard of jewelry most girls have, as others will presumably be envious of her. It has been observed that a number of fine girls who received for their engagement a diamond ring with an exceptionally large stone, did not wear the ring while amongst their friends. They explained that other *kallos* had not received such elaborate rings and they did not want them to feel less fortunate than themselves. Fortunate are the *chasanim* who have *kallos* with such sterling *midos*.

5. EXCESSIVE "LEISURE TIME" LEADS TO VANITY:

(a) Being active and well occupied prevents vanity: Training a girl to make good use of her time, thereby ensuring that her mind is constantly occupied with worthy thoughts, is a most important precondition in raising her to become a true *tznua*. To achieve this all-important requirement a girl must be trained from a young age to be as active and as industrious as possible. If she develops in this way, there is reason to hope that she will become a *tznua* and also a *ba'alas chesed* who gives a helping hand wherever it is called for.

If a girl is trained to be industrious when she is young she will grow into a teenager who has the same quality. Since she will be constantly alive and vibrant, rather than inactive and empty, she will not have the *yetzer horah* of studying other people's clothes and then contemplating how to buy the same or something even more striking. She will also not become overly concerned about her appearance, which in turn would cause her to indulge in large amounts of cosmetics and excessive jewelry. Her mind, being filled with far more important matters, will not be drawn into trivialities.

Chazal have a very grim view of a person who idles his time away. In the *Mishna Kesubos* 59b, they say, בטלה מביאה לידי זימה - "Inactivity leads to immorality." Total inactivity can *chas v'shalom* lead to outright immorality, because when the mind is unoccupied and empty it wanders deep into forbidden territory where the latent base passions of a person find their satisfaction. Even if just part of the day is wasted, the mind is partially unused, and as a result it can wander into poisoned areas that bring the person into close contact with the world of corruption. For example, a person with a lot of spare time on his hands could spend a good part of it reading newspapers and magazines that discuss the foul types of misconduct that are currently in the news. The result of this is that the person's mind absorbs large amounts of grime every day, and this will not leave him unaffected.

(b) Vacation should be fulfilling, not simply "whiling time away": It is important that even during vacation, the day is structured as far as possible, and that a program is made to fill the days and weeks with activities which will enable children to relax and enjoy, such as games, sports, family outings, visits to a safari park, social events and similar experiences. Apart from enjoyable outlets it is good for them to spend some time helping a large family where the mother could do with an extra pair of hands. Such a vacation will end with girls being happy, content and fulfilled, and ready to continue their studies in a healthy frame of mind. In contrast, when the vacation is spent just whiling away the time, doing nothing meaningful, be it for themselves or for others, it leads to frustration and dissatisfaction which are prime initiators of vanity and minor departures from the ways of *tznius*.

(c) People work hard at what they appreciate: The key to encouraging a girl to use her time usefully and valuably, is by ensuring that she appreciates the worth of the work she does. This applies to a young girl who is involved in school work and helps her mother at home with her siblings. It also applies to a young lady engaged in housekeeping and looking after the family, who as a sideline works to earn money to help sustain the family, or who teaches children and infuses into their tender *neshamos* a taste of our holy heritage. If she understands the importance and great value of these undertakings she will throw her heart and soul into them. She will spend every free minute available ensuring that what she does is done to the best of her capability and in the best way possible.

The verse says in *Eishes Chayil*, טעמה כי טוב סחרה לא יכבה בלילה נרה - "She appreciates the worth of her enterprise; her light is not extinguished at night" (*Mishlei* 31:18). Since she appreciates and even values the venture she is involved in, she works diligently and tirelessly on it even until late into the night. The *Eishes Chayil* is particularly enthusiastic about the most significant of her undertakings - bringing up and attending to the needs of her family. Due to her healthy and wholesome attitude, and her correct priorities, even though she might work late into the night she is up bright and early in the morning to look after her family as stated in another verse in *Eishes*

Chayil, ותקם בעוד לילה ותתן טרף לביתה וחוק לנערותיה - "She arises before daybreak to feed her family and attend to the needs of her maidens" (*Mishlei* 31:15). Where there is appreciation there is happiness, and where there is happiness there is a resolution and thrust. Satisfaction invigorates a person and enables him to accomplish an incredible amount.

(d) An industrious person does many types of jobs: In the verses of *Eishes Chayil,* written by Shlomo Hamelech in honor of his mother, it is repeatedly mentioned that the *Eishes Chayil* has a deep sense of responsibility to her husband, family and the poor. It portrays the *Eishes Chayil* as a person who will undertake many types of work, as nothing is unfitting or too difficult for her. Whatever needs doing she is willing and capable of doing. She acquires a field, plants a vineyard, spins thread, weaves cloth, makes clothes either to sell or to dress members of her own family. She trades and if necessary even travels abroad to find ways of sustaining her family. She gives clothes to the poor and extends alms to the needy.

Outstandingly, due to her great love for Torah, she relieves her husband of as many duties as possible, so that he can concentrate his energies to the study of Torah. Hence the verse, נודע בשערים בעלה בשבתו עם זקני ארץ (Mishlei 31:23). [See *Ran*, *Kiddushin* 29b that women in *Bavel* would earn money so that their husbands could devote themselves fully to their Torah studies. The same concept is written in *Aderes Eliyahu* by the *Vilna Gaon, Breishis* 2:18 and in *Chidushei HaGra*, *Brachos* (61a) s.v. *B'tchila*].

These verses demonstrate the need to train girls to be capable and competent in as many fields as possible. With these qualities they will be able to accomplish much good. Also, their husbands and sons are more likely to be given the opportunity of growing into outstanding *Talmidei Chachamim*.

(e) A responsible and industrious person does not seek excuses: The *Eishes Chayil* does not seek excuses to free herself from what she is capable of doing. Realizing the merit of doing *mitzvos* and the will of *Hashem* in general, she tries to achieve as much as possible. The verse says in *Eishes Chayil*, חגרה בעוז מתניה ותאמץ זרועותיה - "She girds her loins with strength and she invigorates her arms" (*Mishlei* 31:17). A person "girds his loins" so that he can walk swiftly without hindrance from the clothes he is wearing (see *Rashi, Shemos* 12:13) and invigorates his arms before undertaking a physical job that is somewhat taxing. The *Eishes Chayil* seeks no excuses. She therefore dresses in a way that her clothes will allow her to undertake the venture efficiently and she flexes her arms so that she can accomplish whatever is within her reach and needs seeing to.

Such are the wonderful ways of the accomplished Jewish woman, whose praises are sung in the beautiful *p'sukim* of the *Eishes Chayil*. It is for us to ensure that our young daughters are raised in a way that they too will one day actualize the great potential that is within each and every one of them.

D. OPPORTUNITIES FOR CHINUCH IN TZNIUS

The following are some of the points concerning habits of *tznius* that must be developed from a very young age.

(a) *Tznius* when dressing and undressing: Even very young children should not get dressed or undressed in a public part of the house such as the morning room if other areas are available, so that the child understands that he must always be fully clothed when in public.

(b) *Tznius* when preparing to bath or shower: When getting ready for a bath, children should be taught to undress in the bathroom and put on their pajamas or bath robe (dressing gown) before leaving the bathroom.

(c) Ensuring knees are covered during play: Young girls should be constantly reminded to sit in a respectable way with their skirts covering their knees at all times, even at play.

(d) Ensuring elbows are covered during play: Young girls should be constantly encouraged to keep their elbows covered. They have an inclination to push their sleeves up when painting, drawing or playing and they must therefore be prompted to keep their arms covered whenever they can. Girls should certainly not be dressed in dresses with short sleeves unless they wear a sweater over them. According to some *Poskim* this is required from the age of three, whilst according to others the obligation starts when the girl is a six/seven year old.

(e) Ensuring neckline is Kosher: Young girls have a tendency to leave the top button of their blouses open, forgetting either to close it or to insert a pin a short way down. Similarly, they may go to school with a pin inserted to stop the blouse opening too far down, but invariably come home without it. Mothers must insist that this does not happen.

(f) Discouraging inordinately loud manner of talking: Children (and particularly girls) should be corrected when they raise their voices to an unseemly level. This is unrefined at home between family and friends and doubly unrefined when it occurs in the street - see 1:B:6 above.

(g) Encouraging girls to skip only in non-public areas: Girls should be encouraged to skip and play similar games only in non-public areas. Apart from problems of momentary minor exposures that can easily occur, it is undesirable for a girl to play such games in a street through which men constantly pass, especially once a girl is a six/seven year old.

(h) Encouraging boys and girls to play separately: Young boys and girls of different families should be encouraged not to play together from as tender an age as possible. This segregation will be found to safely forestall unhealthy feelings of affection developing in more advanced childhood. (*Rabbeinu Yehuda HaChassid, Sefer Chasidim* No. 168 and *Responsa Minchas Yitzchak* 3:109).

(i) Teaching boys and girls in different classrooms: Young boys and girls should be taught in different classes so that they are educated from the earliest age possible that males and females should not mix - except within the family. (See *Meiri Kiddushin* 80b, *Responsa Iggros Moshe*, Y.D. 1:127, 2:104, 3:73 and *Responsa Shevet HaLevi* 1:29).

(j) Jewelry: Young girls may be adorned with jewelry in accordance with their needs. Care should, however, be taken to give them only modest and inexpensive items as befits a young girl, such as a gold plated necklace rather than a real gold necklace. The same applies to a ring, bracelet, watch etc. A child is perfectly happy with pretty looking imitation items which improve her appearance and has no need for real jewelry. For her modesty and general good *midos* it is far better not to give her real jewelry so that she learns to be satisfied with less than the very best.

(k) Earrings: Earrings are ornaments that many adult girls and women do not always wear, as they are extra adornments and differ from basic jewelry such as necklaces, rings, watches etc. Furthermore, in many homes substantial earrings are not worn by young girls before the teen years, because it is felt that if a child is adorned with substantial earrings this could cause her to attach far too much importance to jewelry. It is interesting to note that this was how things were in the times of *Chazal*. Although women and girls wore jewelry, young girls did not wear earrings until they were adults. See *Rashi, Shabbos* 65a s.v. *Habanos,* who writes, בנות קטנות שמנקבות אזניהם ואין עושין נזמים עד שיגדלו - "Young girls had their ears pierced but did not wear earrings until they grew up". However, inserting small decorative rings into the lobes to keep the pierced holes from closing is acceptable to all, as such rings are not substantial pieces of jewelry.

E. GUARDING FROM HARMFUL FRIENDSHIPS

1. THE EFFECT OF FRIENDS ON A PERSON: People and particularly children are considerably affected by the attitude of friends. If they have a low standard of *tznius* this could influence a girl's outlook about a matter which is of supreme importance to her whole future. It is therefore vital that parents keep a watchful eye on the type of girl their daughter associates with. It is best to encourage her from a very young age to play with children of families with correct attitudes to *Yiddishkeit* and *tznius*, so that unhealthy friendships never start. See 2:A concerning the effect of peer-pressure.

2. SOME FRIENDS DO NOT BRING OUT THE BEST IN A CHILD: On the verse in *Eishes Chayil,* דרשה צמר ופשתים - "she sought wool and linen" (*Mishlei* 31:13), the *Midrash* explains that this refers to Sarah. The deeper meaning of this is that Sarah demanded that Yishmael be kept away from her son Yitzchak because the friendship would be detrimental to Yitzchak. She maintained that although Yishmael may be a good person (as was certainly Avraham's view) nevertheless, for the two to associate would be ruinous and they must therefore be separated. Just as wool and linen are both individually permissible but when together form a forbidden combination (*shatnez*), so too there are children who individually are fine but are harmful to one another when brought together (Harav Zvi Hirsh Ferber *zt'l* of London, in his *sefer*, *Eishes Chayil*).

When trying to stop an undesirable friendship, parents who are careful to avoid speaking *lashon horah* whenever possible experience difficulties in explaining to their daughter why she should not be friends with the other child. This is especially so when the problem is just a subtle lack of refinement. As stated, they can explain to her that although the other child is good, nevertheless, a friendship between them would be detrimental to them.

F. BEING SATISFIED WITH WHAT ONE HAS - HISTAPKUS

1. WITH HISTAPKUS A GIRL WILL SEE THE BEAUTY OF TZNIUS: *Histapkus,* being satisfied with what one has, is one of the most important lessons to teach our children. It brings in its wake bountiful *brachos*. Not giving a girl all the luxuries that her heart desires, and instead teaching her to be happy with what she has, enables her to disregard the overly attractive dress and the unrefined jewelry of her contemporaries. This training starts from a very young age indeed, when the child insists on having a sweet, a piece of cake, on wearing a certain item, on going today to a particular friend to play and so on.

Although on many occasions the child's request is justified and no harm is done in responding favorably to it, on many occasions it is unreasonable. In such a case it is most important not to let the child have his way in order that he should learn to be happy with the food, the clothes or the friend offered by the mother and he does not get the feeling that he must have whatever his heart desires.

2. EDUCATING A GIRL TO BE RESPECTFUL TO HER CLOTHES: As stated, a girl has a natural tendency to want more and more pretty clothes because she wishes to be good-looking at all times. Whilst parents must not give in to this desire, they should redirect her craving by encouraging her to look carefully after the clothes she possesses, thereby ensuring that they remain decent and befitting for as long as possible. If she does so she will always feel well dressed and the desire to frequently have new clothes will lessen. Since wanting to appear in new dresses and outfits is the forerunner to a lack of *tznius* and refinement, curbing that desire at an early age is an important investment for the future.

Accordingly, parents should direct their daughters to treat their clothes with care and respect, and to ensure that they remain clean and in good condition. The spirit of the recommendation should be that just as one would be careful with and respectful of any item of real importance, so too a person should be careful with and respectful of clothes. Although clothes should not play a leading role in a girl's life and should certainly not be of paramount importance to her, she should nevertheless have a feeling for them and respect them, since they do an enormous service to her, enabling her to look both respectable and graceful. The respect she should show her clothes is part of the all-important trait of *hakoras hatov* - being grateful.

We are taught by *Chazal* to be respectful to bread although it is an inanimate item, because bread is the most basic of all foods, and foods keep body and soul together. By treating it respectfully we demonstrate our feelings of gratitude to *Hashem* who has given us bread which is so essential to our lives. One must therefore neither throw bread across the table (M.B. 171:9) nor pass a full drink over it lest it spills and spoils the bread (M.B.

171:5). So too, an outfit or dress which does so much for a woman or girl should be treated with respect. It does a great service to her needs of modesty and her general pleasant appearance.

The following is related in *Chazal* (*Yalkut Shimoni*, quoted in *Be'er Moshe, Shmuel* page 283) "Clothes bring respect to a person. There was a very virtuous man, who would take off his outdoor clothes and fold them up himself whenever he came home. He was asked, 'You have many disciples and members of your family, so why do you bother to fold up your clothes yourself?' To this he answered, הבגדים מכבדים אותי בשוק, אף אני מכבד אותם בבית, הוא דכתיב כי מכבדי אכבד - 'The clothes bring me respect in public. It is therefore only fitting that I show respect to the clothes once I am back at home!' This attitude is expressed in the verse, 'I respect that which brings me respect' (*Shmuel* 1:2:30)."

By training a girl to be respectful to her clothes, she will learn to be grateful for what she has, and will be blessed with the trait of *histapkus*. As explained, this in turn will preserve within her the traits of modesty and general *tznius*.

3. WE ARE AFFLICTED BY THE PURSUIT OF LUXURIES: To our dismay, the pursuit of luxuries has gripped our society in an exceedingly harmful manner and is part of the driving force behind much of the pomp and glitter which accompanies *pritzus'dik* clothing. If our daughters were brought up with a degree of the wonderful trait of *histapkus* - making do and being satisfied with what one has, rather than looking for greater and greater improvements to one's comforts and to the image one projects, much of the material in this *sefer* would not have had to be written.

The *Mishna* (*Pirkei Avos* 2:13) discusses the most outstanding character trait man can have. One of the opinions mentioned is that of Rabbi Eliezer who praises a man who is blessed with an עין טובה - "a good eye". This is generally understood to mean a person who has a "magnanimous eye" - he feels for the needs of others and goes out of his way to help them. However, the *Rambam* in his commentary writes that it means a person with a "happy and contented eye". He explains that when a person is happy with all that *Hashem Yisborach* has given him, he will merit to have the *midah* of *histapkus*, since he does not feel that he needs more, איזהו עשיר השמח בחלקו - "Who is wealthy? - he who is content with what he has" (*Pirkei Avos* 4:1).

4. HISTAPKUS IS THE BEDROCK OF CHINUCH AND TZNIUS: In our affluent throwaway society, the delight people have from the gifts they have received (whether directly from *Hashem* or from parents, spouse, friends etc.) is very short-lived. In no time at all they take what they have for granted and are busy eyeing the things they do not yet possess. If we succeed in implanting the trait of עין טובה in our children, many an attempt by the *yetzer horah* will doubtlessly fail because our children will be happy with their lot, happy with what they have and happy to be *Yidden*.

When the great *mechaneches*, Rebbetzen Vichna Kaplan *o.h.,* started the *Beis Yaacov* movement of the United States, she turned to Reb Shraga Feivel Mendelowitz *zt'l* (who had previously started a *Beis Yaacov* and understood the mentality of the American girl) with a request that he advise her where to lay the main stress in the education of the girls. To this he answered that the main stress should be on "being *mistapek b'muat*" - being content with little, because everything evolves from that. If this characteristic can be implanted, the rest will eventually fall into position of its own accord (*Shlucha D'Rachmana* Page 193).

If a girl is very good-looking and at the same time has the positive attribute of *histapkus* - of being satisfied, she will thrive on the fact that she need not concern herself with her looks. She will occupy her mind and time with things that are far more valuable than external looks and will develop into a fine Jewish daughter. However, if a girl is very good looking but has the negative trait of often not being satisfied with what she has, the combination could prove to be a recipe for disaster. Lacking satisfaction with what she has, it could drive her to beautify herself even further although it is totally unnecessary. She might do so to such an extent that her appearance will prove to be a stumbling block to others.

Asher, one of the sons of Yaacov Avinu, was a personification of satisfaction. His very name Asher meant מאושר - "Contented and satisfied" - see *Breishis* 30:13. It is interesting to note what is said about the daughters and granddaughters of such a father. On the verse, ברוך מבנים אשר - "Asher is blessed by children" (*Devarim* 33:24), *Rashi* writes, שהיו בנותיו נאות וכו' נשואות לכהנים גדולים - "His daughters were good-looking and married *Kohanim Gedolim*". Although they were particularly good looking, they developed into the finest and purest *Bnos Yisroel*. They were chosen to be wives of *Kohanim Gedolim* who could only marry maidens and would look for girls of the highest caliber - see comment in *Toras Moshe* by the *Chasam Sofer*. This substantiates what has been said; with the trait of *histapkus*, being satisfied, good looks do not prevent a girl from becoming a fine and outstanding lady. On the contrary, they can help her become a valuable person and a pride to the Jewish people - see *Mekoros* 2:8.

G. CHINUCH ON THE IMPORTANCE OF CLEAN LANGUAGE

1. LANGUAGE AFFECTS BEHAVIOR AND SENSITIVITIES: Cleanliness of language is another most important aspect of *tznius*. *Chazal* tell us that דברו חכמים בלשון נקיה - "The Sages speak with the cleanest language possible" (*Sanhedrin* 68b). Likewise the Torah uses, as far as possible, only positive words such as 'not *tahor*', rather than negative words such as '*tameh*', although *tameh* would be the fitting term and it is somewhat clumsy to say 'not *tahor*' (*Pesachim* 3a). This is to teach us that while *lashon horah* and immoral language are obviously *ossur*, it is also wrong to use harsh or negative words if there is no need for them to be used. Negative language makes the person's outlook and behavior coarse, whilst the care to use the finest and most positive language possible makes the person refined in his outward behavior and in his inner feelings and sensitivities. See 1:B:6 and 1:B:7 above, concerning *tznius* in relationship to speech.

2. DISCUSSING TORAH AND MITZVOS WITH SPECIAL REVERENCE: Using derogatory terms when talking about Torah and *mitzvos* is particularly disturbing, since it demonstrates a fundamental lack of appreciation for *devarim she'bikdusha*. For example, if a person says, "the *Midrash* does not make sense," he has used a derogatory expression about part of *Toras Hashem*. This is unforgivable even though he will claim that all he meant to say was that he cannot understand the hidden meaning behind the words of the *Midrash*.

The *Gemara* (*Pesachim* 3b) relates that once when the *lechem hapanim* was divided out, three *Kohanim* expressed how small a portion each of them had received. One said, "I received as little as a bean". A second said, "I received as little as an olive". A third said, "I received as little as the tail of a small lizard". *Chazal* found the description used by the third person offensive, since he compared the holy *lechem hapanim* to the tail of an unclean creature. They investigated and found that he had generally no regard for *kodshim* and was therefore unfit to do the *avoda*.

3. USING PLEASANT LANGUAGE WHEN DEALING WITH CHILDREN: When dealing with troublesome children some use harsh, coarse or boorish language, such as, "Shut up" (when telling a child to be silent); "You're eating like a pig" (when trying to educate a child to eat with better manners); "You're a liar" (when accusing the child of not saying the truth). Using such terminology is harmful for the children, as it encourages them to use the same language between themselves. Once they use it as children, they will continue using it when they are adults.

With a little foresight a person can say the same things without using derogatory language. For example he can say, "Keep quiet"; "Your manners are atrocious"; "You are not telling the truth" and so on. It is related in the *sefer, P'aer Hador* (Vol. 3, page 20) that the *Chazon Ish* was very sensitive to the language people used. When someone, who had come to the *Chazon Ish* about a dispute, said to him, "The other person is telling lies", the *Chazon Ish* would correct him with, "You mean to say, he is not telling the truth".

4. ENSURING THAT CHILDREN SPEAK ONLY CLEAN LANGUAGE: If parents hear their children talk with coarse or harsh terminology or hear them use rude language they must react in a very forceful manner. They should explain to their children that a person must not let such words cross his lips. They should be given to understand that just as *treife* food may never enter our mouths, so too, *treife* words should never leave our mouths. Just as *treife* foods are *metameh* (defile) our physical body, so too, *treife* words are *metameh* our spiritual body - our mind, the *Kodesh Kodoshim* that is within each one of us. Just as bad-tasting food is harmful to our body, so words of bad taste contaminate our soul. If a child persists in using bad language, he should be punished so that he does not grow up with such a character fault.

In *Sefer Hayirah* (no. 299) *Rabbeinu Yona* writes, יזהר מאוד מאוד שלא יוציא שום נבול ודבר ערוה מפיו אף דרך שחוק - "A person must be extremely careful (*Yizoher meod meod*) not to let out of his mouth any unclean or impure expression, not even in jest".

With girls this is of extreme importance, as their natural way of speaking should be to encourage and speak nicely to their young siblings and eventually to their own young children. Furthermore, *tznius* of speech is a prerequisite for other forms of *tznius*. When explaining the seven characteristics of a *tznua*, *Rabbeinu Yehuda HaChassid* in *Sefer Chassidim* No. 350 enumerates, לשון רכה - a soft spoken tongue, as the very first. When describing the *Eishes Chayil* the verse says, פיה פתחה בחכמה ותורת חסד על לשונה - "She speaks intelligently and teachings of kindness are on her tongue" (*Mishlei* 31:26). To impart such teachings, her own tongue must be a shining example of purity and kindness.

A *Rebbe* at a *cheder* told the author of this *sefer* the following: Every now and then he has trouble with children using words that should not be in the vocabulary of a Jewish person and he has an interesting way of dealing with the problem. He keeps an onion in *cheder*. Whenever one of the boys persistently misbehaves in the manner described, he cuts off a tiny piece of onion and makes the boy chew it. When the child says that he dislikes the taste, the *Rebbe* tells him that he is punishing his tongue for saying such bad words. When the child comes home, his mother notices right away that the child has been chewing onion and out of pity for her child calls the *Rebbe* to find out what happened. The *Rebbe* tells the mother that her son used bad language and that although he does his best to prevent it, it is really up to the parents to educate their child not to speak in this manner and to react strongly whenever he does so. They should even prevent their child from playing with neighboring children whose parents allow them to be lax in this matter, so that the child understands that it is a serious offense.

This has been recorded neither to influence others to do the same nor to give a stamp of approval to this particular method of dealing with the problem. Rather, it has been put on record because of the overall approach.

- A young child who has heard bad language and then uses it, often does not really understand how bad and how hurtful these words are. He must therefore be taught in the most potent way possible that they are very bad and distressing, and that by speaking in this manner he is fouling his mouth.

- He is taught that harsh words hurt for a long time, just as the taste of onion lingers long after it has been removed.

- Parents must be informed that their child persistently uses bad language, since much of this misconduct either stems from home (brothers and sisters) or comes from friends and is not forcefully stopped at home. Since it is often awkward for a teacher to approach parents about a matter that shows a lack of *chinuch* at home, it is a wise move on the part of the teacher to conjure up a means of causing the parents to contact him rather than the reverse.

5. USING FOUL LANGUAGE (NIVUL PEH) - RECIPE FOR DISASTER: *Chazal* say, בעון ניבול פה צרות רבות, וגזירות קשות מתחדשות, ובחורי (שונאי) ישראל מתים, יתומים ואלמנות צועקים ואינן נענים - "As a result of speaking *nivul peh* troubles increase, harsh decrees are made, young people die, orphans and widows cry for help and are not answered" (*Shabbos* 33a). There is almost no other sin for which *Chazal* prescribe such a bitter set of punishments. This shows how damaging this particular sin is to the *nefesh* - the soul of a Jewish person. Indulging in *nivul peh* is nothing short of a recipe for disaster.

The common denominator of all the punishments mentioned is that *Hashem* withdraws His *hashgacha pratis* - His watchful eye, from *Klal Yisroel*. Once there is no *hashgacha*, illness, death, evil decrees and general helplessness become the natural lot of the Jewish people, *rachmana litzlan*. For *Hashem* and His *malachim* to be present and safeguard us, there must at least be some degree of spiritual cleanliness. When people speak *nivul peh* and talk about the lowest forms of misconduct humans can fall to, there is such spiritual contamination in the air that anything which is spiritual cannot exist in its midst.

6. TAKING CARE NOT TO ADOPT THE LANGUAGE ONE HEARS: *Chazal* say, הרואה סוטה בקלקולה יזיר עצמו מן היין - "Whoever sees a *sotah* being punished should become a *nazir* to totally abstain from wine" (*Sotah* 2a). Although this man has just seen the tragic results of *arayos,* he is nevertheless in danger of being affected, for he has come face to face with a woman, at a time when Heaven bore witness that she had done this terrible sin. This visual contact is harmful. His Yiras Shomayim and *Yiras Cheit* therefore require reinforcement which he does through *nezirus* - see *Mekoros* 11:3.

In our day and age, impure and immoral language is directed at us from all forms of media. Ideally, we should neither read nor listen to the media, to prevent hearing, and all the more having visual contact with, the terms and descriptions they use. For this reason many do not allow even a radio into their house. The least we can do is to guard our tongues and not allow words that reflect the sick state of mind of our generation to pass our lips. This is a decisive step towards segregation from the *tumah* of the cultures that surround us.

7. TEFILLOS PRESENTED BY PURE MOUTH ARE WELL RECEIVED: Dovid Hamelech says, מי האיש החפץ חיים וכו׳ נצור לשונך מרע וכו׳ - "Who desires a full life etc.? Guard your tongue from evil etc." (*Tehillim* 34:14,15). All types of evil talk are referred to in this verse including *lashon horah*, *sheker*, *letzonus*, and *nivul peh* in all its forms.

It is noteworthy that the verse uses the uncommon term נצור rather than the far more usual term שמור. The reason for this is that the word שמור is used for guarding something like money or a precious article which would be lost or damaged if not guarded, but will not improve or increase as a result of the guarding. In contrast, the word נצור refers to a guarding which produces positive results, such as guarding a fruit tree from types of damage. This protection bears positive results: The tree will supply him with an abundance of luscious fruits. Hence the verse, נצר תאנה יאכל פריה - "He who guards his fig tree merits to eat its fruits" (*Mishlei* 27:18).

Returning to the verse נצור לשונך מרע. Dovid Hamelech tells us that by guarding our tongues we will reap very positive benefits - our *tefillos* and *tehillim* will be well received. The *Chofetz Chayim* said, "Wine must be served to the king in a clean cup. If the cup is not clean the wine will not only not be appreciated, on the contrary, it will positively anger the king". So too our *tefillos* and *tehillim* must be served from a clean mouth. When delivered from such a mouth, *Hashem Yisborach* delights in them and will speedily answer them.

H. CHOOSING A SCHOOL UNIFORM FOR GIRLS

1. IMPORTANT FOR THE PRESENT AND FUTURE: The uniform a girl's school chooses for its pupils serves an important role. It ensures that the girls are dressed in a Kosher and fully acceptable manner. This applies both to senior girls who are eleven plus and to junior girls from six/seven years and upwards, since all must be dressed in a Kosher manner - see 6:S:2 below. Also, the girls will learn from the clothes the school recommends, what their educators consider as Kosher and refined clothes, especially if this is spoken about at an assembly at the beginning of the year and basic reasons are given.

2. BLOUSES: If a white or light-colored blouse is to be part of the school uniform it is essential that the blouse is of a good quality cotton which is not see-through - see 6:D:3 below. Some schools prefer striped blouses (white and navy-blue stripes) because such blouses are not see-through even when the cotton is not so strong and thick - see 6:E:4(a) below. They are therefore more naturally guaranteed to be Kosher. Also, being thinner, they are cooler and more comfortable in the summer months than the white blouses which must be of a thicker cotton. Furthermore, if the parents purchase the white or light-colored blouses for their daughters it is up to their judgment that the blouses are not see-through. This carries the risk of parents having an inadequate standard.

All these reasons are however only an explanation as to why some prefer striped blouses rather than plain ones, but there is no obligation whatsoever to do the same. It may however be found to be a sensible proposition for the school to supply the blouses if the uniform involves wearing white or light-colored blouses. In this way the *kashrus* of the blouses is guaranteed.

3. SKIRTS: It is recommended that the school demands that the girls wear either a pleated, a gathered or an A-line skirt. If a loose straight skirt is adopted, parents with only a limited understanding in *tznius* will send their daughters to school wearing a tight or semi-tight skirt, which is not Kosher. By not allowing any type of straight skirt to be worn no infringement will occur - see 6:I:2 below.

The following is a quote from an "Information and rules pamphlet" given to each girl on acceptance into a *chareidi* girls' high school in England:

SCHOOL UNIFORM:

This is required at every attendance at school.

(a) Standard all-year-round uniform consists of a plain navy skirt not denim. It should be without fancy trimmings or buttons and long enough to ensure *tznius*.

(b) Only skirts that are flared or pleated from the waist down are acceptable. No tight skirts are allowed even if pleated lower down.

(c) Blouses should be plain white or light blue and care should be taken that they are not see-through.

(d) Sweaters and cardigans should be navy with no fancy trimmings and buttons. All materials should be usual school materials to the exclusion of velvet, denim, silk or chunky knitwear.

(e) Tights should be thick enough not to be see-through and shoes should be standard school-wear, black or navy.

(f) Hair accessories should not be fancy. They should be white, navy, black or silver colored and they should be the minimum size required to keep hair in place.

(g) Coats and jackets should be navy. However, summer jackets may be another color as long as it is a quiet color and the cloth is plain i.e. excluding bright pink etc. and a floral design.

Other schools might have a uniform of a different color, require striped blouses rather than plain ones, and in general stress other points. This has nonetheless been recorded to demonstrate the power a school has to direct its pupils to that which its teaching staff considers to be the ideal manner of dress for a girl in her school-age years.

Concerning *tznius* that is required when girls go swimming - see 9:J:2 below. Concerning the dress that girls should wear when they do exercises (athletic activities) and gymnastics, - see 9:J:3 below.

4. MAKE-UP AND JEWELRY: There is much to be said in favor of not allowing girls to come to school with makeup since young girls have no need for cosmetics. This will teach them that makeup is to be used only sparingly, in accordance with the need. If this message comes across, hopefully when they are adults they will use cosmetics only with moderation and refinement - see 7:K:1 below.

Some schools do not allow girls under the age of fifteen or sixteen to come to school with jewelry (except for a watch and the minimum earrings required for pierced ears), since with young girls jewelry causes much rivalry and jealousy. Resulting from this, if a girl comes to school with excessive jewelry (because her parents capitulated to her desires and allowed it) it can detrimentally affect all the girls in the class - see 7:I:2 below. Hence, enacting a rule not to allow makeup and jewelry in the school could pay handsome dividends. Parents who feel such rules are unjustified can send their daughter to another school that does not have such rules rather than let their daughter spoil the tranquillity of this school.

5. WHAT A SCHOOL ALLOWS, IS TAKEN BY MANY AS A HETER: A considerable responsibility lies on the shoulders of the administration of an

Orthodox school, not only towards their own pupils but also towards the community at large. When a school allows a certain way of dress, ladies in the wider community use this information to justify their personal modes of dress, with the argument that if the school allows it, there must be opinions which permit it.

People take it for granted that an Orthodox school, which has many *heimishe* children amongst its pupils, would not allow its pupils to wear a mode of dress without having first checked up with a competent *halachic* authority as to whether it is alright for girls of this age to dress in this way. Moreover, they argue that even if the administration does not seek a ruling for every *halachic* issue they come across, nevertheless, if all *Rabbanim* held that to dress in this manner was *ossur*, the school would not and could not go against the opinion of all *Rabbanim*. With this way of thinking, whatever the school permits its pupils to wear becomes an automatic *heter* for many to follow suit.

This warning to school authorities is not a theory but unfortunately a stark reality. The writer of this *sefer* has encountered a large and vibrant Orthodox community where exactly what has just been written occurs. When women are approached about their slits, their short and ultra tight skirts, and their wide-open blouses, their response is that since the local *frum* school permits its pupils to dress in this manner, there must be *Rabbanim* who condone this way of dress, as the school would never do something which is against the opinion of all *Rabbanim*. They therefore reason that they too have the right to follow these fictitious lenient opinions, although they understand that others disagree and forbid this way of dress.

Chazal say, כל מי שאפשר לו למחות באנשי עירו נתפס בעון אנשי עירו - "Whoever is in a position to prevent the people in his town from doing wrong and does not do so, is held responsible for their wrongdoings" (*Shabbos* 45b). If not stopping people from sinning is such a crime, can one estimate the responsibility of supplying people with an excuse and proof that they are right in their misdeeds, thereby encouraging them to sin?

In contrast, when a school insists that its rules are a hundred percent *halachically* correct, the reward deserved by those who are in a position of authority within the school is very considerable. They will have the *z'chus* of setting the standard that nothing less than true *halacha* is acceptable, and the healthy example shown by their pupils will extend to the rest of the community. Also, the rules laid down by the school authorities can have a direct bearing on the homes of some of the girls, because some of the mothers will feel that they cannot afford to dress in a way forbidden by the school, as this might cause friction between themselves and their daughter. About such people *Chazal* say, משה זכה וזיכה את הרבים זכות הרבים תלוי בו - "Moshe had the merit to bring others to do the will of *Hashem* - their good deeds are subscribed to him" (*Pirkei Avos* 5:18).

I. CHINUCH LASTS A LIFETIME

1. CHINUCH OF PARENT TO CHILD: When parents have implanted true values into the hearts and minds of their children, they have "put them on the right path" for life. *Chinuch* has hit its mark if children will do as their parents have taught them even when they are out of sight of their parents and even when they are adults and independent people who can do as they please. The *Shloh Hakadosh* (*Sha'ar Haosios*) writes that *chinuch* is like tying a stick to a young tree to ensure that it grows straight. Once the young tree has been straightened it will stay straight forever.

When Shlomo Hamelech writes about the obligation on parents to be *mechanech* their children, he says, חנוך לנער על פי דרכו גם כי יזקין לא יסור ממנה - "Educate the young child in the way suited to him; this will guarantee that even in his old age he will keep to those guidelines" (*Mishlei* 22:6, *See Malbim*). Two critical points are stressed in this verse. Firstly, the fact that the child is young and still free of negative impressions. Secondly, the approach taken with this child is one that suits his nature and educational requirements. The result of this *chinuch* is that it will last him a lifetime. Since the *emes* was planted into the child's heart before anything else, the impression is deep and everlasting.

2. CHINUCH OF REBBE TO TALMID: The great *Rosh Yeshiva* of *Lublin*, Rabbi Meir Shapiro *zt'l* had the beautiful verse, לכו בנים שמעו לי יראת ה' אלמדכם - "Go my sons, listen to me, I will teach you the fear of *Hashem*" (*Tehillim* 34:12) painted onto (or engraved into) the portals of the *Yeshiva*. When asked why he chose this verse he answered, "The verse starts with the words 'Go my sons' rather than, 'Come my sons', implying that a *mechanech* must impart such deep Yiras Shomayim into his students that even when they take leave of him they continue to listen to him". Continued the *Rosh Yeshiva*, "I wish to infuse my *talmidim* with such a strong bond to Torah and *mitzvos* that even when they finally leave the *Yeshiva*, they will nevertheless continue listening to me and serving *Hashem* with zeal and *simcha*".

This statement is true with all forms of *chinuch*, and *tznius* is no exception. The lifelong *tznius* of a daughter and her future family will be an everlasting merit to her parents who lovingly educated her with an ideal set of values.

J. CHINUCH - DEDICATION

1. A CHILD IS DEDICATED TO A LIFE OF TORAH AND MITZVOS: The word *chinuch* is used in two senses. It means "to educate", the meaning for which it is commonly used. It also means "to dedicate" as in the words *chanukas habayis* - dedicating a house to the service of *Hashem*. These two meanings are in fact interlinked - one educates to dedicate, and dedication is born out of a good education.

Just as in *chanukas habayis* the house is dedicated to the service of *Hashem*, so too, parents dedicate their children to the service of *Hashem* by impressing on them the importance and great value of all that has to do with *Yiddishkeit*. They teach them what a Jewish person refrains from because they cause *tumah* and are against the will of *Hashem*. Conversely, they teach them how we perform the many wonderful *mitzvos* that fill our lives. Hence, *chinuch* is an education that leads to dedication. Failing to dedicate is failing to have educated properly.

When parents give their children the correct *chinuch*, everyone stands to gain, not only the children who consequently grow up *b'derech haTorah v'haYirah* but even the parents themselves. *Chinuch* is like a boomerang - that which is dispatched returns to its thrower. For example, the *Yidden* gave away money, gems, precious metals etc. for the *Chanukas ha'Bayis* - the erection and dedication of the *Mishkan* in order to create a fitting abode for the *Shechinah*. Once the *Mishkan* was dedicated it radiated *kedusha* and *bracha* back onto *Klal Yisroel*. Accordingly, the outlay was returned to its donors with considerable dividends.

It is the same with the *chinuch* of children. Parents learn to appreciate the *emes* of the *Derech Hashem* and come much nearer to it, as a result of toiling to impart this way of life to their children. It is human nature that a person becomes very attached to a cause for which he works day and night. Therefore, exerting themselves to create new servants of *Hashem* gives parents a deep feeling for our wonderful heritage. Hence, not only do children benefit from *chinuch* but so do the parents themselves. (Heard from Harav Moshe Schwab *zt'l*, former Mashgiach of Gateshead Yeshiva).

2. A GIRL IS DEDICATED TO BE A WORTHY WIFE AND MOTHER: Educating a daughter to the ways of Torah and *tznius* means dedicating her to be a worthy wife and mother in *Klal Yisroel*. In her teenage years her personality is formed, resulting in the person who will be the wife, confidante and support of her future husband, and mother and educator to her future children. The greater her level during her formative years in good *midos* (*bein adam lachaveiro*) and in *ahavas* Torah *umitzvos* (*bein adam laMakom*) the better a wife and mother she will be in years to come. By acquiring sterling *midos* and true Yiras Shomayim, her husband will have an exemplary *ezer knegdo* at his side and her children an excellent mentor who will raise them into fine *Yidden*.

Avraham Avinu, the great educator of the masses, wore a medallion on which there was an elderly man and woman on the one side, and a boy and girl on the other, מטבע של אברהם אבינו זקן וזקנה מצד אחד בחור בתולה מצד אחר (*Bava Kama* 97a). Avraham taught the world that the qualities found in an elderly man and woman are a direct result of what is put into them in their young and formative years.

His son Yitzchak Avinu, raised under the tutelage of his great father, married a young girl of three, although she would be unable to bear children for at least ten years. He did so in order to enable Rivka to develop into adulthood under his influence rather than allow her to grow into a woman in the house of her father Besuel (*Tiferes Yehonasan* by R' Yehonasan Eybeshitz zt'l, *Parshas Toldos* s.v. *Bas Besuel*). This once again underscores the fact that the future of a woman is greatly dependent on the qualities established in her young and adolescent years.

3. MODESTY IS RICHLY REMUNERATED: Rather than consider such a girl as burdened and restricted with *tznius*, she should be viewed as lucky and most fortunate to have been educated and dedicated by her loving parents to live a life grounded on refinement and modesty. Her parents, like all parents, want her future bliss, and are aware that Yiras Shomayim coupled with these special traits will bring the greatest degree of blessing and happiness into their daughter's future life and fortunes.

The blessings *tznius* brings in its wake are incalculable because *Hashem* has a special love for those who practice a refined style of life and maintain strict privacy in all that involves their personal life and affairs. He feels a special closeness towards them for they live a life of purity. This significant fact is enshrined in a few beautiful words of Chazal. In *Pesikta Rabasi* (also known as *Pesikta D'Rav Kehana*), chapter 46 the following saying is recorded: שאין לך חיבה לפני המקום מן הצניעות [שנאמר] והצנע לכת את ה' אלוקיך - "Nothing is more beloved to *Hashem* than the practice of *tznius*, as is inferred in the verse 'And go with modesty [as you will then merit to be] with *Hashem* your G-d' (Micha 6:8)".

What greater good fortune can a person have than to be aware that Hashem, the greatest dispenser of kindness, loves him and is near to him?

Chapter Four

BRACHOS IN PRESENCE OF ERVAH

INTRODUCTION

From this chapter onwards the *halachos* of *tznius* are recorded as they are presented in the *Shulchan Aruch* and the major *Poskim*. The *halachos* are, of course, adapted to the types of garments that are available to us and to the way clothes are worn nowadays.

As this *sefer* is intended for women, it may seem correct and most natural that garments be discussed from the start. This would mean starting with hair styles for unmarried girls and head-coverings such as *sheitels* for married women and then proceeding from garment to garment. This has, however, not been done, as will be immediately apparent to the reader. Instead, the structure and framework used are the *halachos* of a man saying a *bracha*, *krias shema* or any other *davar shebikdusha* in front of an inadequately-clad female. This approach has been chosen for a number of reasons.

- Firstly, *Chazal*, the *Rambam* and the compiler of *Shulchan Aruch* did not arrange a section on "The *halachos* of *Tznius* Concerning Female Clothing" as such. Their approach was quite different. Within the *halachos* of *krias shema* they wrote a section which deals with a man who wishes to say *krias shema* when there is an inadequately-clad female present in the room at the time. In the context of these *halachos*, almost all *halachic* points concerning what needs to be covered and which clothes are or are not suitable for a *Bas Yisroel* are recorded. Since this is the way *Chazal* and the great *Poskim* presented these essential *halachos* to *Klal Yisroel*, it was felt that it would be correct to do the same. Whether we understand their reasoning or not, this must be the most correct way of laying down these *halachos* and to follow in their footsteps will lead to the best results.

▪ Secondly, there is a very powerful message, even for women, in the *issur* for men to say *krias shema* and *brachos* in front of an inadequately-clad female. From these *halachos*, women and girls can see for themselves the far-reaching effect that even minimal carelessness in dress has on men who catch sight of them. This will make every self-respecting woman aware that we are not dealing here with matters of commendable or preferable conduct, but rather with factors that are of critical significance to the purity and chastity of the Jewish people. When a *bracha* is said by a man facing a woman with semi-uncovered arms, the *bracha* is imperfect and according to some is even invalid and classified a *bracha levatala*. It is therefore most educational for women and girls to be made aware of the pervasive effects of laxness and infringements on matters pertaining to this aspect of *halacha*.

▪ Thirdly, these *halachos* are of immense practical significance to the woman at home even when she is just with her husband. If she sits at the breakfast table with her hair or a *tefach* of her hair uncovered, or if just half the upper sections of her arms are uncovered, and her husband sits facing her, all *brachos* he recites while in that position are imperfect, and according to some are rendered *brachos levatala*. This is so even if he is not actually looking at her while saying the *bracha*.

Therefore, apart from the fact that it is greatly preferred from the *tznius* point of view that she covers herself properly even indoors, it follows from what has been explained, that by being lax in this matter she effectively puts an obstacle in the path of her husband. It is inevitable that he will frequently forget to close his eyes or turn away from her before saying a *bracha* or *dvar* Torah and she will have caused him to do wrong - *see Mishna Berura* 75:10.

In order to explain the *issur* of saying a *bracha* in front of an inadequately-clad female, one must first of all describe the *issur min haTorah* for anyone to say a *bracha* when facing a completely-unclad person (whether male or female). This is the basis on which the *halachos* mentioned are constructed, and if omitted will impede a proper understanding of the *halachos*. Moreover, mothers deal with young children who are sometimes undressed. They must therefore know when it is *ossur* for them to say a *bracha* or anything similar.

[If the *halachos* of "*brachos* in the presence of *ervah*" are found to be too difficult to comprehend, they should be omitted so that the *halachos* of *tznius* that are of direct relevance to women and girls can be learned in a clear and uncomplicated manner. In such a case the whole of Chapter 4 and Chapter 6, Nos. T - W should be omitted].

There are altogether four subjects within this topic that require elaboration. These will be explained in the following chapters. They are:-

איסור דערות דבר - ***Brachos* etc. may not be said when facing *ervah***
- discussed in this Chapter.

שער באשה ערוה - **Exposed hair of a married woman attracts attention**.
- discussed in Chapter Five.

טפח באשה ערוה - **Skin that should be covered attracts attention.**
- discussed in Chapter Six.

קול באשה ערוה - **Singing is a form of exposure and attracts attention.**
- discussed in Chapter Eight.

The names of the latter three subjects have been coined by *Chazal*. The fact that they use such a severe and outspoken noun as ערוה when classifying these matters (although they usually advocate the use of as refined a term as possible - דברה תורה בלשון נקיה) is proof of the extreme severity with which they viewed them. Evidently, the *kedusha* of *Klal Yisroel* largely depends on the mode of dress and public conduct of women and girls. Consequently an improvement in the implementation of these *halachos* is a strengthening of *kedushas Yisroel* in general. With this in mind, let us summon the strength to reverse the present trend and muster the courage to differ from the masses. We will wear our badge of honor and distinction with pride and we will feel elated with the dignity and esteem of *tznius*.

A. BRACHA FACING UNCLAD PERSON - ISSUR MIN HATORAH

1. THE PRINCIPAL ISSUR: From the verse, ולא יראה בך ערות דבר (*Devarim* 23:15) we learn that it is *ossur* to say a *bracha*, a *dvar* Torah and any other type of *davar shebikdusha* in sight of an impurity (*ervah*). This refers to saying a *bracha* in front of a completely unclad male from the age of nine or unclad female from the age of three - M.B. 75:23. Such nakedness is known as *ervah min haTorah* and applies to nakedness of any human-being, Jew and non-Jew alike, but does not apply to the nakedness of an animal - O.C. 75:4 and M.B. 75:20. It is irrelevant whether the person saying the *bracha* and the naked person are both male, both female or one is male and the other female, as the *issur* applies in all cases. Moreover, the *issur* applies whenever the *ervah* is visible. It therefore applies whether the *ervah* is totally uncovered, is covered with a see-through garment or is screened-off by a see-through window - see *Mekoros* 14:1.

Saying a *davar shebikdusha* in such a situation is considered as being grossly disrespectful to *Hashem* with Whom the *davar shebikdusha* is closely identified. It is a transgression which can *chas veshalom* lead to poverty, illness and similar hardships - see *Mekoros* 25-26.

[It should be noted that the *halacha* stated that *ervah* applies only from the age of three or nine, is the opinion of the *Rema* which is followed by *Ashkenazim*. *Sephardim*, however, follow the opinion of the *Beis Yosef* (O.C. 75:4) who is of the opinion that *ervah* applies immediately after birth - *see Chaya Adam* 4:1 *and Graz* 75:7. In fact, according to these *Poskim* it is preferable for everyone, even *Ashkenazim,* to be stringent and comply with the opinion of the *Beis Yosef.* The *Mishna Berura*, however, does not seem to share this opinion.]

2. VERBALIZING TORAH FORBIDDEN - THINKING PERMITTED: The *issur* applies to saying a *bracha*, *Bircas Hamazon*, *Tehillim*, *dvar* Torah, and learning Torah or singing a song containing *p'sukim* or the name of *Hashem* in front of *ervah*. In short, all *devarim shebikdusha* may not be said when facing *ervah*. Concerning songs that praise *Hashem* but do not contain *p'sukim* nor is the name of *Hashem* uttered - see 8:G:3 below.

The *issur* only applies to verbalizing *divrei* Torah in sight of *ervah*, but there is no *issur* in just thinking about *divrei* Torah or just reading from a *sefer* without verbalizing the words. The verse, ולא יראה בך ערות דבר uses the word דבר which alludes to the word דיבור - speech, indicating that speaking *divrei* Torah in sight of *ervah* is forbidden, whilst there is no *issur* in just thinking about *divrei* Torah in this situation (M.B. 75:29).

If a person verbalizes the words but says them silently or covers his mouth with his *siddur* or *sefer*, the words are still considered as being said and the *heter* of "thinking *divrei* Torah" does not apply (*Responsa Salmas Chayim* 1:61). Moreover, writing *divrei* Torah is forbidden when facing *ervah*, even if he does not verbalize the words when writing them down. Only thinking Torah thoughts, which is an inactive form of learning, is subject to the *heter* mentioned, whilst writing is comparable to speaking *divrei* Torah or *tefilla*, and is forbidden - see *Mekoros* 20:5-6.

Just as a person may think *divrei* Torah although he is facing *ervah*, so too, he may hear *divrei* Torah that are being said. Moreover, he may listen intently to the *divrei* Torah in order to understand them. When hearing and even when listening, the person is passive rather than active. It is therefore no different than thinking about Torah which is permitted, as has been explained.

It is, however, forbidden for someone facing *ervah* to listen to a *bracha* with the intention of discharging his obligation (being *yotzeh)* with that *bracha* for a food he is about to eat or a *mitzva* he is about to perform. Since the verbalization of the *bracha* will be attributed also to him (due to the principle of שומע כעונה - "listening is considered as saying it oneself") he will be considered as having verbalized the *bracha* himself. As this will be happening while he is facing an *ervah*, it is forbidden (M.B. 75:29).

3. THE ISSUR APPLIES EVEN WHEN NOT LOOKING AT ERVAH: When stating this *issur* the Torah uses the words ולא יראה בך - "nakedness shall not be seen with you" rather than ולא תראה - "you shall not see". This implies that the *issur* is transgressed even if the person does not actually look at the *ervah* while saying the *bracha* etc. As long as he is in a position where he could see the *ervah* if he looked he is considered to be together with it and in an impure environment. Even if there is quite a distance from the position of the person to the position of the *ervah*, nevertheless, if the *ervah* is ahead of him and he could look at it if he so desired, he is considered to be in one and the same place as the *ervah*. This is the meaning of the verse "nakedness shall not be seen with you" ie. it should not be together with you when you are saying a *davar shebikdusha,* as it would be disrespectful to address *Hashem Yisborach* while in this situation. He may therefore not say a *bracha*, sing *zemiros* etc. when *ervah* is before himself. Similarly, he may not learn Torah while in this situation because he is bringing something extremely holy into an impure setting (M.B. 75:19) - see *Mekoros* 14:1.

However, the *issur* does not apply when the *ervah* is situated to his right, left, or rear since it is out of his area of sight and a person is not considered to be totally together with items which he is unable to see. He is therefore considered to be in a respectable and undefiled location and in a situation fit for saying a *davar shebikdusha*. In such a case he may say a *bracha* even if the unclad person is within his four *amos* (M.B. 75:30).

An unclad person himself may not say a *bracha* or any *davar shebikdusha* because of the exposure of the *ervah*. Even if the person does not look at this area of the body, the *issur* still applies because the person is in a position where "nakedness can be seen with him" (M.B. 75:19).

4. BRACHA MAY BE SAID BY TURNING AWAY FROM THE ERVAH: As stated, if *ervah min haTorah* e.g. an unclad child, is in front of a person who wishes to say a *bracha* etc., he must turn his entire body to face a different direction so that the *ervah* is at his side rather than straight ahead. Since the *ervah* will then be out of sight, he may freely say a *bracha* (M.B. 75:29).

It would be inadequate for him just to close his eyes or put his hands in front of his eyes, because the *ervah* would still be considered to be within his sight. Similarly, the *issur* applies even if it is dark and the *ervah* cannot be seen, because the deciding factor is the position of the *ervah* in relationship to the person - not the actual ability to see it.

Moreover, it is inadequate for the person just to turn his head in a different direction, because the *ervah* will still be regarded as being in sight. This is because a person is considered to be facing the direction his body is facing even if his head is turned in a different direction. He is therefore regarded as facing the *ervah*. For the same reason, the *issur* applies to a blind man who is facing *ervah* although he cannot possibly see it (M.B. 75:29).

B. BRACHA FACING SEMI-CLAD FEMALE - ISSUR D'RABANAN

1. A WOMAN'S OBLIGATION TO DRESS ADEQUATELY: A woman is obligated to ensure that her body is adequately covered whenever she is in public. The details concerning exactly what must be covered and what does not require covering will בע״ה be explained in detail in subsequent chapters.

This obligation is at the very heart of the *halachos* of *tznius*. If a woman continuously refuses to comply with these requirements, the wrongdoing is so serious and the effect it can have is so detrimental that the husband has an obligation to divorce her (*Gittin* 90b). The *Rambam* writes the following (*Hilchos Geirushin* 10:22), אשה רעה בדיעותיה ושאינה צנועה כבנות ישראל הכשרות, מצוה לגרשה שנאמר גרש לץ ויצא מדון. ואשה שנתגרשה משום פריצות אין ראוי לאדם כשר שישאנה, שאין זה מוציא רשעה מביתו וזה מכניסה לתוך ביתו Loosely translated this means, "If a woman has bad pursuits or does not practice *tznius* as do other righteous women, it is a *mitzva* to divorce her..... A good person should not marry a woman who has been divorced because of *pritzus*. Just as the first person was not to have such a wife (i.e. such an influence) in his house, so too, the second man should not have her in his house."

Some areas require covering because of an obligation *min haTorah* whilst other areas because of an obligation *mid'Rabanan*. Thirdly, there are areas that require covering because the local Orthodox women of this generation feel an urge to be stringent and have taken upon themselves to cover them. Since they are particular to cover these areas, they must be covered *mid'Rabanan*. These three levels will now be explained.

(a) Obligation *min haTorah* to cover: It is a Torah obligation to cover the main trunk of the body and some additional areas. For example, a married woman is obliged to have her hair covered whenever she is in public. When an area must be covered due to Torah law, the obligation is called *Das Moshe* (דת משה) - a law transmitted by Moshe Rabbeinu at *Har Sinai*, although not spelt out in explicit terms in the Torah - see *Mekoros* 37:2.

Since these are "covered areas", the laws of *tznius* require that they are covered whenever she can be seen by men other than her most intimate family. Her intimate family includes her father, grandfather, great-grandfather son, grandson, great-grandson, brother and husband - (*Shar Hatzion* 225:2, *Toras Hahistaklus* 14:20 and *Taharas Einayim* 3:3).

The Issur does, however, apply to a cousin, uncle, nephew, father-in-law, brother-in-law, son-in-law, step-father, step-brother and step-son since they are not close blood relatives. The guiding line is the *issur* of *yichud* - see E.H. 22:1. When it applies, the full *halachos* of *tznius* likewise apply - see *Mekoros* 71.

Since these parts of the body are "covered areas" they have been termed *ervah*. The fact that they are called *ervah* is of Rabbinical origin, since the Torah term *ervah* applies only to total nakedness. The *issur* to say a *davar shebikdusha* when facing these areas is therefore a prohibition *mid'Rabanan* but not *min haTorah*. This is an important point to be aware of as otherwise a person learning these *halachos* can become confused.

(b) Obligation mid'Rabanan to cover: There are parts of the body which, although not מקום צנוע - "covered areas" *min haTorah,* have been designated by *Chazal* as "covered areas", such as the upper section of the arms. When an area must be covered due to *Chazal* considering it a "covered area", it is called *Das Yehudis* (דת יהודית) - a law made to preserve the refinement of Jewish women (*Kesubos* 72b) - see *Mekoros* 37:4. Since these are "covered areas" *mid'Rabanan,* they must be covered whenever she can be seen by men. Also, these areas are included in the areas termed *ervah* by *Chazal* with the result that a *davar shebikdusha* may not be said when facing them.

(c) Obligation to cover, due to *minhag:* There are areas which have become "covered areas" due to the accepted practice by Orthodox women to consider them as areas that should be covered. An example would be not to walk outdoors barefoot even in a very hot climate, although the *halacha* does not demand that the foot be covered. Since the feet have become "covered areas" they may not be exposed when she is in public, nor may a *davar shebikdusha* be said facing them - see *Mekoros* 49:12, 54:1.

(d) *Issur* to expose even less than a *tefach:* All areas that have to be covered, whether because of *Das Moshe* or because of *Das Yehudis,* must be covered completely. There is absolutely no *heter* for a woman to leave less than a *tefach* of those areas uncovered. This is because even a minor exposure is provocative and a serious shortcoming of *tznius*. It is therefore *ossur* for the neckline of the garment to extend even half a centimeter beyond the permitted level - (O.C. 75:1 *Rema; Chazon Ish* O.C. 16:7; *Iggros Moshe,* E.H. 1:58 s.v. *V'lachein*).

The term טפח באשה ערוה - "A *tefach* of a woman's body is *ervah*" is used with respect to the *issur* of saying a *bracha* when the person's eyes are closed and he cannot possibly look. If the area is classified *ervah* it is *ossur* to say a *bracha* although his eyes are closed. In this context a distinction is drawn between a *tefach* and less than a *tefach*. A *tefach* is a significant area and classified *ervah,* whereas less than a *tefach* does not have that status.

Hence, the term טפח באשה ערוה must not be misconstrued as a general *heter* for a woman to leave less than a *tefach* uncovered - see *Mekoros* 37:6.

2. AREAS THAT MUST BE COVERED ARE TERMED "ERVAH": As stated above, all areas of a woman's body that must be covered according to the *halachos* of *tznius* whether *min haTorah* or *mid'Rabanan* have been classified as *ervah* by *Chazal.* Since when these areas are uncovered they are provocative and cause immoral conduct, such as men gazing at women, they have been fittingly termed *ervah* by *Chazal* (M.B. 75:1). This is so, irrespective of whether the female is Jewish or non-Jewish, married or single. There is also no distinction made in *halacha* between a young and elderly woman or between an attractive and unattractive person (*Ben Ish Chai*, *Bo,* 12; *Kaf Hachayim* 75:24). Since these areas are *ervah,* it is *ossur* for a man to say a *bracha* or any *davar shebikdusha* in front of them (M.B. 75:1-5) - see *Mekoros* 14:2-6.

These areas have been given the status of *ervah* in relationship to men who are provoked by seeing them. They do not have the status of *ervah* for the woman herself nor for other women since only men are affected by the inadequately covered body of a woman. Women remain unaffected, except when seeing gross misconduct which injects *tumah* into anyone who sees it - see *Mekoros* 12:4. Accordingly, a woman may say a *bracha* even if the upper section of her arm is uncovered or she is looking at another woman whose upper arm is uncovered (M.B. 75:8).

3. A TEFACH EXPOSED HAS THE STATUS OF ERVAH: If a *tefach* (4"x4") of skin is exposed, the *ervah* status is given to that area - see *Mekoros* 15:1-7. A man who wants to say a *davar shebikdusha* should therefore turn away from it just as he must do when *ervah min haTorah* is in front of him - 4:A:4 above. That *ervah* must be the size of a *tefach* is a law, just as it is a law that an "act of eating" refers only to eating a *Kzayis* (*Rosh, Pesachim* 10:25) - see *Bach*, beginning of O.C. 75 and 6:T:1 below. Also, when the substantial area of a full *tefach* is exposed, it is particularly provocative and was therefore given the full status of *ervah* by *Chazal.*

[However, a *tefach* of hair has a more lenient status and is only partial *ervah,* as will be explained. Altogether, hair is more lenient than flesh as can also be seen from the fact that unmarried girls need not cover their hair although they must cover all parts of the body that married women must cover].

If it is difficult for the man to completely turn aside from the "exposed *tefach*", he may rely on opinions which do not give a *tefach* of exposed skin the full status of *ervah*. They maintain that since the *ervah* status is based on the effect seeing the area has on a man, the *issur* applies only when the man is looking in the direction of the exposure and can easily see the exposed area. Accordingly, in cases of difficulty, a man may say a *bracha* by closing his eyes or by looking elsewhere in a way that the woman is out of his field of vision (M.B. 75:1 - *Graz* 75:1). Likewise, if the room is dark, he may, in case of difficulty, say a *bracha* although a *tefach* is exposed and he is facing it.

Similarly, *Bnei* Torah may talk to each other in learning while walking along the street even though they know that there are many indecently-dressed females ahead of them. Since this is a constant ongoing problem and to be stringent would cause considerable *bitul* Torah, one may rely on the opinions which state that the *issur* does not apply when one looks down or elsewhere (see *Responsa Salmas Chayim* 1:57) - see *Mekoros* 33.

It was explained concerning *ervah min haTorah* that only verbalizing the *divrei* Torah is *ossur* but there is no *issur* in thinking about *divrei* Torah (see 4:A:2). The same obviously applies to *ervah d'Rabanan*. There is no *issur* in thinking Torah matters in a place where women are inadequately dressed. Accordingly, a man may think *divrei* Torah or read a *sefer* while traveling on public transport even if he faces indecently dressed women.

4. LESS THAN TEFACH NOT ERVAH, BUT BRACHA OSSUR: If less than a *tefach* of skin is exposed, the exposure is not *ervah*. It is, however, *ossur* for a man to say a *bracha* when looking at such an exposure (even if she is his wife) or when positioned in a way that if he so desired he could see her without having to move his head. Since looking at her can cause thoughts about a woman (הרהורי אשה), *brachos* and *d'varim shebikdusha* may not be said under such conditions. However, if he closes his eyes or the room is dark [and according to some even if he just looks down at the floor or *siddur* rather than directly at the woman] he may say a *bracha* because in all these cases he is not in a direct position to be affected by the exposure (M.B. 75:5, 75:28). See *Mekoros* 17:1-7, 37:1-3.

5. TEFACH SCREENED OFF - SAME AS LESS THAN TEFACH:

(a) Woman dressed in see-through garments: Whenever the *ervah* is screened off by a net kerchief placed over uncovered knees (to take an example) or by a see-through blouse and through it the upper sections of the arms or the chest area are visible, it is sufficient for the man to close his eyes [and according to some, to simply look elsewhere] and say a *bracha* even though a *tefach* is exposed before him. Since the *ervah* is screened off and he is not looking at it, he is detached from it both by location and by sight, and is therefore not considered to be saying the *bracha* in the presence of *ervah*.

This *heter* applies even to total nakedness which is *ervah min haTorah*. Whenever it is behind a screen, closing eyes etc. is adequate. Therefore if a child wearing only a see-through night-dress is in a room, a person facing the child could close his eyes or look downwards to say a *bracha,* even though *ervah min haTorah* can be seen through the garment - see M.B. 75:25 and *Mekoros* 38:1-2.

(b) Man covering his eyes with spectacles or a book: Spectacles worn by the person facing the *ervah* are not considered a screen. This is because the *heter* of a screen is based on the fact that the *ervah* is screened off and the person facing the *ervah* is not considered to be in one and the same place as the *ervah*. Spectacles which cover just the eyes but not the whole person cannot be viewed as a screen or a division between the person and the *ervah*. Therefore, if the person closes his eyes and they are also covered by spectacles it still remains *ossur* for him to say a *bracha* whenever closing eyes alone would not help. Similarly, covering one's eyes with one's hands or a book is not considered as screening off the *ervah* and is no better than simply closing one's eyes - See *Chazon Ish* O.C. 16:7.

(c) The person and the *ervah* are in two different domains: A person may say a *davar shebikdusha* facing an *ervah* that is in a different domain even if no screen divides between himself and the *ervah*. For example, he is standing in front of an open window and a partially dressed woman is walking past outside. Since the *ervah* is in a different domain, and he is not looking at it, he is not considered to be saying a *bracha* whilst in the close proximity of nakedness.

Likewise, if a person stands on a balcony that overlooks a street in which inadequately dressed women walk, he may say a *bracha* by simply closing his eyes, or according to some, by looking straight ahead in a way that the *ervah* is not in his line of vision. Similarly, a man traveling in a bus or car may learn when facing an open window even though inadequately dressed women pass outside. If he looks down in the *sefer* he may even verbalize the Torah he is learning since he is not considered to be learning Torah in the vicinity of *ervah*. See *sefer, Mishmeres Chayim*, Chap. 4 note 9.

This last *heter* applies only to *ervah d'Rabanan* such as an inadequately dressed woman, but not to *ervah min HaTorah* such as a naked child who is in a second room and can be seen through an open door. In such a case one may not say a *davar shebikdusha* even if one closes one's eyes. This is because there is, in fact, a dispute whether being in a different domain creates a *heter* or not. Therefore, one may be lenient concerning *ervah d'Rabanan* but not in cases of *ervah min HaTorah* (see M.B. 75:29 and M.B. 79:14).

C. ADDITIONAL POINTS CONCERNING INADEQUATE DRESS

The following are points that will be dealt with extensively in subsequent chapters. For the sake of clarity they are mentioned here as a short introduction. The principle behind these points is that if the exposure will have no effect on a particular onlooker, then in relation to him the exposed skin does not have the status of *ervah*.

1. A TEFACH EXPOSED - AFFECTS EVEN CLOSE FAMILY: A husband, father, grandfather, son, grandson, and brother may not say a *bracha* when a *tefach* is exposed, whether skin or hair, because a *tefach* is classified as *ervah* by *Chazal* as they say טפח באשה ערוה. Although a woman may say a *bracha* facing a *tefach* exposed on another woman, as for her the exposed flesh of another female is not considered *ervah*, males, even of very close family, are different. This is because females remain totally unaffected by such an exposure, while males that are very close family are slightly provoked by it. Although the provocation is minimal, and it is probably no more than the enticement of a woman's countenance, it nevertheless causes the *tefach* exposed to retain its classified name of *ervah* also concerning them. It is therefore forbidden for them to say a *davar shebikdusha* while facing a *tefach* of a close female relative (O.C. 75:1) - see *Mekoros* 17:8.

2. LESS THAN A TEFACH - DOES NOT AFFECT CLOSE FAMILY: A husband, father, grandfather, son, grandson and brother may say a *bracha* when less than a *tefach* is exposed, whether hair or skin (apart from the upper section of the leg), because less than a *tefach* is not classified as *ervah*. Being close relatives they are only minimally affected by seeing the exposure, and this alone will not cause "הרהור - negative thoughts". There is therefore no *issur* in saying a *davar shebikdusha*.

We similarly find that there is no *issur* of *yichud* between such relatives because there is almost no *arayos* tendency between them (see *Pischei Teshuva* E.H. 22:2 in the name of the *Bach*). So too, seeing a small area on such a close relative is so insignificant that no *issur* on saying a *davar shebikdusha* is caused. [It could even be that close relatives are simply not affected at all by an exposure of less than a *tefach*. They are therefore permitted to say a *davar shebikdusha* facing such an exposure as it is meaningless concerning them.] Accordingly, a son may say a *bracha* even if his mother's *tiechel* is not properly on and less than a *tefach* of her hair is showing. Similarly, a brother may say a *dvar* Torah to his sister even if her sleeve does not fully cover her elbow (see *Biur Halacha* 75:1 s.v. *Tefach* and *Mekoros* 17:8.

3. SPECIAL STATUS OF UPPER SECTIONS OF THE LEGS: A husband, father, grandfather, son, grandson and brother may not say a *bracha* even if just less than a *tefach* of the upper section of the leg is exposed because this area is particularly provocative. This *halacha* is known as שוק באשה ערוה - "the thigh of a woman is *ervah*" (M.B. 75:7). This *halacha* should be taken as a yardstick with which to assess the intense harm caused by a woman or girl wearing a short garment that allows some of the knees (which are part of the upper section of the legs - see 6:H:3) to show.

4. EXPOSURE ON A GIRL UNDER THREE AFFECTS NO ONE: The exposed skin of a girl under three (some say under six/seven) is not *ervah* because it does not affect anyone. Even those who consider nakedness of an under three to be *ervah* and forbid saying a *bracha* when facing such nakedness (see 4:A:1 above) agree that partial nakedness of an under three cannot be considered *ervah d'Rabanan* because the limbs of such a young girl cannot possibly arouse the interest of anyone (*Biur Halacha* 75:1 s.v. *Tefach*).

5. A GIRL UNDER ELEVEN DOES NOT AFFECT CLOSE FAMILY: The exposed skin of a girl under eleven is not *ervah* in relation to her grandfather, father and brother because close relatives are not affected at all by exposure of such a young girl even if more than a *tefach* is visible - *sefer*, *Birur Halacha* 75:1. See *Mekoros* 16:1.

D. ISSUR TO SAY BRACHA WHEN WOMEN SING

1. WOMEN MAY NOT SING WHERE MEN CAN HEAR THEM: When a girl or woman sings, she exposes part of her natural beauty. If a male hears this, it has a similar effect on him as seeing an exposure of a part of her body that is usually covered. The *halachos* of *tznius* therefore require that a woman does not sing where men can hear her.

2. WHEN HEARING A WOMAN SING HE MAY NOT SAY A BRACHA: A man may not hear a woman sing whether she is Jewish or non-Jewish, married or single. However a husband may hear his wife sing just as he may see her hair etc. If any man hears a woman sing he may not say a *davar shebikdusha* at that time. He is in a position to be provoked into thoughts about a woman and a *davar shebikdusha* may not be said at such a time. This *halacha,* known as קול באשה ערוה will בע״ה be explained in detail in Chap. 8.

3. A MAN MAY NOT SAY BRACHA WHEN HEARING HIS WIFE SING: If a man hears his own wife sing which is permitted, he may nevertheless not say a *bracha* at the time, because even his wife's voice is somewhat attractive to him and considered *ervah*, albeit *ervah shel heter* - an attraction to a person permitted to him. Accordingly, a husband may not say *Bircas Hamazon* or learn verbally from a *sefer* if he can hear his wife singing (which women often do when busy in the kitchen or when putting the children to sleep) as will be explained בע״ה (O.C. 75:3 *Rema*). The same applies to a grandfather, father, son, grandson or brother. Although they may hear their close blood relatives sing, they may not then say a *bracha* - see 8:A:2 below.

E. ISSUR TO BE UNCLAD IN FRONT OF SEFORIM

1. THE ISSUR TO APPEAR UNCLAD IN FRONT OF SEFORIM: A *sefer* should not be exposed to *ervah*. It is subject to these *halachos* because the word דבר at the end of the verse of ולא יראה בך ערות דבר refers both to holy words (a *bracha*, *dvar* Torah etc.) and to holy objects (such as *tefillin*, *mezuza*, a *sefer*, *bircas hamazon*, wall chart with verse or *ma'amar Chazal* etc.). This means that the Torah forbids revealing true *ervah* i.e. to undress (oneself or a young child who is old enough to have *ervah*) in front of a *sefer* or similar holy object - see M.B. 45:2-5 and *Mekoros* 19:1.

A woman may be partially dressed in front of a *sefer* even if much more than a *tefach* of her flesh is uncovered. This is permitted because the general flesh of a woman is classified *ervah* only in relationship with a male who can be provoked by it, but not for a female who remains totally unaffected by seeing it. Concerning a *sefer*, the general flesh of a woman is not classified as *ervah*, because it too cannot be provoked. Since the nature of the *halacha* is that a *sefer* must "not see *ervah*" the *halacha* does not apply to women in partial dress and certainly not to men who are only in partial dress. Accordingly, a mother may nurse her baby when there are *seforim* in the room even if she is not taking precautions to cover herself and ensure that the *sefer* cannot "see" her flesh - see M.B. 45:5 and *Mekoros* 20:1-4.

2. THE ISSUR APPLIES TO PLASTIC-COATED WALL CHARTS: The *issur* mentioned applies even if the wall chart is laminated or covered with a plastic sheet. The point of the *issur* is "sight" i.e. the holy article should not see *ervah*, and this will not be prevented by a see-through cover - see M.B. 40:7 concerning a similar matter. See also *Mekoros* 9:2. Many glossed or laminated wall charts exist which should not be hung in a bedroom used by a young girl over the age of three unless she is trained to undress under a cover. For example, there are charts with the text of *shema*, *Bircas Hamapil*, *Asher Yatzar*, and so on. Likewise, if a *mezuzah* is fixed onto the inside frame of the door leading into a children's bedroom, the *mezuzah* should not be covered with see-through plastic since the name of *Hashem* written on the outside of the *mezuzah* will be exposed to the *ervah* - see M.B. 40:7.

If just *Modeh Ani* is pinned up on the wall the *issur* does not apply according to most *Poskim*. They do not consider it to be a *davar shebikdusha* as it is not a *posuk* nor does it contain *Hashem's* name - see 8:G:3 below.

It is forbidden for a boy of nine to expose himself in front of a *sefer*, a holy object such as a pair of *Tefillin* or the name of *Hashem*, irrespective of what it is written on. However, by the age of nine the boy has presumably been educated that he must cover himself while undressing even if no *davar shebikdusha* is in the room. If he does so there should be no need to remove *devarim shebikdusha* from the room - see 6:Q:A below.

Chapter Five

COVERING HAIR - CROWN OF THE JEWISH WOMAN

INTRODUCTION

In this chapter the *halachos* and guidelines of *mitzvas Kisuy Sa'aros* - the *mitzva* for married women to cover their hair - will be explained בע״ה. Although many inroads have unfortunately been made over the last decades to undermine this wonderful and holy *mitzva*, we do not accept the prevailing attitude of people that nothing can be done to restore it to its previous glory. In our day and age, many women are ready to follow the *derech ha'emes* - the road of truth - if only it is explained to them in the correct way.

It should be noted that in the times of *Chazal* even non-Jewish women covered their hair when married (*Sanhedrin* 58b). This demonstrates just how deep-rooted the need for *tznius* is in the constitution of the married woman, and all the more so in the nature of the Jewish married woman. It is, therefore, an unnatural state of affairs that some women no longer feel a need for special modesty once married. Segregation, which is the cornerstone of *kedushas Yisroel* (and in more normal times, was understood to a degree even by the *umos ha'olam*) is particularly indicated for a woman after marriage, as she is an *eishes ish*. See 5:D:2(h) below and *Mekoros* 21:5.

These notes explain the *halachos* with their underlying reasons and relevant *hashkofos* and it is hoped that this elucidation will awaken a dormant spark and help restore the honor and sanctity of the *Bas Yisroel*. *B'ezer Hashem* this great *mitzva* will once again take its rightful place of honor amongst all other *mitzvos* of the Torah.

A. COVERING HAIR IN PUBLIC

1. WOMAN IS IN PUBLIC - OBLIGATION MIN HATORAH: It is an obligation *min haTorah* for a married woman [or a woman who was married in the past - M.B. 75:11] to have her hair covered whenever she is in public area or appears amongst a large number of people. This is derived from the verse, ופרע את ראש האשה - "The *Kohen* shall uncover the hair of the *sotah*" (*Bamidbar* 5:18) which implies that before the action of the *Kohen* her hair was covered, because she was in *Beis din* among many people. See 5:D:2(g-h) for reasons why this *mitzva* was given to married women.

Although it is an obligation *min haTorah* for a married woman to cover her hair when in public, the *ervah* status given to the hair is an innovation by *Chazal*. Consequently, *min haTorah* a man may say a *bracha* when looking at the uncovered hair of his wife or another woman because they are not *ervah*. *Chazal* have however labeled hair of a married woman "*ervah*" and it is therefore *ossur mid'Rabanan* to say a *bracha* when looking at such hair, be it another woman's whose hair he may not see, or his own wife's which he may see - see 4:B:1(a) above, and *Mekoros* 21:16-19.

Hair was given the status of *ervah* by *Chazal* because when any part of the female body that should be covered is uncovered it can affect a man who sees it and can cause him to feel attracted to her.

2. WOMAN CAN BE SEEN BY INDIVIDUALS - MITZVA D'RABANAN: It is an obligation *mid'Rabanan* for a married woman to cover her hair when she is not in the public eye but she could be seen by men who are not part of her intimate family, e.g. when she goes out to the porch or yard. The *issur* applies even if she can only be seen by one individual, such as when she opens the door to a stranger.

As explained previously, obligations related to *tznius* of women's dress that are *min haTorah* are called *Das Moshe* whilst obligations originating from *Chazal* are called *Das Yehudis*. Accordingly, covering hair in public which is an obligation *min haTorah*, is *Das Moshe*, whereas covering hair where only an individual can see her hair is *Das Yehudis* (*Kesubos* 72b).

3. HAIR THAT IS DIFFICULT TO COVER - DEPENDS ON MINHAG: Hair which is difficult to contain in a regular well-fitted hair covering is *halachically* exempt from this obligation. This refers to hair which grows on the temples next to the ear or on an exceptionally low hairline that extends below what a net or *tiechel* would normally contain. These are known as שערות היוצאות חוץ לצמתן. Although the temples are considered as part of the head, the *halachic* obligation to cover is limited to that which is naturally contained in a net-like cover. It is, however *ossur* for a man to gaze with intent at such hair just as he may not gaze at her face (M.B. 75:13).

Although there is no obligation to cover such hair, nevertheless, if local *shomrei mitzvos* are stringent and cover them, the *halacha* obliges all women who live in this locality to behave likewise. In fact, many have adopted the custom to be stringent because Kabbalistically much stress is put on covering all hair of the head without exception (M.B. 75:10 and 551:79). See also *Mekoros* 22:1-2.

If a woman lived in a place that is lenient on this issue but is now (permanently or just temporarily) in a place that is stringent, she is obliged to cover this hair in accordance with the local *minhag* (*Biur Halacha* 75:2 s.v. *Michutz*). It would be considered immodest for her to show hair in a place where people do not usually do so (and local men are not used to seeing even these hairs of married women), even though it is *halachically* permitted for her to do so at home where people are used to it - see 1:G where this concept is explained at length.

It must be made quite clear that the above-mentioned leniency refers only to hair which grows on the temples and is therefore difficult to cover or to contain in a net. There is, however, no *heter* for a lock of hair that comes from the upper head area to descend and protrude from the *tiechel*, snood etc. at the temples or even below them since such hair can easily be contained. Such hair must therefore be covered in line with all other hair. It has unfortunately become fashionable in some circles to allow some locks of hair to show. This is related to the misconduct of window *sheitels*, explained in 5:D:6 below and it should be widely publicized that this is totally incorrect even if the hair that protrudes measures less than a *tefach* - see 5:C:2-3.

4. HAIR THAT GROWS BELOW THE TEMPLES: The two *minhagim* mentioned in the previous point, concern hair that grows below the usual hairline down to the bottom of the temple bone. The temple bone is next to the ear and does not move around when the person opens and closes his mouth, in contrast to the jaw bone which does move. Down to the lowest part of the temple bone, which is identical with the lowest part of the ear tunnel, is part of the head rather than the face. It is called by the Torah, פאת הראש - "the corner of the head" and, concerning a man, hair that grows there is *payos harosh* which he must not cut off completely - see Y.D. 181:1. It is with reference to hair growing in this area, that some have the *minhag* to cover even this hair since it is after all hair of the head whilst others do not have such a *minhag*. However, hair which grows below this point which is hair that grows below the ear tunnel, is not subject to *minhag* at all. It is facial hair rather than head hair, and the obligation to cover refers only to head hair not to hair that comes from a totally different source.

5. HAIR THAT GROWS ON THE NECK: Hair that grows on the neck is exempt from the obligation of being covered, since the Torah obliges hair of the head to be covered (ופרע את ראש האשה - see 5:A:1 above) and the neck is simply not part of the head. Even the *minhag* mentioned (in 3 above) of covering the hair that grows on the temples, does not apply to hair that grows on the neck - see *Mekoros* 22:3.

It has nevertheless become a widespread *minhag* to keep this hair short. This is because if it is long it could appear to people to be hair of the head that is hanging down and is showing at the neck. As explained (at the end of No.3 above) such hair must be covered since it is part of the general hair of the head. If the hairs on the neck are short it is obvious that they have grown on the neck and there is no general *minhag* to make an effort to guarantee that they are concealed - see *Mekoros* 22:4.

6. HAIR OF A MARRIED NON-JEWISH WOMAN: Some *Poskim* write that the hair of a married non-Jewish woman might be considered *ervah* (M.B. 75:12 in the name of the *Chayei Odom*). Their doubt is based on the fact that even non-Jewish women used to cover their hair once they were married (*Sanhedrin* 58b). This indicates that hair-covering is a fundamental requirement for any married woman. There is therefore an element of *pritzus* in not doing so and this might give her hair the status of *ervah*. Other *Poskim*, however, maintain that since non-Jewish women are not obligated to cover their hair after marriage, and nowadays most do not do so, there is no reason for their hair to be considered *ervah* (*Derech Hachayim* No.1, *Kaf Hachayim* 75:16; *Responsa Iggros Moshe* O.H. 4:15; *Yabia Omer* 6:13:5).

B. COVERING HAIR IN PRIVACY

There are four reasons why a married woman should preferably cover her hair even when she is at home and no one besides her husband can see her. They are as follows:-

1. *REASON ONE* -

- OPINIONS THAT HAIR IS COVERED INDOORS, MIDRABANAN: According to most opinions, when a woman is in the total privacy of her home she has no *halachic* obligation to cover her hair. However, some opinions maintain that a woman must cover her hair even in the total privacy of her home, except when her physical needs require that her hair be uncovered e.g. when showering. Since the hair of a married woman has been labeled *ervah* by *Chazal*, they consider it a lack of *tznius* to leave the hair uncovered even in private. The *Mishna Berura* is of the opinion that one should preferably be stringent in this matter (*Biur Halacha* 75:2 s.v. *Michutz*). Accordingly, it is commendable that a woman has her hair covered with a *tiechel* when she goes to sleep at night - see *Mekoros* 23:1-8.

On contemplation, a person must be overwhelmed at the *kedusha* which permeates every aspect of a Jewish person's life. Even when alone, he is aware of a "Presence" and behaves with the same respect and dignity as when other people are around - מי כעמך ישראל גוי אחד בארץ.

2. *REASON TWO* -

- CHAZAL HIGHLY COMMEND TZNIUS PRACTICED IN PRIVACY: The *Poskim* write that even the lenient opinion (that maintains that she is not *halachically* duty-bound to cover her hair in privacy) agrees that it is an extremely praiseworthy act of *tznius* for a woman to cover her hair whenever possible (even in bed). This is evident from the story of Kimchis. This outstanding woman merited having seven sons who all became *Kohanim*

Gedolim. When asked what notable deed she did to merit having such children she answered, "The ceiling beams of my house never saw the hair of my head" (*Yuma* 47a). This means that even when she wished to comb her hair she would avoid exposing the hair properly. For example, she combed the hair under a shawl that lay loosely over her head - see *Mekoros* 83:4.

This was an outstanding act of *tznius* and it is certainly not expected of the average woman. However, the basic idea of reducing the exposure of hair to the absolute minimum is certainly to be learned from Kimchis, and her ways should be emulated as far as possible. As a result of this particular form of *tznius*, a woman could merit to have children who are great *Talmidei Chachamim*.

This recommendation is greatly strengthened by the fact that the *Zohar* lays very great stress on women covering all their hair whenever possible, (as will be mentioned in 5:C:3 below - M.B. 75:14). Therefore, although the average woman is certainly not expected to be like Kimchis, the *Poskim* recommend that she endeavors to follow the words of the *Zohar* and that her hair is kept covered whenever reasonably possible - see *Magen Avraham* 75:5 and *Mekoros* 23:9-12.

3. *REASON THREE* -
- HER HUSBAND MIGHT SAY BRACHOS FACING HER HAIR: According to the opinions that there is no *halachic* obligation to cover the hair when in private, there is still a serious consideration due to which the *Chofetz Chayim* recommends that a woman covers her hair. This is that the hair of a married woman is *ervah* to everyone, even her husband (שער באשה ערוה), and it is *ossur* for any man to say a *bracha* or *davar shebikdusha* when facing the hair even if the woman is in a place where she has no strict obligation to cover her hair (M.B. 75:10). See 6:Q:2 below and *Mekoros* 23:12.

The probability of transgressing the *issur* should not be underestimated. For example, if a husband or son says a *bracha* or sings *zemiros* when facing his wife/mother whose hair is uncovered he has transgressed an *issur*. Moreover, any *dvar* Torah the husband tells his wife will require that he avoids facing her at the time, since when facing her and all the more when looking at her, he is in a position also to look at her uncovered hair. Similarly, if a husband says *krias shema* in his bed while facing his wife whose hair is uncovered he is saying a *davar shebikdusha* in front of *ervah*. Due to the prevalence of these considerable pitfalls, it is highly recommended that a woman covers her hair whenever possible (*Chofetz Chayim* in *Geder Olam*, Chapter Two and letter of the *Chofetz Chayim*, printed in the *sefer*, *Chofetz Chayim Al HaTorah*, page 322).

It is clear from the words of the *Chofetz Chayim*, that he maintains that the opinion which permits a woman to leave her hair uncovered indoors (*Mogen Avraham* 75:5), allows this only for a short time but not that she spends the whole day with her hair uncovered. To do so is wrong according to all opinions because it will inevitably cause her husband and sons to say improper *brachos*. It must also be made clear that even the opinion which is *halachically* lenient quotes the *Zohar* mentioned above, and recommends that one follows the words of the *Zohar*.

4. *REASON FOUR* -
- HER HAIR SHOULD BE COVERED FOR HER OWN BRACHOS: An additional reason why a married woman should keep her hair covered even indoors is the fact that a married woman should not say a *bracha* when her hair is uncovered. This is the opinion of many *Poskim* who maintain that just as a woman's hair must be covered when she is in public, so it must likewise be covered when she says a *bracha*. They surmise that just as a man should not say a *bracha* when his hair is uncovered (O.C. 91:3, O.C. 206:3, M.B. 2:12), so too, a married woman should not say a *bracha* when her hair is uncovered. In their opinion in both cases it is *kalus rosh* (being distinctly disrespectful) to say a *bracha* "with a bare head" as this symbolizes the removal of the Heavenly yoke (*Trumas Hadeshen* 10).

This is the opinion of the *Chesed L'Alafim* O.C. 2:8 (quoted in *Responsa Yabia Omer* 6:15:11)*; the Tzror Hamor* (quoted in *sefer Halichos Beisah* 6:15 and *Taam V'Daas, parshas Nassoh* s.v. *V'Omrah*). This is also the opinion of *Responsa Yaskil Avdi* Vol. 7 page 289. Similarly, the *Ben Ish Chai*, second year, *Shemini* 19 and the *Amoros T'horos* on *Hilchos Tevilah* by the *Gaon MiButchatch* No.20 write that women should cover their hair when saying a *bracha*. They do not, however, state that they have the same severity as a man, as do the first three *Poskim* quoted.

It should furthermore be noted, that even an opinion which holds that women may say a *bracha* with uncovered hair agrees that it is a widely accepted *minhag* that married women cover their hair before saying a *bracha* (*Halichos Bas Yisroel* note 5:6 in the name of Hagaon Harav Shlomo Zalman Auerbach *zt'l*).

In addition, a woman should certainly not *daven* with her hair uncovered. *Davening*, which is an audience with *Hashem*, requires that the person is dressed in a respectable manner, which is in clothes that he would gladly go out in. For example, a person should not *daven* in nightclothes, a bedroom robe (M.B. 91:11), without socks so that part of the foot is visible (M.B. 91:12) or in a yarmulke that is not covered by Tallis or hat (*ibid.*). Similarly, working clothes which a person would not wear when amongst other people, such as an apron, should be removed before *davening* (*ibid.*). Returning to uncovered hair - since it is an embarrassment for a married woman to be seen with her hair exposed (*Rashi*, *Bamidbor* 5:17 s.v. *Uporah* and *Rashi Kesubos* 72a s.v. *Azhara*) it is obvious that her hair must be covered before *davening*.

Since a woman should cover her hair before saying a *bracha*, which is said frequently throughout the day, and before *davening*, it is obvious that her hair should be covered at all times of the day, since otherwise she is bound to err. This reason is in addition to the first three significant reasons stated, due to which hair should be covered even indoors. Apart from all these reasons, one must consider visitors who frequently come to the house such as the *chavrusos* (learning partners) of her husband or grown up sons, school friends of her boys, nephews who come to visit, guests who come for a meal and general callers to whom she regularly opens the front door. If she does not always have her hair covered, the obligation of *kisuy sa'aros* will inevitably be transgressed on many occasions.

5. CLOSING COMMENT: Besides all the valid reasons that have been given above, a major point that concerns the welfare of the Jewish people is associated with this issue. This is directly related to the third reason mentioned above, the *issur* for a man to say a *bracha* facing uncovered hair. It is expressed in a letter by the *Chofetz Chayim*, (printed at the end of *Chofetz Chayim Al HaTorah* page 322). The letter, dated *Tammuz* 5684, was written at a time when great financial difficulties befell the Jewish people and the *Yeshivos* were in desperate financial straits. In his letter the *Chofetz Chayim* attributes all the *tzaros* to the fact that women were lax with matters of *tznius* and walked around their homes with uncovered hair, short sleeves and even sleeveless dresses. This caused their husbands and sons to say many *brachos* in front of *ervah*, which is a profanation of *Hashem*'s name. The *Chofetz Chayim* writes as follows (translated loosely, but as accurately as possible):-

"*Chazal* say that all parts of the female body that should be covered are *ervah*. Today, due to our many sins, serious breaches occur concerning this *halacha*. The *yetzer horah* entices women to go around in their houses with uncovered hair, sleeveless dresses and deeply cut out necklines, in a way that almost wherever a person looks he faces *ervah*. As a result of this, many of the *brachos* he says in his own house or when he *davens* at home facing his wife or grown up daughter are 'improperly made *brachos*', as they are said facing *ervah*.

"As everyone knows, a *bracha* contains the holy name of *Hashem*. When a *bracha* is said properly the *bracha* brings blessings upon the person as the verse says, בכל מקום אשר אזכיר את שמי אבוא אליך וברכתיך - 'Wherever you mention My name [in a respectable manner] I shall come and bless you [with wealth]' (*Shemos* 20:24). The same applies in the reverse, G-d forbid. When *brachos* are said facing *ervah* this causes poverty, as *Chazal* say (*Nedarim* 7b), בכל מקום שהזכרת השם מצויה שם עניות מצויה - 'In all places where the name of *Hashem* is mentioned [improperly] poverty is to be found'. On this *Gemara, Rabbeinu Nissim* writes, 'Since the positive mention of *Hashem*'s Name brings financial benefits, the negative mention of *Hashem*'s Name has the opposite effect and causes the curse of poverty'....... Consequently, it should not surprise us that the Heavenly blessings cease to flow and that people's earnings have dwindled drastically etc."

Such are the bitter fruits of undermining a support pillar of *kedushas Yisroel*. It is exactly as was predicted in the *Zohar* quoted in full in 5:C:3 below.

A change of attitude will certainly help enormously in procuring the correct mode of conduct. Instead of covering the hair being viewed as a restraint and encumbrance, it should be considered as the crown and glory of the Jewish woman, which is what it truly is.

It should be noted that the previous *Rav* of *Komemiyus*, Hagaon Harav Binyamin Mendelson *zt'l* related that he heard the following from the *Chazon Ish*:- **"The extent of a woman's *Yiras Shomayim* can be assessed by the way she covers her hair. As careful as she is with covering her hair, so authentic and genuine is her *Yiras Shomayim*"** (*Pe'er Hador* Vol 3 page 18).

C. LEAVING FRONT OF THE HAIR UNCOVERED

1. THE OPINIONS OF THE POSKIM: According to almost all *Poskim* - amongst them the *Responsa Chasam Sofer* O.C. 36; M.B. 75:10, *Chazon Ish* (quoted in *Responsa Teshuvos V'Hanhagos* 1:62, 2:692) and the *Gedolei ḤaPoskim* of our generation (see their ruling in *Mekoros* 1:6) a woman must cover all her hair when in public and there is no *heter* for even a minor part of the hair to be uncovered over her forehead - see *Mekoros* 24:17-19. Unfortunately, some women have taken the liberty of leaving some of their hair uncovered basing themselves on their understanding of a ruling given in *Responsa Iggros Moshe* (O.C. 4:112). In truth, even in this *Teshuva* (Responsum) no general *heter* was given. This is fully evident from the wording of the *Teshuva* itself. For women to freely leave some hair uncovered on the basis of this *Teshuva* is a departure from the intention of its great author *zt'l* as will be explained - see *Mekoros* 24:1.

This is a matter of paramount importance as it is a violation of an aspect of *tznius* that is spelt out explicitly in the Torah (*Bamidbar* 5:18). Evidently, this aspect of *tznius* infuses considerable *tahara* into the Jewish home. Therefore, to undermine it, is tantamount to ravaging a central pillar of *taharas Yisroel*. To clarify this matter further, the following points should be noted carefully.

2. AN OPINION THAT GIVES A HETER IN SOME CIRCUMSTANCES: As mentioned, there is a general misconception concerning the nature of the *heter* given in the *Iggros Moshe*. People assume that Maran Hagaon Harav Moshe Feinstein *zt'l* allowed women to leave less than a *tefach* uncovered. This is totally incorrect. He allowed this only under pressing circumstances as is evident from the wording at the beginning of the Responsum. To dispel incorrect interpretations the translation of a testimony by Harav Dovid Halpern *shlita*, *Rav* of *Beis Hamidrash* Hendon, London, has been incorporated (see *Mekoros* 24:18 for original text) :-

On the fourth of Shevat 5754 I had an audience with Hagaon Rav Dovid Feinstein שליט״א son of הגאון המפורסם רשכבה״ג מורה״ר ר׳ משה פיינשטיין זצ״ל and we spoke about the ruling of his father zt'l concerning the hair of a married woman. Hagaon Rav Dovid shlita said to me that it is clear from the text of the Teshuva that his father zt'l never intended to give an all-out heter for the exposure of two finger widths of hair. The Teshuva was a personal heter given for an exceptional case - as he writes, 'she [the lady who did not agree to cover her hair] should not be considered a major sinner ח״ו'. This is also indicated from the introductory words of the teshuva. 'In the first place I intended not to answer your query in writing as it is adequate that I give a verbal heter when the circumstances justify it etc.' The Responsum also finishes with the words 'It is correct for women to be stringent and cover their hair completely as the Chasam Sofer held.' All this clearly implies that no general heter was given.

I then showed Hagaon Rav Dovid shlita a letter written by Hagaon Rav Nissim Karelitz shlita of Bnei Brak. In it he writes the following: 'Some justify their action of not covering all their hair by saying that this was the opinion of the great Gaon, the author of the Iggros Moshe zt'l. However, whoever learns the Teshuva from beginning to end will see clearly that it was written only for a special case and it is clear from the wording of the Teshuva that girls and women should be educated to cover all their hair'. Hagaon Rav Dovid shlita agreed to the content of the letter.

I furthermore had the considerable merit of having an audience with Hagaon Rav Avraham Pam shlita on the sixth of Shevat 5754. I showed him the complete text I had written after my visit to Hagaon Rav Dovid shlita. His response was that it is absolutely clear from the Teshuva that this is the true interpretation of it and that no collective heter was given to leave some hair uncovered.

(Harav) Dovid, son of Hagaon Harav Elchanan Halpern shlita.

An inquiry was made concerning the letter written by my esteemed friend Harav Dovid Halpern *shlita*, as to whether the Gaon Harav Dovid Feinstein *shlita* was willing that the testimony contained in the letter be publicized. Harav Hagaon R' Mattisyahu Salomon *shlita*, *Mashgiach Ruchni Yeshivas Gateshead* UK, now of *Beis Medrash Govoha*, *Lakewood*, New Jersey U.S.A. had occasion to be in the United States shortly after the above mentioned letter was written. He visited Hagaon Harav Dovid Feinstein *shlita* and presented him with this question. After the visit, Harav Salomon *shlita* released the following letter. It has been loosely translated from its original in *lashon haKodesh* - see original text in *Mekoros* 24:18. It reads as follows :-

I visited the Gaon Moreinu Harav Dovid Feinstein shlita in the month of Adar, 5754. While I was there, I showed him the letter written by Hagaon Harav Dovid Halpern shlita and asked him whether he grants permission for this letter to be publicized in England. Hagaon Harav Dovid Feinstein shlita took the letter, read it slowly and carefully, and responded that he is in agreement and gives permission.

I then asked him whether he just allows us to publicize the letter or whether he means that there is an obligation and a positive duty to publicize the letter. He responded with a question, 'What will happen if you publicize it in England? Will people actually listen to you and follow the letter?' To this I said, 'There are many people who will not accept it from me, but there are also a large number of people who will accept what I say. They will respond favorably when they hear from a reliable source that they erred in their understanding of the opinion of his father the great Gaon ztl'. To this Hagaon Harav Feinstein shlita responded firmly and resolutely, 'If so, it is a mitzva to publicize this letter as it will hopefully prevent people from stumbling'.

I am hereby fulfilling the instructions of one of the foremost Chachmei HaTorah of our times. I am publicizing his opinion and thereby taking steps to remove a michshol (a stumbling block) from before the Jewish people.

(Harav) Mattisyahu Chayim Salomon.

This matter was also discussed with other *Gedolim* in *Eretz Yisroel,* (Hagaon Harav Nissim Karelitz *shlita* and Hagaon Harav Chayim Pinchas Scheinberg *shlita*) and they too concurred that it is erroneous to construe the ruling as if it is a *heter* for women to do so in the first place. See letter signed by these two Gedolim in *Mekoros* 24:18.

[Apart from all the above, a discrepancy must be pointed out. The ruling mentioned (O.C. 4:112) is written in a Responsum dated 5717 and again in a Responsum (E.H. 1:58) dated 5721. There is, however, a third Responsum (O.C. 4:15) dated 5732 in which it is written explicitly that even less than a *tefach* of hair must be covered in line with other "covered areas" of a woman's body which must be fully covered and even less than a *tefach* may not be exposed. See *Mekoros* 24:12 where this subject is discussed at length].

In addition to all the above, experience has shown that those who are lenient quickly take liberties, willingly or accidentally and expose more of their hair than the *Iggros Moshe* allows even under the most pressing circumstances. The *Iggros Moshe* stipulates that the visible strip which is about two *tefochim* long (18 cm. as wide as the forehead) must be less than half a *tefach* wide (i.e. less than 4.5 cm. wide) because if it is half a *tefach* wide the area showing will be equivalent to a square *tefach*, and this is definitely *ossur*. The facts are that those who leave hair open invariably leave a strip that is 4.5 cm. wide or more and for this there is no justification, as explained. Even if during the first hour of the day the hair showing is less than two inches wide, it easily slips back with the passage of time and during much of the day more hair can be showing than is justifiable according to any opinion.

It follows from all that has been explained that the trend to wear a snood or beret which covers most but not all the hair, is a departure from *halacha* and the *derech hayashar* - the path followed by *Klal Yisroel* from the earliest times. To claim that there is an unqualified *heter* by one of the *Gedolei Hador* of our times to dress in this way, is fallacious as explained above.

3. KABBALAH: GREAT DAMAGE IS DONE BY EXPOSING HAIR: All opinions agree that Kabbalistically a woman harms herself, her husband and children by partially exposing some of her hair. Moreover, those that leave some hair uncovered usually do so in order to look more attractive and from the *Zohar* it is evident that when the hair is uncovered to attract attention, the harm and damage done is even greater.

The importance attached by the *Poskim* to this *Zohar* is quite exceptional. The *Magen Avraham*, *Mishna Berura* and *Chasam Sofer* hardly ever mention Kabbalistic opinions in the context of a *halachic* analysis. In this matter however, they all quote the *Zohar Hakadosh* (*Nossoh,* page 125) and strongly recommend that one heeds its warning. See *Magen Avraham* 75:4, *Mishna Berura* 75:14, and *Chasam Sofer* O.C. 36. The *Zohar* says the following (the original Aramaic can be found in *Mekoros* 25:1-2 :-

> *Rabbi Chizkia said, 'Cursed be the man who allows his wife to expose hairs of her head beyond their covering. Covering the hair is one of the acts of modesty that should be performed even in the home (i.e. not just in public). The woman who allows some of her hair to be uncovered in order to exhibit it causes poverty to descend on her home, her children not to reach the prominence they could have achieved, and an impure spirit to dwell in her home. What precipitates such misfortunes? The hair that she exposed within her house! If the effect of an indoor exposure is*

such, imagine what damage is caused by exposing hair outdoors..... A woman should, therefore, ensure that not even a single hair is uncovered even when she is indoors, and all the more so when she goes outdoors'.

If women would realize the harm they inflict upon themselves by being lenient, they would surely return to the traditional Jewish way of covering all their hair. It is tragic that such an important *Chazal* as this *Zohar* is not more widely known.

4. IF LOCAL WOMEN COVER ALL THE HAIR, ALL MUST DO SO: Those who reveal some of their hair although they live in a place where the general practice is to keep all hair covered [disregarding the warnings of the *Zohar* mentioned in the previous point], are unaware of a *halacha*. The *halacha* states that if the accepted way of Orthodox women is voluntarily to cover a certain area then, even though there is no *halachic* reason to do so, it becomes a binding obligation on every woman in that place, since it becomes מקום שדרכו להיות מכוסה (M.B. 75:2 and *Ben Ish Chai parshas Bo,* 12).

Therefore, if a woman lives in an area where the general way of dress of Orthodox women involves covering the hair entirely, it is *ossur* according to all opinions for her to leave a small part of her hair uncovered when going out in public. By claiming that she is relying on an opinion that is lenient, she is in fact displaying ignorance of *halacha*.

5. CLOSING COMMENT: We live in a time when the importance and far-reaching effect of *kisuy sa'aros* is little understood and is under threat, being presented by some as a matter of little significance. In truth, authentic *Yiddishkeit* and the whole character of the Jewish home are dependent on women practicing all aspects of *tznius* properly. The saying of *Chazal*, כהררים התלוים בשערה - "They are like mountains that hang on a hair" (*Mishna Chagiga* 10a) is highly appropriate to our issue. It is most significant that the great *Chasam Sofer zt'l* and Harav Samson Raphael Hirsch *zt'l* who both succeeded in establishing healthy and vibrant centers of *Yiddishkeit* were great campaigners for this *mitzva* and instilled a deep respect and reverence for it amongst their followers.

The *Navi* says, נפלה עטרת ראשנו אוי נא לנו כי חטאנו - "The crown of our head has fallen; Woe unto us for we have sinned" (*Eichah* 5:16). Due to our sins and lack of *kedusha,* the crown of our heads - the beautiful *mitzva* of *kisuy sa'aros* - has fallen. The crown is however not broken. It is up to us to pick it up and return it once again to its rightful place. With that we will awaken once again within ourselves the deep rooted feelings for real *tznius* and *kedushas Yisroel.*

D. SHEITELS

1. A SHEITEL MADE FROM SYNTHETIC OR REAL HAIR: It has been widely accepted in *Klal Yisroel* that a woman may cover her hair with a *sheitel* (M.B. 75:15) although there are opinions which are strongly opposed to it - see *Mekoros* 28:1. Amongst those who permit a *sheitel* are the *Rema* (O.C. 75:2) and the *Magen Avraham* (75:5). They maintain that although a woman may not go out with her natural hair on display, a *sheitel* is no more than a garment made of hair, and neither the Torah nor *Chazal* forbade wearing such an item. A *sheitel* is therefore permitted according to these opinions whether it is made of synthetic hair or human hair. There are, however, conflicting opinions as to whether a woman may wear a *sheitel* made from her own hair. This should therefore be avoided (M.B. 75:15).

Should a woman settle in a community where women do not wear a *sheitel* because they follow the *Poskim* who forbid it, she is obliged to conduct herself according to the prevailing custom and not wear a *sheitel* - see 1:G above. Amongst those who forbid *sheitels* are the *Be'er Sheva* No.18 and the *Chasam Sofer* in his commentaries on O.C. 75:2 (the *Chasam Sofer* might, however, refer only to human hair *sheitels)* - see 5:D:5(c) below.

When a woman wears a *sheitel* that is the same, or almost the same color as her own hair, she must take special care to ensure that no part of her own hair hangs out and passes as just part of the *sheitel.* It is understood that the longer she allows her hair to be, the greater the danger of this happening. Therefore, once a woman needs a haircut she should not delay it unnecessarily as this can result in some of her hair showing. It should furthermore be noted that the *Chofetz Chayim* writes in *Taharas Yisroel* (Chapter 13, Note 19) that it is praiseworthy practice for married women to keep their hair short, for reasons other than that her hair might show - see *Mekoros* 1:6.

2. THE GREAT EXALTATION OF THE MITZVA OF COVERING HAIR: The head-covering is one of the most cherished pieces of clothing a woman possesses. With it she fulfills a great *mitzva min haTorah* and it bestows on her many exceptional side benefits that emanate from fulfilling a *mitzva* that is founded on *tznius*, the most important characteristic of the *Bas Yisroel*:-

(a) She demonstrates submission to *Hashem*'s wishes: When wearing a head-covering a woman conceals this natural source of attraction from the eye of the public and thereby demonstrates that she is a servant of *Hashem*. She places His wish, that an *eishes ish* (a married woman) covers her hair and conceals it from the view of the public, above her own natural desire to look attractive and enhance her appearance by displaying her natural hair.

(b) She demonstrates the purity of Jewish family life: The head-covering symbolizes the *kedusha* of the Jewish family, in which the wife dedicates her life to her husband to the near-total exclusion of any form of contact with other men. She therefore withholds the *chein* of her hair from the view of the general public (*Trumas Hadeshen* No.10) - see *Mekoros* 21:3, 28:3.

(c) It is a source of *Yiras Shomayim*: When this *mitzva* is kept properly and with the correct attitude it imparts considerable *Yiras Shomayim* to the person. Men cover their head with a *yarmulke* or hat in line with the recommendation of *Chazal*, כסי רישיך כי היכי דתהוי עלך אימתא דשמיא - "Cover your head so that you shall experience the fear of Heaven" (*Shabbos* 156b). If covering just part of the head as is practiced by men has such an effect, how much more must covering the complete head have a deep and far reaching effect on a woman's *Yiras Shomayim*.

(d) It is a source of *Kedusha* and inspiration: Considering that the head is the most distinguished and most significant part of the human body as *Chazal* say, ראש מלך על כל אבריו - "The head is king over all the limbs" (*Shabbos* 61a), the influence of *kedusha* that is transmitted to the whole person by a *mitzva* done continuously with the head must be immeasurable. Significantly, *Chazal* say that when a man wears *tefillin* he has a special defense against serious sin (*Menachos* 43b). Accordingly, a woman who lacks the outstanding *mitzva* of *kisuy sa'aros*, because she does not fulfill its *halachic* requirements, withholds from herself a vital source of spirituality and inspiration.

(e) It protects from illness and pain: Who can assess the physical advantage, in protecting the person from illness and pain, that is gained from an unceasing *mitzva* such as *kisuy sa'aros*. *Chazal* have taught us that a person is protected while he fulfills a *mitzva*, as they say, מצוה בעידנא דעסיק בה מגנא ומצלא - "While a *mitzva* is being carried out it shields and safeguards the person" (*Sotah* 21a). Hence, a *mitzva* that is done over many hours of the day is a highly prized source of protection. Similarly, the *mezuzah*, which is an ongoing *mitzva* fulfilled at all times, is singled out by *Chazal* as a *mitzva* which offers exceptional protection to people (*Shabbos* 32b).

(f) It procures great dividends: The head-covering enables a woman to fulfill the *mitzva* of *kisuy sa'aros* minute by minute throughout the day, thereby enabling her to earn great riches both in this world and in the world to come - see C:3 above. While a man adorns his head with *tefillin* for about an hour a day, a woman has the merit to adorn her head with an article of *mitzva* throughout the length of the day. In fact, one of the great *Rabbanim* of our generation, Hagaon Rav Shimon Schwab *zt'l,* once said that women are not obligated in the *mitzva* of *tefillin* because they wear "their *tefillin*" throughout all hours of the day. They therefore do not require the added sanctification of *tefillin* as in the case of men - (see 6:F:5 below, concerning *Tefillin shel Yad*).

Since the head-covering plays such an important role, it is only fitting that it displays the inner refinement and sensitivities of the *Bas Yisroel*. It should therefore be an article of clothing which adds luster and aristocracy to the royal status of the Jewish woman who is a *Bas Melachim*.

(g) The difference between a married woman and an unmarried girl: The Torah allows a girl to appear in public with her hair uncovered although it adds considerably to her *chein* and demonstrates her natural good looks whilst the Torah considers it *pritzus* for a married woman to do so. As mentioned previously, even the *umos ha'olam* understood this and expected their wives to cover their hair in public - see *Sanhedrin* 58b. A married woman is an *eishes ish* and this warrants that part of her beauty be withheld from the public eye. Although she should dress pleasantly and graciously in a manner which reflects her *simcha* and nobility, she should not display her full natural *chein* for everyone to see. (See this point in *Urah Kavodi* by Hagaon Harav Avigdor Miller *shlita* page 222 and *Mi Yirpeh Lach*, page 203).

On the other hand, an unmarried girl need not mask part of her natural *chein* and may allow her hair to reflect her natural good looks (although not in a way that draws attention to herself). An unmarried girl is not an *eishes ish* and there is therefore no need for her to cover her hair to withhold part of her *chein* from the public eye. Also, her good appearance can aid in finding her future partner in life. There is therefore a positive reason for her hair not to be covered and hidden - see *Kesubos* 52b. See also 1:N:3 above, 7:K:1 below and *Mekoros* 28:3-7.

(h) Additional reasons culled from *Chazal* for this special mitzva: Apart for the reason just given why a married woman must cover her hair, there are at least two additional reasons for this special *mitzva* that can be derived from the teachings of *Chazal*.

- Firstly, "covering and enwrapping the head" symbolizes the desire to be left alone and not wishing to socialize with everyone. For this reason, in the times of *Chazal*, a mourner would sit with his head covered and wrapped, known as עטיפת הראש - see Y.D. 386. In his grief he could not socialize nor did he want to. If people came to visit him and convey their condolence he was grateful, but he was certainly not in a mood to socialize in an enjoyable and lighthearted manner. Similarly, a *metzorah* - a leper, would sit alone with his head covered and enwrapped to help him realize the enormity of the sins he had transgressed - see *Vayikrah* 13:45. He was to sit outside the three camps and also to dress in a way that helped him feel that he was not fit to enjoy proper contact with people.

Although the issues are far from identical, this is one of the prime inner reasons for the *mitzva* of *kisuy sa'aros*. By covering her head, which is a half measure of "covering and enwrapping the head", the married woman is saying to men whom she comes across that she 'wants to be left alone' and is neither available for marriage nor for other types of unnecessary contact. Had Chava not caused Adam to sin, in which case the *yetzer horah* would have been far less intense, this symbol would not have been necessary, and she could have left her hair uncovered. However, now that the *yetzer horah* has been internalized and become a potent force, she must be safeguarded from all forms of immorality by this *mitzva*.

Hence, *Chazal* say in *Eruvin* (100b) that after the sin of the *eitz hadaas* Chava was told that from hereafter she was to be עטופה כאבל - "[partially] covered like a mourner" referring to the *mitzva* of *kisuy saaros*. This does not mean that she should look unpleasant or that she should walk around downhearted like a mourner. It means that she covers her hair as a sign to the public of 'wanting to be left alone', just as this is the message inherent in a mourner covering and enwrapping his head. She is telling the world, "I am a married woman and do not want to be sought after by men other than my husband" (*Responsa Shevus Yaacov* 2:11 and *Birkei Yosef* Y.D. 393:1).

- A further reason for this *mitzva*, which like the first reason is inferred to by *Chazal*, is as follows: We are told in *T'nach* that after Tamar had been assaulted by Amnon she covered her hair. With this she demonstrated her yearning for modesty and chastity - see *Shmuel* 2:13:19.

Since her privacy had been tampered with, there was a danger that this would harm her natural trait of *busha* and *tznius*. To counter this she covered her hair when in public, thereby practicing an act of modesty which is beyond that of other girls. Marriage, in which a girl who had previously had no contact with men now has a husband, has a similar subtle potential of affecting her natural modesty. To prevent this, the married woman performs the additional modesty of covering her hair, which is a refinement beyond that expected of unmarried girls.

Chazal in *Sifri, Parshas Nasoh,* No. 56 bring the story of Tamar covering her hair after the incident with Amnon as a source for the *mitzva* of *kisuy saaros* by every married woman. With the explanation given this is very well understood since in both cases its function is to preserve her modesty. This also explains why the *mitzva* continues even when a woman is widowed and no longer an *eishes ish - Beis Shmuel* E.H. 21:5. This additional modesty is required *min haTorah* only when she is in public, because the modesty lies in withholding from the public the appearance of her full attraction. That being the case, to appear in public in a manner in which she looks no different to her usual self, is a violation of the very purpose of this *mitzva*.

These far reaching explanations should help people who seek the truth understand why it is wholly against the Torah's intention that a woman's head-covering is so well made that men would not know that she is married and that this is not her true hair - see 5:D:4(a) below for further elaboration.

3. THE PLAGUE OF UNREFINED SHEITELS:

(a) *Sheitels* that are unusual, long or eye-catching:

▪ **Wild unkempt look:** To our deep regret, the *yetzer horah* has succeeded in causing impurity of deed and sometimes even of thought to be associated with the *mitzva* of wearing a head-covering. For example, some *sheitels* have an unkempt wild look to them. Such *sheitels* do not comply with the most basic requirement of *midas hatznius,* since a woman wearing such a *sheitel* will be noticed wherever she goes because of her unusual and disarranged appearance. Also, such *sheitels* demonstrate a carefree approach to life. This is totally out of character for a *tznua* who is blessed with *Yiras Shomayim* and is constantly careful. See 1:A:4(c) above and 7:C:1 below concerning clothes that are very casual. Other *sheitels* have been manufactured or set in elaborate immodest styles and are not fit to be worn by *N'shei Yisroel* who are inherently refined and self effacing.

▪ **Long styles:** Some *sheitels* are long and loose, and lie flowingly over the young woman's shoulders or even hang down her back. There could hardly be a more undignified way of fulfilling this *mitzva* than to copy hair styles sported by the common females of the *umos ha'olam*. In fact, many of the greatest *Poskim* maintain that it is *ossur* even for a girl to have long loose hair as it attracts far too much attention to her and lacks *tznius* (*Magen Avraham* 75:3, *Moir Uketziah* 75, *Responsa Shevus Yaacov* 1:103 - see also 5:H:2(a) below). All the more, it is against *tznius* for a married woman to appear with such a hair-style since a married women is expected to dress with more modestly than unmarried girls - see 5:D:2(g-h) above.

In *Eretz Yisrael* and also in many other communities there is a firm ruling that women should not wear long *sheitels* even when the hair is bound together behind the head. They maintain that such *sheitels* are made to style that is girl-like and not used married women and are therefore not *tznius'dik*. In such places it is *ossur* for the individual to disregard the ruling and the local standard of *tznius*, and wear such a *sheitel*. (See *Mekoros* 1:6 for a statement signed by the *Gedolei Eretz Yisroel*, Hagaon Harav Shlomo Zalman Auerbach *zt'l* and *yibodel l'chayim*, Hagaon Harav Yosef Shalom Elyashiv *shlita*). Even in other places where there is no fixed ruling against wearing long *sheitels* provided the hair is bound together, nevertheless, much speaks for keeping *sheitels* no more than shoulder length, as *sheitels* are far more refined and *eidel* when short.

▪ **Conspicuous, lopsided *Sheitels*:** *Sheitels* that have a deliberate and excessive difference in style on the two sides, e.g. on the right side the hair hangs forward over the eye and covers almost half the face, whilst on the left side it is brushed back behind the ear, are unrefined. This type of style is made to be highly conspicuous. To gain that advantage the woman is prepared to suffer the inconvenience of not being able to use one of her eyes properly. Such styles are naturally attention-seeking and contravene the most basic rule of *tznius* which is to shun attraction and attention - *Responsa Shevet HaLevi*, Preface Vol. 1 and 5:H:1 below. The *sheitel*, which is a *mitzva* article that is culled from the sublime world of true Jewish modesty, is severely degraded by having such a style.

Similarly, *sheitels* that are distinctly lopsided and much longer on the one side than the other, are unrefined. Those with a feeling for *tznius* are deeply distressed by these trends and worry what new *yetzer horah* will emerge tomorrow. They yearn for the day when the exterior of the Orthodox Jewish woman will once again reflect her rich and precious interior.

(b) The wrath of *Hashem* at eye-catching hair creations: These derailments from the tracks of *tznius* did not occur yesterday. On the contrary, they are thousands of years old and are part of a malady about which *Hashem* complained bitterly through His *Navi*, Yeshayohu. The verse in *Yeshaya* 3:16 says ויאמר ה' יען כי גבהו בנות ציון וכו' הלוך וטפוף תלכנה - "*Hashem* complains that He is angered by the haughtiness of the Jewish daughter......she walks bloated". *Rashi* explains, הלך וטפוף: היו קושרות פאות נכריות....עם קליעותיהן שיראו גסות וטפופות - "Bloated means that they used to inflate their hair and turn it into an eye-catching creation by binding foreign pieces of hair onto their own hair. This caused their hair to stand tall and look grossly enlarged". They did this in order to exhibit and parade their beauty whilst for basic good-looks and delightful appearance, brushing and styling their natural hair would have been quite adequate.

The condemnation of *Yeshaya HaNavi* refers to unmarried girls who artificially aggrandized their hair by turning it into a grossly enlarged creation. This was so detrimental that it aroused *Hashem*'s wrath with Jewish girls in particular and the Jewish people in general, and contributed towards the *churban habayis*. It is all the more unfitting when a married woman, from whom *Hashem* expects extra modesty, exhibits an inflated eye-catching hair covering. When she does so, she drives away and even expels the *kedusha* that she would have infused into the community through the *mitzva* of *kisuy sa'aros*, which is a central feature in *tznius* and *kedushas Yisroel*.

(c) The distressing association between the wig and foreign cultures: Even the names given to some styles of *sheitels* e.g. "Girly", "Bahama", "Fiji", "Little Rascal", "Rapture" (and some names that are too repulsive to quote) reflect the low standard of morality prevalent in today's society. Although these names may be designed to attract the non-Jewish market, advertising them under these names in the Jewish press and in Jewish *sheitel* stores (and in some cases even in a home with children around, when the mother sells *sheitels* from the house) associates *sheitels* with the fashion houses of Paris rather than *kedushas Yisroel*. It is difficult to remain silent when experiencing how שפחה כי תירש גברתה - "a low maidservant replaces her mistress" (*Mishlei* 30:23). The wig worn by *nochrios* replaces the *sheitel* worn by the *Bas Yisroel*. We have abandoned an item which radiates *tahara* and depicts inner qualities.- an item that is the splendor of *N'shei Yisroel*.

(d) A *sheitel* refined on one woman might not be refined on another: It should be noted that a *sheitel* which looks refined on one person might look unrefined or even girl-like on a second person. Some styles suit a broad face not a narrow face, whilst others are just the opposite. The same applies to the length of any particular *sheitel*. A certain length might look fine on a rounder face but very unrefined or have a girl-like appearance on a longish face, and so on. Accordingly, a woman should be cautious and not buy a *sheitel* of a certain style just because it looks perfect on her friend, since the result might be quite different when she tries it on herself. She should likewise not be led astray by poster pictures of women wearing wigs since that *sheitel* might look quite different when it is on her head.

4. A SHEITEL SO WELL MADE THAT IT IS BARELY DETECTABLE:

(a) It should be immediately apparent that the hair is covered: In our day and age, it has become necessary to stress something which is of a most elementary nature. This is that it is totally incorrect and against the will of the Torah for a woman to wear a *sheitel* that has been manufactured to such perfection that to an onlooker (who does not know she is married) she appears to be an unmarried girl. As is well known, many custom-made *sheitels* are made to this level of undetectability.

Wearing such a *sheitel* contravenes the commandment that a married woman must cover her hair, which the *Poskim* say is so that men other than her husband are not attracted to her when she is an *eishes ish* - see *Trumas Hadeshen* No. 10 and *Rosh, Kesubos* 72a. See also *Mekoros* 28:1-2. It is therefore obvious that it should be immediately evident that she is wearing a *sheitel*, and that the *chein* which is apparent is due to a *sheitel* not to her true hair. To circumvent and outwit this Torah obligation completely violates the spirit of the law and is forbidden.

The following is written in *Responsa Chesed L'Avraham*, E.H. No. 87:- האיסור בגילוי שיער משום פריצות שהיא מתנאית לבני אדם, מה לי שיער עצמן או שיער נכרית שנראין כשערות עצמן, תורה אחת להם ואסור מן התורה - loosely translated this means, "Since it is *ossur* to uncover hair because she thereby displays her beauty to people, what difference does it make whether she reveals her own hair or displays a wig which looks as if it is her own hair etc"?

There are actually some young women who look more "girl-like" in their *sheitels* than real girls. [See *Gemara* (*Nazir* 28b) that there is a way of making a wig to such perfection that it has as much *chein* and beauty as true hair - see *Bigdei Shalom V'emes,* page 43]. This could not be further from the will of *Hashem* Who has indicated that a married woman is to conceal some of her beauty from the public eye by covering her hair. *Rashi* writes (*Kesubos* 72a s.v. *Azhara*) that the hair of the *sotah* was uncovered in *Beis Din* because, כמו שעשתה להתנאות על בועלה - "it is presumed that [if she was *mezaneh*] this is what she did in order to beautify herself in the eyes of her suitor". This *Rashi* is clear proof that a girl with her hair uncovered is more attractive than a married woman with her hair covered. Otherwise, why should it be assumed that the *sotah* uncovered her hair? Therefore, for a married woman to cover her hair in a way that she looks as attractive as a girl violates the essence and character of this *mitzva*.

Apart from the above, there is an obvious reason why it should be immediately apparent that a woman is married and no longer a girl. Although it is forbidden for a man to study the features of a married woman due to the *issur* of *v'lo sosuru acharei eineichem* (*Biur Halacha* 225 s.v. *Afilu*) it is permissible to study the features of an unmarried girl if it is for the sake of marriage. A prospective *chasan* may look at a girl to see if he likes her (*Kiddushin* 41a) and so may a father looking for a *shiduch* for his son, a brother looking for a *shiduch* for his younger brother or anyone who is busy with *shiduchim* (*Avos d'Rebi Nosson* 2:5). All such people may look at the girl's countenance, observe how she talks to people and watch how she reacts to certain situations, since all this is needed to form a true impression. Since looking and studying is permitted in the case of an unmarried girl but not with a married woman, it should be immediately obvious that someone is married and no longer available for a *shiduch*.

See also *sefer, Machanecho Kadosh* No.16 who records that married women in *Yerusholayim* wore longer dresses than girls in order to immediately distinguish between them. It was also to protect the married women with an extra measure of *tznius*, just as the Torah commands her to cover her hair in public - see *Mekoros* 21:3-5.

This Daas Torah is expressed in a statement that appears in *Mekoros* 28:14 signed by the great *Poskim*, Hagaon Harav Shlomo Zalman Auerbach *zt'l*, *lehibodel l'chayim*, Hagaon Harav Yosef Shalom Elyashiv *shlita*, Hagaon Harav Shmuel HaLevi Wosner *shlita* and Hagaon Harav Nissim Karelitz *shlita*). They write particularly bitterly about this matter, as they consider it as a fundamental disloyalty to the *mitzvos* of the Torah. This was also the view of Maran Hagaon Harav Yaacov Yisroel Kanievsky *zt'l*, the Steipler Gaon - see his letter in *K'reina D'igrsa* 2:124. This ruling is also to be found in earlier *Poskim* - see *Responsa Maharil Diskin, Kuntres Acharon* 213 and *Responsa T'shuras Shai* 1:570.

Moreover, see 5:D:2(h) above for reasons culled from *Chazal* for this special *mitzva*. In the light of those reasons it is obvious that it should be fully recognizable to the public that she is a married woman and that she is not being seen in her natural hair.

(b) Lack of pride in a *mitzva* demonstrates a lack of appreciation: To those who know that she is a married woman and can therefore detect that she is in fact wearing a *sheitel*, this barely recognizable *sheitel* demonstrates that she does not deem it a privilege to fulfill this *mitzva*, as she is trying to suppress and neutralize it as far as possible.

Women who wear the *sheitels* mentioned would in fact feel highly embarrassed if their grown up sons walked around with a small, barely noticeable *yarmulke* perched somewhere on the back of their heads so that it did not interfere with their handsome appearance. Similarly, they would feel terrible if for aesthetic reasons their husbands decided one day to embed all *mezuzos* around the house into their respective door posts, so that one could hardly tell that the entrances had *mezuzos*. These women would surely confront their sons and husbands with the argument that a *Yid* should gladly and openly do the *mitzvos* just as a soldier proudly displays the medals a king has given him. (See M.B. 8:26 what the *Chofetz Chayim* has to say about those who go out of their way to totally hide every trace of their Tzitzis). Yet, these very same women camouflage their own "article of *mitzva*" and do everything in their power to disguise it and hide it to ensure they look as natural and as pretty as possible.

A further potent comparison is the following. How would a woman feel if her son had a *yarmulke* made for himself that was like a miniature *sheitel* - gauze on the inside and short man-like hair covering it from on top? When he wears it, his head is of course covered. However, to everyone who sees him, he has nothing on his head (see M.B. 2:12). We can well imagine what his distraught mother would say when trying to convince him that it is wrong to brush one's religion under the carpet. The answer he gives, that when out on the street he is ashamed to show that he is a *Yid* and therefore hides it, will of course find very little sympathy with his mother. However, little does his mother realize that she is doing exactly the same as her son. She, with many of her friends, are ashamed or hurt by the fact that *Yiddishkeit* requires them to cover their hair and that they cannot look as perfect and as natural as a girl. They therefore have a *sheitel* made which looks exactly as their own hair. With it they successfully hide a major part of their *Yiddishkeit*, much to the chagrin of all *erlicher Yidden*.

The following incident was related by the Mashgiach Harav Hagaon R' Don Segal *shlita* in his speech he gave in *Bnei Brak* on *Rosh Chodesh Sivan* 5755. "Thirty years ago I was speaking to Hagaon Harav Shlomo Zalman Auerbach (*shlita*) about the prevailing fashions of *sheitels*. He said to me the following, 'If a woman would have turned up in *Yerusholayim* fifty years ago wearing a *sheitel* she would have been stoned (as they followed the opinions which forbade *sheitels*) and in those days *sheitels* were straw-like and could not be confused with real hair. Nowadays, women come to speak to me and I cannot tell whether it is their natural hair that is visible or whether it is a *sheitel*. To me this is absolutely despicable! It is comparable to a person eating kosher meat who does everything in his power to make it appear as if he is eating *treife* meat. So too, these women want to do the *mitzva* of *kisuy sa'aros* but do everything in their power to give the impression that the hair is uncovered. To me this is extremely abhorrent!' These were the words of the *Gaon*" (*Mi Yirpeh Lach* , page 174).

A highly experienced *kallah* teacher in the United Kingdom told the author of this *sefer* that occasionally when she meets one of her *kallos* a few weeks after the young lady's *chasuna*, she has momentary difficulty remembering whether the girl is already married or not, even though she personally attended the girl's wedding. The young lady looks exactly as she looked before her marriage, to the point that her teacher is confused for a while about her status. Is this the *Ratzon Hashem*?

On this breach in *Yiddishkeit* should we not lament with the verse, ויצא מן בת ציון כל הדרה - "the Daughter of *Tzion* has lost all her splendor" (*Eichah* 1:6) - she no longer understands the *chein* that accompanies *shemiras hamitzvos*.

5. THE ISSUR TO APPEAR AS IF ONE IS DOING AN AVEIRA: A person must not do something which gives the impression that he cannot be bothered to do a certain *mitzva* or that he is transgressing one of the laws of the Torah or even just one of the laws enacted by *Chazal*. Although he knows that there will be no truth in the assumption, he is still *halachically* obligated to desist from causing such a misunderstanding, as will be explained.

(a) The obligation of והייתם נקיים מה' ומישראל: If a custom-made *sheitel* is so well made that women who know her and know she is married would mistakenly think that this is her real hair, she transgresses the *issur* of והייתם נקיים מה' ומישראל (*Bamidbar* 32:22) - a person must neither do an *aveirah* nor do something which appears to people to be an *aveirah*. The former is an *aveirah* in the eyes of *Hashem* and the latter is an *aveirah* in the eyes of *Yisroel* - hence the two terms מה׳ ומישראל in the verse. Therefore, if local people would think that she is not wearing a *sheitel* she would transgress the *issur* mentioned - see *Mekoros* 30:1-3.

(b) The *issur* of *chillul Hashem*: Furthermore, by wearing such a *sheitel* she will be responsible for making a considerable *chillul Hashem*. People will say that the emphasis placed by others on covering hair is overstressed and exaggerated, as there are some *frum* young ladies who do not bother to cover their hair at all. Lessening the severity of an *issur* in the eyes of people is a distinct form of *chillul Hashem*, as the Torah of *Hashem* is thereby being profaned (*Yuma* 86a) - see *Mekoros* 9:1.

It may seem that nowadays undetectable custom-made *sheitels* have become so widespread in some communities that everyone in those circles knows that a lady could be wearing a *sheitel* even though they cannot detect it. Should this be correct, neither of the two *issurim* just mentioned would apply (but the two points explained in 5:D:4 would, of course, still apply). The truth of the matter is, however, that at present only a small number of custom-made *sheitels* are so perfect that they are really undetectable. Therefore, when someone has a really undetectable *sheitel* it would still be natural for people to suspect her of not having covered her hair at all.

Furthermore, this can lead to individuals who lack *Yiras Shomayim* taking advantage of custom-made *sheitels* and not covering their hair at all, knowing that they will be able to "get away with it" as people will think they are surely wearing a high-class custom-made *sheitel*. Such deception is recorded in *Chazal* - see *Bava Metziah* 61b and *Rashi, Bamidbar* 15:41 that people who lacked *Yiras Shomayim* would sometimes color a thread of their *tzitzis* with a color that was very similar to *techeiles*, to deceive people into thinking that they had applied true *techeiles* as the *Torah* commands.

To demonstrate just how far removed the ideals and aspirations of those who wear the *sheitels* mentioned are from the attitudes of the Torah as portrayed by *Chazal*, it should be noted that *Rashi* writes in *Kesubos* 72a that a married woman feels disgraced when people see her hair. Similarly, *Rashi* writes in *Bamidbar* 5:18 in the name of *Chazal*, מכאן לבנות ישראל שגילוי הראש גנאי להן - "[From the fact that the hair of the *sotah* is exposed] it is apparent that it is a disgrace for a married woman to have her hair displayed". It is therefore incredible that some married women do everything in their power to cause people to think that the hair which is visible is in fact their own hair. If this is not making a "sham and farce" of the Holy Torah, what is?

(c) Many early *Poskim* were worried that *sheitels* would be misused: It should be noted that over the last four centuries many *Poskim* have maintained that it is *ossur* to wear a *sheitel* altogether (unless concealed under a cover) because it can be mistaken for real hair and the wearer appears not to have her head covered (See *Be'er Sheva* 18, *Divrei Chayim* Y.D. 1:30, 2:59, *Teshuva Meiahava* 48). Even to this day, quite a number of communities do not allow *sheitels* due to the many *Poskim* who forbid it. This was also the *minhag* of the old *yishuv* of *Yerusholayim*. The *Poskim* who nevertheless permitted them were of the opinion that it is immediately apparent that a woman is wearing a *sheitel* and no misunderstanding could occur (*Magen Avraham* 75:5, M.B. 75:15. *Responsa Shnos Chayim* 316 - see *Otzar HaPoskim* 21:24:5). Their *heter* is, of course, invalid if the *sheitel* is made so expertly that it passes for real hair.

(d) Many who do wrong, do so quite innocently: Many who perpetrate these and other wrongdoings are certainly totally unaware of how wrong these misdeeds are, and the negative image they project by behaving in these ways. It could even be that some people will feel offended by the harsh terms that have been used, when in fact, they have done these deeds and worn these garments in total innocence and ignorance. However, the wrongdoings themselves must be condemned in most forthright terms, even though the perpetrators very likely do not deserve such censure. This has to be done because only by exposing the offenses and showing the attitude they project, and by revealing the conscious or subconscious thoughts of those who started off these wrongdoings, will people truly understand how incorrect these ways of dress are, and how detrimental they are to the delicate fabric of *kedushas Yisroel*.

6. THE ISSUR TO WEAR A "WINDOW SHEITEL": We must place on record a most unpleasant *pirtza bechomas hadas* - breach in the fortress of *Yiddishkeit*. This is the "window *sheitel*", which is a *sheitel* with a hole in it. Through it the woman pulls out a section of her own hair. This she mingles with the hair of the *sheitel* that is in the majority, claiming that although her hair improves the appearance of the *sheitel*, her hair is annulled in the majority of synthetic hairs (בטל ברוב). Some do the same without having a hole in the *sheitel*, by drawing some of their hair out from under the side or the back of the *sheitel* and then brushing it over the *sheitel* to give it a "more natural" look. This exposure of hair is totally and absolutely forbidden for the reason just explained. Apart from this, the very desire to ensure that the *sheitel* has a more "natural look" and could pass as her true hair is a *treif* concept. It is totally against the spirit of this *mitzva* and has been roundly condemned by our *Gedolim* - see 5:D:4 above and *Mekoros* 27:1-5.

This conduct, in which the person pounces on any apparent loophole to circumvent the laws of the Torah, reeks of a dislike for this *mitzva*. The *mitzva* of covering hair was given to the daughters of *Yisroel* to bolster their dignity and esteem. Unfortunately, that which is a badge of honor and distinction is looked down upon and is viewed as a sign of enslavement to an age-old ritual. Let us take courage and halt this steady erosion of true Jewish values!

It must be emphasized that women have a pivotal and exalted role in the Torah-life of our communities. When they display a love and affection for *Yiddishkeit*, it does wonders to the whole fabric of Jewish society. Whereas, if they react with apathy and lethargy to central features of our heritage, it is calamitous and sows seeds of estrangement in society as a whole and is particularly harmful to their own children and families.

Hagaon Harav Yosef Lis *zt'l*, a close associate of the holy Brisker Rav *zt'l*, mentions in one of his letters a remarkable statement by the great Gaon Harav Yaacov MiSlutzk *zt'l* (the author of the *Ridvaz* on the *Yerushalmi*). He said the following words, כל העליות ביראת שמים אצל כלל ישראל, וכן להיפך כל הירידות רח״ל, הכל החל אצל הנשים - "All general improvements in the *Yiras Shomayim* throughout the history of the Jewish people and all general declines in *Yiras Shomayim* that have occurred, all started with women" (*Yosef Daas*, letter 18). Women have a far more central position in the history and development of the Jewish people than they readily appreciate!

E. TIECHELS AND OTHER HAIR COVERINGS

1. TIECHELS:

(a) Communities in which women wear only a *tiechel* not a *sheitel*: It has been mentioned in 5:D:1 above that some communities are particular that women do not wear *sheitels*. They follow opinions which consider a *sheitel* an inappropriate cover as it displays hair, and the Torah requires that a married woman does not display hair. The fact that a *sheitel* is not her true hair is immaterial according to their opinion. Those who wear a *tiechel*, either for the reason mentioned or because they wish to wear the original head-wear of the Jewish woman, demonstrate that they happily accede to covering their hair as *Hashem* wants them to. They are not perturbed by the fact that covering hair in this manner is only practiced by Orthodox Jewry and is otherwise totally unheard of in the outside world.

(b) Even a *tiechel* can be worn in an unrefined manner: Although this is so, women who wear *tiechels* and similar hair coverings are not exempt from the *yetzer horah* of unrefined and even ostentatious head-wear. They must therefore take care that the color and the style of the *tiechel* is calm and *b'cheint*, not loud and coarse. Particular mention must be made of the color fuschia which is a deep very rich pink that is commonly very bright and eye-catching. Neither a *tiechel* (that is to be seen by others) nor a dress that is of this very bright pink should be worn.

Some styles of *tiechels* and ways of wearing *tiechels* have evolved that stem from a desire to look sophisticated and be noticed, such as those secured by an exceptionally large, elaborate and eye-catching bow situated at the side of the head. The head has a lopsided look due to the gigantic sized bow which is situated on one of its sides. It is unfitting for the otherwise noble bearing of *N'shei Yisroel* to wear such an unrefined head-covering. It is also *ossur* for a woman to dress in a way which causes men to look at her. A woman may, however, cover her hair with a colorful *tiechel* or other type of head-covering which is very *b'cheint* but not eye-catching. Provided it covers her hair fully, a cheerful head-covering is fine.

(c) Strange, lopsided creations are eye-catching and unrefined: It should be noted that in the irregular and turbulent world in which we live, lopsided creations are often considered pretty. This is in line with modern art which has no symmetry whatsoever and is nevertheless admired. For example, between the *umos haolom* there are strange types who adorn themselves with a large earring on the one ear and nothing on the other. Also, there are girls who have distinctly long hair on the one side of the head and short hair on the other side. Likewise, there are those who will appear with a sweater in which one arm and half the body is black or some other dark color while the other arm and half the body is white or similar light color. Everything of this nature looks very strange and wrong to anyone who is not used to it, because it is distinctly uneven and unbalanced.

In contrast we find in the Torah that when something is lopsided it is considered blemished and damaged. See verse *Vayikra* 21:18 where the Torah states that a *Kohen* who has one large and one small eye, or any other irregularity between corresponding limbs is a *ba'al mum* and may not do

Avoda in the *Beis Hamikdash*. On the other hand the beautiful maiden described in *Shir Hashirim* is praised for the perfect symmetry of her teeth and other parts of her body - (see verse 4:2 and 4:5).

Whilst there is of course a great difference between the body itself and adornments of the body, as the latter need not be perfectly symmetrical e.g. women have rings, bracelets, brooches etc. on the one side and not on the other, nevertheless, when an adornment gives the wearer a totally lopsided and irregular look, it is foreign to *Am Yisroel*. Such an item is in fact not an adornment at all, as it has no true *Chein* and serves only to attract attention, since the person looks unusual. To us Yidden attracting attention is always wrong, and in the case of a girl or woman is a form of *pritzus*.

People who have seen unfitting and unsymmetrical modes of dress for some time become used to them and sometimes can no longer see why they are considered unrefined. It is therefore fitting at this point to mention a general guide for defining refined and unrefined modes of dress: A mode of dress which when seen for the first time looks distinctly unpleasant and even detrimental to the person's appearance (rather than just unusual) is usually an unrefined way of dress. It has been created so that its wearer stands out and is noticed by all and sundry, and it is just with the passage of time that people have become used to it and no longer find it unsightly.

(d) A *tiechel* should not be drab, somber and cheerless: Having warned against overly conspicuous and flamboyant *tiechels*, it is important to stress that a *tiechel* should also not be drab and dreary. Firstly, a woman must at all times look appealing to her husband, and head-wear has an enormous bearing on the woman's general appearance. Secondly, it is wrong for her to give the impression that *Yiddishkeit* is restrictive, somber and gloomy, when in fact *Yiddishkeit* is a most delightful and joyous way of life.

2. CROCHETED HAIR COVERINGS: Some women wear crocheted head-coverings which have large holes throughout and do not cover the hair adequately. To make them Kosher, many are lined with a light colored inner lining. With this type of lining, it is recognizable to everyone that the hair is fully covered. Such hair coverings are therefore acceptable, (provided the lining is not see-through because if the hair can be somewhat seen through, the cover is inadequate - see *Mekor Chayim* O.C. 75:2 in *Kitzur Halachos)*.

Some line their crocheted head-coverings with a dark-colored lining which is colored exactly like their own hair and is therefore not noticed. This gives the impression that the woman's hair is showing through. It appears that she is transgressing the *halacha* which states that in public a woman's hair must be totally covered and to cover just the majority is inadequate.

Those who wear this type of crocheted head-covering are unaware that we must not do something that gives the impression of being an *issur*. To do so is a transgression of the *halacha* of והייתם נקיים מה' ומישראל - (see 5:D:5 where this *halacha* is explained). Women must therefore cover their hair in such a way that the onlooker can tell that they have complied with the *halachic* requirements of covering their hair properly - see *Mekoros* 30.

Head-coverings should have a band of foam or something similar sewn on the inside to prevent them from slipping back. This is particularly necessary with silk head scarves which are very slippery and easily move out of position if they do not have a grip. It is similarly important to ensure that a head-wear which is held in position by an elasticized band is sufficiently firm around the head to prevent it moving back or to the side with ease.

3. HAIR COVERING THAT EXTENDS FAR DOWN THE BACK: Snoods and other head-coverings that have a long part which hangs far down the back are not recommended, even if they are well made and cover the head completely. The added weight caused by the excessive part hanging down pulls the covering back and can reveal the front of the hair, which is *ossur* as explained earlier. Although with constant care it can be kept in position, it is still far better to wear other safe and trouble-free types of head- coverings.

Moreover, even if a certain woman will be careful at all times to ensure that her hair remains properly covered, the fact that she wears such a hair covering will encourage others also to wear it, and amongst them there will certainly be women who will not be adequately careful. She will therefore indirectly cause a lessening in the fulfillment of the *mitzva of kisuy sa'aros.*

4. UNDERSTANDING THE DAMAGE CAUSED BY AN AVEIRA: The *Chazon Ish zt'l* used to say: "One still finds people with *Yiras Hashem*, but very few people have *yiras cheit!*". (Harav Hagaon R' Zalman Rotberg *shlita*, *Rosh Yeshivas Beis Meir*, *Bnei Brak*, quoted in *Pe'er Hador* 3 page note 18). With this he meant that there are many G-d fearing people who understand that *Hashem* is aware of all their deeds and that there is a reward for *mitzvos* and punishment for *aveiros*. There are, however, only very few people who appreciate the actual harm caused by an *aveira* (even when transgressed by mistake), the damage it inflicts on the person's *neshama* and how negatively the *tumah* affects him in general. People who truly have such an understanding are *yorei cheit.* They are, however, few and far between.

A *mitzva* such as *kisuy sa'aros* is best supported with both *Yiras Shomayim* and *yiras cheit - Yiras Shomayim* to make every effort to fulfill the will of *Hashem* and cover the hair properly, and *yiras cheit* to understand the damage caused when men see the hair or say *brachos* under forbidden circumstances. This applies also to general tznius. Appreciating the harm caused by a lack of tznius will encourage girls to dress appropriately, and will be the criterion by which garments are selected for a wardrobe.

Yiras cheit goes even further. *R' Yochanan* says (*Sotah* 22a) that we can learn *Yiras cheit* - the fear of sin - from a young lady who was overheard praying as follows: **רבונו של עולם בראת גן עדן ובראת גהינם, בראת צדיקים ובראת רשעים, יהי רצון מלפניך שלא יכשלו בי בני אדם** - **"*Ribbono Shel Olam*," she implored, "You have created *Gan Eden* and You have created *Gehinom.* You create people that become *tzadikim* and You create people that become *reshoim.* May it be Your will that no one stumbles (into the sin of gazing at me and deserves *Gehinom*) because of me".**

The meaning of her *tefilla* is as follows: Although there are and there will be sinners amongst *Klal Yisrael* and it is not within her power to prevent this phenomenon, nevertheless, she begs *Hashem* that He protects her that she is not used as a tool by others to sin (by gazing at her). She pleads for this because if she were associated with such an *aveira* it would soil her *neshama* even though she would not be responsible for the sin as she dresses with full *tznius.* This *tefilla* was a feature of true *yiras cheit* - she understood the far reaching harm caused by an *aveira,* both to the transgressor himself and to others involved.

F. HATS

1. EXTRA REFINEMENT OF WEARING A HAT OVER THE SHEITEL: In some communities, an extra refinement is practiced. Women cover their *sheitels* with a hat to prevent anyone mistakenly thinking that the *sheitel* is the woman's real hair and that her hair is uncovered. Women look extremely refined and regal with such double head-wear. The practice of wearing such hats is indicative of the deep feeling these people have for *tznius.* By concealing their hair beyond the requirements of the Torah, they show in a most beautiful way a willingness and pleasure to do this *mitzva.* Some even have a *halachic* basis for wearing such hats. According to them the obligation to have an upper covering (רדיד) when going out amongst the public (*Kesubos* 72b) applies even when the lower covering is in itself complete. This is, however, not the opinion of most *Poskim* - see *Responsa Chasam Sofer* O.C. 36. *Apei Zutoh* E.H. 21:9 and *Responsa Teshuva Meiahava* 1:48. See also *Mekoros* 31:1-8.

2. THE UNFORTUNATE TREND OF WEARING EYE-CATCHING HATS: As is the way of the *yetzer horah* to take advantage of every situation, some have unfortunately misused the concept of hats on *sheitels* and don large, high-standing or turban-like, ostentatious hats that are exceptionally eye-catching. These hats are often heavily adorned with large flowers or bows, or the hats are made with very bright colors. They are so eye-catching that when a woman wearing one of these hats boards a bus, all the women and a large proportion of the men notice her and continue to gaze at her as she walks down the aisle. Is this *tznius*? Wearing such a hat can only be interpreted as a means of obtaining grandeur and admiration. Can it be said about this woman that she has a modest demeanor and a regal bearing? - see *Mekoros* 31:9-10.

The eye-catching hats worn by some, has caused a further departure from *tznius'dik* conduct that was the hallmark of these very women until recent times. Amongst the wearers of these ostentatious hats there are quite a few who also have their *sheitels* styled in an unrefined manner. The *sheitel* is done up in a way that a woman from her type of background would never have worn, and only now that she is wearing a hat has such a style become acceptable. These women seem to think that since they are stringent and don a hat over their *sheitel* they have the right to allow themselves the liberty of wearing *sheitels* that are far from refined.

One must, however, acknowledge that these women have a point. A refined *sheitel* covered by an unrefined hat looks rather odd! To even things out, the *yetzer horah* has devised a way by which both the *sheitel* and the hat are in unison. Maybe, an alternative way to regulate things could be recommended. This is to change the prevailing hats, for hats that are *eidel* and befitting for *N'shei Yisroel*. Once this has been done, both the *sheitels* and the hats will look refined, and will fit one another perfectly.

3. BEING OTHERWISE 'CORRECTLY DRESSED' IS NO EXCUSE: It must be mentioned that many women who wear these ostentatious hats otherwise dress well and wear garments that cover them entirely. In reality, being dressed in a "Kosher" way can itself be a ploy by the *yetzer horah* to justify misconduct. It can be part of the same syndrome as the person who keeps Shabbos, does *mitzvos*, gives *tzedaka* etc. and considers himself a *frum* person but at the same time has distinctly immoral papers and magazines mailed to the house. Does his *Yiddishkeit* compensate for the devastation he brings to himself and his family by having such newspapers around?

Not only are her Kosher clothes no excuse, but they actively cause others who are not so perceptive to be influenced and to perpetrate the same misdeed. These women reason to themselves that if a woman from such a background and family, and who dresses with such *tznius*, wears such a hat, there is surely nothing wrong with it, even though it would have seemed to them to be somewhat ostentatious. The same happens whenever a woman dresses in a Kosher manner in all ways except one. For example, all her clothes are refined and of adequate length and her hair is well covered but her hosiery is see-through and most inadequate. All her Kosher clothes serve the negative role of encouraging others to be lax in this area of *tznius*. Since they see that a person who is obviously careful about *tznius* attaches no importance to covering the legs properly, this matter becomes insignificant in their eyes.

Hence, doing wrong has the effect of devaluing everything. When the *yetzer horah* is given a foothold, even the good deeds turn sour and foul. Accordingly, a maxim that dominates our life must be, בכל הדרך אשר צוה ה' אלוקיכם תלכו - "You shall go in the ways of **all** the *mitzvos* that *Hashem* has commanded you" (*Devarim* 5:30) because only then are any of the *mitzvos* really complete. By doing all His *mitzvos* we shall be granted to experience the end of the verse, למען תחיון וטוב לכם והארכתם ימים בארץ אשר תירשון - "So that you will merit to live; experience only good; and live long on the land you inherit". As a result of adhering to all the *mitzvos* without exception, *Hashem* will love us and grant us a long life replete with contentment and happiness.

4. SOMETHING WORN ONLY BY YIDDEN CAN STILL BE UNFITTING: Some women justify wearing such hats because they are worn only by Jewish ladies. This is a complete fallacy, and the fact that *nochrim* might not wear this head-wear has no bearing on the issue. It neither transforms it into a "Jewish type of dress" nor justifies wearing it in any way whatsoever. As a matter of fact, these hats project the antithesis to *Yiddishe chein*. The word *tznius* means "hidden", and any form of dress that is eye-catching is devoid of any element of *tznius* - the emblem of the Jewish woman. The same applies to a *tiechel* which is not worn with fitting modesty. Although an item worn exclusively by Jewish women, if it is unusual and eye-catching it is *treife* - see 5:E:1 above.

It is doubtlessly hurtful to the many women who wear refined and *eidel* hats that such a beautiful and praiseworthy practice has been misappropriated and misused by some. Hopefully, as a result of steadfast adherence to the original custom by the many who wear only modest and refined hats, the appreciation of the original *Yiddishe chein* will quickly find its way back.

5. A REFINED WOMAN IS ADORNED BY HER HEAD-WEAR: The *bracha* of עוטר ישראל בתפארה - "He who crowns *Yisroel* with splendor" - said every morning by men and women alike, refers to head-wear. In the context of male Jewish dress it refers to the hat which naturally completes the person's dress. It represents the personality of its wearer and a refined person is adorned by his hat as if it were a crown of nobility. With this in mind we thank *Hashem* every morning for "crowning us with splendor". Similarly, a woman completes her attire with head-wear that is impressive in its refinement, and reflects the regal and virtuous character of *N'shei Yisroel* - see *Mekoros* 32:1.

G. SAYING A BRACHA FACING UNCOVERED HAIR

1. THE ISSUR APPLIES EVEN TO A HUSBAND AND CLOSE FAMILY: As mentioned, since a married woman's hair must be covered, her hair has the status of *ervah* (שער באשה ערוה). It is, therefore, *ossur* for a man to say a *bracha* etc. when looking at a woman with uncovered hair - (See 4:B:4 above). Her hair has the status of *ervah* even to her husband (albeit *ervah shel heter* as he is allowed to see it) because hair attracts and whatever attracts males is *ervah* (O.C. 75:2). The same applies to a father, son or brother who sees the uncovered hair of his married daughter (letter by the *Chofetz Chayim, Chofetz Chayim Al HaTorah*, page 322).

2. LOOKING AWAY WHEN SAYING THE BRACHA: If a woman with uncovered hair is seated at the table, ideally the men should face a different direction or close their eyes for *Bircas Hamazon* etc. If it is difficult to do so, they should at least look down or in a slightly different direction so that she is not in their line of vision - see 6:T below and *Mekoros* 33:1-4.

H. GIRLS' HAIR STYLES

1. A GIRL'S HAIR STYLE SHOULD BE NEAT AND REFINED: Unmarried girls must strive to strike the right balance. On the one hand, they should be particular to keep their hair-styles neat and refined and not arrange their hair in extravagant and attention-seeking styles, as there is serious lack of *tznius* in doing so. The damage it can cause is all too evident from the way Yeshaya HaNavi condemned the grossly inflated hair styles that prevailed amongst girls of his times, (as has been recorded in 5:D:3(b) above). On the other hand, a girl must not disregard her appearance and hair plays a major role in the overall appearance of a girl.

Her hair should therefore be neat and tidy and neither be overly long or inflated nor be unkempt and give an untidy impression. Instead of going to either extreme, her hair should be appealing and pleasing, and should make a respectable and even *b'cheint* impression. She is, after all, of royal descent and her appearance should bear witness to that.

2. THE LENGTH AND STYLE OF A GIRL'S HAIR:

(a) Untied hair should preferably be only shoulder length: Many *Poskim* maintain that long loose hair that hangs over the shoulders and down the back is unrefined and subject to an *issur d'Rabanan*. According to their opinion, when a girl has hair that is long enough to be braided it should be braided or tied together and not be left to hang wide open. Sporting long loose hair is overly attractive which is inconsistent with *tznius*.

Furthermore, it gives the impression that she wants her beautiful hair to be noticed and admired, and such aspirations are inconsistent with *tznius*. Even if this is not her intention, the impression is still made to her detriment and detriment of others. (*Maharil, Hilchos Nisuin* No. 11; *Magen Avraham* 75:3; *Moir Uketziah* 75; *Responsa Sh'vus Yaacov* 1:103 and *Responsa Shevet Halevi* 6:199 who are stringent in this matter. See also M.B. 75:12; *Otzar HaPoskim* 21:26:1 and *Mekoros* 1:6 and 29 for further opinions). Since many *Poskim* are stringent and girls nowadays tend not to have braids, it is strongly recommended that their hair is no more than shoulder length.

In *Eretz Yisroel* considerable stress is put on girl's hair not being both long and unbraided, as is well known. It is hoped that *frum* girls world-wide follow the example of their *Eretz Yisroel* contemporaries, as this apparently minor point is in fact a foremost detail which adds much to the general refinement of the girl. It is, however, self understood that should a girl wish to have long hair and bind it back or braid it together, she may of course do so. This is in fact the ongoing *minhag* of the old *yishuv* of *Yerusholayim*.

(b) Hair dangling over the face is not a Jewish way of dress: The above refers to long hair which is secured to stay away from the face with a head band, clips etc. Concerning such hair there are diverse opinions in the *Poskim* whether it is right to let it hang loosely over the shoulders and upper back or not, as explained. However, for hair to be totally untied and to hang loosely over the face is not even spoken about in the *Poskim*. This is because allowing the hair to descend down the back of the head or over the face in a casual way was not the done thing and was simply not a Jewish way of dress.

Chazal, in fact, state quite explicitly that hair which is held away from the face is far prettier and *b'cheint* than long loose hair that dangles over the face. On the verse, מבעד לצמתיך שערך - "Your hair is held together by a kerchief" (*Shir HaShirim* 4:1 see *Rashi*) the *Midrash* says as follows, האשה הזאת כשמצמת שערה לאחוריה הוא תכשיט לה - "The female figure is beautified by her hair being tied back" (*Midrash Shir Hashirim,* 4:3).

Moreover, the same verse in *Shir HaShirim* (4:1) sings praise of the Jewish daughter with the words שערך כעדר העזים שגלשו מהר גלעד - "Your hair is like that of a herd of goats as they swiftly descend the slopes of Mount Gilod". The *S'forno* explains: "The hair of the Jewish daughter is like that of goats descending the slopes, with the wind rushing past them and their hair firmly blown back". Thus, it is stated in the *Midrash* and the *S'forno* that a girl's hair is tidily behind her head in a pleasing and noble manner.

Apart from the above, the Gemara (*Shabbos* 95a) relates that Chava, the first woman to be created, was beautified by *Hashem* before bringing her to Adam. *Hashem* did this by plaiting her hair rather than leaving it loose as it was after she was formed. According to present day attitudes one wonders why *Hashem* did not just let her long hair hang loosely down her back and over her shoulders. Evidently, *Hashem* was of the opinion that a woman looks far better when her hair is secured than when it is left to dangle freely.

(c) The strange trend of long hair being left totally untied: Nowadays many adult girls use no hair-bands nor alternative type of accessory to hold down their hair. Due to this, their hair (whether long or short) hangs loosely in all directions and requires continuous flicking back to prevent it descending and covering part of the face. Girls are so busy flicking, that as time goes on, more and more advanced forms of flicking are being developed. At present this strange hair style is the "in thing", and to leave one's hair untied and totally loose is part of being a sophisticated young lady.

If for the sake of beauty a girl is prepared to undertake the trouble of having to continuously flick the hair back she is evidently indulging in an unnatural form of beautification. It is the same with all other worldly pleasures. For example, if the amount the person eats causes him indigestion he is obviously eating immoderately and if his drinking causes drunkenness the person is obviously over-indulging in drink. Similarly, if high-heeled shoes cause walking difficulties (see 6:O:2 below) or if a hair-style requires continuous tossing the head back, the girl is over-reacting in her pursuit of beautification. See 5:D:3(a) above, concerning *sheitels* with such styles.

Although, it may be hard to change this widely accepted trend (until fashions change) the fact is that this casual hair style lacks refinement and has no *Yiddishe ta'am*. This is compounded by the fact that when the hair is long and loose there is a *halachic* objection according to some opinions, as mentioned above. If only, that the aristocratic, refined and uncomplicated forms of dress and hair-styles that were common just a few decades ago were once again appreciated and embraced by our daughters and sisters.

(d) Long, loose hair is a spiritual disadvantage: Finally, it must be mentioned that there is a *Kabbalistic* disadvantage in girls leaving their long hair completely open and undone. Human hair, in the mystics of the Torah, is related to *midas hadin* - "it demands a strict rather than lenient assessment of the person's deeds" (*Zohar HaKadosh, Bamidbar* 151). The more the dominance of the hair, the greater the power of the *midas hadin*. For this reason, men, who would be very affected by hair, are advised to keep their hair short (apart from the *payos*). The *Ari HaKadosh* writes in *Sha'ar Ta'amei Hamitzvos* that this is alluded to in the verse, ואיש כי ימרט ראשו טהור הוא - "And a man whose hair is removed is purified" (*Vayikra* 13:40).

Women, on the other hand, are not affected by having long hair. However, the *Sifrei Kabbalah* write that it should be bound. The binding symbolizes that the *din* is contained and not allowed to extend excessively as is signified by long open hair which has a tendency to "spread out far and wide". It follows that for hair to be bound is an advisable investment, and can bring in its wake great salvation. (See *Ben Yehoyada*, *Shabbos* 95a, and *Yuma* 47a, by the Sefardi Gaon Rabbeinu Yosef Chayim - the *Ben Ish Chai*).

(e) Summary: To retain clarity it is best to reiterate the main points once again. They are as follows:- (1) The hair, whether long or short, should be secured in a way that it does not hang over much of the face. (2) If the hair is secured not to descend on the face but is otherwise loose, it is best that it is no more than shoulder length which is too short to be braided. (3) If the hair is long it should preferably be braided or held together in some other way.

3. HAIR ACCESSORIES - PRETTY BUT NOT OSTENTATIOUS: Hair accessories such as ribbons, head bands (plastic) and hair bands (cloth) may certainly be pretty and colorful. It was in fact common practice in the times of *Chazal* to have decorations in the hair (*Shabbos* 57b) - see *Mekoros* 63:14. It is, however, incorrect for girls to sport large gaudily-colored bows and hair bands, or massive bows that are quite out of proportion to the head. Similarly, while silver or gold colored head bands are often fine, if they are studded with numerous large colored stones they are sometimes overdone and showy. Such headbands are therefore unfitting for a *Bas Yisroel* even when young and just a school girl. When an adult girl wears a gaudily colored or ostentatious hair band or head band it is particularly unpleasant, since she is evidently showing herself off to everyone.

4. HAIR HAS A CONSIDERABLE POWER OF ATTRACTION: The intense power of attraction and even enticement inherent in a girl and woman's hair is repeatedly highlighted in Torah literature. At the very start of the Torah we find that Chava, the one and only woman in the world, was beautified by *Hashem Yisborach* before he brought her for the first time to Adam. This was done by doing up her hair in an attractive and appealing manner. Although clothes were of no importance at that time, nevertheless, *Hashem* knew that her hairstyle would be so meaningful that He completed the creation of Chava with this additional act of kindness (*Shabbos* 95a).

Likewise, the power of enticement of hair is vividly described in a *Rashi* on the Torah. We are told that whilst Yosef was in the house of his master Potifera, the lady of the house developed a considerable yearning for him. This was caused by Yosef paying excessive attention to his appearance. The verse says ויהי יוסף יפה תואר ויפה מראה. ויהי אחר הדברים האלה ותשא אשת אדוניו את עיניה אל יוסף - "Yosef had a beautiful figure and beautiful appearance. After these events, the wife of his master lifted her eyes to Yosef" (*Breishis* 39:6,7). *Rashi* explains that these two statements are put together because, ראה עצמו מושל, התחיל אוכל ושותה ומסלסל בשערו - "When Yosef realized that he was the chief executive of his master's house he started cultivating his figure - he ate and drank to have a healthier appearance - and he would groom his hair until it looked beautiful". His improved appearance had such an alluring effect on the wife of his master that from then on she knew no rest. She would prevail upon him and even coax him to show an interest in her. We see from here the effect that hair beautification can have to arouse unwelcome appeal.

Similarly, we are taught in the Torah that a woman who is suspected of having had an illicit affair is assumed to have removed her hair covering and beautified her appearance by uncovering and arranging her hair in a provocative and suggestive manner. She is therefore put to shame by having her hair revealed before all when in the *Beth Din* (*Kesubos* 72a *Rashi* s.v. *Azhara*). Here again, hair is viewed as a major means of enticement.

In a comparable vein, the *yefas toar*, with whom the Jewish soldier has become enamored, has her hair cut off to lessen her attraction in his eyes (*Devarim* 21:12). Although her beautiful garments are removed from her and she sits in his house in the drab and dull clothes of a mourner, this alone will not cause him to retract from his intention to marry her. However, with the removal of her attractive hair he will finally submit to the will of *Hashem Yisborach* and find the strength to tear himself away from this woman. In an identical way, a *nazir*, who is in danger of descending into bad ways as a result of his handsome appearance and good-looking hair, is instructed to first let his hair grow long without being groomed and when the *nezirus* comes to an end to cut it all off (*Nedarim* 9b). This is the Torah's powerful remedy to help bring him back onto an even keel and guarantee the safety of a man who is in spiritual danger.

All this underscores the immense power of appeal and captivation ingrained in hair and particularly in the hair of a girl or woman. It is little wonder that the Torah commands the married woman to conceal her hair from the eyes of strangers so that they are not attracted to her - see *Mekoros* 21:3-5. Accordingly, when a girl wears an unpretentious, refined and genteel hair-style rather than a highly conspicuous one, she presents an image of modesty and self-effacement. Whereas, if she sports a striking hair-style, this is considered *pritzus* and her appearance is shameful to the otherwise cultured and gracious personality of the Jewish woman.

Chapter Six

TZNIUS IN DRESS - HALACHOS AND REQUISITES

A. THE PRINCIPAL HALACHA

1. AREAS THAT MUST BE COVERED: All women and girls, married or unmarried, must cover all parts of their main body (torso) plus parts of their arms and legs when in public or in the presence of individuals outside their immediate family. Under no circumstances may even a small part of these areas be uncovered in the presence of men or boys. These areas naturally provoke attention (with the upper section of the leg even more provocative than other areas - See 4:C above and 6:U:4 below) and must therefore be covered by decree of *halacha* - see *Chidushei HaMeiri*, *Berachos* 24a and *Levush* O.C. 75:1. Their status as *ervah* has been established by *Chazal* and is not dependent on the local or prevailing custom. Accordingly, even if most Jewish women would *chas v'shalom* not cover these areas properly, the *halacha* would still remain the same (M.B. 75:2) - see *Mekoros* 37.

2. ISSUR TO REVEAL A MINIMAL PART OF "COVERED AREA": As explained (in 4:B:1(d) above), all areas of the body that may not be exposed must be covered completely. The *halachic* allowance of less than a *tefach* (4" x 4") implied in the term טפח באשה ערוה, applies only to the husband and very close family saying a *bracha* when facing such an area that happens to be exposed. For example, she has rolled up her sleeve revealing a small part of her upper arm. Since it is less than a *tefach* it has not been given the *ervah* status by *Chazal* and they may say a *bracha* while facing her. However, with regard to the general public, any amount is considered provocative and must be covered completely, and there is absolutely no difference between a *tefach* and less than a *tefach* - see *Iggros Moshe* E.H. 1:58 and *Mekoros* 37:6.

Accordingly, whenever a woman can be seen by a man other than her closest blood-relations she must ensure that her main body and similar areas are completely covered (O.C. 75:1) - see *Mekoros* 24:13-14, 54:8. The *halachos* concerning a man who wishes to say a *bracha* or *dvar Torah* but faces an immodestly dressed female, will be explained in 6:T below.

3. BOY OF THREE SHOULD NOT SEE WOMEN IN PARTIAL ATTIRE: Women and girls who go to a Kosher beach which is designated at certain times for women only, may take with them boys that are under the age of three. However, once three years old they should not be taken, because a child of that age might already be impressionable and a male must not see an improperly dressed female. Although the impression will apparently do him no harm at this very young age, it can nevertheless prove to be harmful once he is older and recalls seeing certain sights when he was much younger. The same applies to mothers who go swimming in a public swimming pool at a time which is only for females. Boys under three may accompany their mother but not boys who are three or over (*Halichos Bas Yisroel* 7:39 citing Hagaon Harav Shlomo Zalman Auerbach *zt'l.* The same is quoted in *sefer, Raboseinu* in the name of the *Chazon Ish zt'l*). Mothers should take this ruling into consideration when dressing in the presence of a young boy.

When a man goes swimming, either in the sea or in a public swimming pool, he may take along his small daughter with him as a spectator even if she is over three (till the age of five/six), since she will not see total nakedness, and a female may see men in partial attire (*ibid.*). She should however not go once she is above this age as it is unfitting for a girl to be in a place occupied by men as this is a form of intermingling.

4. BOY UNDER THREE SHOULD NOT SEE FULLY UNCLAD WOMEN: Although a boy who is under three may see his mother or other women in a swimming pool for the reason explained, he should not see his mother shower when she is in a totally unclad state. This is because, from the point of view of the mother, it is wrong for her to do something which impinges on her natural modesty, even if it is not harmful to the very young child. See a similar issue in *Bechoros* 44b and M.B. 3:22.

Also, it is spiritually harmful for a male to see *ervah min haTorah* of a female even if he is far too young to understand or remember anything in adult years. The *Gemara* (*Brachos* 10a) relates the following, "When Dovid Hamelech sucked from his mother, he looked at the place from which he sucked and sang the following praise: ברכי נפשי את ה׳ ואל תשכחי כל גמוליו - 'My soul blesses *Hashem* as He does not forget the young children who suck' (*Tehillim* 103:2). *Rav Avahu* said that the praise was said for the fact that, in a woman, nursing takes place in an area that is near the heart and far removed from that of *ervah min haTorah*, in contrast to animals - *Rav Yehuda* explained the significance of this - *Hashem* especially changed the anatomy of a human being so that the baby does not see the *ervah* area when feeding." From this remarkable *Chazal* we learn once again how seeing "forbidden sights" burns a hole into the *neshama* of the person even if no bad thoughts or passions are aroused by what he sees - see 2:B:3 above.

B. THE NECKLINE

1. THE HALACHIC STATUS OF THE NECK - ITS BOUNDARIES: The neckline of the garment must cover everything that is below the actual neck. Although a woman need not cover her neck - see *Mekoros* 34:1-5 - she must cover the whole of her main body (the torso). She must, therefore, cover whatever is *halachically* not considered to be part of the neck. It is imperative that women and girls know the true guidelines and do not mistakenly consider areas that are beyond the neck as just extended parts of the neck that may be left uncovered. Some people have straight shoulders and when that is the case it is very obvious where the neck ends and the shoulders start. Others, however, have slanting shoulders and without guidance they can easily err and attribute to the neck that which is in fact part of the shoulder - see *Mekoros* 35:1-3.

The following are the boundaries of the neck - all that is beyond these demarcation lines belongs to the main body:

(a) At the front - At the front, the neck ends just above the collar-bones; the collar-bones form the frontal uppermost part of the main body (the torso). As the collar-bones are part of the main body, they must be properly covered, in line with all other parts of the main body - see *Magen Avraham* 4:23 and M.B. 4:53. If a person puts his hand onto the area just below the neck he cannot fail to feel the top of the collar-bones. Consequently, even without the aid of a mirror a woman can feel whether the front part of her neckline is covered and Kosher or not. A mirror can, however, prevent general errors concerning the neckline - see 1:J:3 above.

At the center of this frontal area, the neck extends slightly downwards between the collar bones in a small V-shaped dip. This is due to the fact that the collar bones do not join one another, but rather leave a soft fleshy area between them. This area is an extended part of the neck and need not be covered. It is however only a small area, and is identical to the place where a man's tie-knot sits (Hagaon Harav Moshe Feinstein *zt'l* and Hagaon Harav Shlomo Zalman Auerbach *zt'l*) - see *Mekoros* 1:5.

(b) At the sides - At the sides the neck gives way and becomes shoulder when it curves outward, or is at least more horizontal than vertical. Since this area is shoulder, it is an integral part of the main body and must be completely covered. Many people mistakenly consider part of the shoulders as extended parts of the neck. This has no *halachic* foundation and is quite incorrect, as explained in *Mekoros* 35:2.

As stated, with some people the neck ends and the shoulders turn abruptly to the right and left, and it is very obvious what is neck and what is shoulder. However, with others the neck curves very gradually and eventually becomes shoulder. For such people it is important to note that by definition a neck is upright - see *Mekoros* 35:2. Therefore, once the curve is more horizontal than vertical, the area is not neck but shoulder and must be covered.

(c) At the back - At the rear, the neck ends and the upper back starts from a point that is level with the highest point of the shoulders. This is above the second projecting bone of the spine which can be seen very well on a young child when he bends his head forward. When a necklace lies at its lowest natural point across the back of the neck, it will hang from what is still considered neck. Below this point the upper back starts, which must be covered as explained. A necklace can also be used to help determine the boundaries of the neck to the right and left. (*Malbushei Kavod* page 33 in name of Hagaon Harav Shlomo Zalman Auerbach *zt'l* - see *Mekoros* 36:1-2).

2. EXTRA REFINEMENT: In some circles, women and girls practice an extra refinement and do not reveal even the small V-shaped lower front-part of the neck. Furthermore, in some circles women and girls are particular always to wear a collar (or a collar piece) so that the neck is partially covered - see *Mekoros* 34:4-5. Some opinions even maintain that *halachically* the lower part of the neck must be covered, and according to their opinion it is *ossur* to expose the complete neck - see *Responsa Shevet Halevi* 5:197:4 and 7:10:1. This is, however, not the opinion of most *Poskim*, although all would agree that it is an extra refinement to do so. See *Rambam, Hilchos Chovel Umazik* 4:15, *Shulchan Aruch* E.H. 83:1 and *Mekoros* 34:1-3.

The refinement of covering part of the neck is particularly fitting when the woman or girl has a long neck rather than a short one. See *Nedarim* 66b where the difference between an extended neck which beautifies the person and a short one which has no such effect is pointed out. Similarly, when describing the features of a beautiful maiden, the verse says in *Shir Hashirim* (4:4) כמגדל דוד צוארך בנוי תלפיות - "Your neck is prominent like the tower of Dovid, built as an ornament" (Rashi: like an ornament that attracts onlookers). Moreover, *Chazal* say, מה צואר שפירא דכולי גופא, הכי נמי בי מקדשא איהו שפירו דכל עלמא - "Just as the neck is the most graceful part of the entire body, so too the *Beis Hamikdash* is the most graceful place in the entire world" (*Zohar HaKadosh, Breishis* 99b). Since an extended neck contributes so much to the beauty of the woman or girl, it is certainly an act of extra refinement to cover part of it.

To cover part of the neck does not usually make the person uncomfortably warm or give a feeling of being restricted. In fact this is exactly how most men dress, both in the winter and the summer. They wear a shirt that has a collar which covers part of the neck (rather than a tee-shirt which is collarless and exposes the complete neck) and do not complain of feeling uncomfortably warm or restricted!

3. LOOSE COLLARS THAT STAND AWAY FROM THE NECK: A collar is sometimes perfect as far as size and position around the neck is concerned but is nevertheless not Kosher. This happens when the collar is the right height but is very loose and stands away from the neck. Although the woman's appearance from a distance will be alright, it will not be Kosher for those who stand near to her, especially for someone who happens to be talking to her. Since the collar is very loose and stands away from the body, areas that must be covered are fully visible to that person, albeit from a side or downward view. This problem is compounded by the fact that looking in the mirror will often not reveal the problem, and certainly not its full extent, because a mirror only projects a frontal view of the person, whilst the problem of these exposures are due to side or downwards views that are visible to a person standing near to her.

Due to this, care must be taken to ensure that the collar fits neatly around the neck rather than just loosely around it. This problem can usually be rectified by inserting a slightly elasticized narrow band or thread into the top of the garment. This has the effect of 'pulling' the neck area together without spoiling the garment's overall appearance. Alternatively, when a dress or sweater has a collar, an elasticized band can be tied into a closed circular band. This can be put under the collar to pull it in and keep it close to the neck, as will be explained in 6:C:1 below. The band is hidden by the collar but does a first class job of keeping the neckline Kosher. Many who have tried this method have found it excellent.

Should a husband notice that his wife's collar does not conceal "covered parts" properly, it is his duty to inform her, since, as stated, the wearer is often completely unaware that this problem exists. The same of course applies to a father and mother who realize that their daughter's collar stands away and reveals areas that should be well covered.

C. ENSURING THAT THE NECKLINE IS IN ORDER

1. THE SECOND BUTTON DOWN IS USUALLY TOO LOW: The *halachos* concerning the neckline are often overlooked and even very Orthodox women are frequently unaware of the incorrect state of their necklines. When the top button of a blouse or dress is left open this will invariably expose much more than just the neck, because the second button is generally too far down. It will be noticed that one can feel the collar-bones inside the area of the opening. This is part of the main body and may not be exposed, as explained. Should a woman or girl wish to leave the top button open, she must insert a pin to prevent the garment opening as far as the second button. Alternatively, a dress-maker can add an additional button and button hole between the first and second button down. Often, no more than a pair of snaps (press-studs) is required, and these can be sewn on by anyone.

Even when the top button of a dress or blouse is closed, this does not always ensure a Kosher neckline. If the woman or girl has a thin neck, a dress or blouse which is otherwise her size could hang limply around the neck since it was designed for a person with a somewhat broader neck. As a result of this, either the front droops down in a way that some of the collar-bone can be seen or the collar moves away from the side of the neck in a way that part of the shoulder is visible.

When the problem is just minor, moving the top button can help. However, such a small correction is often insufficient. Instead, a dressmaker might be able to alter the collar and thereby correct the neckline. Alternatively, some women tie a 9"-10" long piece of elasticized band into a closed circle. This band is hidden under the collar and encircles the complete neck - the tiny bit that crosses the center front area where there is no collar, goes unnoticed. This pulls the collar slightly in, making it Kosher. Although these suggestions for correcting the loose collar can be employed, it is obvious that in the first place those who are liable to experience this problem should make doubly sure when purchasing a dress or blouse that the collar fits well and will give a Kosher neckline.

A heavy shoulder-bag strapped over the shoulder can cause the shoulder area of a garment to be pulled down in line with the movement of the strap. If this happens, a substantial part of the shoulder will become uncovered, which is forbidden as explained. Pulling the shoulder area of the garment towards the neck after the bag is already in position might help prevent this problem to a degree. This must, however, be continuously monitored as such a strap has a tendency to pull downwards taking the garment with it and causing a *tznius* problem. It is therefore better to avoid carrying a heavy weight in a shoulder bag.

2. ENSURING THAT THE BACK CLOSURE IS FULLY EFFECTIVE: The buttons, snaps (press-studs) or 'hooks and eyes' at the back of the garment must be checked, because a garment will sometimes open up quite considerably between one button and the next. When fastened with ribbons, there is a particular danger of this happening, because a 'knot and bow' easily loosens. Even if no flesh can be seen through the opening, it is still *ossur,* because inner garments must also not to be seen - See 6:D:1 below and *Mekoros* 39. With a dress or sweater the most effective solution is to fix a zipper into the opening. A zipper closes completely and is therefore ideal.

3. PROBLEMS WITH SWEATERS AND COLLARLESS DRESSES: Those who wear a pullover, sweater or collarless dress (without a blouse) must ensure that the top of their garment is close fitting and that it lies firmly around the neck. If it sits just tenderly around the neck it will inevitably reveal part of the woman's shoulder, as it will veer over to the right or left with the slightest movement, particularly when she leans over to one side while sitting at a table. Also, the strap of an ordinary bag hanging from the shoulder will tug at the shoulder of such a dress or sweater and pull it down with the effect of exposing the shoulder at that side. One must therefore reinforce the neck area with the insertion of an elasticized band.

If no correction has been made, such a pullover or sweater may only be worn together with a blouse which covers the area that would otherwise have been exposed. If a dress has the above mentioned problem, it can be worn with a wide inset collar piece (a "dickie") which will adequately cover the front, back and shoulder areas.

A garment with a boat-shaped (or oval-shaped) opening is usually fine at the front and back, but reveals part of both shoulders - hence it's name 'boat shaped', see *Mekoros* 1:5 and 34:6. Such a garment can only be worn together with a blouse or only after its collar area has been rectified.

A necklace worn as a choker cannot be relied upon to make an inadequate neckline Kosher. Although such a necklace certainly improves matters, it does not completely cover the area. It also often moves out of position, revealing part of the shoulder that should be properly covered. Therefore, while a choker is a welcome addition to a Kosher neckline, it is not capable of making an inadequate neckline Kosher.

4. NECKLINE OF SWEATERS TEND TO STRETCH SUBSTANTIALLY: Pullovers and sweaters are precarious even if they are definitely Kosher when the garment is bought. This is because they have a tendency to stretch within a comparatively short period of time as a result of the wearer forcing her head through its rather narrow opening or due to laundering. These types of garments must therefore be kept under continuous surveillance and must be checked regularly to ensure that the neckline has not stretched in a way which renders the garment unfit to be worn until corrected. An elasticized band inserted into the casing of the neck area soon after purchase will prevent this type of problem from occurring.

When a woman or girl has been dieting and has lost about half a stone, the neckline of her sweater or dress which used to sit snugly in position around her neck will often hang limply around the neck in a way that is no longer Kosher. The danger is of course much greater when items are collarless, and minor movement out of position reveals that which is part of the main body. It is therefore important to check frequently while losing weight that the neckline remains in order.

As stated, an enormous amount of oversight exists concerning this subject. It is therefore strongly recommended that people make each other aware when their neckline is inadequate. Experience has shown that women do not take offense concerning this matter (as they sometimes do when other faults are pointed out) because it is obvious that oversights can occur as the wearer cannot properly see the front, sides and back of the collar area.

5. INADEQUATE NECKLINES CAUSE FORBIDDEN SIGHTINGS: *Halachically*, a man may see a woman's face and hands as he talks to her, but must not intentionally gaze at them. It is, however, *ossur* for him to see (even just in passing) areas that should be covered, since these areas are provocative (M.B. 75:7 - See 6:T:1 below). Hence, a partially revealed shoulder presents a stumbling block to a man who happens to see the woman or girl. It is essential that women and girls realize that it is their responsibility to ensure that men do not transgress these *issurim* even inadvertently. This realization should give them fresh motivation to dress as is required.

6. THE HAZARD CAUSED BY SOME "INSETS": Many present day outfits are worn with an inset. This is to fill in the whole top chest area which the outfit does not cover. It must be pointed out that these insets are often not Kosher, although people are not aware of it. The top of these insets is usually absolutely straight, rather than shaped to hug the neck. Although the center-point of these insets sits firmly up against the neck, the two sides of the inset are usually far too low and therefore inadequate. Sometimes the inset is "just right", but the moment the woman or girl bends slightly forward, one or both of the corners of the jacket open up, exposing part of the upper chest or part of an inner garment that should be covered. With what has been explained, it is understood that this is totally unacceptable.

Experience has shown that, even if the husband or father warns his wife or daughter about this exposure and she tries to pin the inset into the dress or outfit in a more efficient way, it usually does not achieve adequate results and remains not Kosher. It is therefore recommended that the top of these insets are not straight. Rather they should be shaped in a way that the front of the neck sits snugly inside the inset. If this is done, the sides of the inset rise high enough around the neck that nothing will be showing.

This warning applies to outfits and jackets that have wide openings which are fitted with an inset to fill in the space. As explained, these insets are very wide and prominent, and if the top of the inset is straight the right and left corners are often far too low down. There are, however, many dresses with comparatively small openings which have small insets to close them up properly. If the tops of these insets are straight they usually do not present a problem as the space is narrow and the outer corners of the inset do not become exposed. Each case should, however, be checked out individually.

7. SKIN-COLORED INSETS: The inset of an outfit, jacket, or dress should not be skin-colored, particularly if the garment is dark colored. When an inset is skin-colored, the impression given from the distance is that the area has not been covered at all. Even though this is of course not the case, it is nevertheless wrong to do something which causes even just a momentary misunderstanding. This is part of our obligation of והייתם נקיים - "to have a clean record" - see 6:M:6 below. Also, wearing such a difficult-to-recognize inset gives the impression of "trying to circumvent the *halacha*". To give such an impression is a *chillul Hashem,* as it educates people to view *tznius* as a hardship and inconvenience rather than a privilege and merit.

D. THE PROBLEM OF SEE-THROUGH GARMENTS

1. NEITHER THE BODY NOR INNER GARMENTS MAY BE VISIBLE:

(a) *Halachically* forbidden and also against basic decency: A woman's body must be totally covered with a garment that does not allow anything worn underneath to be seen. The *issur* applies both to seeing the skin and to seeing the outline of the body. It also applies to all inner garments including the slip (see (d) below), as it is against *tznius* for all such items to be seen in any way - *Bach* Y.D. 340 s.v. *Al.* See also *Mekoros* 38:1-2

The following is a statement by the great *Sefardi Gaon* the *Ben Ish Chai* in his *sefer, Chukei Nashim,* Chapter 17 - וכן אסור לאשה ללבוש מלבוש דק אשר ייראה דרכו הלבוש הפנימי, ומחוץ לחוקי הדת דבר זה בושה וחרפה ומחוץ לנימוסי נשים - "It is *ossur* for a woman to wear a thin garment through which inner-garments can be seen; apart from this being against the laws of *tznius,* it is shameful and disgraceful, and contrary to the accepted conduct of women". The same is stated in *Responsa Torah Lishmah* No. 400, where he discusses the steps a husband must take to ensure that his wife does not appear in public wearing a see-through garment.

It is actually evident from *Chazal* that it is against the principles of *tznius* for part of the flesh to be seen through the outer garments. *Chazal* say (*Bava Basra* 57b) that the garment of a *Talmid Chacham* should not be see-through, as the *Rambam*, *Hilchos Deios* 5:9 writes, ולא יהא בשרו נראה מתחת מדיו כמו בגדי הפשתן הקלים ביותר שעושים במצרים. Although *tznius* is not generally a prime characteristic of men, nevertheless *Talmidei Chachamim* are singled out as having *tznius* - see *Derech Eretz Zuta* 7, *Midrash Tanchuma, Ki Sisah* 15 and *Rambam Hilchos Deios* 5:6. Therefore, a *Talmid Chacham*, being a *tznua,* is expected not to wear a garment which allows any part of his flesh to be discernible.

In reference to women, although mentioned in the *Poskim, Chazal* themselves do not mention explicitly that women may not wear see-through garments. This is because, being obviously against all that *tznius* stand for, it speaks for itself that women must not dress in such a way. See *Biur Halacha* 339:3 s.v. *Lehakel,* that something which is obviously *ossur*, such as the *issur* of mixed dancing, is not stated explicitly by *Chazal*. Furthermore, in the case of women where their flesh has the status of *ervah,* it is obvious that their garments may not be see-through, since this will cause men to see their flesh which is forbidden (M.B. 75:7) or say a *bracha* while facing their visible flesh which is likewise forbidden (M.B. 75:25).

Due to this *halacha,* there are many blouses that are unacceptable, unless the woman wears a cardigan or sweater on top of them or an additional shield under them, as will be explained - see *Mekoros* 1:7 and 39:1.

When a woman tears *kriah*, *rachmana litzlan*, the *halacha* states that she should immediately pin up the torn part of the dress or blouse. Otherwise part of an inner garment will be visible, and for that to occur is an infringement on the requirements of *tznius*, as stated (*Moed Katan* 22b; Y.D. 340:11).

(b) Flesh is considered visible even if just its color shows through: A garment is considered see-through even if just the beige-pink color of the flesh or the white color of the inner garment can be seen through, but not the shape of the limbs or the actual inner garments themselves.

Rabbeinu Yaacov Emden *ztl* in his *sefer, Mor Uketziah* O.C. 75 proves this from the *Gemara* (*Yuma* 35b) where we are informed that the mother of a certain *kohen* made a *kesones* (vest) for her son out of very precious material, but his peer would not let him wear it during the *avoda* in the *Beis Hamikdash* because it was see-through. The *Gemara* explains that the cloth was actually quite thick, but also somewhat translucent, due to which his flesh could be seen through the cloth "just as red wine can be seen through an opaque glass decanter" (see *Rashi*). Just as only the red color of the wine can be seen through such glass but not the actual fluid itself, so too the color of the skin could be seen through the vest but not the skin itself, nor the shape of the limbs. Although just the color could be seen, it was considered see-through and unfitting to be worn by a *kohen* while doing the *avoda*.

However, if no true color shows through, and all one notices is a darkening due to the background, this would not be considered see-through, since one is neither seeing the shape of the limb nor the color of the flesh.

(c) Defective clothing harmful to every type of observer: At this point it is appropriate to mention that many women and girls harbor a mistaken assumption. They are under the impression that when a woman or girl is inadequately clad it is only marginally harmful - as only men with low morals notice and are detrimentally affected by such ways of dress. They are quite convinced that all other men would not even notice, and certainly not be affected by inadequate dress.

The truth of the matter is not so at all, and in fact all classes of men (including *tzadikim*) are affected by a lack of *tznius*, since *Hashem* implanted attraction to members of the other gender into the very make-up of mankind. He did so, so that people have trials and challenges in their lives over which they can successfully triumph. They can thereby earn themselves the great reward *Hashem* has in store for those who have withstood the tests He puts in their path - see *Mekoros* 2:3 and 4:1-5. This is such a universal truth that those who are convinced that it is not the case (and therefore do not take *tznius* of dress seriously) are grossly out of touch with reality. A good *chinuch,* both at home and in school, should ensure that girls grow up aware of the constant care they must take (see 1:H:1 for further elaboration).

(d) An underblouse that is discernible through the top blouse. Due to problems of see-through garments, many wear an underblouse or other type of inner shield, as will be explained later. Since an underblouse is not worn as an under garment but as a second blouse and as a protective shield, no *issur* is transgressed if it can be seen and even slightly recognized through the top blouse. There is, however, an advantage if even this type of item does not show through.

Although a slip should not be seen, as stated in (a) above, an underblouse is very different, in spite of the fact that both items are worn for protection. A full slip is a 'cut out' piece of clothing and therefore by definition a private item that should not to be seen by others. Even a half slip, although not a 'cut out' item, is nevertheless a distinctly feminine piece of clothing as it has lace trimmings or is made of a net type of material etc. Many women would, in fact, be embarrassed to hang a full slip or a half slip on a washing line that is on full view, just as they would feel concerning other types of inner garments.

An under-blouse is, however, totally different as it is neither a 'cut out' item nor is it a distinctly feminine item. One must also consider the fact that apart from Jewish women who are particular about *tznius,* an underblouse is not generally worn. It is therefore not viewed as a typical female piece of clothing. In fact women would not feel embarrassed to hang an underblouse to dry where they would hang a top blouse. As a result of these far-reaching differences between a slip and an under blouse, there is no *issur* when an underblouse is discernible through the top blouse.

It has, however, been mentioned, that there is a very definite advantage in the underblouse not showing through, and certainly in being no more than slightly discernible. Since it is after all not an outer garment, keeping it out of sight is an advantage and would be viewed as extra refinement. Also, since people have become insensitive to the lack of *tznius* in wearing real see-through garments, the more effort put into countering this attitude the better it is.

2. NON-WHITE INNER ITEMS - LESS LIKELY TO SHOW THROUGH: Considering the difficulties that can be experienced in obtaining proper non-see-through blouses, it should be noted that white is visually very powerful, and, if the inner garments are white, they might show through an outer garment which would have masked a milder color. It is thus advisable to avoid purchasing white inner garments if possible. Light beige is recommended as it is a very mild color. Also, the color is similar to skin and it will therefore not show up in contrast to the skin. [In some cases one may be able to dye bright white inner garments with a mild beige color. In fact some have found that adding a couple of granules of tea concentrate to a wash has the effect of permanently coloring the item a light beige]. Alternatively, if an outer blouse is colored rather than white - and particularly if it is multi-colored - the problem of see-through will be far less acute.

In this context it must be mentioned that when a blouse or dress is white or a color close to white the undershirt should not fasten with dark colored buttons, or by means of a clearly evident zipper, as these are easily detected from the outside. Instead, it should be secured by white ribbons or white buttons that cannot be seen through the blouse or dress.

The two suggestions given above, that either the inner garment or the outer blouse should not be stark white, are often not possible to implement, and for many women see-through blouses present a serious problem. The following notes analyze the problem and recommend ways of overcoming it:-

3. RULES CONCERNING DIFFERENT GRADES OF OPAQUENESS: Blouses are made of materials of very different grades. This affects their opaqueness considerably. The rules are as follows:-

(a) Non-see-through: There are "non-see-through" white blouses. This means that the material (usually cotton or high quality polycotton) is so solid that even the outline of bright white inner garments does not show through these blouses. Since nothing shows through these blouses, they may be worn irrespective of what is underneath. As explained in No.2 above, some items that might have been partially see-through can be worn when the outer garments or the inner garments are colored, as this itself will sometimes remedy the problem and make them like non-see-through blouses.

(b) Partially see-through: There are "partially see-through" blouses (usually white polycotton of average quality, or very good quality polyester) through which, even though one can neither see skin color nor white. However, the outlines of white inner garments show up, because of the sharp contrast between the white inner garments and the human skin which is much darker. Such blouses may be worn by implementing one of the following recommendations:-

- **With cardigan or sweater:** They should be worn with a cardigan or sweater which closes high enough to cover the point where the outline of the white inner garment would be seen against the skin.

- **Worn over beige items:** They should be worn with beige inner garments. Since beige and skin color are similar colors, the outline of the inner garment will not show up against the skin.

- **With underblouse that covers main body:** They should be worn with an underblouse that reaches close to the neck. The underblouse should either have elbow-length sleeves (when the color of the flesh shows through and the arms are a problem) or no sleeves at all (when the color of flesh does not show through, and the problem is just the white inner garments). In the latter case the arms do not show up due to the contrasting colors of the arms and the white inner items, because almost no contrast is noticed between the main body to the arms.

(c) See-through: There are real "see-through" blouses (usually made of fine spun nylon or polyester) through which one can see white, skin color and often even beige. Such blouses may not be worn (without a sweater or inner shield - see below) even on top of beige inner garments that close up to the neck and have full sleeves, because the inner garments can be seen through the blouse. Such a blouse should preferably not be purchased, but if bought, must be worn with a sweater or inner shield, as stated.

A woman or girl should obtain the most comfortable and appropriate type of 'shield' for her personal needs. In this way she will wear the shield not only when it obviously needed but also in borderline cases. The *kashrus* of her dress will therefore be guaranteed. There are three alternatives:-

- **With a sweater that gives full cover:** It can be worn with a cardigan or sweater, provided that covers it her so substantially that nothing of her main body, arms or inner garments will be visible.

- **With an undershirt that gives full cover:** The first alternative is to wear an undershirt (known in the U.K. as a vest) that is made of very soft knitted cotton and shaped to give full cover. It covers the chest until close to the neck and has long sleeves. Being soft and shaped to fit around the body it is not bulky, as many find underblouses that are made of blouse-like cotton to be. Since the inner garment sits snugly around the body rather than against the inner surface of the top blouse, its white color is not so pronounced and other inner items hidden under it. It can therefore be worn under a see-through blouse without being noticed.

Wearing this type of undershirt is ideal for a cool or temperate climate, whereas in a hot climate this type of undershirt might be too warm, particularly as it has long sleeves. However, others find they can wear it even in hot weather. [Should an undershirt that gives the main body full cover exist with no sleeves, it can be used when the blouse is only partially see-through but not when it is fully see-through, as explained in the next point].

- **With an underblouse that gives full cover:** The second alternative is to wear an underblouse that is made of usual blouse cotton. This item is worn just under the outer blouse or dress. The underblouse covers the full front and back of the person, until just under the neck, thus screening off all that must be covered. Some underblouses have sleeves whilst others have no sleeves. As explained, if the upper blouse is properly see-through it requires an underblouse with sleeves, so that the arms are not seen through, whilst if the blouse is only partially see-through, sleeves are not required. Such an underblouse is worn by many even in hot climates. Those who find them uncomfortable should rather use the third method.

For maternity wear, a long inner-dress, instead of a slip, can be made of cotton batiste material (a very fine cotton). If it hangs from the shoulder to the knees it will solve problems of transparency and will also help conceal the figure. The latter could be necessary if the outer dress is made of a silky material that tends to cling to the body.

- **With a cotton lining that gives full cover:** The third alternative is to line the outer blouse or dress with a cotton batiste material. It should line the outer garment from shoulder to waist. If worn without an undershirt people find it comfortable even in hot weather. [Inspecting garments whether they are see-through - see 6:E:4(c) below].

4. DISORDER OF IGNORING THAT A GARMENT IS SEE-THROUGH:

(a) Regrettably, what was once shameful has become acceptable: Having explained what steps should be taken to prevent degrees of see-through, a distress signal must be sounded. This is that there are quite a number of women in the *chareidi* circle who would not purposefully display that which should be covered. They have, however, become insensitive to the personal degradation and the obvious provocation that is involved in allowing such items to be seen. This is evident from the fact that even when told and made aware that their dress or blouse is see-through, they ignore the information and are unconcerned about it. This is a level of insensitivity that shocks whoever feels for *tznius* and the upkeep of basic respectability.

It has always been a constituent of elementary self-respect that a woman conceals all inner items and ensures that nothing can be seen of them. This iron-clad rule of human conduct has, however, taken a number of severe blows. One was when the infamous slit-above-the-knee came into existence. Often part of the slip or the lining of the dress was visible when the woman walked, much to the chagrin of decent people. Secondly, when the see-through blouses and dresses first came onto the market with the development of nylons and other man-made fabrics they caused the inner garments to be detected and sometimes even seen quite clearly through the outer garment.

The Jewish woman and girl would at the beginning take every precaution not to fall victim to this major lack of *tznius*. However, seeing these breaches in decent conduct relentlessly, even in the dress of elegant shop assistants, female bank clerks, has taken its toll, and previous sensitivities have now turned into callous insensitivities. To some women, for the outline or the veiled image of an inner item to be visible is no longer a disgrace and an infringement on personal privacy. In their affected way of thinking, if the sleeves are of ample length and the dress has a decent neckline, all is well. The truth, however, is that these qualities do not compensate for the disorder of the garment. On the contrary, they add to its disorder, as its apparent 'signs of kashrus" encourage Jewish women to wear it and overlook its serious fault. Such a dress is comparable to the animal that displays its cloven hooves, professing to be Kosher, whilst in fact this is not the case at all.

The swift decline in values, and the way in which what was impossible and outrageous just a short while ago, has suddenly become acceptable and fashionable, is a special feature of the *yetzer horah* of *arayos* of our times. The *nisyonos* of the times preceding the coming of *Moshiach* are of a nature that people are confronted with a fast declining slide into all forms of exhibitionism. This, together with many other symptoms, signifies just how devastating the influence is, and that everyone has to practice constant vigilance not to be swept away by the tide of unbridled and indecent behavior that engulfs us. This tidal wave of indecency has the potential of drawing almost anyone along, if he does not watch each and every step he takes.

(b) Declines that once took decades, now happen rapidly: Already seventy years ago, the holy *Chofetz Chayim* saw the emergence of the "pattern of swift decline" that has just been explained. The following is the translation of part of a letter that he wrote on *Rosh Chodesh Tammuz* 5684. It is printed in the *Chofetz Chayim al HaTorah*, page 324:-

"Although we appeal to *Hashem*, אל תשליכנו מלפניך ורוח קדשך אל תקח ממנו - 'Do not reject us and do not take Your spirit of sanctity from us' (*Tehillim* 51:13), the *Satan* outwits us and dispels sanctity from the Jewish people. How does he do this? He arouses the *yetzer horah* of lust, so that girls walk around partially unclad ..... This was the idea of Bilam the wicked, who encouraged the daughters of Moab to present themselves in an unclad state which in turn caused the Jewish people to stumble...... The verse states והיה מחניך קדוש ולא יראה בך ערות דבר - 'Your camp should be holy, *ervah* should not be seen with you'. Clearly, the sanctity of *Yisroel* depends on all that is *ervah* being covered and not visible".

The *Chofetz Chayim* finishes off with the following statement: ומה שהיה צריך היצר הרע מלפנים לעמול כמה שנים התחכם היום ועושה זאת בזמן קצר - "That which used to take the *yetzer horah* many years to achieve, he now cunningly manages in just a short time". The truth of these words is borne out before our eyes. The atrocious dress worn by many nowadays and the defilement that fills even the higher-class newspapers, is a result of a sudden decline to a level of immorality and depravity that was unknown just a few decades ago. Most middle-aged adults remember the days when high-class newspapers were undefiled and could be read by all without a worry. Today, hardly a newspaper can be found that is fit for a *shomer mitzvos* or indeed any respectable person to allow into his house.

As time goes on, *pritzus* becomes worse, and what was impossible last year is accepted as natural behavior and the norm this year. What was a punishable offense just a few short years ago, is so commonplace amongst the *nochrim* of today that as far as they are concerned there is nothing whatsoever wrong with it. These misdeeds are too terrible and deplorable to mention in a *sefer* that is to be read by *Yidden*. However, the existence of such corruption underscores the truth of the *Chofetz Chayim's* statement. Towards the end of days the moral decline will be very swift - and will therefore be exceedingly threatening.

5. OUTFITS THAT MUST HAVE AN ACCOMPANYING BLOUSE: There is a certain oversight that many may not have come across. If not for the fact that this has been noticed in a number of localities, one would have preferred to leave it out of the *sefer* so as not to display the carelessness that prevails even in *chareidi* circles in matters of *tznius*. With this we refer to a refined two-piece outfit that looks absolutely perfect both in the front and back. It closes so well at the upper front that it is worn by some without a blouse.

The problem is that the jacket covers the top of the skirt by no more than a few inches, as is usual for all outfits. As a result of this, when the wearer bends somewhat forward or raises her arms to put something onto a shelf, the two parts of the outfit separate from one another revealing inner clothes or in some cases the flesh itself. This is something which dare not happen. In fact, it is quite amazing that women who see this glaring defect on another woman's outfit, do not inform her as soon as possible in order to save her from future embarrassment and from appearing in public in such a way. Regretfully, our *midas ha'busha* (bashfulness) is often badly misplaced. See *sefer, Malbushei Kavod* (page 54) which similarly warns about this hazard.

E. DRESSES AND BLOUSES

1. WHAT TO LOOK OUT FOR WHEN BUYING A GARMENT:

(a) Ensuring that the general look of the garment is refined: Concerning the main outer garments that women and girls wear, it is appropriate to state that everyone buys a garment with an eye on how pleasing the garment will look on them. They consider whether the size, color and style will enhance their general appearance or not. Sadly, many do not stop to think, "How Jewish will this garment look on me?" or, "How obvious will it be on first sight that I am Torah observant?" This is what every Jewish person should consider before buying an item which will affect his or her whole appearance.

(b) Making certain that the buttons keep the front properly closed: On some blouses the buttons are too far apart, causing the blouse to frequently open up when the person is sitting or just not in a fully upright position. The same happens when a blouse is made of a very soft material. The cloth will sometimes buckle up when the person leans slightly forward, causing the space between the buttons to open up, even though the buttons are not excessively spaced out. In these cases, the opening of the front of the garment may reveal part of the chest or part of an inner garment, both of which are *ossur*.

Such blouses may not be worn unless secured in a way that ensures that they will not inadvertently open up during wear. The way to correct the problem and render them Kosher, is to fix snaps (press-studs) at the vulnerable areas. They will not be seen and will not spoil the appearance of the garment in any way - but will ensure that the garment is closed in a way that nothing shows.

Some blouses have only scant closing facilities down the front - just one or two buttons near the top. Under the buttons the right side of the blouse just overlaps the left side by an inch or two all the way down, and is kept closed by its lower end being tucked firmly into the top of the skirt. Obviously, such blouses may not be worn unless extensively secured with snaps, as described. Ideally, however, such blouses should not be worn at all, because they are usually totally unsuitable. Also, wearing such blouses could encourage other women and girls to wear them as well, and they might lack the sensitivity to secure the front in a fully adequate way.

2. DRESSES AND BLOUSES MUST NOT BE TIGHT-FITTING:

(a) The nature of this *issur*: It is against elementary *tznius* and refinement to wear tight-fitting dresses or blouses that accentuate the chest area (see *Brachos* 10b and *Midrash, Shir HaShirim* 4:1:5 about the effect this area has on the female appearance). Similarly, it is *ossur* to wear tight-fitting skirts which emphasize the thigh area - see 6:L:4 below and *Mekoros* 40. Regrettably, in our times, some of those who still have a strong sense of commitment to Torah learning, to giving *tzedaka*, to *kashrus* and to almost all other facets of *Yiddishkeit,* no longer have an understanding nor sensitivity for true *tznius*. This is a direct result of the secular manner of dress which includes items such as slacks (trousers) and ultra-tight skirts which emphasize the shape of the body. We pray that just as there is an inspiration from Heaven to bring thousands of previously non-religious people to *teshuva*, so too our religious sisters should be inspired to understand and admire true *tznius* and refined behavior, even though they are surrounded by many who have no feeling for it - see *Mekoros* 4:13-14 and 40:1-7.

(b) With a change of figure, loose garments can become tight-fitting: It frequently happens that a dress or blouse that was well-fitting when bought becomes tight fitting at some later stage. This can be due to the garment having shrunk; being worn with a thermal undershirt instead of a summer undershirt for which it was bought; the girl having grown; the person having put on weight; or pregnancy. Since the item used to fit perfectly, the woman or girl might not realize that the change has occurred. It would therefore be appropriate for a good friend to make her aware that the dress or blouse does not fit her at present.

(c) Tight-fitting clothes were not worn even at home: The extent to which Jewish women and girls would feel uncomfortable and not properly dressed when wearing tight-fitting clothes can be seen from the *Gemara* (*Shabbos* 112a). There, the Shabbos *issur* of "tying a knot-and-bow that is to remain for 24 hours" is discussed. In that context it is stated that a woman or girl may gird herself on Shabbos with a broad waistband, because she will certainly untie it to take it off once again and the knot will therefore definitely last less than a day.

The *Rishonim* ask that this need not be so. Since a waistband is only moderately tight round the waist, a woman or girl can remove it without undoing the knot, by simply pulling it downwards over her legs or upwards over her head (*Rashi*, *Meiri* and *Chidushei HaRan)*. To this they answer that Jewish women and girls would on principle not remove a waistband in such a way because of the lack of *tznius* that would be involved. Removing it in such a way would mean squeezing it over the thighs or across the upper part of the body, and such unrefined appearances (even on top of other clothes) were avoided when possible even at home between the family and even for just a short moment.

This was the standard of the average *Bas Yisroel* in the times of *Chazal*! It brings feelings of shame over us when we know that some of our sisters and daughters wear tight-fitting blouses, dresses and skirts, and present themselves in such clothes all day long, both at home and amongst the public. [See 6:H:7-8 and 6:I:1-2 below concerning tight-fitting skirts.] See also 6:R:1 below in the name of Hagaon Harav Shmuel Halevi Wosner *shlita* and Hagaon Harav Yosef Shalom Elyashiv *shlita* that for this reason girls who wear pajama trousers should not walk around in them even between bedrooms. Trousers display the shape of the body and to walk around in them is a distinct lack of *tznius*. Instead, they should robe themselves with a night robe or a house coat as soon as they rise from bed.

3. BLOUSES SHOULD NOT CLING TO THE WEARER:

(a) Reasons why blouses should not cling: It is *ossur* to wear a blouse which, although not tight-fitting as far as size is concerned, contracts and clings tightly to the upper part of the body. The same applies to dresses and skirts made of a crinkled material that contracts to fit closely to the lower part of the body. These garments are doubly defective. Firstly, they show every contour of the body and it is *ossur* for the body to be displayed in any way, and all the more for its shape to be stressed. Secondly, the outlines of the inner garments are often noticeable through such tight-fitting materials - see 6:D:1 above. Such garments must therefore not find their way into our society. Wearing such tightly clinging clothes emanates from the desire to exhibit that prevails in the modern world, while the goal of *tznius* is to be as unobtrusive as possible - see *Kevuda Bas Melech,* Chapter 2 note 39, 6:I:2 and see 6:I:3(h) below. See also *Mekoros* 40:4.

(b) Man-made fabrics are likely to cling - remedy to problem: All synthetic man-made fabrics such as nylon, terylene, polyester, acetate, tricel and acrylics develop an electro-static charge as they are worn and as a result have a tendency to cling to the body. The consequence is that the garment becomes a closely fitted item, even though as far as size is concerned it is far from tight fitting. This problem is discussed in 6:I:3(a-f) below. It is explained there that the remedy for this problem is to rinse the garment in fabric conditioner which effectively prevents this problem from occurring. There are, however, some women and girls who know from experience that for certain reasons they are not affected by this problem - see 6:I:3(e) where this point is explained.

4. GUIDANCE FOR BUYING A GARMENT OR CLOTH: For further guidance on the above points, the following text has been excerpted from a letter written to the author of this *sefer* by the Rebbetzen of a highly respected *mashpia* in *Yerusholayim*. It is particularly relevant to the types of materials sold in *Eretz Yisroel*:

(a) Print and color helps camouflage: When shopping for fabrics or for clothing in general, printed materials will provide more effective camouflage than solid colors, both for preventing a see-through effect and for concealing general shape e.g. maternity wear. Furthermore, medium colors are often more camouflaging than dark colors of the same weave.

(b) Cloth sometimes shrinks: Washable materials should be washed and if possible dried in a clothes-drier before being sewn into a garment. Cottons, viscose, rayons and challis material can shrink up to 10%. This in turn can make a significant difference in the size or length of a newly sewn garment. [On the other hand, if a finished garment was not pre-shrunk care should be taken not to put it into a clothes-drier].

(c) Checking for see-through against the sun: Questionable materials or garments should be checked against sunlight i.e. the woman wearing the blouse or dress should stand facing the person who is to check the garment on her. The woman's arms should hang loosely slightly away from the body. Sunlight (or some other good source of light) should be at the rear of the woman wearing the blouse etc. and the checker should stand a few feet away out of the glare of the sun. One would sometimes be amazed how see-through clothes are when checked in this manner! [Also surprising is the fact that even moderate sunshine (as is usual in England) rather than bright sunshine can cause a garment to be see-through]. It should be noted that Hagaon Harav Shmuel HaLevi Wosner *shlita* signed a proclamation in *Tammuz* 5747 - see *Mekoros* 40:5 - in which he states that garments should be checked against the sunlight for transparency.

(d) Checking for see-through against an artificial light: If a dress, blouse or skirt is checked for translucency in a room illuminated by an electric light, the reading need not be correct. The power of an electric light is usually much weaker than that of sunlight (especially when not very close to the source of the light) and although the garment seems not to be see-through, it could well be that in sunlight this would not be the case. It is therefore essential that a garment is checked carefully in sunlight (or inside a store but close to strip lights that are fixed down a wall e.g. on either side of a full length mirror. If Kosher there, it is likely to be Kosher in sunlight, although this is not guaranteed, as explained above).

(e) Length of inner protection, when the skirt is see-through: If a dress or skirt is see-through, it must be lined with a material that makes the garment opaque. Alternatively, a suitable slip should be worn under the dress or skirt. In either case it should ideally be just a couple of inches shorter than the outer garment. This is to ensure that what is seen through the outer garment (when in sunlight) appears to be the lining of the dress rather than a slip, as a lining is usually almost as long as the outer garment. Also, if the lining or slip is just knee length, a movement that lifts the garment slightly will cause her knees etc. to show (in sunlight) through the outer garment, since the lowest part of the garment is not protected by a lining or slip.

5. GEMACHS FOR KOSHER DESIGNS: A MULTI-FACETED CHESED: A special note of gratitude must be expressed to women who have taken upon themselves to provide the Orthodox community with *gemachs* for patterns of dresses and outfits. Their focus is not just on saving people money, but also so that women produce for themselves and their daughters garments that are really refined. This type of venture spreads *tahara* in *Klal Yisroel* in three ways - practically, educationally and spiritually.

(a) Practical advantage: The *gemachs* enable women and girls to have clothes made to true Jewish taste and with full adherence to *Hilchos Tznius*. Many find great difficulty in finding such clothes in a store. Even if they do find the right style, they have difficulties in finding clothes suitable for their size or their build. These patterns solve this problem. Also, when making their own clothes, they can ensure that the position of the second button down is such that the neckline will remain Kosher when the top button is open - something rarely found nowadays (see 6:C:1 above). Moreover, they can see to it that the buttons are close enough to eliminate the possibility of innergarments being seen through the spaces between the buttons (see 6:E:1(b) above).

(b) Educational value: By distributing only the right types of patterns and discussing with the borrower how the patterns should be used, those who run these *gemachs* educate the borrower (and also those who will see them dressed in the new garments) to understand the difference between Jewish dress and what others try to achieve when designing a garment. In the wider world, the impure science of dress designing seeks to ensure that the item is as "eye-catching" and glamorous as possible. Furthermore, the dress or outfit is made to highlight certain parts of the body or subtly to cause the onlooker to focus on them. *Lehavdil*, the Jewish science of dressmaking is exactly the opposite. The garment is designed to be pleasant and *b'cheint* but not to be eye-catching in any way. The emphasis in the design is placed on streamlining the garment in a way that the body is camouflaged as far as possible - see 6:L:4 below for more on this point.

There are far too many women and girls who innocently buy almost any style as long as the color and size are right, without checking carefully that the garment is free of the '*pritzus* of style' mentioned. We are therefore grateful that there are around the world women who yearn for an awakening of *tznius* in *Klal Yisroel* and have the enterprising spirit to set up *gemachs* and supply ideal patterns at little or no charge. וזכות הרבים תלויה בהן.

(c) Prevents looking at immodest pictures: A further advantage of such *gemachs* is the fact that many patterns and most clothing magazines contain indecent pictures that may not be seen even by females, whether young or old. As has been stressed elsewhere, people mistakenly think that females are exempt of the *issur* of watching indecent conduct or of looking at pictures of it. This is not the case at all, and such contact, apart from the serious *issur* involved, is extremely harmful to the attitudes of a young girl - see 2:B:2 above. *Gemachs* will hopefully take due precautions to ensure that material that has *treife* pictures does not pass through their hands -/ even if the actual pattern or design would have been appropriate.

6. TRAINING GIRLS IN DRESSMAKING - HIGHLY COMMENDABLE: In our times, it is highly recommendable to train girls in the art of dressmaking and general sewing. Lessons should be given on this subject in schools and, if necessary, also in seminaries. With the general deterioration of modesty and refinement and the present day attitude about openness, it has become exceedingly difficult to find clothes that are Kosher and refined. Even if the material and style are suitable, and as far as length is concerned the garment is appropriate, there is still every likelihood that the neckline will be far from acceptable. Similarly, if a garment has a good neckline, it is likely to be too short or too tight, and so on. In many cases, if a girl or woman can sew, she will be able to rectify a garment that would otherwise have been unwearable. Sometimes, a beautiful and refined garment emerges from such treatment.

If the girl becomes really expert, she will even be able to make garments for herself, and later on, when married also for her daughters. Also she could take up dressmaking as a profession. In that case, apart from earning money which might prove to be a *bracha*, she can be of enormous assistance to others who require help to obtain Kosher clothing.

A certain seminary which only teaches *Kodesh* and has no program for general subjects, nevertheless runs a training course for dressmaking. The *menahel* explained: The *Hannah* of the seminary consider this particular subject as "*kodesh*". With it, the girl will be able to make for herself clothes that are really Kosher and refined. At the very least, she will be able to improve manufactured garments and render them Kosher. See 3:B:5 concerning the type of teacher that should be employed for this subject.

In the praises Shlomo Hamelech sings about the *Eishes Chayil*, he points out that מרבדים עשתה לה שש וארגמן לבושה - "She made for herself pleasant-looking bed covers; she also made herself white (linen) and purple garments to wear" (*Mishlei* 31:22). Moreover, סדין עשתה ותמכור - "She manufactured robes and sold them" (*Mishlei* 31:24). Evidently, it is commendable for woman to be knowledgeable in these arts.

F. UPPER SECTION OF THE ARMS - SLEEVES

1. UPPER SECTION OF ARMS MUST BE COMPLETELY COVERED:

(a) This obligation is part of *Das Yehudis*: The complete upper sections of the arms are covered parts of the body. This is stated in *Kesubos* 72b where *Chazal* say that a woman violates דת יהודית - "fitting Jewish behavior" - if she is טווה בשוק ומגלה זרועותיה לבני אדם - "spins in public and reveals her arms to people" - see *Mekoros* 74:10. Since the upper section of the arms have a powerful potential to arouse attention, they must be completely covered whenever she can be seen by anyone other than her close blood relatives and her husband - see 4:B:1(a) above. The *issur* to uncover the arms or even just part of the arms in public applies even if Jewish women in her locality act wrongly and do not cover their upper arms at all - see M.B. 75:2 in the name of the *Rokeach*, section 324.

(b) Sleeves must ensure proper cover: It is imperative that a woman wear a garment which can be relied upon to always cover the upper sections of her arms even when they are bent, since a woman is liable to bend her arms whilst out on the street or in her garden where she can be seen by men. Also, the sleeves must be long enough, so that when boarding a bus or taking an item off a shelf, she can expect her upper arms to remain safely covered even though they are stretched upwards. Sleeves should therefore extend to at least three inches (7-8 centimeters) beyond the elbow - or more according to circumstances. Furthermore, women and girls should not wear dresses, tee-shirts and sweaters that have wide sleeves (unless the sleeves are full length and will not ride up the whole lower arm) and could cause the upper arms to be revealed either when sitting with folded arms or when carrying an item with both her arms etc. - see 1:F above and *Mekoros* 41:1 and 42:3-5.

(c) The attraction caused by uncovered arms: Since the power of attraction of uncovered arms is not realized by all, the following *Midrash* (*Breishis* 80:5) is most informative:- וירא אותה שכם בן חמור, ר' שמואל בר נחמן אמר שגלה בה דרועה - loosely translated this means, "Shechem, who forcibly took Dinah the daughter of Yaacov, was attracted to her by procuring a glimpse of her arms and this aroused his distressing interest in her" [דרועה is Aramaic for זרועה]. This *Chazal* shows the effect uncovered arms can have, and how bitter the result of carelessness in this matter can be.

It should be noted that when *tznius* in dress was lax in certain countries, both the *Chofetz Chayim zt'l* and the *Gerer Rebbe zt'l* (the *Imrei Emes*) wrote letters to the public about *tznius* and mentioned in particular the evil of uncovered arms. See the letter of the *Chofetz Chayim* from year 5684, printed at the end of *Chofetz Chayim Al Hatorah* page 322 and the letter of the *Gerer Rebbe* in *Osef Michtavim*, Vol 1, letter one, from year 5666. This should strengthen our realization that a woman's arms have a powerful effect of inviting undesirable attention.

(d) The way men avoided coming into the proximity of sin: We are told in the *Gemara* that people would sometimes allow a woman of the neighborhood to bake in their house, as not everyone had the means to bake in their own home. When such permission was granted, the *baal habayis* would keep away from that part of the house - because the woman would roll up her sleeves and reveal her arms and he would not want to be in the close proximity of a woman with uncovered arms - see *Bava Kama* 48a. Similarly, we are told by *Chazal* that when Korach's messengers came to fetch On Ben Peles to join Korach's revolt against Moshe Rabbeinu, they stopped short in their tracks. They saw the wife of On Ben Peles combing her hair in the hallway of her home and under such circumstances would not enter the house in spite of the urgency - see *Sanhedrin* 110a and 1:Q:2(d) above. On ben Peles was thereby saved from the terrible death that befell Korach.

People would simply not go near uncovered arms or other areas that have been labeled *ervah* by *Chazal.* Such was the natural *tahara* and *kedusha* of *Klal Yisroel* of old. A person naturally felt he was endangered if he came into close proximity with sin. In contrast, we today are assaulted by females with short sleeves and short skirts whenever we venture out of our front doors. This bitter reflection arouses us to beseech *Hashem,* השיבנו ה׳ אליך ונשובה חדש ימינו כקדם - "Bring us back to you O *Hashem* and we shall return" - we beg of you to "re-establish the *klal Yisroel* of old" by enabling us to live in an environment that is conducive and suited to a *Torah'dik* life (*Eicha* 5:21).

2. ELBOWS ARE PART OF UPPER ARMS AND MUST BE COVERED: The elbow has the same *halachos* as the upper section of the arm and must be completely covered - *Beis Yosef* O.C. 92 and M.B. 4:54. This is contrary to the opinion mistakenly held by many that only the upper arm must be covered but not the elbow itself. This is an error because the elbow is a part of the body that *halachically* must be covered. Also, the elbow is not an independent bone as is widely thought (although there are two minor additional bones in that area - see *Mishnayos Ohalos* 1:8). Rather, the upper limb of the arm (the humerus) ends right inside the elbow area where it is locked into position with the bones of the lower section of the arm (the radius and the ulna). In fact, the elbow is a "ball and socket" area, the "ball" being the rounded end of the bone of the upper arm, and the "socket" the top end of one of the lower bones of the arm (the radius). Hence the upper limb of the arm occupies a substantial part of the elbow. Since the upper section of the arm must be covered and it extends into the elbow, it is understood that the complete elbow must be covered - see *Mekoros* 1:1 and 42:1-2.

Many people who have heard the term טפח באשה ערוה have mistakenly concluded from it that it is permissible to leave less than a *tefach* of a forbidden area uncovered. They therefore allow their wives to leave the last inch or two of the upper arm uncovered and certainly the elbow. This is a serious mistake (as has already been explained in 6:A:2 above) since the *halacha* requires complete covering of forbidden areas. The *tefach* measurement was given only in connection with the husband saying a *bracha* when his wife is not fully-covered, but there is no *heter* whatsoever to leave a small amount uncovered in the presence of a stranger.

3. ISSUR APPLIES EVEN IF THE EXPOSURE IS UNINTENTIONAL: The *issur* to appear in public with any part of the upper sections of the arms uncovered applies even if this is not done to draw attention to her arms or because she desires to wear a fashionable short-sleeved dress. Moreover, even if it is obvious to the observer that she has done so with no negative intentions, it still remains *ossur*. The arms naturally attract attention and *Hilchos Tznius* demands that this should not happen. Also, the very fact that she does not care that a covered part of the body is on display is a serious lack of modesty and is itself a form of *pritzus*.

This is evident from *Chazal* who say that a woman is a *prutza* if she is טוה בשוק - "spins in public" (*Kesubos* 72b), because while spinning, part of her upper arms are exposed. The *Poskim* write that the exposure occurs by itself in the process of spinning and is unintentional - not that she pushes up her sleeves before starting to spin. It is nevertheless considered *pritzus* because she is aware that it will occur and regardlessly goes ahead and spins in public (*Hafla'ah, Kuntres Acharon*, E.H. 115). Accordingly, when girls play ball in a place where they can be seen, they must be careful that their arms do not become uncovered as a result of excessive stretching to catch the ball. Also, they should have sleeves which are long enough that during normal play the upper arms will not become revealed - see 9:J:3(h) below.

Even if such an exposure is a one time occurrence and hardly ever happens to her, it is still wrong and considered *pritzus*, because even a one-time sighting of a covered part of a woman's body is an *aveirah* and is harmful - *Chelkas Mechokek* E.H. 115:11. Accordingly, if a mother carries her child through the streets or inside a hotel where she is amongst the public, she must be careful to ensure that her upper arms do not become uncovered in the process.

It is related that the Chazon Ish was once visited by a young couple belonging to a family with which he had a very close connection. They came to ask whether he recommends that the husband undergo a serious operation which the doctors advised him to have. The Chazon Ish listened to all the facts, and after careful consideration, recommended that the young man go along with the advice of the doctors and have the operation. The Chazon Ish added his warmest *brocho,* wishing the young man a heartfelt *refuah shleima.*

After giving the *bracha,* the Chazon Ish requested the husband to leave the room so that he could speak privately to his wife. When the husband was out of the room the Chazon Ish said to the young woman, "*Ich volt gebeten die arbel*' - "I would like to ask for the sleeves [to be lengthened]". Although her sleeves extended over her elbow, the Chazon Ish was not satisfied. He wanted her to lengthen the sleeves.

The young woman was totally taken aback. The Chazon Ish had been discussing with them a problem of life and death. He had nevertheless noticed her sleeves, was disturbed by them and had even found a way to tell her that he did not consider her sleeves long enough (without embarrassing her husband who had allowed her to dress in this manner). She learned to appreciate that *tznius* was a matter of paramount importance to the Chazon Ish, as he did not overlook this even in the face of the very serious matter he had been discussing with them (*B'mechitzos HaChazon Ish,* page 127. The author heard it from the couple who are his close relatives).

4. UPPER ARMS MAY NOT BE VISIBLE THROUGH THE SLEEVES: Since the upper sections of the arms and the elbows must be covered, if a woman or girl wears a semi see-through blouse which enables the observer to see the part of her upper arms, she is inadequately covered. To appear in public she must wear either a sweater over the blouse or an undershirt or underblouse with long sleeves under the blouse to shield everything in an adequate manner - see 6:D:3(c) above. Some women who are careful as far as the problem of see-through garments are concerned when out in the street, but do not take the same precautions when indoors even though visitors frequent her home. This is incorrect, since the *halachic* requirements of *tznius* must be practiced even in the presence of individuals.

5. WE ALL WEAR A "SIGN OF ALLEGIANCE" ON OUR UPPER ARM: It was stated previously in the name of one of the great Rabbonim of this generation that, although women do not have the *mitzva* to wear *tefillin,* they do have a counterpart to *tefillin.* This is the great *mitzva* of "covering the hair" which sanctifies the woman similar to the sanctification *tefillin shel rosh* bestows on a man - see 5:D:2(f) above. Both are crowns on the head of the Jewish person and both prevent *arayos*-related misconduct - see *Rambam, Hilchos Tefillin* 4:25 who stresses this aspect of the *kedusha* of *tefillin* when he writes, כל זמן שתפילין בראשו של אדם ועל זרועו...אינו נמשך בשחוק ובשיחה בטילה ואינו מהרהר מחשבות רעות - "As long as *tefillin* are on the person's head and arm he....is not drawn to levity and idle talk nor will he entertain evil thoughts". That is as far as *tefillin shel rosh* - "*tefillin* of the head" is concerned.

A man, however, also dons *tefillin shel Yad,* "*tefillin* of the arm". Here again women have their complementary *mitzva.* This is the *mitzva* of *tznius* concerning "covering the arm" - a *mitzva* both for married women and unmarried girls. The predominant position of this *mitzva* is on the upper section of the arms, but many apply this *tznius* also to the forearm (see 6:G:1 below), similar to the straps of *tefillin* that are wrapped onto the forearm.

Just as *tefillin* is identified by the Torah as a "a sign of allegiance" to *Hashem* (לאות על ידיך - *Devarim* 6:8), so too, covering the arm in the correct manner is a "sign of allegiance" on the part of the girl and woman to the will of *Hashem* that *kedusha* should prevail amongst the Jewish people. Although, other parts of the body are also covered, they are obvious necessities, called for by basic modesty and expected even from non-Jewish women. However, covering hair and the upper arm, are acts of *tznius* done only by Jewish women, and are therefore "signs of allegiance" to *Hashem.*

These two forms of *tznius* are therefore very special - and fittingly correspond to the great *mitzva* of *tefillin* of men. Both symbolize the fact that our intellect (the head) and physique (muscular part of the arm) are fully submitted to the will of *Hashem Yisborach.*

There is a *halacha* concerning *tefillin* - a man may not be מסיח דעת, "become totally oblivious of the fact that he is wearing *tefillin*" because he is liable to neglect treating the *tefillin* with the care they require (O.C. 44:1). Hair covering and arm covering are subject to a very similar recommendation, as both can easily move and the area become somewhat uncovered. A woman or girl should therefore never become oblivious of her hair covering or her sleeves. On the contrary, she should be constantly on the alert to ensure that they are fully covered, as is *halachically* required.

G. FOREARMS - SLEEVES

1. THE HALACHIC STATUS OF THE FOREARMS:

(a) According to most *Poskim* the forearms need not be covered: Most *Poskim* maintain that the *halacha* does not require women to cover their arms below the elbow. [This is the opinion of *Rashi, Shabbos* 63b s.v *Etzada; Rambam, Hilchos Chovel Umazik* 4:15; *Shulchan Aruch,* E.H. 83:1; *Od Yosef Chai* (by the *Ben Ish Chai*), *parshas Bo,* number 1; *Mishna Berura* 4:54 and *Chazon Ish* O.C. 16:8.]

Although there is an opinion which maintains that the forearms require covering [the *Chavas Yair* in his *sefer, Mekor Chayim* 75:1], the consensus of opinion amongst both previous and present-day *Gedolei HaPoskim* is that *halachically* the forearm need not be covered - see *Mekoros* 1:1.

Although there is a dispute concerning the forearms, all opinions agree that women need not cover their hands or fingers in public, as is written explicitly in the *Rambam* and *Shulchan Aruch* just mentioned. This is so although women used to wear outdoor garments that covered the hands. Due to this it was quite usual never to see a woman's hands. [See *Shabbos* 53b, *Rashi* s.v. *Darkoh bekach* that people would not get to know when a woman had no hand or similar blemish because they never usually saw a woman's hands]. This was, however, definitely not a matter of *halacha* - and they exposed their hands when necessary. For example, when a person handed money to a woman she would put out her hand to receive it - *see Brachos* 61a. Also, rings are called by *Chazal* תכשיטין שבחוץ - "Ornaments that are visible externally" (*Shabbos* 64b), because rings adorn fingers which are *halachically* uncovered limbs.

(b) The extra refinement in covering the forearms: Although there is no *halachic* obligation to cover the forearms, nevertheless, this part of the arms offer an opportunity for a woman or girl to exercise her own instinctive feeling for refinement, where *halacha* has not demanded it of her.

Harav Hagaon Rabbi Moshe Sternbuch *shlita* relates that he heard from his grandmother, Rebbetzen Pines *o.h.* that she personally asked Maran Hagaon Harav Reb Chayim Soloveitchik *zt'l* (known as Reb Chayim Brisker) whether a woman must cover the lower section of her arms. To this his answer was, "The obligation to cover extends only to past the elbow. However, to cover the complete arm is a הידור - a considerable enhancement of the *mitzva* of *tznius*" - see *Mekoros* 41:2-9, 43:1-3 and 44:1-2.

The Rebbetzen of the *Steipler Gaon*, Rebbetzen Miriam Kanievsky *o.h.* used to say that "covering the lower sections of the arms is a *segula* for having sons who are real *talmidei chachamim*" - see *Mekoros* 43:2. She was of the opinion that when a woman or girl voluntarily covers her arms completely, she demonstrates with this a warmth for *tznius* and an appreciation for full refinement of dress. This is a *segula* for children who are *talmidei chachamim*, as will be explained in 10:A, 10:B and *Mekoros* 25:3-6.

(c) In some communities women cover almost all their forearms: Although women are not obligated to cover their forearms, as explained, it is nevertheless the custom of many to cover most of the forearms. This could be a reaction to the serious *pritzus* that prevails nowadays and engulfs us all. To counter this assault, those who feel deeply for *tznius* take upon themselves to be stringent, even though it is not a *halachic* obligation.

There could, however, be a deeper reason behind the fact that many prefer to cover most of their forearms nowadays. All parts of a woman's body potentially attract attention, even areas that are always uncovered, as the *Rambam, Hilchos Krias Shema* 3:16 writes, וכל גוף האשה ערוה - "The entire body of a woman attracts attention" (see *Aruch Hashulchan* O.C. 75:1 that the *halachic* significance of this statement is that a man may not say a *bracha* while gazing with pleasure at his wife's or daughter's face). Similarly, the *Rambam, Hilchos Issurei Biah* 21:2 writes that a man may not gaze even at a woman's little finger, since pleasure can be derived from every part of the body - see *Od Yosef Chai*, *Parshas Bo*, No.2.

Since they can cause a man to stumble, the *Shloh Hakadosh, Sha'ar Ha'Osyos*, section '*Tznius*' recommends that "a woman cover all parts of her body so that they do not cause people to sin". [Apart from her face as she communicates with her face and to cover it would be a major inconvenience. Similarly, to cover hands would be an enormous inconvenience - see 7:K:3(a) below.]

Moreover, in the *Chorev*, Chapter 69 Section 458, Hagaon Hatzadik Harav Samson Raphael Hirsch *zt'l* writes concerning general feelings of *tznius*, "Only parts of the body which primarily serve as instruments of work should be visible". This means that it is characteristic of someone possessing healthy feelings for *tznius* to cover whatever he can cover without causing himself discomfort. It seems that this is the core reason why *Talmidei Chachamim* would wear longer garments than other people, as stated in the *Gemara Bava Basra* 57b . A *Talmid Chacham* has a stronger sense of *tznius* than other people - see 6:D:1(a), and correspondingly has a strong urge to cover himself with a long loose hanging garment.

Forearms were left uncovered, because women did a lot of physical work that continuously required the use of the forearms. For example, they scrubbed the floor, heated the hearth with wood or coal, kneaded dough, grated vegetables, squeezed fruit juices by hand, laundered and wrung all items by hand, sewed by hand, etc. Virtually all these jobs require the use of the hands and the forearms. The forearms were therefore left uncovered like the hands. About these industrious women the verse says, חגרה בעוז מתניה ותאמץ זרועותיה - "She girds herself with strength and she invigorates her arms" (*Mishlei* 31:17).

Nowadays, however, covering the forearms is hardly an inconvenience as we have food processors, liquidizers, dough makers, cookers and ovens, washing machines, clothes dryers, sewing machines, carpet cleaners and many similar gadgets. Since the need for forearms to be bared has decreased considerably, many women and girls happily cover all or most of the arm, although it is not a *halachic* obligation, as stated.

2. PLACES WHERE WOMEN COVER THEIR FOREARMS: As stated, in some *chareidi* circles it has become customary that women and girls cover most of the lower section of the forearms - and some go even further and cover the whole lower section of the arm (except where the bracelet or watch is worn). If one is in such a place, one must do likewise, because the individual woman is *halachically* required to keep the standard set by women of that time and place. For men of these places to see the lower section of a woman's arm uncovered is almost as harmful as seeing the upper sections uncovered, because as far as these men are concerned the forearms are covered areas - *Biur Halacha* 75:2 s.v. *Mi'Bachutz* and 1:G:2 above.

If covering most or all of the forearm has not become the local *minhag,* an individual may, of course, do so herself. She has, however, no right to insist that other women and girls do so (except the principal of a school or seminary who can insist on a special standard of dress from those who are in their institution).

If a woman, belonging to a community that is particular on covering the forearms, is temporarily away from home, and is amongst people who are not stringent concerning this issue, she is obligated to keep the stringent *minhag* that prevails at home. She must therefore cover her forearms even though the other Orthodox women who live in this place do not - see 1:G:5 where this subject is explained.

3. RUTH COVERED FAR MORE THAN WAS MANDATORY ON HER: Due to her difficult circumstances, Ruth was forced to gather fallen stalks from a field in which male workers were harvesting. Ruth dressed and conducted herself with perfect *tznius* at all times. However, now that she was in a situation where she might be observed (especially as she was exceptionally good-looking, as stated in the *Midrash* on the verse ויקר מקרה - Ruth 2:3), she went far beyond the normal *halachos* of *tznius* and even covered her hands. The *Midrash* (*Ruth Zutah* 2:6) records what the lad said to Boaz in response to his query as to who Ruth was: יש כמה ימים שהיא עמנו

שלא נראית אפילו אחת מאצבעות ידיה ורגליה, ואין אנו יודעים אם אלמת היא או דברנית - "She has been with us for quite a few days but we have neither seen any of her fingers or toes nor have we heard her speak, and we do not know whether she is dumb or capable of speech". Ruth, in her great piety, practiced a level of *tznius* that was well beyond the letter of the law, so as to maintain her purity in this unhealthy situation.

This is also the meaning of *Rashi* (*Ruth* 2:5) who writes that Boaz was impressed with the conduct of Ruth because, דברי צניעות ראה בה, מלקטת עומדות מעומד ושוכבות מיושב כדי שלא תשחה - "He noticed that Ruth stood up to pick the upright stalks and sat down to pick the low lying ones [so as not to have to bend down]". Since *Rashi* mentions that she stood up whenever she picked upright stalks, it seems that there was an act of sanctity and *tznius* in doing so. What is special about standing up?. The answer is that her extreme modesty of not allowing even her hands to show would have been jeopardized had she picked upright stalks from a sitting position. To do so would have required that she stretch her arms upwards to snap off the upper parts of the stalks where the kernels were located, and this could have caused her hands or even her forearms to become uncovered. To ensure that this does not happen, she stood up to pick those stalks.

Her outstanding *tznius*, of going beyond the *halacha* because circumstances called for it, was richly rewarded. There are many present-day women who feel that with *tznius* being at such a low ebb in our day and age, it is highly desirable to partially emulate Ruth and cover the lower section of the arms even though this is not *halachically* required. They too will certainly enjoy the rich reward *Hashem* has in store for those who foster and promote *tznius*.

H. UPPER SECTION OF THE LEGS - SKIRTS

1. SKIRTS MUST COVER THE KNEES COMPLETELY: It has been explained (in 6:A:1 above) that the upper sections of the arms and the upper sections of the legs must be covered when in public by decree of *halacha*, due to their proximity to the main body. Therefore, even if most women would wear short sleeves or short skirts, it would still remain strictly against the *halacha* to do so (M.B. 75:2) - see *Mekoros* 44:1 and 45:1-5.

To wear a short skirt (and all the more so a mini-skirt) is probably the worst form of *pritzus* that has found its way into the dress of people who are otherwise *shomrei mitzvos*. [See *Taz* O:C 75:1 who stresses how extremely harmful it is when any part of the upper sections of the legs is uncovered.] For many years our greatest *Poskim* and *Rabbanim* have announced again and again that this is a major violation of the requirements of *tznius* and a total defacement of the refined image the Jewish woman usually projects.

It is a painful sight to see a couple walking along with the husband dressed in true Jewish garb, evidently happy to look like a *Yid*. He is almost a copy of the way his grandfather looked years ago. Next to him walks his wife dressed in a way that would make her grandmother turn over in her grave!

Our lives are *b'Yad Hashem*. We constantly pray and hope for His protection against illness. If we "protect our bodies" by dressing in accordance with the ways of the Torah, we can hope that *Hashem* will likewise "protect our bodies" and grant us good health. However, if we display insensitivity to *kedushas* and *taharas Yisroel*, how can we expect His protection? - see *Mekoros* 26.

2. DYNAMIC LETTER BY MARAN HAGAON RAV MOSHE FEINSTEIN: The following is the translation of a highly authoritative letter signed by Maran Hagaon Harav Moshe Feinstein *zt'l* on this issue. (The original is printed at the end of the *sefer*, *Kummi Ori* and in *kuntres*, *Am Segula*) - see *Mekoros* 45:1.

> *The subject of Tznius for women is a major Biblical obligation. It applies not just to married women to whom the Torah forbade even the exposure of hair and all the more so areas of their bodies that should be covered, but even to unmarried girls...... They have the same issurim as married women and these issurim are of the gravest nature.*
>
> *Lately the urge for pritzus has found its way even into homes of shomrei Torah luring them into wearing short garments, rachmana litzlan. I have come to announce and proclaim in public that this is one of the most serious* aveiros. *Those who transgress it will be severely punished, whilst those who do not give in to this urge will be richly rewarded both in this world and in the next. I want to make it known that it is an obligation on the Bas Yisroel to wear Kosher clothes which do not allow even the most minimal part of her knee to show, chas veshalom, whether at the time of walking or when she sits down. Even if she wears thick hosiery it is still forbidden, because it is an immense pritzus [to show the shape of the knee] even when no flesh can be seen. All the more so when sheer*

> *hosiery is worn through which the flesh can be seen and the covering is therefore reckoned as non-existent.*
>
> *It is an obligation on each and every man to supervise the members of his family and ensure that they do not violate the halacha by wearing short garments, chas veshalom. They will then fulfill the verse of Vehaya Machanecho Kadosh and will be worthy of having upright and blessed children who engage in the study of Torah and the fulfillment of mitzvos.*
>
> *We turn to the heads of educational institutions for girls and request of them to be strong in this difficult struggle and not to allow pupils to wear short garments. In the merit of Tznius and kedushas Yisroel we should soon merit the redemption!*

Those who are familiar with the *Teshuvos* of Reb Moshe *zt'l* will bear witness that this is an uncharacteristically strong letter for him to sign. It demonstrates just how strongly this great *Gadol* felt about the issue.

3. LENGTH MUST GUARANTEE COVER OF KNEES AT ALL TIMES: A woman or girl must cover the upper sections of the legs including the knees (M.B. 75:2). This is because the knee is not an independent bone (apart from the slim knee cap). Instead, it contains the rounded lower end of the upper section of the leg - the femur. This upper bone extends through to the lowest point of the knee to the extent that when a person who is sitting puts his hands onto his knees he is touching the rounded lower end of the femur bone. The lower leg (the tibia) which is slightly indented to comfortably support the rounded end of the upper section is situated just below the knee. Since the upper section of the leg must be completely covered as has been explained, and the upper sections of the legs extend down the complete knee, it is obvious that the knee must be completely covered. (See 6:F:2 where a similar but not identical point was explained concerning the elbows).

A woman must ensure that her knees remain fully covered at all times, even when she is sitting, stretching, ascending stairs and so on. The skirt length must therefore ensure that her knees will not be uncovered even for a moment, since she could be seen just then - see *Mekoros* 1:2 and 45:1.

A skirt which on sitting down must first be pulled forward to cover the knees, is not long enough, since the knees will often not be covered at the moment of sitting down. Furthermore, such a skirt can ride up at any time, without the woman immediately realizing it - see letter of the *Steipler Gaon* in the *Kreina D'igrsa* 1:200 where he stresses that for a skirt to be just knee-length is grossly inadequate.

4. SKIRTS SHOULD EXTEND A TEFACH (4 INCHES) BELOW KNEES:

(a) Four inches below the lowest point of the knee cap: It has been carefully assessed that dresses and skirts must hang at least four inches (10 cm.) below the lowest point of the knee cap to guarantee that the knees will be covered at all times. This is particularly necessary in the case of straight skirts which have a tendency to ride up. The *halacha* that dresses must extend to 4" (10 cm.) below the knee is the ruling of Hagaon Harav Shlomo Zalman Auerbach *zt'l, yibodel l'chayim* Hagaon Harav Yosef Shalom Elyashiv *shlita*, Hagaon Harav Shmuel HaLevi Wosner *shlita* and has been endorsed by many other great *Poskim* - see *Mekoros* 1:2. In fact no authoritative *Posek* has voiced a contrary opinion.

(b) Four inches is sometimes insufficient: If a skirt extends 4" below the knee but is still unreliable and will at times ride up when sitting down (until pulled forward) or when getting onto a bus, this is usually because the skirt is too tight. Before a correction has been made, such a garment is unfit to be worn for two independent reasons - it is too tight around the thigh (see 6:L:2 below) and it is not long enough to cover the upper limbs properly (see 6:H:3 above). However, sometimes due to the person's figure the 4" addition below the knee is insufficient, even though the garment is not too tight. When that is the case the skirt must be lengthened to the appropriate size, to ensure that the knees remain covered at all times.

(c) Advantage of garments extending beyond the four inches: Nowadays, many women and girls in Orthodox circles wear dresses and skirts that extend to more than four inches (10cm.) below the knees. This trend is to be given as much support as possible, because many situations exist nowadays that cause a *tznius* hazard, and these are best averted with a longer garment. [See 9:I where such situations are described, and 9:I:6 where it is pointed out how a longer garment is safer in certain situations.]

(d) Hazards that occur when girls run in the street: Women and girls should avoid running in the street whenever possible. If they have to run, they must be careful that it does not cause the skirt to rise above the permitted level or the slip to show. Obviously, a long dress is safer than one of average length. A further drawback in running is the noise that is usually made when running. This noise announces the presence of the woman or girl and even attracts people to look at her as she runs, and is far from *tznius'dik* conduct - see 6:O:4 below. Both these problems can, however, be avoided if due care is taken. Nevertheless, since running usually infringes on *tznius*, it is best to refrain from it whenever possible. Ideally, teachers should teach their pupils about the hazards of running, since parents do not think of warning their daughters about these types of pitfalls. [As to the problem of girls running down the stairs when wearing a very flared skirt - see 9:J:4(b).]

5. ENSURING THAT THE SKIRT HAS THE RIGHT LENGTH:

(a) When in doubt, seeking advice from someone else: Occasionally, a woman or girl finds a garment that is very much to her taste. She likes the material and the style suits her well. After going from store to store with no success, she is delighted to have found an item which is just right on her. However, to her dismay, it is rather short with nothing in the hem to let down. She is in a dilemma. On the one hand this is just what she can do with and is very *tznius'dik* as far as the general garment is concerned. On the other hand it is rather short. In such cases she must be strong and not give in. If in doubt whether the garment is suitable she should ask a second person who is unbiased to advice her. She should reassure herself that as a reward for not taking that garment *Hashem* will probably give her something that is even more suitable than the previous one.

(b) What fits one person might be totally unfit for a second person: If an outfit, dress or skirt looks perfect and *tznius'dik* on one person, it does not follow that it will be the same on another person, although they seem to be the same size. Even a slight difference in a person's size, height or build can make a lovely garment totally unacceptable. One must therefore not rush to buy an item that looks exceptionally nice on one's friend.

(c) Trying to minimize an inadequacy by saying, "It will be alright": When buying clothes people have a tendency to say, "It will be alright" or, "It will pass!" This means, "True it is a bit short or tight, but being only minimal I think I can get away with it". Although this is a widespread way of thinking, it is wrong and has no place in *halacha*. In *halacha* there is a cut-off point which is the minimum requirement to be Kosher. If a centimeter or half a centimeter of the knee can sometimes be seen the garment is *posul* although people attach no importance to such a small amount.

The same is true in all fields of *halacha*. For example, in *shechita* a bird is Kosher if most of the wind-pipe has been cut through. If just half has been cut it is *neveila* and the meat *treif*, even though to the eye of the observer there is hardly a difference between half and a millimeter over half (Y.D.

21:1). Similarly, a dough which has stood for seventeen minutes and fifty nine seconds is Kosher for *Pesach* and suitable for *matzo*, whilst if it stood eighteen minutes it is *chometz* and may not even be owned on *Pesach* (M.B. 459:14). The same applies to clothes. If they cover the area surrounding the neck, the arms and the knees they are Kosher, whilst if they almost cover these areas but not fully, they are *treif.*

(d) A growing girl's skirt should preferably have a deep hem: When buying a dress or skirt for a girl who has not yet grown to her full height, one should try if possible to ensure that the garment has a deep hem. This will allow the item to be lengthened as she grows taller and the need to lengthen the garment will arise. When such a hem is not available, there is a danger that the girl will continue wearing the garment even once she has grown taller and it no longer fits her.

The expense and bother involved in obtaining a replacement item, plus the attachment the girl might have to this particular dress or skirt may well blind her, and even her parents, as to the inadequacy of the garment, which is a fault that will gradually become worse and worse. Since the extra hem could make all the difference, it is of considerable advantage to procure it. When having a dress or outfit made for such a girl, one should ensure that a substantial hem is left to be let out in the future.

Apart from the advantage from the point of view of *tznius*, it is also far better for the education of a girl that she wears her clothes for quite some time, rather than to be regularly buying new clothes. See 3:F about the role *histapkus* (being contented with little) has on the overall *chinuch* of a child.

It is particularly upsetting that Orthodox clothes manufactures who often produce beautifully Kosher and *b'cheint* garments for growing girls, usually do not leave a substantial hem inside the garments. If they would, they would have the merit of encouraging and aiding this all important aspect of *tznius*.

(e) A Skirt that at first sight looks like a mini-skirt: There exists a straight fitted skirt which has an outer frilled lace skirt attached to it which hangs right away from the main skirt that is below it. This outer skirt hangs to about six inches above the knees, and has the appearance of a mini-skirt because it strikes the eye and is the first thing noticed when the girl comes into a room. Instead of this additional layer adorning the main skirt, it makes the garment highly distasteful, as it is a specimen from the world of *pritzus* that surrounds us at all times.

Although this girl is covered by a full length skirt (i.e. the lower one), it is nevertheless abhorrent to wear something which on first sight looks like a mini-skirt. The mini-skirt has brought so much *tumah* to the world and even to *Klal Yisroel*, that a person who has minimal sensitivity for *tahara* cannot wear a garment on which a (mock) mini-skirt is very much on display. It is self-understood that the older the girl, the worse such a garment is on her.

This does not refer to most "balloon-skirts" where the additional piece lies limply against the main garment. It furthermore does not apply to multi-tiered dresses as bridesmaids wear, because in these the different sections combine as part of one continuous skirt. In the above mentioned skirt, however, the upper frilled mini-skirt and the lower straight long skirt do not blend into one unified garment. Due to this, on first sight it appears as if she is wearing a mini-skirt.

6. VERY LONG SKIRTS AND DRESSES: Very long skirts and dresses that reach right down to the ankle or almost to the ankle ('maxis') are not recommended nowadays, even though they could be viewed as exceptionally modest garments, covering virtually the complete lower leg. There are a number of reasons for this:-

(a) Objection one - In many areas such skirts are conspicuous: It is wrong for an individual to wear a garment that is very different from what the local Orthodox women wear, even if the item is exceptionally *tznius'dik*. By dressing differently to everyone else she attracts attention to herself, which is not in accordance with *tznius* and refined behavior. Although it might be far from her intention to attract attention to herself, and on the contrary, she may be wearing this item in pursuit of extra refinement, this is nevertheless incorrect - see 1:D:6 above. See also *Mekoros* 3:2 and 69:6.

This rule does not apply when there is a *halachic* requirement to dress in a certain way. Therefore, if local Jewish women wear just knee-length skirts, whoever knows better and is aware that a skirt has to extend to four inches below the knee, must do so, as this is *halachically* required, even though it is quite different from the way other people dress - see 1:G:5.

(b) Objection two - She appears to be copying the latest styles: A woman or girl must avoid giving the impression that she is copying the latest trends, because such copying causes grave oversights and infringements in *tznius* to occur. It is even wrong to adopt an extra degree of *tznius*, over and above the *halacha*, if this will mean wearing a garment which is in the height of fashion. Since these very long skirts and dresses are generally worn only when they are at the height of fashion, it is incorrect to wear them. See 1:H:6 above, *Malbushei Kavod*, page 29, and *Mekoros* 58.

A *Bas Yisroel* must, however, not deviate from that which the *halacha* requires even if it happens to have become the prevailing taste. For example, the area around the neck must be covered even if it has become very fashionable to wear close fitting collars, and everyone is sporting a "very Kosher neckline". Since it is *halachically* required, there can be no question of doing otherwise.

(c) Objection three - Such skirts are not worn because of modesty: There is something distinctly distasteful about the very long skirts produced nowadays. In fact it is incorrect to view them as exceptionally *tznius'dik* garments. The point will be best understood by first referring to a strange phenomenon that was to be found at a time when Jewish women slipped to a very low level in *tznius* and were roundly admonished by *Yeshaya HaNavi*.

One of the items he mentions that women wore at that time was a face-kerchief called a רעלה, which hung over the face with just slits cut out for the two eyes. This is of course a mystery - how could it be that women who were *prutzos* wore an item as *tznius'dik* as this? *Rashi* offers the answer. He writes in *Yeshaya* 3:19, והרעלות, צניף שמצניפות כל פרצופיהם חוץ מגלגל העין, כדי שיתאוה אדם ליזון במראות הלסתות - "Women wore these kerchiefs which covered their faces in order to provoke men and arouse within them a passion to see their cheeks". As a result of this, when the kerchief would lift due to a bit in the wind, the appearance of the cheeks presented an enticement to those who saw it. In other words this excessive covering was done to heighten the attraction to themselves, and was part of the unholy crusade that they had undertaken to entice and provoke men to desire and admire them as much as possible - see 6:J:2 below.

This is one underlying reason in depth why the face, which is usually the most beautiful part of the person, need not be covered, whilst other limbs must be kept covered even though they are much less attractive - see 9:V:9(b) that a casual sighting of a covered part of the body is forbidden whilst it is an act of piety to avoid a casual sighting of the face. Since the face is always on display, its power of attraction is less than that of other limbs which are usually covered. See *Maharal MiPrague, Gur Aryeh*, *Breishis* 12:11 s.v. *v'Achshov,* where he writes the following: שהפנים כיון שהוא מגולה לכל, אין האדם מתפעל ביופי שלו ולא נכנס יצר היופי בלבו וכו׳ - "Since the face is revealed to all, its beauty does not powerfully affect a person who sees it [as do other parts of the body]".

This is the psychology that lies behind these ultra-long garments. When the fashion designers feel that the provocation generated by exposing the legs is beginning to wane, they create a garment which covers the legs completely. This garment usually has a slit in it (see 6:J:2) or is a wraparound (see 6:I:2) which serves to complete what they are trying to achieve. Eventually, they consider it time to return to the fashion of very short garments, and the cycle repeats itself over the years. There is, therefore, not much *tahara* or *tznius* in this garment. As the function of these garments is to achieve the exact opposite of *tznius*, they are not for a *Bas Yisroel.*

This teaches us an important lesson. An item which at first sight looks very *tznius'dik,* might be very far from that, and could in fact have been manufactured to achieve just the opposite. When the designer of the item is not known to have any feeling for modesty, its *tznius'dik* appearance should be viewed with considerable suspicion.

(d) Objection four - Such skirts are often extreme casual wear: Very long garments are often introduced as just another aspect of extreme casual wear. This is evident by the fact that many of these garments do not have a decent hem, and instead finish off as if torn from some other material or have threads and the like dangling down. It will be explained (in 7:C:1 below) that casual wear is distinctly non-*tznius'dik,* as it is designed to lessen the feelings of shame and privacy. Feelings of shame and privacy together comprise the substructure that underpins *tznius* - see *Mekoros* 59:4-5.

7. THE SKIRT MUST EFFECT A TOTAL DISGUISE OF THE AREA: Even though the upper sections of the arms and legs are both *ervah* by decree of *halacha* (as explained in 6:A:1 above), there is an important difference between them. The upper arms must be covered but there is no *halachic* obligation to disguise and mask their shape by covering them with a shawl etc. The upper sections of the legs, however, are governed by a far more stringent *halacha*. They must be covered in such a way that the limbs are totally disguised and the shape of the thigh and upper sections of the legs cannot be seen.

The verse says in *Shir HaShirim* (7:2), מה יפו פעמיך בנעלים בת נדיב, חמוקי ירכיך - "How beautiful are your shoe-clad footsteps O daughter of [Avraham Avinu] the nobleman; [how refined is your dress in that] your thigh is hidden and obscured". חמוקי means "to make disappear" as in the verse חמק עבר לו (*Shir HaShirim* 5:6. See *Ibn Ezra, Shir HaShirim* (7:2) and *Rashi*, *Moed Koton* 16a s.v. *Chamukei*). The verse חמוקי ירכיך therefore means hidden or disguised, which is far more than just being very well covered.

As explained, the verse states that the dress of the *Bas Yisroel* is sufficiently loose that the thigh area is hidden. Based on this verse, the *Gemara* says in *Moed Katan* (16a), מה ירך בסתר - "Just as the thigh is hidden". *Chazal* do not say that ירך מכוסה - the thigh is covered - but that it is hidden, implying that it is dressed in a loose fitting garment and the thigh is therefore hidden and goes unnoticed.

The damage caused by the thigh area not being hidden properly is spelt out by *Chazal* in no uncertain terms. The *Gemara* (*Nedarim* 20a) quotes a statement by one of the great *Amoraim,* כל המסתכל בעקבה של אשה הויין לו בנים שאינם מהוגנים - "Whoever gazes at the heel of a woman will have bad children". The Gemara goes on to explain that the statement actually refers to the thigh area, which is much higher up on the body than the heel. However, because of 'refinement of language' *Chazal* referred to the 'heel' since the thigh area is above the heels (see *Beis Habechira-Meiri ibid*). The *issur* of gazing at that part of the female body and the painful consequences that result from doing so, should be reason enough for women to dress in a way that ensures that this form of gazing does not happen, and certainly that it is not encouraged, as is the case when close-fitting skirts are worn.

8. SLACKS AND TROUSERS: Slacks and trousers are absolutely forbidden and wearing such clothing is viewed as gross *pritzus*. Not only do they display the general outline of the upper sections of the legs (the point mentioned in the previous paragraph), but they exhibit and emphasize the full shape of each of those limbs - see *Rashi*, *Pesochim* 3a s.v. *b'Zov and Responsa Shevet Halevi* 6:118.2 about the *pritzus* of פיסוק רגלים - displaying the division of the upper sections of the legs. They are therefore one of the worst pieces of female clothing in existence - see *Mekoros* 46:1-7.

According to some *Poskim* when wearing trousers a woman also transgresses the *issur min haTorah* of *lo yehi kli gever al ishah* (usually referred to as *lo silbash*) - "a woman may not wear clothes suited and worn only by men" (*Devarim* 22:5). This is so although many non-Jewish women wear trousers nowadays and they are shaped quite differently to male trousers. These *Poskim* maintain that a garment which is intrinsically not suited to a female (either due to *pritzus* or some other reason) is subject to this *issur,* even if the world at large has deteriorated and the garment is widely worn by women. (See *Responsa Minchas Yitzchak* 2:108, *Responsa Shevet HaLevi* 2:63 and *Responsa Tzitz Eliezer* 11:62. See also *Halichos Bas Yisroel,* note 7:7 for those who disagree with this ruling).

This issue is comparable to the *issur* for a man to dye or pull out a white hair from his head or beard that is otherwise dark, which is an act of beautification typical of women (תיקוני אתתא) and remains *ossur* even if in these times many men also do this - (see Y.D. 182:6, *Biur HaGra* Y.D. 156:7, *Responsa Shevet HaLevi* 2:111 and *Responsa Lehoros Noson* 2:70) - see *Mekoros* 46:3-7.

The *Chazon Ish zt'l* was asked whether nowadays it is possible to consider slacks as not such a forbidden garment, since so many women wear them. To this the *Chazon Ish* responded that in spite of it being worn by many, it is absolute *pritzus* to walk around in such a garment, adding that he was convinced that if at the time of the *Sanhedrin* a woman would have appeared in public in slacks, she would have been brought to *Beth Din* and stoned for behaving with gross indecency - see *Orchos Rabbeinu,* Vol. One, page 226 and *Mekoros* 46:2.

To many of us who have had our values and standards battered by our daily experiences, such a response seems an overreaction. The *Chazon Ish*, the leader of his generation, was, however, not prone to overreacting. Rather, being a great Torah authority, he saw matters in their true perspective and understood what *tznius* really is and what it stands for. To him, dressing in this manner was equal to doing one of the worst *aveiros* possible. [See 6:E:2(c) concerning the care women and girls took in the times of *Chazal* to avoid tight-fitting clothes.]

9. CULOTTES: It is *ossur* to wear culottes (a flared skirt that is joined between the legs at approximately half-way down). Although these garments do not emphasize the shape of the body as do slacks and trousers, they are nevertheless garments of considerable *pritzus*. As the woman walks, the skirt she is wearing "opens up" every now and again. Since this happens, the garment is very eye-catching. Such a garment is therefore no better than a skirt with a slit which is roundly condemned by all *halachic* authorities even when the slit is above the knees, because of the measure in which a slit attracts the eye. Eye-catching items are always *pritzus'dik*. They are all the more so when they direct the observer to a part of the body which in Jewish ethics should be camouflaged so that it is not noticed at all - see 6:J:1 below.

There is also a further consideration due to which culottes can not be permitted. This is to ensure that no advances are made towards wearing slacks and pants. Culottes and slacks are both trouser-like garments and if culottes were permitted it would erode the *issur* on slacks and pants. It follows, that for two independent reasons wearing culottes is a major infringement of *tznius*.

I. FLARED, STRAIGHT AND WRAP-AROUND SKIRTS

1. EPIDEMIC OF TIGHT FITTING SKIRTS CAUSES INSENSITIVITY: Being slim has become such an important feature in the world of fashion that women wear tight-fitting, slim and sometimes even pipe-like dresses to emphasize how slim they are. They do so in spite of the discomfort involved in walking around in such tight-fitting garments, because nothing is more important to them than to find acclaim and admiration for their figure and general appearance. In contrast, the Torah teaches us that a woman and girl are to look pleasant and gracious but should not engage in showing-off (כבודה בת מלך פנימה - "the honor of the *Bas Melech* is internal" - at home not on public display - *Tehillim* 45:14). It involves dressing in a way that one's outward appearance is not conspicuous, but is a display of *eidelkeit* and modesty. When reading *Megillas Esther* and seeing Esther's dislike for excessive beautification (*Esther* 2:15), we have an insight into how a true *Bas Yisroel* feels about these matters.

As stated (in 6:H:7 above), in Jewish law the dress or skirt must cover and also screen-off completely the upper sections of the legs. It has already been mentioned (*ibid.*) that when describing the *tznius* of the *Bas Yisroel* the verse writes חמוקי ירכיך - "Your thigh is obscured and disguised" (*Shir HaShirim* 7:2) which means much more than just "covered". Hence the complete thigh bone, which ends at the lower end of the knee (as explained in 6:H:3 above) must be hidden behind a loose skirt so that it is obscured.

Only a loose-fitting garment will camouflage the limbs to that extent and hence only such a garment may be worn. We must not allow the secular fashions of female pants and tight-fitting skirts, which diametrically oppose all that modesty and *tznius* stand for, to set standards for our wives and daughters. It is lamentable that men and women alike encounter slacks and tight-fitting skirts whenever they venture out of their houses, because this type of dress is part of the culture and way of life of the society amongst which we live. As a result of this, many have become insensitive to the extreme lack of *tznius* in outlining these limbs.

Some women dress in outfits that are Kosher as far as size and material is concerned but are tight-fitting. Sometimes, these garments are even longer than is *halachically* required, but tight around the body. A person with keen insight said that these women make every endeavor to "dress as immodestly as possible within the confines of *halacha*". Unfortunately, this 'appraisal' is accurate, even though transgressors are often unaware that they entertain, albeit almost sub-consciously, such intentions. As is usual with enticements of the *yetzer horah*, the idea he puts forward that this is within the confines of *halacha* is false - because to dress immodestly is totally against *halacha* and such garments cannot be worn "within the confines of *halacha*". Just as *treife* meat is forbidden to be eaten even if it is cow meat rather than horse meat, so too, such tight-fitting clothes are forbidden to be worn even if the garments are of the correct length and the correct type of material.

2. LOOSE SKIRTS, KOSHER; OTHER SKIRTS, NOT KOSHER:

(a) The guidelines: The following skirts are Kosher as they screen off the body and upper sections of the legs: fully pleated skirts, flared skirts (that have plenty of cloth and hang graciously and loosely), straight skirts if they are loose fitting, and A-line skirts (which broaden gradually as they descend). However, tight-fitting skirts, close-fitting skirts, straight narrow skirts (pencil skirts) and all the more V-line skirts (which gradually become narrower as they descend, also known as tapered skirts) are not Kosher, as they show and emphasize the shape of the body (the hips) - see *Mekoros* 40. Some refrain from wearing straight skirts altogether, even those that would be a loose-fit on their figure, because they are afraid that they will be taken as an example by others, and they will wear tight fitting skirts or V-shaped skirts, without realizing that a close fit or V-shaped skirt is not Kosher.

Straight skirts that have a single pleat at the back, starting about half way down the garment; straight skirts with a number of pleats clustered together (known as concertina) and jumpers (called in England pinafore skirts) that are straight but have frills or pleats at the lower end of the garment, are not always Kosher. If the upper part of these skirts is close-fitting, the skirts emphasize the shape of the body, and are not Kosher, even when the lower part of the garment is loose to allow for leg movement. Many girls are not aware that there is anything wrong with these garments until they are told. Once they are told and they understand the issue, they are usually only too happy to comply with the requirements of the *halacha*. Teachers of girls should make a point of explaining to their pupils which skirts are Kosher and which not. See 6:E:2 concerning tight-fitting blouses and dresses.

It has been assessed by Orthodox professional seamstresses that for a skirt or dress to mask the shape of the body, the garment should have at least 3-4 in. (8-11 cm.) more material on the widest part of the thigh area (which is approx. 7 in. - 18cm. down from the waist) than the measurement of the body itself. Therefore, if the circumference of the body in that area is 38 in. (95 cm.), the circumference of the garment should be at least 41-42 in. (98-99 cm.) This is a ruling by Hagaon Harav Shmuel Halevi Wosner *shlita* and Hagaon Harav Nissim Krelitz *shlita* and signed by them. See *sefer, Hatzne'ah Leches*, page 50.

(b) The deterioration in the attitudes of present-day society: Present-day society, with its serious dearth of *tznius*, considers tight-fitting clothes to be both becoming and tasteful. Some of our wives and daughters have learned to think the same, and there are present-day *shomrei mitzvos*, male and female alike, who are fully convinced that straight pencil-like skirts and dresses are far more graceful than gathered or pleated ones. This is just one of the many instances in which we have become products of the prevailing degenerate social order. We have, in fact, no idea to what extent our views and attitudes are cultivated and molded by the opinions and practices of the *umos ha'olam* amongst whom we reside. This is a natural phenomenon, as it is natural and typical for people to be deeply affected by the ideas and ideals of the people who surround them and amongst whom they live. It is exactly as the *Rambam* write, דרך בני אדם וכו׳ להיות נוהג כמנהג אנשי מדינתו - "It is part of human nature for a person to emulate the conduct of his immediate society" (*Rambam, Hilchos Deios* 6:1).

To counter these attitudes it should be noted that in the times of *Chazal*, when the world was far less corrupt than it is today and *Klal Yisroel* was on a much higher standard than nowadays, women had the opposite attitude to nowadays. They considered flared garments, with plenty of spare cloth, to be far more elegant and graceful than tight-fitting, slim-line clothes. This is mentioned in the *Gemara* (*Kesubos* 48a) where *Chazal* say that a husband is obliged to buy his wife the type of clothes she needs. On this *Rashi,* s.v. *Lfum she'eiroh,* writes, זקינה קשה לה משאוי ואינה יכולה לסבול בגדים רחבים וילדה צריכה בגדים רחבים להתנאות בהם - "Elderly women find the weight of extra cloth a problem and therefore cannot wear very flared clothes. On the other hand young women are not disturbed by the weight of the cloth and the husband must therefore supply them with wide flared clothes which enhance their beauty." The same is mentioned in *Shabbos* 12a, *Rashi* s.v. *Aval d'Yaldos*.

This information should serve as an eye-opener to many. Through it they will realize that present-day conceptions of grace and charm are often totally different from those held in former times. This in turn may encourage women and girls to maintain their true Jewish dignity, and refrain from wearing tight-fitting clothes that not only lack *tznius* but also basic respectability and grace - see *Mekoros* 40:7.

3. SKIRTS THAT HAVE A TENDENCY TO CLING TO THE BODY:

(a) Skirts that develop an electro-static charge: Many skirts are made of non-absorbent man-made fabrics that become charged with static electricity. While walking, the material rubs against a nylon slip or the body, and this generates electricity which in turn causes them to cling. Due to this, as the wearer walks the skirt will sometimes cling to the body in a way that the shape of the upper leg is evident. To understand how this problem is overcome, it is appropriate to explain in short the cause and nature of this phenomenon.

(b) Problem occurs when synthetics rub against synthetics or skin: When a material made of a natural fiber rubs against a skin or a cloth surface, no electricity is formed. Therefore, a skirt made of wool, linen, cotton and viscose (an absorbent silk-like material made from a wood or the cotton fibers of the ginned seed), does not present a problem. Moreover, if a garment made of synthetic material, such as some types of nylon, rubs against a natural material no electricity is formed, as only friction between two synthetic materials or between a synthetic material and the body will generate an electric charge in the cloth. People therefore find that when a nylon or terylene dress is worn without the inner protection of a cotton slip, the dress is drawn to the legs as the person walks.

(c) Problem occurs only when synthetics are dry: As stated, a garment made of synthetic fiber, such as nylon, polyester (terylene), crimplene (a knitted polyester) and acrylics, that rubs against the body or against another synthetic material, becomes electro-statically charged. This phenomenon does not occur when the synthetics are wet or even just slightly damp. Water is a conductor of electricity. Therefore, if the material is moist the electricity is conducted away whilst if it is dry the electro-static charge remains and causes clinginess.

(d) Three remedies for the problem of static electricity: The most recommended remedy to this problem is to add "fabric conditioner" to the final rinse of the garment. Fabric conditioner acts as a "wetting" agent for synthetics. With this on its surface the fabric will not cling. Alternatively, the garment can be sprayed with an anti-static spray to prevent this problem occurring. The latter is, however, less effective than conditioner. A third way to prevent electro-static charge is, as mentioned, to wear a cotton slip. A half-slip, that only covers from the waist and below, will do for a skirt but will be inadequate for a dress of synthetic material because the upper part of the dress can still cling to the upper part of the body, just as a blouse made of synthetics needs protection to prevent clinginess - see 6:E:3 above.

(e) An electric charge only develops under certain circumstances: The level of static electricity is far greater when the garment has been dried in an electric clothes-drier than when it has been hung to dry on a washing line. There appears to be two reasons for this. The item is drier when dried in a machine than when hung indoors or outdoors where the air will usually contain some humidity. Secondly, when dried in a machine, the garment has been rubbed very extensively as it is tossed around the interior of the drier and this causes the cloth to have a considerable level of electro-static charge.

One woman may be less affected by static electricity than another. This is because she perspires more than the other or works in a damper environment. Her garments are therefore slightly damp and this in turn conducts the electricity away. Accordingly, a mother who knows from experience that she does not require conditioner for her own clothes, must not take it for granted that her daughter's clothes do not require it. It could be that since she, the mother, cooks and spends much of the time in the kitchen her clothes become lightly dampened and therefore unaffected, whilst her daughter's would be affected.

Finally, it must be mentioned that the problem is much greater in the summer when clothes are thoroughly dry than in the winter when the atmosphere has more humidity. Therefore, having worn a dress or skirt in the winter and not having experienced any trouble does not mean that when wearing it in the height of summer or in a hot country such as *Eretz Yisroel* there will likewise be no need to use fabric conditioner.

(f) An electro-static charge occurs in quite a few garments : The problem of clingy clothes is a modern problem which the previous generation did not have to contend with. Due to this, some people do not realize the extent of this problem - that it applies to all items of clothing made of synthetic fabrics, such as blouses, dresses, tights, and slips. All such items cling at times to the body and to other garments made of synthetics. Fabric conditioner on one synthetic fiber garment does not prevent a second item made of synthetic fiber from clinging to it.

Accordingly, all such items should be rinsed in fabric conditioner. Many women, sensibly, rinse every family wash in fabric conditioner to ensure that this problem does not arise. If one does not do so, the blouse could cling and accentuate the shape of the upper part of the body (apart from being uncomfortable for the wearer). So too, a slip can ride up with the result that there is no slip where it is needed, and a skirt that requires a slip to prevent it being see-through, will be without that protection. All such problems can be prevented by rinsing the items mentioned in fabric conditioner. Finally it must be mentioned that it is important to request from personnel at a launderette that washes clothes for women and girls that they put fabric conditioner into the final rinse of the clothes, as many would not automatically do so.

(g) Skirts made of crepe or chiffon fabric: Skirts made from very lightweight fabric such as chiffon are first of all extremely see-through. They must therefore have a lining whether the skirt is straight, gathered or pleated. The same applies to certain types of crepe fabrics. Secondly, these fabrics are extremely soft. Due to this, when the wearer walks outdoors and the wind blows on her, forcing the dress against the body, the dress clings to the body and reveals its shape in an *untznius'dik* manner. Accordingly, when going outdoors with such a dress one should wear a coat over it.

This problem is of less concern when the chiffon skirt is gathered or pleated. Due to the large amount of extra fabric, it hangs freely and is not likely to cling to the body. An extra precaution would be to add a deep hem to the garment. Such a hem adds weight to the garment and helps to ensure that it hangs away from the body - see 6:E:3 and *Mekoros* 40.

(h) Skirts made of a stretch fabric: Stretch fabrics are largely used in a manner that is totally unsuitable for *Bnos Yisroel.* Skirts that are made of this material are invariably very close fitting and display the shape of the body in an inappropriate manner. They fit closely around the legs, stretching and contracting as the person walks. Although such skirts are very fashionable nowadays they are part of בגדי עשו החמדת - "The desirable and fashionable clothes of Eisav" (*Breishis* 27:15) which simply do not belong in the wardrobe of *Bnos Yisroel.* The same applies to pullovers and sweaters made of stretch fabrics, that are manufactured as maternity wear. These pullovers characterize the depths of immodesty that exist in our generation and must not be worn by Jewish women - see 7:F below.

However, a loose hanging or gathered skirt that is made of this fabric, which is a strong hard-wearing material that lasts for years, is perfectly in order, provided the woman is careful not to continue wearing it during pregnancy when it will inevitably become close fitting.

4. WRAP-AROUND SKIRTS - A SHAMEFUL SIGN OF THE TIMES: Wrap-around skirts (skirts that are like kilts without the pins) are another product of our times and Jewish women must be fully aware of their serious faults. They are as follows:-

(a) It is *pritzus* if an inner garment can be seen: Firstly, when stretched (and the overlap is average, not exceptionally large), they open to reveal what is beneath them. This happens when getting into or out of a car and when it is windy. It can even happen when simply sitting down indoors, if due care is not taken to prevent the garment opening. This is certainly the worst aspect of these skirts. Such a garment is so wrong to wear and so contemptible, that a generation ago even those who were not Jewish would not have worn a garment such as this, since to allow the slip to show was considered as being semi-undressed. In spite of this, since the *umos ha'olam* have not been blessed with the *midos* of *busha* and *tznius*, it has become acceptable to them to walk around in a state of indecency, such as being only partially clothed or with inner garments on display.

It is, however, astonishing that *Bnos Yisroel*, for whom *eidelkeit* and *tznius* are hallmarks and intrinsic parts of their innate character, have become so insensitive to *pritzus* that they too are agreeable to wear a wrap-around, in spite of its glaring fault. See 6:D:4 about insensitivities that have developed regarding see-through blouses and dresses. See also the heartfelt cry of the *Mishna Berura* (*Biur Halacha* 339:3) concerning the unbelievable lack of understanding some people display concerning even very serious *pritzus* such as mixed dancing.

(b) It is *pritzus* if the skirt has a slit-like opening: Secondly, even if the skirt has a large overlap due to which it cannot open properly even when stretched, it is still improper to wear the garment if when sitting down the skirt opens up to reveal part of the lower leg that would otherwise have been covered by the garment. Such an opening is associated with a slit which must not be allowed under any circumstances.

Moreover, wearing a wrap-around that has an exceptionally large overlap will be viewed as a license, and will cause others to wear wrap-arounds that have only average overlaps. The resulting *pritzus* will be the fault of those who cause people to think that they are acceptable items to wear.

(c) It is *pritzus* if the skirt gives the impression that it opens: Thirdly, even if the skirt has been stitched closed from the inside so that when the flap opens the garment does not reveal anything, not even part of the lower legs, this garment is nevertheless forbidden because it is sinful to walk around with a skirt that gives the impression of being capable of opening up. Since the onlooker does not know that the garment has been secured from the inside, the opening of the flap is highly provocative since he assumes that the skirt is like all other wrap-arounds.

Although, skirts with loose flaps were worn by the finest women before wrap-arounds appeared on the scene, nowadays that wrap-arounds are around and have become so prevalent, the onlooker will automatically assume that the garment worn is a wrap-around and the loose flap is therefore considered provocative.

(d) Making a wrap-around skirt suitable to wear: For a wrap-around skirt to be put right and to be suitable to wear it must be secured in a way that it no longer has a loose flap. This can be done by inserting a couple of safety-pins on the inside of the garment half way down and near the lower end of the garment. They will effectively prevent it from opening and give the skirt the character of all other skirts. Alternatively and more preferably, the flap should be sown down. This should be done either all the way down or at least for two thirds of the way down the length of the skirt. The lower third that will not be sewn down will not present a problem as it will have the character of a pleat rather than a slit, since it will have a full cloth backing and will reveal only more of the same material.

(e) Wearing a skirt that has an additional flap: There are some skirts that do not open up at all but have an additional loose flap. The style and shape of the flap bears evidence to the fact that the garment does not open up and that instead the flap is just an additional piece of cloth added on for style. Such a skirt may be worn even if the flap is not sewn down because whoever sees it understands immediately that it is not a wrap-around. The loose flap is therefore of no concern.

(f) Wearing a kilt: Kilts, which are wrap-arounds that are very well secured externally by a large safety-pin are permitted, as none of the above-mentioned problems exist with them. They may be worn provided that they do not open up below the pin to form a slit-like opening. Usually this will not happen as the top layer extends far past the start of the lower level which in turn ensures that the garment does not open up to form a slit. It is understood that a kilt which is predominantly a bright red color cannot be worn, because bright red garments are eye-catching and forbidden - see 7:B:1 below.

J. SLITS - DECORATIONS ON SKIRTS - BELTS ETC.

1. SLITS ARE FORBIDDEN EVEN WHEN BELOW THE KNEES: All leading *Poskim* of our generation have ruled that a slit in a skirt or dress is absolutely forbidden, even if it is completely below the knee and even if it stops at four inches under the knee. A slit attracts attention to the legs because as the wearer walks her legs continuously appear and disappear. In some strides, more shows, while in others, less shows. All this has a powerful beckoning effect on male passersby, even though this is far from the woman's intention. Just as an advertisement that continuously lights up, switches off and lights up again catches people's attention, so legs that continuously appear and disappear are highly conspicuous. See *Responsa HaRadvaz* (2:770) that a man may not walk behind a woman because the man is drawn to observe her movements and this is forbidden under the *issurim* of *pritzus* - see 9:F:10(c) and 9:H:5(a) below.

A further reason for forbidding a slit even if well below the knee, is that the only way to safeguard *Bnos Yisroel* from the "*tumah* of slits" is to instruct them not to have any form of opening at the bottom of a skirt or dress wherever it should be. This is the typical *Torah'dik* approach. For example, due to the severe *issur* of paying interest, *Chazal* decreed that a borrower must not even pay a verbal compliment to the creditor out of gratitude for the loan (known as *ribis devarim*), as this could precipitate more serious forms of interest - see Y.D. 160:11. For this reason, plus the first reason given, *Gedolim* have totally forbidden a slit even if under the knees and even if it is not particularly eye-catching.

The excuse given by many that with the tight skirts worn nowadays a woman cannot stretch her legs when there is no slit, is totally invalid and unacceptable. Women who give this excuse should be told that if they would only wear a Kosher skirt that is loose around the body and is not narrower around the legs than higher up, they would not experience these difficulties. Furthermore, instead of having a slit, the garment could have a pleat (a lined slit) which would allow the garment to expand without revealing the legs in any way.

The following is the wording of a statement by *Gedolei HaPoskim* released in 5748: **"A slit in a garment is forbidden because of *pritzus*. It is forbidden even if thick tights are being worn. It is forbidden even if the complete slit is below the knee."** The statement is signed by Hagaonim Harav Shlomo Zalman Auerbach *zt'l* and *yibodel l'chayim* Harav Yosef Shalom Elyashiv *shlita*, Harav Ben-Zion Abba Shaul *shlita*, Harav Shmuel HaLevi Wosner *shlita* and Harav Nissim Karelitz *shlita* amongst others - see *Mekoros* 1:3.

In a statement released during *Aseres Yemei Teshuva* 5742 in Lakewood, New Jersey, USA, the following is written: "A dress or skirt may not have any slit that reveals any part of the knee or leg". It is signed by Hagaon Harav Shneur Kotler *zt'l* and *yibodel l'chayim* by the *Mashgiach* Hagaon Harav Nosson Wachtfogel *shlita* - see *Mekoros* 24:19:6 and 46:8.

2. A SLIT ABOVE THE KNEES - MANIFESTATION OF PRITZUS: A slit that extends above the knee is one of the worst forms of *pritzus* in clothes that have been invented and is by its very nature a vulgar and immodest way of dress in the extreme. The severity of this matter and the fact that not all women understand what is so wrong with it makes it a necessity to explain the nature of this wrongdoing. This is so even though it is a contravention of *tznius* to explain more than is absolutely essential for a clear understanding of the *halacha*. The evil of such a slit is threefold:-

- Firstly, a slit has a powerful beckoning effect on the person who sees it, as has been explained in 1 above concerning a slit that is below the knee. This applies also, and to an even greater extent, to a slit that is above the knee - see *Mekoros* 46:8.

- Secondly, the slit exposes part of the upper section of the legs. This is severe indecency because if any part of the upper section of the legs is exposed it presents a major provocation to any man who might notice it (as stated in the *Taz* O.C. 75:1) - see *Mekoros* 44:1.

- Thirdly, the originators of this uncivilized form of dress knew that a slit above the knee has a particular potential to incite passersby. It is a fact of human nature that curiosity is aroused when the person is given just a fleeting glimpse but cannot see the subject matter properly. (See *Rashi, Yeshaya* 3:19 already mentioned in 6:H:6(c) above). Since the sight is partially withheld, what is seen is particularly provocative. This is part of the inner meaning of the verse מים גנובים ימתקו - "Stolen waters are appealing" (*Mishlei* 9:17).

It should be noted, that many men are more troubled when they have to walk near a woman with a slit than a woman who wears other types of *pritzus'dik* clothes. A *Rav* speaking in *Bnei Brak* in *Kislev* 5753 about this problem said the following: "It used to be possible for an '*ubgehieter Yid*' who did not want to see the face of women to look down rather than straight ahead. Nowadays, when he does so, he is in danger of unwittingly seeing one of the worst types of *pritzus* - the slit."

The very word "*pritzus*" means to be "*poretz geder*" - to breach the wall or fence. There is no more absolute form of this *aveirah* than making a slit in a garment that encloses the body - one is literally breaching the wall. *Rabbanim* and *mechanchim* must make a stand for the honor of *Klal Yisroel* and eradicate this scourge from our midst.

As a matter of fact, when a woman or girl walks around dressed in a garment that has a slit she is a serious public hazard and she will be held responsible for causing many people to sin, *chas veshalom*. If those who perpetrate this wrongdoing knew the extent to which they endanger their own health by behaving in this manner they would surely reconsider their actions (see No. 4 below). The Torah commands us to ensure the safety of the community by removing public hazards (*Shemos* 21:33 concerning a pit left uncovered in a public domain). Likewise, since the Jewish population deserves to be safeguarded from this public hazard, the *midas hadin* could, G-d forbid, demand that she should be prevented from harming the public. (See 7:K:3 below concerning a woman's responsibility not to cause men to sin). See *Mekoros* 26:2-3, 69:1 and 69:5.

Our fervent *tefilla* is יתמו חטאים מן הארץ - "sin should be eradicated from the world" (*Tehillim* 104:35) on which *Chazal* say (*Midrash Tehillim*) חטאים ולא חוטאים - "the sins should be uprooted, not *chas v'shalom* the sinners". We pray that the perpetrators of this sin learn to appreciate that the key to *kedushas Yisroel* is in the hands of women. If their dress is deplorable, it eradicates whatever *kedusha* men have derived from their *tefilla* and Torah learning. On the other hand, if their conduct and dress is exemplary, it projects *Yiras Shomayim as cheit* to all who come into contact with them.

3. THE ABSURDITY OF SAYING "MIND YOUR OWN BUSINESS!": When some women and girls are told by a *Talmid Chacham* that they must not walk around with a slit, especially when it is above the knee, they reply impudently, "Mind your own business!" or "Don't look!" and similar answers. The *chutzpah* in such responses is beyond description. They first of all contaminate the streets by walking around in a totally inadequate manner of dress, igniting the *yetzer horah* of men wherever they go. They then have the impudence to say that they are not harming anyone - men should look away.

In fact, when a man complains, he is very much minding "his own business" which is to be able to walk along the street without being tripped up or without having to keep his eyes absolutely glued to the ground. The following parable (mentioned in *Vayikra Rabba* 4:6) comes to mind. A passenger on a boat started to drill a hole in the floor of his cabin. When the alarmed co-passengers tried to stop him he argued, "Mind your own business. I am making a hole in my cabin and this has nothing to do with anyone else". The absurdity of the answer speaks for itself since he was putting everyone's life at risk. It is just as absurd for a woman to walk around in *pritzus'dik* dress and then to say, "It's my personal affair. If you don't like it, don't look!" It may be her personal clothing but it puts everyone at risk. As stated, slits are one of the worst public hazards that exist in female clothing.

Those who have the audacity to reply, "Mind your own business!" should be informed about a *Gemara* in *Brachos* (20a) which relates that the *Amora*, *Rav Ada Bar Ahava* saw a woman walking along the street with a provocative coat. Thinking she was Jewish he went up to her and tore off her coat, thereby bringing the act of *pritzus* to an immediate end. The *Gemara* praises this great *Amora* for the courage he displayed, by ripping a *pritzus'dik* coat off a woman. It states that his deed was considered so meritorious that in its wake *Klal Yisroel* could be granted major *yeshuos*.

This great *Amora* knew that some men would inevitably be provoked by a woman wearing *pritzus'dik* clothes. He went about "minding his own business" which was the maintenance of *kedusha* and *tahara* in *Klal Yisroel* by stripping the garment from its wearer. Similarly, if a *Talmid Chacham* remarks or reacts to a provocative way of dress, rather than turning a blind eye and ignoring it, he is minding his own business which is to ensure that the *kedusha* of the society is maintained.

The offenders who shamelessly shout back, "Don't look!" are reacting in a way that is not just gross insolence but is completely flawed, as it does not address the problem at all. The *issur* involved is not a question of looking but of seeing or accidentally noticing an uncovered part. By the time the passing man realizes that he must "not look" in her direction the damage has been done (M.B. 75:7, M.B. 225 *Biur Halacha* s.v. *Afilu*) - See 6:T:1 below.

4. CONDEMNATION BY ONE OF THE GREATEST POSKIM: The following is the translation of a statement released by Maran Hagaon Harav Yitzchak Yaacov Weiss *zt'l, Rav Av Beis Din* of *Yerusholayim* and author of *Responsa Minchas Yitzchak* together with his *Beis Din*:-

> *We are alarmed to hear of a new dreadful breach in the wall of tznius in relation to female dress. The fire has already caught hold of the periphery of the camp of shomrei Torah umitzvos. This is to wear dresses that have slits either at their sides or in the center, which is a manner of dress that represents pritzus and rebellion. A Bas Yisroel who wears such a garment transgresses das Yehudis and encroaches on the cardinal issur of giluy arayos.*
>
> *Lately, Heaven has been shocking us with dreadful accidents and illnesses within our community. The pain and suffering rachmana litzlan have been very great. The women who wear the pritzus'dik garments mentioned are to blame for this. They cause many to sin and it is they who thereby invite serious retribution on the community, as the Torah says, 'ervah should not appear amongst you as it will cause Me to withdraw My protection from you.'*
>
> *We hereby decree with the force of the Holy Torah that it is absolutely ossur for a Bas Yisroel to wear the above-mentioned disgusting clothes. This is forbidden even in a way that the flesh is not visible as one is obligated to distance oneself from impurity. Upright and refined N'shei Yisroel must react sharply and protest against those who wear these forbidden forms of clothing. In the merit of standing guard on the watchtowers of tznius, the Guardian of Yisroel will stand guard and protect His vineyard from all mishaps and illnesses, rachmana litzlan. All of us should merit having a gemar chasima tovah and experience the everlasting redemption with the coming of Moshiach speedily in our days.*

The statement is signed by the *Ra'avad* and his *Beis Din*. The Hebrew original can be found in the *Mekoros* 46:8.

The *Navi* laments in *Eicha* (1:9), טומאתה בשוליה לא זכרה אחריתה - "Her impurity was visible on her hems: she disregarded the consequences". Metaphorically, this verse hints at the problems of short skirts and slits that afflict our generation. It bemoans the state of the Jewish daughter: טומאתה בשוליה - "Her impurity is evident at the lower end of her garment" - its totally inadequate length and its unforgivable slit - לא זכרה אחריתה - "She has not taken note that she will be accused before the Heavenly Court for having caused men to sin".

Our consolation is that despite the above, it is never too late for a girl or woman to change her ways and display the strength of character that Jewish women are capable of mustering. Although she may have erred until now, she is willing to change her ways completely and with her new mode of dress will spread *kedusha* and *tahara* in *Klal Yisroel*. Moreover, her new image will be a *kiddush Hashem* as it will demonstrate to her many friends and associates what authentic Jewish conduct really is and what change she has undergone to attain it.

5. A SLIT SHOULD BE SEWN UP, NOT JUST BUTTONED UP: A slit should preferably be sewn up so that it is completely sealed. It is generally insufficient to just close the slit with buttons or snaps (press studs) because they are unreliable and easily become undone. This happens especially when pressure is exerted against them, such as when getting in and out of a car. However, if one is sure that the buttons are reliable and close together there is no need to stitch the area closed. It should be noted that buttons on a skirt that are made during manufacture are generally more reliable than buttons added to a garment to close a slit. The latter is often done by an amateur or semi-amateur and does not keep the slit securely closed.

Also, the pressure that will often exist to force the slit open, eg. when climbing steep stairs or when getting in and out of a car, renders buttons and particularly snaps unreliable, even though in other areas such buttons or snaps will usually keep things together very well indeed.

As an alternative to sewing up a slit, one could add in a piece of cloth which is either of the material from which the garment is made or something that looks very similar. This will effectively turn the slit into a pleat. It should, however, not be sewn up with a piece of silk lining if slips are also made from such silk, because to the onlooker (who could see the slit open when she sits down, climbs stairs etc.) it might seem that the slit is in fact open and that part of the slip is showing through. Concerning adding a cloth lining of a different color than the garment - see No. 7 below.

6. PRECAUTIONS NEEDED WITH BUTTON-UP SKIRTS: Whenever a garment is closed by buttons, be it a full dress or a skirt, it is essential to ensure that the spaces between one button and the next are short enough not to open and reveal the inner garment. In our times nothing is too "unfitting" for the general market, and there are garments available that do not close properly. If the dress or skirt has this problem the ideal solution is to sew everything up from the inside so that nothing can show. If snaps can be relied upon they can be used as an alternative to secure the skirt. Should a garment button down well, and has no problem with the spaces between the buttons or that the lower end opens, it may be worn - see *Responsa Panim Meiros* 2:183 that in the times of *Chazal* dresses opened right down the front.

Should a button-up garment extend four inches below the knee (i.e. the required length) but the last button is not very near the bottom of the garment, the opening should be sewn up, or be secured with snaps if one knows they will be reliable. This is because all dresses and skirts must extend four inches below the knee to ensure that the knees remain covered when climbing stairs and when sitting down. If these four inches open up easily it is as if there is a slit in that area since when climbing stairs or when sitting down the knees are visible through the opening.

Should the button be at the lower end of the four inches past the knee, but the garment is long and there is a substantial opening below this point, even this should be sewn up because such an opening is like a slit that is below the knees, and to be lenient can cause people to be lenient with real slits - see No.1 above. In this case as in the previous one, should one know that only minimal pressure is exerted against the openings, then instead of sewing the ends together one could simply fix in some snaps and they can be relied upon to keep the area closed.

7. DARK SKIRTS WITH PLEATS THAT REVEAL A LIGHT LINING: It must also be mentioned that dark-colored dresses and skirts that have a large pleat lined with white, gold or similar light-colored materials are unrefined garments. As the woman walks, the white or gold cloth shows, disappears and then shows again, thereby attracting attention in a very unpleasant manner. Such garments are the product of modern society which seeks garments that are eye-catching, assertive, loud and ostentatious, whilst Jewish women seek garments that are gracious, quiet and unobtrusive.

Also, when a white lining appears in such a pleat it can sometimes be mistaken as a slip showing through a slit, and whenever a thought such as this can cross the casual observer's mind, the garment is unrefined. For this reason light colored garments with a black lining showing can be unfitting, since there too, the lining can be mistaken as a black slip showing through.

8. SKIRTS AND DRESSES WITH LACE ADDED ONTO THE HEM: Dresses which have white lace added to the hem are not always tasteful and refined. If the onlooker's first impression could be that some of the slip (petticoat) is hanging out, the garment cannot be classed as *eidel*. It is self-understood that the older the girl, the more unpleasant this is. Although these remarks apply to many places, if in some areas wearing such garments has become so widespread that no one would have the above-mentioned impression, the criticism stated would not apply.

9. DECORATIONS ON SKIRTS AND DRESSES: A final point to mention concerns decorations on skirts. A skirt may certainly be decorated with embroidery. It is, however, unrefined to have a prominent flower, a prominent design or a cluster of decorative buttons positioned just in the center of the upper front of a skirt. The decorations draw attention to that part of the person and are therefore distinctly unrefined. [Hagaon Harav Shmuel Halevi Wosner shlita and Hagaon Harav Nissim Krelitz *shlita*, *sefer*, *Hatzne'ah Leches*, page 50]. It goes without saying that similar decorations on the upper rear of a skirt are grossly distasteful.

Jewish women and girls who wear garments with the faults mentioned certainly do so with total innocence, and would be horrified if it were suggested that they wish to draw people's attention to their physique. Nevertheless, the *tumah'dik* intentions of the secular designers is harmful and such a garment has the opposite affect of a *tznius'dik* piece of clothing. Have we not been told to keep a distance of a least four *amos* from a house of *Avoda Zarah* or of a *Zonah* (see *Mishlei* 5:8 and *Avoda Zarah* 17a) so as not to be affected? Jewish sensitivities are very far reaching.

10. BELTS AND WAISTBANDS:

(a) Refined decorative belts: Women and girls may wear decorative and pretty looking belts provided they are refined and are neither highly ornamental nor eye-catching. See *Mishna Berura* 301:134 who mentions that there were places where women wore two belts on top of each other. The lower one was strong and girded the person well, whilst the upper one was decorative and gave a delightful finish to the garment it was worn upon. The

Mishna Berura states there that two such belts may be worn on Shabbos in the street, even though two identical belts may generally not be worn on top of one another, because in this case each belt serves its own function. It is clear from this statement that just as a dress may be pretty and decorative, so too, a belt may be pretty and decorative, and add luster to the garment on which it is worn.

(b) Eye-catching belts: There are however some highly provocative belts and waistbands in existence. These are belts etc. with accessories hanging from them or bright beads and stones embedded in them, that make the belt very striking and eye-catching. Furthermore, there are cloth belts which have heavy individual pieces of gold attached around the belt giving it a high-shine unrefined look. Similarly, there are distasteful belts which have the name of the manufacturer in large pronounced gold letters attached to the outer surface of the belt. Such a belt is very showy and begging for attention. Also, although there are refined gold chain belts that are suitable to be worn even by the finest women, there are others that are a very heavy gold chain with the added accessory of golden hearts dangling from the chain at intervals. Such belts are מוקצה מחמת מיאוס - "they are unfit to be touched, never mind worn because of their extreme unpleasantness"!

A belt is a highly effective accessory of a person's dress. If refined it can have a wonderful effect on the person's dress. Alternatively, it can have a devastating effect on the complete dress of that person. In fact a girl wearing a plain decent dress but with the addition of one of the belts mentioned will turn her complete person into a symbol of *pritzus* and coarseness.

Amongst the wrongdoings of the women at the time of Yeshaya HaNavi he mentions that they wore highly decorative belts that were very eye-catching. See *Shabbos* (62b) where *Chazal* bring a verse in *Yeshaya* 3:24 warning transgressors that ותחת חגורה נקפה - "Where the highly decorative belts (called צלצול) were worn the flesh shall become cancerous and develop holes". The *Maharsha* quotes the *Gemara* in *Sotah* (8b) where it is mentioned that a *zonah* would gird herself with a belt called a צלצול to attract the attention of men to herself. We gratefully acknowledge the fact that Orthodox women and girls generally know to keep right away from such items as they are grossly distasteful and bring impurity over their wearer.

(c) Excessively wide belts: It is furthermore incorrect to wear an excessively wide belt which is like a sash if it binds the dress or skirt much lower down than usual and has the effect of pronouncing the thigh area, or alternatively binds the dress or blouse closely to the body well above the waistline and therefore pronounces the chest area, Such an item must not be worn because neither the thigh nor the chest areas may be pronounced.

K. HOUSECOATS

In some places women go out to the street dressed in a housecoat which is often worn in place of regular garments. Even those who do not go out wearing it will occasionally invite a person who has come to the door into the house although they are dressed just in a housecoat. A number of points must be made in connection with this, since when this is done without due care it can easily lead to an infringement on many points of *tznius*.

1. TOP BUTTON: The top button of these garments is sometimes left open, especially when the weather is hot, and reveals much more than is permissible because the second button is too far down.

2. NECKLINE: The neckline of these garments is often not Kosher and part of the shoulder is exposed if no dress or blouse is worn under them. These coats are often made to be worn on top of a dress or blouse and the collar area is therefore usually quite loose.

3. SLEEVES: The sleeves of these coats are often very wide. When such sleeves cover only three-quarters of the arm they can easily ride up and reveal part of the upper section of the arm.

4. THE CLOSURE: The bottom of the garment is frequently inadequately closed, with the last button eight inches (20 cm) from the lower end. Also, there can be large gaps between one button and another. If such problems exist, extra buttons should be fixed so that the garment closes properly.

5. SEE-THROUGH: A very serious problem with housecoats is the fact that some are made of a type of thin partially see-through material. The silhouette of the body of the wearer can often be seen terribly clearly when sunlight shines through the housecoat or at night when the light is behind her. Since these are worn with very little else, this can of course be a dreadful exposure.

This is a most serious point because women often do not realize that their garment is see-through.

Since many women prefer to wear housecoats in hot weather as they are light and comfortable, it would be advisable to arrange with the manufacturers that they make housecoats to specifications which would render them suitable for both indoor and outdoor wear.

L. LOWER SECTIONS OF THE LEGS - TIGHTS (HOSIERY)

1. HALACHIC STATUS OF THE LOWER SECTION OF THE LEGS: The lower section of the legs must be fully covered with hosiery (tights or stockings) which masks the legs and covers them very well - see *Mekoros* 1:4. There are two independent reasons why the lower sections of the legs must be covered in this manner:-

- Firstly, *Chazal* state that שוק באשה ערוה - "the leg of a woman is *ervah*" (*Brachos* 24a). According to many *Poskim*, *Chazal* are referring to the lower sections of the legs. Since the lower section of the legs is labeled *ervah* by *Chazal,* they must be very well covered in much the same way as the upper sections of the arms. (*Mekor Chayim* by the *Chavas Yoir* 75:1 and many present-day *Poskim* - amongst them *Responsa Shevet Halevi* 1:1 and *Responsa Be'er Moshe* 4:143). See *Mekoros* 47.

- Secondly, it is fully-accepted Orthodox practice that the lower sections of the legs are covered whenever a woman or girl is in public to lessen their visibility and render them indistinct. The legs are therefore אברים שדרכם להיות מכוסה - limbs which are generally covered and obscured and as such it is an obligation on everyone not to deviate from this practice, as has been explained in 1:G and 6:G:2 above. (See M.B. 75:2, *Responsa Salmas Chayim* 1:66 and *Iggros Moshe* E.H. 4:100 who state this reason for the obligation for covering the lower part of the legs).

According to both reasons see-through tights are unacceptable because when such tights are worn the legs remain fully visible and even more attractive than legs that are not covered at all. (See also *Mekoros* 47-49 for an in-depth study and elaboration on both reasons given).

Although the lower sections of the legs must be very well covered as stated, there is no obligation to screen off the legs so that they cannot be seen - in contrast with the upper section of the legs which must be hidden and disguised behind a dress or skirt - see 6:H:7 above. The upper sections of the legs contain the thigh, and the thigh and all that belongs to that area must be completely screened off. This obligation does not apply to the lower sections of the legs which are not part of the thigh area. For this reason women need not wear dresses down to their ankles.

Since the entire leg surface must be well covered, it is obvious that the tights may not be of a laced or patterned fabric that has numerous holes throughout its surface, because part of the leg can be seen through the holes - (see ruling by Maran Hagaon Harav Shlomo Zalman Auerbach *zt'l* and *yibodel lechayim* Maran Hagaon Harav Yosef Shalom Elyashiv *shlita* in *Mekoros* 1:4). Moreover, such tights are usually designed to lure the observer and as such are highly *pritzus'dik.* See 6:M:8 below concerning tights that have tiny insignificant holes through which nothing can be seen.

2. THE HARM CAUSED BY INADEQUATE COVERING OF THE LEGS:

(a) The far reaching effect of such a wrongdoing: It is essential that women and girls be aware that to inadequately cover the legs is tantamount to displaying them and causing people to look at them, which is a *pritzus'dik* way of dress. Moreover, covering the legs inadequately gives the impression that the woman or girl wants her legs to be seen, in line with the conduct of present day society. Although these effects might be far from her intention, they are nevertheless likely to occur, and she will be responsible for them.

The following is a statement by a British hosiery consultant taken from an article that discusses the way to promote the sale of tights during the summer months when people would not buy them for warmth. "We tend to recommend hosiery over the summer as a way to color the legs very quickly without tanning them" (*Hosiery Report, September '96*). This is their viewpoint. We do not share their distasteful interest in leg beautification, be it by causing a tanned look, by causing the legs to shimmer in the light, or by giving them a very smooth, matt-like look, which are all designed to arouse an interest to look at the legs. On the contrary, our reason for wearing tights or stockings is as an act of *tznius*, to distinctly lessen the noticeability of the legs and thereby lessen any natural appeal there may be to look at the legs.

On reflection the situation with tights is closely comparable to that of wigs. Wigs are worn by many of the *umos ha'olam* to beautify themselves and change their appearance at will. In contrast, they are worn by *N'shei Yisroel* as an act of *tznius* to cover their own hair in a respectful and pleasant manner. Due to this, the *sheitel* of the refined *Bas Yisroel* is quite different from the glamorous wig worn by the *umos ha'olam*. So too, tights are worn by *nochrios* to improve the appeal of the legs whilst *N'shei Yisroel* wear them for the absolute opposite purpose. Due to this, the tights *N'shei Yisroel* wear are not the same see-through tights that suit the interests of the *umos ha'olam*.

The more stringent a woman or girl is in covering her legs well, the more she underpins *Kedushas Yisroel*. Such conduct will intensify the quality of her own *Yiddishkeit* and commitment to *halacha*. Also, other women or girls will take note of the way she dresses and if they are inclined to *tznius* will emulate her example. She will therefore reinforce the *Yiddishkeit* of other people apart from her own.

(b) The Halacha is not "suspended" during summer or vacation: During the summer months or when on vacation a woman or girl must not relax her values of *tznius*. Therefore, to wear Kosher tights throughout the winter but see-through tights in the summer or when on vacation is wholly incorrect. As lack of refinement in dress is one of the major ailments of the Orthodox and otherwise devout part of *Klal Yisroel* of this generation, it must be countered by adhering fully to the *halachos* of *tznius* at all times and in all situations. Also, being strong on issues of *tznius* at times of test, when she may be looked down upon by others, makes an all round *kiddush Hashem*. She thereby displays the sterling qualities and inner strength typical of a true *Bas Yisroel*.

(c) Tights should be "checked on the legs" to see if adequate: In all cases (except when tights are totally opaque) it is important that women and girls check tights (that they have not previously worn) on their own legs to ensure that they give the legs adequate cover and look *tznius'dik*. The camouflaging potential of tights depends on many factors, some related to the tights; others to the wearer, as will be explained. It can therefore happen that two people wear the same tights and they are alright on one person but totally inadequate on the other. There are four points to consider:-

- Firstly, the camouflaging potential of tights lessens considerably when they are stretched unnaturally. Therefore if the person's legs are too large for these tights, they lose much of their obscuring and screening effect. This is even more so when the person is too tall or their hips too large for these tights and they have to be stretched unnaturally lengthwise to fit. This is because tights are woven to allow for quite some stretching in the width but not to allow for excessive stretching in the length. They therefore become much thinner when stretched lengthwise. Accordingly, two people might both wear the same average-size tights. However, since one is taller than the other, the tights are virtually see-through on her legs whilst they are opaque and fine on their friend's legs.

- Secondly, the camouflaging potential depends considerably on the color and shade of the tights. Also of major significance is the natural color of the legs, because light colored skin is more difficult to cover adequately than darker skin. Therefore, a pair of tights may be alright on one girl but no good for her peer who has lighter skin than her.

- Thirdly, the camouflage potential depends on the density of the weave of the tights i.e. how many threads there are per square inch. In fact, two manufacturers in the same country will produce tights of the same denier (an international measure of the thickness of the actual thread but not of the cloth in general) and the tights of one manufacturer camouflage the legs whilst those of the other manufacturer do not, as is very well known. This is due either to a difference in the shade or in the density of weave. Also, more recently (since strengthened by Lycra - see next point) tights are made with a very plain weave in which just horizontal and vertical threads are used, creating a very thin cloth, whereas previously the weave was strengthened by additional threads that ran diagonally across the cloth, which in turn thickened the cloth considerably.

- Fourthly, many up-to-date tights and stockings contain Lycra or a similar product throughout - not just in the upper area which surrounds the body but all the way down the leg. When Lycra is present, the tights may appear to be a good grade because Lycra is a cloth stiffener and when held in the hands the cloth feels very substantial. However a second property of Lycra is that it is highly elastic, and when stretched in a normal manner it could become very thin. This problem did not exist until recently. It is therefore essential that people are aware that tights and stockings containing Lycra (in the leg area) must be checked carefully.

Accordingly, the fact that a woman or girl has worn similar tights or stockings in the past and they were fine, cannot be taken as proof that this new type will likewise be alright. Also, the fact that another woman or girl looks alright in these tights cannot be taken as evidence that they will likewise look alright on her. It is therefore essential that when changing to a different type (even of the same manufacturer) one checks the new tights carefully to ensure that they cover the leg well and look *tznius'dik*.

3. INTENSE FEELING OF A GADOL B'YISROEL ON THIS MATTER: The following story illustrates the intense feelings that one of our great *Gedolim zt'l* had about this holy obligation. After the passing of the Klausenberger Rebbe, Harav Hagaon R' Yekusiel Yehuda Halberstam *zt'l* a woman came to visit the family during the *shiva* and brought with her a pair of black socks. She related the following story. Shortly after the Second World War the Klausenberger Rebbe *zt'l* was in a D.P. (displaced-persons) camp in Germany. One day, as the Rebbe walked along the street he noticed an Orthodox Jewish girl whose legs were evidently not covered. The Rebbe approached the girl saying, "*Mein Kind! Vie kumt dos as a Yiddishe meidel geht ohn socken?* (My child! How can a Jewish girl walk around without stockings?). "Rebbe!" answered the girl, "*Vos ken ich tohn - ich hob poshet nisht*" (Rebbe, what can I do, I simply don't have any.)

The Rebbe bent down, removed his shoes and started taking off his black socks. As he did so he said to the girl, "*Kum, ich gib dir meine*! (Come, I'll give you mine!) The Rebbe then added, "*Ich meg gehen ohn socken, ober a Yiddische tochter - der Torah farlangt az eirer fies darfen zein tzugedekt*". (I may go without socks, but the Torah demands that a Jewish girl must have her legs covered!). With this he handed his socks to her - although he, a highly-respected Rav, would have to walk around with bare legs. The girl in this incident was the very woman who came to visit the family during the *shiva*. She had cherished these socks for fifty years and now brought them along to the *shiva* to show the family the *tzidkus* of their father even under the most trying conditions. (*Heard from Rebbetzen Weiss of Yerusholayim, daughter of the late Klausenberger Rebbe zt'l*).

Let us hope that our wives and daughters who have been granted a much better and much calmer life than was the lot of those who lived through the terrible camps fifty years ago, take this story to heart and implement modesty and refinement of the legs in its fullest sense.

4. DRESS SHOULD BE TASTEFUL; HOSIERY SHOULD BE DECENT: Some people mistakenly think that whatever is suitable for a dress, outfit, and coat is likewise suitable for tights and other forms of leg-wear. This is not the case and such an attitude is fundamentally against the Jewish outlook. While the main body should be tastefully and gracefully dressed, as this projects the image of the person and it is wrong for a girl or woman to look drab and somber, legs should be decent and respectable but not pretty and tasteful. For this reason a dress or outfit may be floral or laced whilst if tights are floral or laced, this is considered a *pritzus'dik* way of dress. We will now explain בע״ה the reason for this distinction.

A pretty dress (that is not a tight fit) camouflages the real body rather than shows it off, as it focuses attention on the *chein* of the dress itself, rather than onto the personal beauty of its wearer. When Avimelech released Sarah from his palace after mistakenly thinking she was available for marriage he gave her a כסות עינים (*Breishis* 20:16). The *Midrash* explains that this was a pretty garment - see also *Seforno*. Avimelech gave Sarah, who was extremely beautiful, such a dress for the following reason: - אמר רבי יוחנן עשה לה כסות שיהיו מביטין בה ולא בנויה - "R' Yochanan explains that the purpose of the dress was so that if the local people gazed at her they would gaze at her dress rather than at her personal beauty" (*Midrash Breishis* 52:12, *Megilla* 15a). See 3:B:2 above and *Mekoros* 66:4.

This *Chazal* conveys a very insightful message. A pretty dress deflects attention from the main body of the person. It is therefore fine for a dress to be floral or pretty in some other way, provided it is not outstandingly beautiful and does not attract undue attention. Leg coverings are, however, totally different as they fit tightly round the legs and affect the appearance of the legs themselves. Therefore, if they are pretty they become a beautification of the leg itself, which is wrong. *Tznius* calls for the natural attraction of the legs to be diminished, whilst these coverings do just the opposite - they beautify the legs and increase their power of attraction. [This is also a reason why it is wrong to wear tight-fitting clothes - such clothes beautify the body rather than deflect attention from it - see 6:E:2 above for further reasons.]

It should also be noted that in the times of *Chazal*, Jewish women wore dresses almost down to the ground, in a way that the legs could not be seen at all. See *Tshuvos HaRadvaz* (2:770) who states that this is how women used to dress and so is also evident from the *Gemara* in *Shabbos* 98b - see *Mekoros* 49:3. This means that although they wore בגדי צבעונים - colorful garments in the times of *Chazal* to look pretty, they did not expose their legs and enhance their legs' appearance.

In a similar vein, the *Midrash Shir HaShirim* (7:3:1) asks on the verse מה יפו פעמיך - "How beautiful are your steps", והלא אפילו ההדיוט כשמקלס בלשון זה גנאי הוא לו ואת אמרת מה יפו פעמיך בנעלים - this means: "How can the verse utter such praise? If even an ignoble and unworthy man would praise the appearance of a girl's legs or her footsteps he would be held in contempt for having stooped so low. If so, how can the verse praise a woman's footsteps?" [The answer given by the *Midrash* is not relevant to our issue.]

We see from this *Chazal* that although an ignoble man frequently gazes at females (*Bava Basra* 168a) and discusses their appearance and charm, nevertheless, to pronounce that a woman legs or footsteps are beautiful is a level of immodesty that is not expected even of such a person!

This all points to the fact that according to the *Torah'dik* way of conduct, which is wholesome and upright, legs are to look decent and respectable, but not attractive or appealing. Accordingly, although nowadays legs are not hidden under a long dress as they were in the olden times, they must nevertheless not be given prominence in dress. This is a significant point which mothers should transmit to their daughters and teachers to their students as understanding the Torah viewpoint helps the person accept the relevant *halachos*.

5. PRITZUS OF THE LEGS - MALADY OF THE LAST FEW DECADES:

(a) Recognizing a new front in the *yetzer horah's* battle: Against the backdrop of the previous piece, a further far-reaching point concerning the covering of legs must be made. Women and girls must be made aware that in this generation the *yetzer horah* of *pritzus* in relationship to female dress has targeted itself with all its might onto the area of the legs. This is evident from the numerous forms of exposure and exhibition concerning the upper and lower parts of the leg that have come into existence over the last few decades. In the times of Yeshaya, women would show off their height with high heeled shoes and beauty by using excessive cosmetics and perfumes - see *Mekoros* 2:1. In the times of the *Gemara,* women would expose their arms when spinning wool in public (*Kesubos* 72b). In the eighteenth century women exposed more than just the neck - see *Mekoros* 34:4. In still more recent times (before World War Two), in some communities women did not cover their hair properly - see *Mekoros* 21:7-11.

There is, however, almost no mention in *T'nach*, *Shas* or the early *Poskim* of *pritzus* concerning either the upper or lower sections of the legs. To our dismay, in our times the *yetzer horah* has succeeded in creating a whole array of *pritzus'dik* modes in relationship to the covering of these parts. He has forged ahead and created the mini-skirt, slacks, the slit at the back, at the front and at the side of a dress and skirt, wrap-around skirts some of which open in a most detestable way, tight immodest skirts, see-through tights, patterned and shiny hosiery of the most eye-catching styles possible, colored or fluorescent tights and many other outrageous displays of immodesty, designed to suit every type of *yetzer horah* - see *Mekoros* 45:6.

(b) This powerful *yetzer horah* may be hinted to in the Torah: This powerful *yetzer horah* is hinted to in the verse (*Breishis* 32:26) ויגע בכף ירכו ותקע כף ירך יעקב בהאבקו עמו - "And he reached the inner thigh of Yaacov and dislocated it in his struggle with him". The *Satan*, the angel of Eisov, struggled all night with Yaacov to bring about his downfall. He was basically unsuccessful. However, just before dawn he cunningly struck Yaacov in the thigh causing him serious injury. The struggle through the night represents the struggle between *Klal Yisroel* and Eisov throughout *golus* which is compared to a long dark night. After much effort, the *Satan* finally found a way to do great harm to the Jewish people. He smote them by dislocating the "thigh of Yaacov" - causing women and girls (who are termed as Yaacov) to lessen their standards of *tznius* concerning this area of the body. As we sadly see - he has been mightily successful and the Jewish people limp under the effect of this serious assault (Heard from a *Talmid Chacham*).

(c) Extra effort to counter prevailing weakness: Since exposure and beautification of legs is the focal *yetzer horah* of present-day *pritzus*, the more we do to counter this by covering these limbs in a substantial manner, the more we demonstrate that our way of life and our aspirations are at total variance to the life-style and aspirations of those to whom the Torah was not given. It is our yearning that more and more of our daughters live up to the standards of *tznius* they are most certainly capable of. In their honor we will sing the verse, מה יפו פעמיך בנעלים בת נדיב - "How sublime and refined are your shoe-clad footsteps, O daughter of Avraham Avinu the nobleman" (*Shir HaShirim* 7:2). See 6:O:4 below for the meaning of "shoe-clad footsteps" and 6:H:7 above for the meaning of other parts of that verse.

(d) How Rachel countered the weaknesses of her civilization: In line with this, an interesting explanation is given in the *Od Yosef Chai* by the *Gaon* and *Tzaddik* Harav Yosef Chayim *zt'l* from Baghdad. When Yaacov saw Rachel for the first time, she was leading her father's flock to the well. The verse relates that the shepherds said to Yaacov, והנה היא באה עם הצאן - "behold she is coming with the sheep" (*Breishis* 29:6). More naturally it should have said, והנה היא מביאה את הצאן - "Behold she is bringing the sheep" which would mean that she was in front of the sheep or behind them as is typical of a shepherd. "Coming with the sheep" implies that she was amongst the sheep and was walking along with them.

The *Od Yosef Chai* writes that this was in fact so. Rachel neither went ahead of the sheep nor behind them, and instead walked amongst them. She used the natural opportunity available to her to hide the lower part of her body from the eyes of the local boys and men, by surrounding herself on all sides with the sheep. The words of the *Od Yosef Chai* are, היתה הולכת בתוך הצאן באופן שתהיה מוקפת מן הצאן מכל צדדיה, כדי שיתכסו פסיעות הנאות שלה בצאן מכל צד, ולא יהא נראה חצי התחתון של גופה לעוברים ושבים וההולכים במדבר - "She walked between the sheep so that she would be encircled by them. Thereby her appealing footsteps would not be seen. Also, the lower part of her body would be hidden from the sight of wayfarers and desert travelers." These were our *Imahos*. It is our obligation and privilege to live in their shadow and enrich our lives by learning from their example. While it is not for us to wear dresses down to the ground (see 6:H:6 above) we can at least emulate the spirit of their ways.

M. TIGHTS (HOSIERY) - COLORS AND PATTERNS

1. COMMUNITIES WHERE DARK TIGHTS ARE NOT WORN: In some communities only light-colored tights are allowed. This refers to light or medium brown, beige, light or dark gray and mild shades of off-white. They do not allow dark colors such as black because they are viewed as modern, fashion-seeking and a departure from established standards in dress. They furthermore forbid dark colors because the leg is noticeable through dark tights that are not fully opaque. Although the tights are the same thickness as light-colored ones that are Kosher, they are more see-through and inadequate. Since the tights are dark and the leg light, the leg shows through in a more meaningful way than through light-colored tights. On the other hand, with light-colored tights, since the tights are similar to the color of skin, the legs do not show through and the legs are considered well covered.

2. COMMUNITIES IN WHICH DARK TIGHTS ARE WORN: In other communities, black tights and in some places even dark navy-blue tights are worn, provided they cover the leg well as will be explained. They have become so common in these places that wearing them is neither viewed as "being modern" nor as copying the dress of the *nochrim* as they have become part of the standard dress of Jewish girls and to some degree of Jewish women. In response to the second complaint mentioned, those who permit dark tights require that dark tights are more tightly textured than is required of lighter colored tights thereby lessening the visibility of the leg - see 4(a) below.

Wearing such tights is not an infringement of the *issur* of בחוקותיהם לא תלכו - "one must not follow the ways of *nochrim*", although the trend of dark colored tights was started by the *nochrim*. This is because that *issur* applies only to ways of dress that are distinctly *darkei nochrim*, such as clothes that project a feeling of self-pride or a lack of *tznius* which is not the case with these tights, since when worn correctly they will not infringe on *tznius*. See 1:H:6 above where this subject matter is explained in detail.

3. COMPLYING WITH THE OPINION FOLLOWED LOCALLY: In a case such as this where there are two diverse opinions, each community must follow the *p'sak* of their *halachic* authorities. It is imperative that those who wear black or blue tights do not do so in communities that do not allow them. There are a number of reasons for this.

Firstly, they would stand out, as people notice when someone is dressed differently from everyone else, and this itself is not *tznius'dik* - see *Mekoros* 69. Secondly, it is wrong to walk around in a way which is not *tznius'dik* according to the feelings of the local people. Since according to their way of thinking this way of dress is incorrect, one is harming them by displaying insensitivity to *tznius* in front of them - see *Mekoros* 30:2. Thirdly, wearing dark tights in these areas will inevitably lead to the spread of this way of dress into their community and according to the local *halachic* opinion this way of dress is forbidden. See 1:G:2-3 where this matter is discussed in more detail.

4. PRECAUTIONS NEEDED WHEN WEARING DARK TIGHTS: Dark tights in contrast with light-colored ones present a number of dangers to accepted standards of *tznius*. It is imperative that maximum care is taken not to lessen the *kedusha* and *tahara* of *Am Yisroel* by walking around in a provocative or even just a marginally provocative way. The following are four points that must be heeded:-

(a) Ensuring that the calf of the leg is well covered: There is a serious problem with dark tights that does not exist with light-colored tights. Being dark but not totally opaque the light color of the legs can show through part of the tights in a way that would not happen with cream, brown, gray or other light tights of the same grade. This is likely to occur in the area of the calf where the tights are stretched and hence thinner than elsewhere. Due to this, a woman or girl might be wearing tights that have become see-through in that area to the extent that they cannot be considered *tznius'dik*. [If the dress extends beyond most of the calf this problem will not exist, but dresses and skirts are not always quite so long.]

It is therefore necessary that women and girls who wear dark tights buy tights that are more tightly textured than they would have required if they were wearing light-colored tights. Alternatively, they can wear tights that are "large size" and are therefore distinctly larger than what they would have personally needed. It has been proven that this helps considerably in making these dark tights more opaque. As they are much less stretched they are far more closely textured.

(b) Extra need for skirt to have the right length: The need for skirts and dresses to extend to at least four inches below the lowest point of the knee (see 6:H:3 above) takes on an added dimension when dark-colored tights are worn. These tights are distinctly not *tznius'dik* and even eye-catching when worn with a skirt that is just knee length. Black is a strong color and it is most unsatisfactory for the full dark leg to be on display. As stated above, the skirt must hang to at least 4" (10 cm) below the knee. This length is adequate but it is even more refined to wear a garment that is a couple of inches longer than this.

(c) Must be accompanied by a skirt of an appropriate color: Often, dark tights look right only when worn with a dark colored skirt such as a black, navy-blue, dark green, or maroon skirt. When such a skirt is worn, the dark-colored tights blend well with the skirt and the person looks refined as the legs are not pronounced. However, when a light-colored skirt is worn with such tights, the dark legs often become very conspicuous (as black shows up against a light background) and are not *tznius'dik*.

The observation just stated is not always relevant, and sometimes dark tights are suitable even with light-colored garments, especially when the garment is long and covers over half the lower leg. These facts have been stated so that a correct assessment can be made. This is part of tznius'dik conduct - to be continuously on the lookout that one's dress is refined and modest.

(d) Black and navy blue tights: Although black and dark blue tights are worn in some circles, this must not be taken as a license to branch out to many other dark or light colors. Black and blue have a distinct advantage in that black is a refined color and the *Poskim* generally encourage the choice of black for a garment (*Shach* Y.D. 178:3) - see *Mekoros* 63:1. Likewise, dark blue is basically like black (*Biur Halacha* 32:3 s.v. *Yichteveim*). It is also a refined color as is well recognized and as stated by *Rabbeinu Bachya*

(*Shemos* 28:15) - see *Mekoros* 63:3. There is a danger of colored tights becoming a "free for all". This must not be allowed to happen as there are many unrefined tights both in dark and in light colors on the market. Therefore, women and girls should only wear tights that are fully accepted and look refined.

5. FULLY-OPAQUE BLACK TIGHTS: Fully-opaque black tights are a most difficult subject to write about. If not for the fact that *nochrios* wear them and that they are nowadays the height of fashion in many places they would be the ideal tights to wear, as they cover the legs completely. It is well known that women in *Meoh Shearim* and in some very *Chassidishe* communities wear black opaque tights or stockings because they are very *tznius'dik* and refined, when worn with a long skirt. It would therefore be wonderful if one could recommend these tights for everyone, girls and women alike. However, when girls from other backgrounds wear these tights they often do not project a *tznius'dik* image at all. It would seem there are two reasons for this.

- Firstly, the girls wear them because they are very much in fashion and are attractive. Even if this is not their motive, it appears to the onlooker that this is the reason for wearing them. It is understood that once wearing black opaque tights has become very widespread amongst the *frum* girls of a certain community and is viewed as the norm, the stigma of being "worn to be fashionable" no longer applies and they will no longer project a *non-tznius'dik* image. At the present time, different communities have very diverse opinions and feelings about these tights and it is impossible to give a general ruling on them.

- Secondly, when opaque tights are worn with a skirt that is only of average length, the large amount of "black" that is visible causes the leg to be conspicuous rather than reserved and refined. This is likely to be the main reason why the women of *Meah Shearim* look refined in opaque tights whilst others often look unrefined.

It has been stressed many times that in communities where a certain mode of dress is considered *pritzus* it is *ossur* for an individual to dress in such a way even though she comes from a town or educational *mosad* where this mode of dress is permitted. Opaque tights are prime candidates for this warning because they are considered offensive in places where *frum* girls do not wear them. It must also be mentioned that the color and length of the skirt worn with opaque tights has an enormous bearing on whether they look refined or not. (The guidelines detailed in No. 4 above, also apply to opaque tights).

6. SKIN-COLORED TIGHTS: Skin-colored tights, which give the impression (to anyone who is a little distance away from the wearer) that the woman or girl is not wearing tights at all, must not be worn irrespective of their thickness. As they give the impression that the legs are uncovered, they attract attention to the leg in exactly the same way as do truly uncovered legs. In fact they are even more attractive than uncovered legs, because the tights have the effect of hiding any discoloration of the legs and giving the legs a perfect appearance which is obviously especially attractive.

Since it is unanimously agreed by all *Poskim* that legs must be covered so that they do not attract attention, skin-colored tights are obviously *ossur*, as they attract attention and defeat the purpose of covering the legs. See *sefer, Yesodos Shel Beis Yehudi,* page 571, where a *halachic* statement from the year 5687, signed by Harav Hagaon R' Yosef Chayim Sonnenfeld *zt'l* is reprinted. Amongst other points it forbids the wearing of skin-colored tights.

Apart from the obvious lack of *tznius* in wearing such tights in a place where people are not used to seeing them, they are *ossur* because they can lead to a misunderstanding, as the onlooker could think this woman or girl has not covered her legs. If this is the case she transgresses the *issur* of והייתם נקיים - a person must not do something that causes people to think that he is sinning - see 5:D:5 above and *Mekoros* 30.

7. PATTERNED TIGHTS: As is the case with all areas of female clothing, tights are available that are the personification of *pritzus* and must not be worn by our wives and daughters. These are dark, heavily patterned tights which are designed to attract attention to the legs - see *Mekoros* 1:4. In the non-Jewish world much emphasis and effort is put by women into the appearance of their legs, and these patterned tights are just part of that lowly and immoral pursuit. In contrast, in the Torah-orientated world great emphasis and effort is made by women to be as inconspicuous as possible in public so as not to cause males to stumble and transgress the Torah prohibition of ולא תתורו אחרי עיניכם. When one considers the difference between these two types of women, one cannot help but exclaim, ברוך אלוקינו שבראנו לכבודו והבדילנו מן התועים ונתן לנו תורת אמת.

As stated, heavily-patterned tights should not be worn because they attract attention to the legs and are often highly provocative. They are therefore a most immodest piece of clothing. Apart from the patterns, many of these tights sport numerous sizable holes and wherever there is such a hole the skin is uncovered and on display. These patterned tights are forbidden even if locally it is common practice to wear them, since by their very nature they are designed to attract attention.

Heavily-patterned tights should not be worn even by girls once they are six/seven years old since all girls must be dressed in *tznius'dik* clothes. It is likewise wrong to allow young girls to wear dark tights that are patterned with large black criss-cross stitches. This is the very design that is worn by the *nochrios* who are the lowest of society. Also, when such tights are worn the legs are exceptionally conspicuous. To dress a girl in such a way is wrong on two counts. Firstly, the legs attract attention and this is *pritzus'dik* once she is a six/seven-year old (and according to some already once she is a three-year old). Secondly, parents are obligated to educate their daughter to a Kosher mode of dress once she has reached the age mentioned - see 6:S:2 below. To dress them in tights that are despicable on a teenage girl can hardly be considered as giving the girl a healthy *chinuch* - see *Mekoros* 1:4.

8. LIGHTLY-PATTERNED TIGHTS: Tights that have a light colorless pattern created by tiny holes in the cloth, may be worn provided local Orthodox women or girls wear such tights. Light patterns such as these are not attractive and the tights are therefore not considered immodest. The tiny holes that accompany such light patterns are usually too insignificant for the skin to show through. They are therefore permitted in places where it is the norm to wear tights of such material. However, in places where it is unusual to wear any type of patterned tights, they will naturally attract attention, since people are not accustomed to women wearing such tights.

If only young girls wear lightly-patterned tights, it is *ossur* for a woman or older girl to wear them, since people notice whatever is unusual. It must be mentioned that small holes may be significant in dark-colored lightly-patterned tights, and might render them unsuitable.

Light colored tights with embroidered patterns of the identical color are alright for a young girl, provided the pattern is not pronounced against the rest of the material which darkens somewhat as it is dressed on the leg. Sometimes, wearing another plain pair of tights under the patterned ones ensures that the patterns are not overly noticeable.

9. SHINY TIGHTS: Tights that have a very distinct shine on them should not be worn. They are made with such a sheen so that as they are worn light reflects from them. As a result the legs are more noticeable than usual and could even attract attention. Such tights are therefore unrefined and serve a purpose which is wrong according to the Jewish outlook explained in 6:L:4 above. However, tights that have only a minor sheen hardly reflect light and are considered refined. They are permitted, provided the local standard of *tznius* has not excluded wearing such tights because they are afraid that wearing them could introduce the more shiny and forbidden types.

10. SOCKS ON TOP OF TIGHTS: In some places ladies and girls wear short brown or sandy-colored socks in addition to their tights for extra warmth and comfort. Since the local Jewish population is used to it there is nothing wrong with dressing in this way as it does not look unusual (except in the eyes of those who are not familiar with it).

However, should a lady or girl from such a place move to or even just visit a community where this way of dress is unknown, it would be a lack of *tznius* for her to wear socks over her tights even though it was fine to dress in this way at home. To the local people this could appear as casual wear, lacking the refinement that is to be expected of a *Bas Yisroel*. Furthermore, she will inevitably be very conspicuous in her socks and draw attention to herself as others do not dress in this way. On each of these counts independently it would be wrong for her to wear these socks in this community - see 1:G:2 above.

Brightly-colored short socks that are worn on top of tights are distinctly unrefined and even *pritzus'dik* leg-wear. They create a powerful contrast of color on the leg and are obviously not worn just for extra warmth or comfort. They have the effect of attracting attention to the wearer's legs and fall under the same category as patterned tights which are *pritzus'dik* leg-wear. They are *ossur* even if they have become widespread and people who have become contaminated by the ways of the *umos ha'olam* to "beautify the legs" do not understand what is wrong with them. This lack of understanding is a phenomenon we must contend with in our misguided generation. It does not give us the right to sanction that which is quite obviously a wrongdoing.

N. THIGH-HIGHS AND KNEE-HIGHS

1. THIGH-HIGHS FINE; KNEE-HIGHS VERY RISKY: Women and girls may wear thigh-highs that extend upwards and cover the knees. However, knee-highs that stop below the knee should generally not be worn because they cannot be relied upon to cover the lower leg and knee properly at all times. This statement is a *psak halacha* of Hagaon Harav Shlomo Zalman Auerbach *zt'l* (*Malbushei Kavod* p.55). In a subsequent ruling, Hagaon Harav Yosef Shalom Elyashiv *shlita*, Hagaon Harav Shmuel Halevi Wosner *shlita* and other *Gedolei Eretz Yisroel* signed the statement - see *Mekoros* 1:4. It is unjustified to consider the obligation to wear tights, stockings or thigh-highs rather than knee-highs a hardship and as something almost unbearable, since stockings were worn without complaint by all Orthodox women until recently.

Even if a skirt hangs past the knee as is required, exposure of uncovered areas can still easily occur if knee-highs are worn. This can happen due to the movement of the garment in windy weather, when running along the street, when sitting down, when ascending stairs and especially when getting in and out of a car. Also, people sitting in a hotel dining room have encountered women wearing knee-highs sitting at another table some meters away with the area below the knees (and sometimes the bare knees themselves) on total display, because the women were wearing knee-highs.

Some claim that when wearing a flared skirt that is a bit longer than 4" below the knee the danger of exposure is virtually non-existent. They therefore claim that knee-highs can be permitted when worn with such a garment. An honest assessment of this claim has, however, shown it to be far from accurate. It has consistently been found that when a woman or girl wears knee-highs under a flared skirt that is longer than the four inches required, exposure still occurs all too frequently. It happens when sitting cross-legged, when entering or leaving a car, when stretching to take an item off a shelf and during similar situations - see 9:I:6 below. Furthermore, in spite of the Kosher length of the skirt people are often careless and sit in a way that their knees can be seen (which is wrong even when the knees are covered by stockings or tights - see 6:H:7 above). The *issur* in displaying the knees is greatly intensified when the knees are bare, because they are far more conspicuous when uncovered. These mishaps occur all the more frequently when the skirt is straight, as such skirts ride up considerably.

When a long skirt (that hangs six inches or more over the knee-highs) is worn, the danger of exposure is minimal, since there is a six inch overlap. It would therefore seem safe to permit women to wear knee-highs with such long skirts. The *Gedolei HaTorah* of Eretz Yisrael are however against giving any *heter* because many people will assume that knee-highs may also be worn with average length skirts. Their wisdom and accurate assessment of human nature has been proven right time and time again - see *Mekoros* 1:4.

2. GIRLS WHO SKIP IN PUBLIC SHOULD WEAR PROPER TIGHTS: When girls skip with a skipping rope (jump-rope), jump over a 'scoobie' (elastic rope) or sway to and fro on a swing, it is almost inevitable that their skirts fly up every now and then. These games are played by girls up to the age of ten or twelve, and children do not always play in discreet places, although they have been encouraged to do so. It is therefore essential that they are dressed in a way that even when this happens it will be as inconspicuous as possible. Since the sudden appearance of the actual leg will attract the attention of a passerby, this must be avoided at all costs.

Accordingly, young girls who engage in these and similar games should only wear proper tights. Even thigh-highs cannot be relied upon under these circumstances, although they extend above the knee.

O. FOOTWEAR

1. FEET MUST BE COVERED AS PER THE ACCEPTED NORM: According to the rules laid down by *Chazal*, a woman need not cover her feet. In some hot countries, such as India, women actually walked around with dresses down to their ankles and left their feet uncovered, and this was perfectly acceptable - (see *Bach* O.C. 75, s.v. *U'mah* and *Badei Hashulchon* Y.D. 195:7 *Biurim* s.v. *V'lo b'mekomos*). Nowadays, in virtually all Orthodox circles, hosiery is worn to cover the legs, as dresses are not ankle length, and it has become an accepted norm to cover the feet with the same thickness as the legs - see L1-L3 above. The feet are therefore a מקום שדרכו להיות מכוסה - a place which people cover and it is *ossur* for a woman or girl to reveal her feet when she is in public (M.B. 75:2; *Kaf HaChayim* 75:2).

Either shoes or sandals may be worn. Although it is customary to wear a foot covering and not walk around barefooted, there is no general custom to wear only shoes that totally enclose the foot and toes. However, as with all other items of female clothing, care must be taken that the sandals do not project an overly sporty and leisurely appearance which detracts from the refinement expected of the Jewish woman and girl.

Painting toe-nails is a distinctly non-Jewish practice and is to be strongly discouraged. To do so belongs to the "excessive beautification" about which Yeshaya HaNavi laments so bitterly - see *Mekoros* 2:1-2 and 53:3. Similarly, ankle jewelry such as a ankle-chains is a beautification of the leg which is incorrect and out of place in our society, as was explained in 6:L:4 above.

2. AVOIDING IMMODEST SHOE-STYLES: The trend towards immodesty that has engulfed the world affects every aspect of female dress. Even shoes are made with such bright colors or immodest designs that a woman or girl with an elementary degree of *tznius* would not buy them. It is understood that the older the girl, the quieter the color and the more refined the shoe should be. Moreover, there are some shoe-styles that are unsuitable, such as excessively high-heeled shoes. If it is obvious to the observer that it must be uncomfortable to walk in such shoes, then doing so announces that the wearer is prepared to sacrifice elementary comfort for the sake of greater height and additional beauty. This is vanity and unfit for a person of quality and value such as the *Bas Yisroel*. This conduct is referred to by Yeshaya HaNavi (*Yeshaya* 3:16) when he complains יען כי גבהו בנות ציון - "[I am angered] because Jewish girls go to all extremes to make themselves taller."

One of the most unpleasant shoe styles that has once again surfaced is the shoe with extremely thick soles. This type of shoe existed already in the days of Yeshaya HaNavi. He writes concerning the Jewish girls of his times, הלוך וטפוף תלכנה - "She walks in a bloated way" (*Yeshaya* 3:16). The *Midrash* explains, כשהיתה אחת מהן קצרה היתה לובשת קרקוסין עבים כדי שתראה ארוכה - "When a girl was short she would wear very thick-soled shoes so that she looked tall" (*Midrash Eichah* 4:18). Yeshaya HaNavi considered such footwear as vanity at its worst, as it meant going to all lengths just to look beautiful or tall. She would even wear heavy (as they were in the olden days) and clumsy shoes, just to ensure that she had "caught up" with other girls who were taller than her. The display of bad taste and bad *midos* that is involved in wearing such shoes should make a *Bas Yisroel* cringe at the thought that in places where *tznius* has deteriorated girls who keep Shabbos and *kashrus* will walk around with these unsightly pieces of footwear.

3. EXCESSIVE GOLD ON SHOES IS PRETENTIOUS: There is certainly nothing wrong with some gold here and there on shoes. However, shoes that have excessive amounts of gold on them are eye-catching and immodest. Just as a moderate amount of finery on an outfit or dress is perfect and adds a lot to the woman's *chein*, whereas an inappropriate amount of jewelry is immodest and pretentious, so too, the right measure of gold can be an improvement to shoes and make them more *b'cheint*, but too much glitter is unpleasant and counter-productive as far as *chein* and refinement is concerned.

Accordingly, if the complete front part of the shoe or the total rear of the shoes is a bright shiny gold, the shoes cannot be considered refined footwear. On the contrary, they are showy and immodest items. This is particularly so when worn by women or teen-age girls although not recommended even for young school girls. Regrettably, as with all items of clothing, there are many who are perplexed and think that the more spectacular and striking an item is, the more it is a prized piece of clothing.

4. NOT TO WALK WITH LOUD OR SOPHISTICATED FOOTSTEPS: It is important to mention an age-old immodest use of shoes. This is to wear shoes that have heels which clatter against the street surface and "announce" that Miss... is walking along the road. The *Navi* Yeshaya (3:16) complained, וברגליהם תעכסנה - "*Hashem* is angered by the manner of walk adopted by the Jewish girls" - see *Mekoros* 2:1:5. A true *Bas Yisroel* walks along the road in a quiet and refined manner. This is consistent with the way she talks and laughs - she neither talks very loudly nor laughs out aloud when in public (and preferably not even in private). Such boisterous and coarse behavior is simply unfitting for the royal status of a *Bas Yisroel*.

Similarly, if a woman or girl walks quietly but in a sophisticated and haughty manner it is a lack of *tznius* that is closely comparable to walking with loud and coarse footsteps. This incorrect conduct is mentioned by Yeshaya HaNavi amongst the many complaints that he voiced about the women of his time. On the verse (*Yeshaya* 3:16) הלוך וטפוף תלכנה (which refers to a number of different wrongdoings that are all incorporated in these words of rebuke), the *Gemara* explains, שהיו מהלכות עקב בצד גודל - "They walked with slow, deliberate footsteps, in a way that the heel of one foot was just ahead of the other foot" (*Shabbos* 62b). This involved walking in a purposeful and calculated way, designed to be noticed and arouse attention. Instead a woman and girl should walk in a quiet, natural and pleasant manner, which does not catch the eye or attract undue attention.

Also, it is wrong to walk in a distinctly proud and overly important manner. Pride is an unpleasant trait in every person, but particularly so in women and girls for whom *tznius* and refinement is the hallmark - see 1:D:2 above. As above, this fault is mentioned by Yeshaya HaNavi (*Yeshaya* 3:16) in his rebuke of the Jewish woman and girl of his time. He says, יען כי גבהו בנות ציון ותלכנה נטויות גרון - "The anger of *Hashem* has been aroused because the daughters of *Tzion* walk with their heads high in the air, in a conceited and haughty manner" (*Midrash Eichah* 4:18). *Rabbeinu Dovid* writes (in the *Taz* Y.D. 198:38) that a woman should not walk in an erect posture with her hands placed on her waist, as this is unpleasant and boastful. Even if this is not her intention, the pose is still unrefined and therefore unfitting for the natural *eidelkeit* and regal bearing of the *Bas Yisroel*. [However, if this is done as part of exercises there is probably nothing wrong with it, even if other women see her].

Rather than being a target for the harsh rebukes uttered by Yeshaya HaNavi (יען כי גבהו בנות ציון, הלוך ותפוף תלכנה, וברגליהם תעכסנה) let us become worthy of the delightful and encouraging compliment uttered by Shlomo Hamelech, מה יפו פעמיך בנעלים בת נדיב - "How sublime and refined are your shoe-clad footsteps O daughter of (Avraham Avinu) the nobleman" - (*Shir HaShirim* 7:2). This verse mentions shoes to symbolize that rather than walking barefooted as is typical of the primitive and lowly life-style of a desert dweller, you walk with "graceful footsteps in shoes". This denotes a cultivated and elite way of life. It is up to us to ensure that our shoes, and the way we walk in them, project the right image, and bear testimony to the quality and substance of our lives. (See 6:H:7 and 6:L:5 above, concerning this verse).

5. MILDLY COLORED SNEAKERS PREFERRED TO WHITE ONES: Women have a problem concerning their foot-wear. Most ladies' shoes that are stylish and have a pleasing look are distinctly uncomfortable, especially when they are worn all day. Comfortable ladies' shoes do exist but nearly all of them look old-fashioned, and understandably women and girls do not want to wear them. The solution that many have found is to wear sneakers. Sneakers are very comfortable and do not have the stigma of being old-fashioned.

Some women wear white sneakers which are sports and leisure wear that have a distinct casual look. It is regrettable that they have found no alternative solution, because it is unfitting for Jewish women and adult

Jewish girls to walk around from morning to night in very conspicuous white casual sportswear. Similarly, brightly colored ones can be highly conspicuous and coarse. Many feel that to wear such items would be an intrusion into the refinement of the Jewish woman's dress. They therefore refuse to wear them and have found a much more acceptable solution. This is to wear sneakers that are brown, gray, blue, black or some other mild (not bright) color, rather than white ones. These do not have such a sporty and casual look, and not being white, are not so conspicuous. Since they are comfortable and do not look "old-fashioned" they serve the needs of women and girls well.

Although it is not ideal to wear white sneakers, there is nothing wrong with women wearing white conventional shoes even though they are noticeable, because shoes are decent and refined pieces of footwear. There is also nothing wrong in wearing white sneakers on the odd occasion, such as on *Yom Kippur*, *Tisha B'av*, when rambling or when going on a hike, since it is usual on such occasions not to be dressed in fully presentable and ideal clothes. However, the regular appearance of women should be in keeping with their highly respected status within society.

6. TZNIUS INVOLVES THE COMPLETE PERSON: There is a special feature that is found with "*tznius* in dress" that is not found in any other *mitzva*. This is that there is no Torah issue which actively involves serving *Hashem* with each and every limb of the body. Torah learning, *tefilla* and eating *matzoh* are done with the mouth; *tefillin* are put onto the head and arm; *shiluach hakan*, *arba minim* and *tzedaka* are done with the hand, *aliya l'regel* and *levoyas hameis* are done with the feet; Similarly, *yeshivas succah* is done with the feet when coming into the *succah* [although the whole body is involved, this is only passive], to mention but a few. In contrast, *tznius* is an area where the woman or girl dresses, covers or adorns every part of her external body in accordance with the requirements of *Hilchos Tznius*.

A married woman covers her hair completely. She ensures that the *sheitel* or *tiechel* is a refined and fitting headgear for a *Bas Yisroel*. The unmarried girl has either short hair, or if long has it tied back or arranged in a refined manner. Her spectacles and earrings are tasteful and refined, adding luster to her *chein* and *tznius'dik* countenance. Her neckline is perfect and adorned by a graceful necklace that embellishes her precious character. Her body is dressed with a garment that covers all the main body and the complete upper sections of the arms and legs. The dress or outfit is colorful, pretty and of aesthetic style and taste but not alluring or ostentatious. The lower sections of the arms are covered if that is the local *minhag* or she feels happy to add this to her general *tznius*. The bracelet, watch and rings which adorn her are quality ornaments that add to her overall distinction. Her fingernails are short and respectable. Her legs are well covered by tights which ensure that the legs have a decent, modest and unobtrusive appearance. Her shoes are handsome and neat but not showy. They are neither very high-heeled to the extent that her manner of walking is affected, nor do they have metal studs which clatter as she walks. It follows that the *mitzva* of *tznius* has a very unique character. It is an all encompassing *mitzva* which lifts and sanctifies the whole person.

Yeshaya HaNavi complained about the all-encompassing sins of the *Klal Yisroel* of his time. He used the descriptive words מכף רגל עד ראש אין לו מתום - "From the underside of the foot to the head there is no part which is unblemished" (*Yeshaya* 1:6). In contrast, we can happily say about many of our present-day women and daughters who practice a high standard of *tznius,* כולך יפה רעיתי ומום אין בך - "Everything about you is beautiful; you are totally unblemished" (*Shir HaShirim* 4:7). Every part of your physique and attire represents the *chein* and the modesty which make *Bnos Yisroel* beautiful.

7. "ALL MY LIMBS SAY HASHEM WHO IS LIKE YOU": Dovid Hamelech says in *Tehillim*, כל עצמותי תאמרנה ה' מי כמוך - "All my limbs proclaim, *Hashem*! Who is like You!" (*Tehillim* 35:10). On this verse the *Yalkut Shimoni* (723) cites a remarkable *Chazal* which at first sight would seem to be the envy of women as most of the *mitzvos* do not apply to them:-

"Dovid Hamelech said to *Hashem* I serve You with all my limbs. With my mind I *daven* to you; with my hair I fulfill the commandment of leaving *peyos*; on my head I don *tefillin*; around my neck I wrap a *tallis*; with my eyes I do the *mitzva* of seeing *tzitzis* (וראיתם אותו); my mouth I fill with Your praise; with my beard I fulfill the law of not shaving with a razor;... around my body hang four *tzitzis*; my right hand writes and points to Torah text; onto my left arm I bind *tefillin*; with my nail I kill the *chattos haof* (*melika*); my kidneys worry whether I serve you correctly (אף לילות יסרוני כליותי); my innards store your Torah (ותורתך בתוך מעי);... my knees serve as *Sandek* for a *Bris Milah*. Hence, all my limbs join me in saying *Hashem*! Who is like You!"

Women should not feel "left out" as if they have not merited to serve *Hashem* with all their limbs. They should not for a moment think that the beautiful verse, כל עצמותי תאמרנה ה' מי כמוך does not apply to them, since this is not the case at all. On the contrary, as explained, with the all encompassing *mitzva* of *tznius*, they serve *Hashem* with all their limbs. They do so during all hours of the day and on every single day of the year. Hence, with *tznius* their whole being is sanctified to the service of *Hashem* and to the fulfillment of His wishes.

P. COATS

1. COATS HAVE DIFFERENT RULES THAN OTHER GARMENTS: Coats are worn over other clothing. Therefore, provided the clothes beneath are Kosher, warnings concerning partial exposure do not apply to coats. It is perfectly natural for a coat not to close right up to the neck because even when open only the dress or blouse shows. For this reason, a short coat is of no concern as it is totally different to a short skirt. Similarly, an opening in the lower half of a coat is totally different to a slit because a coat is just an additional garment worn on top of a dress or skirt and in no way does the opening cause people to look at her legs as is caused by a slit in a skirt.

There are however a number of points concerning coats that should be mentioned with respect to their being ostentatious or eye-catching. Coats are prime targets of the fashion designers and generally in the world of fashion as they are garments specified for public appearance. Points to be noted are as follows:-

2. SUITABLE MATERIALS AND COLORS: Coats should be of calm and refined colors since bright colors such as bright red, bright yellow, bright purple etc. are immodest. This applies to coats for adults and to coats for children. (See 7:B where the subject of colors is discussed in detail. See also *Mekoros* 1:8 and 63:18-20).

Shiny black, brown, gray or blue leather and plastic coats are worn nowadays by many women and girls even in some very Orthodox circles. Since they are widely worn, they are generally considered by people to be in order even though some of them are very shiny. Even metallic coats are worn by many with the claim that, being so widespread, they should not be viewed as ostentatious and are therefore permitted. This generalization is however not quite so simple. The assumption that when something is widely worn it is not to be considered eye-catching is far from accurate. That rule applies only to items that are refined in themselves but were not allowed until now due to being unusual in this environment and therefore very noticeable. Once these items become widespread, their stigma falls away and everyone may wear them. On the other hand, a red garment, to take one example, is forbidden even if the whole town wears red, because red is a loud and aggressive color and inherently *pritzus'dik* - see 7:B.

With the coats just mentioned one must be very careful, since some of them could fall under the latter classification in which case they are *ossur* even if wearing them has become very widespread. Some coats may be acceptable on a child but not on an adult. Others may be alright on a young person but not on a middle-aged or elderly person. Moreover, some types of shiny coats give their wearer a distinctly non-Jewish look. Each type of coat must therefore be judged with a discerning eye. The criterion must be whether the coat is refined and looks right on this particular wearer.

In a place where it is uncommon to wear any (or all) of the coats mentioned and to the local population they are flashy and flamboyant, they must not be worn, since as far as this location in concerned they are most definitely eye-catching garments - see 1:G above.

Shiny gold-colored coats and coats made of a glittery material that shine brightly in the sun cannot be considered as refined garments even if they become very widespread. They are made in order to solicit attention and as such are diametrically opposed to all that *tznius* stands for.

3. UNPRETENTIOUS AND REFINED STYLES: Quiet, unpretentious and graceful styles are evidence of the *eidelkeit* of the wearer. Being dressed in such a garment gives the wearer an air of dignity and nobility. Such coats are therefore ideal for a person described as a *Bas Melachim*.

On the other hand, flamboyant styles or strikingly unusual styles are ostentatious and unrefined. Alternatively, coats that are very coarse and are typically worn by the lowest of society, are undignified and it is degrading to wear them. The wish to wear such coats is usually related to an unfulfilled life and lack of self-respect. Such coats are therefore not for the Orthodox Jewish community. If the wearer is indifferent to the fact that others dislike this type of garment this in itself is due to a diminished sense of *tznius*.

Concerning a King, the Torah writes that he must possess two *Sifrei* Torah, one for home use and one to accompany him when he goes out. So too, the Jewish woman or girl who is a *Bas Melachim* must possess two codes of law - a refined and cheerful dress for inside the home, with a refined and more regal manner of dress for when she goes out.

4. DIGNIFIED BUTTONS AND STUDS: Coats may certainly be enhanced with graceful buttons that add luster and *chein* to the coat. Here again, in the right measure they are fine but if overdone are counter-productive. Large showy studs or large gaudy buttons that stand out spoil a coat that would otherwise have been ideal. Fortunately, if one buys a coat with such excessive decorations they can usually be removed or the buttons exchanged for others that have the dignity and finesse associated with the clothes worn by *N'shei Yisroel.*

5. GRACEFUL BUT NOT OVERLY ELEGANT: Overly elegant coats are unrefined and do not reflect the *pashtus* (lack of sophistication) and humility which is the way a *Yid* is to feel, especially as we are in *golus*. Such coats are also capable of awakening anti-Semitic feelings in those of the *umos ha'olam* who are jealous of the wealth that is displayed by the higher classes. No one is suggesting that women should not have beautiful Shabbos clothes but there is a point which is beyond *kavod* Shabbos. It causes feelings of grandeur and of being exceptionally important.

It goes without saying that extremely luxurious fur coats that stand out as being extravagantly expensive and appear to have cost thousands of dollars, are unduly conspicuous and are not recommended. Even if it was normal to wear such magnificent coats in the last generation, and women wearing such coats were not particularly conspicuous, times have changed, and to wear them nowadays in public raises eyebrows and does no one any good, particularly as the society in which we live has generally cut down on wearing furs, as many people are against killing animals for their furs. Therefore, the Jewish lady who wears an outstandingly luxurious fur garment is particularly conspicuous. This is especially relevant today when in a number of countries animal-rights campaigners are looking for excuses to attack *shechita*. Being over-complacent that such reasons are far-fetched is a folly that has, in our long sad history, brought much suffering to the Jewish people.

Even if the fur of the coat is artificial fur (known as simulated fur) which is an excellent imitation of very expensive fur, the above mentioned forms of damage could still occur. Many people are not aware that there are cheap imitations of real fur, and will therefore naturally assume that the coat is made of real luxurious furs. Also, amongst the *umos ha'olam* there are many who think that all *Yidden* are rich and will assume that a Jewish woman buys the real thing, not an artificial replacement of it.

In some places, wealth (i.e. proof that you can be trusted with substantial credit - see *Rashi, Bava Metzia* 96a s.v. *Liro'ous*) is demonstrated by the expensive clothes worn by "the wife". This is a *ma'aseh soton* - a trap laid down by the *yetzer horah* to justify behavior which destroys the traits of *tznius* and humility both in herself and in others who admire her. Also, little does the woman realize how much she may, *chas veshalom*, be inviting an *ayin horah* upon herself and her husband's business. *Chazal* say, בינה יתירה נתן הקב"ה באשה - "*Hashem* endowed a woman with an extra measure of intuition" (*Niddah* 45b). Let her use it to find a more suitable way of convincing potential creditors of her husband's financial worth.

Q. IN THE PRIVACY OF HER HOME

1. KEEPING COVERED WHAT CHAZAL CLASSIFIED AS "ERVAH" :

(a) When she has no need to uncover the area: It has been mentioned (in 5:B) that quite a few *Poskim* maintain that a woman should cover her hair even in the privacy of her home whenever she can, without causing major inconvenience to herself, even though no other person is present. *Chazal* have labeled hair as *ervah* (שער באשה ערוה - *Brachos* 24a) and *ervah* should (according to these opinions) be covered whenever possible. The same applies to a *tefach* of areas of the body that must be covered as that too has been labeled *ervah* by *Chazal* (טפח באשה ערוה - *ibid).*

In fact, flesh has an even stricter *ervah* status than hair, as can be seen from the fact that the stringent opinion which requires a man to turn away from a *tefach* of flesh before saying a *bracha* agrees that in the case of hair, closing the eyes is adequate - see 4:B:3-4 above. See *Meiri, Bava Kama* 82a and *sefer, Yaros Dvash* by Hagaon R' Yehonasan Eybeshitz *ztl,* Vol.1 page 43. The latter writes explicitly that a woman must be covered and must dress *tznius'dik* even indoors. The same is evident from *Responsa Chasam Sofer* O.C. 36 end of s.v. *V'daas.*

Similarly, *Tosfos, Pesachim* 50b s.v. *Maskulta* writes in the name of *Rabbeinu Channanel* that it is distasteful for a woman to make a living by engaging in a form of spinning that involves working with her upper arms bare. This is so even though she works indoors and cannot be seen by men.

Although, if she has a need to do so no *issur* is involved, it still remains undesirable to spend lengths of time with her arms uncovered.

Accordingly, whenever possible a woman should be dressed even at home in such a way that the main body and the upper sections of the arms are covered so that a *tefach* is not revealed. It is therefore incorrect for her to walk around with short sleeves, a wide open neck or a see-through garment etc. Even if she and many others would not be ashamed to be seen by their children and close family with short sleeves or a wide open neck, nevertheless, since these areas are *ervah,* it is incorrect in the first place to leave them uncovered - see *Mekoros* 50.

(b) When she needs to uncover the area: When kneading dough by hand or when performing similar jobs, a woman may, if necessary, roll up her sleeves even above the elbow although this area is *ervah d'Rabanan* because this is a necessity for personal hygiene. It is comparable to exposing hair and body when showering, swimming etc. However, if a woman has visitors or lodgers in her house, she must of course be dressed just as she would be when going to a public place. Dough making, scrubbing for *Pesach* etc. are not a *heter* to relax the standards of *tznius* - see *Mekoros* 50:1-3 and 51:1-4.

(c) Uncovering less than a *tefach*: Although there is definitely no *halachic* obligation to cover less than a *tefach* of flesh in the privacy of her home where she will not be seen by men, as it is not classified *ervah* by *Chazal,* there is nevertheless one area which according to many *Poskim* is considered *ervah* even when less then a *tefach* of it is uncovered. This is the knee and upper sections of the legs. *Chazal* have said that שוק באשה ערוה (*Brachos* 24a) and the *Taz* O.C. 75:1 maintains that this area is labeled *ervah* even when the overall size is less than a *tefach* - see also M.B. 75:7. Accordingly, a woman and girl should ensure that the dress, skirt, night dress and the like that she wears in the privacy of her house covers her knees properly. Concerning the lower sections of the legs - whether they must be covered in the privacy of the home - see *Halichos Bas Yisroel,* Chap. 4, note 28 and *Responsa Minchas Yitzchak* 6:10 and 11:5.

It should be noted that the *Yerushalmi* (*Megilla* 1:10) states that Kimchis who had seven sons that all served as *Kohanim Gedolim,* said about herself that she merited this because, לא ראו קורות ביתי שערות ראשי ואימרת חלוקי מימי - "the beams of my home never saw my hair nor did they see the hem of the inner garment I was wearing". With this she meant that she was always careful to cover both her hair and her body with an alternative item before removing what she had worn until now, so that her hair and her body would not be uncovered even for a short moment. The extreme caution taken by Kimchis, never to allow anything to show, is not expected of most of us, as explained in 5:B:2 above. However, we can learn from this *Chazal* that just as it is a praiseworthy *midas chassidus* to cover all the hair in privacy whenever possible (as recommended in the M.B. 75:14) so too, it is a praiseworthy *midas chassidus* for a woman or girl to cover even less than a *tefach* (of areas which when a *tefach* is exposed are *ervah)* even in privacy.

2. UNCOVERING WHAT IS USUALLY COVERED DUE TO CUSTOM: Areas that *Chazal* have not actually classified as *ervah,* but women voluntarily cover and have made them into covered areas (דרכן להיות מכוסה) need not be covered in the privacy of her home; for example, the lower sections of the arms, in places where in public they are covered. Even though these areas have become *ervah* in those places because women have taken upon themselves to cover them, they have a more lenient status than areas which *Chazal* labeled as *ervah*. Thus, they do not have to be covered at home - see *Mekoros* 50:7 and 53:1-2.

Accordingly, the feet from the ankles and below (including the toes) need not be covered indoors because the feet are not "labeled *ervah* by *Chazal*" and must be covered in public only because they are דרכן להיות מכוסה. A woman or girl may therefore walk around with a long house robe (to accommodate both opinions in 6:L:1 above) even though her feet, including her ankles and toes, can be seen as she is not wearing tights or stockings.

[A *bracha* may, however, not be said when facing the feet and similar area. This is because it is *ossur* to say a *bracha* when facing an area that people are particular to cover when outdoors amongst the public. Since they feel that it is right to cover these areas when outdoors, these areas adopt the "*ervah*" status, whenever a *tefach* or more is exposed and retain this status even indoors although the same people are not particular to cover these areas indoors (M.B. 75:10). See *Halichos Bas Yisroel* (Chap.4. end of note 28) in the name of Hagaon Harav Yosef Shalom Elyashiv *shlita* that due to this *halacha* it is *ossur* according to all opinions to say a *bracha* facing a woman's uncovered legs even in the privacy of the home (see 6:L:1 above).

What has just been mentioned is similar to the *halacha* that a husband may not say a *bracha* when facing his wife's uncovered hair although he may see his wife's hair, and according to some opinions she has no obligation to cover it in private (M.B. 75:10). Since her hair must be covered when in public, it has the status of *ervah* for all places and for all people without distinction. Therefore, no man may say a *bracha* without either closing his eyes or at least turning his head away - see 5:B:3 and *Mekoros* 54:3-8.]

3. AREAS THAT WOULD EMBARRASS HER IF SEEN BY FAMILY: The *halacha* mentioned, that feet and similar areas need not be covered indoors, has an important condition attached to it. It is permitted only if Jewish women in that locality would actually not mind to go around in the bedroom part of their houses with these areas uncovered. Whereas, if they would not like to be seen by their children with these areas uncovered, they are obligated to cover them even when no one is there to see them (O.C. 2:1). This is because it is ossur for both men and women to reveal areas of their body in the privacy of their home if they would be embarrassed to be seen by members of the family in such a state of undress. For example, a grown boy may not walk around in underwear because he would be ashamed if seen by other members of the family in such an undressed state.

The reason for this *halacha* is that *Hashem* is constantly present everywhere, and even if no human being is in the house the *Shechinah* is there. If one would be ashamed to appear in front of human beings in this manner, all the more so one should be embarrassed to appear like this in front of *Hashem*, Whose Honor fills the world - מלא כל הארץ כבודו. As a result of this, a person must take care to cover as much as possible while getting dressed or undressed, e.g. to use a dressing-gown or robe to cover his body as much as possible - see 7:M:3 below and *Mekoros* 52:1-3.

In most places women would not be ashamed to appear in front of their family with their feet only partially covered by slippers. It is therefore perfectly in order for this area to be uncovered provided she has slippers on. Her gown/robe should be full length to cover the legs which would otherwise be uncovered (thereby accommodating both opinions in 6:L:1 above) - see *Mekoros* 53:1.

4. TZNIUS IS WAY OF LIFE, NOT JUST "IDEAL PUBLIC CONDUCT": A far-reaching message can be learned from the *halacha* mentioned. *Tznius* is not just a form of public conduct. Rather, it is a style of life that is to be practiced even in privacy.

We learn that Ruth impressed Boaz by her *tznius* and he therefore chose her as a wife (*Ruth* 2:5). *Rashi* explains that the *tznius* Boaz saw was that Ruth crouched to pick up the sheaves rather than bend forward. Apparently, this is a most elementary act of decency and it is hard to see what it was that so impressed Boaz.

The answer lies in a minor point mentioned at the beginning of this incident. The verse mentions that Ruth said: ואספתי בעמרים אחרי הקוצרים - "And I shall gather among the sheaves behind the harvesters" (*Ruth* 2:7). It is interesting to note that she said אחרי. *Chazal* say, אחר סמוך, אחרי מופלג - "When the term אחר is used it means 'closely after' or 'closely behind'. When the term אחרי is used it means 'far after' or 'far behind'" (*Breishis Rabba* 44:5 *and Rashi, Devarim* 11:30). Since Ruth used the term אחרי she clearly kept far behind all the harvesters so that no intermingling could possibly occur and so that she would not be observed while she picked the stalks and gathered fallen bundles.

The fact that even when in a deserted part of the field she was particular to crouch rather than bend forward demonstrated her refined conduct even when out of the public eye. It was this that deeply impressed Boaz. Her noble and sensitive character and her deep *Yiras Shomayim* was worthy of producing a descendant who would compose the beautiful chapters of *Tehillim,* which due to their depth and sensitivity inspire us to *tefilla* and *Yiras Shomayim* till this very day - see 1:N:4 and 9:I:7.

R. NIGHTCLOTHES

There are different opinions amongst the *Poskim* concerning the nightclothes that complies with the requisites of *tznius* and is recommended for women and girls. The opinions are recorded here without stating that one is correct or incorrect. Since there are *Poskim* who support each opinion, everyone should follow the way accepted in their community or should find out what their *Rav* recommends.

1. PAJAMAS: It was explained (in 6:H:8) that it is gross *pritzus* for a female to wear trousers. This does not apply to night clothes such as pajamas although they comprise a top-piece and trousers. They are not regarded as "garments of *pritzus*" even though they fit around the body. Since even when the wearer steps out of bed she is seen by no one other than her closest family (or in the case of a girls' educational institution, by room-mates) the fact that they are trouser-like does not matter.

Such garments are not subject to לא תלבש - the *issur* for women to wear garments intended for men, even though clothes subject to this *issur* may not be worn even indoors where no man can see her according to some opinions - see *Responsa Minchas Yitzchak* 2:8 and *sefer, Malbushei Kovod v'Tiferes* 2:15. This is because pajamas have been female nightclothes for many years and are worn exclusively in the privacy of the home. Moreover, these garments are specifically made for women and girls and their shape and pattern is quite different from the garments worn by men. (See *Mekoros* 46:11 that Hagaon Harav Yosef Shalom Elyashiv *shlita* and Hagaon Harav Shmuel HaLevi Wosner *shlita* have both stated that there is no issur of *lo silbash)*.

Even though this opinion allows pajamas to be worn, it is wrong for a girl or a woman to walk around the house in pajamas (Hagaon Harav Yosef Shalom Elyashiv *shlita* and Hagaon Harav Shmuel HaLevi Wosner *shlita*, - see 6:E:2 above). She should ideally avoid leaving the bedroom in pajamas if she is not robed. Trousers are garments so distinctly unfit for females that a woman or girl should feel "less than minimally dressed" when walking around in such a garment. If she does not feel so, there is a shortcoming in her sensitivities for *tznius*. Accordingly, she should robe herself in a night-robe (dressing-gown) or a housecoat so that she will walk around in a respectable manner - see *Mekoros* 46:11.

2. NIGHTGOWNS: Some are of the opinion that pajamas are not permitted for females. They maintain that all trousers, even those worn in bed, are "garments of *pritzus*" for a female - See *Kevuda Bas Melech* 2:54 and *Responsa Vay'varech Dovid* 1:104. They therefore allow women and girls to wear only a nightgown. This opinion is widely accepted in *Chassidishe* circles and there is definitely greater *eidelkeit* in this type of nightclothes as it hangs completely loose on the person. In fact, it is clear from early sources that women always used to sleep just with a nightgown with no close fitting garment of any description - Yoreh Deah 182:5. (See *Responsa Shevet HaLevi* 3:128:2 and *Mekoros* 46:12).

Some are particular that the nightgown should be full-length, especially if it is fully opaque (non-see-through) and she might walk around in it. A full-size nightgown covers also the lower sections of the legs and being a loose-hanging garment is a very refined form of nightclothes. Although the above is commendable there is no obligation to have a nightgown of this length. A nightgown must however at least cover the knees comfortably, so that the upper sections of the legs are not exposed when getting up until one is covered in a night robe or housecoat - see 6:Q:1 above.

It should be noted that if the nightgown is somewhat see-through it would be incorrect to walk around the house without the addition of a robe because to be dressed in such an item is "less than minimally dressed". Moreover, if others who are not members of the family can see her, she should be robed even if the nightgown is totally opaque - see 7:D:2.

It is obvious that many styles of nightgowns that exist nowadays are unfit for the *Bas Yisroel,* whether married or unmarried. Highly see-through nightgowns, and gowns that are cut out to expose large areas have been manufactured to serve and cultivate a *pritzus'dik* way of life. Garments such as these, that lack the slightest vestige of refinement, should not be worn even as bed-wear, as they promote and foster an attitude that is in total contrast to all that *tznius* stands for. Finally, it should go without saying that a night-shirt, which is a nightgown that does not reach the knees, is a *treife* garment (unless worn together with pajama trousers) because the person is partially uncovered when leaving bed - see *Mekoros* 46:9.

3. NIGHTGOWNS OVER PAJAMA TROUSERS: A third opinion maintains that pajamas are "garments of *pritzus*" as far as females are concerned (just as is held by the second opinion). However, they recommend a compromise, because pajama trousers serve a valuable function. When wearing just a nightgown, limbs can become uncovered during sleep as a result of the quilt moving. This, however, will not happen if under the nightgown pajama trousers are worn. For this reason, they feel that rather than forbid pajama trousers they should be encouraged. They allow pajama trousers together with a nightdress because in this way the trousers are mostly hidden and totally different from trousers that are worn as part of a pair of pajamas. (See *Responsa Vay'varech Dovid* 1:104 and *Responsa Shevet Hakhasi* 3:33:2 for a full discussion on this subject. See also *Mekoros* 46:3).

4. CHILDREN: Small children up to the age of six or seven (depending on their size) are allowed both to wear pajamas and to walk around in them. Since some *Poskim* hold that *chinuch* to dress in full accordance with the *halachos* of *tznius* only starts at six or seven (see 6:S:2 below) one may certainly follow their opinion in this case when the girl is fully-covered and indoors where no one can see her - compare with 7:B:1 below. Once a girl is six or seven (and all the more so when ten or eleven) she should be taught to put on a gown/robe when she gets up, so that she does not walk around the house in pajama trousers. If there are boarders or visitors in the house it is particularly important that girls only appear robed - see *Mekoros* 46:14.

5. THE NEED FOR TZNIUS EVEN IN NIGHTCLOTHES: Some mistakenly think that for nightclothes, *tznius* does not apply because it is totally out of sight of men. They therefore buy themselves pajamas and other nightclothes of loud unrefined colors; pajamas that have two bright contrasting colors such as a garment that is half-red and half-yellow. Some sport *pritzus'dik,* coarse or foolish designs and slogans on their nightclothes. Those who do so are mistaken, because coarse or boorish behavior practiced anywhere is detrimental to the person's personality and *Yiras Shomayim*.

The *Gemara* says in *Brachos* (62a), אין קורין צנוע אלא למי שצנוע בבית הכסא - "A person cannot be considered a *tznua* unless he is refined when in the bathroom". This goes to show that a person who is aware that מלא כל הארץ כבודו - *Hashem Yisborach* is Omnipresent - always conducts activities related to his body with utmost modesty and refinement. This aspect of *tznius* is one of the areas where the distinction between *Klal Yisroel* and the *umos ha'olam* concerning refinement and bashfulness is profoundly evident (*Sanhedrin* 104b, *Rashi* s.v. *Nifneh; Rash, T'haros* 4:5). However, to a degree this can be found even by the *umos ha'olam* as the *Gemara* says in *Brachos* 8b, "*Rabban Gamliel* said, I appreciate the Persians because they have refined eating manners, are refined in the bathroom and in other concerns" - see 1:A:4(c), 2:E:2 and 7:M:4.

By behaving in the negative way described and wearing coarse unrefined clothes, the person displays a total indifference to the fact that we are surrounded and exposed to severe *pritzus*. Whoever yearns for a sheltered *tznius'dik* life would not wear clothes that identify their wearer with the lowest of the *umos ha'olam*.

6. THE EXTENT TO WHICH NIGHTCLOTHES SHOULD COVER: It has been explained (in 6:Q:1) that, although not an absolute obligation, it is highly commended if in the seclusion of her home a woman or girl covers whatever *Chazal* have labeled as Ervah so that a Tefach is not exposed - see 6:Q:1(c). It is comparable to the *Zohar Hakadosh* which gives enormous credit to a woman covering her hair in the privacy of her home and even in bed. It will also save her husband from saying *devarim shebikdusha* (*Shema, hamapil* etc.) when facing a *tefach* of uncovered flesh - see 5:B:3 above.

It is therefore correct and ideal *tznius'dik* conduct for a woman or girl to ensure that when out of bed and even when in bed her neckline is basically Kosher and that sleeves cover the upper section of the arms. Although, when her arms are under the bed covers they are obviously covered, they can easily become uncovered and if her nightdress or pajama top has short sleeves she could be lying in bed for extended periods of time with her upper arms partially uncovered. See *sefer*, *Bnei Beischa* Chapter 13 note 76 who quotes a ruling from the *Gaon* and *Tzaddik* the *Satmar Rav zt'l* that nightclothes should not be see-through and should cover in an adequate manner.

Accordingly, it is appropriate that night garments have a correct neckline and sleeves which cover the complete upper arms. If it is difficult for her to obtain such nightclothes she should at least endeavor to don a Kosher robe/gown as soon as she gets up, so that she does not walk around the house in short sleeves and with part of her shoulder and upper frontal area uncovered. As stated, even this is not an obligation according to most *Poskim*. However, all agree that it is highly commendable for a woman and girl to conduct herself in this way.

S. A GIRL UNDER BAS-MITZVA

1. AN UNDER BAS-MITZVA MUST DRESS IN TZNIUS'DIK CLOTHES: A girl below the age of *Bas-mitzva* must also be dressed in the way described for adults since uncovered parts of a girl's body can attract attention. Such a girl must therefore be dressed in a manner that totally covers her body (the torso). The neckline must be Kosher. Her upper arms must be fully and reliably covered. She must wear tights to cover her legs. If these areas are uncovered they are classed as *ervah*. Accordingly, it is *ossur* to say a *bracha* or any *davar shebikdusha* while facing her if she is inadequately dressed.

A father may say a *bracha* if his daughter who is under eleven years old is inadequately dressed because a father is usually not affected by this. The same applies to a brother who like a father is usually unaffected until his sister reaches the age of eleven - see 4:C:5 above and *Mekoros* 16:1.

2. CONFLICTING OPINIONS IF AGE IS THREE OR SIX/SEVEN:

(a) The unresolved dispute: There are two basic opinions concerning the minimum age at which a girl must be dressed properly. Some *Poskim* maintain that the obligation begins when she is three years old just as it is an *issur min haTorah* to be in a state of *yichud* with a girl of this age who is an *ervah* (E.H. 22:11) - see *Biur Halacha* 75:1 in the name of the *Shulchan Shleima.* See also *sefer, Malbushei Kavod* p.84. This is in fact the opinion of most *Poskim* - see *Mekoros* 55.

Others, however, maintain that this obligation begins only when she has reached the size of an average seven year old, which is when her female charm starts to become apparent. From then on, the sight of her uncovered arms etc. can be slightly provocative and cause sinful thoughts. The arms must therefore be covered since they are considered *ervah* - *Chazon Ish* O.C. 16:8, see *sefer, Halichos Bas Yisroel* 4:4 and *sefer, Ohr LeTzion* by Hagaon Harav Ben Tzion Abba-Shaul *shlita* 6:12. This was also the opinion of Maran HaGaon Harav Moshe Feinstein *zt'l* as cited in his name in the footnotes on the book, Children in Halacha (7:4). If a six year old is tall and has the size of a seven year old she must be treated as one. Conversely, if a seven year old is small and looks like a six year old the *issur* does not apply to her - see *Mekoros* 56:1.

It is difficult to state a ruling concerning this dispute as some *kehillos* are stringent and follow the first opinion whilst others are lenient and follow the second. [Also, some maintain that the *Chazon Ish* agreed that there is a *chinuch* obligation to dress her properly even before her body is provocative - see *Malbushei Kovod* page 83 and the incident recorded in (b) below.]

It should however be noted that according to both opinions if a girl is tall enough to pas as a seven year old she must have long sleeves and be careful with her neckline etc. It is furthermore important to note that Maran Hagaon Rav Yosef Shalom Elyashiv *shlita* of *Yerusholayim* has ruled that once a girl is seven her skirt must cover her knees; it is not sufficient that her knees are just covered by tights (*Malbushei Kavod* p. 85) - see *Mekoros* 55:2. Concerning tights for a young girl - see *Mekoros* 56:10-12.

(b) The Chazon Ish encouraged his sister to be stringent: The *Steipler Gaon zt'l* insisted that his young daughters wear skirts that cover their knees, as he considered this a *halachic* requirement. This was shortly after he arrived in *Eretz Yisroel* and his daughters looked rather odd among the populace of the district in which he lived at the time. People even remarked to the Rebbetzen *o.h.* about how peculiar and old-fashioned her children looked. The Rebbetzen was hurt and quite upset by the way people reacted and went to her brother, the *Chazon Ish zt'l,* to pour out her heart.

The *Chazon Ish* responded with the following words: "Why should what they say upset you? You know that you are dressing your daughters as is *halachically* correct, and in a fitting manner. The others who do not dress their daughters in this way and allow them to go around partially naked are strange people who dress their children in an unfitting and unusual way. Why take note of what strange people think or have to say?" - *Leshichno Tidreshu* Vol 1 page 160. See *Mekoros* 57:1.

The *Chazon Ish* taught his sister (who was in fact a great *tzaddekes* in her own right) that being proud of one's adherence to *darkei* Torah on the one hand, while disregarding and even pitying those who make nasty and hurtful remarks on the other hand, enables the person to be strong. With that strength he will not be affected or even influenced by the ill-founded remarks and viewpoints of others.

3. IT IS NO HARDSHIP FOR A YOUNG GIRL TO DRESS B'TZNIUS: Some people feel that to dress a young girl in tights or long sleeves is a hardship for the child. They believe that if there is an opinion which is lenient until the age of seven it is only fair to the child to follow it. This argument is unfounded since young children are perfectly happy in any garment as long as it is comfortable.

If a young girl does occasionally protest against wearing tights etc. this is only because she lives in an area where many young girls do not wear them and she is afraid that her friends will mock her about the way she dresses. With the correct attitude on the part of the parents, and encouragement when necessary, a child will be just as happy and comfortable with long sleeves and tights as with short sleeves and socks.

4. POINTS CONCERNING THE OPINIONS MENTIONED: Three important points must be made concerning the two opinions mentioned:

(a) Not to mock someone who is stringent: If an individual is stringent and dresses his three year old in a way that the upper sections of her arms and legs are covered even though everyone else is lenient in this matter until the age of six/seven, it would be wrong to mock such a person or his child. What he has done is in fact commendable as it is right to ensure that what one does is correct according to most *Poskim*. This certainly applies in this instance, as the *Mishna Berura* (whose authority as final *p'sak* is rarely challenged) and most other *Poskim* are stringent. Therefore, much is to be said in favor of being stringent and dressing very young girls in as refined a manner as possible. Accordingly, if someone is stringent he should be encouraged, not sneered at - see *Mekoros* 57:1.

(b) Not to bring a little girl with short sleeves into a men's *shul*: It is preferable not to bring a girl under the age of seven who is not fully clothed into the men's *shul* if there are individuals in the community who are stringent in this matter. This would cause hardship to them since they are particular not to say a *davar shebikdusha* when facing a three year old girl who is not fully clothed. The minority, however, cannot force the majority not to bring such young girls to *shul* in inadequate dress. On the other hand, if the majority of people in the *shul* are particular on this issue it is *ossur* to bring an inadequately dressed girl into *shul* (*Halichos Bas Yisroel* 4:13 in the name of Maran Hagaon Harav Yosef Shalom Elyashiv shlita).

[It is appropriate to mention that in some circles there is a dislike for the bringing of three year old girls into the men's *shul* although they are dressed *b'tznius*. In a *shul* there must be total segregation between males and females (see *Succah* 51b and *Mekoros* 78:1) and even a three year old is a young female whose presence would be an infringement of the segregation required. This viewpoint is substantiated by the opinion which holds that three year olds must be properly dressed, because they are after all young females. Similarly, there is an *issur* of *yichud* even with a three year old girl (E.H. 22:11). Others are however of a different opinion and do not view bringing such a small child to *shul* as an infringement of the required segregation.]

(c) Not to be lenient when the local people are stringent: If one lives in a district where most families follow the stringent opinion, an individual should not dress her child differently. This is because people who follow the stringent opinion are sorely disturbed when seeing a five year old girl walk around in public with short sleeves, a short skirt and short socks. Their feelings should be taken into account, especially since deep-rooted principles of *tznius* are involved. To disregard their sensitivities on these matters is selfish and egoistic and displays an attitude which should have no place in our lives - see 1:G above.

T. ERVAH STATUS OF AREAS THAT SHOULD BE COVERED

Some of the following *halachos* have already been explained in Chapter Four. They have nevertheless been repeated here in conjunction with many additional *halachos*, and after it has been explained what parts of the female body must be covered and to what extent, to give as complete a picture as possible of these little-known *halachos*. It is hoped that as a result of learning these *halachos*, women and girls will become aware of the immense importance attached by *Chazal* to *tznius*. They will also see that *brachos*, *divrei* Torah etc. can easily be said under forbidden circumstances due to laxity in *tznius* of dress within the home. This in turn will בע״ה give a new impetus to this area of *shemiras hamitzvos* and infuse a renewed *kedusha* into our way of life.

1. ERVAH DUE TO RULING BY CHAZAL - WILL ALWAYS BE ERVAH: It has been explained that the hair of a married woman, the main part of a woman's body (the torso), the upper sections of the arms and legs, and according to some also the lower sections of the legs, are *ervah* by decree of *Chazal* since they are areas that have a potential to invite the unwelcome attention of men. They have the status of *ervah* irrespective of whether local women generally cover them as they are supposed to, or are lax on this matter and do not do so. Accordingly, if local women do not cover their hair, or women and girls wear wide open-necked blouses and dresses that expose part of the chest or shoulders, or they have short sleeves or short skirts, the areas exposed remain *ervah* even though the local inhabitants are used to seeing women and girls in this state. See 4:B:1(a) why the *ervah* status is of Rabbinical origin although many areas must be covered *min HaTorah*.

The status of *ervah* applies only when a *tefach* is exposed. Just as there are Torah measurements (*shiurim*) of a *k'zayis*, a *k'beitzah* etc., so too, *ervah* has a size and this is a *tefach*. However, all people who are affected by an exposure that is smaller than a *tefach,* may not say a *bracha* when in such a presence, because it is unfitting to say a *davar shebikdusho* in the presence of that which causes sinful thoughts. This applies to everyone who is not a close blood relative, whilst a husband, father, son and brother are unaffected by less than a *tefach.* For them the *issur* only starts when an area of a *tefach* is uncovered because that area is *ervah* - see No. 4 and 5 below.

Accordingly, if when nursing her baby a woman is not fully clad, her husband may say a *bracha* or a *dvar* Torah even when facing her, provided that less than a *tefach* is revealed. However, if this area is exposed to a male who is not a close relative, the issur applies even if less than a *tefach* is uncovered.

[It is of course totally *ossur* for a woman to expose such an area in the presence of a man who is not a very close relative (M.B. 75:3). In fact, even just nursing a baby with the area well covered in the presence of a man who is not of her closest family is very far from *tznius'dik* conduct. Part of the general break-down of the innate feelings of true modesty manifests itself in the ease with which women feed in places where they might be seen by men.]

Since a girl who is a six/seven year old is subject to these *halachos*, both according to the *Mishna Berura* and *Chazon Ish* (see 6:S:2 above), an exposure of her chest, arms and legs will have the status of *ervah* for everyone other than her close blood relatives - see 6:T:4-5 below.

2. ERVAH DUE TO MINHAG - DEPENDS ON PRESENT CUSTOM: Areas of a woman's body that *Chazal* have not said must be covered but Orthodox women have taken upon themselves to cover (known as דרכן להיות מכוסה) are classified *ervah d'Rabanan* when uncovered. Since they are *ervah*, no man may say a *bracha* or *dvar* Torah while facing them in an uncovered state - see *Mekoros* 14:2 and 54:1. For example, nowadays women have firmly accepted to cover their feet when in public. As a result of this, it is *ossur* even for a husband to say a *bracha* etc. when directly facing the uncovered feet of his wife - see 6:O for details. Likewise, in communities where women and girls are particular to cover almost all the lower section of their arms, it is *ossur* for a man to say a *bracha* when facing a female with uncovered forearms. See 6:G:2 above and *Mekoros* 54.

3. AREA ONLY COVERED IN PUBLIC - "ERVAH" EVEN INDOORS: An area which must *halachically* be covered when in public, has the status of *ervah* even at home (see 5:B above) e.g. the hair of a married woman. Even a husband may not say a *davar shebikdusha* when facing her when such an area is uncovered although they are inside the home. Consequently, he must not say a *dvar* Torah to his wife at the breakfast table if her hair is uncovered, since he is facing hair which is *ervah* (*Chofetz Chayim, Geder Olam*, Chapter Two).

Moreover, an area that has not been named *ervah* by *Chazal* but is generally covered by women when they are out in public, has the status of *ervah* although women do not cover it when they are at home. Since it is covered when outdoors, it has the status of דרכן להיות מכוסה and is considered *ervah* everywhere, whether outdoors or indoors. As above, it is *ervah* to everyone, even to the people with whom she lives (such as her husband, father or son) although they regularly see this area uncovered. Since it is an area which people feel should be covered in public, it has the status of *ervah* everywhere and for everyone (M.B. 75:10) - see *Mekoros* 54:3-6.

Accordingly, if it is the local *minhag* to cover the full arm when in public but at home women are only particular to cover beyond the elbow, the forearm is *ervah*. Consequently, no man (not even her husband or close family) may say a *bracha* when looking at her arm or even just a *tefach* of it. Similarly, although a woman may walk around the house with a long night-robe and slippers in a way that her uncovered feet can be seen, no one may say a *bracha* when looking at her uncovered feet since they are an area which is דרכן להיות מכוסה when in public.

4. TO HUSBAND - ISSUR ONLY WHEN TEFACH EXPOSED: If a woman is nursing her baby and a *tefach* or more is uncovered, her husband must turn away before saying a *bracha*, a *dvar* Torah, *halacha* or anything similar (M.B. 75:3). This applies even if he is not actually looking at her, as has been explained. However, if less than a *tefach* is uncovered he need not turn away, because in the case of a husband the *issur* applies only when a *tefach* or more is uncovered as a husband is not provoked by less than a *tefach* (O.H. 75:1 *Rema*) - see *Mekoros* 17:8 and 54:8.

The *halacha* that an exposure of less than a *tefach* causes no *issurim* to a husband, applies to most parts of the body, but not to the knees and upper sections of the legs. These limbs are so provocative that they effect everyone even when just less than a *tefach* is exposed (M.B. 75:7) - see 4:C:3 above.

5. TO CLOSE RELATIVES - ISSUR ONLY WHEN TEFACH EXPOSED: If a father faces his daughter, a grandfather his granddaughter, or a brother his sister whilst they are in an inadequate state of dress, the *issur* of saying a *bracha* applies only if a *tefach* is exposed - see *Mekoros* 17:8. This applies when the female is an eleven year old or even an adult, because close blood-relatives are unaffected by an exposed area that is less than a *tefach* - see 4:C:5 above.

If more than a *tefach* is exposed, the area is *ervah* and even close relatives may not say *dvarim shebikdusha.* Moreover, if part of the upper sections of the legs are exposed one must be stringent even if the exposure is less than a *tefach*, as explained in a previous point. These two stringencies apply only if the girl is an eleven year old, because an exposure on a girl younger than this will not affect close blood relatives - see *Mekoros* 16.

U. SAYING BRACHA FACING TEFACH OR LESS THAN TEFACH

1. HOW TO SAY BRACHA IF TEFACH IS EXPOSED: A man may not say a *bracha, Tefilla* or *dvar* Torah (whether in Hebrew or any other language) when facing an inadequately dressed woman on whom *ervah d'Rabanan* is visible, even though he is not actually looking at her (except under very exceptional circumstances - see 6:V:8). Exposed parts of the body are *ervah d'Rabanan* and the holiness and sensitivity of *devarim shebikdusha* requires that anything classed *ervah* is not together with the person who is about to say them (*Bach* O.C 75). Even if there are many meters between the person wishing to say the *bracha* and the inadequately dressed woman the *Issur* still applies, as long as she is within the range of vision of the man (*Chayei Adam* 4:2) - see *Mekoros* 14:1.

Generally, only an exposed *tefach* (approx. 4"x 4" - see *Mekor Chayim* 75:1) of the body has the status of *ervah*. There is however one exception. This is that according to many *Poskim* an exposure of part of the thigh has the status of *ervah* even if the area is less than a *tefach* (see M.B. 75:7 and 6:T:4 above). The knee is the lowest part of the thigh and this stringency therefore applies to it - see 6:H:3 above.

If a man wishes to say a *bracha* or a *davar shebikdusha* in the presence of flesh which has the status of *ervah*, there are three opinions as to what he should do:-

(a) Stringent opinion - he should turn his whole body away: The most stringent opinion holds that he should turn his whole body away in a different direction, so that the *ervah* is to the side or rear of the person (M.B. 75:1 and *Biur Halacha* in name of the *S'mag*, the *Vilna Gaon* and *Nishmas Odom*) - see *Mekoros* 33:1-3.

(b) Middle opinion - he should close his eyes: A second opinion holds that it would be sufficient for him to close his eyes (ibid. in name of *Bach* and *Pri Megodim*. This is also the opinion of the *Maharsha, Makos* 24a). Looking slightly away so that the *ervah* is not in the direct line of vision is inadequate, because there is no guarantee that he will not look back. Closing the eyes is however a definite abstention from looking - see *Mekoros* 33:4.

(c) Lenient opinion - he should look away: A third opinion holds that he need just direct his focus elsewhere so that the *ervah* is not in his line of vision. This opinion maintains that although it would just require a slight adjustment for the *ervah* to be once again in his line of vision this is nevertheless adequate (*Chazon Ish* O.C. 16:7) - see *Mekoros* 33:8.

Ideally, when *ervah* is in front of a person, he should turn in a different direction in order to comply with the first opinion. However, if this is difficult as it will cause major embarrassment to the woman, he should try at least to comply with the second opinion. If even this is too difficult he may rely on the third opinion mentioned - see 6:V:1 below.

2. HOW TO SAY BRACHA IF LESS THAN TEFACH IS EXPOSED: As stated in 6:U:2 above, if the exposure is less than a *tefach* or if the *ervah* is uncovered hair (which is less severe than skin as can be seen from the fact that an unmarried girl may reveal her hair) all opinions agree that he need not turn away. It is sufficient for him to just close his eyes (M.B. 75:5) or if necessary to face slightly away from it in a way that it is out of his field of vision (*Chazon Ish* O.C. 16:7).

V. PROBLEMS OF BRACHOS WHEN FACING IMMODEST DRESS

In the light of the *halachic* principles mentioned in the previous points the rules are as follows:-

1. SAYING BRACHA ON A BUS, TRAIN OR AIRCRAFT: When saying a *bracha* or *tefilla* on a train or plane and *ervah d'Rabanan* is in front of him (for example, women with exposed arms and shoulders are among the crowd) the man should preferably turn his body to face the window, so that the *ervah* is out of sight (to accommodate the first opinion mentioned in U:1 above). Should he be sitting in an aisle seat and facing the window will not help, he should close his eyes or at least look down into a *Siddur* or at the floor so that the *ervah* is out of vision. If an indecent film is being screened, he need not try to turn away. A film is similar to seeing *ervah* through a window and in such a case even in the first place he need just close his eyes or look downwards so that the picture is not in his line of vision - as explained in 6:V:5 below.

2. SHEMONE ESREI ON AN AIRCRAFT: When *davening Shemone Esrei* on a plane a man should stand at the back (if this is possible and will not overly disturb his concentration - see *Responsa Iggros Moshe* O.C. 4:2) and face a window rather than the passengers. Even if this means not facing the east, this is still preferable because facing the east towards *Yerusholayim* is only a preferred way of *davening*, whilst not to *daven* when facing *ervah* even with closed eyes is proper *halacha* according to some opinions (M.B. 90:19, *Responsa MaHarsham* 4:126).

Moreover, people sometimes look around while *davening* and if he would do so he would certainly transgress an *issur* if he looked at partially uncovered hair etc. while *davening*. Also, it is incorrect for a person to *daven* behind people who are sitting as it appears as if he is bowing down to them (M.B. 102:8), unless the seat backs are ten *tefochim* high (about one meter high) and reach down to within less than three *tefachim* of the floor, which is not usually the case in an aircraft (M.B. 102:2). Due to all these considerations he should face a window when *davening* rather than the people (see *sefer, Oz Nidberu* 12:27). Even a woman to whom the first two reasons do not apply (as uncovered flesh of a woman is not *ervah* to another woman - M.B. 75:8) should *daven* towards the window because of the third reason mentioned.

Before starting to *daven* he should look through the window up to heaven. This will help him feel humbled and daven with earnest to *Hashem* (M.B. 95:4). However, once davening he should look down into his *siddur* (or *daven* with his eyes closed) except when wanting to look up to the heaven to experience once again the greatness and majesty of *Hashem* and arouse himself to renewed concentration in his *davening* (M.B. 90:8).

3. FACING SEE-THROUGH CLOTHES - SHOULD CLOSE EYES: If a woman is dressed in a see-through blouse, see-through dress, has a see-through shawl on her hair or is wearing any other sheer piece of clothing, it is *ossur* to say a *bracha* when facing her, because her skin and inner clothes which are both provocative can be seen, and whenever a provocative area can be seen it is *ossur* to say a *bracha*. However, since the skin and inner clothes are covered (albeit by very thin see-through material) they have a more lenient *halacha* than when they are totally uncovered. As long as the man closes his eyes (according to the stringent opinion) or looks down or just away and she is out of his field of vision (according to the more lenient opinion) and is not in a position to be provoked he may say a *bracha*, even though he faces her (according to the more lenient opinion).

This is sufficient even if more than a *tefach* can be seen and had such an amount not been covered he would in the first place have had to turn away. Since it is covered, the person saying the *bracha* is not considered to be in one and the same place as the *ervah* and the *issur* does not apply. Similarly, if she wears a very short garment and the upper sections of her legs are covered by see-through tights he may say a *bracha* by just closing his eyes (M.B. 75:25) - see *Mekoros* 39:2.

4. ERVAH SEEN THROUGH WINDOW - SHOULD CLOSE EYES: If a man looks through a window (whether through the glass or completely open) at a crowd of people amongst whom there are inadequately-clad women, he need only close his eyes or look elsewhere to say the *bracha* because he is looking at *ervah* that is in a second domain (M.B. 75:29, 79:14) - see *Mekoros* 38:1. The same applies when a man sees an inadequately dressed woman through a mirror. Since the actual person is not in the same domain as him, nor is he looking at the person, closing his eyes or just looking elsewhere is sufficient. (See *sefer, Mishmeres Chayim,* Chapter 4 note 9 and 4:B:5(c) above).

If a man has a need to, he may look out of a window although there are inadequately-clad women among the crowd, provided he is only scanning the view generally but is not focusing on an individual. For example, if he is looking out for someone or wants to see if a car has arrived, he may look at the crowd in general. Although the women are within vision (and due to that he may not say a *bracha* when looking in their direction) he is not considered to truly see them - 6:V:9(c) below. However, if he has no need to look out of the window he should not do so because this could cause him to focus on *ervah* - see *Bava Basra* (57b) and 6:T:1 above.

5. FACING IMMODEST PICTURE - SHOULD CLOSE EYES: The same *halacha* applies when facing a picture of an inadequately-clad woman or girl or seeing such a person in a mirror. Just as it is *ossur* for a man to look at a female who is not properly dressed so also it is *ossur* for him to look at a picture or image of a female in such a state - (*Responsa Minchas Elazar* 3:25; *Minchas Yitzchak* 2:84; *Be'er Moshe* 4:147:21,22; *Yabia Omer* 1:7. 6:12). See *Mekoros* 39:3-10 and 40:6.

Moreover, many *Poskim* maintain that just as it is *ossur* for a man to say a *bracha* if there is an inadequately-clad female within vision (even if he is not looking at her) so it is *ossur* for a man to say a *bracha* when facing such a picture unless he closes his eyes or at least looks downwards so that the picture is not within his line of vision (*ibid.*). This can be relevant at the breakfast table when there may be an indecent picture in a morning paper. Not only may a man not look at these pictures but he must make sure that they are out of his sight when saying a *bracha*. In fact, a morning paper which carries such pictures, is not the type of paper to read or to let into the house.

A man may say a *bracha* when facing a picture of a fully-dressed lady just as he may say a *bracha* when an adequately-dressed woman is in front of him. It is, however, *ossur* for anybody to *daven Shemone Esrei* in front of a painting or photograph of a person, whether man or woman, or of any other interesting scene because the picture can easily disturb his concentration (M.B. 90:71). In the case of pictures of people there is an additional reason: it appears that he is bowing and praying to the person who is in the picture (*Taz,* Y.D. 141:14).

Many people are unaware of this *halacha*. It is particularly relevant to women who *daven* at home, and pictures of *Gedolim* or of the family are commonly positioned around the rooms of the house. Women must be careful not to face such pictures when *davening*. However, if pictures are above the height of the head the *issur* does not apply, because a person is not disturbed by a picture that is above his head. Also, when the picture is at that height, bowing down does not give the impression as bowing to those who are in the picture - see *Mekoros* 38:4.

6. FACING IMMODESTLY DRESSED NON-JEWISH WOMEN: If the woman in front of the person wishing to say a *bracha* is not Jewish, the *halachos* are similar but not identical. If part of the main body or the upper sections of the arm or legs are uncovered, it is *ossur* to say a *bracha* facing her. Since these areas are classified *ervah* by *Chazal*, they are provocative parts of the body and *ervah* in every case.

This is most important for a man who works in an office together with non-Jewish ladies - see 9F. If they have short sleeves or short skirts the man must turn to face a different direction before saying a *bracha*. Similarly, if he buys a drink at a kiosk and the lady serving has a dress revealing a *tefach* of an area that is not just the neck, the man must, if possible, turn the other way before saying a *bracha* - (see O.C. 75:4 that *ervah min HaTorah* applies even to non-Jews, and M.B. 75:17 where it is spelled out that *ervah d'Rabanan* applies even to non-Jewish women, *Ben Ish Chai, Parshas Bo,* No.8).

If a non-Jewish woman wears no tights and the lower sections of her legs are visible from where the man stands, according to some *Poskim* it would be permissible for him to say a *bracha* when looking in her direction. They maintain that the lower sections of the leg must be covered because it is an excepted *minhag* to do so and non-Jewish women do not have a *minhag* to cover these sections - see 6:L:1 above. However, according to the opinion which considers the lower sections of the leg to be *ervah* classified by *Chazal* this *heter* would not apply, unless she was sitting at a desk and her uncovered legs could not be seen from the standing or sitting position of the man, in which case all agree that he may say a *bracha* even when facing her.

7. PROBLEMS OF BRACHOS AT CHUPAH: *Rabbanim* who officiate at *chupos* that are attended by ladies whose hair is uncovered must not look at any of these ladies when saying the *brachos*, but need not turn to face a different direction since looking into the *Siddur* excludes the women from their field of vision. However, if women with uncovered arms or deeply cut necklines attend the *chupos*, the *Rav* should if possible turn to face a different direction before saying any of the *brachos*, as explained - *Responsa Yabia Omer* 3:7. See *Mekoros* 33:13.

8. LECTURING TO WOMEN WHO ARE IMMODESTLY DRESSED: When speeches and *shiurim* are given to people who are not yet committed to *Yiddishkeit*, the ladies who attend these speeches and *shiurim* are often not dressed to the minimum *halachic* standard. The upper sections of their arms are sometimes partially uncovered, their necklines can be far from Kosher and although married their hair is uncovered. This presents a serious dilemma because it is *ossur* to say *devarim shebikdusha* when facing *ervah*. On the other hand, in order to reach these people and influence them, they must hear inspiring and stimulating *divrei* Torah. Their entire future as committed *Yidden* could depend on these speeches and *shiurim* and if these cannot be given, they and their children would be left without *Yiddishkeit* forever.

There is a ruling by the *Chazon Ish* for this situation. Basing himself on a precedent of a similar though not identical situation recorded in the *Rishonim*, he rules that the speeches and *shiurim* may be given. The *heter* is founded on a principle known as עת לעשות לה' - A Torah law may occasionally be violated in order to enable a much greater measure of Torah law to be observed in the future. The person giving the speech or *shiur* should however make every effort not to look at these exposed areas so that although they are in his field of vision he is not actually looking at them (*Chazon Ish* O.C. 16:11).It must be stressed that the principle of עת לעשות לה' is used only on very exceptional cases and requires a precedent from *Chazal* or the *Rishonim* so that it may be applied to a particular set of circumstances.

9. LOOKING AT WOMEN AND GIRLS: To prevent confusion between the *issur* of saying a *bracha*, singing *zemiros* or speaking Torah when facing *ervah d'Rabanan* and the general *issur* for a man to look at women and girls, it is essential to lay down the most basic guidelines of these *halachos*. There are three levels of "looking" in reference to the general *issur* of looking at females:-

(a) Looking (הסתכלות) - Gazing with pleasure and interest at the face or movements of a female is forbidden even if she is dressed perfectly (M.B. 75:7, M.B. 225 *Biur Halacha* s.v. *Afilu*). To do so is an *issur min haTorah* learned from the verse ולא תתורו אחרי עיניכם (*Bamidbar* 15:39). This applies to all women except the closest blood relatives such as one's mother, grandmother, daughter, granddaughter, and sister (see M.B. 225:1 and *Shaar HaTzion* 2). Concerning a young girl who is still under *Bas-mitzva* - see 6:V:10 below.

(b) Seeing (ראיה) - Looking at a female without any specific interest e.g. looking casually at a woman when talking to her, is permitted provided the woman is properly dressed and one is just casually looking at her face or hands whilst talking to her. There is however a *midas chassidus* (an act of extra piety) to avoid looking even casually at a woman (apart from the closest blood relatives) although she is fully dressed (M.B. 75:7).

Areas of the female body that should be covered but are exposed have a much more severe status than face and hands. Such areas must not be seen even in a casual manner with no special interest on the part of the man - M.B. 75:7. The *Chazon Ish* (O.C. 16:7) explains that being an area that is usually covered, even a casual sighting will attract the man to look with interest. This will turn the casual sighting into an act of הסתכלות - gazing which is *ossur* - see 6:C:5 above.

(c) Within line of vision (בתוך המבט) - The female is in the man's line of vision (and he could in theory focus on her from this position) but he is not focusing his eyes on her. This is permitted, even when the female is inadequately dressed, provided he has a need to be in this place and has no real alternative. For example, walking through a crowd in a normal manner without focusing on any particular inadequately dressed woman. Similarly, speaking to an audience, at which time the speaker generally does not look at any particular person but they are all within his field of vision (*Rashbam*, *Bava Basra* 57b starting *L'mianes Nafshei*; *Bach*, O.C. 75 end of piece starting *Tefach*. See also *Mekoros* 70 for an in-depth study of this subject). Saying a *bracha* is, however, not permitted when ervah is within the person's line of vision - as explained in 6:U:1 above.

10. LOOKING AT A YOUNG GIRL:

(a) Her face etc.: The *issur* of הסתכלות - gazing, applies to a female who has the status of *ervah* to this man, and he will be considered as deriving pleasure from an *ervah* which is forbidden. The *issur* therefore applies to a girl who is twelve and has presumably reached puberty and become an *ervah* (M.B. 75:17 and *Toras Hahistaklus* 14:17). It also applies to the man's sister-in-law (sister of his wife) who is *ervah* to him even when she is very young. He may therefore not gaze at her features.

A man may, however, look at the face of a young girl who is not an *ervah* to him although he enjoys looking at her features. Since she is not an *ervah* and her face is something people constantly seen, which in turn minimizes the intensity of the pleasure derived, no *halachic issur* is involved.

That is as far as strict *halacha* is concerned. It is, however, an act of piety not to gaze even at a young girl who at present is not *ervah* (*Rambam, Pirush HaMishnayos, Sanhedrin* 54a). This is learned from Iyov who said, ומה אתבונן על בתולה - "Why should I gaze at a maiden" (*Iyov* 31:1). The reason for this piety is that one day the girl will be married, and if this man has developed an interest in her, this might harmfully linger on into a time when she is a married woman (*Avos D'Reb Nosson* 2:5). [There is, however, an opinion which maintains that *Chazal* have obligated us to keep this act of piety and it is therefore an *issur d'Rabanon* - See *Beis Shmuel* 21:2.]

(b) An area that should be covered: It is *halachically ossur* for a man to look at parts of a young girl's body that should be covered but are now exposed, even though the girl is not an *ervah* to him and the problem of 'benefiting from *ervah*' does not apply in her case. Seeing an area that is usually not on display can motivate a thought process that can be harmful to the person. This case is similar to purposefully listening and enjoying the singing of a young girl - M.B. 75:17. Such pleasure can arouse a feeling of wanting to indulge into further types of pleasures - see 8:E:2 below. To pursue such pleasure is therefore an *issur d'Rabanan* of לא תקרבו לגלות ערוה - "Do not cultivate within yourself a desire for immorality" (*Vayikra* 18:6) - (see *Rambam, Hilchos Issurei Biah* 21:2-5).

It is similarly *ossur* to kiss, hug, stroke the hair of, or sit on one's lap, a girl who is over three (or according to some six/seven) who is not an *ervah.* Being an activity that can give a man feelings of enjoyment it is no different to listening with intent to a girl sing or looking at otherwise covered parts of her body - see *sefer, Oz Nidberu* 13:57 and *Responsa Avnei Yoshpeh* 2:89:7.

W. VALIDITY OF BRACHA SAID FACING ERVAH

1. BRACHA SAID FACING ERVAH MIN HATORAH:

(a) If aware of *ervah* - *bracha* invalid: The essential factor is the person's awareness that the *ervah* was present when he said the *bracha.* Therefore, if a man or woman said a *bracha* facing a completely unclothed person (*ervah min haTorah*), whether male or female, and was aware of the fact that the unclothed person was there or was likely to be there, the *bracha* is invalid. Even if he did not actually look at the unclothed person while saying the *bracha* it is nevertheless invalid because even then he has transgressed the *issur min HaTorah.* Since he knew or suspected that an unclad person was in the room, he is regarded as having been grossly disrespectful in saying a *bracha* under such circumstances. The *bracha* is consequently invalid. (*See Introduction of Biur Halacha* 74 point 4 and M.B. 75:4 concerning *brachos* and *krias Shema*) - see *Mekoros* 18:1.

Even if he was ignorant of the *halacha* that it is *ossur* to say a *bracha* when facing *ervah,* the *bracha* is still invalid as even in such a case he is considered to have been very disrespectful. The mere fact that he said a *bracha* in front of *ervah* and assumed that in spite of this situation it was permissible to say a *bracha* is regarded as being presumptuous - (compare to M.B. 76:31 and 185:7) - see *Mekoros* 18:3-5.

(b) If unaware of *ervah* - *bracha* valid: If someone said a *bracha* not knowing that *ervah min haTorah* was in front of him, and also had no reason to suspect that it was there, the *bracha* is valid. Since he was unaware of the circumstances he was not disrespectful and the *bracha* is valid - (similar to M.B. 76:8) - see *Mekoros* 18:6.

2. BRACHA SAID FACING ERVAH D'RABANAN:

(a) Looked at *tefach* - *bracha* valid, *shema* invalid: If a person said a *bracha* when looking at a *tefach* of exposed flesh (*ervah d'Rabanan*) e.g. at his wife who had not covered the upper section of her arms or whose hair was uncovered, the *bracha* is valid. Uncovered flesh and hair are given the name "*ervah*" by *Chazal* in only a partial sense i.e. that it is *ossur* to say *devarim shebikdusha* in front of them. However, they are not truly classified as *ervah*, as is evident from the fact that a second woman may say a *bracha* when facing them. It is therefore questionable whether saying a *bracha* in front of them is considered as being grossly disrespectful. Thus, a *bracha* said in front of them should not be repeated because it may be unwarranted and consequently a *bracha levatala* - a *bracha* in vain - which is a major *issur*. *Shema* must however be repeated in such a case as there is no *issur* of *bracha levatala* in the case of repeating *shema* - (similar to M.B. 73:4 and M.B. 74:5) - see *Mekoros* 18:7.

(b) Did not look purposefully at *tefach* - even *shema* valid: If a person said *shema* in front of an exposed *tefach* (*ervah d'Rabanan*) but did not purposefully look at the uncovered flesh or uncovered hair at the time, the *shema* is valid. Similarly, if while saying *shema* he heard a woman sing but paid no attention to it, the *shema* is valid. Since there is an opinion (not mentioned above) that maintains that when the person is "not looking" or "not listening", the *issur* of saying *devarim shebikdusha* in front of *ervah d'Rabanan* does not apply, *shema* need not be repeated, even though it is incorrect to rely on this lenient opinion (M.B. 75:4) - see *Mekoros* 18:10.

(c) Looked at less than *tefach* - even *shema* valid: If a person said *shema* when looking at less than a *tefach* of exposed flesh he does not have to repeat the *shema*. If the woman in question is his own wife the *bracha* is obviously valid because he may even in the first place say a *bracha* or recite *krias shema* in front of less than a *tefach* (O.C. 75:1). However, even if the woman whose flesh is exposed is not his wife he need not repeat the *shema* because according to many opinions there is no *issur* in saying a *davar shebikdusha* in front of an exposure that is less than a *tefach*. See O.C. 75:1 and *Elya Rabba* 75:1 in name of the *Bach*. See also *Mekoros* 18:10.

Chapter Seven

REFINED CLOTHES, JEWELRY AND COSMETICS

A. OVERDRESSING - OSTENTATIOUS CLOTHES

While the Jewish woman should dress pleasantly and tastefully, it is wrong for her to dress during the week in clothes fit for Shabbos or *Yomtov*, or to dress on Shabbos and *Yomtov* to an exceptionally high standard. This holds true even if the garments are not ostentatious. This also refers to having an extraordinary amount of dresses and outfits, due to which this woman or girl appears constantly in different clothes - see *Mekoros* 59:1. There are many reasons for this. Amongst them are the following:-

1. FIRST OBJECTION - DAMAGING TO WEARER'S CHARACTER: The attribute of modesty, which is essentially part of *tznius* (see 1:D), is detrimentally affected by too high a standard of dress. Being very well-dressed gives a person a feeling of perfection, and we are all unfortunately very far from attaining that grade. It is therefore simply bad for one's *midos* to dress at all times in such a way. Mothers dressing their little daughters in clothes fit for a princess should realize that this is not good for the child's development - see *Mekoros* 59:1.

A further problem that can arise from over-dressing is that this can lead to jealousy and envy. The woman or girl will gradually require better-looking and more costly clothes, and unless she is exceptionally rich, it could come to a point when she will not be able to afford them. She will then become jealous and envious of those who are very wealthy and wear the clothes she cannot afford. In short, one shortcoming and weakness leads to the other, and untold harm is done to the person.

Rabbi Moshe Chayim Luzzato writes the following in *Mesilas Yesharim* (chapter 13):- **"Indulgence in any type of pleasure invariably leads to sin. For example, ...concerning clothes and jewelry, the Torah does not state any limits as to how beautiful they may be. All the Torah insists on is that they must not contain *shatnez* and that if a man's garment is four-cornered it should have *tzitzis*. Once these two points are taken care of, there are no further *issurim* in the Torah. Nevertheless, who does not know that wearing ostentatious and highly embroidered clothes leads a person to haughtiness? Even immorality can be a consequence of wearing such clothes. Apart from this, jealousy, indulgence and deceit result from arousing the desire within oneself for something one will eventually find hard to obtain. Have not *Chazal* said, 'When the *yetzer horah* sees that a person is easy prey, he encourages him to over-indulge in exquisite clothes and to beautify his hair. He knows that these activities lead to all forms of sin' "** (see 2:G:2 above). These are the critical but painfully true words of the *Mesilas Yesharim*.

2. SECOND OBJECTION - DRAWS AYIN HORAH TO HERSELF:

(a) The harm caused by *ayin horah*: Displaying excessively expensive clothing and jewelry is not only harmful from the *tznius* point of view but is also an act of gross folly as she, G-d forbid, invites harm upon herself. The *Ribbono Shel Olam* established two opposing forces in the world. *Ayin Tovah* (literally, a good eye) with which one person imparts blessing onto a second person, and in contrast, *ayin horah* (literally, an evil eye) with which a person can do considerable harm to a second person.

It is our duty to love another *Yid* and view all that he has and all his successes with an *ayin Tovah*. The *ayin Tovah* is a source of blessing and is one of the ways one *Yid* can help another. On the other hand, *ayin horah* is like a curse and causes harm and destruction (*Bava Metziah* 107a, *Choshen Mishpat* 378:5). It is given as a test for people to avoid harming others by being envious and resentful of their good fortune. It is very important to understand the danger of *ayin horah* since appreciating this danger keeps a person, who might otherwise have behaved in an ostentatious manner, very much in check.

(b) Not to cause oneself or others to have an *ayin horah*: The woman of worth makes it her business to prevent others from having to cope with jealousy. She avoids "*shteching* (poking) others in the eye" and does not exhibit the many blessings *Hashem Yisborach* has bestowed upon her for all to see. She knows that to do so is grossly unfair towards others. She also understands that it would be a major disservice towards herself since by doing so she attracts *ayin horah* upon herself and her family, *rachmana litzlan*.

In contrast, the refined and benevolent *Bas Yisroel* is very careful not to put an *ayin horah* on others, *chas v'shalom*. When she sees another woman dressed in a delightful new dress or outfit, her immediate reaction is to tell her friend how nice the garment is and how well it suits her. She also wishes her to wear it "*gezunte heit*" and to have many *simchos* in it. As a result of reacting in this way, she safeguards herself from the pitfalls of jealousy and its unfortunate consequences. [See *Rema* O.C. 223:6 that it is an established *minhag* to wish the one who is wearing a new garment תתחדש, meaning, תבלה ותתחדש - "you should merit to wear it out and replace it".]

(c) Saying "*bli ayin horah*" wherever appropriate: When telling family or friends about a *simcha* in another family such as the engagement or the birth of a child she will always add "*bli ayin horah*" so as to wish the other family well with all her heart and not to allow personal yearnings to interfere. By reacting in this manner, she imparts these wonderful traits to her children so that they too become people who view the blessings of others with an *ayin tovah* and are truly happy with other people's *simchos*. (See the words of the Gaon the *Chida zt'l* in *Tziporen Shamir* No.172, that it is an obligation to say *bli ayin horah*. See also *sefer*, *Shemiras Haguf V'Hanefesh* 241:1 who cites the *Minchas Elazar*).

(d) *Tznius* naturally prevents *ayin horah*: Just as a lack of *tznius* causes *ayin horah*, so too, keeping *tznius* properly prevents *ayin horah*. This is a natural result of not arousing those who could be enticed into giving an *ayin horah*. This point is mentioned in *Chazal* concerning the breaking of the *Luchos* (the Tablets) - one of the greatest losses the Jewish people ever sustained. *Chazal* say, לוחות הראשונות שנתנו בפומבי שלטה בהם עין הרע ונשתברו, אמר הקב״ה אין לך יפה מן הצניעות - "The first *Luchos* which were given with much publicity were subjected to an *ayin horah* and were broken. *Hashem* then said that 'there is nothing more beautiful than privacy'. As a result the second *Luchos* were given quietly, between *Hashem* and the Jewish people with the exclusion of the *umos ha'olam*" (*Midrash Tanchuma, Ki Sisah* No.31).

The first *Luchos* were given amidst major publicity to beautify the occasion. This, however, led to *ayin horah* and disaster. *Hashem* then said that rather than beautify the *Luchos* in a physical way by doing so before a multitude of people, we will beautify the giving of the *Luchos* in a spiritual manner, by giving it amidst the finest and most cherished good *midah* that exists - the *midah* of *tznius*, which will certainly not arouse an *ayin horah* - אין לך יפה מן הצניעות - "no trait is as beautiful as *tznius*". The second *Luchos* were therefore given privately, just within the "family circle" of *Hashem Yisborach* and *Klal Yisroel*.

It is for us to take note of this remarkable *Chazal*. Rather than beautify ourselves in a way that begs for public acclaim, which can cause *ayin horah,* let us enhance ourselves with the most beautiful and cherished of traits - that of privacy, modesty and *tznius*, which adds so much luster to a person's appearance and to the essence of his life. Over a hundred years ago *Harav Samson Raphael Hirsch* wrote the following in "*Choreb*", Chapter 67: "We have thus paid dearly with our most costly treasure (*tznius*) for the inflow of European culture, which the century has brought into our circle. Our homes, youths and maidens are no longer models of sublime, chaste, moral purity - which they used to be in former generations." This was the cry from the heart of a man who sought to save *Klal Yisroel* from destruction.

Today would certainly seem to be no better. However, we have reason to hope that just as there is an enormous awakening to *teshuva* in our times, so too *b'ezer Hashem*, many of our youth and many of our girls and young women will return to the ways and attitudes of *Klal Yisroel* of old, appreciating that אין לך יפה מן הצניעות.

(e) *Tznius* effects a Heavenly protection from *ayin horah*: Apart from *ayin horah* being naturally prevented by the *tznius* of keeping one's affairs and successes private, there is also a special Heavenly protection from *ayin horah* that is given as a reward for practicing a high level of *tznius*. This is based on the principle that *Hashem* repays *midah k'neged midah* - measure for measure. In the merit of the person covering and concealing that which should not be seen, he is protected that others do not see his successes and do not pay them their unwanted attention.

The *Maharal* in *Nesivos Olam* (*Nesiv HaTznius,* Chapter One, paragraph s.v. *Ub'Bava Basra*) remarks that Rachel who was distinguished by *tznius* (as stated in *Megilla* 13b) was rewarded with a firstborn son Yosef who received the blessing of עלי עין - "to be above the eye", which is that he would be immune from the threat of Evil Eye (*Breishis* 49:22). In the same vein, Yosef was given a blessing that his children would be "as fish in their multitude in the midst of the land," וידגו לרוב בקרב הארץ (*Breishis* 48:16). Just as fish of the sea are not menaced by the Evil Eye, so the descendants of Yosef will be shielded from it. This heavenly protection was afforded them as a direct result of the exemplary *tznius* of their grandmother Rachel.

3. THIRD OBJECTION - CAUSES NOCHRIM TO BE JEALOUS OF US: When Jewish women walk around in the most expensive clothes, adorned in their best finery and jewelry and painted with excessive makeup, the envy of the *nochrim* among whom we live is exceedingly aroused. This is not a far-fetched theory but an explicit statement by *Chazal* in the *Gemara* (*Shabbos* 139a) אמר רב פפא אי בטלי יהירי בטלי אמגושי - "If we would cease exhibiting ourselves with eye-catching hair-styles and costly garments, persecutions from those who dislike us and stir up trouble against us would likewise cease" (*See Rashi*).

The following is a quote from the *Responsa Teshuva Mei'ahava* (by the greatest disciple of the *Noda BiYehuda*) Vol 1, *Responsa* 48: **"Our ancestor Yaacov, to whom *Hashem* said, הנה אנכי עמך ושמרתיך בכל אשר תלך - 'Behold I am with you and shall guard you wherever you go' (*Breishis* 28:15), nevertheless said to his sons, למה תתראו - 'Why do you aggravate your neighbors?' (*Breishis* 42:1). We who live in exile must be all the more careful. It is a fact that all the persecutions and expulsions that have occurred to the Jewish people until this day in Spain, Portugal and many other countries, were all caused by jealousy and envy aroused by our ostentatious mode of dress. During these times there was no difference between the dress of a Jewish person and that of the highest classes of non-Jewish nobility."**

Let us take this frightful testimony to heart and prevent calamity from befalling *Klal Yisroel* once again, *chas veshalom* - see *Mekoros* 61:1.

4. FOURTH OBJECTION - CLOTHES BECOME TOO IMPORTANT:

(a) Clothes are not to be a cult and goal in themselves: Importance should be attached to dress, as a person's self-image is greatly enhanced by being well-dressed and this in turn brings *simcha* into the home. However, it is wrong to attach excessive significance to the whole subject of dress. There are many more meaningful things in life than dress, and to put excessive emphasis on the external is an act of vanity. Just as eating, which is most important for a person's health, must be understood as a means, not as a goal, i.e. a person should "eat to live" and not "live to eat", so too, clothes should be regarded as a means to improve one's self-image and bring *simcha* into one's home, but they must not become a cult and a goal in themselves. People who talk about nothing but clothes and food all day are evidently obsessed by these aspects of life to an unhealthy degree.

(b) Harm to person's *ruchnius* when clothes are overly important: The destructive power of being "captivated by dress" is expressed in no uncertain terms in a letter by one of the foremost *Roshei Yeshiva* of our times, Harav Hagaon R' Aharon Leib Steinman *shlita*, *Rosh Yeshivas Gaon Yaacov* and author of the "*Ayeles HaShachar*" on *Shas*. The letter is actually about young men who attach far more importance than is justified to their hats, shirts, ties, suits and shoes to the great detriment of their learning and their true growth. Although it is about men, it reflects the view of a *Gadol b'Yisroel* on the gravity of this matter. The letter reads as follows:-

> *Peace to you!*
>
> *Distressingly there are not many who earnestly wish to know the correct way a person should go, although everyone claims they do. They fool themselves because they do not delve deeply into the course of their lives, and when looking from a superficial viewpoint a person can easily deceive himself.*
>
> *I am writing at present in connection with what I hear affects a sizable part of the Yeshiva world. This is that many have started paying excessive attention to their clothes, applying their heart and mind to them. They try to dress in the latest fashion, and are extremely particular about their appearance. There can be no doubt that such people lack Yiras Shomayim. Furthermore, whoever turns his mind to such things cannot be successful in his learning. Even if it seems to the observer that these bachurim make a name for themselves in the Yeshiva, the truth is that it is impossible for them*

to be truly matzliach in their learning; for those who have no Yiras Shomayim must, in the course of time, deteriorate in their understanding of Torah. Those who indulge in the above are striding towards becoming the opposite of true Bnei Torah for whom Torah is their portion in life and fills their whole existence.

Do not fall into the trap of those who scoff at people who conduct themselves correctly and do not follow their ways. On the contrary, a person should escape and distance himself from conduct which diametrically opposes all that a Ben Torah should be.

Hashem will not deny good from those who follow Him with purity; they shall merit a special measure of siyata d'shmaya.

Signature,

Teves 5753

On the same note, the Chasam Sofer *zt'l* writes:- על פי דרך הטבע המנהיג בניו בבגדי שש ורקמה כדרך השרים אין דברי תורה מתקיים בהם - loosely translated this means, "If parents dress their sons in garments of exceptionally fine material or that have fine embroidery, which are clothes typically worn by a prince, it is natural that the Torah their sons learn dissipate and they do not become *Talmidei Chachamim*" (*Drashos Chasam Sofer*, page 333).

(c) The harm caused when priorities are wrong: By developing a wrong sense of priorities and by putting far too much stress on external beauty, a person may similarly become overly house-proud. This could lead to not wanting a large family because with children around one cannot keep the house perfectly tidy and sparklingly clean at all times. In real Jewish values, the greatest treasure a woman can have is a family of *y'reim* and *Talmidei Chachamim*. Her home is no more than a vehicle to enable her to do so. In response to the woman who ascribes undue significance to external appearance, Shlomo Hamelech says in *Mishlei* (31:30), שקר החן והבל היופי אשה יראת ה' היא תתהלל - "Charm is false and beauty is trivial, the woman who has *Yiras Shomayim* is worthy of praise and admiration".

(d) Correct priorities are evident around the house: When a woman has the correct attitude, she will want her house to be tastefully decorated and aesthetically pleasing but with moderation so that a true *Yiddishe* atmosphere prevails. She may decide to hang up pictures of things that we *chareidim* admire, such as pictures of *Gedolei Yisroel*, a *Rebbe* learning with his pupil and so on. She considers *seforim* and their bookcases as an ornamentation of her home rather than an unpleasantness. They are given a place of honor in her home and adorn her best room rather than being relegated to a secondary room where their presence is not so readily noticed.

5. FIFTH OBJECTION- SHABBOS CLOTHES ARE TO BE SUPERIOR: The verse says, וקראת לשבת עונג לקדוש ה׳ מכובד - "You shall call Shabbos a delight; the holy day of *Hashem* honored" (*Yeshaya* 58:13). From this verse we learn the *mitzva* of *Kavod Shabbos* of which one of the main features is the *halacha* that לא יהא מלבושך של שבת כמלבושך של חול - "Your Shabbos clothes should not be the same as your weekday ones" (*Shabbos* 113b).

Since the function of changing clothes is to bestow honor on Shabbos, it is obvious that Shabbos garments must not only be different to those worn during the week, but also distinctly better (M.B. 262:5). By doing so, the person gives honor and prestige to this very special day. It is therefore incorrect to dress on weekdays to an unnecessarily high standard. With such weekday clothes the person's Shabbos clothes will hardly be better than the clothes he wears during the week, and they will therefore detract from the *Kavod* of Shabbos - see *Mekoros* 60:1-2.

6. SIXTH OBJECTION - COST INVOLVED IN SUCH CONDUCT: Such conduct results in the wife continually needing new outfits and dresses. This can put considerable strain on the family finances. The same, of course, applies to daughters who can also put a financial burden on their fathers. Often important issues are neglected, such as paying school and *shul* fees, because money has to be available to finance other unjustifiable needs (*Biur Halacha*. 529: s.v. *V'al tzamzam*).

Klal Yisroel has suffered greatly from the effect of women constantly nagging their husbands for more money so that they can buy all that their hearts desire. When the *Navi* Yeshaya states the reasons for the *galus*, he says, מלכם תדכאו את עמי וכו׳ ויאמר ה׳ יען כי גבהו בנות ציון וכו׳ - The *Malbim* translates these *p'sukim* as follows: "Their princes oppressed and swindled my people. This was caused by the haughtiness of the Jewish daughters whose appetite for fancy and ostentatious dress knew no limits" (*Yeshaya* 3:15). The *Malbim* explains that the princes stole and swindled because they were in desperate need of money. This in turn was caused by their haughty wives who strained and eventually consumed the financial assets of their husbands in pursuit of their ceaseless desires for fancy clothes and jewelry.

In *Shulchan Aruch* O.C. 529:1 it says ואל יצמצם בהוצאת יום טוב - "a person should not be sparing when it comes to Yom *Tov* expenses". On this the *Mishna Berura* writes in the *Biur Halacha*:- **"However, a person must be sparing with expenses of other days (*Tur*). The source of this is the *Gemara* (*Beitzah* 16a) which states, 'A person's sustenance is decided from one *Rosh Hashana* to the next' to which *Rashi* says, 'A person must therefore be careful with his expenditure, because if he overspends he will run short and he will be given no more than the fixed amount'.**

"This should serve as a strong censure in our times when regrettably people are very liberal with home expenses. They indulge in excesses and buy unnecessary luxuries. This misconduct causes many casualties. It eventually drives the person to theft or dishonesty and brings him discredit and shame. There are many causes for this ignominious behavior. However, the prime cause is that women do not foresee the consequences and therefore desire more and more. Praiseworthy is the husband who stands firm and does not fall prey to continuous persuasion. Rather, he insists on running his household according to his means" - see *Mekoros* 62:1-3.

7. SEVENTH OBJECTION - CONSIDERABLE WASTE OF MONEY: Even if someone is personally blessed with wealth, it is nevertheless wrong to set an unnecessarily high standard of dress, particularly as large amounts of money must inevitably be spent on numerous head-wear, outfits and dresses of the latest fashions and designs. Wasting money is an *issur* of בל תשחית - being wasteful. Many needy families could be helped and much Torah learning could be made possible if this money was not wasted on closets full of the latest fashions. Instead of thanking *Hashem* for the livelihood He gives, His kindness is repaid by infringing on *tznius* - one of the most cherished aspects of *Yiddishkeit*.

The numerical value of ממון (money) is 136, the same as that of סולם (a ladder). Money is like a ladder. With money a person can ascend to great heights, or descend to a world of trivialities. Spending money correctly can elevate a person to lofty heights of supporting Torah-learning and the furtherance of *kedusha*. Money becomes a ladder standing on the earth and reaching up to the heavens - סולם מוצב ארצה וראשו מגיע השמימה (*Breishis* 28:12). Conversely, money wrongly spent causes a person to fall from the loftiest heights to seek vanity and pursue a frivolous way of life. If we appreciate and remember this, we will spend our money sensibly and wisely, with farsightedness, and in accordance with the *Ratzon Hashem*.

8. EXCEPTIONALLY RICH-LOOKING, OSTENTATIOUS CLOTHES:

(a) Such clothes cause men to gaze at her: Dressing in exceptionally expensive, high-class clothes is contrary to the ways of *tznius*, if this is beyond the way women and girls generally dress in one's circle. By wearing an ostentatious outfit or coat, she attracts considerable attention to herself, as people are not used to seeing others dressed in this way. As has been mentioned before, attracting attention is irreconcilable with *tznius* which stands for refinement and self-effacement.

It is remarkable that when the wife of Potifera tried to entice Yosef to sin, one of the methods she used was to constantly change her clothes. The *Gemara* says (*Yuma* 35b), בגדים שלבשה לו שחרית לא לבשה לו ערבית בגדים שלבשה לו ערבית לא לבשה לו שחרית - "The clothes she wore (to impress him) in the morning she no longer wore in the evening. Those she wore in the evening she did not wear next morning." She knew that although she had so far not been successful in influencing Yosef, this could well change once she was wearing clothes that would really attract Yosef (or she would impress him by appearing in a large variety of colorful clothes, which can have an alluring effect similar to that of highly attractive clothes). With this in mind, she constantly changed the clothes she wore. Hence, we see the impact and enticement of exceptionally beautiful garments on the observer. They have this potential even if the wearer is far from harboring negative intentions.

(b) A man may not gaze at a woman's colorful garments: Even if those who are attracted by the appearance of the clothes gaze only at the clothes and not at the wearer herself, they will still have stumbled into an *issur* of *histaklus* (the *issur* of gazing at women) because the *issur* of *histaklus* applies even to gazing at the pretty garments of a woman. The *Halacha*, in fact, goes even further. A man may not gaze at a colorful dress of a woman he knows even when she is not wearing it, see E.H. 21:1 where the *Shulchan Aruch* writes, ואסור להסתכל בבגדי צבעונים של אשה שהוא מכירה אפילו אינם עליה שמא יבא להרהר בה. Therefore, if a woman wears a highly eye-catching garment, she will be a stumbling block to many.

(c) She teaches others a mode of conduct harmful to *tznius*: An additional problem with such clothes is that by allowing herself the liberty to dress very differently to everyone else, she "opens the door" for others to do the same. If some of those who copy her lack a feeling for *tznius*, they will buy themselves clothes that are not worn by others (the liberty they have learnt from her) and are also very unsatisfactory from the point of view of *tznius*. It is part of society's built-in security that people are directed to do what is right, at least in public, because they do not want to, or cannot afford to "step out of line". Once this principle is overturned, many serious wrongdoings and incorrect ways of dress will suddenly surface. The responsibility for this erosion will lie on the shoulders of the one who wore ostentatious clothes that were out of line with the usual ways of dress.

(d) The importance of preventing this type of misconduct: The *Gemara* (*Brachos* 20a) relates that *Rav Ada Bar Ahava* saw a woman dressed in an inappropriate coat. Thinking she was a Jewish woman who had the audacity to parade in public in such an item, thereby breaking the accepted boundaries of *tznius*, he went up to her and tore the coat off her. It later transpired that she was not Jewish and he was fined by the non-Jewish courts 400 *Zuz* for shaming the woman. He reacted by saying that the heavy fine was well worth while, since people would thereby hear of the incident and the desired lesson would be learnt.

The *Gemara* relates this incident to illustrate the intense feeling people had for *tznius*, and the way in which a great person who saw a harmful breach reacted firmly to prevent it spreading. *Rashi* explains that the garment concerned was not outrageous in size or style. Rather it was an exceptionally rich and ostentatious coat which was far beyond the normal type of garment worn in those times. Even such a garment warranted such a severe reaction as to rip the garment off the woman. (Others, however, explain that the garment was bright red - see 6:J:3 and 7:B:1).

9. DRESSING IN THE LATEST FASHIONS:

(a) Garments of the latest fashions are usually eye-catching: It has been explained (in 1:I:4 above) that the *issur* of בחוקותיהם לא תלכו - "adopting alien cultures" - does not apply to general clothes manufactured by non-Jewish designers. This must not be understood as a license to become "highly fashionable" and to persistently buy garments that fit the latest styles and trends. Such garments will often attract considerable attention to the woman or girl as others are not accustomed to this type of dress, and when that is the case the garment is wholly *untznius'dik*. Regrettably, this pursuit has a strong hold in our affluent society, and even some who dress *b'tznius* have been caught up in it. They insist that whatever they wear in public must be of the very latest fashion and style. This trend is all-encompassing and involves literally everything from hair accessories down to shoes - (see 1:I:6-10 above, where many of the pitfalls of being excessively fashionable are described) - see *Mekoros* 58:1-3.

(b) Preventing one's daughter slipping into fashion addiction: Insisting that all clothes are of the latest fashion often starts harmlessly by the wearer thinking how pretty the latest styles are, but develops within a short time into a habit or even an obsession. A triviality turns into a major issue that occupies the person's thoughts and their spare time. Parents must therefore guard their daughter from taking the first or second wrong step. If she has bought herself a type of item that no-one else in the community wears, this could well be a daring step in the direction of becoming hyper-modern. To prevent her slipping into this harmful style of life, they should encourage her to return it and change it for something appropriate. It is sometimes helpful to tell her that if necessary when changing it she may buy an outfit that is somewhat more expensive, as long as it is refined and respectable on her.

(c) Fashion preoccupation is a form of vanity: The dress or outfit of a woman and girl should certainly be of very good taste. It should be *b'cheint* so that she looks pleasant and graceful wearing it. There is, however, no need for her to insist that everything, from head to toe, resembles only the latest fashion magazines, with the consequence of possessing closets-full of unworn clothes. Wearing only the latest fashions is a pursuit of vanity as it usually stems from an urge to show off one's good looks, one's good taste or one's financial means. Insistence on this standard is wrong even for Shabbos clothes, and unequivocally wrong when it comes to weekday wear.

(d) Time, money and effort are wasted in the pursuit of fashions: Apart from the fact that wearing highly fashionable garments often arouses attention, the very effort involved in dressing at all times "to perfection" makes the person extremely clothes conscious and in danger of wearing clothes that are really not *tznius'dik*. If one considers the amount of energy and time involved in keeping up insistently with the very latest styles and trends, one must appreciate that this cannot but affect the girl detrimentally. It has been stated elsewhere that excessive fashion consciousness creates *nisyonos* (tests) and even paves the way for *pritzus* - see 1:I:7 above. This is obvious, because if the latest fashion involves a garment that does not meet the standards called for by *tznius*, she, who is allured and captivated by fashions, will find it hard to muster the strength to withstand the pressure.

(e) *Gedolei Yisroel* warn about the pursuit of fashions: The problem of fashions is certainly not a new one and *Gedolei Yisroel* constantly speak about the great harm it causes and the great dangers it presents - see 1:I:10 above. The following is a quote from the *sefer,*, *Chorev* by the staunch supporter of pure *Yiddishkeit*, Hagaon Harav Samson Raphael Hirsch *zt'l*, Chapter 67, **"The most beautiful ornament of woman is modesty and moral purity. This should also be apparent in her attire, in her demeanor. The purpose of your clothing should not be to make yourself noticeable, but modest covering. Your demeanor and glance should be modest. A married woman should not be seen with her hair uncovered. Not everything which "fashion" decrees is good, O youth and maiden! If your greatest treasure is precious to you, then listen to the call of the Torah, avoid everything which borders upon immorality, even if "fashion" has consecrated it a thousand times. Nothing unholy, nothing which can rob you of your holiness and purity, can be made holy and pure by "fashion". Let the coteries of the impure reject you, let them mock at you; that is better than that *Hashem*, who has summoned you to holiness, should reject you from His holy proximity".**

10. CLOSING COMMENT: The verse says in *Shir HaShirim* (2:14), הראיני את מראיך השמיעני את קולך - "Let me see your appearance; let me hear your voice". A *Gadol* remarked on this verse that *Hashem* pleads with the Jewish woman, "Let me see your refined and modest appearance; I will then gladly hear your *tefillos*". *Hashem Yisborach* is only too pleased to grant health and financial assistance to those who use these gifts for the benefit of Torah and *mitzvos*. Since the woman's outer appearance bears witness to her attitude to health and financial means, if they are as befits the *Bas Yisroel* she will find a kind and warm response to her *tefillos* and supplications - see 7:L:6 below.

B. BRIGHT RED AND HIGHLY CONSPICUOUS COLORS

1. THE ISSUR TO WEAR PROVOCATIVELY COLORED CLOTHES:

(a) Bright red is singled out by the *Rishonim* as provocative: The *Rishonim* and the later *Poskim* write that a woman must not wear a bright red garment in public, be it a blouse, jacket, cardigan, skirt, dress or coat (*Brachos* 20a - *Shach* Y.D. 178:3 - *Responsa Shevet HaLevi* 6:24:2). The following are the words of the *Rabbeinu Nosson ba'al Ha'Aruch* (one of the *Rishonim*) quoted in the *Gilyon* of *Brachos* 20a, בגד אדום כגון כרבלתא דתרנגולתא, שאין דרך בנות ישראל להתכסות בו, שהוא פריצות ומביא לידי עבירה - "A red garment, similar to the comb of a rooster, is not worn by Jewish girls because it attracts attention and can cause sin" - see *Mekoros* 63:1-17.

(b) Bright red was and still is an attention-seeking color: Bright red is an eye-catching color even nowadays when very bright fluorescent colors are available and are widely used. This can be seen from the fact that bright red is used extensively the world over on vehicles, structures and announcements that should be noticed by the public. For example, in most countries fire-engines, the "stop" lights on traffic lights, "braking" lights on cars and the warning lights of police cars and ambulances are bright red. Also, when a store is painted bright red it sticks out amongst all surrounding stores. Evidently, when something is this color it is conspicuous and causes people to look at it. Since bright red is a loud and exhibitionist color it is unsuitable for the clothes of a Jewish woman or girl for whom being unpretentious, refined and modest is part of the very essence of her personality.

(c) When only part of the garment is red: The *issur* applies when the whole or a large part of the garment is red - see *Mekoros* 63:17. Moreover, even if the red area covers only the minority of the garment but is large enough to be bright and eye-catching the garment should not be worn. However, if the cloth just has red stripes, the garment has a moderate red pattern on it, or the garment is made of checked material which has red squares within it the red is usually not eye-catching and the garment is therefore permitted - *see Malbushei Kavod,* page 24.

(d) The status of colors other than bright red: This and similar ways of dress are loud and attention-seeking, rendering them unfit for a *Bas Yisroel.* All very bright or fluorescent colors are included in this. The Jewish woman and girl is referred to as a *Bas Melachim*. Fittingly, her dress is regal, tasteful and refined. Once a girl has reached the age of six/seven she should not be dressed in bright red clothes or other brightly colored garments. However, under the age of six she is so small that her red clothes would not affect anyone - see *Mekoros* 1:8 and 63:18-20.

Maroon is a permitted color. It is brownish red and is certainly not a loud and bright color, even though it is part of the family of red (*Halichos Bas Yisroel* 7:3 in the name of Hagaon Harav Elyashiv *shlita.* See also *Responsa*

Shevet HaLevi 6:24:2). Dusky pink, deep apricot, plum and salmon are also all certainly permitted. However, fuchsia (a deep rich pink) is a very bright eye-catching color that should not be worn whether for a major garment such as a dress, outfit and coat or a minor item such as a *tiechel* - see 5:E:1 and *Mekoros* 63:26-28.

2. BRIGHTLY COLORED INDOOR WEAR: The *issur* applies to garments that the woman or girl would wear when going out of the house. If such garments are very brightly colored they should not be worn even indoors because the garments themselves are unrefined. There is however no *issur* in wearing distinctively indoor clothes such as an apron (or a housecoat in places where one does not step into the street with it) which are brightly colored, since the garment will not attract the attention of people who are not her immediate family - see *Mekoros* 63:21-25. It is, however, incorrect to open the door to a caller when dressed in a red indoor garment.

This will explain the bright red garments the *Eishes* Chayil made for all members of the family (*Mishlei* 31:21 - כל ביתה לבוש שנים) and the red garments Shaul *Hamelech* made for the wives of those who went to war on behalf of *Klal Yisroel* (*Shmuel* 2:1:24 - המלבשכם שני). There could, however, be an alternative explanation. It could be that these garments were worn even outdoors but only under some other protective garments.

3. GAUDILY DECORATED SWEATERS: In some places, sweaters and tee-shirts are available that are decorated with numerous large colored glass beads, gold studs, tinsel tassels and similar glittery items, to a point that they are quite spectacular. Such garments are exceedingly loud and far more captivating than the red clothes which *Chazal* forbade, as explained. Wearing this type of garment gives the impression that the person is begging to be noticed amongst other women. Incredible as it may sound, even some apparently *choshuveh* ladies have been caught up with this fashion and have appeared in public wearing these types of garments. All that can be said is - the amazing power of the *yetzer horah* at confusing and misleading people is quite astounding. The more we realize this, the more capable we are of guarding ourselves from his tactics.

Yeshaya HaNavi chastises the Jewish woman of his time for her lack of *tznius*. Amongst the main points he complains about is the effort she made to be in the spotlight, to be noticed and observed by all. He complains, הלוך וטפוף תלכנה - "These females stride along with their height artificially increased" (*Yeshaya* 3:16). The *Midrash* (*Eichah* 4:18) explains this in two ways. A tall woman would engage two shorter women to walk on either side of her. She did so in order to exhibit her height and ensure that everyone noticed it. Alternatively, she would wear shoes with abnormally thick soles and heels to increase her height - see 6:O:2 above. Height was regarded as a form of beauty and these women did whatever they could to ensure that their height would be as conspicuous and as noticeable as possible. This type of conduct is such a serious departure from modesty that the *Navi* attributes much of *Klal Yisroel's* downfall to it - see *Mekoros* 2:1-4.

Wearing tee-shirts (even if long sleeved and with Kosher necklines) and sweaters that have loud, gaudy colors and large immodest displays is in line with the conduct of the women mentioned in *Yeshaya*. Can wearing such garments be reconciled with the character of *tznius* and the refinement expected of the Jewish woman and girl? Would walking around in such items not render the wearer a prime target for the scathing rebuke of the *Navi*?

4. COLOR IS A BLESSING WHEN USED CORRECTLY: Color is a heaven-sent gift that we are surrounded with all the time. It adds considerably to the delights *Hashem* has put into the world. Without it, everything would just be different shades of a monotonous single color.

Hashem has handed color to the world in a most wonderfully balanced way. On the one hand, wherever we look outdoors we see different shades of green - a placid and tranquil color. Grass, vegetation and leaves of almost all trees are green. To a degree, brown is visible on the tree trunks and autumn leaves. Finally, the sky is a calm light blue. All three colors, green, brown and light blue are tranquil and mild, imparting peace of mind to the person who sees them. As a result of this, when a person ventures out of his house in a rural area he is in a peaceful environment and enveloped in a sea of serenity.

On the other hand, *Hashem* gave certain creatures and plants a striking range of color for specific purposes. *Chazal* state (*Midrash Tanchuma, Tazria* 2; *and Breishis Rabba* 7:4) that the feathers of the peacock have 365 shades of different colors, as many as the days in a solar year. With this display of color the bird's appearance is pleasing to its partner. Similarly, colorful flowers are to decorate the inner home environment of people. See *Vayikra Rabba* 23:6 where *Chazal* say, מה שושנה זו עולה על שולחן מלכים - "The rose is brought onto the table of Royalty". A little further on the *Midrash* says, שושנה זו מתוקנת לשבתות לימים טובים - "The rose exists to beautify the Shabbos and *Yom Tov*". Moreover, some flowers have medicinal properties and their bright colors serve to direct people to them - (see *S'forno* and *Ohr HaChayim, Breishis* 30:14).

From all this we learn that color should be used in a balanced and fitting manner; calm and peaceful colors for public outdoor wear and a wider variety of color for the private domain of our homes. We pray that Hashem allow us to use the gift of color to decorate our homes and ourselves with taste and finesse to develop a warm and comfortable setting for the family we endeavor to bring up *b'derech haTorah VeHayirah* - see 1:R:6 above.

5. A BAS YISROEL IS A GEM, REQUIRING A PERFECT SETTING: The verse in *Tehillim* (45:14) says, כל כבודה בת מלך פנימה ממשבצות זהב לבושה - "All the glory of the princess is within; her garments are like the settings of a gold ring". Gold is a precious but soft metal. When a setting is formed on a gold ring, it is essential that all parts of the setting are made perfectly, to ensure that the diamond is totally secure within it. The number of clasps, their length and their shape are all critical factors in guaranteeing the safety of the diamond. When set, the diamond blends beautifully with its gold surroundings. Together they become a superb piece of jewelry.

In this analogy, the Jewish woman's *tznius* is compared to a precious diamond, which can *chas v'shalom* be lost without proper care. For garments to offer proper and reliable protection, it is essential that they are of the right length and suitable design. When her finely designed garments have a pleasant and refined color, they greatly enhance the woman's gracious appearance. (Developed from commentary in ArtScroll Tehillim).

6. VERY COLORFUL CLOTHES WORN BY PEOPLE FROM ORIENT: In Oriental countries, Orthodox Jewish women dress in much more colorful clothes than those worn by Orthodox women in Western countries. Similarly, they adorn themselves with much more jewelry than others are used to. In the Orient itself, there is nothing wrong in wearing such colorful clothes or such an amount of jewelry because they are worn by everyone, even the most *tznius'dik* women, and are therefore considered refined. However, if a woman from the Orient lives in a town which is totally or predominantly Western, it would be wrong for her to go about in very colorful dress or for her to send her girls to school dressed in such clothes, because according to Western Orthodox Jewish standards such garments are ostentatious and unsuitable - see 1:G:2. She may, however, wear them at home among the family circle because for Oriental people these are usual everyday garments and as such would be considered refined.

C. COARSE GARMENTS - EXTREME CASUAL WEAR

1. UNSUITABLE FOR A CONSCIENTIOUS AND REFINED PERSON: It has already been stated in 1:A:4(c) that coarse garments and extreme casual wear are unsuitable for Jewish people in general and for Jewish women in particular. Only basic reasons were given, whilst here the subject is dealt with from a much wider perspective and with many important applications. The following are reasons why coarse garments are unfit for a *Bas Yisroel*:

(a) Reason one - Refined dress prevents mingling in wrong society: A coarse garment is not the type of dress that befits a Jewish girl. A *Bas Yisroel* with *Yiras Shomayim* is constantly on guard against assaults on her purity, whilst wearing coarse garments is related to a free, "I don't care" Bohemian way of life, which is very much in contrast with the *Bas Yisroel's* style of life. Being constantly cautious and wary prevents her befriending people who have low morals and from going to places where *pritzus* prevails - that are both very harmful to an impressionable young person - see 1:A:4(c).

Therefore, skirts and jackets that are made of very coarse material or that have coarse bulky seams, simply do not suit her. Similarly, heavyweight (stonewash) denim, which is a coarse denim with a faded pale blue appearance, that looks even worse in the hem and seam areas, is unfit for the clothes of men and all the more for the clothes of women and girls. [In some specially refined circles women and girls do not wear any type of denim although it is hard-wearing and practical because it is related by name and basic appearance to the rough types of denim which stand for uncivilized and outlandish styles of life. They do not wear denim skirts even when the skirts are quite different from those worn by the lower classes, being dark colored rather than a light faded blue, and sewn with unobtrusive stitches instead of the usual prominent and coarse stitches]. See *Mekoros* 59:4-7.

(b) Reason two - Self-respect calls for respectable manner of dress: Moreover, coarse clothes demonstrate a distinct lack of self-esteem and self-respect. It is the way the youth likes to dress nowadays and is in line with their lifestyle which is likewise slipshod and untidy. A *Bas Yisroel*, in contrast, is particular about her dress and the dignity of her appearance, in line with her neat and dignified style of life. She is aware of the significance of the *Bas Yisroel* and her obligation to ensure that her qualities are properly preserved. In association with *tznius*, the Jewish woman is referred to as a princess (כל כבודה בת מלך פנימה - *Tehillim* 45:14). This is to indicate that *tznius* requires that the Jewish woman is fully aware of her royal status.

A person with refinement and self-respect feels uncomfortable when dressed in clothes that are coarse and suited to the lowest type of person. We are taught by *Chazal* to safeguard our own dignity and refrain from doing things that are repulsive (בל תשקצו) or things that cause embarrassment or emotional discomfort, because *Yiras Shomayim* and good *midos* can only be cultivated in a setting of refinement and sensitivity (*Brachos* 19b).

The shawl worn by a *Talmid Chacham* is called a סודר. *Chazal* say (*Shabbos* 77b) that this word is an abbreviation of the words סוד ה' ליראיו - "The secrets of *Hashem* are known to *Yirei Hashem*" (*Tehillim* 25:14). Rabbeinu Shmuel Eidelish *zt'l* in his commentary *Maharsha* explains this saying with the following words:- בגדי אדם מרמזים על מדותיו של אדם ובמעלות המדות היא היראה וכו' - "A person's clothes portray his *midos*. Since *Yiras Hashem* is one of the greatest *midos,* it is natural that the garments of a *Talmid Chacham* represent the trait of *Yiras Hashem*". The garment projects such an image of virtue and integrity, that an observer would naturally feel that *Hashem* can trust this person with His most sensitive secrets. Hence, the garment worn by the true *Talmid Chacham* stands for סוד ה' ליראיו - "The secrets of *Hashem* are known to *Yirei Hashem*".

This offers a perfect explanation as to why present day youth wear uncivilized looking tee-shirts sporting huge pictures and slogans, bedraggled, torn, and thread-bare jeans, and the like. As stated, clothes represent the *midos* of a person. Since these people are empty, suffer from internal disarray and are emotionally torn asunder from within, this is powerfully reflected and portrayed on their outer garments. In contrast, the more life is fulfilled and tranquil, the more this shows in the respectability and quality of the clothes.

(c) Reason three - If no self-respect, in greater danger of sinning: A person without self-respect is far more liable to sin than someone who possesses a healthy measure of respectability. This fact is high-lighted by the ruling of *Chazal*, האוכל בשוק פסול לעדות - "He who eats in a public market place is disqualified from testifying in court" (*Kiddushin* 40b). This *halacha* is recorded by the *Rambam* (*Hilchos Eidus* 11:5) with the words שהבזויים פסולים לעדות - "The despicable are disqualified from testifying". Since the person lacks basic self-respect his testimony is not to be trusted. In *'Mishnas*

Reb Aharon' Vol 1 page 157-158, Maran Hagaon Harav Aharon Kotler *zt'l* explains the justification of this *halacha:-*

"If a respectable person has an urge to give false evidence for some sort of gain, his conscience would prevent him from doing so. He will reason to himself, 'How can I lower myself to behave like a common criminal in such a contemptuous manner?' This reflection will occur whenever the person possesses dignity and self-respect. However, if he has no self-respect, this powerful and essential source of self-discipline and restraint will be missing and he is liable to be dishonest to secure a gain. He therefore cannot be trusted to bear witness, particularly not against a second person".

This axiom applies to all spheres, because a person who has no self-respect is liable to fall into any type of sin or wrongdoing. Moreover, when the lack of self-respect is displayed in clothing it is particularly conducive to a lack of *tznius* in clothing and related issues.

(d) Reason four - Garments affect person's spiritual standard: It should be noted that in the Jewish way of thinking, clothes, both for men or for women, should be designed to give dignity and respectability to their wearer. The *Gemara* (*Shabbos* 113a) relates that ר׳ יוחנן קרי למאניה מכבדותי - "Rabbi Yochanan referred to his clothes as articles of honor" because they brought him honor and dignity. Similarly, *Chazal* say כבודו של אדם בגדו - "The prestige of a person depends on his garb" (*Shemos Rabba* 18:5). Evidently, the inner person is deeply affected by the person's outer manner of dress - see 1:I:11 above. Therefore, clothes that are coarse, which are degrading and ignoble, are unfit to be worn by anyone and particularly by women. When those who do not at first realize the effect clothes have on a person adopt finesse of dress and conduct, they quickly realize that their personalities are improving as a result of their better manner of dress.

The *Shloh Hakadosh* (*Shar Ha'Osios* 9) writes, המלבושים לבוש הגוף והגוף לבוש הנפש. ובטהרת המלבושים יעורר טהרת הגוף, ובטהרת הגוף תעורר טהרת הנפש - "Garments are the clothes of the body, and the body, the clothes of the soul. Unsullied clothes lead to an unsullied body and an unsullied body leads to an unsullied soul". This beautiful quote speaks for itself as to the importance of respectable clothes.

(e) Convincing girls that coarse garments are inappropriate: Some girls and young women cannot see anything wrong with coarse forms of dress. They should be asked how they would feel if the wife of a *Rav* or *Rosh Yeshiva* wore these clothes. They will probably concede that for such special people these clothes are not fitting. Following this response, one should explain to the girl or young woman that she too is a very special person, and that she too has the potential to become an outstanding individual in *Klal Yisroel*. It is therefore unfitting for her to wear these clothes. The verse עוז והדר לבושה - "She dresses in clothes of strength and regality" (*Mishlei* 31:25) describes the attire of the *Bas Yisrael* as anything but casual and improper.

(f) *Umos ha'olam* concede that casual wear projects a low image: It is interesting to note that at times even the *umos ha'olam* do not allow young women to dress in casual dress. For example, stewardesses on aircraft of many high-class airlines and attendants in some high-class stores dress in a very respectable manner. Their hair is short or neatly tied back, their necklines are usually close to "Kosher", they do not wear denim skirts and they do not sport long dangling earrings etc. These better class airlines and prestigious firms want the young women who represent them to project a highly respectable image. They know that casual dress is cheap and incompatible with the image they seek.

Our daughters are *Bnos Melachim* at all times. They are stewardesses not just during a five hour flight when they are in the eye of the public but for twenty four hours a day, day in day out. Their royal status is authentic and real. As they are *Bnos Melachim*, casual dress is cheap and unfitting for them. Instead it behooves them to dress in a *b'kavod* manner even in the sanctuaries of their homes.

(g) The "honor of a *Bas Melachim*" is not a girl's private property: Even if a *Bas Melachim* is prepared to forgo the prestige her special status bestows upon her, she remains obliged to maintain her reputable image. Just as a king cannot forgo the honor of his high office, מלך שמחל על כבודו אין כבודו מחול (*Kesubos* 17a) because the honor of his high office is a requirement of the Jewish people, so too, a *Bas Melachim* must maintain her dignity and royalty of dress for the sake of the rest of *Klal Yisroel*. Also, it is detrimental for her personal self-image to dress in a distinctively low manner of dress in common with the simplest of people. This in turn can cause a serious erosion in her standard of *tznius*, as explained.

When the *Rambam* describes the conduct of a *Talmid Chacham* he first writes, צניעות גדולה נוהגים תלמידי חכמים בעצמן - "*Talmidei chachamim* conduct themselves with very considerable *tznius*". He then goes on to say, ולא ילבש לא מלבוש מלכים כגון בגדי זהב וארגמן שהכל מסתכלין בהן, ולא מלבוש עניים שהוא מבזה את לובשיו, אלא בגדים בינונים נאים - this means:- "He should not wear clothes worn by royalty such as clothes made of gold or purple as they would cause people to look at him. He should also not wear the undignified clothes of the poor as they shame their wearer and project him in a bad image. Rather he should wear standard clothes that are pleasant-looking" (*Rambam Hilchos Deios* 5:9). Here we have the effect of extreme casual wear spelled out clearly. Accordingly, if a woman or girl dresses in an undignified manner she does an injustice to the status of the Jewish daughter.

(h) Streaks of casual wear that are found even in formal clothes: It is similarly most unrefined and even repulsive to wear "extreme casual wear" such as slouches (known in the UK as 'leg warmers'). These are thick thigh-highs which do not sit firmly on the leg. They therefore wrinkle up and hang limply on the legs giving the wearer a bedraggled look. Such unbecoming wear should neither be worn alone nor on top of tights (except when playing tennis or some other sport in a secluded place).

Likewise, it is unfitting for the zipper on a skirt to be uncovered and fully visible. A zipper is not displayed on a man's trousers. Why should a distinction be made and it be allowed to be displayed on a skirt? A zipper is to enable the garment to be fastened or removed, and it is most undignified to display this facility for everyone to see. Since zippers are usually covered or at least partially hidden, elementary refinement calls for them to be concealed as far as possible. Buttons on a skirt do not have this stigma because buttons are not usually covered. Furthermore, they often serve also as a type of an ornament for a garment and therefore have a dual function. There is therefore nothing wrong in displaying buttons on a skirt. (For a similar sentiment see *Peleh Yoetz*, under title "*tznius*") - see *Mekoros* 59:5.

2. LARGE SCRIPT, HEART ETC. - COARSE AND IMPROPER:

(a) Large letters and pictures: It is unfitting for a *Bas Yisroel* to wear a sweater that has large letters or numbers printed on it, whether on the front or the back. It is irrelevant whether the letters make up words or are just abbreviations. The same applies when a large picture of a teddy-bear (which is childish and degrading for an adult) or something similar is embroidered onto a sweater. Such sweaters are unrefined, to say the least, and are not the type of garment an older girl who appreciates her true worth would wear.

(b) A large heart: Worst of all is a garment with the design of a large heart right across the front or back of the garment, or a medium-sized heart with an arrow crossing through it, which are symbols of *pritzus* of the *umos ha'olam*. These represent an attitude and way of life that is diametrically opposed to all that *kedushas Yisroel* stands for. Also, to wear such a garment would be a transgression of the *issur* of בחוקותיהם לא תלכו since whatever is made to advocate *pritzus* is forbidden under this *issur* - See 1:H:6-9. Even if the wearer is totally indifferent to the emblem and has bought the garment only because no other garment of the right size and color was available in the stores, it is still wrong to wear a garment which, due to the design that is on it, is an embodiment of *pritzus* - see *Mekoros* 5.

(c) A bright red heart: Similarly, prominent bright-red hearts embroidered or printed onto a sweater or tee-shirt are *pritzus'dik* designs, that belong to the culture or lack of culture of the *umos ha'olam*. This applies even if the heart is just the size of a small apple. As above, it is unfitting for Jewish women and girls to sport such hearts on their garments even though they disassociate themselves from all that they stand for. A *tznua* keeps away from that which belongs to the world of *tumah* and *pritzus*, so as not to be affected by it, and so as not to give the impression of giving it approval in any way. These emblems are far more disturbing and distasteful on the outfit of an adult girl. However, they should not appear even on the dress of a young girl so that she knows not to wear them once she is an adolescent.

(d) Hearts in other colors: Hearts in colors other than red, and particularly those that are of a similar color to their background and do not stand out, are not forbidden. They are not made to symbolize anything and are just as a harmless design. Similarly, a pendant and small earrings in the shape of hearts cannot be considered as unrefined items and as such are not forbidden. It must, however, be noted that they are not to everyone's taste, as some find all heart-shapes items unrefined (being of the same basic design as those that stand for *pritzus*). If a daughter knows her father disapproves of them or if local *frum* people disapprove of them, they should not be worn.

Feelings of *eidelkeit* and how far to distance oneself from *pritzus,* differ greatly in different *kehillos.* What could be fine to people of one background might be very disturbing to others from a different background.

(e) To us, the heart is devoted to the service of *Hashem*: The heart is the center of a person's emotions and passions. Those who have not merited to be in the league of the 'servants of *Hashem*' are carried away by their emotions and passions and this they advertise with the large hearts that they paint on their garments. We pray to *Hashem* that He purify our hearts that we understand to direct our emotions and passions as He wishes them to be. Dovid Hamelech says, לב טהור ברא לי אלוקים ורוח נכון חדש בקרבי - "*Hashem* create a pure heart for me; let this lead to the upsurge of a new spirit within me" (*Tehillim* 51:12). We too, beg that we be granted a pure heart that leads to a new spirit of *tahara* and *tznius*, a spirit in which our emotions and passions are fully directed to the will of *Hashem*.

3. DRESSING DRABLY IS INCORRECT FOR MANY REASONS: There are women who dress drably and somberly, and take almost no interest in their appearance. Some will even do so because of a misplaced feeling of *tznius* and modesty. For example, they do not care how slip-shod their *sheitel* looks and will leave their homes with their *sheitels* totally uncombed and unkempt. Moreover, they wear colorless, styleless or drab dresses that have no *chein* whatsoever. Such ways of dress are distressing to most women who admire good taste and aesthetic garb, and as a minimum they expect a woman to have a pleasing appearance.

Dressing shabbily is not only distressing and unsociable, but there are some very positive reasons why women and girls should look pleasing and well dressed at all times. They are as follows:-

(a) A woman should look *b'cheint* to her husband: *Hashem* gave women a natural *chein* and implanted within them an instinctive desire to look pretty. This is for very understandable reasons. The appearance of a girl is a significant help in enabling her to find a husband with whom she can establish a family. Also, the appearance of a wife has a major impact on the *shalom bayis* which is the mainstay of the home. It prevents the husband looking for satisfaction elsewhere and is therefore a major buttress to *kedushas Yisroel*. For this reason the *Gemara* (*Kesubos* 17a) records that at a wedding in *Eretz Yisroel* verses were sang to the *chasan* in which he was told in no uncertain terms that his *kallah* was good-looking and very *b'cheint* - the actual wording they would use is recorded in 7:M:2 below. See 1:R above where this point has already been expounded upon.

Finding *chein* in the eyes of her husband is of such importance, that in cases when the natural appearance of a woman might not have been conducive to "finding *chein*", *Hashem* in His kindness ensured that the husband nevertheless sees *chein* in her. *Chazal* say, חן אשה על בעלה - "A husband discerns and sees a charm in his wife" (*Sotah* 47a - *see Rashi*). Since her appearance is of such importance, it is her responsibility to consolidate and enhance this *chein* by caring about her appearance and by being meticulous about the types of clothes she wears. The extent of this issue can be learned from *Kesubos* 71b *Rashi* s.v. *Bigdei Tzivonim*. *Rashi* writes there that for a woman to dress drably is גנאי ובזיון הוא לה ומתגנה על בעלה - "To dress in a drab manner is unworthy and shameful for her. Also, it will make her distasteful to her husband".

(b) *B'cheint* dress fosters *Shalom Bayis*: The pleasant appearance of a wife helps create the harmonious atmosphere that exists in the home of *shomrei* Torah *umitzvos*, since, when a woman looks after her appearance, her husband becomes aware how much his wife cares for his feelings. The verse says in *Eishes Chayil*, מרבדים עשתה לה שש וארגמן לבושה - "She made tasteful divan covers for herself; her garments are of fine linen and purple wool" (*Mishlei* 31:22). Amidst the many praises expressed in these beautiful verses about the *Eishes Chayil* she is commended for manufacturing good-looking divan covers for her home, and colorful and aesthetic garments for herself. It is a great compliment to her that her home looks attractive and inviting, and that her clothes are cheerful and of quality. Being particular that her dress and her home are welcoming to her husband befits her reputation as an *Eishes Chayil.*

It is noteworthy that this verse is followed by a verse stating that her husband is a *Talmid Chacham* of repute (נודע בשערים בעלה). Caring about her appearance brings happiness and contentment to her home and this in turn is conducive to total devotion to *limud haTorah*. (See 1:R above, where this is explained in much greater detail).

(c) For the sake of *tznius* it is essential that a woman looks *b'cheint*: Apart from the reasons for not dressing drably given so far, to dress in such a way is distinctly counter-productive to *tznius*. It discourages others from the very ideals of *tznius*. Those who need encouragement to improve in *tznius*, see in dreary and shabby forms of dress a confirmation of what their *yetzer horah* has long been telling them - "dressing with *tznius* means dressing in a dismal manner and looking like a drudge". We must be on guard neither to justify the untrue arguments of the *yetzer horah* nor to supply him with ammunition or evidence.

In contrast, if a woman dresses gracefully and with true *chein*, she disarms the *yetzer horah* with her very way of dress and proves him utterly wrong. She, and others who dress like her, have the *zechus* of spreading and encouraging *tznius* in *Klal Yisroel*.

D. OPENING A DOOR WHEN NOT PROPERLY DRESSED

1. THE DANGER OF OVERSIGHTS: When opening the door early in the morning to a caller, a woman might not yet be fully dressed. Similarly, if she has a guest in the house, she may be seen by him during the early hours of the morning when she is attending to the children but has not yet had a chance to dress properly. The same applies when staying in a hotel; a woman may come down to fetch an early morning coffee before she is properly dressed. It is important that the laws of *tznius* are kept in such semi-domestic situations as it is forbidden for a woman to expose areas which should be covered even if she can only be seen by one or two individuals.

Before leaving her house to go shopping, a woman carefully checks herself and makes sure that she is perfectly dressed. She even looks into a mirror to check her appearance and to ensure that no hair hangs out of her *sheitel* or other type of hair-covering. However, when answering the door to a caller, a woman is in a hurry since she does not want to keep the caller waiting or cause the caller to leave thinking no one is in. She therefore feels obliged to compromise on her standard of dress, even though she knows it is not ideal. There is a danger that in her hurry she will omit elementary *tznius* requirements. The caller can wait a minute but the *issur* of having appeared in non-*tznius'dik* attire is irrevocable. If one is afraid that the caller will leave, shouting, "I'm coming" or "Just a minute!" will help to keep the person there.

This subject is of such importance that the previous *Rosh Yeshiva* of Lakewood N.J. Hagaon Harav Shneur Kotler *zt'l* and *lehavdil* the *Mashgiach* of Lakewood Yeshiva, Hagaon Harav Nosson Wachtfogel *shlita* mentioned this point specifically in a circular bearing their signatures that was distributed during *Aseres Yemei Teshuva 5742*. The wording is as follows, "A woman answering the door of her home is responsible that her appearance be fitting even for the presence of a stranger".

2. POINTS ABOUT WHICH TO BE CAREFUL: The following short checklist is presented as a guide to what must not be overlooked:-

(a) Head-covering: She must ensure that her head-covering covers her hair properly without allowing hair to show at the front, sides or back. On the spur of the moment, it may be simplest to pull it further down than may be necessary to ensure that the hair is properly covered.

(b) Wearing a robe: She must be wearing a robe (dressing gown) before opening the door because she must never be seen by others in her true nightclothes, irrespective of how non-see-through they may be and how well they cover her body. There is little difference between nightclothes and inner-clothes about which the *Poskim* state that they may not be visible at all (see 6:D:1 above). She must ensure that the robe is closed so as not to display her night clothes.

(This does not refer to the far outer edges of the nightclothes which may be seen beyond the sleeves and length of the robe she is wearing. Since this excess covers areas of the body which do not require covering it is totally different to inner-clothes).

(c) Closing the top button: The neck opening of the robe must be closed so that the collar-bones and shoulder are not visible. If there is a button, it should be used. Otherwise the collar should be turned up so that the area is closed. Due to this point, it is essential to procure a robe that can be closed at the upper front in one of the two ways mentioned.

(d) Length of robe: The robe she wears when she opens the front door should reach the ankles and thereby hide both the upper and lower sections of the legs which are at present uncovered (See *Responsa Minchas Yitzchak* 6:10). It is important to ensure that the buttons extend far down the garment since otherwise, with the slightest movement her uncovered legs or nightclothes will appear. This ankle length is required when she is not wearing tights. However, if she is wearing tights, it would be permissible to open the front door wearing a robe that covers her legs in the same way as a Kosher skirt.

Some practice an act of extra refinement and make a principle of opening the door only when the robe is ankle-long (irrespective of whether they are wearing tights). Firstly, this encloses the complete length of the nightgown. Secondly, since she is evidently not dressed at present, it is an act of *tznius* to compensate for this, by appearing only with a full length garment which gives maximum cover.

(e) The robe should be of the right material: A woman must possess a robe that is respectable enough to use for opening the door, or when she might be seen by a guest at home or in a hotel. Some robes or dressing gowns are made of thin cotton-like material and are more like nightgowns than robes. They are completely unsuitable, because whenever a woman appears in distinctive bedroom attire or that which closely resembles it, there is a severe lack of *tznius*.

(f) Footwear: She should wear slippers or other type of footwear so that she does not appear in front of a stranger in bare feet. She may appear in slippers although her feet are not completely covered by tights as they are when she goes out, because there is no set rule that a woman will not be seen in her own home with minimal foot wear. It would be incorrect to appear without any footwear at all because people do not generally walk around the house bare-footed.

3. EXTRA REFINEMENT - OPENING DOOR ONLY FULLY DRESSED: It must be put on record that some women would not answer the door when dressed in a robe even if all the precautions mentioned had been taken. They would likewise neither be seen within their house by a stranger who happens to be there nor would they emerge from their quarters in a hotel when in a robe. These women feel it is immodest to be seen in anything related to nightclothes (even if not bed-wear) and will therefore not answer the door until they are fully dressed. Their feeling is admirable and they should certainly follow the standard of *tznius* that they instinctively feel or that they saw in their mother's home. However, for those who do not practice this extra refinement, the guidelines mentioned above are the minimum.

4. FOLLOWING ONE'S INTUITIVE STRINGENCIES FOR TZNIUS: *Tznius* has minimum requirements but there is no maximum. The more refined and *eidel* the person is, the greater will be her feelings for modesty of dress and behavior. Elsewhere (in 1:C:5 above) the words of the *Chazon Ish zt'l* were recorded. He said that a woman should work lifelong on improving her *tznius* to greater and greater standards just as a man toils throughout his life at understanding Torah to greater and greater depths. As her instinct becomes stronger her tznius is expected to become even more refined. See *Bava Metziah* (83a) and commentary of the *Vilna Gaon, Mishlei* 2:20 that a *Tzadik* is obligated to conduct himself in a more stringent way than is ruled in *Shulchan Aruch* for most people.

Due to this, if a woman has an instinctive feeling that to do something or to dress in a certain garment is unrefined, she should follow her instinct and refrain from that action or from wearing that garment, even though *halachically* the action or garment is allowed. If she were to strictly follow the letter of the law and do things or wear things which cannot be reconciled with her innate feelings, she would thereby weaken and even impair the standard of *tznius* she has attained. It may even be that Kimchis had such an exceptionally refined sense of *tznius,* that she had a personal obligation to ensure that the beams of her house never saw her hair - see 1:B:1(b).

Correspondingly, the *Midrash* (*Bamidbar Rabba* 4:20) writes that Michal, daughter of Shaul Hamelech, informed her husband Dovid Hamelech about the outstanding *tznius* of her father's family. She illustrated it with the following fact, כל בית אבי היו צנועים וקדושים שלא נראה מהם לא עקב ולא גודל - "All members of my father's family were exceptional in their *tznius* and *kedusha* to the extent that neither heel nor large toe was visible at any time". With this she was saying that they wore long, loose garments almost down to the ground. As a result of this neither the heel, which is first to show on the back of the foot, nor the big toe, which is first to show on the front of the foot, were seen at any time. This was of course extreme *tznius* and far beyond the letter of the law. Nevertheless, since they had reached such sensitivity and refinement, it would have been wrong for them to uncover what they instinctively felt they had to cover.

Standards laid out in this *sefer,* are either minimum requirements or recommendations of improved refinement that a woman should strive for. There is, however, always place for greater *tznius,* provided it is genuine and not done to impress others (see 1:D:6) and is a pleasure to those who see it rather than something disturbing and unpleasant (see 1:M:3 and 7:C:3).

E. GOING OUT IN A ROBE

1. NIGHT-ROBES: The so-called openness and informality of the society in which we live has frayed and weakened the thin cords that bind us to the *Klal Yisroel* of old. For them, modesty was in the very air they breathed and part of their very existence. Today, it is a struggle to maintain even just a slight measure of *tznius* and natural Jewish refinement. As a result of this, one will find individuals doing things that would have been out of question until recent times. If these misdeeds are not stopped they will make further and further inroads into our society, as people quickly copy one another.

An example of this is a woman going from her house to a neighboring house or even across the road while dressed in a night-robe (known in England as a dressing gown). To "bring the home out to the street" is a form of *pritzus* since by doing so one is breaching the natural boundaries within which this garment is fit to be worn. Some have even taken the liberty to venture out to a nearby store while dressed in a full-length housecoat which is in effect a night-robe. Whoever sees this cannot but feel that this woman has just 'rolled out of bed' and 'popped out' to the store to purchase something.

This is totally unacceptable behavior. A night-robe is worn when a person is undressed and is ready to go to bed or has just come out of bed. A woman is simply "not dressed" when she wears such garb. If so, how can a woman appear in the street through which men pass with such an item? Is this not a serious lack of privacy and *tznius*? This misconduct has led individuals to go even a step further and stand at their front door or even go out (to see off their children on a school bus) while just in a nightgown (known in England as a nightdress or nighty). To do this is, of course, absolute *pritzus* and must be condemned in the strongest terms possible. This type of development is exactly what *Chazal* have taught us, עבירה גוררת עבירה - "one transgression leads to another" (*Avos* 4:2).

It may seem unnecessary to specify misdeeds that are so obviously wrong. However, in our times, people's attitudes have become so impaired that the only safe course to take is to state categorically when something is totally incorrect and to explain why this is so. Shlomo Hamelech in his wisdom said, עת לחשות ועת לדבר - "There is a time to be silent and a time to speak" (*Koheles* 3:7) - different times call for different reactions. Today, when people are so perplexed about the *emes* it is a "time to speak" about true *tznius* of dress and conduct, even though issues concerning *tznius* were treated until recently with the full privacy and confidentiality they deserve.

2. SHABBOS-ROBES: The above refers to night-robes which are bedroom-related clothes and there is therefore a serious lack of *tznius* in walking with them in the street. There are, however "Shabbos-robes" which are comfortable long robes that many women wear indoors throughout Shabbos to keep their true Shabbos clothes clean for special occasions. Shabbos-robes are usually much better quality garments than the night-robes referred to above, and many look quite different to them. They are more elaborately designed and are usually closed with a zipper that runs all the way up and closes the garment properly, rather than with snaps as is the case with night-robes. Also, Shabbos-robes usually have a proper Kosher neckline which covers the wearer well. It would therefore appear to be quite different than a night-robe and permissible. This is on condition that any slit the item may have, even if just below the knee, has been sewn up - see 6:J:1 above.

In spite of these advantages it is wrong to appear in public in some types of Shabbos-robes, as will be explained shortly. In fact, after extensive research, it seems that many have a subtle feeling that there is something wrong in going out to the street with some types of Shabbos-robe. However, not being able to define what is wrong with an article that covers the woman completely, they have themselves started walking out on Shabbos dressed in these robes. Hopefully, they will realize that the subtle feelings they were unable to define are in fact the very reasons mentioned below. *B'ezras Hashem*, as a result of these clarifications, they will desist from wearing unsuitable types of robes in public in the future. The points are as follows:-

Point one -

(a) If it has much in common with a night-robe, it is unfitting: If the Shabbos-robe looks very much like a night-robe as it is made of the same type of material and is shaped very similarly, it is unrefined and even distasteful to go out in the street dressed in it, as the garment shares a common name and basic characteristics with a night-robe. This should be felt by any person with a healthy perception of *tznius*. Furthermore, when someone outside the Orthodox Jewish community sees a woman walking in the street in this robe he automatically thinks that she is walking around in her bedroom wear. Can a way of dress that gives such an impression be Kosher and wearing it be an "honor for Shabbos"?

Point two -

(b) If highly decorated and could cause men to look, it is unfitting: Some Shabbos-robes are heavily embroidered with gold. Being on a rich velvet background they sometimes look exceptionally beautiful. As time goes on, fancier and even more expensive-looking Shabbos-robes appear. Some even have multiple studs and similar glistening decorations on them. As a result of this, these robes are very eye-catching, highly attractive and even captivating. Since, a man may not gaze at a woman or her pretty dress, these robes precipitate the transgression of the *issur* of *histaklus*. It has been mentioned (in 7:A:8) that it is *ossur* to gaze at a garment even when it is not being worn - all the more it is *ossur* to gaze at a dress when it is actually being worn. Such robes are therefore an obstacle to many.

For a woman to parade with such a highly embroidered item in front of men and *bachurim*, whether in a main street or a side street, could well involve the *issur* of *Lifnei iver* (the *issur* of causing others to stumble - see 4:B:1 above), as it incites men to gaze at her or her dress.

Point three -

(c) If made to have special feminine appeal, it is unfitting : Some of these robes are very feminine pieces of clothing, designed to find considerable appeal in the eyes of the husband. This is due to the bright color of the garment, the way in which it has been styled and its decorations and accessories. Dresses are worn when women are to mingle between people and as such they are of calm colors and are decorated in a moderate way, whilst these robes are personal, feminine garments and highly appealing. It is therefore unfiting for a woman to be seen dressed in such a robe outdoors.

It is likewise unfitting to wear a garment that is very feminine by nature or very decorative in the public areas of a hotel or holiday colony, since it will be in the presence of men other than the immediate family. People tend to relax both physically and spiritually once they are in a hotel or on vacation. The danger of *pritzus* in womens' dress is therefore particularly great in a hotel and similar situations. Some women consider themselves to be 'on show' when in a hotel. They therefore turn up with three or four outfits for a single Shabbos, whilst at home they would wear at the most two outfits on a single Shabbos. Walking around in a very feminine or highly decorative Shabbos-robe is just another example of the same phenomenon.

The praise, מה טובו אוהלך יעקב - "How beautiful are your tents Yaacov" (*Bamidbar* 24:11) was said because the entrances of their tents did not face each other, so that people would not look into one another's abode - (see 1:B:9 above). This was to prevent people seeing anything that had an element of privacy to it. Surely, a highly decorative feminine robe, has more than an element of privacy about it.

(d) Not to be misled by a misrepresentation of *Kavod* Shabbos: It is a ploy of the *yetzer horah* to create an aura of "*Kavod* Shabbos" around wearing in public an item which has the above mentioned faults, whilst in fact such items undermine the natural walls of *tznius* which protect both the Jewish people and the holiness of the day of Shabbos. We must be aware of this ruse and steel ourselves against him.

It is high time that we unmasked the *yetzer horah* of all the "great deeds" he does "in honor" of this or that *mitzva*. Once he recommends *shmoozing* during *davening* so that the *shul* is a "*heimishe*" place and a pleasure to go to. Another time he recommends that a Kosher Pizza shop is opened where boys and girls can meet until late into the night, all in order "to ensure that the youth eats Kosher". A third time he recommends *chasunas* be extremely elaborate and flamboyant affairs, for no reason other than to "honor *chasan* and *kallah* in a fitting manner". He is ever so holy and well meaning!!

He likewise goes out of his way to cater for "*Kavod* Shabbos". No amount of make-up or finery is too much for the great *mitzva* of honoring Shabbos. Similarly, in our case - he misleads the public into thinking that when these stunning robes are worn outdoors they add luster and splendor to the day of Shabbos. The truth is far from that. Since they are designed to make women look very beautiful, to display such an item in public detracts from the *kedusha* and *tahara* that are the hallmarks of Shabbos.

(e) Not to go out with Shabbos-robes where not yet customary: Shabbos-robes should not be worn in areas where they have so far not become the local custom. When only a few individuals wear these ankle-long garments, the general public are unaccustomed to seeing a woman in such garb and to them it seems that she is walking along the street in an elaborate night-robe and it is obviously immodest to appear in public in a garment which gives the impression of being bedroom wear. Also, experience has shown that many people turn that which could have been a refined item into a most unrefined and even *pritzus'dik* piece of clothing.

It is recommended that no type of robe is introduced, irrespective of whether it is made of velvet, cotton, polyester etc. because once this trend starts one type of item leads to the other and ultimately the serious immodest forms of Shabbos-robes will be worn. Therefore even those that look just like extra long housecoats rather than elaborate night-robes should not be introduced. Prevention is always a far safer policy that attempting to harness a process that has already been set into motion.

Apart from all that has been mentioned, there are *yerei'im* who are not in favor of going out in Shabbos-robes even when they would neither be confused with bedroom robes nor are they highly decorated or overly feminine. Since the robe is full length and completely loose, it "encloses" the woman rather than "dresses" her, in contrast to a dress or outfit which dresses her. They maintain that the observer sees her as an undressed person, just as he would consider her to be if he saw her wearing a night-robe which is likewise ankle length to cover and hide all that is unclothed. Viewed in this way, such a item is an infringement of her privacy and *tznius,* and unfit to be worn outdoors on Shabbos. Even if those who are very much used to it do not agree with this sentiment, it is nevertheless the way it is seen by those to whom it is not so common. This therefore underscores the recommendation that it should not be introduced into places where it is not commonly worn.

Note: The section on Shabbos-robes was written only after careful consideration. Knowing that in some circles women go out in the street and walk around in hotels in very luxurious Shabbos-robes, there is a possibility that some people will turn a blind eye to the compelling reasons that have been explained, and instead accuse the *sefer* of demanding unjustified *chumros*. As such, it would appear more sensible not to say anything about this subject. However, since silence can be interpreted as a form of consent, it was felt that the *emes* must be said. In this way those who look for true *tznius* will appreciate the great *emes* in what has been written, and will not be swayed by those who do differently.

Due to the subtle hard-to-define nature of this issue, the detrimental feelings that can be aroused by wearing this gown in public have been explained and clarified to a greater degree than has generally been done. Experience has shown that only by pin-pointing the hidden *tumah* of this and similar evasive issues can one hope to convince those who seek the *emes*.

F. MATERNITY WEAR

1. CLOSE-FITTING MATERNITY WEAR SHOULD NOT BE WORN: Mention must be made of an incredible lack of sensitivity that has found its way even into good homes. This refers to close-fitting or even semi-tight maternity wear which discloses the shape of the body. Such exposure should be unacceptable to any decent person and is a gross violation on *tznius*. This is compounded by the fact that everyone understands that an extended abdomen is unsightly, as *Chazal* say in *Nedarim* (66b). Displaying the shape of the body during pregnancy is therefore proof of a coarsening of the woman's sensitivities. We are warned in the Torah not to learn from the ways of the *nochrim* by following their civilization, culture and philosophies. Who would have thought that our sisters would admire the fashions and fads of the rest of the world to such an extent that they would follow them blindly into wearing garments that are abhorrent?

Regrettably, the view of many women has become so distorted that even when told how non-Jewish such garments are, they fail to see anything wrong in them. This demonstrates how far fashion magazines have affected the judgment and attitudes of women. ביישנות (bashfulness) is one of the three hallmarks of the Jewish people, whereas these clothes reflect the assertive and impudent character of the "modern woman".

Although it is self understood that the Jewish attitude concerning maternity wear is as has been stated, it is nevertheless bolstered and rendered irrefutable when it is seen spelt out explicitly in *Chazal* or in one of the *Rishonim*. The verse in *Shir HaShirim* (7:3), בטנך כערימת החטים סוגה בשושנים is explained by the *Ibn Ezra* (in his second elucidation) as referring to an expectant mother. Shlomo Hamelech says that during advanced pregnancy the abdomen is comparable to a mound of grain - narrow towards the top and broad further down. The *Ibn Ezra* then goes on to explain that the end of the verse describes how the expectant mother dresses, סוגה בשושנים - "the mound of grain is surrounded by a hedge of roses and is thereby disguised and protected from theft". So too, the expectant mother dons a broad garment that camouflages her shape, and shrouds it as far as possible. This in turn serves to protect her privacy and modesty.

2. BEING MINDFUL THAT CLOTHES WILL BECOME UNSUITABLE: In many cases a woman dons a maternity garment at an early stage of pregnancy when the garment looks fine on her. However, she inadvertently continues wearing it into later stages of pregnancy when it becomes more and more unsuitable. Women must be careful not to fall into this trap. They should change into appropriate garments as soon as the necessity arises. Let us not forget "oversights are no excuse!" We know that for an oversight that has led to *chillul* Shabbos a person brings a *korban chatos* - a *korban* that is so significant that it is *Kodshei Kodshim*. All this is because a person is held responsible for oversights, since if he had really cared and appreciated the gravity of the issue, the error would not have occurred.

3. THE IDEAL GARMENTS TO WEAR: The original one-piece garment which hung loosely over the whole front of the body and the present day two-piece outfit that has a loose hanging tent-like top, are both perfectly suitable. It is essential that the two-piece outfit is well made and allows for expansion without the garment going out of shape as a garment that is out of shape will not camouflage the person properly. Since tops must be loose they should not have a ribbed band as this will inevitably accentuate the figure as time goes on. If the top has a draw-string it can be tied during early pregnancy but be left undone (or extremely loose) during the latter months.

4. RECOMMENDATIONS TO THOSE WHO SELL MATERNITY WEAR: Those who sell maternity clothes to the Jewish public should not allow unsuitable garments to pass through their hands. Furthermore, when they sell a garment that is not fully expandable to a woman who is in early pregnancy, they should tell her that this garment will be suitable for the next few months but no longer. Such sales-people should realize that it is in their hands to redirect the current trend and to re-educate people to wear refined and tasteful maternity wear. The *zechus* of doing so is immeasurable.

5. IF NECESSARY, ONE SHOULD HAVE GARMENTS MADE: If a woman cannot buy maternity garments loose enough to mask the contours of the body, she should have them custom made. For *simchos*, many people go to dressmakers and have all types of outfits made. So too, with the dignity and respect of *Am Yisroel* and particularly the honor of *N'shei Yisroel* at stake, it is proper to go to the trouble and expense of having an appropriate garment made.

An expectant mother has much to be grateful for, considering how many people long for children, ה' ירחם עליהם. She also has much to pray for - that all goes well through to a healthy birth and that the child she bears becomes a true עבד ה'. It is therefore fitting that her demeanor reflects the very special qualities and virtues of the *Bas Yisroel*.

It should be noted that *Rabbeinu Bachya* writes (*Breishis* 34:1) that *tznius* is a *segula* to prevent miscarriages. The verse compares the children of a *tznua* (אשתך כגפן פוריה בירכתי ביתך) to the fruits of an olive (בניך כשתילי זיתים - *Tehillim* 128:3) and olives develop on the tree for a full nine months. This is to indicate that the children of the *tznua* will likewise develop a full nine months and not arrive prematurely. Children of a mother who is a *tznua* are special. They are so dear to *Hashem* that He offers His extra protection. Similarly, a person may be given children in the merit of *tznius* - see 10:A:5.

G. CHECKING FOR SHATNEZ

1. WEARING SHATNEZ CAUSES UNTOLD DAMAGE: One of the most important Torah precepts concerning clothes is the *issur* to wear *shatnez* - a garment that contains both wool and linen. Proportions are immaterial and the *issur min haTorah* of *shatnez* is transgressed even if just one thread of linen is used in a woolen garment. Although the intricacies of *hilchos shatnez* are not within the scope of this *sefer,*, nevertheless, in a *sefer,* that deals with the *Kashrus* of clothes it is appropriate to mention that garments must be tested to ensure that they are *shatnez* free (Y.D. 301:2).

The word שעטנז is a combination of the two words שטן עז, meaning that the wearer will be under pressure to sin by a powerful and mighty *yetzer horah* (*Rabbeinu Menachem Rikanti*, *Vayikra* 19:19). Hence, when a piece of clothing is Kosher it deserves the title עוז והדר since it represents strength and grace. In contrast, when a garment contains *shatnez* it is subject to the ignominious title of שטן עז, as it exerts an extremely negative influence over the person. Clearly, the *tumah* involved in this particular *issur* harms the person immensely and prevents him attaining any real standard of *Avodas Hashem*.

2. WHILE WEARING SHATNEZ, TEFILLOS ARE NOT ACCEPTED: The *sefer, Shalmei Tzibur* (*Dinei Netilas Yadayim Shacharis* No. 2.) writes that nothing prevents the acceptance of a person's *tefillos* more than wearing a garment that contains *shatnez* during *tefillos*, even if he is doing so inadvertently. In the *sefer, "Nes Hatzalah shel Yeshivas Mir"* Chapter 28, Rabbi Elchanan Yosef Hartzman records the following incident that happened during the years the *yeshiva* was located in Shanghai.

"On weekdays the students wore suits that they brought with them from Lithuania. However, for Shabbos and *Yom Tov* they were given new suits. One *Yom Kippur*, a student suddenly left the *Beis Hamidrash* in the middle of *davening* and returned shortly afterwards. To everyone's surprise he had changed into his weekday suit. When asked later why he had changed his suit, he answered that he found himself unable to *daven* with his usual *kavana* and *dveikus*. It occurred to him that his suit might have *shatnez* in it although it had been checked.

"He remembered that the *seforim* write that *shatnez* can prevent a person's *tefillos* from being accepted and presumably it can likewise stop the person *davening* properly. He therefore changed to his weekday clothes. To his great relief, from then on he *davened* much better. After *Yom Kippur* his Shabbos suit was checked carefully and *shatnez* was in fact found in a most unexpected and secluded place. It transpired that although the garment was previously checked the *shatnez* had escaped detection."

3. WHILE WEARING SHATNEZ, YESHUOS ARE IMPEDED: Apart from standing in the way of *midas harachmim*, wearing *shatnez* can actually cause a strengthening of *midas hadin* (strict judgment). The *Mekubalim* write that if certain *Malachim* of prosecution would combine forces they would level very forceful accusations against *Klal Yisroel*. However, *Hashem* in His mercy holds them apart so that they cannot combine forces. This kind intervention on the part of *Hashem* occurs when *Klal Yisroel* themselves keep apart what they have been commanded to keep unmixed. However, if they wear *shatnez* and mix together what should have been kept apart, *Hashem* likewise allows the negative *Malachim* to join forces - to the detriment of *Klal Yisroel* - See *Meam Loez*, *Vayikra* page 213 in the name of *Maharam Rikanti*.

The following incident happened to a *Kollel* man in Gateshead. When in London to raise funds for the *Kollel* in which he learns, he periodically visited a traditionally Orthodox couple and over the years became very friendly with them. This couple always kept Shabbos, *taharas hamishpacha* and *Kashrus* to the best of their ability, amongst other *mitzvos* about which they learned more and more as time went on. They had been married for six and a half years and had no children although they were very eager to have a family. They sought the best medical advice available but to no avail. The young woman poured out her heart to this *Kollel* man, weeping bitterly that they seemed to be destined to have no children. The *Kollel* man was very moved and on his return to Gateshead discussed the matter with a good friend.

After some thought, the latter recommended that the couple be encouraged to undertake an additional *mitzva* that they had presumably hitherto not kept, in the merit of which they might be blessed with a child. The *Kollel* man found it a good idea and after some consideration decided to suggest the *mitzva* of *shatnez*. The husband's immediate reaction was that he knew all about *shatnez*. He had even had his suits and coats tested for *shatnez* and they were perfectly Kosher. He was then asked if his wife's outfits and coats were tested. The husband reacted with surprise. They had been under the impression that this *mitzva* was only for men and did not apply to women.

On realizing their error, they took the wife's clothes to be tested and on inspection her coat was found to be full of *shatnez*. The *shatnez* was promptly removed and the garment rendered Kosher. This incident happened in mid-*Ellul* 5753. In *Tammuz* 5754, just nine months later, she gave birth to a healthy baby boy. The delight of the couple was indescribable and they are eternally grateful to *Hashem Yisborach* for having answered their *tefillos*.

Let us take this story to heart and appreciate the *kedusha* of a *mitzva* and the *tumah* generated by an *aveirah* even when transgressed inadvertently.

Note: So that no misunderstanding occurs as a result of this story, it must be stressed that the meaning of this story is as follows: It may be decreed on a couple (for a reason known to *Hashem*) that they must wait some years before their family begins. To this decree a clause is added that if a substantial *zechus* (merit) materializes it can override the decree. The *zechus* can be in the form of *tefilla*, *tzedaka*, *gemilus chasadim*, *limud haTorah*, the *bracha* of an outstanding *tzaddik* and the like. At this point *shatnez* comes in. Even if a merit is produced, nevertheless *shatnez* is such a powerful "obstruction" that it can stand in the way and prevent the salvation from coming. As soon as this "obstruction" is removed, the *zechus* comes into effect, enabling the *yeshuah* to materialize quickly.

4. A TZNUA DOES MITZVOS WITH FULL DEDICATION:

(a) A *tznua* does *mitzvos* without compromise: It is appropriate to mention that when *Chazal* refer to a person who is scrupulous about the *mitzva* of *shatnez* they call him a *tznua* - See *Mishna Klayim* 9:5. This is because *tznius* is a title given by *Chazal* to people who are deeply attached to *mitzvos* and fulfill them without half measures or compromise (*Bava Kama* 69a, *Mishna Dmai* 6:6). This is spelled out explicitly in the *Rambam*, *Pirush HaMishnayos Maaser Sheini* 5:1, where he writes, "*Tznuim* are people who are particular to do the *mitzvos* of the Torah properly, exactly as they are *halachically* required".

The person is given this title which stands for privacy because his whole being yearns to do the *Ratzon Hashem*. Since his secret innards are aglow with *Ahavas Hashem* (*Kochov MiYaacov*, *Haftora Balak, s.v. V'hatzneia*) he looks for opportunities to please and give pleasure to his Master. His first concern is, of course, to ensure that every *mitzva* he does is done properly and fully in accordance with the *halacha*. He is also involved in *mitzvos* and *ma'asim tovim* that are voluntary - beyond the letter of the law and beyond the call of duty.

(b) A *tznua* does *mitzvos* as privately as possible: When a *tznua* does *mitzvos* (between man and *Hashem*) or *chasadim* (between man and man) he does them as privately as possible (*Succah* 49b, *Rashi*, s.v. *Hotzoas*). With this he demonstrates that he performs the deeds with a *penimius* - they are born out of an appreciation for their importance and significance. Also, that his very being is attached to *Hashem Yisborach* and that he delights in doing what he knows gives pleasure to the *Ribbono Shel Olam*. He therefore shuns the praise he would get from others, feeling that such praise would only detract from his devotion to the will of *Hashem*.

(c) *Mitzvos* performed with *tznius* are done with greater *penimius*: Performing *mitzvos* and *chasadim* privately increases and consolidates the person's *penimius* even further, because a *mitzva* done with a pure motive causes a great attachment to *Hashem*. Hence the verse in the *Navi*, ומה ה׳ דורש ממך כי עם עשות משפט ואהבת חסד והצנע לכת את אלוקיך - "What does *Hashem* request of you? Just that you keep the *mitzvos* (*Redak*), that you love being kind and that you go with *Hashem* privately" (*Micha* 6:8). By doing *mitzvos* privately the person "goes with *Hashem*" and is deeply attached to Him.

(d) Even highly publicized *mitzvos* can be done with *tznius*: Even *mitzvos* and good deeds that must basically be done in public can in fact be done with a great deal of *tznius*. If the person secretly gives substantial financial support, or he does the *mitzvos* with deep inner feelings and very pure intentions and he keeps the financial aid and his feelings and intentions away from the eye of the public, he is performing these *mitzvos* with great privacy and *tznius*. This is what *Chazal* mean when they say (Succos 49b) on the verse just mentioned, והצנע לכת זה הוצאת המת והכנסת כלה - "Doing *mitzvos* privately applies when attending to the burial of the dead and when assisting engaged couples to get married". These are of course *mitzvos* that are naturally done in public. We are nevertheless commanded to do even these *mitzvos* with a deep privacy so that we walk privately with our Creator when performing any type of *mitzva*.

H. PERFUMES

1. THE SIGNIFICANCE OF SWEET SCENTS AND FRAGRANCES: Aromas and pleasant smells are greatly valued pleasures. *Chazal* established that a *bracha* should be said on fragrances, although smell does not nourish the body, because the *neshama* experiences great pleasure and elation from a pleasant scent (*Brachos* 43b). It is for this reason that *b'samim* is used during *Havdala*. The *neshama* feels deflated and is saddened with the departure of Shabbos. Inhaling the fragrance of *b'samim* revives the *neshama* and raises the person's spirits once again - (M.B. 297:2).

It is remarkable that there are almost as many *brachos* on *b'samim* as there are on all foods and drinks put together. There are five *brachos* on *b'samim*: *Borei atzei b'samim*, *Borei isvei b'samim*, *Shenasan reiach tov l'peiros*, *Borei shemen areiv* and *Borei minei b'samim*. On foods and drinks there are six *brachos*; *Hamotzi*, *Mezonos*, *Hagofen*, *Haeitz*, *Ho'adamah* and *Shehakol*. The fact that there is such a range of different *brachos* on fragrances demonstrates the inner significance of *b'samim* and the great benefit people derive from them.

2. PERFUMES ARE PRINCIPALLY FOR HOME USE:

(a) *Chazal* considered this an important requirement: In line with other fragrances, perfumes that are used only by women have been put into the world for a very beneficial purpose. Their main objective is in the context of *shalom bayis*; to ensure that the husband enjoys the presence and company of his wife. Just as a woman must dress pleasantly and appealingly for her husband to consolidate the affection they have for one another, so too, if necessary, it is appropriate for her to use perfume in this context, provided it is used in the right measure and is not over-applied.

When used in this way it is considered so important that *Ezra HaSofer* made an amendment in the framework of Rabbinical law that peddlers who sold perfumes should not be hindered from traveling from village to village to sell their goods. He ordered local *b'samim* vendors not to stop their traveling rivals from coming to their villages. He did so in order to ensure that an adequate variety would be available and that women could buy the type of scent they required (*Bava Basra* 22a, see *Rashi*).

(b) How scents were available to the women in the wilderness: On a similar note *Chazal* ask, "What perfume was available to the married women during the forty years they were in the wilderness?" - *Midrash Shir HaShirim* (4:14). To this the *Midrash* gives two answers each based on evidence from *p'sukim*. Rabbi Yochanan said it came up together with the water from the *be'er*, whilst Rabbi Avahu said it came down from heaven together with the *mon*. [This could mean that fragrant oils which were fluid perfume came up with the water from the *be'er* whilst sweet smelling spices which were solids descended together with the *mon* from heaven. See *Yoma* 75a where the *Gemara* states that the scent that came down with the *mon* required pounding to release the scent. Clearly, it was a dry type].

We see from this *Chazal*, that the outstanding *nissim* of the *be'er* and *mon* were used by *Hashem* as a supply point for something that the world associates with vanity. Evidently, when used correctly by servants of *Hashem*, perfume is related to anything but vanity. It is comparable to the mirrors which women used in the *midbar* to beautify themselves and were found fitting to be used as part of a holy vessel in the *Mishkan* - See 1:H:C(3) and 1:R:7 above.

(c) Scents used correctly are associated with *kedusha*: When a scent is used in the way intended by the Master Planner יתב״ש, it is to be considered a source of *kedusha*. It may even be fitting to apply the words uttered by Yitzchak Avinu about a sweet fragrance, in response to the fragrance that was in the room after Yaacov Avinu had made his entry. Yitzchak Avinu said, ראה ריח בני כריח השדה אשר בירכו ה׳ - "behold the scent of my son is as precious as the scent that is found in the field that *Hashem* blessed - *Gan Eden*" (see *Rashi*, *Breishis* 27:27).

3. OUTSIDE THE HOME, PERFUME MUST BE USED SPARINGLY:

(a) No more than mild scents should be used outside the house: As previously stated, the place for perfume is mainly in the home. Outside the home, perfume should be used very sparingly and carefully. Women and girls should use just mild scents or fresheners which have a pleasant effect on their most immediate environment but are not overly noticeable and certainly not alluring in any way. It should be noted that *Rashi* (*Yuma* 75a s.v. *Tachshitei*) writes concerning perfume, בשמים וכו׳ להיות ריחן ערב לבעליהן - "Scents that women use as a pleasure for their husbands". *Rashi* specially adds the last word לבעליהן - "their husbands", because as far as others are concerned scents are not for enjoyment, as mentioned previously - see *Mekoros* 64:1-4.

(b) The devastating power of misused fragrances: Regrettably, the quantity of perfume and the choice of scents used by some are attractive and even somewhat alluring. The harm and damage this does is indescribable. *Chazal* (*Shabbos* 62b) compare the overpowering effect that perfume can have to that of poison. Just as a person need ingest just a few drops of poison for it to have a devastating effect, so too, a few drops of perfume can have a detrimental effect on men that are nearby. Not that total immorality need *chas v'shalom* result, but it definitely arouses considerable attention and devastates *kedushas Yisroel*. Little wonder that Eisav's wife was called "Bosmas" (*Breishis* 36:3) - her very name stands for perfume. Apparently, she was the "personification of perfume" as one would expect of the low-life wife of a *rasha* such as Eisav.

(c) Girls used perfume to entice - sin caused *churban habayis*: The *Navi* Yeshaya (*Yeshaya* 3:16) castigated the Jewish girls of his time about their many iniquities. Amongst them he mentions that ברגליהם תעכסנה -

"With their steps they anger me". The *Gemara* (*Shabbos* 62b) explains that they had small soft containers of perfume concealed in their shoes. When they approached a group of men they would press their foot onto the container so that scent was released and the air around them was highly perfumed. This misdeed was termed by *Chazal* as "poisoning the environment". Doing this in order to arouse the interest of men was so utterly wrong and such a source of *tumah* that this, together with similar sins, became a contributory factor in the destruction of the *Beis Hamikdash* - the source of *kedusha* in *Klal Yisroel*.

Sadly, many women and girls do not realize that in Torah terms, when a woman misuses perfume it is as if she is distributing poison to her immediate surroundings. Those who within minutes of entering the office have filled the room with their scent, making everyone immediately and constantly aware of their presence, are in fact polluting the atmosphere. These may be harsh words but those who seek the *emes* must acknowledge that they are very much the truth.

(d) A man may not intentionally smell other women's fragrances: In addition to the above it must be mentioned that just as it is *ossur* for a man to gaze at the face or features of a woman, so it is *ossur* for him to intentionally smell her perfume. See E.H. 21:1 where the *Shulchan Aruch* writes, ואפילו להריח הבשמים שעליה אסור - "It is *ossur* even to smell the scent that is on a woman" just as it is *ossur* to look intently at her. In both cases, he is deriving a physical pleasure from *ervah* and as such these are forms of *znus* - "*znus* of the eye" and "*znus* of the nose" - See *Mesilas Yesharim* Chapter 11 who writes so explicitly - See also 9:C:1 and 9:C:8 below.

(e) He may not smell her fragrances even when they are not on her: The *Mishna Berura* 217:17 adds in the name of the *Taz* that it is even forbidden for a man to intentionally smell perfume that had been on a woman or girl he knows, but is not on her at present i.e. to smell a garment belonging to a woman or girl he knows, that has a distinct scent of perfume. [Some *Poskim* maintain that he may, however, smell a bottle of perfume belonging to her since what is in the bottle has never been on her body - *Aruch Hashulchan* Y.D. 195:23]. This is *ossur* just as he may not gaze at a pretty garment that belongs to a woman he knows even if she is not wearing it at present, as even this can arouse his interest in her - see 7:A:8 above.

If women would only appreciate what harm is done and what a stumbling block enticing scents can be for men, they would use only very sparing amounts of refined perfume when in public, as stated above.

4. SCENT THAT IS APPROPRIATE FOR JEWISH WOMEN TO USE: Women should endeavor to use only delicate and sensitive scents. Even if they intend using the perfume just inside their home, it is nevertheless preferable that types that are unrefined and alluring are not used. For the maintenance of "feelings and sentiments of *tznius*" a person should at all times do what is refined and *eidel* and avoid the opposite. Since many of the perfumes that are available are unrefined and uncultured they should not be used - see *Mekoros* 64:5.

Music that is refined, sensitive and deep uplifts a person, whilst music which is coarse has a negative effect on the person's complete outlook as it blunts his sensitivities and can even arouse passions that are latent within a person and should have been left dormant - see 9:F:7(d) and 9:J:3(f) below. Similarly, perfume that is refined can give much pleasure and as mentioned, even the *neshama* enjoys it, whilst if it is unrefined it can have a very negative effect on the person. Instead of benefiting the *neshama*, it can arouse the urge to read and see forbidden literature and the like - urges which *tznius* constantly subdues and controls. It should be noted that *Chazal* state that some scents have such a negative effect on man that they can arouse in him an urge for immorality (*Bava Kama* 16b).

It is highly significant that *Chazal* say, שלושה דברים משיבים דעתו של אדם קול מראה וריח - "Three phenomena revive the spirit of man: sound, sight and smell" (*Brachos* 57b). This means enjoying music and sweet song (*Rashi*), an exquisite scenery or sight, and a beautiful fragrance. All these sensations exist both in a dignified and soul-lifting manner and in an ignoble and unworthy way. The spirit of man is revived and invigorated by the former and is put into disarray and negativity by the latter. Just as *tznius* calls for purity of sight, so too, it calls for purity of music and scent.

It is related in the *Gemara* (*Yoma* 39b) that the rich and deeply aromatic smell of the *ketores* that was sacrificed in the *Beis Hamikdash* was so exceptionally fragrant that a woman, whether in *Yerusholayim* or in far away *Yericho*, had no need to use any form of perfume to find *chein* in the eyes of her husband. (This does not mean that the perfume could not be detected due to the overwhelming fragrances of the *Ketores*, but that there was just no need for it - see *Tosfos Yeshanim* s.v. *Kallah*). The fact that the *ketores* could substitute for perfume, indicates that the fragrances women used in those times were of a similar refinement and sensitivity to that of the *ketores*. When buying perfume, women should take guidance from this remarkable *Chazal*.

5. USING PERFUMES ON SHABBOS: It is an *issur d'Rabanan* to apply perfume or other scents to a garment on Shabbos. Improving a garment by adding a pleasant scent to it is called *moled reiach* and to do so on Shabbos is forbidden *mid'Rabanan* under the *melacha* of *Makeh b'Patish* (M.B. 322:18). The *issur* applies to a garment such as a blouse, dress and outfit, and even to a piece of cloth such as a handkerchief, towel, tablecloth and bed-sheet. It is therefore *ossur* to dab perfume onto any of these items on Shabbos. Even a *sheitel* is a garment, albeit somewhat different to other garments, and subject to the *issur* of *moled reiach*. Accordingly, it is *ossur* to spray a perfumed spray onto a *sheitel* on Shabbos.

If an item already has this scent or perfume on it from before Shabbos, it is *ossur* to apply more of the same scent or perfume to it on Shabbos. This too is considered a significant improvement to the item, as the smell will be enriched by the additional scent or perfume - (M.B. 511:26).

Although perfume may not be applied to a garment or piece of cloth on Shabbos, it may be applied to the human body (M.B. 128:23, *Responsa Mishna Halachos* 7:46) and according to some *Poskim* even to a girl's hair (*Responsa Ginas Veradim* O.C. 3:16). Although others disagree with this *heter* (*Responsa Be'er Moshe* 8:24 and *Minchas Yitzchak* 6:26) the general custom is to be lenient and allow it.

As stated, there are some who do not allow perfume to be sprayed onto the hair on Shabbos. This is either because they consider hair to be like a garment (*Responsa Halachos Ketanos* 2:20) or because the scent lasts longer on the hair than on the body and giving hair a scent is therefore a more significant type of improvement (*Responsa Rav Pealim* 2:51). However, even these opinions agree that scented deodorants may be sprayed under the arms on Shabbos although many a person will thereby be giving scent to hair. This is permitted because the purpose of the deodorant (even when scented) is to prevent or nullify the odor of perspiration, not in order to produce a positively pleasant scent. It is therefore not considered a positive improvement to the area, and does not fall under the *issur*. (*Responsa Sheilas Ya'avetz* 2:42, *Be'er Moshe* 1:34. See also O.C. 328:26).

I. JEWELRY

1. JEWELRY - A NATURAL PART OF A WOMAN'S ATTIRE: Jewelry is a natural part of a woman's attire provided it is pleasant and refined. It may even be worn in public because, as stated, it is part of the female dress. Just as she may wear a graceful dress, so she may adorn herself with jewelry that improves her appearance - see *Mekoros* 65:1-3. In fact, we find in *Chazal* that even the most worthy women, such as the wife of Rabbi Akiva, wore jewelry. Furthermore, jewelry was specifically given by the husband to his outstanding wife as a sign of appreciation for the great qualities and the special acts of *chesed* she had performed. See *Nedarim* 50a, *Yerushalmi Shabbos* 4:1, *Vilna Gaon* on *Mishlei* 1:9 and *Mekoros* 66:2-3.

2. THE HARM TO TZNIUS CAUSED BY EXCESSIVE JEWELRY: It is incorrect for a woman to wear exorbitantly expensive jewelry, unusually large pieces of jewelry, or to bedeck and adorn herself with an excessive amount of jewelry. Accordingly, massive gold or diamond-studded rings, bracelets and belts that are designed to show off wealth, are not suitable for the *Bas Yisroel*. For a girl or woman to adorn herself in any of these ways also entails a serious lack of *tznius* as it attracts unwarranted attention.

It has been mentioned that it is *ossur* for a man to gaze at the colorful clothes of a woman he knows, even if the clothes are not currently being worn - see 7:A:8 above. The same applies to a woman's jewelry - see *Chochmas Adam* 125:3. Accordingly, not only is it *ossur* to look at jewelry that at present adorns a woman and enjoy the effect it has in adorning her, but it is *ossur* even just to look at the piece of jewelry itself without considering its effect in beautifying the person. It follows that if a woman or girl wears jewelry that is excessively large or eye-catching, she will be held responsible for causing men to gaze at her or at the jewelry that adorns her - see *Mekoros* 65:5-6.

3. EXTRAVAGANT JEWELRY ENDANGERS THE PERSON: Apart from attracting undue attention, adorning oneself in this way causes many evils. If really excessive, it is boastful and arouses the jealousy of both peers and neighbors. This in turn often precipitates unintentional *ayin horah* which causes untold damage (see 7:A:2 above). It also arouses the jealousy of non-Jews and causes unnecessary tension between them and us (see 7:A:3 above) see *Mekoros* 61. To our detriment, anti-Semitic literature often depicts the wealthy Jewess showing off her ridiculous display of jewelry.

Moreover, extravagant jewelry can put a woman or young lady in danger. As everyone knows, there are people around who will readily attack women or follow them home in order to steal their expensive jewelry. Intelligent people have the foresight to avoid doing things that can be harmful both to themselves and others. Hence the verse in *Mishlei* 14:1, חכמות נשים בנתה ביתה ואולת בידיה תהרסנה - "The intelligent woman behaves in a way that secures her home, whilst the foolish one destroys everything by her ill-considered deeds".

4. LAVISH JEWELRY CHEAPENS THE PERSON: A lavish and excessive display of jewelry is unrefined even if the jewelry is inexpensive. Over-decoration is coarse and detracts from the natural *chein* of a Jewish woman or girl. On the one hand, moderate, dignified and well-placed jewelry shows the woman's good taste, her feeling for *eidelkeit* and her general nobility. On the other hand, excessive decoration reflects a lack of dignity and finesse. It also has the effect of cheapening the person in the eyes of others because the implication of lavish jewelry is that gold, glitter and gems are appropriate substitutes when true values are absent. A *Bas Yisroel* is far too precious to be degraded in this way.

5. SPECTACLES AND EARRINGS - ENSURING THEIR REFINEMENT: Vigilance must be exercised before purchasing any part of one's attire or adornment to ensure that one keeps on the right side of the demarcation line. This line divides between articles that enhance her natural *chein* which are fine and those which cause glamorization which are not to be worn. Earrings and simple articles such as spectacles, if chosen with due care, can add a lot of *chein* and much needed color to the person's face, whilst, if the ways of the world are taken as guidelines, they can be ostentatious and unfitting in size, style or color.

Although earrings and spectacles are relatively small items in comparison to garments, their highly prominent position on and around the person's face makes them exceedingly conspicuous. They can be a welcome supplement to a pleasant way of dress, or ruin the effect of an apparel which is otherwise both pretty and refined.

The *Gaon* and *Tzaddik* Harav Nosson Zvi Finkel *zt'l*, the great *Mashgiach* of *Slabodka* (known as the *Alter* of *Slabodka*) used to say, "a person's face is a *reshus harabim* (a public domain)," since it is on display for everyone to see. He would therefore berate someone who walked around with a sullen face thereby spreading misery to his onlookers. In line with his definition, let us make sure that our faces project refinement, sweetness of character and *simchas hachayim* to the pleasure of others, rather than present them with an appearance which projects insensitivity and weakness.

6. CLOSE-FITTING EARRINGS AND DANGLING EARRINGS:

(a) Refined close-fitting earrings: Two types of earrings are mentioned in the Torah - נזמים and עגילים. נזמים (*Breishis* 35:4) were gold rings that hung from the lobe of the ear. They shared a name with nose rings that were likewise called נזמים (*Breishis* 24:47) because they too were rings that hung from the central part of the nose (see *Malbim Mishlei* 25:12). The other ornament was called עגילים (*Bamidbar* 31:50) - the root being the word עיגול - a circular item. These earrings were apparently circular disk-like items similar to present-day studs. Such earrings can add much *chein* to a woman or girl without being in any way obtrusive. These two types of earrings are mentioned in the Torah. However, the modern creation of a long ornament that dangles far from the ear is not mentioned. Since they dangle far from the ear they are unrefined, catching the eye with their glitter and continuous forward and backward movement. Only short drop-earrings are refined as their glitter and movement is minimal - see *Mishna Keillim* 11:9 where such earrings are mentioned.

Studs and similar close-fitting earrings, which are small or of moderate size, are refined types of jewelry and a natural part of a woman's attire (see *Rashi*, *Shabbos* 65a s.v. *Habanos*, that in the times of *Chazal* girls would have their ears pierced so that they could wear earrings when adults - see also 3:D(k) above). Stud-like earrings especially can add a lot of *chein* to a woman or girl without being in any way overly prominent.

(b) Long drop-earrings and large hoops: Long drop-earrings and large hoops are unrefined items, irrespective of whether they are made completely of gold or are predominantly pearl. There are girls that dress in a fully respectable manner who wear drop-earrings that extend to an inch or even two inches below the lobe. They obviously do not realize that these ornaments are very eye-catching and in effect spoil the otherwise *tznius'dik* dress and appearance of the girl.

It must be mentioned that sometimes a fine girl looks alright when wearing long slim drop-earrings. They do not look ostentatious, because they are slim and do not appear to be very expensive. They also do not overly attract attention to her because, due to her hair style, they are mostly covered by her hair and are not on constant display. Such a girl must, however, realize that if she wears these earrings she is giving a "*hechsher* label" to such jewelry, and many others are likely to follow her example. They will think to themselves that if such a fine girl wears long drop-earrings there is surely nothing wrong with them.

This type of thinking can prove to be very harmful, and her wearing such earrings might turn out to be a considerable stumbling block to others. When long drop-earrings are worn they are often very showy. Whilst her earrings are mostly hidden under her hair, theirs could well be on full display. Whilst she wears long slim drop-earrings, others who always add their own flavor to a *heter*, might wear long drop-earrings that are substantially heavier than hers and very unrefined. This fine girl is therefore well advised not to wear such earrings, although in her case they look alright, so as not to inadvertently mislead others.

7. TASTEFUL JEWELRY ADDS A LOT TO A WOMAN'S CHEIN: The *Midrash* gives the following unusual parable: יאה מסכנותא לברתיה דיעקב כערקא סומקא בקדלא דסוסיא חיורא, "Scarcity [of jewelry] is apt for the Jewish daughter; it is comparable to a red band tied around the neck of a white horse" (*Vayikra Rabba* 13:4 and quoted by *Tosfos Chagiga* 9b). *Chazal* appear to be saying the following: A white horse is one of the most graceful creatures that exists. It is a shame to excessively decorate such a creature to the point that the horse's natural beauty is camouflaged and disguised. However, to tie a red band near the head of a white horse is fine and even commendable. A band is but a small item and has the effect of highlighting the natural grace and beauty of the white horse, since white looks exceptionally pretty when contrasted with a small measure of red.

So too, scarcity in the use of jewelry rather than over indulgence, is the ideal way for a woman or girl to adorn herself. The *chein* and modesty of the *Bas Yisroel* are not disguised or shrouded when tasteful jewelry is worn - on the contrary, the jewelry contributes to the existing *chein*, grace and general good looks which have been given in great measure to the daughters of the Jewish people.

J. JEWELRY ON SHABBOS

The following are a number of important points that concern jewelry on Shabbos.

1. ISSUR TO BEND A CLASP SO THAT IT CLOSES ONCE AGAIN: If the clasp of a bracelet or watch has stretched and no longer catches, it is *ossur* to bend the clasp (even with one's fingers) so that it will catch once again and close. To do so is an act of repair and an *issur min haTorah* of מכה בפטיש, since this minor change enables the article to be worn once again. Similarly, if the pin of a brooch has bent and will not catch, it is *ossur* to straighten it and enable it to close once again (*Magen Avraham* 340:11, *Orach Chayim* 509:1).

2. WEARING AN ORNAMENTAL KEY-BROOCH IN THE STREET: A keybrooch (a gold key made into a brooch) may be worn in the street on Shabbos if it is so decorative and pretty that the woman would (if necessary) wear it as a brooch even if she had no door to open. This can be assessed by considering what she would she do if over a Shabbos she was in a different town and the key would not be needed to open a door. If she would nevertheless wear this brooch (should she have no prettier brooch to wear), the brooch is evidently a true תכשיט - ornament, and may be worn on Shabbos. Otherwise, it is just a pretty key but not a true תכשיט and may not be worn in the street on Shabbos (O.C 301:11).

Even when it is considered a true piece of jewelry, it may be worn only if her purpose for wearing it is both for use and also for decoration. However, if her purpose is only for use and she has no interest at present in the decorative qualities of the brooch, as she would not have bothered to wear a brooch on this outfit, wearing it would be considered an act of transportation (*ibid Sha'ar Hatzion* 38). Actually, since the intention of the wearer is not so evident, some *Poskim* totally forbid wearing it on Shabbos. However, the *minhag* is to be lenient and wear such key-brooches (M.B. 301:42, *Biur Halacha* s.v. *B'zeh*).

3. ISSUR TO WEAR A NECKLACE UNDER A DRESS: Some women wear their very expensive necklace totally hidden under their blouse or dress when on the street, so as not to arouse jealousy or be exposed to the danger of theft. On arrival at their destination they pull out the necklace so that it sits on the blouse or dress where it can be seen. Similarly, some wear a pearl necklace under their blouse for a certain length of time so that the pearls are rejuvenated by contact with the skin.

This practice is forbidden on Shabbos because a necklace is not a garment but a piece of jewelry for enhancing one's outer appearance, and when it is totally under a dress or blouse it is not in a position to serve that function at all. Since a necklace (in contrast to the items mentioned in M.B. 303:53 that are for personal feelings of adornment) is a piece of jewelry intended for external use, to wear it under clothes is an act of transportation (הוצאה) and forbidden, similar to the *Biur Halacha* 301:11, s.v. *b'zeh,* concerning a watch attached to a visible gold chain but the watch itself is inside a pocket.

This case should not be confused with a קמיע - an amulet (such as a necklace with a ruby that is worn by some women during pregnancy as a safeguard against miscarriage - see *Rabbeinu Bachya*, *Shemos* 28:15 and O.C. 303:25) that may be worn even under the main garments. An amulet is not intended for decoration and therefore need not be worn where it can be viewed (O.C. 301:25), whilst a necklace is purely a piece of decoration. [Note: Apart from the amulet mentioned, a *shaaloh* must be asked concerning wearing in the street other types of amulets which are not ornaments - see O.C. 301:25].

A necklace may be worn on a dress even in the dark of night and even under a coat although it cannot be seen. This does not contradict the *halacha* just stated because when it is on a dress it is in a position to function as a decoration, given the right circumstances ie. if it were light or there was no coat on top of it. This is therefore a normal act of adornment and is not viewed as transportation. The same applies to a bracelet that is in the right position on the wrist but cannot be seen at present because a sleeve covers it or an overcoat is worn over it - see *Mekoros* 65:8-9.

A necklace under a dress, or a bracelet pushed high up the arm are, however, different, because they are in a wrong position and as long as they are in this position they are totally useless. A man may certainly not wear his tie (which is likewise an adornment rather than a garment) under his shirt because it is in a totally wrong place, and if he does so he is considered as carrying it, albeit in an unusual manner. Similarly, it is *ossur* to wear spectacles on the forehead or up on the head while walking along the road. So too, a necklace that is under the blouse is being transported in an unusual manner and is not considered as being worn - see *Mekoros* 65:10.

4. UNDOING A KNOT THAT OCCURRED IN A FINE NECKLACE: Thin necklaces quite often become accidentally knotted with a type of knot that may generally not be tied nor untied on Shabbos, see *Rema* O.C. 317:1. The knot in the necklace may nevertheless be undone, because it came about accidentally, and an overhand knot (the name of the knot referred to in this instance) or a double knot that came about unintentionally does not have the status of "a knot" and may be undone on Shabbos. This is because any form of bonding (be it gluing or knotting) that occurs unintentionally is not considered a bond, and may therefore be undone (M.B. 317:23 citing the *Chayei Adam*, *Chazon Ish* O.C. 52:17 and compare to M.B. 340:44). Similarly, if an unintentional knot occurs on shoelaces or on a coat or dress belt, it may be undone on Shabbos.

K. COSMETICS

1. COSMETICS ARE TO BE USED WITH MODERATION:

(a) General guidelines: Cosmetics exist to be used in a moderate and refined manner when the need arises. A woman could require cosmetics to improve her appeal to her husband (*Shabbos* 64b) and an adult girl might need it so that she looks graceful and *b'cheint*, and *shidduchim* are suggested for her (*Kesubos* 52b). Moreover, an *Eishes Chayil* spreads *simcha* to her surroundings and this requires a healthy and cheerful countenance which can necessitate the use of minor, well placed makeup.

She may even go out in the street with a moderate and unobtrusive complement of cosmetic, if necessitated by the reasons mentioned. This is proven from *Shabbos* 80a, כדי לכחול עין אחת and Y.D. 198:17- see *Mekoros* 67:1-2. This is also the opinion of *Responsa Shevet Halevi* 6:33:2.

In this vein the *Mishna* says in *Pirkei Avos* (6:8), הנוי והכח וכו' נאה לצדיקים ונאה לעולם - "Good appearance, physical strength etc. befit the righteous and befit the world". When the right people use these gifts in the right way the right recipients benefit from it and all is fine.

The ideal way of using cosmetics is to apply them with such moderation, and to use colors that are so close to natural, that an observer would not realize that cosmetics have been used. Instead, they would presume that the color is due to her natural good appearance. When the cosmetics are obvious, the woman displays the effort she is making to look more attractive. Since this effort is often misdirected and inappropriate, the less she announces the fact that she uses cosmetics the better. This is, however, only the ideal and has been mentioned for those who can live up to this level of refinement. The true *halachic* requirements are that "excessive paint" is not used because it attracts attention and to attract attention violates the standard of *tznius* expected of a *Bas Yisroel* - see (b) below and *Mekoros* 67:6. As stated, refined colors may be used in a careful measure to enhance the appearance of the woman or adult girl.

Furthermore, due to the prevailing gross misuse of cosmetics that prevails in the world, many who have an acute feeling for *tznius* and refinement keep the use of cosmetics to a bare minimum. This is a typical reaction to a wrongdoing - those who wish to stem the tide refrain from the activity altogether or minimize it as far as possible.

(b) Cosmetics of the face and eyes: The excessive use of cosmetics is an area in which the *yetzer horah* has reaped enormous triumph even in religious circles. This temptation does not originate in the twentieth century. Long ago the *Navi* Yeshaya (3.16) bemoaned this trend with the words ויאמר ה׳ יען כי גבהו בנות ציון ותלכנה נטיות גרון ומשקרות עינים - "And *Hashem* said (He brought the *churban* upon *Klal Yisrael*) because the daughters of *Tzion* are haughty, they walk with a proud posture and they color their eyes". On the last two words *Rashi* writes, צובעות עיניהם בסקרא ובכחול - "They color their eyes with red and blue colorants" - see *Mekoros* 2:3.

▪ **Eye shadow**: The *Navi* apparently refers to a substantial application of eye-shadow, in which the upper eyelids are unnaturally colored red, blue, green, purple etc. (See *Gemara Niddah* 67b, *Yoreh Deah* 198:8 and *Badei Hashulchan* 198:63). The *Navi* disapproves of transforming one's appearance in such a way and considers doing so an indulgence which involves a serious lack of *tznius*. It is a misuse of cosmetics since whatever is done to arouse attention and cause people to look at her is forbidden under *pritzus* - see *Rabbeinu Yona* quoted in 7:K:3(a) below and *Mekoros* 69:1-2. Living amongst the *umos ha'olam,* reading their literature, hearing their broadcasts and consequently being influenced by their way of thinking, is the reason why some people are unable to see what is wrong with women and girls coloring their eyes in a substantial manner. This is just as the verse predicts, ויתערבו בגוים וילמדו מעשיהם - "And they mingled with the *umos ha'olam* and they learned from their ways" (*Tehillim* 106:35).

▪ **Eye-liner:** Eye-liner, (a cosmetic applied as a line onto the lower eyelids, usually next to the eye-lashes) is mostly used to accentuate the eyes. Therefore if it is used this must be with extreme moderation so that it is hardly noticeable, that the face remains *eidel* and that the *Yiddishe chein* is not lost under a mask designed to draw attention to themselves. A woman should use it only if she needs this type of makeup and that it is the accepted practice of refined women of her area to use it when necessary.

- **Mascara:** Mascara, an eye makeup in which the eye-lashes are darkened (without changing the color) is the safest of the different types of eye makeup, as it is used to darken eye-lashes that are already dark colored. It therefore serves as an enhancement rather than a transformation. However, even this type of eye makeup can be misapplied, as excessive blackening has the effect of making the eyes highly conspicuous. When this is the case, the person has indulged in immoderate beautification, which as stated, is not just a departure from *tznius'dik* and refined conduct but is a form of *pritzus*.

Before using mascara in a moderate manner, care should be taken to ensure that local *Rabbanim* and local refined women do not oppose its use, because one must never lessen the prevailing standard of refinement that exists generally in one's district. In our generation, the need to set standards is greater than ever before. To be one of those who move the boundaries of these standards is an awesome responsibility because the consequences of changing *tznius'dik* attitudes are unforeseeable.

- **Blush and Rouge:** Of all forms of facial cosmetics, face powders such as blush and rouge that are used just to produce a natural healthy complexion are the most acceptable since they are solely used to supplement missing color and are usually unnoticed or almost unnoticed (M.B. 303:79). It is however wrong to apply a distinct change of color such as a reddening, when the result will be unnatural because, as stated, to make the face conspicuous and is *pritzus'dik* (see *Tosfos Kesubos* 72b s.v. *B'toveh*).

(c) Cosmetics used for excessive beautification: It has been explained elsewhere that a woman and girl should wear a graceful dress, and adorn herself with appropriate jewelry so that she projects a *b'cheint* image. It is, however, incorrect to wear a brightly-colored dress, an outstandingly beautiful outfit, or adorn herself with large eye-catching jewelry, as over beautification leads to vanity and pride. It is similarly incorrect for a very good-looking woman or girl to make herself even more beautiful by adding cosmetics to her eyes, lips, cheeks and nails. Adding beautification to that which is already highly attractive and very good-looking stems from a craving for acclaim (unless this is normal for local standards). If, as a result of the cosmetics, her appearance is eye-catching or even sensational, her application is diametrically opposed to all that *tznius* stands for. Since cosmetics are prone to overuse and misuse, mothers and *mechanchos* must guide girls to use cosmetics (in places where it is the norm to use this type, see 7:K:6 below) in a modest and carefully-controlled manner.

(d) Indulgence by few, causes others to copy innocently: As stated by the *Navi* [quoted in (b) above] 'acclaim-seeking' is usually the original cause for over-indulgence in cosmetics. The desire to be regarded as exceptionally attractive, precipitates extravagance in this area. However, as is the case with many indulgences, once something is done by many, the individual who is not an 'acclaim-seeking' type will feel an urge to follow suit so as not to be considered unworldly and simple. Therefore, many women and girls will imitate the over-indulgence of the initiators even though they personally are not conceited. If not for a blindness caused by the worry of contempt, these otherwise refined and modest women would have been perfectly happy with their natural *chein* and good looks, and would feel no need to accentuate their appearance with exceptional amounts of makeup.

(e) Different communities have different standards: In different parts of *Klal Yisroel* there are, in fact, very different "levels of norm" as far as the use of cosmetics is concerned. In some communities women use cosmetics only occasionally and very sparingly, while in other communities it is the norm for cosmetics to be used by almost all ladies. In the latter type of environment, a wife must of course use cosmetics for the sake of her husband, since that is what he expects. Even in circles where cosmetics are used only occasionally, it is sometimes appropriate for a woman to add color to her cheeks and improve her appearance and appeal to her husband, particularly if she looks pale and fatigued.

2. COSMETICS ARE TO ENHANCE - NOT TO 'BE CONSPICUOUS':

(a) Cosmetics should not be used to attract attention: The following guidelines should be taught to girls who are likely to use cosmetics before or after marriage. Cosmetics are used by people in two totally different ways. (1) To improve their image and enhance their looks. (2) To make the person conspicuous and striking (either by over beautification or by a transformation that is not necessarily pretty, such as applying excessive or deep color to the area of the eyes). The former is Kosher, the latter is *treife*. This means that cosmetics are correctly used when they improve a woman's appearance, so that she projects a healthy, happy and pleasing appearance. They are, however, incorrectly used when they attract attention to her and lure males and females alike to look at her - see *Mekoros* 67:1-5.

A verse in *Tehillim* (45:12) reads, ויתאו המלך יפיך כי הוא אדניך והשתחוי לו - "The King will desire your beauty, for He is your Master and you bow to Him". The King of Kings, the *Ribbono Shel Olam*, will love your beauty knowing that you are His loyal subject who pursues physical beauty in the right spirit and with virtuous aspirations. You attend to your beauty in a controlled and balanced measure. You do so to bring pleasantness to your environment, *simcha* to your home and delight to your husband, not to gain the admiration of all and sundry for your charm and engaging looks.

(b) Some use cosmetics to do nothing but attract attention: As explained, apart from the malady of over beautification, cosmetics are used by many to attract attention to themselves as women of high society (rather than to actually beautify themselves). Adjectives such as beautiful, pretty and attractive are used nowadays to describe a woman who projects an image of being a lady of wealth or leisure, although all would agree that the excessive cosmetics does not beautify her at all. Many facial cosmetics and many extravagant pieces of jewelry fall under this classification and in the false world we live in these two effects are confused with one another. Whilst it is natural and appropriate for a woman to enhance her appearance, it is improper and inappropriate for her to use cosmetics to seek acclaim - see *Mekoros* 58:4.

(c) 'Application of lipstick' and 'eyebrow plucking' often improper: Lipstick is a prime candidate for the two ways in which cosmetics are used. If a close-to-natural colored lipstick is added with finesse to pale lips it gives color where it is needed and can prove to be an enhancement to the woman's appearance. However, if a bright or deep red lipstick is applied, it is often no beautification at all, especially if applied liberally and lavishly. The lips are a bright or deep unnatural color, causing the face to lose all *Yiddishe chein*.

Moreover, a lavish application of dark unnatural color causes the lips to look enlarged. When praising the maiden, the verse says, כחוט השני שפתותיך - "Your lips are like red threads" (*Shir HaShirim* 4:3), indicating that lips are beautiful when they are slim. Moreover, *Chazal* (*Nedarim* 66b) say explicitly that שפתיים עבות - thick lips are not complimentary for a woman. In truth, lavish, dark lipstick is not used as an honest enhancement but to be considered a "lady of elegance" who has plenty of time to decorate herself - see *Mekoros* 67:3. Since this cosmetic is all too frequently misused, many refrain from using it altogether, as mentioned in 7:K:1(c) above.

Plucking eyebrows to thin them down a little is widely practiced, and is considered a normal form of facial improvement. However, it is very far from *eidel* to pluck the eyebrows into an unnatural thin line, so that instead of eyebrows there is a slim dark brown line. All that is unnatural is coarse and improper, and subtracts from the person's refined facial features. A further positively *pritzus'dik* way of eyebrow plucking is to pluck them into a thin arch-like shape. This is very crude and unrefined and can even project a vulgar look. Sadly, there are Jewish women and girls who follow methods of facial improvement they see in the wider society, without considering whether they will improve their image or will have the adverse effect of giving them a thoroughly graceless and even *pritzus'dik* look.

(d) Deception is charming and frivolity beautiful - today's world: The great *Rebbe*, Reb Baruch MiMezovitz *zt'l* once interpreted the verse, שקר החן והבל היופי אשה יראת ה׳ היא תתהלל (*Mishlei* 31:30) in the following metaphorical manner: "When deception is considered charming (שקר החן), and frivolity is viewed as beautiful (והבל היופי) the woman who has *Yiras Shomayim* and refuses to be drawn into these types of misconduct deserves praise (אשה יראת ה׳ היא תתהלל)". In our day and age, where there is an enormous amount of misconduct around, women and girls who steadfastly remain uncontaminated are deserving of great commendation for their dedication and loyalty to preserving the purity and sanctity of *Klal Yisroel*.

3. THE ISSUR FOR WOMEN TO CAUSE MEN TO GAZE AT THEM:

(a) Diametrical opposite of *tznius*: The excessive use of cosmetics is provocative and the absolute opposite of *tznius* and refinement. The *Rishonim* write that just as a man is expected not to gaze at women, so a woman must not cause men to gaze at her. Using excessive cosmetics is in direct conflict with this edict and is also forbidden under the issur of *Lifnei iver lo sitain michshol* - the Torah prohibition against causing others to sin (*Vayikra* 19:14) - see 1:A:5, 1:J:1, 4:B:1(e) and 7:E:2 above.

Rabbeinu Yona writes exceptionally strongly about a woman's responsibility in this field. In *Iggeres HaTeshuva,* Chap. 78, he writes: וצריכה האשה שתהא צנועה ונזהרת שלא יסתכלו בה בני אדם חוץ מבעלה, מפני שהמסתכלים בפניה או בידיה יורדין לגהינום, והיא ענושה בעונש כל אחד ואחד מהם, מפני שהחטיאה אותם ולא נהגה צניעות בעצמה ונכשלו בה - freely translated this means: "A woman must be modest and mindful that men (other than her husband) should not gaze at her. If as a result of over beautification they gaze at her face or hands, they will be severely punished. She too will be punished for each and every one of them because she led them astray by not behaving with due restraint and modesty" - see *Mekoros* 69:1 and 69:5.

It should be noted that the Rambam writes in *Hilchos Krias Shema* 3:16, כל גוף האשה ערוה - "All parts of the female body are liable to attract unwarranted attention" and the face is certainly no exception - see 6:G:1(c) above. As such it would seem that the face should be covered when she is in public, since it has the power to attract. To this the *Tzemach Tzedek* (*Responsa, Shaar Hamiluim* 45) writes that women need not cover their faces when in public because "the ways of the Torah are pleasant" and to impose an obligation on women to cover their faces would violate that edict. [A further reason could be that blurring the natural identification of a person could be seriously misused and would enable weak individuals to go to illicit places - see *Sanhedrin* 38a where this type of idea is mentioned]. Accordingly, it is self understood that to add fully unnecessary beautification to the face, which is far beyond the needs of a woman, is forbidden, because with such a beautified face she is presenting a hazard to the public.

It should also be noted that the *Od Yosef Chai, Parshas Bo,* No.2. writes that if hands or face are beautified well beyond what people are used to, they have the status of *ervah* and a man facing such a decorated woman may not say a *bracha*. Although this exceptional ruling might not be everyone's opinion, it demonstrates the harm caused by excessive beautification.

(b) Causes problems of *shalom bayis*: Apart from the above, we have no idea how many unhappy marriages (which afflict the Jewish people at the present time to a much greater degree than ever before) are a direct result of this irresponsible behavior - when the wife is not as glamorous as other women who decorate themselves with excessive makeup. There are many who engage nowadays in the great *mitzva* of promoting matrimonial harmony (שלום בית). Little do women realize that many of them are unwittingly engaged in causing matrimonial disharmony (חורבן הבית) by the way they appear in public.

4. COSMETICS CAN CAUSE CONFLICT WITH SHEMIRAS SHABBOS:

(a) Creates a strong urge to use cosmetics on Shabbos: Quite apart from the *tznius* problem involved in the use of excessive cosmetics, attention should be paid to the fact that most forms of makeup are forbidden on Shabbos. For example, lipstick, nail varnish and almost all facial colorants are subject to the *issur* of צובע - coloring (see 7:L for full treatment of this subject). A sensible person takes this into consideration when using cosmetics during the week, and uses makeup just to improve but not to transform her appearance completely. If one regularly changes one's entire appearance, it can become so embarrassing to appear without makeup and without one's usual appearance on display, that one will be sorely tempted to use forbidden forms of makeup on Shabbos, *chas v'shalom* (O.C. 303:25) - see *Mekoros* 68.

(b) Makes Shabbos a dull day in comparison to weekdays: Even a person who has *Yiras Shomayim* and will definitely not transgress Shabbos should still avoid regularly putting on excessive makeup during the week. This is because it is a *mitzva* to make Shabbos a delightful day - וקראת לשבת עונג (*Yeshaya* 58) - See M.B. 242:4, 250:2. It is therefore incorrect to do something on weekdays which will inevitably cause the person to feel a let down on Shabbos. Instead of delighting in Shabbos, she will constantly be looking forward to *motzoei* Shabbos when makeup will be permitted once again. Therefore, it is improper to beautify oneself during the week to the extent that one will sorely miss it on Shabbos.

A person wanted to install an air conditioner in the apartment of the holy *Steipler Gaon*, Harav Yaacov Yisroel Kanievsky *zt'l*, so that the *Steipler Gaon* who suffered from asthma would be less bothered by the humid heat of *Bnei Brak*. The *Steipler Gaon* refused the offer. He explained that since he did not use the general electricity on Shabbos (as it is generated by *mechalelei* Shabbos) and would therefore not use the air conditioner on Shabbos, he did not want it at all. He said that he did not want to have a convenience which would make the weekdays more comfortable for him than Shabbos, as he would thereby undermine the *mitzva* of making Shabbos a delightful day - וקראת לשבת עונג (*Toldos Yaacov*, page 170).

5. OVER-INDULGENCE CORRUPTS A PERSON: As stated previously, over-beautification causes men to look and even gaze at women, and is therefore a transgression of the *issur* of *lifnei iver*, "do not cause others to sin" - see 4:B:1(e). Apart from this there is also an intrinsic wrongdoing in all forms of over-indulgence. The Torah commands us קדושים תהיו - "Be a holy people" (*Vayikra* 19:2). The *Ramban* writes that this refers to activities such as eating, drinking, dressing, and self beautification. These are of course permitted. However, they should be done with moderation, since over--indulgence in them makes the person boorish and coarse.

The *Ramban* writes that wallowing in the pursuit of such pleasures can detrimentally affect a person to a point that he would be considered a נבל ברשות התורה - "as leading an ugly life although not transgressing any particular *issur*". To prevent this happening the Torah forbade over-indulgence. Therefore, eating and drinking is permitted but it is *ossur* to be a glutton or a drunkard. Similarly, whilst a woman or girl should look after her appearance she must not over-indulge and pamper herself with excessive jewelry or cosmetics.

The importance of the *mitzva* of קדושים תהיו is apparent from the fact that this *mitzva* was said at the gathering of *Hakhel* - in the presence of everyone (*Vayikra* 19:1). This meant all men and women came together to be instructed about this particular issue. Since the very essence of the Jewish person depends on living by this edict, everyone had to be present to hear it. Moreover, *Rashi* writes that the *mitzva* of קדושים תהיו refers in particular to that which can cause immorality and a degree of corruption. We are commanded to abstain from doing anything which can cause inroads into this forbidden area.

In this context it should be mentioned that a woman may dress at home in clothes that give her husband pleasure even if they are unsuitable for appearance in public. Similarly, she may adorn herself at home with jewelry that would be inappropriate to wear outdoors. Since this dress and adornment does not attract unwanted eyes, there is nothing fundamentally wrong with it. Moreover, if the clothes and jewelry are needed to increase the fondness of her husband for her, they are indeed in place. However, if her husband does not need them, for a woman to overly beautify herself with no valid reason, is in truth just a form of over indulgence which is never correct, as explained.

6. YOUNG GIRLS SHOULD PREFERABLY NOT USE COSMETICS: It is important to note that although there is no *halachic issur* for a young girl to use a minor amount of makeup, this should be discouraged if possible. It should be explained to young girls who might desire to use it that this practice is a prime candidate for the advice of *Chazal*: קדש עצמך במותר לך - "Sanctify yourself by restraining yourself from certain permitted things - as indulgence can mislead you" (*Yevamos* 20a). The advice is based on the verse קדושים תהיו (*Vayikra* 19:2) mentioned in the previous point. This is because those who indulge in cosmetics from a young age develop a craving for it and when they become young women they often over-paint themselves.

In the case of young girls, for whom looking attractive could be of prime importance, makeup is highly addictive. Not only do they find it exceedingly difficult to reduce the amount of makeup used hitherto, but experience has shown that they develop a need to apply more and more makeup with the passage of time. It will be noticed that after a year or two they substantially increase the amount of color they put on. This happens because they feel that what they have been using until now is not enhancing their appearance any more, and that their faces lack the special color they envisage. As a result of this, by the time they are married they could be painting themselves to an unacceptable degree. For this reason, it is preferable that until a girl is close to marriageable age she avoids cosmetics altogether or uses just a very minimal amount. A well known *mechanech* when speaking to girls about this topic said to them subtly, "I paint my house when it looks dilapidated!" implying, why should a girl who looks perfect paint herself with cosmetics and thereby change or mask her natural good appearance?

In conclusion, it must be put on record that in some circles girls are brought up in a way that even when they reach marriageable age they manage perfectly well with no cosmetics at all. These girls are as eligible for a good *shidduch* as anyone else, and often even more so, due to their obvious refinement. In our day and age, when *chitzonius* plays such a prominent role in people's lives and cosmetics are so often misused, parents feel that if they can raise their daughters to manage without cosmetics they are bolstering the fortress of *taharas Yisroel*. Furthermore, they are saving their daughters from the trials and tribulations of over-painting and excessive beautification, and instead encouraging them to concentrate on real values.

7. LONG NAILS: Some people regard long finger-nails as an object of beauty. In truth they are considered the opposite from the Torah viewpoint. The verse says concerning the maiden taken captive in war (the *yefas toar*) ועשתה את צפרניה - "She shall let her nails grow" (*Devarim* 21:12). On this *Rashi* comments, תגדלם כדי שתתנוול - "she shall let them grow long so that she becomes repulsive". Hopefully, as a result of this her captor will agree to send her away. The source of *Rashi* is a statement by Rabbi Akiva in *Yevamos* 48a.

We see from here that from the Jewish point of view long nails are coarse and repulsive. The practice of allowing nails to grow long should therefore be discouraged. It goes without saying that false finger-nails and false eye-lashes are extraneous forms of cosmetics that should be alien to the *Bas Yisroel* (See *Responsa Achiezer* 3:33:1 and *Responsa Iggros Moshe* Y.D. 3:62 about other problems that can arise due to long nails or false eye-lashes).

8. NAIL POLISH: If a girl or woman lives in a society where it is common to use nail-polish, she may use it but she must be careful not to apply a color that is coarse and undignified. The color should therefore be kept as close to the natural coloring as possible, thus excluding bright red, purple, blue .etc. (See *Ketzos Hashulchan* Chap.146 end of paragraph s.v. *Tzoveia*, *Responsa Be'er Moshe* 4:147:14). As with many other forms of cosmetics, there are many who do not use nail varnish at all, being happy with the beauty and *chein Hashem* has given them (except for an occasional enhancement of their face when they are tired and a bit short of color) and see no need to engage in elaborate forms of manicure and nail varnishing. This is one of the areas where no law has been laid down. Instead, it has been left to the refinement of each woman to assess what is and what is not right for her.

It has been explained elsewhere, that an individual must not depart from the standard of *tznius* upheld by the rest of the local Orthodox population. Accordingly, for an individual to apply nail varnish or similar type of cosmetic within a *kehilla* where these cosmetics are considered unrefined is comparable to "overdressing". Even though it may be the norm in some other places, it is forbidden in that place because it is a departure from the locally accepted standard of refinement and *tznius*. See 1:G above where this subject is discussed at length. See also *Shiurei Shevet HaLevi* 198:17 par. s.v. *Tzoveia*.

9. ARTIFICIAL TANNING OF THE SKIN: In the world at large, women brown their skin by using a sun-bed (a portable solarium) or artificial means such as lotions that have a tanning effect, to give the impression that they have just been sunbathing in the most glorious sunshine. This is not the practice of Orthodox women and is considered as excessive indulgence into the sphere of cosmetics (even though for skin to be slightly browned is additional beauty - see *Pirkei d'Rebbi Eliezer* Chapter 24, note no. 3 and *Mekoros* 67:9-11). It should be explained what is wrong with this practice so that women understand why this and similar types of elegance-seeking activities are undesirable, and should be firmly kept out of our midst.

Whoever sees a woman or girl beautified in this manner is immediately aware that she is going to all lengths to beautify herself. She obviously spends a considerable amount of time and effort (either by tanning or by applying lotions) on maintaining her golden brown color. Evidently, female beautification has an extremely prominent place in her scale of values.

For a Jewish woman to indulge in this type of makeup is harmful not only to herself but also to others who see her, particularly if they are young impressionable girls. Also, Shabbos would become a serious problem because artificial means of color-restoration that could be needed to keep everything well painted are forbidden on Shabbos. This type of glamorization is therefore totally unfitting for the *Bas Yisroel* and we should gladly leave it to others who do not have our set of values.

10. INSIDE HOUSE MORE DECORATED THAN OUTSIDE - PARABLE: The following is a quote from the *Sefer HaMesholim* by one of the *Rishonim*, Rabbeinu Yosef Giktilia *zt'l* (the author of the *sefer, Sharei Orah* - mentioned in the *Beis Yosef Orach Chayim* section 25). He writes as follows in Section 136:- "Concerning beautification, a woman is like a house. People do not excessively paint the exterior of their houses. Instead they retain the comprehensive and substantial decoration for the interior of the house. So too, when a woman goes outdoors she should wear jewelry and use cosmetics with moderation. However, indoors where she is with her husband and family she should decorate herself as appropriate."

The comparison he makes is most interesting and well-suited. People paint the exterior of their homes so that the house looks pleasing and enhances the area. They do not, however, decorate their house in a way that people are powerfully attracted to the house and develop a desire to take possession of it. This should also be the attitude of a woman. She should be seen in public in a pleasing attire and *b'cheint* appearance but not in such a way that she is highly-decorated which in turn attracts people to her.

11. BEAUTY EXISTS WHEN NESHAMA SHINES THROUGH BODY: Man has a spiritual inner core surrounded by a physical outer shell. The spiritual inner core is the Holy *neshama* which is within each and every one of us. We refer to it each morning in the *bracha* of *Elokai neshama*, when we say נשמה שנתת בי טהורה היא - "the *neshama* that You have put into me is pure". The physical outer shell is the body which is a sanctuary for the *neshama* as long as it is to be in this world. It is the duty of the person to ensure that his body serves the *neshama* and enriches it with Torah and good deeds, rather than causing it distress at being kept in this world for no valid purpose.

True beauty exists when the purity of the inner *neshama* shines through the outer shell - the body. The serene facial expression of the person bears witness to the quality of the *neshama* and the purity of the body, since for the light of the *neshama* to penetrate the body, the *neshama* must be radiant and the body unsoiled and translucent, allowing the rays of the *neshama* to shine through. Hence when the Torah tells us about the outstanding beauty of our *Imahos*, the true meaning of this praise is that both the inner and the outer being of these great women were of the most exceptional standard. See *Yisroel Kedoshim* by Hagaon R' Zadok HaKohen *zt'l* page 49-50 and *Pachad Yitzchak* by Hagaon R' Yitzchak Hutner *zt'l*, *Chanukah* 7:4-5. See 3:B:1 above where this idea has already been mentioned.

When a Jewish woman uses cosmetics to enhance her appearance, her purpose should be so that her *chein* is enhanced and the qualities of her true person more readily evident. It is sad when the paint is so excessive that not only does it not bring out her *chein* and display her qualities, but on the contrary, it covers everything over. One will find, for example, a woman who has very special attributes and is exceptionally kind and considerate. In spite of this, due to the veneer that hides her true features, it is very difficult for those who do not know her personally to detect these qualities and to believe that she is such an exceptionally warm person, since she looks so common and inferior. Sadly, instead of looking her true self, she truly looks like anyone but herself. See 7:L:6 below about the word פנים.

12. A FACE THAT "PROJECTS PURITY" IS BEAUTIFUL: When the verse relates the age of Sarah Imeinu it states that she lived, מאה שנה ועשרים שנה ושבע שנים - "A hundred years, twenty years and seven years" (*Breishis* 23:1). *Rashi* explains that the unusual presentation of the numbers is due to the fact that each unit had its own significance. In that context *Rashi* states, "When she was twenty years old she was as beautiful as a seven year old". A well known difficulty on this saying is that generally a twenty year old girl has a more becoming countenance than a seven year old.

The answer to this is that in the "dictionary of *Chazal*", יופי - good-looks - entails not just a pretty face but also the "pure facial expression of the innocent". Usually a seven year old has greater innocence and therefore also a purer facial expression than a twenty year old. However, Sarah Imeinu was so pure and perfect that at twenty years old she had the same innocence and purity as she had when she was a seven year old (Harav Hagaon R' Mattisyahu Salomon *shlita*, *Mashgiach* of *Yeshivas Gateshead,* now of *Beth Medrash Govoha,* Lakewood U.S.A.).

13. "MY HEART AND MY FLESH SHALL SING TO *HASHEM*": The verse says לבי ובשרי ירננו אל קל חי - "My heart and my flesh shall sing a song of praise unto You, O living G-d" (*Tehillim* 84:3). This heartening verse should be taken by the Jewish woman and girl as a guiding light. When considering cosmetics and similar forms of beautification she should recall this verse - "My heart and my flesh shall sing a song of praise to You *Hashem*" - It is inadequate that I acclaim and admire *Yiddishkeit* with my heart alone. My flesh must join me in pronouncing the greatness of *Hashem* and the perfection of His Torah and *mitzvos*. The refinement of my bearing and the serenity of my countenance must bear witness to my being wholeheartedly Torah orientated and *mitzva* observant. With such obvious purity, my flesh joins my heart in producing a sweet and beautiful melody to the honor of *Hashem* - לבי ובשרי ירננו אל קל חי.

L. COSMETICS ON SHABBOS

1. THE MELACHA OF TZOVEIA - COLORING AND DYEING: Many people do not fully understand the problems involved with the use of cosmetics on Shabbos. It is therefore appropriate to explain this issue as simply as possible. A few introductory points must be made. Firstly, to paint a surface with durable paint is a *melacha min haTorah* of *Tzoveia*, whilst to use a temporary paint that can easily be wiped off is an *issur d'Rabanan* (M.B. 320:59).

Secondly, painting a wall or an article etc. with permanent paint is a *melacha min haTorah* as the color lasts indefinitely, whereas to apply color to the human body is an *issur d'Rabanan*, as the body rejects the color after a day or so. Since it is no more than a temporary form of coloring, it is only *ossur mid'Rabanan* (M.B. 303:79).

2. USING A POWDER THAT HAS A "VERY WEAK ADHERENCE": What has not been explicitly spelt out by *Chazal* is what the *halacha* would be when a color that can easily be wiped away is applied to the human body. In such a case the color is doubly "non-permanent" - the actual paint being used and the surface which is being colored are both causes for it to be temporary, and it could be that *Chazal* would not have forbidden this at all.

Maran Hagaon Harav Moshe Feinstein *zt'l* is lenient on this issue (*Iggros Moshe* O.C. 1:114) whilst Maran Hagaon Harav Shlomo Zalman Auerbach *zt'l* (*Shemiras Shabbos Kehilchaso* Sec.14 Note 158) and *yibodel lechayim* Maran Hagaon Harav Shmuel Wosner *shlita* (6:33:1) are stringent. The lenient opinion has been widely accepted in many circles in America (but to a much lesser degree in *Eretz Yisroel* and England). According to the lenient opinion, if a woman has small red spots on her face she may cover them up with a white chalk powder. Similarly, if she has a pale complexion she may dab a plain pink powder onto her face - see *Mekoros* 68:1-8.

3. IF "RUBBED IN" ALL AGREE THE COSMETIC IS OSSUR: Maran Hagaon Rabbi Moshe Feinstein *zt'l* writes that his *heter* applies when the powder is dabbed lightly onto the face but not when it is rubbed in. This is because by rubbing it into the skin the color mixes with the oils and greases of the skin and becomes oil-based. Once a colorant is oil-based, it cleaves firmly to the skin and will not come off by simply rubbing a towel firmly over the face. Coloring with a color that sticks to the skin is considered as using a true paint on the skin which *Chazal* explicitly forbade.

It follows from this reasoning, that even if a woman dabs the color onto her face, it will only be permitted if the color is oil-free. Accordingly, the *heter* applies only when:- (a) the powder does not have an oil base; (b) the powder is dabbed but not rubbed into the skin.

4. MOST FACE-POWDERS ARE OSSUR ON SHABBOS: Nearly all present-day cosmetic powders have an oil base and are therefore forbidden on Shabbos according to all opinions, even if they are only to be dabbed onto the face e.g. rouge, foundation, blush, (eye-shadow, mascara, eye-liner etc. are obviously forbidden). When Maran Hagaon Rabbi Moshe Feinstein *zt'l* was shown (some ten years ago) the effect of dabbing rouge onto the hand, he responded by saying that his *heter* referred to powders that could be wiped off the face with a towel, but not to substances such as rouge which once in contact with the skin can only be removed by washing them away. His *heter* was only given for colorants available forty years ago that were not oil based. He even wrote a letter to this effect which was widely publicized at the time and has since been printed in *Responsa Iggros Moshe* O.C.5:27.

5. FACE-POWDER MADE FOR SHABBOS - SUBJECT TO DEBATE: There is a powder especially formulated for use on Shabbos. It could in theory be used (by those who follow the lenient opinion) **provided it is just dabbed onto the face with a brush and not rubbed into the skin in any**

way. It may only be dabbed on with the bristles of a brush, not with a sponge pad, because the actual powder is a powerful colorant and if pressed firmly against the skin will stain the skin even if oil is not mixed with it. In fact, the author of the *sefer, "Gefen Poriah*", who sanctioned the use of this special cosmetic for Shabbos, writes concerning its use (in the sources to Section Eight, No. 44), "Only a brush applicator and not a sponge applicator should be used to apply the powder to the face". In practice, many women seem to use this product in a forbidden way. They rub it into the skin which is forbidden, and many do not know that it should not be applied with a sponge or pad.

To summarize, even according to the lenient opinion, rouge etc. may not be used under any circumstances. A cosmetic especially formulated for Shabbos may be used, but only by dabbing it on lightly with a brush. Rubbing it in, dabbing it on with pressure, and dabbing it on with a sponge are all forbidden. In addition, many feel that since present-day powders are powerful colorants and can so easily be misused, it is debatable whether they should be allowed even according to the lenient opinion.

6. SHEMIRAS SHABBOS GIVES CHEIN TO FACE OF BAS YISROEL: It follows from all that has been explained that using cosmetics on Shabbos is a precarious and doubt-ridden exercise. Fortunate is the woman whose love for Shabbos and strength of character enable her to avoid using cosmetics on Shabbos altogether.

(a) A *chein* radiates from a face not painted because of Shabbos: A person's face is called "פנים" (*panim*) and is spelled the same as the word פנים (*p'nim*), "interior". This is because the inner feelings and character of a person are displayed on his face (see *Rashi*, *Breishis* 13:8 and *Maharal MiPrague, Gur Aryeh*, *Breishis* 19:29 note 81). The *Or HaChayim* (*Breishis* 19:17) writes that Lot and his family were told not to turn round and look at Sodom because if their countenance would face Sodom, the Angels that were sent to destroy the wicked inhabitants of Sodom would see their faces. Since the face reveals the inner self, the Angels would detect the corruption of Lot and his family and destroy them together with Sodom. Conversely, but based on the same principle, the verse says והיו עיניך רואות את מוריך - "Your eyes should behold the countenance of your teachers" (*Yeshaya* 30:20), because the inner *kedusha* of the *Rebbe* is revealed on his face (see *Eruvin* 13b).

In line with this, the *Bas Yisroel* is affectionately addressed with the words הראיני את מראיך - "Let me see your appearance" (*Shir HaShirim* 2:14). Her facial appearance and her outer expression are a window with which to probe her inner soul. Special beauty and *chein* radiate from the face of the woman and girl who does not use cosmetics to enhance her appearance on Shabbos. Her face is aglow with her פנים - *p'nim* - her inner soul, which sparkles with the radiance of Shabbos. About such women Shlomo Hamelech says, אשה יראת ה' היא תתהלל - "The praise and admiration of an *Eishes Chayil* is the *Yiras Shomayim* displayed on her countenance" (*Mishlei* 31:30).

(b) *Yiras Shomayim* adds a beautiful glow to the face: In truth, *Yiras Shomayim* gives so much to a woman's appearance that it is the best of all cosmetics. If our daughters knew and appreciated this fact, the *nisayon* of refraining from using cosmetics on Shabbos would diminish considerably. The following are the words of the *Midrash* (*Breishis* 11:2): ברכו באור פניו של אדם, וקדשו באור פניו של אדם, לא דומה אור פניו של אדם כל ימות השבת כמו שהוא דומה בשבת - "The blessings and *kedusha* of Shabbos add a gleam and sparkle to a person's face. His face has a special glow on Shabbos that it does not have during the week". The *simcha* and the *kedusha* of Shabbos have such a profound effect on a person that they refine and even illuminate the person's facial features. Since *shemiras* Shabbos enhances the person's appearance, a woman or girl who finds she must use cosmetics on an ordinary weekday could well find that she does not need cosmetics on Shabbos.

(c) Spiritual beauty is real - it surpasses physical beauty: A further *chizuk* to refrain from cosmetics on Shabbos can be derived from the following: The *Chasam Sofer zt'l* writes (in *Succah* 36a) that a communal *esrog* that has got many brown marks due to the many hands that have held it to do the *mitzva*, is considered an אתרג מהודר - "a beautiful *Esrog*" and remains Kosher, even though discoloration generally renders an *esrog possul*. In the case of this *esrog*, the discoloration bears witness to the great merit the *Esrog* has had of being used so extensively for the service of *Hashem*. This "discoloration" is therefore a beautification rather than a shortcoming. So too, a face that lacks color due to *Shemiras* Shabbos is in fact a "beautiful face" that finds favor in the eyes of *Hashem* and man. True, there is some "discoloration" or, to be more accurate, slight lack of color. This is however testimony of *Yiras Shomayim* and quality, and should be viewed as a special badge of distinction.

7. LONG-TERM COSMETICS: Those who are very much in need of cosmetics should inquire from their *Rav* whether he sees fit to allow them to use long-term colorants that last for at least 24 hours. These could be applied before Shabbos and will last throughout Shabbos. As it is generally known that such cosmetics exist there is be no *issur* of מראית העין or והייתם נקיים in using them. However, if they are obvious and fully noticeable it is preferably to do without them because some people do not know that long-term cosmetics exist. When the face of a *Bas Yisroel* bears witness to her dedication to *shemiras* Shabbos and *kiyum hamitzvos* this is the greatest possible enhancement and beautification to her appearance.

A long-term lipstick which a woman rejuvenates after it has been on for about half a day by passing her tongue over it (thereby releasing microscopic capsules of color) may not be rejuvenated in this way on Shabbos. To do so is considered צובע because this particular substance is made to change to a deeper and improved color by her action. Since this act of צובע can very easily be done, it is to be recommended that this type of lipstick is not used for Shabbos - see *Mekoros* 68:9.

8. IMPROVING COMPLEXION OF SKIN - BUT NOT COLORING: One may use on Shabbos a skin colored face-powder even if it is oil based if the sole purpose of using it is to improve the complexion of the face i.e. just so that the skin has a smooth matt-like appearance but not to add color. Similarly, a woman may use a white talc powder just to smoothen her face. Since she is not changing the color of her face, no צובע is involved, even though the powder is rubbed into the skin and sticks firmly to it. These powders may, however, not be used to conceal red spots and flecks since in such a case they are being used to color the marks and change them back to usual skin color.

Only a powder may be used to smoothen the skin. A cream which has the same effect is forbidden due to the *issur* of *Memareiach* - the *issur* of smoothing out substances on Shabbos. For this reason, hair creams, that produce a shine but do not change the color of the hair, may not be used on Shabbos (M.B. 303:81).

In line with what has been explained, a woman may use “Papier Poudre” which are small pieces of powder-impregnated paper that remove both the dust and the shine from the skin, and gives the skin a clean matt-like finish. The same would apply if slightly damp papers were available to bring about this effect. Since no liquid is squeezed from the paper there can be no question of סחיטה - squeezing (see M.B. 613:25), and from the point of view of coloring - the woman is simply not coloring anything. Such paper may therefore be used on Shabbos. The papers must, however, be torn from their pad before Shabbos, if that is how they are sold, since otherwise an *issur* of קורע - tearing, is involved - see M.B. 340:41.

9. NAIL POLISH - APPLICATION OSSUR, REMOVAL PERMITTED: If it is Shabbos and the nail-polish has become scratched and no longer looks respectable it will have to be removed. To paint it over or even just to touch it up is an *issur* of צובע - coloring (O.C. 303:25). It is even *ossur* to use a transparent lacquer since it has the effect of causing the nails to look somewhat darker and is viewed as coloring (M.B. 327:12). It also cannot simply be ignored, as the woman cannot do *netilas yadayim* with scratched nail-varnish because the damaged polish is a *chatzitzah* - an obstruction to the water, which in turn would invalidate the washing (See O.C. 161:2).

Such scratched polish must therefore be removed and the removal may be done even with a varnish remover - see *Mekoros* 68:10-11. The solvent should be rubbed over the polish with one's fingers because to use cotton-wool would involve the *issur* of סחיטה - squeezing (O.C. 320:18).

M. INSPIRING LETTERS CONCERNING TZNIUS

1. A GREAT MECHANECH PLEADS FOR LESS COSMETICS:

The following is a letter sent by the great *mechanech* and *mezakeh es harabim,* Reb Avraham Dov Kohn *zt'l,* founder and principal of the Gateshead Seminary, to his many *talmidos*. He brought Torah and *Yiras Shomayim* into thousands of homes. The letter speaks for itself:-

בס״ד

I would like to speak to you on a matter of supreme importance to all of us and hope you will give it your willing attention. It is about tznius.

I am not referring to failures concerning the proper covering of the hair of our married ex-students, to improper necklines on dresses, to pritzus re stockings and sleeves. We all know that no proper past or present Sem-girl would disgrace herself and harm the reputation of our Seminary in any of these points.

I am referring to matters which belong to the category of קדש עצמך במותר לך - "sanctify yourself by not overindulging in permitted things" and to matters that fall under the rule of דברים המותרים ואחרים נהגו בה איסור, אי אתה רשאי להתירן לפניהם - "Things that are permitted but some people are stringent and do not do them: you have no right to be lenient in their presence" (Pesachim 50a). These matters present one of our biggest problems.

My dear friends. I know very well that there is no issur to paint one's nails with colored nail varnish, to apply bright lipstick, to paint one's eye-lashes etc... No issur, and yet these things do not agree with the dignity of the Bas Torah we wish to educate.

I know very well the argument that these things need not necessarily be a contradiction to the Yiras Shomayim of the person. However, they become of such arresting importance, that sooner or later they are bound to take a vital position in the life of that girl or woman. This must cause loss of moral stature of mind and spirit - in the chinuch atmosphere of her home and place of activity.

If things go well for her family in respect of Torah and Yiras Shomayim it will be in spite of her, not because of her. Does not להיות אם בישראל - "to be a mother in Yisroel", which is the real task of a woman, mean that everything should be just because of her? The future and the success of her family is in her hands! In a time like ours there is a particular need for גדרים וסייגים - precautions and safety measures. Who should have more appreciation for this than girls who have had such a chinuch! I would be most unhappy to meet one of the former pupils whether single or married who does not live up to the Seminary standards in these points.

I would like to meet everyone of you as often as possible and nothing should prevent me doing so. You know very well that we in the Seminary stress very much the importance of tidiness and respectability. We take care that the girls should not lose their sense for all that is essential - for a pleasant appearance as much as for self-respect. The girls live up to an ideal of רוח הבריות נוחה הימנה - "her conduct and ways are pleasing to people". But this must never lead to an over-emphasis of fashion on those above-mentioned matters, which turns into a digression and must then be labeled as glamorous. This we must never tolerate.

I have touched on a delicate matter, which cuts deeply into the personal affairs of some of you. You might argue that I should have waited to discuss this point personally in Chugim sessions. You might be right in principle. However, I feel it is a matter of urgency that cannot be left to the chance of a possible meeting. I am also confident that no-one will be angry with me for a bit of old Sem. mussar.

Our Bnos Eretz Yisroel who are privileged to live on Admas HaKodesh have special responsibilities of giving the lead to others in these matters.

I do not see at the moment the likelihood of meeting all the chugim in the various countries on this problem. But should it be necessary לטובת הענין to pay a personal visit to one place or another, I shall not hesitate to undertake any journey irrespective of expenses and physical strain.

You surely remember the Yalkut in Yeshaya 3:- כל שאפשר לו למחות באנשי ביתו ואינו מוחה נתפס באנשי ביתו - "Whoever can prevent members of his household from sinning and does not bother to do so, is held responsible for the sins they commit" and we are all one בית, one big family!

These matters are of immense significance in our times because they pertain to the very upkeep of Torah in the Jewish people. I pray that the One who grants mankind intellect assigns us the understanding to embark on the righteous path of הצנע לכת את ה' אלוקיך - "Walking modestly in the ways of Hashem Your G-d".

ענינים אלו הן הן גופי תורה בזמננו אנו. ואני תפלה שהחונן לאדם דעת ידריככן בדרך נכונה של הצנע לכת לפני ה' אלוקיך.

בברכת נחמת ציון,

הק' אברהם דוב הכהן

2. A GREAT MECHANECHES CALLS FOR IMPROVED TZNIUS:

The following is a translation of Rebbetzen Kaplan's last letter in the Alumnae Bulletin of *Beis Yaacov* of America - the great Torah institution that she founded and headed for many years. She expressed her wish that this letter be translated and printed in that bulletin. It is a most wonderful letter as must be apparent to whoever reads it. From it gushes forth a heartfelt cry from a mother to her daughters imploring them not to abandon nor forsake the most valuable and most important part of their heritage.

To My Dear Spiritual Daughters לאי״ט.

Greetings upon the renewal of the Alumnae bulletin! May Hashem help that the bulletin serve as a bond to unite our entire Beis Yaacov family. It should help inspire us in Yiras Shomayim and fulfillment of mitzvos.

The Gemara in Brachos (20b) relates the following: The Malachim said to Hashem, "Ribbono Shel Olam, it says in Your Torah, אשר לא ישא פנים ולא יקח שוחד - 'Who does not show favoritism and does not take bribery' (Devarim 10:17). But don't You show favoritism to Bnei Yisroel, as it says in Bircas Kohanim, ישא ה׳ פניו אליך - 'Hashem shall show you favoritism' (Bamidbar 6:26)?" Hashem answered, "How can I not be noseh panim? They do mitzvos with so much love. For instance, I commanded them to bentch when they had eaten enough to be satisfied. But their Chachamim made a takonoh that they bentch even if they only ate a piece of bread the size of an olive or egg."

The Talmud is full of examples where the Chachamim added stringencies onto the mitzvos that Hashem commanded. This they have done because of their great yearning to please Hashem. Naturally, we are obligated to fulfill all the takonos of our Chachamim. In fact, listening to the Chachamim is a mitzva of the Torah as it says in Devarim (17:11) ועשית על פי התורה אשר יורוך ועל המשפט אשר יאמרו לך תעשה - "And you shall conduct yourself by the laws they teach you, and you shall react according to the judgments of which they inform you".

The Vilna Gaon explains in his commentary on Mishlei (22:9) as follows: Hashem manages the world with a system of midah kneged midah. When Yidden carry out mitzvos only to the degree that is absolutely necessary, only to the letter of the law and no more,

Hashem acts with the same strictness - He treats them just by the letter of the law. When that is the case the relationship of Hashem to Am Yisroel is that of "lo yisah panim v'lo yikach shochad" - He does not show favoritism. However, when Yidden carry out the will of Hashem to its utmost, when they take upon themselves extra precautions to themselves from sinning, Hashem acts likewise towards them with extra consideration. Then He is "noseh panim l'Yisroel" - He shows us favoritism and compassion. He is not over particular and instead of judging with strictness He judges with kindness and mercy.

Lately, there have been a number of tragedies both here and in Eretz Yisroel that really shook everyone up. Chazal say that in a time of tragedy one should search himself and his actions. In a time like this we must study ourselves carefully and see what is being demanded of us in Heaven. For what must we collectively do teshuva?

As far as Yiddishkeit is concerned it seems that the situation is much better today than it used to be. We are baruch Hashem zocheh to see a great revival of Torah in our generation. It is wonderful to see how women love to do mitzvos. There are countless organizations for the strengthening of Torah and chesed. It makes one want to call out together with Shlomo Hamelech *the words from Shir HaShirim (4:3) כפלת הרמון רקתך,* on which Rashi *comments, אפילו ריקנים שבך מלאים מצות כרמון - "Even your empty ones, even those who are on a low standard, are as full of mitzvos as the pomegranate is full of seeds".*

However, the yetzer horah has interfered and led our daughters astray in one specific area. It is this that I want to bring to your attention. Your lofty p'nimius, dearest Yiddishe techter, is not always matched by your chitzonius. Your appearance and style of dress sometimes lack the ואבדיל אתכם מן העמים להיות לי - "I will segregate you from other nations, to be Mine". The tznius and chein of the Bas Yisroel is sometimes not apparent in the clothing that is being worn. It is not enough that a dress is not cut out and is of decent length. The designers make clothes in a way that they arouse inappropriate thoughts, even though as far as size is concerned the piece of clothing is within the boundaries of halacha.

Likewise, the plague of makeup on the face and eyes is so widespread that many do not see what is wrong with it anymore. Sadly, it has even entered some of the finest homes. People think, "If this choshuveh Rebbetzen or this Talmid Chacham's wife does it, it's probably permissible". I do not mean to criticize anyone. The women of our generation are bli ayin horah on a very high standard. In many ways they are equal to the women of previous generations. However, in this one area הצליח מעשה שטן - "The Satan has regretfully been successful".

I believe that the main reason for this is that we don't consider the consequences. Nowadays, women are in business, at work, out shopping and so on. It is no good to go out over dressed and made-up, as this is machshil many people by arousing the wrong kinds of thoughts. Consider, even for a wedding one shouldn't dress in a very eye-catching manner. The Chofetz Chayim was once sitting at a meeting and a young girl came in a few times to serve refreshments. He requested that she should not come in anymore saying, "Are we sitting among Malachim?" I have mentioned on a number of occasions in the name of the Gemara that one of the Chachamim said that he learned Yiras cheit from a young girl. He overheard her davening and beseeching Hashem that she should not be guilty of causing anyone to sin.

We must be careful how we dress and act, so that no harm is caused by bringing people to inappropriate and forbidden thoughts. We are commanded לפני עור לא תתן מכשול - "Do not put a stumbling-block before the blind". Dressing up is only for one's husband. אין תכשיטין אלא לבעלה - "A woman should wear jewelry only for her husband". Sadly, many women do just the opposite. In the house they are always dressed in a duster and tiechel but they dress up when they go out.

In the introduction of the Mesilas Yesharim, the author writes that a person has to attain Ahavas Hashem. This means that we should strive with our whole heart to please Hashem, just as we strive with all our heart to please our parents. If we wish to know what pleases Hashem, let us hearken to the way Chazal praise the Jewish daughter. The Gemara says (Kesubos 17a), "How does one sing the praises of a kallah? לא כחל ולא שרק ולא פרכוס ויעלת חן - She does not paint herself up and she does not arrange her hair in an outstanding way - and she is nevertheless full of charm". This is the way Chazal praise the Jewish daughter. We must bring back the old natural Yiddishe chein. With that we will strengthen the kedusha of our camp and fulfill the pasuk's command, "והיה מחניך קדוש".

Who knows if we are not being judged in Heaven because of our negligence of tznius. Who knows if this is not ח״ו a result of ולא יראה בך ערות דבר ושב מאחריך - "Immorality should not be seen with you, lest I step back and depart from you" ח״ו.

My dear ones! Let us be mechazek this aspect of our lives. It is certainly hard to go against the tide and not follow the styles, but it is not impossible. A style is a man-made creation. If a person is determined, he can b'ezer Hashem create other styles, and then one person follows the other. Let there arise from among you the first group of Nachshan Ben Aminadavs. Just as he gathered his courage and was the first to jump into the water, so you should have the courage to be the first to stand up against the tide and declare war on all forms of pritzus. Many will follow you, and you will have the wonderful zechus of being mezakeh es harabim.

Let us strengthen ourselves and bring as much kedusha and tahara as possible into our lives. With that we will give tremendous pleasure to our Father in Heaven and He will say to the Malachim וכי לא אשא פנים לישראל, "How can I not show favoritism towards the Bnei Yisroel? Are they not fighting a war on My behalf?" As a result of Hashem's satisfaction with our deeds, He will conduct His dealings with us in a merciful manner. All gezeiros against us will b'ezer Hashem be canceled. We won't hear of any more tragedies and sickness ל״ע. All the sick will be healed and all the healthy will remain well. There will be peace among Yidden as we merit the fulfillment of the pasuk, ישא ה׳ פניו אליך וישם לך שלום.

With love, Yours,

W. Kaplan

[A number of points that are written in this letter have been mentioned elsewhere in the *sefer*. They have nevertheless been retained, so that the complete letter is presented. Fortunate is *Klal Yisroel* to have been granted such *mechanchim* and *mechanchos*. It is our duty to make full use of their legacy elucidated in these letters. We can give them no greater *nachas* in *Olam HaEmes*.]

---

3. A LETTER ABOUT DRESSING IN "HONOR OF SHABBOS":

The following is a letter written to seminary girls outlining the correct approach to dressing for Shabbos. Much can be achieved if those responsible for the education of girls would place "striving for *tznius*" high on their list of priorities. If a complete generation of seminary graduates were educated to cherish and deeply appreciate *tznius* in dress and conduct, they would have an extraordinary impact on their homes and upon the next generation as a whole. They would strengthen the Jewish people in these trying times and safeguard them from the enticements that endanger their very existence.

At *Matan Torah*, *Hashem Yisborach* instructed Moshe Rabbeinu to approach the women before the men - כה תאמר לבית יעקב ותגיד לבני ישראל - "So you shall say to the house of Yaacov (the women) and instruct the sons of *Yisroel* (the men)" (*Shemos* 19:3 and *Shemos Rabba* 28:2). Why were the women spoken to before the men? Rabbeinu Shmuel Eidelish *zt'l* explains in his commentary, *Maharsha* (*Sotah* 21b) that once women appreciate Torah and *mitzvos*, they can be relied upon to encourage others and ensure that the rest of *Klal Yisroel* also accepts them. It was therefore of utmost importance to first win the appreciation of the women for the Torah that was to be given to the Jewish people. Accordingly, educating girls to *tznius* and similar qualities is tantamount to educating a large cross-section of the community to the ways of *Hashem*. For this reason *Chazal* say, אין הדורות נגאלים אלא בשכר נשים צדקניות שבדור - "Salvations come to the Jewish people in the merit of righteous women of the generation" (*Yalkut Ruth* 606). With righteous women as our mothers and wives, there is a hope for the future.

בס״ד

יום ג׳ לפרשת תרומה שנת תשנ״ו לפ״ק

To my devoted Talmidos שתחי׳.

After much consideration I have decided to write to you about a subject that would generally have been mentioned in a shiur. I feel that in this instance the written word may have a deeper impact and reach further than the spoken word and have therefore made an exception. The subject is kedushas Shabbos and the way it can be enhanced both at home and in Seminary. Before coming to the point, I wish to put on record that over the years much headway has been made in improving the refinement of dress and general tznius of our students, and with gratitude to Hashem we are aware that the vast majority of our students dress at all times in a way that complies with the spirit and the halachic requirements of tznius.

However in one area some are lacking direction. This concerns what we do in "honor of Shabbos". Even on this issue the majority of girls are not to be faulted, and their appearance on Shabbos is as befits the sanctity of the day. However, since there are some who err, it is important that we state clearly our hashkofoh on this matter. In this way all girls will know what is not within the spirit of the chinuch we offer our girls. Our chinuch has been successful, if, when nisyonos arise after leaving Seminary a girl will know the derech hayashar a Bas Yisroel is to follow.

Now for the main letter. It is written in a firm and forthright manner (although only some err as stated) as befits the importance of the issues it addresses:-

Some girls are under the impression that dressing for Shabbos for adult girls involves more than dressing into Shabbos clothes and effecting some minor physical enhancements. They therefore engage in beautifications that far surpass the needs of Shabbos. For example, they brush their hair in a way that it hangs loosely and flowingly over their shoulders. Also, they apply substantial facial cosmetics, such as different forms of eye makeup, bright lipstick etc. Those who do so are, however, very mistaken, and have a distorted vision of what a Bas Yisroel should look like on Shabbos. Whilst their manner of dress might be the authentic way of honoring Shabbos, their ways of beautification are foreign implants. They have confused 'self beautification' with 'beautifying Shabbos'.

If these girls are asked, "For whom are you beautifying yourselves?" they will surely answer in all earnestness, "In honor of Shabbos!" The following must, however, be asked: What would the holy day of Shabbos consider 'an honor' - hair that is kept short or bound together and made up in a b'cheint and eidel manner, or long hair that lies loosely over the shoulders in a way typical of non-Jewish girls? Such a hair style projects the image of a girl who wants her beautiful hair to be noticed and admired. Since this is the impression created, it lacks any vestige of kedusha, even if in fact this is not the girl's intention. We say in Tefillas Mussaf of Shabbos, עם מקדשי שביעי - "We Yidden are a people who sanctify the Shabbos". Can there be any doubt as to which type of hair style adds to kedushas Shabbos?

There are girls who throughout the week do not allow their hair to dangle freely because they are busy writing notes all day and loose hair would get in the way. However, on Shabbos, when no writing takes place and loose hair will not disturb, they leave their hair undone and open. What should we say to the trickery of the Soton. As always, he uses every means available to achieve his goal. He commissions our very Shemiras Shabbos and the fact that on Shabbos we do not write, and causes Bnos Yisroel to appear with long open unrefined hair on Shabbos, although these very girls look fine throughout the week.

Additionally, is Shabbos enhanced by applying substantial makeup, which paints over the true face of the Jewish princess and detracts from the Yiddishe chein of a Bas Yisroel, or does a face that shines with the natural beauty and purity of the neshama of a Yid, add luster to this very special day? What confers onto Shabbos Kodesh the honor and prestige it deserves?

Another point that regrettably needs mention concerns the length of skirts. You have learnt in the name of all Gedolei HaPoskim that a skirt must reach four inches below the lowest point of the knee to guarantee proper cover of the knees and above. There are those who comply fully with this ruling during the week, when they wear their usual everyday clothes. However, when it comes to Shabbos they feel that "l'chvod Shabbos" their skirts should be shorter, because shorter skirts have a more pleasing look. What can be more hurtful than to see tznius lessened in honor of Shabbos! (Altogether, the whole basis of the nisayon needs investigation. Where does the feeling that 'shorter skirts have a more pleasing look' come from? Has this not been culled from wholly impure sources such as the substandard ways of dress we come across in the streets).

There are girls who throughout the week wear a loose-fitting skirt. They, however, improve their dress for Shabbos and wear a close-fitting straight skirt as it is a more classy way of dress. These skirts are often shorter than the fuller types of skirts mentioned and are commonly less than the required length. There is of course no heter to be lax with any of the fundamentals of tznius. It is similarly wholly incorrect that some of these straight skirts are tight fitting, pronouncing parts of the body. Other skirts are distinctly narrower further down than higher up. This is very wrong even if it is a loose fitting skirt as this too displays the hips and general shape of the body and is therefore an immodest manner of dress.

Let us stop and reflect for a moment. How can we possibly view wearing such clothes as giving Kovod to the Shabbos and to Hashem who gave us the Shabbos? Whilst these mistakes are of course oversights, they would not occur if we internalized the feelings for tznius and made them part of our lives.

Finally, it must be pointed out that there are girls who wear on Shabbos thin tights that add no tznius or refinement to the legs whatsoever. The institution of covering the legs is totally defeated when the tights do not lessen the visibility of the leg in a meaningful way. There can be no prospect of honoring Shabbos while dressed in a manner that contravenes modesty and care for kedushas Yisroel - the symbols and endorsements of the Jewish daughter. Once again, not intending to do wrong does not correct the damage caused.

In the song Mah Yedidus we sing, כשושנים סוגה בו ינוחו בן ובת - "Just as rose bushes protect a garden, so Shabbos brings calm and protection to its sons and daughters". If we protect that which has been entrusted into our hands, we will be deserving of the protection that is granted in the merit of honoring the holy day of Shabbos!

To summarize: The overall appearance of the Bas Yisroel on Shabbos is that of nobility, chein and purity. Her clothes are majestic and aristocratic. Her hair is refined and eidel looking, and the beauty of Shabbos as it blends with her tznius which is internalized shine forth from her tranquil face. If girls accept these great truths they will find that Shabbos will become quite a different day for them. Its uplifting ruach will extend to all the days of the week.

I sincerely hope this matter receives your earnest and immediate attention. Wishing each one of you the multiple brachos of Shabbos, as we sing in the zemiros of Shabbos, כל שומר שבת כראוי לו וכו׳ שכרו הרבה מאוד על פי פעלו - "Whoever keeps Shabbos as befits it etc. shall be richly rewarded in accordance to his deeds". The brachos of

Shabbos are plentiful as Chazal say, כל המענג את השבת נותנים לו משאלות לבו - "Whoever makes Shabbos a delightful day shall be granted all the requests of his heart!" (Shabbos 118a). Our future happiness lies in our hands!

בברכת כל טוב והצלחה רבה לכל אחת ואחת מכן,

Rabbi ....

---

4. A LETTER FROM A LADY WHO LONGED TO FEEL FOR TZNIUS:

The following is one of the most moving and heartfelt letters sent to the author of this *sefer*. It was written after a number of excerpts from this *sefer* had been published. The letter reflects the conflicts a woman might feel at times concerning the demands of *tznius* in relationship to makeup and general dress. It then goes on to demonstrate how, as a result of searching for guidance, inspiration and *chizuk*, this woman obtained great encouragement from the insights she read and they had a profound effect on her complete life style. This underscores the enormous contribution made by a woman's positive attitude. It creates an acute awareness in the person and directs her to where *chizuk* can be found:-

Manchester

To Harav ....,

I have been reading the excerpts from "Modesty - An Adornment for Life" and it is with sheer gratitude that I put pen to paper to express the following...

Being a "makeup wearer" and an artistic person, I have over the past years been trying to refine certain areas regarding the halachos of tznius. I have wanted to "prove" that a person can be "arty" yet at the same time conform to the norms of our society without losing one's individual touch. I have been encouraged by the idea that a woman should be pleasing. Her strength comes from her ability to conform to the halachos. This, however, does not have to rob her of her own individuality.

An area that presented great difficulty to me was keeping my hair covered at home (not just general covering, rather the scrupulous way.) I really tried to work out why this required such a great effort on my part, even though a Rebbetzen I really admire stressed so much the importance of this mitzva and also I have heard so many times about the sons of Kimchis etc. Of course I want good children so why was I having such a conflict in this area?

Then, one day I came across a book with the story of Kimchis. I read it once again and was overcome by the words - Kimchis did not keep the mitzva because she was 'makpid' that even the walls should not see her hair - but because she was aware of Hashem's presence and because of that could not help but cover it so scrupulously. I felt thrilled, as finally the Kimchis story "hit home". I realized that if I would have a far deeper commitment to being aware of Hashem's presence it would help me in this area. This however in itself requires so much "hard work". I felt on the way Baruch Hashem (but a long journey still).

When word "got around" that Harav... was bringing out not just a booklet but a proper sefer on the halachos concerning tznius, I had the following mixed feelings, even though I would like to improve in this area.

(1) I wonder when this sefer will be available so that I can see what I'm doing wrong (defensive).

(2) I felt I was getting geared for the "Yes but" Syndrome (defensive).

(3) I loved the introduction to the initial book on tznius so I really look forward to seeing the new sefer (excited).

(4) Oi! I wonder what demands will be placed on me!

Well, when I read the excerpts from 'Modesty - An Adornment for Life', I did not want them to finish. Feelings of hisorerus in this area just gushed forth. I know why. The excerpts involved our whole selves, not 'just' the doing or not doing, but our thoughts, feelings, ancestors, children and aspirations, all interwoven to present this worthy concept in the most becoming way.

My first "shock" was reading that tznius is to a girl what Torah learning is to a boy (being aware of the efforts carried out for Torah). These words have been another turning point for me and have helped me translate the words into actions. How would I feel if my husband spent hours reading about the importance of learning, the beauty etc. yet seldom picked up a sefer!

Therefore I thank Harav .... for initiating this gush of inspiration. As I once heard in the name of Harav Simcha Wasserman zt'l, "If a person wants someone to do something - the request should be in a way that the person will want to do what is asked of him/her".

Thank you for writing a sefer which does just this.

Mrs ....

---

5. A SEMINARY GRADUATE FACES A WORLD HOSTILE TO TZNIUS:

The following is a heartfelt letter from an ex-seminary girl. In it she expresses her appreciation for all that she gained spiritually. She also requests her *Rav* to *daven* for her so that she should stay strong and retain the standard of *tznius* she gained during her time in the seminary. The letter powerfully demonstrates the dilemma of the *Bas Yisroel* - after learning to love and admire *tznius* she is engulfed by a world that is hostile and estranged to *tznius* and all that it stands for. She begs her *Rav* to *daven* for her, because she understands that *Hashem* comes to the aid of those who turn to him with sincerity - קרוב ה׳ לכל קוראיו לכל אשר יקראוהו באמת. Her letter is reproduced here so that it can be a source of *chizuk* to the many cherished *Bnos Yisroel* who find themselves in similar situations. With strength and *tefilla* they will be able to retain what they gained, build on it and even pass it on to future generations.

בס״ד

אלול תשנ״ה

London

Dear Rabbi ....

To say a mere thank you for all that you have done for us I feel is totally inadequate. Not only did you teach us the halachos but you instilled within us a true desire to do the right thing. I must admit that before I came to Sem I often resented being constantly corrected concerning halachic matters. However, after my first shiur with the Rav that feeling left me, never to return. This is because you showed us the beauty of each halacha as you gave over the facts as well as imbuing us with a love for living a life totally centered around תורה. For this I am forever indebted to you.

I must also say that .... inspired many of us. I can say quite confidently that for me as well as for many of my friends (if not all) the shiur was one of the highlights of the week. We went away uplifted, with a strong desire to truly keep and put into practice what we learnt.

I have now returned home to a distorted world full of turbulence and confusion. It hits one as one walks on the streets. We feel so alone away from our precious haven. Yet as the Rav said in his departing speech - לכו ונלכה באור ה׳ - all that we have acquired from you goes with us.

I therefore ask you to daven for us, that ה׳ should give us סייעתא דשמייא to overcome these difficult נסיונות and the ability to retain the high level of צניעות the Torah requires of us - thus not falling prey to the poisonous influences of society.

May הקב״ה give the esteemed Rav the כח to continue his invaluable work עד מאה ועשרים שנה.

כתיבה וחתימה טובה,

.... (Signature)

---

6. A FROM A LADY WHO TEACHES "TZNIUS" TO LOCAL WOMEN:

The following letter is a precious gem and much can be learnt from it. (1) It is heartwarming to see the intense and deeply sincere love for *tznius* that is within reach of an *erlicher Bas Yisroel*. From the first to the last word the letter demonstrates the great aspirations of the writer. (2) It demonstrates what a single sincere person can achieve even without a team of co-workers. The writer set up a *shiur*. Also, she is so enthusiastic about this cherished *mitzva* that she yearns to overcome the problem of *pritzus* in the wider community and even suggests how this can be done. (3) The positive response of the participants in the *shiur* is heartening. It is testimony to the fact that with the correct approach the *halachos* of *tznius* and the conduct it calls for, are acceptable even to women of our times. (4) The writer shows concern for the finest detail of *halacha* - to ensure that it is correctly understood and that it is neither under nor over emphasized. (5) The letter shows how deep sensitivities related to *tznius* can be. It could be that once mothers have made a *chizuk* in *tznius*, the children are immediately affected by the extra *kedusha* in the household. They *daven* better as a result of it and are hurt by forms of *pritzus* they come across. Now for the letter itself:

London

Ellul 5755

לכבוד ....

I have to try, with words which will never be enough, to thank the Rav *for the loan of the precious Sefer, עוז והדר לבושה. The magnitude of help given by the Sefer is beyond description.*

One cries over the Sefer with deep regret over shortcomings and missed opportunities. This is followed by a wish to help others avoid pitfalls and similar suffering. Having begun in a happy hour, our shiur is into its third week בעי"ה with a small group of ladies. Hakadosh Baruch Hu *should help us to continue after the* Yomim Tovim *אי"ה. The shiur seems well received ב"ה. On the first occasion one lady offered to sew up anyone's skirt which needed attention, and on the second occasion, another lady offered to help elasticize necklines. In this way, we are all able to support and help each other.*

I am very worried about the quality of giving over this shiur, of chas v'shalom misrepresenting anything or not encouraging anyone enough who comes to learn and work on their tznius. I wish there was a tefillah similar to that of ר' נחוניא בן הקנה not to be machshil chas v'shalom anyone with one's mistakes! Could there be such a tefillah? Since I'm worried about what I'm giving over, I may send one gloss of it at some point, to receive some advice, if it's possible.

The rewards of working on tznius are immediate and awe-inspiring, together with the inner simcha and serenity which follows, and the improved תפלות of the children, just as the Sefer promises. A young teenage daughter (13), previously famous for her speedy Shacharis, told me on her return from camp, she had decided to make a greater effort with tefillah and would try and daven Mincha and Maariv as well. My joy was indescribable.

We often wonder why we do so poorly in comparison to the wonderful achievements of the previous generation. Surely it was the superior tznius of the mothers which underpinned these achievements. May it be Hashem Yisborach's will that we recover by learning your Sefer until we become the Sefer.

It seems ב״ה very valuable to have a group of women learning and working on their צניעות together. There is that warm support and encouragement within the group, the ease of asking and answering questions together, and of teaching halachos which benefit from a small amount of demonstration. This in no way replaces the major התעוררות of a שיעור by a Rav, but it is a useful working addition. It would be helpful if all the Batei Midrash in London could have small groups learning together. Then the battle would be fought on many fronts, and so many loyal foot soldiers would quickly overrun the enemy, פריצות.

I have to give endless thanks for the enormous help this precious sefer has rendered to me and my family and the school that is kind enough to have me teach. There are numerous children of all ages (in school) and the damage that could be incurred by my inadequate dress is a frightful and frightening specter. For this reason it's best for me to adopt as much מדת חסידות as possible. I'm, however, careful to emphasize in the Shiur, basic halachos which you bring down that everyone is mechuyov to keep, clearly distinguished from מדת חסידות. We gratefully learn from your holy sefer where the dinim are distilled with such perfect clarity, ב״ה.

With heartfelt wishes for a כתיבה וחתימה טובה to all the family and all Klal Yisroel.

בברכת כל טוב,

Mrs ....

Chapter Eight

SINGING IN THE PRESENCE OF MEN

A. THE HALACHA OF KOL B'ISHA ERVAH

1. THE ISSUR FOR MEN TO HEAR WOMEN SINGING: A woman may not sing in the presence of a man (other than her closest family - see below), because with this she exposes part of her inner beauty, which in turn provokes undue attention. Hence *Chazal* established the *halacha* that קול באשה ערוה - the voice of a woman who sings is *ervah*.

A woman and girl may therefore not sing in the presence of a male visitor or a relation such as an uncle, cousin, nephew, father-in-law, brother-in-law, son-in-law, step-father, step-brother or step-son. (The *issur* applies once a boy is nine - *Halichos Bas Yisrael* Chapter 6 note 1, in the name of Hagaon Harav Shlomo Zalman Auerbach zt'l). A *kallah* may likewise not sing in the presence of her *chasan* because before marriage she is not yet related to him, and it is *ossur* for him to hear her sing (O.C. 75:3).

2. STATUS OF BLOOD RELATIVES CONCERNING THIS ISSUR: A woman may sing in the presence of her husband although her voice attracts his attention. Since a wife is permitted to her husband she may certainly be attractive to him. Her voice is therefore *ervah shel heter* to him.

She may also sing in the presence of her close blood relatives i.e. her father, grandfather, great-grandfather, son, grandson, great-grandson. She may sing in the presence of these relatives although she is of course forbidden to them and must not cause them to be attracted to her. This is because attraction between close blood relatives is minimal (and such relatives may even kiss - E.H. 21:7). Therefore, for attraction to be caused by hearing her sing is out of the question. Since relatives are unaffected by the singing it is permitted.

Some opinions are stringent and do not allow a brother to hear his sister sing - this is quoted in the name of the *Chazon Ish zt'l*. Many are, however, of the opinion that this is permitted provided he is not listening out to enjoy her singing. See *Mishbetzos Zahav Levusho*, page 156 point 6, in the name of the *Brisker Rav,* Maran Hagaon Harav Yitzchak Zev Soloveitchik *zt'l* and Hagaon Harav Shlomo Zalman Auerbach *zt'l* who maintain that a brother may hear his sister sing. This is also the opinion of *Responsa Teshuvos V'Hanhagos* 2:138 - see *Mekoros* 71:3-14 for elaboration. (Concerning a man hearing a girl that is under *Bas-mitzva* - see 8:E) .

3. THE ISSUR APPLIES EVEN WHEN SHE SINGS A BRACHA: The *issur* of *kol ishah* applies even when the female sings a *davar shebikdusha*, such as part of *davening, Bircas Hamazon* and the like (*Sefer Kolbo* 45; M.B. 479:9). This is because the urge of *arayos* exists even when a *mitzva* is performed as can be seen from the fact that a *mechitza* is required in a *shul,* although it is a place set aside for *devarim shebikdusha.*

Moreover, intermingling occurred in the *Beis Hamikdash* during the *Simchas Beis Hashoeivah* which drew large crowds. To prevent this, they built an upper gallery for women. This is referred to by *Chazal* as a תיקון גדול - "A major rectification" - due to the great improvement in *kedushas Yisroel* which it brought about (*Succah* 51b). This intermingling took place not only in an exceptionally holy place as the *Beis Hamikdash*, but during a celebration of the highest spiritual order called "*Hashoeivah*" (which literally means "drawing") because משם שואבים רוח הקודש - "From there people drew *Ruach HaKodesh*" (*Breishis Rabba* 70:8).

In spite of the outstanding holiness of the place and the intense sacredness of the occasion, the *yetzer horah* did not consider himself a *persona-non-grata* and caused intermingling to occur in the midst of this very *simcha*. He manipulated the high spirits generated by the fervent *kedusha* of the occasion to achieve the very opposite of that which drew the people together in the first place. Similarly, if a female sings a *bracha*, part of *davening* or a chapter of *Hallel* in the presence of men, it will be just as harmful as all other instances of *kol b'ishah ervah* - see *Mekoros* 4:3.

B. SINGING THAT CAN BE HEARD FROM ANOTHER ROOM

1. ENSURING THAT A NEIGHBOR CANNOT HEAR HER SING: The *issur* of *kol b'isha ervah* applies even if the woman is in a different room than the man - see *Responsa Chasam Sofer, Choshen Mishpat* 190. People living in apartment blocks must therefore be particularly careful not to violate this *issur*. As they are in very close proximity to one another, a girl or woman may not sing in a way that a man in an apartment near to hers can hear her. Should she wish to sing, she must close the windows, and thereby confine her voice. Similarly, if a mother sings a lullaby to her baby to calm him and help him sleep, she must ensure that people who are not close blood relatives but live nearby are not capable of hearing her voice - M.B. 560, *Shar Hatzion* 25.

Occasionally, a woman sings in her apartment with the windows closed, but due to the power or pitch of her voice (or the thinness of the wall), the man who lives next door (or just above or below her) can hear her clearly. In such a case he must find a way to make her aware of this problem, so that she sings in a way that he does not hear her.

2. WOMEN SINGING WITH CHAZAN - MUST KEEP VERY LOW TONE: If women *davening* in a ladies' *shul* wish to accompany the singing of the *Chazan*, they may do so but only in a low tone. It should be low enough that even if many women and girls are involved, their collective voices will not be audible in the men's *shul*. The same applies at a *chasuna* or *sheva brachos* where the men and women are together in one large hall which is subdivided by a full size *mechitza*. When dancing, the girls might wish to sing with the orchestra. This would require that they sing in such an undertone that their singing cannot be heard from the men's part of the hall.

C. THE ISSUR APPLIES TO ALL FORMS OF SINGING

1. SAYING VERSES IN A VERY TUNEFUL WAY: The *issur* of hearing a female sing applies whether the woman sings a proper song or just recites verses in a tuneful way, such as the tune of *leining*. Accordingly, if there are visitors at the *seder* table (see 8:H:1 below) women may join in but only quietly whether it is a part of the *Hagadah* that is sung properly or a part that is just recited in a melodious way. Similarly, if a girl comes late for a Shabbos meal and must say *Kiddush* herself (and there are people who are not family in the room) she should either say the *Kiddush* quietly or without a melodious tune (M.B. 479:9; *Mateh Efrayim, Hilchos Kaddish, Elef L'mateh* 9; *Otzar HaPoskim* 21:20:2 - see *Mekoros* 73:2).

Wailing and chanting in a sad voice (similar to that of a *hesped*) does not attract people to her and therefore does not fall under the *issur* of *kol isha*. See *Yirmiya* 9:16 where the Novi says, התבוננו וקראו למקוננות ותבואינה - "Consider and call female wailers and they should come". Evidently, wailing and chanting in a sad tone does not fall under this *issur*. See also *Tiferes Yisroel*, on *Mishnayos Moed Katan* 3:68.

The *issur* of *kol isha* applies whether one hears a Jewess or a non-Jewess sing, just as all other forms of exposure may not be seen even on a non-Jewess (M.B. 75:17). Accordingly, it is *ossur* for a man to go to an opera if there are female singers or even to watch a film on which a female sings.

2. HUMMING AND WHISTLING: It is *ossur* for a woman or girl to hum a tune in the presence of men. Humming is in fact singing (as she is using her vocal chords), but instead of the voice coming out of her mouth she produces it through her nose. It is therefore the "voice of the woman" and subject to the *issur* of קול באשה ערוה - see *Mekoros* 73:3.

Whistling is not forbidden under the *issur* of *kol isha* because no true voice is involved. It is no different than creating music with a musical instrument which is permitted - see *Magen Avraham* 338:2, who writes that whistling is similar to producing music with an instrument. However, although whistling is permitted and in previous generations it was practiced by even the greatest (see *Rema* O.C. 338:1 and *Kaf Hachayim* 338:7), nowadays, in many circles, it is practiced only by the low class. Accordingly, it is unrefined for girls who belong to these circles to whistle. Moreover, to produce an exceptionally melodious form of whistling is a special talent, and women should not display special talents in public, as is explained in 8:C:5.

3. FEMALE CHOIR: There is no difference whether a man hears just one woman singing or a group of women, because a man is attracted by a collective female voice just as he is attracted by an individual female voice. Men may therefore not listen to a choir of women or girls. See *Sotah* (48a) where *Chazal* say, זמרי נשי ועני גברא כאש בנערות - "When a group of women sing and a group of men respond in song, it is like setting fire to flax", meaning that listening to the song of women can cause the *yetzer horah* of the men to flare up - see *Mekoros* 72:1. Just as a man must not listen to a choir of women even though he cannot single out the voice of any particular woman, so too it is *ossur* for a man to listen to a choir that involves both males and females singing together - see *Megilla* 21b and 8:G:1 below.

Even if all the men that are present are in the choir, and there are therefore no male bystanders who are just listening to the choir, the *issur* of *kol b'ishah ervah* still applies to the males in the choir. Due to the attraction female voices has on males, the men could derive pleasure from hearing females even when the female voices are interlaced with male voices. See 8:H:1 below for a further reason why this is forbidden. See *Mekoros* 77:3.

When a group of girls travels on a bus or coach with a Jewish man in the driver's seat, it is *ossur* for the girls to sing, as they will caused the Jewish man to hear *Kol Ishah*, (which, as stated, is *ossur* even when there are many female voices together and even if they cannot be seen at the time - See *Responsa Chasam Sofer*, *Choshen Mishpat* 190). However, if the driver is a non-Jew, who does not have an *issur* to hear women sing, they may sing (just as Jewish girls may talk to a non-Jew even if he gazes at their faces), provided they are not singing for him or in response to his request, since it is against *tznius* for a female to purposefully present any of her beauty to a man - 9:J:2(b).

4. TAPE RECORDINGS ETC: Many *Poskim* maintain that a recording of a female voice cannot be termed as *ervah* because only the female body, or song that comes directly from a female body, can be classified as *ervah*. Nevertheless, according to many *Poskim* it is *ossur* for a man to hear a tape of a woman or group of women singing. See *Responsa Beis Shearim* O.C. 33, *Chelkas Yaacov* 1:163, *P'ri HaSadeh* 3:32 and *Shevet HaLevi* 3:181, 5:197. They maintain that this is *ossur* (especially to someone who personally knows the woman or one has seen a photograph of her) because hearing her female voice can bring a man to forbidden thoughts. It is comparable to looking intently at a woman's colorful dress which is *ossur* although it is not human flesh because it can attract a man's attention - E.H. 21:1.

It is therefore incorrect practice for a man to listen to women singing on the radio or a tape. When a woman plays a tape of women singing, she should ensure that it cannot be heard by the men in her household or in neighboring apartments. Furthermore, if a private tape-recording is made of women or girls singing at a party, *siyum* etc., it is important that the tape be clearly marked, so men who should not hear these women sing know that this tape is not for them - see *Mekoros* 73:1-2.

5. WOMEN DOING JOBS THAT ATTRACT MALE SPECTATORS: A man may hear music produced with musical instruments by a woman or a group of women. Since no female voice is involved, the *issur* of קול באשה ערוה does not apply (*Aruch Hashulchan* 75:8). It is, however, *ossur* for men to observe women playing musical instruments because there is a general *issur* for women to exercise special skills in front of men as they thereby attract attention to their movements - see *Teshuvas HoRadvaz* 2:770 and *Responsa Mishnah Halachos* 6:25.

Due to this, a woman should not act in a play, paint a mural, weave a complex tapestry or play a sophisticated game etc. in a place where men can see her. She may however sew, knit, type, operate a computer, play well-known games etc. although men can see her, because these are skills that many people have and therefore do not attract attention - see *Mekoros* 74:1.

The *Chasam Sofer* (*Shabbos* 21b) writes that in theory it would be a *hidur mitzva* (a welcomed voluntary deed) for women and girls not to be *yotzeh* on *Chanukah* with the *menorah* lit by the *baal habayis,* and instead to light the *menorah* themselves just as males do. *The Chasam Sofer* goes on to explain that women and girls nevertheless do not do so because of *tznius* (unless she is a single woman who is obligated to light - see O.C. 675:3). Originally, everyone lit the *menorah* outside the entrance of the house in full view of the public, and it was unfitting for females to light a *menorah* which attracts attention when everyone is outdoors and they could be observed by by-passers and males of the neighborhood.

Since women did not actively participate in this *mitzva* when it was originally given they retained this *minhag* even once the lighting of the *menorah* was moved from the exterior to the interior of the house. [Evidently, the merit of *tznius* is so great that it is preferable to retain a memory of an act of *tznius* rather than do a *hidur mitzva*].

We see from here that women and girls should forgo doing a *hidur mitzva* if it will attract attention to themselves. It therefore goes without saying that where no *hidur mitzva* is involved it is all the more incorrect for women and girls to behave in public in a way that draws the attention of people to them.

D. RECITING A BRACHA WHILE HEARING A WOMAN SING

1. BRACHA WHILE A CLOSE FEMALE BLOOD RELATIVE SINGS: As stated, a woman may sing in the presence of her most intimate family, such as father, grandfather, brother, son, grandson and husband, as close blood relatives are hardly attracted to her. For this reason, they may generally hear her sing even when she is an adult. However, once she is an adult or eleven years old and close to adulthood, a slight pleasure is derived from hearing her female voice. It is therefore forbidden for such relatives to recite a *bracha* whilst hearing her sing (see 8:F:2), just as they may not say a *bracha* when seeing her in inadequate dress, (see 6:U:5). [*Mimishbetzos Zahav Levusho* page 156:7 in the name of Hagaon Harav Shlomo Zalman Auerbach *zt'l*].

If the man puts his fingers into his ears or uses ear-plugs and is therefore unable to hear the female sing, he may say a *bracha*. Just as turning away from a semi-clad woman enables a man to say a *bracha*, because the *ervah* has been removed from before his eyes, so too, blocking his ears removes the *kol ishah* from his hearing and he may say a *bracha* - see *Mekoros* 73:4.

2. BRACHA WHILE HEARING WIFE SING: A husband naturally enjoys hearing his wife sing and it is therefore considered *ervah* to him - albeit permitted *ervah*. It has been explained earlier that it is *ossur* to recite a *bracha* in the presence of *ervah* even if it is permitted *ervah*. Accordingly, when a husband is *benching*, learning or discussing *divrei* Torah, his wife must not sing within his earshot (O.C. 75:3 *Rema*). This *halacha* is hardly known and would surprise many otherwise observant people. He may, however, continue learning without verbalizing what he learns because only spoken *divrei* Torah are forbidden. See 4:A:2 and 4:B:3 above.

Even if he regularly hears her sing, the *issur* still applies, just as he may not say a *bracha* when she is not properly dressed or her hair is uncovered even if it is common for him to see those areas. Her song and uncovered limbs are natural attractions, and can therefore affect the husband although he frequently hears and sees them - see *Mekoros* 73:5-10.

If a wife must say *Kiddush* on behalf of her husband who is not well, or for some other reason (M.B. 271:4), the wife should not sing any part of the *Kiddush*. When hearing her the husband will be considered as saying the *Kiddush* himself (due to the principal of שומע כעונה). Therefore, just as he may not say a *bracha* himself when hearing his wife sing, so too, he may not say a *bracha* "by hearing" whilst he hears his wife sing (M.B.75:29). The fact that his wife is the very person who is reciting the *bracha* on his behalf is immaterial.

3. BRACHA WHILE A WOMAN PERSISTENTLY SINGS NEARBY: It happens sometimes that a man cannot help hearing women sing, e.g. there is a club near the house and women sing there to an audience, a neighbor's wife sings and he cannot stop her, a neighbor plays his radio so loudly that he cannot help but hear females singing. Should it be a short term problem the man could block his ears as explained above. This is, however, not a solution for an ongoing problem. In all such cases, the *halacha* for saying *brachos* is somewhat more lenient. Since he cannot help himself, and this condition will cause major *bitul* Torah, he has a *heter* to say *brachos* etc. provided he does not pay attention to the women singing.

Since he is concentrating on the *bracha*, he will most probably not hear the song at all. Even if he does hear the song, it will not enter his thought processes because he is thinking about the *bracha*. He has thereby removed the element of attraction from the song he hears. Hearing a song in such a way is comparable to facing a woman with uncovered hair but not looking at her. In both cases, the element of attraction is missing, and the usual *issur* of *ervah* does not apply. This *heter* must, however, not be relied upon in the first place. Instead, reasonable steps should be taken to move away or to stop the women singing when men can hear them (M.B. 75:17).

4. REACTION OF A GADOL WHEN IN A DILEMMA: The Slutzker *Rosh Yeshiva*, Hagaon Hagadol Harav Isser Zalman Meltzer *zt'l* lived during the latter part of his life in *Yerusholayim* where he was *Rosh Yeshiva* of *Yeshivas Eitz Chayim.* He was once seen walking to and fro outside his house, and was evidently reluctant to enter his own home for some reason. A *Yeshiva bachur* who saw him, approached the *Rosh Yeshiva* and asked him if he could help the *Rosh Yeshiva* in some way. The *Rosh Yeshiva* declined the offer, saying he needed no help. Since he continued pacing to and fro, the *bachur* approached him once again, and begged the *Rosh Yeshiva* to allow him to be of assistance. The *Rosh Yeshiva* reiterated that he required no help.

He explained that he had already entered his house and saw that the Jewish maid, who was a poor and lonely individual, was in the house washing the floor. He continued, "While she works she loves singing to herself. However, she knows that I must not hear her sing. She therefore stops singing the moment she realizes that I have entered the house. Since I do not want to deprive this unfortunate woman of her enjoyment, I would rather let her finish her work and only then enter the house. Until then I will gladly wait out here".

Reb Isser Zalman could not slip quietly into the house, as the maid would continue singing and he was not allowed to hear her due to the *issur* of *kol b'isha ervah.* On the other hand, he did not want to stop her singing due to his sensitivities for her feelings. Therefore, although time was precious to him, he did not enter his own home until she had finished and was ready to leave. (Hagaon Reb Moshe Mordchai Schulzinger *shlita* in his *sefer*, *P'ninim V'igros Toras Ze'ev*, page 40).

Such are the ways of the great sages of our people. Their concern for fulfillment of *halacha* (*bein adam l'makom*) and their concern for their fellow Jew (*bein adam l'chaveiro*) are both perfect and exemplary. They furthermore do not sacrifice one because of the other. Instead, they invariably find a way to accommodate both obligations, often at the expense of personal comfort.

E. HEARING A GIRL UNDER BAS-MITZVA SING

1. HETER TO HEAR A GIRL UNDER BAS-MITZVA SING: A man may hear a young girl sing but may not purposely listen to enjoy it. Hearing a female singing is a lesser cause of sinful thoughts than seeing exposed parts of a female's body. Therefore, although a ten year old girl may not walk around inadequately dressed because catching sight of her can be provocative, she may sing within earshot of men and one is not afraid that this will cause unwarranted attraction - see M.B. 75:17 - *Responsa Iggros Moshe* O.C. 1:26 and *Mekoros* 75:1.

[It must be mentioned that if a girl has developed the physical signs of adulthood (puberty) before the age of twelve, she has the full status of an adult and must be treated with the laws of a twelve-year-old (*ibid.*). Nowadays, it is quite common for an eleven-year-old to have reached this state. When this is the case, she must be careful not to sing where men can hear her even though she is under twelve].

2. ISSUR TO LISTEN AND ENJOY AN UNDER BAS-MITZVA SING: Listening to a young girl (who is not his daughter) in order to enjoy the singing is forbidden because, once proper attention is paid, even the singing of a minor can have the detrimental affect stated. Accordingly, men may not listen to a choir of young girls (six/seven year olds) because it involves 'intentional listening' which is forbidden - see M.B. 75:17 and *Mekoros* 75:2. If a school that has a prize-giving day at which young girls sing in a choir experiences great difficulty in preventing some fathers from coming, a *shaaloh* should be asked - see *Responsa Iggros Moshe* O.C 1:26.

3. ISSUR TO HEAR YOUNG SISTER-IN-LAW SING: A man may not hear his sister-in-law who is a minor sing even if he is not saying a *davar shebikdusha* at the time. A sister-in-law (sister of his wife) has a strict *ervah* status to him as the Torah forbids him to marry her as long as his wife lives - (Vayikrah 18:18). When a young girl has such a strict *ervah* status, her singing is forbidden even from the tender age of six/seven. Accordingly, a young girl may not sing the מה נשתנה at the *seder* when her brother-in-law is seated at the table. The same applies to any other song she wishes to sing in an audible tone with the rest of the family in the presence of her brother-in-law whether on *Pesach* or at any other time. However, if only other guests (who would not be forbidden to marry her) are there she may sing the מה נשתנה in their presence as long as they are not personally interested in hearing her sing (M.B. 75:17).

A step-daughter is an *ervah* to her step-father as her mother is the wife of her step-father - (*Vayikra* 18:17). Accordingly, all that has been stated concerning a sister-in-law applies also to a step daughter. Therefore, from the young age of six, and all the more so when she is an adult, she may not sing in the presence of her step-father.

F. RECITING A BRACHA WHILE UNDER BAS-MITZVA SINGS

1. ISSUR TO SAY BRACHA WHEN HEARING YOUNG GIRL SING: Although a man may hear a girl who is under *Bas-mitzva* sing he may not at that time recite a *bracha* or sing *zemiros*. This is forbidden because female singing is, after all, classified as *ervah* and can cause sinful thoughts when "listened to". It is therefore an unfit setting for a *bracha* (M.B. 75:17) - see *Mekoros* 75:1. This applies only if the girl is at least six/seven years old since from that age her voice is distinctly feminine (*Ben Ish Chai - parshas Bo* No.13) - see *Mekoros* 75:6.

2. ISSUR TO SAY BRACHA WHEN 11 YEAR OLD DAUGHTER SINGS: Although a father may hear his daughter sing whether she is a minor or an adult, he may not recite a *bracha* while hearing his daughter who is eleven--years-old sing (see 4:C:5) because her female voice could slightly affect him. However, if she is younger than this, the father may recite a *bracha* although he hears her sing because a father is totally unaffected when hearing his young daughter sing. Therefore, as far as he is concerned, her voice is simply not considered *ervah* (just as it is not *ervah* for women). The same applies when a brother hears his sister sing - he may not say a *bracha* if he hears her sing once she is an eleven-year-old (*Biur Halacha* 75:1) - see *Mekoros* 75:5.

Accordingly, if a husband hears his wife, eleven-year-old daughter or a six-year-old who is not his daughter sing a lullaby to a baby, he must stop *benching* or learning (verbally). He may, however, continue reading (visually) from a *sefer* and he may simply "think in learning" - (see 4:A:2 where this is explained). If a girl under six is singing to the baby, he may ignore her singing completely and carry on *benching* or learning as usual.

G. WOMEN SINGING ZEMIROS WITH THEIR FAMILY

1. THE DIVERSE OPINIONS AMONGST THE POSKIM: In some communities, the whole family, including the women, sing *Zemiros*, *Shir Hama'alos* and *Bircas Hamazon* together, although as a result of this men are saying *devarim shebikdusha* while women are singing. The justification given for the custom is that when they all sing together the men presumably have no particular interest in hearing the voices of the women. Being close family whose voices the men have heard many times, they do not hear the female voices when interlaced with male voices. This is in accordance with the principle found in *Chazal* concerning a similar situation, תרי קלי לא משתמעי - "when two people say the same thing simultaneously, their individual voices cannot be discerned" (*Megilla* 21b).

Furthermore, they reason that even though a husband is usually attracted to his wife's song [and in cases of special attraction the principle of תרי קלי לא משתמעי does not apply because the person listens out for the voice he has a special wish to hear - איידי דחביבא ליה משתמעי - (*ibid*)] nevertheless when he sings together with her it is to be assumed that attraction will be virtually non-existent, since he wants to hear a "collection of voices" rather than an individual voice. Moreover, *Tosfos, Sotah* 39b s.v. *Ad.* writes that a person cannot hear a second voice when he is singing himself even if it holds a special attraction to him. He will, therefore, not hear his wife's voice when he sings together with her and the rest of the family.

Although she may of course sing with a slightly different timing to him ie. start before him or finish after him, this does not matter, because he is allowed to hear his wife or daughter sing. It is only whilst he is personally saying a *davar shebikdusha* that he must not her a *kol isha* and in this case he will not hear her whilst he is singing himself. See the *Otzer HaPoskim* 21:20:4 in the name of the *Chasan Sofer* and *Responsa Seridei Eish* 2:8 who writes that Hagaon Harav Samson Raphael Hirsch *zt'l* and Hagaon Harav Ezriel Hildersheimer *zt'l* agreed to the lenient opinion (and claims that they allowed even more than is written in these notes) - see *Mekoros* 76:1-12. This was also the opinion of Hagaon Harav Shlomo Zalman Auerbach *zt'l* as he states in a Responsum printed in the *sefer, Chazon Dovid* (in memory of HaRav Dovid Miller *zt'l*) page 93. This is also the opinion of Hagaon Harav Yosef Shalom Elyashiv *shlita* as stated in his name in the *sefer*, *Imrei Shefer* (by Harav Efrayim Landau *shlita*) on *Rosh Hashana*, page 38. It is recommended that the husband and sons sing in a distinctly louder voice than the females to ensure that they will not hear her sing (*ibid*).

Other *Poskim* disagree with this *heter*. Amongst them are Hagaon Harav Moshe Feinstein ztl as stated in his name in the *sefer, Rivevos Efrayim* 2:122, *Responsa Tzitz Eliezer* 7:28:3 and *Responsa Oz Nidberu* 3:71. Therefore, if one does not have the *minhag* to be lenient and sing together, it should not be introduced - see *Mekoros* 76:10.

2. IF FEMALE HARMONIZES ALL AGREE IT IS OSSUR: It is self understood that all opinions agree that the *heter* mentioned does not apply if the wife or eleven-year-old daughter harmonizes as the family sing. In such a case the *heter* of תרי קלי cannot apply because the men want to hear the female voice. Furthermore, when someone harmonizes, their voice is heard independently of the other voices. However, if the daughter who is harmonizing is under eleven, no *issur* is involved - see 8:F:2 above.

3. ZEMIROS NOT CONTAINING TORAH NOR NAME OF HASHEM: Some of the *Poskim* who do not accept the *heter* of תרי קלי לא משתמעי for saying *Shir Hama'alos* or *Bircas Hamazon* when the family sing together, nevertheless permit singing *zemiros* together when there are no *p'sukim* or *divrei Torah* involved nor is the name of *Hashem* mentioned properly, as they do not consider such *zemiros* to be *devarim shebikdusha.* Similarly, they would allow a man to sing *zemiros* quietly while his wife or daughter sing them loudly, although in such a case there can certainly not be a *heter* of תרי קלי לא משתמעי (*Halichos Bas Yisroel* 6:8 in the name of Hagaon Harav Yosef Shalom Elyashiv *shlita*).

Proof for this idea can be brought from *Modeh Ani* which is said in the morning on waking up even before washing *negel wasser* although *dvarim shebikdusha* may not be said before *negel wasser* (*Magen Avraham* 4:28 in name of *Seder Hayom* and M.B. 1:8). Evidently, these *Poskim* hold that a praise to *Hashem* that does not contain *p'sukim* nor the proper name of *Hashem* is not considered a *davar shebikdusha* and may therefore be said with unwashed hands. It may similarly be said even in the presence of *ervah*.

There are however other *Poskim* who consider "singing praises to *Hashem*" a *davar shebikdusha,* even if the song involves neither *p'sukim, divrei Torah* nor the name of *Hashem* (*sefer*, *Mekor Chayim* 75:1 and *sefer*, *Be'er Sheva,* in the part called *Be'er Mayim Chayim* No. 3). Concerning the proof from *Modeh Ani* - it should be noted that the *Yavetz* in his *Sefer*, *Mor Uketziah* end of chap. 4 and the *Sefer*, *Olas Tamid* 4:15 are of the opinion that it should not be said until after washing - see *Mekoros* 76:10.

H. WOMEN SINGING ZEMIROS IF NON-FAMILY ARE PRESENT

1. WOMEN MUST ENSURE THAT THEY CANNOT BE HEARD: When a man who is not part of the close family is at the Shabbos table, the above-mentioned justification does not apply, and all women and girls must refrain from singing in an audible voice. This is because such a man is powerfully attracted to the sweet voice of the women. Their singing voices are therefore *ervah* to him and forbidden, even when he is not saying a *bracha*. It is consequently unjustifiable to base a *heter* on the principle of תרי קלי לא משתמע - since there will surely be moments when they will sing but not he, for example, they start a bit ahead of him or finish a bit after him. Since he must not hear these females sing at all, there is no way of permitting this. Furthermore, due to the power of the attraction, the man might well hear the female voices even when they have blended with the male voices - see 8:C:3. This is also the opinion of the *Badei Hashulchan* Y.D. 195 note 219.

Therefore, the *heter* mentioned does not apply when strangers or far relatives are at the table. This is of particular importance on *seder* night when many have guests at the table. The females may sing, but only in such a low voice that they cannot be heard by the men present - see *Mekoros* 77:1-3.

2. THE SHIRAS HAYAM - THE PROBLEM OF KOL ISHAH: After the miraculous crossing of the Red Sea, the *Bnei Yisroel* sang the *Shiras Hayam*. The women did not join the men singing and instead sang a *Shirah* on their own (*Shemos* 15:20). One of the *Rishonim*, the *Rokeiach,* explains that they did not sing with the men because of the *issur* of *kol b'ishah ervah*, as the men would inevitably have heard the women sing. As stated, even the opinion which is lenient concerning a family singing together agrees that if the males and females are not all of one immediate family the *issur* of *kol ishah* applies. Therefore, since the whole of *Klal Yisroel* were there at the time, it was *ossur* for the men and women to sing the *Shirah* together. Instead, Miriam *HaNeviah* led the women to a place where they could not be heard by the men, so that they could sing their own *Shirah*.

The *Atzei Chayim* (quoted in *Meam Loez*, page 360) writes that the women used musical instruments to ensure that their voices would not be heard by the men,. The loud volume of the instruments completely drowned their voices, especially as they were some distance from the men. The verse therefore writes ותצאנה כל הנשים אחריה בתופים ובמחולות - "And all the women followed her with musical instruments and dance" (*Shemos* 15:2O).

I. A DOMESTIC SHOULD NOT SING OR DRESS PRITZUS'DIK

1. A DOMESTIC SHOULD NOT BRING PRITZUS INTO THE HOUSE: Some domestics (whether Jewish or non-Jewish), are inclined to sing softly or hum to themselves as they work. If all the males are out of the house at the time there may be no problem in her doing so (provided no words are involved, as they are usually indecent). However, she must be instructed not to sing or hum when the *ba'al habayis*, his sons or male visitors are around. One can explain to the non-Jewish domestic that in Jewish law there are strict laws of segregation between males and females. Within this context a man may not hear a female (other than his wife or close relative) sing, as he will be benefiting from part of her inner beauty and talent.

2. ONE IS FULLY ENTITLED TO DEMAND CONFORMITY: Some people feel that a request such as this cannot be asked of a non-Jewish domestic. Due to this, they allow domestics to sing softly to themselves. They even allow them to walk around with distinctly bad forms of dress, such as a blouse with the upper front deeply cut out or a skirt that is far too short, although when a female walks around in such dress it is detrimental to the males in the house and causes problems with *brachos* they make. This assumption is, however, totally incorrect, and the employer has every right to demand that she arrives at work dressed in a certain way or (if she prefers) that she wears a housecoat over her clothes during work.

In fact, hotels lay down very specific rules as to how their staff are to dress. It is highly informative to read what the author of this *sefer* saw hanging in the office of a prestigious non-Jewish hotel in the city of Liverpool, U.K. It concerns their female staff and reads as follows:

May 1993.

The Gladstone Hotel Banqueting Department Uniform Standard.

Head; Long hair should be tied back. No colored hair clips or combs.
Discreet make-up. No overpowering perfume.

Hands; Short clean nails. Clear nail varnish.

Jewelry;	No excessive jewelry. Only studs or small earrings. No charm bracelets or bangles.
Dress;	Plain white blouse, preferably with collar, and long or three quarter length sleeves. Black skirt, length not above the knee.
Shoes;	All black sensible shoes; No sandals, boots, stilettos or slippers.

Much can be learnt from this statement. Evidently, even the *umos haolom* know what is a refined mode of dress. As such, are we demanding too much of our daughters when we ask them to dress in a similar refined manner? It also underscores the right every employer has to demand a mode of dress of his employee. One can even request a modest and refined standard although in their home surroundings these women dress very differently.

3. GUESTS CAN BE REQUESTED TO COME IN MODEST ATTIRE: Every story related in the Torah contains far-reaching lessons. We find that Avraham brought three non-Jewish guests into his abode and attended to them in a princely manner. However, before granting them entry he said, יוקח נא מעט מים ורחצו רגליכם - "Let a small amount of water be brought so that you can wash your feet" (*Breishis* 18:4). *Rashi* explains that this was because he thought that they were idol worshipers who bow down to the dust of their feet. So that this dust is not brought into his abode (which is not a Halachic requirement, see *Kli Yakar*) he requested them to wash their feet before entering. Avraham did not feel he was asking too much of his guests in requesting them not to bring into his house something which would disturb him. All the more so, a person is entitled to demand that a woman does not walk around his house in distinctly *pritzus'dik* attire.

When Reb Yaacov Yosef Herman *zt'l* married off a child in New York in 1922, he added at the bottom of the invitation the words "Ladies, please come dressed according to the Jewish law". Although feelings for *tznius* were much weaker at that time than now, and these people were his guests, he nevertheless felt it right to request of those who wish to attend his *simcha* that they come in respectable and modest clothes (*All for the Boss*, page 93).

Just as guests can be requested to dress in a certain manner, so too, an employed woman can be told to come to work in a basically modest manner of dress and can be requested not to sing even softly to herself if this will disturb members of the household by whom she works.

Chapter Nine

SAFEGUARDING KEDUSHAS YISROEL

A. DENYING THE YETZER HORAH THE SLIGHTEST FOOTHOLD

1. THE YETZER HORAH IS EASILY AROUSED: The central feature and prime motive for all *halachos* concerning female dress and public conduct is the concept of *ervah* - שער באשה ערוה (5:A:1 above) טפח באשה ערוה (6:A:1 above) שוק באשה ערוה (6:L:1 above) and קול באשה ערוה (8:A:1 above). This means that if there is exposure or even just inadequate cover, her appearance has the potential to draw the attention of a male to her physique and arouse within him inappropriate and even forbidden thoughts, termed by *Chazal* as הרהורי עבירה - "sinful thoughts". A forbidden thought need be no more than that the man derives a degree of pleasure from the sight he sees or the singing he hears. This pleasure is sinful because the female is an *ervah* to him and to have any type of enjoyment from the physique of an *ervah* is an *issur* of לא תקרבו לגלות ערוה - "do not draw near to *arayos*" (*Vayikra* 18:6).

We see from these *halachos* just how weak and vulnerable human beings are, and how easily they are drawn to *arayos* - illicit contact of any description. It requires no more than an inappropriate visual contact between man and woman to precipitate their spiritual destruction. Just as dry straw needs no more than a spark to ignite it, so too, the passion of man needs no more than a slight incitement to arouse it. For this reason, when discussing the *issur* of קול באשה ערוה, *Chazal* (*Sotah* 48a) compare the situation of a man hearing a woman sing sweetly and beautifully to אש בנעורת - "putting fire to flax", as the emotions of man are easily aroused and excited - see *Mekoros* 4:6.

2. FAMILIARITY - FIRST NAME TERMS:

(a) The danger inherent in being very friendly towards everybody: Being friendly to people is very Jewish conduct and is to be very much encouraged. Indeed, *Chazal* say, הוי מקדים לשלום כל אדם - "Greet every person even before they have greeted you" (*Avos* 4:15). It is nevertheless wrong and exceedingly harmful for people of the opposite genders to greet one another with great familiarity and warmth, as if they are happy to once again cross paths with such a close friend and associate. This creates a feeling of familiarity and closeness that can do great harm.

In the open and informal society that prevails there will be those who are of the opinion that all people should converse free and easily with everyone else without distinction. We, however, live by the motto of Dovid Hamelech, נר לרגלי דבריך ואור לנתבתי - "Your words are a lamp for my feet, and a light for my path" (*Tehillim* 119:104). Rather than lend an ear to what people have to say, we will seek guidance from the words of *Hashem*, as recorded in His holy Torah.

We read in the Torah (*Vayikra* 24:11) that *Shlomis Bas Divri* fell prey to an Egyptian man who took a liking to her. This happened because she was a very outgoing person and displayed a very friendly disposition to women and men alike. Due to this, she would greet everyone with a cheery 'good morning' and engage them in an affectionate chat.

This is hinted to in her name. *Rashi* (*ibid*) writes as follows: שלומית, דהות פטפטה שלם עלך שלם עליכון מפטפטת בדברים שואלת בשלום הכל. בת דברי, דברנית היתה מדברת עם כל אדם לפיכך קלקלה - "Her name was *Shlomis* for she would greet everyone with a warm *Shalom Aloch* ('peace unto you' in a singular form) and a group of people with a broad *Shalom Aleichem* (in a plural form). She was always greeting and befriending people.

Her name was *Bas Divri* because she would speak to everyone. As a result of greeting and talking to everyone a certain Egyptian was attracted to her with the result that her spiritual life lay in ruins". She is held so heavily responsible for the tragic results, that she is actually called a *zonah* although she never willingly lived with the Egyptian, as is explained in *Rashi, Shemos* 2:11 s.v. *Makeh.* See *sefer, Levush Haorah* on *Rashi* and *Sifsei Chachamim, Vayikra* 24:11.

In the climate of the present day world, people would consider such an easy-going young woman to be a warm, outgoing and even charming young lady, who is a pleasure and an asset to society. Not so the Holy Torah. From the Torah point of view such warmth and open affection to all and sundry is poisonous. It creates feelings of affinity and fondness where none should exist and the eventual results can be most tragic.

(b) Addressing by the first name is a sign of familiarity: Once a person truly grasps the extreme vulnerability of man to *arayos*-related *issurim*, he will understand that certain ways of conduct which are thought of by many as just "being *heimish*", are in fact very far from correct practice. For example, people address other people's wives by their first names e.g. they answer the phone with, "Good morning! How are you, Judy?" or when meeting a woman on the street they say, "How are things, Hadassa?" and so on. Since she is neither the sister nor very close relative etc. of this man, to be on first name terms with her is an infringement of *tznius*, as it displays feelings of familiarity (*Taz*, Even HaEzer 21:1 in the name of the *Mahrshal*). See also *Mekoros* 81:1.

It is of course, possible that in earlier times when people did not have surnames women were addressed and referred to by their true name. Even if this were proven to be the case, this would have no bearing on what has just been stated. When a name is used by everyone, using it contains no element of familiarity. It would therefore be all right for anyone to refer to her by name. However, when a woman or girl has a general name that is used by the wider public, and a more specific name that is used only by those close to her, then should a male neighbor use this specific name he demonstrates that he considers himself close to her and even one of her personal friends. In this demonstration of closeness lies the germ for further forms of familiarity and the break-down of *kedushas Yisroel*.

(c) *Chazal* say that using the first name is a sign of affection: It is written explicitly in *Chazal* that calling someone by their personal name is an act of endearment. On the verse, ויקרא אל משה וידבר ה' אליו - "And He called to Moshe and *Hashem* spoke to him" (*Vayikra* 1:1) *Rashi* quotes *Chazal* that *Hashem* always addressed Moshe by name as this is a קריאה של חיבה - "a call of endearment".

Similarly, the *Toras Kohanim, Vayikra* 1:3 writes that whenever a name is called twice, such as משה משה they are קריאה של חיבה וקריאה של זירוז - "The first is an expression of endearment and the second of encouragement to react swiftly without delay" - see *Malbim*. Finally, the following are the words of the *Maharal MiPrague* in *Gur Aryeh* (*Vayikra* 1:1) אם לא יקרא אותו בשמו רוצה לדבר אליו. אבל כשקורא אליו בשמו לומר 'משה' מורה על שהוא מחבב הנקרא וידוע אצלו - "Calling a person without using his name indicates that the caller wants to speak to him. However, if the caller uses his name (Moshe) this means that he is dear to the caller and he is fond of him".

We see from these sources that calling someone by his personal name, when he could be addressed without the use of the name, is a sign of affection and fondness. Since that is so, addressing a woman or girl by her first name when there is no need for it is out of place and a lack of *tznius*.

(d) Laxity with names leads to other harmful forms of laxity: Being lax with issues such as first name terms, is conducive to similar forms of misconduct, and causes men to go as far as complimenting women on their beautiful outfit or voicing similar remarks. Those who do so have inadvertently strayed from the Torah's ways which instructs men not to look intently at women, see 7:E:2 above, and all the more, not to be "*heimish*" and overly familiar with them. They do not realize that it is *ossur* for a man to praise a woman for her beauty as such praise causes affection and falls under the *issur* of "greeting women affectionately", explained in 9:F:4 below.

The harm in such talk goes so far that the *Rishonim* state that, whenever there is no valid reason, a man should refrain from mentioning the beauty of a woman even to another man, as even this has the potential of causing an unhealthy interest in her to develop - see *Sefer Hayirah L'Rabbeinu Yona* No. 254 and *sefer, Orchos Chayim L'Rosh* No. 98.

(e) Close relatives are not subject to this restriction: The objection to first-name terms holds true when the man has no need to address the girl or woman by her first name. In such a case, using her first name is a demonstration of familiarity, closeness and even endearment, or at least has the potential for cultivating such feelings. However, when the girl or woman is a close relative and it would be expected and fully natural for him to call her by her first name even if he had no particular feelings of affection for her, the use of it is not viewed as a sign of over-familiarity nor a cause for over-familiarity to arise. A man may therefore call his step-daughter, half-sister, daughter-in-law etc. by their first name. In all such cases this is fully expected due to close family connections and one need not estrange them by calling them Mrs.... or Miss.....Concerning a sister-in-law, many men practice a praiseworthy compromise. Just as their children refer to her by name after uttering the prefix Aunt, they too refer to her as "Aunt .....".

It should be noted that in *kiruv* work there can be a need to use first names. Some couples become like "adopted children" to those who have been *mekarev* them to *Yiddishkeit.* As such, they would feel alienated if they were addressed only by their formal titles.

(f) Can result in major complications with the *issur* of *yichud*: In connection with this, it must be pointed out that in many cases the *issur* of *yichud* [which is that a male and female, other than husband and wife and the closest blood relatives, may not be together in a secluded area - see 9:C:2 and 9:J:10 below] will almost certainly be transgressed as a result of using first-name terms. This is because of a clause in the *halachos* of *yichud.* בעלה בעיר - "the fact that her husband is local", which usually prevents the *issur* of *yichud* from applying, does not help once the male is very familiar with the female (E.H. 22:8). Furthermore, according to many, the *heter* of פתח פתוח - "that the door is unlocked", does not help once the male is on very close terms with the female (E.H. 22, *Beis Shmuel* 13, *Chelkas Mechokek* 13).

This condition is known as לבו גס בה - "He is very familiar with her" and is a malady which can easily develop between an employer and his female secretary or between a man and his female neighbor. When an employer or male neighbor purposefully "keeps a safe distance" by addressing the woman or girl by Mrs... or Miss..., close familiarity will not develop. Whereas, if he calls her Chana or Sarah, and all the more so if he calls her Chana'leh or Soro'leh, it is almost inevitable that he will become very familiar with her. As a result the *yichud* problem mentioned will arise, making it *ossur* for the boss to be in the office with her although her husband is in town and the door is unlocked. See *sefer Dvar Halacha, Hilchos yichud* 7:18.

See 9:F:7 concerning the use of first names in offices and places of work. Furthermore, see 9:J:10(b) about doctors addressing their female patients.

3. ADVERTISEMENTS MUST NOT UNDERMINE TZNIUS:

It is fitting at this juncture to mention another malady that has become acceptable practice in the wider community but is harmful to the cause of *tznius*. This refers to adverts in a national or local Jewish newspaper for the sale of items such as *sheitels*, outfits, dresses and coats. They are sometimes described as dazzling, sensational, stunning and as turning those who wear them into beauty queens. When adverts describe the glamour and the great beautification that results from wearing such exquisite items, this sets a standard which is subconsciously implanted into the minds of all who read the adverts week after week. The opinion formed is that a woman or girl is well dressed only when as a result of her clothes she looks stunning, glamorous and outstandingly beautiful. The modesty and refinement of the Jewish daughter are projected as something of the past, that is simply not for the modern woman with her sophistication.

The same applies to jewelry that is advertised as being highly attractive and as having the potential for turning their wearers into the envy of the townspeople. Likewise, children's clothes are advertised as being worthy of being worn by a millionaire's daughter or that they are so regal and becoming that they will turn a young girl into a princess. This sets a standard that is harmful to the child and to society as a whole - see 7:A:1 above. All such adverts drive the readership away from refined and tasteful clothes that befit the noble nature of the Jewish woman or girl.

Further departures from *tznius'dik* practice involve using adjectives to describe types of maternity wear, night clothes etc. that are not fitting for an Orthodox Jewish newspaper and certainly not for the male readership of the paper, many of whom will glance through all parts of the paper. Although these adverts are intended for women only, they must nevertheless be suitable for men as well, because all parts of a newspaper can be seen and even read by anyone.

It is heart-warming when every now and again someone has the strength to advertise as a Torah committed person would. They will describe their stock as, "Beautiful in appearance and beautifully Kosher", "We do not compromise our *Yiddishkeit*", "*tznius* is our hallmark". Just as a bad example affects others, so too, a good example leaves its mark and will be copied by others, to the advantage of *Klal Yisroel*.

4. DEPRIVATIONS DUE TO TZNIUS ARE ONLY IMAGINARY:

Those who are blessed with true refinement know that refraining from the points mentioned is not an infringement of human rights. Rather, it brings *kedusha* and *tahara* to one's life and considerably underpins one's own *shalom bayis*. The Torah informs us that when strangers came to the home of שרה אמנו she modestly stayed within her tent (הנה באהל) since there was no need for her presence. This exemplary behavior increased the admiration and love of her husband for her, as stated in *Rashi (Breishis* 18:9*)*. It is our fervent wish that our daughters, who are great grand-daughters of Sarah Imeinu, emulate her conduct.

Also, the esteem people have for her is not jeopardized by her modesty and the way she keeps out of the limelight. On the contrary, her modesty turns into a source of admiration and is one of the greatest praises that can be said about a girl - see 1:N:4 above. It is actually the way of *Hashem* to repay good deeds not just by rewarding the person handsomely, but by ensuring that the very "sacrifice" he brought for the sake of the *mitzva* is returned with dividends. This is similar to the saying of *Chazal*, עשר בשביל שתתעשר - "Separate *ma'aser* and you will become wealthy" - meaning, that the *ma'aser* money you give away will be refunded with rich dividends, ensuring that you will be in a far better financial position having given the *ma'aser* than you were beforehand.

It is the same with every *mitzva* that entails some personal sacrifice - after a time it becomes evident that there was no sacrifice at all. For example, to become Jewish, Ruth who came from the royal house of Eglon, King of Moab, sacrificed her position as a princess. She was surely under the impression that she would never again come anywhere near royalty. However, following the trail of history we find that she once again became a royal person and became the grandmother of Dovid Hamelech and Shlomo Hamelech. She, in fact, became far more than a princess and even had a throne of her own in the throne room of Shlomo Hamelech - see *Melochim* 1:2:19 and *Bava Basra* 91b. This vividly demonstrates how *mitzvos* and keeping the *ratzon Hashem* do not cause any loss at all.

Accordingly, modesty and refinement will not cause a girl to remain unnoticed and ignored. On the contrary her good name, due to her humility and refinement will be well recognized by all who should know about her. Have we not been taught by Shlomo Hamelech, טוב שם משמן טוב - "A good name is better than sweet smelling oils" (*Koheles* 7:1)? For the fragrance of sweet smelling oils to spread, the oils must be exposed. Not so a good name - it is known without its owner having to exhibit himself in any way. On the contrary, the greater the modesty the more it is appreciated and the higher the regard in which it is held.

5. APPRECIATING THE 'BEAUTY OF TZNIUS' ENSURES IT IS KEPT: The *issurim* of the Torah and particularly the *issurim* of *arayos* are compared to a "hedge of roses" - סוגה בשושנים (*Rashi*, *Shir HaShirim* 7:3 and *Gemara*, *Sanhedrin* 37a). A 'hedge of roses' with its thorns symbolizes a barrier which a person could easily breach if he so wished, but decides not to and instead allows it to exercise full control over his life. So too are the numerous *issurim* of the Torah. There is no one to force the person to do what is right nor is there an immediate retribution for transgressing its *issurim*, and *Klal Yisrael* nevertheless allows its laws to control their lives.

The term used in the verse to describe the *issurim* of *arayos* seems rather strange. It would be more fitting to describe these *issurim* as a fence of thorns rather than a hedge of roses, since it is the thorns of the rosebush that serve as the barrier, not the flowers that grow on these bushes. Hagaon Harav Mordechai Gifter *shlita*, *Rosh Yeshivas Telz*, U.S.A., in the name of one of the *Gedolim* of Telz explained as follows. Rosebushes hardly present an imposing barrier as they can easily be trampled by anyone disposed to do so. They are nonetheless effective. Their effectiveness lies in their very beauty, as only a callous person would trample beautiful roses. Accordingly, it is the roses not the thorns that are the true barrier. Such a hedge will deter whoever appreciates its beauty; for the one who has no aesthetic perception of beauty, it is almost no barrier at all.

Similarly, *issurim* are effective to deter he who understands their beauty and perfection. He who sees the *kedusha* and the purity that lies deeply embedded in the *issurim* of the Torah, and understands that this code of conduct leads to a blissful and wonderful life, appreciates the "hedge of roses" and would never consider trampling upon them - see *Mekoros* 4:7.

This applies to all *arayos*-related *issurim* and especially to *tznius*, a major feature amongst *arayos*-related *issurim*. *Tznius* is beautiful, offering women, girls and the people who come into contact with them the protection they require. It injects *kedusha* into our everyday life whilst not lessening the *chein* and warm disposition that goes with being a *Bas Yisroel*. When a woman or girl appreciates that this is genuinely so, she will happily practice *tznius* and all that it stands for, whether in her public or personal life.

B. GEZEIROS ARE AN INTRINSIC PART OF THE MAIN ISSUR

1. GEZEIROS COMPLEMENT THE ISSURIM MIN HATORAH: Now that the *halachos* and attitudes of *tznius* in public have בע״ה been explained, it is in place to expound an insight into the vital role of *gezeiros* (precautionary *issurim*) which comprise the major body of the laws of *tznius* (as they are to safeguard against immorality). This refer to all *gezeiros* whether *min haTorah* or *mid'Rabanan*. We tend to underestimate the enormous impact *gezeiros* have on the whole character of the parent *issur*. *Gezeiros*, in fact complement and complete the parent *issur* as will be explained בע"ה. Therefore to treat them lightly is tantamount to treating the parent *issur* lightly.

Hashem Yisborach wants a person to refrain not only from the main *issur* but also from everything related to it, so that he has such purity concerning this issue that no connection with the *issur* whatsoever. Anything that leads to the main *issur* is regarded as related and affiliated to it. Accordingly, *gezeiros*, whether *min haTorah* or *mid'Rabanan*, are not to be understood just as "safeguards" for the *issur*, merely preventing a person stumbling into the main *aveirah* itself. Rather, they are *issurim* in their own right, because doing these actions would form an attachment to the main *issur*.

For example, a *nozir* is forbidden to drink wine. As a precautionary measure, he must not eat grapes. If he does eat grapes he has committed two wrong-doings. Firstly, he has put the main *issur* of drinking wine at risk because eating grapes can lead to drinking wine. This is a serious *issur* in its own right. Secondly, he has made an incursion into the "territory of drinking wine" by partaking of something that is associated with wine while the Torah expected him to keep the "*issur* of drinking wine" to such an extent that he does not even eat grapes which are related to wine.

2. IF NOT TZNIUS'DIK, IT BELONGS TO WORLD OF IMMORALITY: The same applies to all *halachos* appertaining to *tznius*. They are not only safeguards but are *issurim* in their own right, of central importance to our survival. They exist so that a Jewish person has no association with immorality at all. To transgress any of these *issurim* is tantamount to having made an incursion into the territory of immorality and corruption.

This principle goes so far that the *Mesilas Yesharim* writes (in Chapter Eleven) that just as there is "real *znus*" by committing the cardinal sin, so there is "*znus* of the eyes" by feasting one's eyes on what one should not see (i.e. שער באשה ערוה, טפח באשה ערוה); "*znus* of speech" when using obscene language; "*znus* of the ears" when hearing a woman sing (i.e. קול באשה ערוה). Just as *znus* means to "feast on something forbidden" and is a source of terrible *tumah*, so also these infringements on *tznius* are forms of "feasting on something forbidden" and bring *tumah* into *Klal Yisroel*. See text of *Mesilas Yesharim* in *Mekoros* 75:3.

3. THE KEDUSHA GENERATED BY GEZEIROS: *Gezeiros* are of such significance and importance that the "spirit of *kedusha*" results mainly from the *gezeiros* and abstaining from the precautionary measures rather than from the parent *issur* itself. Concerning *arayos*, many precautionary measures are in fact *issurim min haTorah*, as the verse states, ולא תקרבו לגלות ערוה - "Do not make inroads into immorality" (*Vayikra* 18:6), one of them being to dress *pritzus'dik* - 4:B:1(e). To these, *Chazal* added further *issurim* which are *mid'Rabanan*. In contrast, with most other *issurim*, such as the *issur* of cooking milk and meat together, the *gezeiros* that accompany the main *issur* are entirely *mid'Rabanan*. In all cases, the *kedusha* is generated predominantly by abstaining from the *gezeiros*, as will be explained.

4. WHAT WOULD SHABBOS BE LIKE WITHOUT ISSUREI CHAZAL? Let us take Shabbos as an example. *Min haTorah* a Jewish person may not do any one of the thirty-nine *melachos* in the regular manner. That is the beginning and end of the *issurei* Shabbos as far as *issurei* Torah are concerned. *Chazal* forbade (1) having a non-Jew do a *melacha*, because one might do it oneself, (2) doing the *melachos* in an unusual manner, because one might do it in the normal way, (3) certain activities as a safeguard to the *melachos* e.g. movement of *muktza*, because the article might be used for a *melacha*; business, because it could lead to writing. They also told us to wear Shabbos clothes in honor of Shabbos and not to prepare on Shabbos for after Shabbos, so as to preserve the honor of Shabbos.

Let us try and imagine Shabbos without the *issurei Chazal* (if it is at all imaginable). People would get up in the morning and dress in their weekday clothes. Men would go to business just as on a weekday. They would switch the lights on with their elbows or by asking a non-Jew to do so. Money could be handled. Business would be as usual, selling to Jews and non-Jews alike. At the end of the day all the day's earnings would be taken home by stuffing them into the brim of the hat thereby transporting them in an unusual manner. If there is no *reshus harabim min haTorah* in that area, the money could be taken home even in the normal way. This would happen every single Shabbos. The lady of the house would do almost all her cooking by switching on the cooker with her two small fingers or with the help of a maid. After the meal she would do all the washing up although not needed for Shabbos and could even use the dishwasher by operating it in an unusual way or with the aid of a maid.

We need go no further to realize that this is simply no Shabbos at all! The "spirit" of Shabbos is created by abstaining not just from the thirty-nine *melachos* themselves but also by abstaining from all that *Chazal* connected to them. To put it simply, our *Chachamim* (with Heavenly inspiration) gave us Shabbos as we know it! In fact the original design of *Hashem Yisborach* was that *Klal Yisroel* should totally abstain from the *melachos* and it was an integral part of His plan that *Chazal* would make these *gezeiros*.

5. KEDUSHA IS BORN OUT OF TOTAL COMMITMENT TO TZNIUS: What has been explained is true with all *issurei Chazal*. In particular, it applies to the laws of *tznius* which are to safeguard the Jewish people from corruption. Accordingly, all forms of *pritzus* are *ossur*, not just because the person could, G-d forbid, come to do a most serious sin, but because only then is there total and absolute abstention from immorality. Just as *kedushas* Shabbos is born out of total abstention from the *melachos*, so *kedushas Yisroel* is born out of total abstention from all that has to do with *arayos*.

When *Chazal* added to the Torah obligation of covering the main body that a woman should also cover the upper sections of her arms, they thereby reinforced *kedushas Yisroel* to an immeasurable degree. Whoever transgresses this decree is sinning not just by violating the words of *Chazal*, and not only because she may be starting a downhill slide to serious sins, but because she has made an incursion into the world of corruption, as uncovering the upper section of the arm has become related to the ultimate *issur*. Conversely, when a woman takes her own precautions, she brings an extra degree of *kedusha* to the world.

We are to be eternally grateful to *Chazal*, for they, with the help of *Hashem Yisborach*, gave us almost everything *Yiddishkeit* stands for. They made our Shabbos into what we know it to be; they made *Kashrus* into a style of life where the mundane act of cooking dinner is elevated to a day-by-day exercise of *yiras cheit*, and it is they who directed the *Bas Yisroel* to wear only that which befits her dignity, her nobility and her outstanding ancestry.

We have much to be thankful for!

C. THE ISSUR FOR MEN AND WOMEN TO INTERMINGLE

1. THE HARM CAUSED BY INTERMINGLING: *Kedushas Yisroel* calls for segregation between men and women whenever possible. *Arayos* in all its shades is the cardinal *yetzer horah* of mankind. There is a craving even for subtle forms of contact between males and females, such as looking at, talking to and joking with one another. As stated in 9:B:2 above in the name of the *Mesilas Yesharim* Chapter 11, in Torah terms, looking at, talking to and joking with women are all subtle forms of *znus*. Furthermore, the mingling itself generates a degree of pleasure which, being derived from an *ervah*, is a subtle form of *znus*. For this reason alone, all forms of contact are viewed as very serious matters, even if it were guaranteed that they would not lead to any form of forbidden relationship.

Even if the person feels no particular pleasure from being in such a situation, it is still wrong and grossly unhealthy, because intermingling has the potential of breaking down the natural barriers that must exist between men and women. Hence, intermingling in all its forms is forbidden and should be considered as a major breach in *tznius* (O.C. 529:4; M.B. 529:22; *Biur Halacha* 339 s.v. *Lehakel*).

Even in the *Beis Hamikdash*, a women's gallery was eventually erected because men and women intermingled during the *Simchas Beis Hashoeiva* and behaved somewhat immodestly. This was necessary although the *yetzer horah* for *arayos* existed in a greatly reduced form in the *Beis Hamikdash* due to the prevailing *kedusha* (see *Succah* 51b, 52a). Even there, although surrounded by *kedusha*, there was no guarantee against *arayos*-orientated *aveiros*. If so, what right do we have to be so confident of our strength and purity? - see *Mekoros* 78:1-2.

2. THE DISCERNING PERSPECTIVE OF CHAZAL:

(a) Stopping a breach at the earliest point: We tend to brush admonition about these things aside, claiming that when mingling no one has any bad intentions, *chas v'shalom*, so why make a mountain out of a molehill? The truth of the matter, however, is that only due to our shortsightedness and to the devious methods of the *yetzer horah* do we think in this way. We are so convinced of our moral integrity that we are amazed by the *issur* in *Hilchos Yichud* that a man may not baby-sit for a young girl of three nor may a woman or adult girl child-mind a nine-year-old boy, to take but two examples - see E.H. 22:11 and 9:J:10 below).

Chazal knew and understood human nature down to the finest detail. They were capable of seeing the beginnings of a breach long before we are able to see it ourselves. In their capacity as Guardians of the Jewish people they alert us and direct us to safe conduct. If we are careful with *kedushas Yisroel* we merit at least to understand the warnings of *Chazal* and appreciate the truth in their words. However, if there is a breakdown of *kedusha*-inspired behavior, we are deaf to *Chazal*'s warnings and will not realize that we are slipping further and further from the purity that is the lifeblood and animating force of *Klal Yisroel*.

The lowest a woman can fall is to become a *sotah* and commit *znus*, *rachmana litzlan*. When starting the chapter about the *sotah*, the Torah introduces it with the verse, איש כי תשטה אשתו ומעלה בו מעל - "A man whose wife deviated from the correct path and is gravely disloyal to him" (*Bamidbar* 5:12). The Torah states that her wrongdoing started by "deviating from the correct path". This departure eventually led from one thing to another until she committed one of the worst *aveiros* possible. The *S'forno* explains the word תשטה - "She deviated from" with the words תשטה מדרכי הצניעות - "She deviated from the ways of *tznius* and usual modesty". Her inappropriate dress, her unfitting conduct and her mingling with men brought about her downfall. What the world at large would have considered as trivial, is pointed to by the Torah as being the true cause and initiation of the dreadful descent that followed thereafter.

In this capacity, the *Mishna* says in *Pirkei Avos* (3:17), אמר רבי עקיבא שחוק וקלות ראש מרגילין את האדם לערוה - "Rabbi Akiva said: Jesting and frivolous light-headedness lead a man to immorality". To many, jesting and distasteful *letzonus* seem very far removed from acts of immorality. However, *Chachmei HaTorah* are described as עיני העדה - "The eyes of the congregation" (*Bamidbar* 15:24 and *Shir HaShirim Rabba* 1:23). They see the very harmful outcome of a mode of conduct at a point when everyone else is totally blind to it and considers it to be harmless.

(b) "Fire" in the Hebrew names of man and woman: *Chazal* state that, י' דאיש ה' דאשה הרי השם מוטל ביניהם וכו' מסתלק מביניהם נשאר אש אש - "The name of *Hashem* appears in the Hebrew names of both man and woman - *yud* in the name of man (איש) and *hey* in the name of woman (אשה). If the name of *Hashem* is removed what remains is אש אש - fire and fire - each one is a fire that consumes the other" (*Kallah Rabosi*, 1). *Chazal* are telling us: if there is holiness in the association of the two genders, they merit having the presence of *Hashem* in their midst. Whereas, when their association is unholy, they are both fire - they consume and destroy one another. Not only does a lack of *tznius* incite an unholy fire in man, but it becomes a fire and source of destruction to both man and woman alike.

(c) Shaking hands: A *yeshiva* student from England refused to shake hands with his step-mother when greeting her. His father was extremely upset about his refusal. He demanded that his son display basic "*derech eretz*" towards his step-mother and shake hands with her whenever appropriate. The son refused, as he had been told that it is forbidden to shake hands with a woman who is not a close blood relative. The son persisted in his refusal and his father eventually became extremely annoyed with him, to the extent that this affected their relationship. Some well-meaning relatives advised the son to capitulate for the sake of *shalom bayis*. In his quandary the son turned to the *Chazon Ish zt'l* and asked him what to do. The *Chazon Ish* responded with a short and sharp answer, חוק ולא יעבור, איסור גמור - **"It is a prohibition that one dare not violate. It is absolutely forbidden".**

In spite of both *shalom bayis* and *kibud av* being at stake, it was out of question to the *Chazon Ish* to violate a fundamental *halacha*, which is what he considered this to be - see 1:N:1 above that *kibud av* is waived when it clashes with *halacha*. [Harav Hagaon R' Binyamin Posen *shlita*, *Yeshivas* Luzern, Switzerland, quoted in *Pe'er Hador*, Vol. 3 page 39.]

See *Responsa Iggros Moshe* O.C. 1:113; E.H. 1:56 and E.H. 4:32(9) who likewise forbids shaking hands with a woman as it is to be assumed that the male will derive at least some degree of pleasure from the physical contact and when that is the case it has the character of *kirvah l'arayos*. See also outspoken letters by the *Steipler Gaon zt'l* printed in *Kreina D'igrsa* 1:162163; *Responsa Be'er Moshe* 4:130 and *Od Yosef Chai* (by the Gaon *Ben Ish Chai zt'l*) *Shoftim* No. 22 where they too maintain that this is totally forbidden. See also *Sefer Chassidim* No. 1090 who writes that one should not shake hands even when the person of the opposite gender is not Jewish. One can explain to the non-Jew that the strict Jewish laws of segregation between males and females forbids any physical contact that accompanies a degree of affection.

3. THE PRUDENT VIEW OF GEDOLEI YISROEL: The *Rav* of *Komemiyus*, Harav Hagaon R' Binyamin Mendelson *zt'l* was previously *Rav* of K'far Ata. While he was *Rav* there, he was once invited to speak to the youth in the local *Bnei Akiva* organization. Harav Mendelson flatly rejected the offer, stating that he would never speak in a place where there was mixed seating. To his surprise, the members of the *Bnei Akiva* were prepared to remedy the problem. They agreed to arrange separate seating during his *shiur* (possibly even with a *mechitza*, see M.B. 315:5. This point is not recorded). However, even after they had agreed to rectify his complaint, Harav Mendelson was still very reluctant to speak within the walls of the *Bnei Akiva* as this could be construed by some to be a tacit sanction of an organization of which he thoroughly disapproved. There was, however, a second viewpoint - speaking there could be beneficial to their *Yiddishkeit*.

Being in a quandary and not knowing which consideration carried more weight, he paid a visit to the *Chazon Ish* and presented him with his problem. To his surprise the *Chazon Ish* responded with the following: *Chazal* say, אלוקיהם של אלו שונא זימה הוא - 'The G-d of these hates immorality' (*Sanhedrin* 93a). "If you speak in the *Bnei Akiva* for an hour, the boys and girls will be prevented from socializing and intermingling for that hour. In spite of all negative considerations, it is worthwhile that you speak there, just to prevent the intermingling for that one hour!" (*Pe'er HaDor* Vol. 2, page 193). Who can plumb the depth of wisdom and purity of a *Gadol* such as the *Chazon Ish zt'l*?

4. A TZNUA IS PROTECTED BY HER MORALITY AND DIGNITY: It must be mentioned that when intermingling does occur, both parties are to blame, irrespective of whether the male or the female is the instigator. If not that the second party were willing to indulge in a lightheaded conversation or were interested in the familiarity, it would speedily grind to a halt. Even if the girl were too shy or too refined to say outright that she is uncomfortable in this situation, the male would quickly sense that it does not suit her and would desist. In truth, when a girl is a true *tznua* there is a natural aura of nobility and privacy that surrounds her that keeps men and youth away from her, as they inherently feel that this girl is not the type who is prepared to behave with familiarity. Hence, her dignity and nobility assist considerably in keeping lurking dangers far away.

The verse (*Breishis* 24:16) describes our mother Rivka with the words והנערה טובת מראה וכו' ואיש לא ידעה - "And the maiden was very beautiful etc. and no man was familiar with her". On this Harav Samson Raphael Hirsch *zt'l* writes the following: "She was so extraordinarily modest that no man dared to become intimately friendly with her. The true modest Jewish girl has such high innate morality and dignity that quite unconsciously she makes such an impression that the lowest boy does not dare to make nasty remarks in her presence nor approach her even with improper looks." These are the words of Harav Samson Raphael Hirsch *zt'l* - the campaigner for unadulterated *Yiddishkeit*. It follows that not only does the Jewish woman dress *b'tznius* and thereby not "invite trouble" upon herself, but her very refinement and *eidelkeit* positively keep those who are "looking for trouble" away from her!

5. EXERCISING MODEST BEHAVIOR WHEN IN A CAB: When a woman or girl takes a taxi or mini-cab driven by a man, it is elementary *tznius* that she sits in the back, not next to the driver (unless all the back seats are taken) which is the typical seating arrangement for husband and wife. Apart from this, while she should be polite and courteous to the driver, she should remain somewhat remote so that he does not draw her into a personal conversation for which some of these drivers are notorious.

Some women and girls try to obtain a cab driven by a woman when available, which is certainly an act of refinement. However, even with a female driver she should be wary not to impart any information that should not become general knowledge because many drivers spread gossip and cannot be trusted however friendly they are.

6. ENSURING THAT VACATION DOES NOT LEAD TO PRITZUS:

(a) Warning in *Shulchan Aruch* that *Yomtov* can lead to *pritzus*: The following illuminating words are written in *Shulchan Aruch, Hilchos Yom Tov* (529:4), חייבים בית דין להעמיד שוטרים ברגלים, שיהיו משוטטים ומחפשים בגנות ובפרדסים ועל הנהרות שלא יתקבצו שם לאכול ולשתות אנשים ונשים ויבואו לידי עבירה, וכן יזהירו בדבר זה לכל העם שלא יתערבו אנשים ונשים בבתיהם בשמחה, ולא ימשכו ביין, שמא יבואו לידי עבירה, אלא יהיו כולם קדושים - "*Beis Din* is responsible for engaging guards over the *Yom Tov* period to walk the streets, search the parks, the orchards and the river-sides to prevent men and women having a party together, as this can lead to sin. The guards should also warn people not to make mixed parties at home, especially if they involve drinking wine, as this can lead to sin."

On this the *Mishna Berura* writes (in *Shaar Hatzion* 21), ובעונותינו הרבים נתפרץ קלקול זה בזמנינו באיזה מקומות גם בימות החול, ועון גדול הוא, ומי שיש בידו למחות בודאי מחויב למחות - "Unfortunately, this malady has spread in our times and occurs even during weekdays (not just on *Yom Tov*). It is a serious sin and whoever is capable of protesting and preventing it, is obligated to do so." As we know, things have not changed for the better since the *Chofetz Chayim* wrote these words.

(b) Being aware of the danger that lurks in certain localities: One of the most dangerous places for lightheaded intermingling to occur in a forbidden manner is a holiday resort or a hotel dining room and lounge environment. When men and women intermingle in a lightheaded atmosphere, a breeding ground exists for all secondary forms of *znus* described above. This is apart from the possibility of such contact leading to very serious misdeeds. To use holidays to erode the very essence of our lives - our *Yiddishkeit* - is a serious misuse of an opportunity given to enable us to invigorate ourselves for a new lease of life.

We must not be party to those who view vacation as a time to relax both in the physical sense and also in their commitment to Torah and *mitzvos*. Those suffering from misdirection will visit a *treife* beach (which is *ossur* both for men and for women - see 2:B:2 above), go to mixed swimming (again forbidden for both men and women - *Gittin* 90b and *Biur Halacha* 339 s.v. *Lhakel*), watch television and engage in similar activities. Conversely, when a true Torah observant person goes on vacation, he relaxes in order to revitalize his body and mind, and prepare himself for a further term of living a productive and holy life, replete with Torah, *mitzvos* and good deeds.

(c) A couple should not openly display affection for one another: In line with the *issur* of males and females intermingling, it is appropriate to mention a further point. This is that it is indicative of *tznius* and segregation that couples do not display obvious affection for one another in the presence of others (*Rema*, E.H. 21:5). This is one of the many *halachos* of *tznius* that are unfortunately very little known. Young couples sometimes exhibit far too much affection for each other at the table of their parents, parents-in-law and sometimes even at the table of a host who has invited them for a meal.

It goes without saying that it is *ossur* for a young couple to walk along the street holding hands, as is typical conduct amongst *nochrim*. (This does not include an elderly couple who are obviously just supporting one another). If not for the fact that this is done by some who are part of the *frum* community, it would not have been mentioned in this *sefer*, which is addressed to the fully observant. It is a *mitzva* to ensure that the words of the *Rema*, E.H. 21:5 are more widely known. [The fact that in some communities the *chasan* and *kallah* emerge from the *chupah* hand in hand, has nothing to do with the above. It is obvious that this is done in order to "break the natural barrier" and is not a public display of affection. It is therefore unrelated to the above].

7. HACHNASAS ORCHIM MUST NOT LEAD TO INTERMINGLING: When a young couple invite a *bachur* to their Shabbos table, they may well be doing a great *mitzva* of *hachnasas orchim*, as this may be just what the *bachur* needs. Care must, however, be exercised that the three of them do not turn into a "happy trio" talking and laughing together without restraint. The *bachur* and the lady of the house may, of course, speak to one another, but there must be a constant awareness that she is an *eishes ish* and that he has been invited to enjoy the company of the young man and not that of his wife.

The same applies when a girl is a guest at the table of a couple. While she may be drawn into a conversation which will enable her to feel at ease, it is wrong and against *tznius* for the young husband to chat and joke freely at his table to the point that he plays the role of "entertaining two young ladies" - one his wife and the other a girl who is a stranger to him. If she becomes as relaxed and as talkative at this couple's table as she is when among her close friends, he has obviously overstepped the mark.

The *Mishna* in *Pirkei Avos* (1:5) says, יהי ביתך פתוח לרוחה ויהיו עניים בני ביתך ואל תרבה שיחה עם האשה - "Your home should be wide open, poor people should feel at home in your house and do not engage in light conversation with a woman". The connection between the two first statements and the last one is the following: Although it is a great *mitzva* to make everyone feel at home in your house, this must not be taken as a license for males and females to engage in enjoyable light talk. This is so, irrespective of whether the visitor is a male and he engages the lady of the house in light conversation or the visitor is female and the man of the house engages her in light conversation (*Chasid Ya'avetz* and *Abarbanel*). Those who practice this elementary segregation know that this does not diminish the quality of the *hachnasas orchim* at all. On the contrary, apart from receiving physical nourishment, the guest will leave the house with a warmth that only a spiritual experience can offer - see *Mekoros* 80:1.

In some places, adult girls go to local people's homes, either in the evening to help settle the small children, or to help with the preparations of food for Shabbos. The husband may greet her when she arrives, especially as she has come to help his family. Also on leaving he should thank her for the help she has extended. It is however wrong for the husband to chat freely and extensively with the girl. She is an *ervah* to him and an enjoyable ongoing friendly chat is *ossur*.

8. THE ISSUR INVOLVED IN COUPLES SOCIALIZING TOGETHER:

(a) Enjoying a light chat with one's friend's wife is *kirvah l'arayos*: Young couples socializing together, by one of them inviting two or three families to join them on a *motzoei* Shabbos or similar time for a social get-together at which they chat and joke together, is just another ploy of the *yetzer horah* to undermine *kedushas Yisroel*. At first sight, such socializing looks like nothing more than a harmless act of friendship. Apparently, it increases the affection between the families, and for families to feel close to one another is a state of *achdus* which is always to be greatly encouraged.

The truth, however, is that socializing in this manner is *treife* and has nothing to do with *achdus*. Since the men relax and chat with the wives of the other men as if they were their own wives, this is nothing short of males and females intermingling and totally against all principles of *kedushas Yisroel*. As always, no good emerges from what is wrong. In the pursuit of friendliness between the families, they run the serious risk of causing an unhealthy interest to develop which can do untold damage to one or more of the families for ever after. Furthermore, if the husbands are friendly with some unmarried young men, it would be natural for them to invite one or two of them over to enjoy the party - once again all in the name of *chesed* and *achdus*. It goes without saying how poisonous such a get-together would be for their spiritual well-being.

Even if it could be ensured that no mishap will emerge from these parties, the very situation of enjoying the contact with another person's wife or a girl is a totally forbidden type of enjoyment. As stated in 9:C:1 above, the *Mesilas Yesharim* (Chap.11) has very stern and potent words to say about men looking at women and talking to them to relax and enjoy themselves. He calls looking at women in this way "*znus ho'einayim*" - adultery of the eye, and chatting and joking with them "*znus ha'peh*" - adultery of the mouth. He does not differentiate between men who are single and men who are married, and there is no foundation to the belief of many, that once a man is married he is exempt from these *halachos*. The Hebrew name for socializing in this manner is קלות ראש - "flirting, that undermines the intellect". It demonstrates the loss of self control that evolves from such undesirable conduct.

(b) In *kiruv*, women should work with women as far as possible: If we wish to help others and show friendliness to them let us look back to the very first *yehudi* and see how he did it. *Chazal* say about Avraham Avinu and Sarah Imeinu, אברהם מגייר את האנשים ושרה מגיירת את הנשים - "Avraham influenced and worked with men while Sarah influenced and worked with women" (*Breishis Rabba* 84:4). Each worked in their own sphere. When Avraham came to his tent with just three men, and his wife was not needed in the dining area, she was nowhere to be seen.

Similarly, we find that although Moshe was the supreme leader of the Jewish people and in a position comparable to that of a king, Aharon was the personal leader of the men and Miriam of the women. The verse says concerning the *Shiras Hayam*, ותקח מרים הנביאה אחות אהרן את התוף בידה ותצאן כל הנשים אחריה - "And Miriam the prophetess, sister of Aharon, took the timbrel in her hand and all the women went out after her" (*Shemos* 15:20). Rabbi Samson Raphael Hirsch writes that the verse mentions that she was a sister of Aharon, which is apparently superfluous, because "Miriam occupied amongst the women the same position as Aharon held amongst the men. Just as Aharon spread the words of *Hashem* amongst the men (as Aharon was the teacher of Torah - יורו משפטיך ליעקב ותורתך לישראל), so too Miriam spread the words of *Hashem* amongst the women". Since she was their leader, she led the women in song after the splitting of the *Yam Suf*. Here again, we see that ideally men are led by men and women by women.

It is our privilege to follow the path of our *Avos* and great teachers, and not forge different and often precarious ways of our own. They are called our *Avos* and *Imahos* (fathers and mothers) so that we follow in their footsteps, just as a child follows the ways of his parents. We fortunately own springs that have pure and sweet waters. Why, oh why, do we foolishly abandon them and draw contaminated waters from unclean sources? - see *Mekoros* 80:1.

D. INTERMINGLING WHEN MANY PEOPLE STAND TOGETHER

1. OUTSIDE A SHUL, AT A SIMCHAS BEIS HASHOEVA ETC: It is characteristic of the *yetzer horah* to use the veneer of a *mitzva* to encourage the intermingling of men and women since people do not suspect the *yetzer horah* of *arayos* to be involved against such a "holy" backdrop; for example, at a *chasuna* where men and women sometimes stand around in the forecourt laughing and joking both before sitting down and towards the end; mixed seating at a lecture about an important topic; at a *Simchas Beis Hashoeva* and similar occasions.

Particular mention needs to be made of the "after *shul* come-together" when women and girls stand clustered outside the men's exit awaiting their husbands or fathers. Such a gathering and intermingling is wrong in itself. It leads to looking at women who are dressed in their best clothes and finery, and also results in chatting with familiarity with other people's wives and daughters. Alas, the *kedusha* derived from the *tefilla* might be lost by the lack of *kedusha* that occurs on exit from the *shul*.

To prevent this problem, women should stand to the side so that when the men come out of *shul* men and women will not mix with one another. Similarly when just one woman waits for her husband outside a *beis hamedrash*, she should stand to the side so that she is not on display to every man leaving the *beis hamedrash* - see *Mekoros* 78:3.

It is instructive to see what *Rabbeinu Yehuda HaChassid* writes in *Sefer Chassidim* No. 991 on the verse, הוקר רגלך מבית רעך - "Keep your feet away from the home of your friend" (*Mishlei* 25:17). Amongst various explanations he writes that it means, "Try not to cross paths with the family of your friend". He explains this with the following recommendation: שהרב יעשה בית המדרש מצד אחר, שלא יסתכלו הנכנסים והיוצאים באשתו או בבתו או בכלתו - loosely translated this means "The *Rav* should see to it that the entrance to his *beis hamedrash* is on a different side of the building than the entrance into his own dwelling. In this way those who enter or leave the *beis hamedrash* do not come across his wife, daughter or daughter-in-law and be tempted to observe them".

Rabbeinu Yehuda HaChassid was referring to Torah students who frequent the *beis hamedrash*. Also, he was referring to the moment before the student enters the *beis hamedrash* to learn Torah or the moment after he leaves, having learned Torah. He nevertheless deemed it important to recommend that the position of the *beis hamedrash* be carefully planned so that the *nisayon* be removed or at least minimized. Quite clearly, *tznius* (modesty) and *zehirus* (taking precautions) are closely related.

2. FULL SEGREGATION BETWEEN MALE AND FEMALE YOUTH: In some places where there is a concentration of *mosdos haTorah*, involving *Yeshivos* and seminaries, it is an advantage if it is arranged that times of travel to and from the different *mosdos* do not overlap. This means arranging that the terms do not start and finish on exactly the same day and time. In this way, large groups of *bachurim* and girls will not meet in the stations, trains, airports, aircraft, and long distance coaches. Although there will, of course, still be some overlap, in this way at least the mass overlap will be eliminated. Apart from the obvious segregation that results from such foresight, it has the advantage of giving the *bachurim* and girls a sample of *kedushas Yisroel* before they arrive at their respective *mosad* for the new *z'man*. If the heads of the different *mosdos* work together in unison, such and similar healthy forms of segregation can easily be arranged - see *Mekoros* 78:4.

Likewise, if there are times when a certain store or kiosk is expected to be visited by *bachurim*, a *tznua* will make it her business not to be there at that time. Similarly, if there are times when the store or kiosk is expected to be full of girls, a virtuous *bachur* will make sure to avoid visiting the store or kiosk at that time.

With reference to praising *Hashem*, the verse says, בחורים וגם בתולות זקנים עם נערים יהללו את שם השם - "*bachurim* and also girls, the elderly together with the youth shall praise the name of *Hashem*" (*Tehillim* 148:11). The *Chofetz Chayim* in *Biur Halacha* (339:4) writes in the name of the *Zichron Yosef* that the verse purposefully differentiates between the latter pair mentioned and the pair mentioned at the beginning of the verse. Concerning the elderly and the youth, it says that they should unite together and praise *Hashem* for His loving-kindness. By uniting together each gains from the presence of the other. The elderly gain from the youthful and vigorous spirit of the youth, and the youth gain from the wisdom and experience of the elderly. In contrast, *bachurim* and girls are distinctly not to go together. Rather, "*bachurim*" praise alone and "girls" praise alone as there would only be a negative input from any type of union between them (except, of course in marriage). When *kedusha* is maintained, the praises uttered to *Hashem* are pure and sublime, and a beautiful relationship develops between *Hashem* and those who praise Him.

3. A MAN PASSING BETWEEN TWO WOMEN, AND THE REVERSE:

(a) The nature of this issue: If people carelessly intermingle they will inevitably violate *Chazal's* warning that a man should not pass between two women, nor should a woman pass between two men. *Chazal* state that to do so can cause the people involved to forget some of their learning (*Horiyos* 13b) and in some cases could even cause them considerable physical harm

(*Pesachim* 111a). [This is quoted *Halachically* by the *Kitzur Shulchan Aruch 4:8; Shulchan Aruch HaRav, Choshen Mishpat, page 1774; Shemiras Haguf 9; Aruch Hashulchan* O.C.2:6; *Menoras Hamaor, Ner 4, Klal 1, Chelek 3, Perek 1; Reishis Chachmah, Sha'ar Hakedusha, Chap.5* and *Maharal MiPrague Baer Hagola, Baer Sheini*.]

We are, of course, unable to understand the nature of the harm caused by walking between people of the opposite gender. However, since *Chazal*, who had a superior understanding of the physical and spiritual aspects of the world, warn us to avoid this situation, it would be an act of folly to disregard their warning as stated by all the authorities mentioned above. It should be noted that when someone said to the *Chazon Ish zt'l* that they find it difficult to heed this cautionary note of *Chazal*, they were greeted with the sharp reply, "Would you also carelessly walk through fire?" (*Ta'ame D'krah* by his nephew, Hagaon Harav Chayim Kanievsky *shlita*, Page 108 No.29).

(b) Certainties concerning this issue: The following are points that are definite concerning the warning of *Chazal*. (Points that are uncertain concerning this warning will be mentioned in (c) below) :-

(1) A man should not pass between two stationary women unless there are four *amos* (approx. 7.5 feet - 2.3 meters) between them (*Ben Ish Chei*, second year, *Pinchos* 17 and Responsa *Salmas Chayim* 503).

(2) A woman should not pass between two stationary men if there is less that four *amos* between them (*ibid*). [For this reason, no *shurah* is made for an *aveilah* after a *levayah rl.* A *shurah* consists of two rows of men facing one another. The *ovel* (mourner) walks through the rows and the men say words of condolence when the *ovel* passes where they stand - *Gesher HaChayim* page 152].

(3) When there are four *amos* or more between the two outer people they are viewed as two separate individuals and the person passing between them is not considered to be passing between two women or two men (*Ben Ish Chai, ibid*).

(4) When two men pass simultaneously between two women or two women pass simultaneously between two men the warning of *Chazal* does not apply and no harm will occur - (*ibid).*

(5) When the outer people are standing or walking in a way that they cannot be considered as associated with one another, the advice of *Chazal* does not apply. For example, they are within four amos of one

another but one is distinctly further ahead than the other. In such a case there is no connection between the two outer people and the middle person is not considered as 'crossing between them' *(ibid)*. This, however, does not include women standing behind one another in a queue. They are connected by being 'together the queue' and it would therefore be wrong for a man to stand or pass between them.

(6) When a 'man, woman and man' walk unintentionally together (such as a husband and wife walking along and a second man walks unintentionally alongside the wife) the warning of Chazal does not apply. Since a) they are all mobile and b) their being together is unintentional, the central person is not considered as walking between the two outer persons *(Responsa Salmas Chayim* 503 - see *sefer, Dover Shalom* 4:21). However, when the three walk together intentionally the issur might apply - see (c) point 4 below.

(c) Uncertainties concerning this issue: There are many uncertainties concerning the application of this warning. For example, it is unclear:-

(1) Whether it applies when the girls are under *Bas-mitzva* (*Sefer Zikaron*, by Hagaon Harav Chayim Kanievsky *shlita* No.19).

(2) Whether it applies within close family eg. a father walking between his wife and adult daughter (see *Beis Baruch* Vol. 1 page 402 and *Shemiras Haguf V'hanefesh* 111 note 12. The latter quotes the *Chazon Ish* who held that it applies even to close family).

(3) Whether it applies to non-Jewish women (*Responsa Maharsham* 4:148). However, *Shemiras Haguf V'hanefesh* 111 note 11 quotes *Poskim* who write that it certainly applies also to non-Jewish women.

(4) Whether it applies when all three people are standing, walking or sitting together, or only when the inner person crosses through the outer ones (*Responsa Salmas Chayim* 504 writes that it applies, see *Responsa Vay'varech Dovid* no.122 s.v. *Ub'nogeia* and *Shemiras Haguf V'hanefesh* 111:(4). However, *Sefer Zikaron* No. 16, *Minchas Yitzchak* 10:68 and *Beis Baruch* Vol. 1 page 402 are in doubt).

(5) Whether it applies when one of the outer two people is sitting and the other is standing (as can happen on a bus) and a person of the opposite gender walks between them. Since the two outer people are totally different positions to one another, it could be that the middle person is not considered as "passing between two people" (see similar query in *Responsa Vay'varech Dovid* 122 s.v. *Od zos*).

(6) Whether it applies when two men pass along either side of a standing woman or two women along either side of a stationary man. This is because the harm might be caused only when by a person passing 'between' two people, not when the reverse is done (see *Halichos Beisoh* 28 note 15).

(7) Some maintain that if the man passing in the middle carries an article such as an umbrella or a *sefer*, he is not considered to be passing alone between the two women and the warning does not apply (*Tiv Yehoshua* 2:12, *Beis Baruch* Vol. 1 page 402, *Zichron Tov* letter 28, *Lev Eliyahu*, *Breishis*, Introduction page 27. This is, however, not unanimously held - *Responsa Vay'varech Dovid* 122 and *Chazon Ish* quoted in *Shemiras Haguf V'Hanefesh* page 334).

(d) Undoing any harm caused: If a person passed between two people of the opposite gender when it was wrong to do so he should say a verse which starts with a statement containing *lo* and finishes with a statement containing *lo*, such as לא איש קל ויכזב ובן אדם ויתנחם, ההוא אמר ולא יעשה ודיבר ולא יקימנו - *Bamidbar* 23:19. Alternatively, he should say a verse that starts with the word *keil* and finishes with the word *keil*, such as קל מוציאם ממצרים כתועפות ראם לו כי לא נחש ביעקב ולא קסם בישראל כעת יאמר ליעקב ולישראל מה פעל קל - *Bamidbar* 23:22-23.

E. RAISING FUNDS FOR TZEDAKA - NO HETER TO MINGLE

1. A PLOY OF THE YETZER HORAH: When the intermingling is done under the facade and guise of "*tzedaka*", the wrongdoing is viewed as a *mitzva* and the people involved are quite convinced that only the over-zealous oppose their activities. These people mistakenly believe that everything is acceptable when done for the sake of a *mitzva*, such as to raise funds for the upkeep of a *mikvah*, a *shul*, *hachnasas kallah*, a *gemach* for loans and so on. Concerts are therefore organized in which men and women, and teenage boys and girls intermingle before and after the event and in some cases even during the event by having a section for mixed seating. This is quite apart from the unhealthy excitement and adoration of the celebrity which usually accompanies these events - see *Mekoros* 12:4-6.

The justification given, that in this way large sums can be raised and that the organizers are doing it *l'shem shomayim*, as all proceeds go to *tzedaka*, is totally irrelevant and absolutely unacceptable. Just as it is *ossur* to steal *matzo* in order to fulfill the *mitzva* of eating *matzo*, and if someone does steal it *Hashem* has an aversion to that person's *mitzva*, so too, *Hashem* does not want and even dislikes *mitzvos* which are born out of affairs that smack of *pritzus*. It is to our great shame that we, the descendants of the *Avos* and a people blessed with ביישנות - bashfulness, have fallen prey to the blatant trickery of the *yetzer hara*.

From the Torah outlook, the place of the Jewish woman is inside the house rather than out on the street. It is such a natural part of her existence that the Torah refers to women as בית יעקב - "the house of Yaacov" (*Shemos* 19:3) rather than בנות יעקב - "daughters of Yaacov". Moreover, the *Gemara* (*Shabbos* 118b) relates that when *Reb Yossi* spoke about his wife he referred to her as "his home" rather than "his wife". She is part of her home and her home is charged by a *Yiddishkeit* and happiness that emanates from her.

It will be observed that in our times when *tznius* is so inadequate, it has become fashionable and even part of life for women to be out of their homes for a large part of the day in pursuit of all types of work and occupations. If she does not need more money she might pursue *mitzvos*, such as working for nominal pay in the office of a *tzedaka* or health organization, a Jewish newspaper or a Jewish magazine and the like. Being a *mitzva* purpose she will come to terms with the fact that there is a problem in the office as far as segregation between males and females is concerned.

One of the most prominent American *Roshei Yeshiva* of our times related the following incident to the author of this *Sefer*. When in *Eretz Yisroel* as a young man he had reason to frequently go into the head office of a major Torah organization. Once when speaking to the director of the organization, a booklet they had published was needed from another part of the building. The director, who was a young man at the time, just called over one of the secretaries and said to her with the greatest familiarity, "Rivka'le! You like being helpful! Do me a favor and fetch a copy of such and such a booklet from the bookshelves on the top floor". The visitor, who was a budding Torah personality brought up in a home of outstanding *tznius* and *eidelkiet*, was so taken aback by the familiar tone with which the director addressed the girl that, (to voice his protest) he spontaneously asked the director whether the secretary was his daughter or younger sister that he talked to her with such familiarity?

The *yetzer horah* knows that the ultimate *mitzva* for women is *tznius*, which calls for healthy segregation between men and women (apart from within the immediate family). Since *tznius* is the corner-stone of *kedushas Yisroel*, the *yetzer horah* will do everything in his power to undermine it. He will therefore encourage all types of *mitzvos* other than this one - see *Mekoros* 80:4.

2. MONEY RAISED BY TREIFE MEANS WILL NOT AID KEDUSHA: When the saintly *Gaon* and *Tzaddik* Reb Elchanan Wasserman *zt'l* was in the United States to raise funds for his *yeshiva* in Baranovitch which was in desperate financial straits, the following incident occurred. A lady who was a relative of the family where Reb Elchanan stayed decided that she wanted to help this great Rabbi in his mission. She therefore arranged a ball on behalf of the Baranovitch *yeshiva* without consulting Reb Elchanan beforehand. Tickets were printed and all arrangements were in hand. Some days before the ball was to take place, someone visited Reb Elchanan bringing with him all the tickets that had been printed so that Reb Elchanan should bless the tickets. With this he hoped to guarantee that the sale of the tickets and the ball itself would be a success.

On hearing the word "ball" Reb Elchanan inquired, "What is a ball?" to which the answer was given that it is a leisurely get-together where there is mixed dancing, light entertainment and refreshments. On hearing the response, the shocked Reb Elchanan took the tickets that were lying on the table and started tearing them up one by one until they were all torn to shreds. While tearing them he kept saying to himself with bewilderment, "Can Torah be built with such money?" A short time later the lady who had arranged the ball and had printed the tickets came to Reb Elchanan in a state of distress. She tried to explain to him how much money could have been raised had the tickets not been destroyed. To this Reb Elchanan responded once again, "Even if the ball would have raised a sizable amount of money, can Torah be built or sustained from such money?" (*Ohr Elchanan* Vol. 2. page 186).

A similar event took place with another one of the great personages of *Klal Yisroel*. One day a woman presented a check of $2000 to Reb Shraga Feivel Mendlowitz *zt'l* for his *yeshiva*. In those days, this was an enormous sum of money, and sufficient to clear all the debts of *Yeshivas Torah Vodaas*. He gladly accepted the money and immediately paid off all the outstanding money owed by his *yeshiva*. On the very next day, *Reb* Shraga Feivel heard that all the money had been raised from a theater party. He immediately borrowed $2000 and returned the entire sum of money to the woman who had presented it to him. He explained that he could not accept it as "*Yeshivos* are not built on theater parties!"

When the Bnos National Council was short of funds, they too considered raising the badly needed funds by putting on a theater party. Reb Elimelech Tress *zt'l* informed them of the incident that had happened with Reb Shraga Feivel some years earlier, and the way in which he had flatly refused such ill-earned money. Upon hearing the attitude of this true Torah personality, they were dissuaded from bringing their intention to fruition (biography of Reb Elimelech Tress *zt'l*, page 173).

3. WOMEN SHOULD DO CHESED EVEN WITH NEEDY MEN: Although women should not mingle with men even for the sake of *chesed*, women should of course give *tzedaka* and practice *chesed* with everyone including men. The verse, כפה פרשה לעני (*Mishlei* 31:20) refers to the woman of valor giving *tzedaka* to a poor man. *Hachnasas orchim* to men and women alike is high on the list of *mitzvos* for which women are praised and encouraged (see *Brachos* 10b) - see *Mekoros* 80:1.

A visitor is brought into the house, made to feel welcome and is given food. The house is a family domain where all members of the household are at home. It is therefore a perfect setting for a woman to help the needy without any danger of intermingling taking place. Provided the lady of the house is not over familiar with her visitor, and merely welcomes him warmly so that he relaxes and regains his strength, she is emulating the conduct of Avraham and Sarah who spent a large part of their days feeding and being of assistance to whoever was in need. Concerning women going out to collect money from families they are acquainted with - see *Mekoros* 79:1-5 that there is nothing intrinsically wrong in doing so, provided the people they go to are known to them to be refined and decent people.

F. OFFICE AND SECRETARIAL JOBS - DANGER TO TZNIUS

1. AN OFFICE JOB IS AN AWESOME HAZARD TO TZNIUS: One of the greatest misfortunes that have befallen our generation as far as *tznius* is concerned is the fact that many Orthodox women and girls work in offices or as secretaries. Many take these jobs to help sustain the family rather than just as an occupation or as a means to earn some extra money. The need for the job is therefore very great but likewise the perils involved are of the most worrying nature. The dangers and pitfalls in such jobs are of such proportion and magnitude that a large part of the material in this *sefer* is directly relevant to it. The woman or girl works many hours a day in an environment that has every potential to destroy *tznius* and all that it stands for, for herself, for her employer and for all males and females that work together in a large office - see *Mekoros* 82:1.

2. URGE TO BE CHARMING AND A "DELIGHT TO HAVE AROUND": Even if we had not seen and heard of the outcome of this dangerous type of melting-pot, it should be obvious that the trials and tribulations that confront such a person can be enormous. So that she is appreciated and so that she feels her job is secure, the woman or girl will have many difficult *nisyonos*. She will have a natural urge to overdress, to wear ostentatious jewelry, to over-apply cosmetics and to use scents and perfumes that are enjoyed by those who are with her in the same room, and she will be a pleasure to have around.

Dovid Hamelech says in the very first verse of *Tehillim*, אשרי האיש אשר לא הלך בעצת רשעים ובדרך חטאים לא עמד ובמושב ליצים לא ישב - "Fortunate is the man who has not walked in the ways of the wicked, has not stood in the path of sinners and has not sat in the environment of scoffers". The *Ibn Ezra* writes that the verse is written in a manner of progression - walking, standing and sitting. To come into contact with evil whilst walking is harmful since everything one sees or hears makes an impression. Worse still is to behold evil while standing. Being unoccupied, one absorbs more of the negative influence and the damage is therefore greater. Worst of all is to sit in the company of evil. When sitting, a person is relaxed and highly receptive to the atmosphere that prevails around him. The effect and damage caused by sitting amongst wrongdoers is therefore very severe and far-reaching.

With this introduction, it is obvious that *pritzus* that occurs in an office, in which a man sees overdress, exceptionally attractive makeup and smells the scent of those who are heavily perfumed, is far more destructive to him than when he comes across the same while walking along the street or when waiting at a train station, at an airport etc. In an office he relaxes and is surrounded by *pritzus* for many hours a day, most days of the week. This exposure to *pritzus* must be extremely detrimental and defiling.

3. URGE TO SOCIALIZE WITH CO-WORKERS: While at work, she will feel compelled to be very friendly with everyone, particularly her superiors and employer, and engage with them at any time of the day in light talk, about anything and everything. In addition, the relaxed office atmosphere is conducive to everyone being on first name terms with one another. The considerable familiarity that develops between the employer and his secretary, or between the males and females working together in a large office, is of such arresting severity and such an infringement of the Torah law of והיה מחניך קדוש - "Your locality shall be holy", that there is practically no comparable situation in which an Orthodox Jewish person can be.

Such conduct is *ossur* even if the alternative would mean that she and her family would be on the poverty line, with nothing to eat. It is of course ridiculous to imagine that any of the above forms of misconduct can be condoned so that "her husband or children can sit and learn". It is as if the family buys cheap *treife* meat so that money is available to be able to "sit and learn".

To see the problem in its true perspective, she should imagine for a moment that the only way she can make a living is to be an actress or a fashion model. Would she for a moment consider disgracing herself and engaging in such a career? She would surely rather work as a maid or live off unemployment benefit than lower herself to such degradation. Having established that, she must know that for a woman or girl to work with a group of people with whom she strikes up a warm and enjoyable relationship, is no better.

4. ISSUR TO GREET WOMEN IN AN AFFECTIONATE MANNER: *Chazal*, had an in-depth gauge to assess the effect things have on a person's emotions, and the response that minor arousals can precipitate. They ruled that אין שואלים בשלום אשה - "It is *ossur* to affectionately and heartily greet a woman" (*Kiddushin* 70b and *Shulchan Aruch* E.H. 21:6). The *Poskim* explain that it is permissible to greet a woman with a warm good-morning, good-bye, *refuoh shleimo* and the like. Such greetings are intended as salutations, signs of respect, giving sincere *brachos*, or forms of encouragement and as such will do no harm. (See *Aruch Hashulchan*, E.H. 21:8 and *Otzar HaPoskim*, 21:48).

However, it is *ossur* for a man to greet a woman in a very affectionate and personal manner. Similarly, it is *ossur* for a man to send regards to a woman or girl through her friend, father or husband, because the woman feels the tenderness and deep personal friendship that is being extended to her. Such expressions of affection are forbidden under the *issur* of ולא תקרבו לגלות ערוה - which translated loosely means, "Do not act in a way that fosters closeness and fondness between people who are *ervah* to one another" (*Rambam Issurei Biah* 21:1-2).

Hearing this *halacha* on the one hand, and considering the affable greetings and effusive conversation that take place in offices on the other hand, gives us an idea of the consternation and alarm with which our Sages would react if they were witness to typical office jobs of our times.

5. CONVINCING OTHERS ABOUT THESE DANGERS: No doubt, many employers and male co-workers will ridicule the apprehension expressed about the effect of female secretaries and typists upon male members of staff. Rather than trying to convince them, they should be asked a very simple question: "If the secretaries and female typists do not turn up one day due to sickness or something similar, does the office seem dull, tedious and uninteresting because the "sparkle" is missing?" If the employer or worker is honest, he is likely to concede that this is indeed the case.

He should then be given to understand that to "enjoy the presence of an *ervah*" is *ossur* even if it develops no further, since this itself is קירבה לעריות - "associating with *ervah*" which is a form of *znus*. See 9:C:1 that to enjoy talking to an *ervah* is *znus hapeh v'haozen*, to enjoy their scents is *znus ho'af*, to enjoy their facial appearance or their dress is *znus ho'ayin* and so on. (Parents who enjoy having their married children and their spouses in their home, are not enjoying "having females around". Instead they are enjoying having "their children around" and this feeling has nothing to do with the gender of their in-laws - see *Breishis Rabba* 70:12 on the verse, וישק יעקב לרחל).

6. THE DETRIMENT OF HEARING FOUL LANGUAGE: The problem with office jobs extends even further. Even if a girl or young lady is a true *tznua*, and carefully avoids all the misdeeds mentioned, should she work in an office with typical present-day *nochrim* or many *non-shomrei mitzvos* she will still be exposed for many hours a day to *nivul peh* that such people usually speak between themselves. Also, if a female in the office seriously lacks *tznius* in her relationship with the male staff, the *tznius'dik* woman or girl will be a daily observer of *pritzus'dik* behavior. As has been stated elsewhere, a person cannot hear and see *pritzus* and remain untarnished. The *tumah* penetrates into his system and great damage is done, even if he is not immediately aware of it.

7. IMPORTANT GUIDELINES: Considering the terrible dilemma our cherished young wives and daughters are in, it is best to lay down a number of guidelines to help them protect themselves if they must work in an office.

(a) Men and women working in separate rooms: It is to be strongly recommended that women work in a room set aside for them within the office complex, rather than in one large room with the men. By sitting in two different rooms, many pitfalls will be eliminated or at least greatly lessened. The contact between male and female will be reduced to the minimum and the danger of over-familiarity largely contained. Furthermore, just being in different rooms because of *tznius*, will serve as a constant reminder to them about the *issur* of intermingling and of all forms of familiarity, however minor they may seem to be.

Should it not be possible to have a separate room, they should at least have a part of the office to themselves, so that they do not work in close proximity of the men. Even then, this is acceptable only in an office of *frum Yidden* where she will not be exposed to obscene language and conduct.

Rabbeinu Dovid Ben Zimrah in his famous *sefer, T'shuvas HaRadvaz* (3:481) warned about men and women working in close proximity, already in his time which was about six hundred years ago. He writes: ומה שיכולנו לתקן הוא שלא ישבו על שולחן אחד לעשות מלאכת הרקום אנשים ונשים כאשר היה בתחלה, אלא שהאנשים לעצמן והנשים לעצמן - "We were able to institute that men and women should not sit and weave at one and the same table, as they used to. Instead, the men would work by themselves and the women by themselves." If this enactment was necessary in those days, the need for it has become much greater in our times when the boundaries of *tznius* have been ruptured and fragmented.

When Boaz addressed Ruth as she collected wheat in one of his fields, he said to her, אל תלכי ללקוט בשדה אחר, וגם לא תעברי מזה, וכה תדקבון עם נערותי - The *Vilna Gaon* translates this verse as follows: "Do not collect in other people's fields. Also, do not cross into another one of my fields. Rather, continue collecting in this very field because in this field I have a group of female workers and you will be able to work amongst them, whilst in other fields I do not have female workers and you would be working amongst males" (*Ruth* 2:8). Such a passage has been recorded for all time, so that we learn from it the ways of *tznius* and *kedusha*.

(b) The problem of first-name terms: If a girl works for a Jewish boss, it is strongly recommended that he and other male workers address her only by her official name e.g. Miss Cohen, Miss Chana Cohen, Chana Cohen and the like, but not by her first name alone. Although, as a result of their 'working association' it might not be absolutely wrong to address an unmarried girl by her first name (as people address those who are much younger than themselves by their first name) avoiding doing so is a powerful means of preventing familiarity. It is therefore to be advocated in a setting that is extremely conducive to familiarity that one avoids addressing even girls by their first names. See 9:A:2 above where the serious problem of *yichud* that arises once an employer becomes very familiar with his secretary is discussed.

It is all the more wrong to address a married woman by her first name, as one must keep a considerable distance from a married woman. Moreover, it is unquestionably wrong to address either a woman or a girl by a name that has been changed to give it a special affectionate sound. It is therefore wrong to use names such as Channah'leh, Soreleh, Suri, Esti, Yocheved'el and the like. Even if they are called so by everyone else, men who address her should not use such terms - see 9:A:2 above.

The Manchester *Rosh Yeshiva*, Hagaon Hatzadik Harav Yehuda Zev Segal *zt'l*, told a *talmid* of his who owns a business in London and has branches in the provincial towns of England, that whenever he calls one of the branches and speaks to the women he should never address them by their first name. He blessed his *talmid* with good *parnasa* on condition that he kept his 'distance' from the women working for him. The writer of this *sefer* heard from one of these women that well over ten years have passed and her boss has never addressed her by her first name, but always, "Hello, is that Mrs...", "Good morning Mrs..." etc. This business experienced much success over the years in keeping with the *bracha* given - see *Mekoros* 81:1-3.

The affection that can be inherent in calling someone by their first-name is powerfully demonstrated in a testimony of a disciple of one of the last of the *Rishonim*, the *Maharil* (*Rabbeinu Yaacov HaLevi zt'l*, d.5187) on whose teachings most of *minhag Ashkenaz* is based. At the end of the *sefer, Maharil* there is a section named *Likutim*. The first item in this section reads as follows: "Whenever the *Maharil* mentioned his wife to others he would not refer to her by name". Apparently, the *Maharil* refrained from mentioning his wife by name because, in his great sensitivity for *tznius* and holiness, he felt that if he spoke of her by name he would be displaying part of his affection for her, and it was unfitting for him to do so. This has not been recorded as a *halacha* and is far beyond what is asked of ordinary people (although it must be put on record that in many *Chassidishe* circles this fine level of *tznius* is practiced to our present day) but to underscore the endearment that can result from using a first-name at a time or setting where it is uncalled for and even unhealthy.

(c) If possible to work in an office of *frum Yidden*: A woman and girl should work in the office of a *frum* person if at all possible, as it is difficult (with present-day tendencies) to see a justification to work elsewhere. A person who flouts *tznius* will be tempted to spend time with the women even if they are in a different room. Should this not be possible, the woman or girl should discuss the proposed place of work with her *Rav*, to hear his opinion whether she can take such a job or not.

The most harmful condition of all is when the employer himself lacks decency and morality. Shlomo Hamelech wisely established that when a man is a servant to a slanderer who enjoys hearing *lashon horah* and lies, he will inevitably become a slanderer himself, because only through tale-bearing will he find favor in the eyes of his superior. He says in *Mishlei* (29:12), מושל מקשיב על דבר שקר, כל משרתיו רשעים - "A governor who hearkens to lies and fabrications, all his servants are sure to be bad people" [because they will endeavor to satisfy and delight their master - *Ralbag*]. Accordingly, working for a man who lacks morality must detrimentally influence the workers.

(d) Not to remain in a job if exposed to ongoing *pritzus*: If when working, the women or girls realize that one particular person does not behave correctly towards them, the matter should be brought to the attention of the employer. In some cases women wishing to conduct themselves with *tznius* will find that the men in the office do not have the most elementary feeling for *tznius*. When this is the case there might be no alternative but to leave and seek alternative employment. The same applies if a radio is kept on in the office, and the music or the features are laced with immorality and depravity that are toxic to the *nishmas Yisroel*. She must consider a place of work that exposes her to *pritzus* to be the same as a place of work which demands *chillul* Shabbos of her - hard as it may be, she must not barter her *Yiddishkeit* for anything.

Furthermore, she must know that since every cent earned is predetermined from Heaven, it cannot be that to obtain the financial help allotted to her she must work in a place where *Hashem* surely does not want her to work. Her *parnasa* must therefore be predestined to come from elsewhere.

Hearing corruption and immoral talk will have a far reaching negative effect even on the finest woman or girl. Although she is totally uninterested in what is being said and turns a deaf ear to it, it will nevertheless be extremely harmful to her. Since her ears constantly hear *tumah*, it must stain her mind and perception although she might not be aware of it. We are told by *Chazal* that one of the greatest *Tanaim*, *R' Yehoshua Ben Chananya*, became a great and saintly man as a direct consequence of what his mother did with him whilst he was still a baby. From the day he was born, she would bring his crib into the *beis hamedrash* so that he would hear the words of Torah spoken by *Talmidei Chachamim* (*Talmud Yerushalmi*, *Yevamos* 1:6).

As a result of this, his mother is praised in *Pirkei Avos* 2:8 with the words ר׳ יהושע, אשרי יולדתו - "*R' Yehoshua*, happy and fortunate is the one who bore him". The credit for all that he became goes to his mother. If hearing *divrei* Torah, when the mind is still far too young to understand anything, brings such *kedusha* and *tahara* over the child, can we possibly assess the degree of *tumah* that is imbibed by the person when they constantly hear *nivul peh* and depravity of the worst type? Concerning impure music, see 7:H:4 and 9:J:3(f) and the *Mishna Berura*, *Shar Hatzion* 560:25 where he warns about the harm caused to a baby if he hears impure song even though he does not yet understand anything.

(e) Ensuring that the *issur* of *yichud* is not transgressed: If males and females work in an office, and outsiders cannot just walk in because the entrance is kept locked, a *shaaloh* must be asked to ensure they do not transgress the *issur* of *yichud* - the *issur* for a male and female to be closeted inside a secluded area. The *issur* of *yichud* could apply even if a number of females (whether Jewish or non-Jewish), or a number of non-Jewish males, work in the office - see E.H. 22:5. See *Mekoros* 82 for further elaborations.

8. WORKING ONLY WITH REFINED WOMEN AND GIRLS:

(a) The harm in associating daily with unrefined girls: The conditions under which a woman or girl may work in an office have been explained. It must, however, be stressed and made abundantly clear, that even when all the above mentioned *tznius*-related problems have been eliminated, working in an office with just females can be far from ideal. Even if there is no direct *tznius* problem, there are threats to other aspects of conduct and attitude. Therefore, fortunate is the one who finds her *parnasa* elsewhere.

The perspective of a girl concerning money, comfort, clothes and *shidduchim*, and her appreciation of *tefilla* and *limud haTorah*, are often adversely affected and even badly eroded in the environment of an office. Often women and girls with whom she works will have come from a weak background. Furthermore, they could have been educated in schools to which her parents would never have sent her. It could even turn out that she will be working from morning to evening with people for whom money, comfort, clothes and good looks are the most important things in the world.

The soul-depleting effect of a day by day exposure to people who lack valued ideals is such that she loses much of the *ahavas haTorah* and *Yiras Shomayim* that had been instilled in her at home, school and seminary. To the critical observer it is heart-rending that in a matter of a year or two, seventeen or eighteen years of careful nurturing is ripped asunder.

The *Brisker Rav*, Maran Hagaon Harav Yitzchak Zev Soloveitchik *zt'l*, was once asked whether it is advisable for a *bachur* to go into a *shidduch* that had been suggested in *Eretz Yisroel* with a *Beis Yaacov* girl who worked in a firm belonging to a nationalistic employer. He replied that if all other girls who work in this firm are *Beis Yaacov* girls one need not worry, and the family could go into the *shidduch*. However, if even just one of the girls is nationalistic like her employer they should desist from entering into the *shidduch*. (Heard from Hagaon R' Avraham Erlanger *shlita*, *Yerusholayim*, author of the *sefer, Bircas Avraham*). This incident demonstrates the opinion of *Gedolei Yisroel* concerning the ease with which a person can be negatively influenced by the attitude, conduct and way of dress of just a single co-worker with whom they come into close contact.

(b) Looking for the most ideal way to earn money: Due to above considerations, it is advisable for a young woman or girl to work in an office which employs only women and girls of the finest and highest caliber. Alternatively, she could teach Torah subjects to children of any age. To do so is very rewarding as she is engaged in *avodas hakodesh* whilst earning a living. Also, a woman and girl can gain considerably from teaching girls the *halachos* and attitudes of *tznius* and true Jewish refinement - see 1:O:1(c) above.

Apart from teaching, there are types of work that she can do in the privacy of her home such as sewing, typing, word-processing, book-keeping, proof-reading, private tuition, speech-therapy, music lessons and the like. When anything of this nature is possible, it has the great advantage over an office job that the woman or girl remains in the safe sanctuary of her home, which is by far the ideal. If she needs to take additional help, she can employ exactly the right type of co-worker, and is not at the mercy of others.

(c) Women going to work - like person crossing the sea: Shlomo Hamelech describes the way the *Eishes Chayil* earned a living for her family with the verse, היתה כאניות סוחר ממרחק תביא לחמה - "She was like a trading ship in her pursuit of finances; she brought her bread from afar" (*Mishlei* 31:14). When sailors travel by ship across the ocean they take many precautions to guarantee their safety. They avoid particularly dangerous areas of the sea where the water is very turbulent and as they travel, they are constantly on guard to ensure that they do not collide with another vessel or other hazards of the sea.

The *Eishes Chayil*, who is forced to leave the safety of her home in order to seek a living, is compared to a sea-going ship. She will not accept employment in places where the "waters are choppy" and the lack of modesty of others threatens her purity. Furthermore, even when she works or trades amongst decent people she is constantly on guard to ensure that no slip concerning *tznius* occurs. She realizes that if a man sees a woman who is not in full Kosher dress a spiritual collision has occurred that is harmful to both parties involved.

The verse concludes with, "She brought her bread from afar". With all the necessary precautions she takes, the *Eishes Chayil* will not leave her home and mingle with people just to earn extra money so that she can buy luxuries and have more comforts at home. Since she can manage without these things, she does not leave the protection of her home in pursuit of such earnings. The verse therefore stresses that she travels away to bring "bread" to her family - bread symbolizing essentials, rather than extras. Naturally, the husband and sons of this wonderful woman are people who are a pride to *Klal Yisroel*.

9. AN EMPLOYER MUST NOT ALLOW PRITZUS IN HIS OFFICE: A Jewish employer is obligated to ensure that *pritzus* is not tolerated in his office or factory. He employs the workers and it is therefore his responsibility to set a standard of dress that is not detrimental to himself or to others who work for him. Even *nochrios* who work for him should not be allowed to appear in such forms of dress and such heavy applications of scent that will inevitably arouse unwelcome interest or foster improper conduct - see E.H. 21:1.

Dovid Hamelech says in *Tehillim* (101:6), עיני בנאמני ארץ לשבת עמדי הולך בדרך תמים הוא ישרתני - "My eyes shall behold the faithful of the land, and they shall reside with me; Only he who goes on the path of purity and innocence shall serve me". Dovid, the most righteous of men, was anxious that his companions and servants should be people of the highest caliber. He prayed that his eyes should not come into contact with the perfidious and the corrupt, because even he would be affected by such contact. This plea must send a chill down our spines when we consider the devastating effect a short skirted, highly scented, sophisticated young secretary must have on her Jewish employer, her male co-workers and anyone who spends many hours a day in her company.

A good employer will endeavor to create a relaxed and tranquil atmosphere in his office. He must not endeavor to create such an atmosphere by allowing males and females to socialize with one another or engage in similar infringements of *tznius*. Earning a living does not grant a dispensation to transgress even the most minor of the *issurim*. All the more so it does not override a wrongdoing related to one of the three cardinal sins of the Torah - *giluy arayos*. In fact, if an office is run on such lines, it attracts weak elements who relish the atmosphere of immorality. This will cause an even greater spirit of *pritzus* in the office, to the detriment of all concerned.

Rather than exploiting such illicit methods to create a relaxed atmosphere, the employer should generate this by treating his employees respectfully; by behaving with all employees with the utmost honesty and fairness; and by keeping calm even when under pressure due to excessive work or due to things not having gone the way he had envisaged.

Note: After all that has been written in this section, it is superfluous to write about the intense harm and far-reaching dangers that result from having an au-pair girl in the house who dresses scantily and enticingly, brings in all types of literature, plays the latest popular music etc. See also 8:I above.

10. SOMETHING DONE BY MANY CAN STILL BE TOTALLY WRONG:

(a) Passions blind people - they do not see a hazard to *tznius*: Some people might feel that it is wrong to maintain that something done by many *frum Yidden*, such as girls working in an office together with men, is distinctly not *tznius'dik*. They will contend that since it is done by many *shomrei mitzvos* it cannot possibly be a form of *pritzus*, because *pritzus* is revolting to *shomrei mitzvos*. This is, however, a totally wrong assumption as can be seen from the many *shomrei mitzvos* who wear garments that do not have Kosher necklines or hemlines, that have slits and that are very tight-fitting - faults that are forms of *pritzus*. Evidently, without proper guidance, not just the individual but whole congregations of *frum Yidden*, can err badly. This is particularly so in issues related to *tznius* because *tznius* is up against strong drives for beauty, recognition, money making, being able to do all that the opposite gender can do, and many other urges and passions.

(b) Strange custom - women were *sandek* at a *bris milah*: To demonstrate just how far people are capable of misjudging a situation, it is appropriate to mention a wrongdoing that is, *Baruch Hashem*, no longer practiced nowadays. From it one can see that a wrongdoing can be practiced by many and be thought of as being perfectly acceptable. Incredibly, it became a wide-spread custom in the times of the *Rishonim* for women to be the *sandek* at a *bris milah*, although this meant men standing around her during the *bris* and the woman being right at the center of the activity. Women would even perform this function when the *bris* was in *shul*, although this involved sitting inside the men's *shul* and being surrounded throughout the *bris* by men.

(c) Difficulties *Maharam MiRuttenburg* had to stop this custom: One of the greatest *Rishonim* of the time, *Rabbeinu Meir zt'l*, known as the *Maharam miRuttenburg*, fought tooth and nail to stop this custom. Although to us such practice seems revolting, the *Maharam* encountered great difficulty in influencing the general populace to desist from this custom. His objections are written in a statement preserved in the *sefer* of his great *talmid*, *Rabbeinu Shimshon Ben Tzadok zt'l* in his *sefer*, *Tashbatz HaKatan*, No. 397. The following is a loose translation of the *Maharam's* statements:

"In my opinion it is a defective *minhag* that in many places a woman sits in the *shul* with men around her and the baby is circumcised while lying on her lap. Even if her husband, father or son is the *mohel* it is still wrong, because it is not right that an adorned woman enters between men and into a *shul*. In this vein, *Chazal* say (*Kiddushin* 52b) אשה בעזרה מנין - "Is a woman to be seen in the courtyard of the *Beis Hamikdash*?" - young *Kohanim* are there and they could be affected by her presence etc. Therefore, whoever can stop this *minhag* should do so and those who desist from following this *minhag* shall be blessed - Peace to you - *Meir son of Rabbi Baruch*."

In a follow-on letter about this matter the *Maharam* writes again, "I have complained about this matter for a long time but my words go unheeded. I maintain that it is a very incorrect practice. Although the *mohel* is busy with the *bris* and is not interested in gazing at the woman, the spectators might not be aware of this. Even if the *mohel* is her husband, not everyone knows that this is the case. Also, was there an *ezras nashim* in the *Beis Hamikdash* for no purpose? Was it not because women are not to mingle with men? I feel that in this case the whole *mitzva* of the *bris milah* is a *mitzva haba b'aveirah* - a *mitzva* that has evolved from an *aveirah*.

"Therefore, whoever is G-d fearing should leave the *shul* not to be there at the time, lest he will be like an accomplice in the *aveirah*...... Moreover, *Chazal* say a person should avoid walking behind a woman and that if he happens to find himself in that situation he should bring it to an end as quickly as possible. They also say that Manoach was an *am ha'aretz* because he walked behind his wife. If mild contact such as walking behind a woman in the street is wrong, all the more so is contact with her as she sits in a *shul* and with a job that is done on her lap - Peace to you - *Meir son of Rabbi Baruch*." This ruling was subsequently quoted in the *Rema*, Y.D. 265:11.

(d) The message - we must take guidance from *Gedolei Yisroel*: This strange episode that can hardly be imagined nowadays, should be a lesson to all of us, just how far people can slip and lose their feel and understanding for *tznius*. Even a *mitzva* as dear and as holy as *bris milah* can turn into a public platform for something distinctly not *tznius'dik*. At the same time people are so convinced that there is nothing wrong in what they are doing that even after the *Gadol Hador* has given out a statement condemning it, people remain unconvinced and continue in their crooked ways.

We see from this that only after developing deep feelings for true *tznius* and personal refinement are we able to see things correctly. Also, we are to learn from this that it is essential that we hearken to the reproach of *Gedolei Yisroel* and allow them to lead us. Even if we are at present unable to understand their reasoning or the justification for their directives, once we do right we will see only too clearly the rationalization for what they say.

(e) The reason why a husband and wife are joint *k'vaters*: To conclude, it is interesting to note that as a result of *Rabbeinu Meir's* guidance, not only were women no longer *sandek*, but the whole manner by which a baby is brought to his *bris* was arranged in the way we know it today. *Rabbeinu Meir* had maintained that it is against the principles of *tznius* for a woman to enter a place that is full of men. It is understood that it is likewise wrong for a man to enter a place occupied by many women.

Accordingly, it would be wrong for the job of transporting the baby from the mother to the place of the *bris* (*k'vatershaft*) to be done completely by a man, because in order to fetch the baby he would have to enter into the place of the mother where she and other women are usually congregated. On the other hand, it would be wrong for a woman to do the complete job of the *k'vater* alone because this would mean that she enters the place where the *bris* is to take place which is fully occupied by men.

It was therefore instituted that a couple (husband and wife) do the job of *k'vater'shaft* between themselves, with the wife fetching the baby from the mother and the husband bringing it into the place of the *bris*. *Rabbeinu Yaacov Mulin zt'l* in *sefer, Maharil, Hilchos Milah* No. 22, quoted in *Darkei Moshe* Y.D. 265:11 and the *Mateh Moshe, Hilchos Milah* 5:5.

It is gratifying to see what *kedusha* and *tahara* lie behind seemingly insignificant *minhagim* that have been done for generations by all *shomrei mitzvos*. Concerning such *minhagim* we are taught, מנהג אבותינו תורה היא - "A *minhag* handed down from our fathers is an integral part of the Torah" (*Menachos* 20b, *Tosfos* s.v. *Nifsal*).

G. SEGREGATION GENERATES KEDUSHA AND HAPPINESS

1. SEGREGATION GENERATES KEDUSHA: An aura of *kedusha* permeates people who keep the requirements of *tznius* and particularly segregation. They learn to cherish not only the *tznius* itself but also the *kedusha* that radiates from it. Moreover, they delight when others live by a similar standard of *tznius* and refinement, as this spreads an atmosphere of *kedusha* in the entire community, affecting young and old alike.

A remarkable facet of segregation is the fact that although it does not involve a positive deed it nevertheless leads to *kedusha*. As a general rule, doing *mitzvos* creates *kedusha* and transgressing *aveiros* creates *tumah*. Not doing a *mitzva*, although very wrong, does not create *tumah*. Similarly, abstaining from an *aveirah*, although good conduct, does not create *kedusha*. In both these cases the person is left in a "plateau state" that involves neither of the two extremes. Concerning *arayos*, however, abstention has such a positive effect on the person that it actually brings *kedusha* over him. See *Maharal MiPrague*, *Gur Aryeh*, *Breishis* 46:10 and *Shemos* 22:30, note 241 [See also approbation by Maran Hagaon Harav Isser Zalman Meltzer *zt'l* on the *sefer, "Ikrei Dinim"* where he writes that *shemiras halashon* - abstention from all types of *lashon horah* - has the same exceptional power].

At the start of the section on *arayos*, the Torah writes, קדושים תהיו - "Sanctify yourselves" (*Vayikra* 19:2). On this *Rashi* comments in the name of *Chazal*, כל מקום שאתה מוצא גדר ערוה אתה מוצא קדושה - "Wherever you find abstention from *arayos* you will find *kedusha*". The *Gur Aryeh*, *Shemos* 22:30 mentioned above and the *Chofetz Chayim* in his *sefer*, *Nidchei Yisroel* (Chap. 23) points out that we are being told that by refraining from *arayos*, *kedusha* is generated although it is an abstention.

With this it can be well understood why usually no *bracha* is made on an abstention, as the term אשר קדשנו במצותיו - "He sanctified us with His *mitzvos*" is out of place, since abstaining does not create positive *kedusha*. Nevertheless, under the *chupah* we thank *Hashem* with the words אשר קדשנו במצותיו וצונו על העריות - "Who has sanctified us with His *mitzvos* and He forbade us to have illicit relationships". Since this form of abstention generates positive *kedusha*, it has the same properties as a *mitzva* and it is fitting to say a *bracha* on it.

2. SEGREGATION GENERATES CONTENTMENT AND HAPPINESS: Segregation not only disarms the *yetzer horah* but also has a most positive effect. It strengthens the complete *Yiddishkeit* of those who practice it and enables them to bask in a deep inner contentment and happiness known only to the servants of *Hashem*. Dovid Hamelech says in *Tehillim* (119:162) שש אנכי על אמרתיך כמוצא שלל רב - "I rejoice over Your word like one who finds abundant spoil". *Chazal* (*Shabbos* 130a) state that this verse refers to the *mitzva* of *bris milah* which has the effect of lessening the sensual drive in man to pursue activities related to immorality.

This *mitzva* and similar ones such as *tznius* and segregation appear to hamper and impede man from doing what he wants, thereby barring excitement from his life and making it dull. To this the verse replies: Although one would imagine the *mitzva* has such a negative effect, in fact, this is not the case at all. On the contrary, once man practices these precepts he instinctively feels how upright and correct they are, and how they improve his life in every way possible. Rather than being restrictive and oppressive as they appear to be, they enable the person and those who live with him to enjoy a life enriched by deep values and considerable fulfillment and *simcha*.

In the verse mentioned, Dovid Hamelech compares these *mitzvos* to שלל - spoil taken from an enemy during a successful military campaign. As has already been explained in 1:R:3 above, when a victorious army takes spoil they are doubly delighted. By losing the spoil the defeated enemy has been considerably weakened, whilst the victors, by obtaining the spoil, have been greatly strengthened for the future. The comparison to *mitzvos* that maintain *kedushas Yisroel* is clear. The natural result of *tznius* and virtuous conduct is twofold. On the one hand, the intensity of the drive of the *yetzer horah* is lessened. Whilst on the other hand, the quality of their lives is greatly enhanced, as living a holy life brings in its wake peace of mind and deep contentment. Those who live by the regulations of the Torah joyfully proclaim, פקודי ה' ישרים משמחי לב - "The precepts of *Hashem* are upright and proper, they gladden the heart" (*Tehillim* 19:9).

H. GUARDING KEDUSHAS YISROEL AT WEDDINGS

1. A KALLAH SHOULD USE COSMETICS WITH MODERATION:

(a) Appearing on this holy day in a fitting manner: On the day of her *chupah*, a *kallah* is a queen and very much in the limelight. On this day, she, together with her *chasan*, will establish a home in *Klal Yisroel*, and as such, there can be no greater or holier day in her life. She should look beautiful on this special day so that her *chasan* is delighted and even ecstatic with his new bride. Her appearance and demeanor should reflect her purity, her kind disposition and her sterling qualities. To this end, it is appropriate for her to use such cosmetics as are needed to enhance her appearance. This is very much in place as *Chazal* say, כלה מקשטין ומבשמין אותה - "A *kallah* should be adorned with jewelry and be made delightful by the application of a pleasant fragrance" (*Shemos Rabba* 23:5).

(b) The unjustified and harmful excesses practiced by some *kallos*: It is, however, a sad symptom of our times that some *kallos* (even in very Orthodox circles) deem it fitting to go under the *chupah* heavily made-up and over-painted. They cover their faces with excessive cosmetics and employ so much paint on their cheeks, eyes, eyelashes and eyebrows that their natural *chein* is completely hidden under a veil of artificial color. As a result of this, these *kallos* step under the *chupah* looking like models or film stars rather than the embodiment of purity and virtue, which is how a *kallah* should appear on the holiest day of her life.

When a *kallah* appears in such a way, it cheapens her image in the eyes of those who look for true values. She will also be responsible for advocating the over-use of cosmetics. Her close friends are likely to learn from her to do the same when their wedding day arrives, and possibly even when they are to meet someone on a prospective *shidduch*. With these excesses, this *kallah* is regrettably starting her new life that will hopefully be conducted *b'kedusha* with a considerable step in the wrong direction - see *Mekoros* 67:6-8.

(c) *Hashem* gives a *kallah* exceptional natural *chein*. It is mystifying why the natural *chein* given to the *Bas Yisroel* and particularly to a *kallah* at the time of her wedding is held in contempt to the point that it is disguised under a veneer of paint. The following *Gemara* (*Kesubos* 17a) illustrates just how far we have slipped from the correct *derech*: "*Rav Dimi* (an *Amora* from *Eretz Yisroel* who was at that time in *Bavel*) reported that the following verse was sung in *Eretz Yisroel* in the presence of *kallos*: לא כחל ולא שרק ולא פרכוס ויעלת חן - 'She has such special *chein* that she has no need for cosmetics, nor does she require a substance that reddens the face, nor has she a need for a special hair-do'". Even though many of our *kallos* do require a degree of make-up, it is wrong to over-stress cosmetics and underrate the true natural *chein* and refinement of the *Bas Yisroel*.

(d) Obligations of *tznius* apply to the *kallah* on her wedding day: A *kallah* should not mistakenly assume that *tznius* does not apply on her wedding day. Although a *kallah* is on public display at her wedding (to publicize that she is becoming an *Eishes Ish* - a married woman) she practices exceptional *tznius* at the very same time. She comes under the *chupah* veiled as a sign of *tznius*, which is beyond the *tznius'dik* dress of any other woman - see *Rashi*, *Trumah* 26:9, and E.H. *Rema* 31:2.

The significance of the *tznius* of a *kallah* on her wedding day goes so far that on the verse, ויתן אל משה ככלותו לדבר אתו - "And *Hashem* gave the *Luchos* to Moshe when He finished speaking to him" (*Shemos* 31:18) *Chazal* say that the giving of the Torah is compared to a wedding - hence the word ככלותו, the root of which is the word כלה - a bride. *Chazal* say that one of the points of this comparison is that כשם שכלה מצנעת עצמה תחת חופתה כך היו ישראל במדבר צנועים באהליהם - "Just as a *kallah* is modest when under the *chupah* although she is in the limelight, so those who received the Torah were modest in the wilderness although they were on public display due to their wondrous existence" (*Yalkut*, *Shir HaShirim* No. 988). The fact that our holy Torah is compared to a *kallah* reflects on the considerable *kedusha* involved in a *chasuna* which is blessed with the right measure of *tznius*.

(e) At her wedding a *kallah* projects all her past *chinuch*: Concerning the *Chazal* just mentioned, it is an interesting observation that the word כלה (*kallah*) - bride is basically the same word as כלה (*kolloh*) - to conclude and complete. Wherein lies the connection? On her wedding day, a *kallah* has completed the first stage of her life. What she is at her wedding is the culmination of the *chinuch* she has had and her personal efforts to acquire good *midos*, *Yiras Shomayim*, *tznius*, *ahavas haTorah* and *ahavas chesed*. Hence a *kallah* is the completed product of many years of preparation, and her future life will reflect the value and worth of this groundwork.

Just as Shabbos is described as a *kallah* (בואי כלה בואי כלה) and the quality of a Shabbos certainly results from the effort that is put into preparing for it, so too, the quality of a bride is the result of all that has gone into preparing her for her future role as a wife and mother in *Klal Yisroel*. It is these great riches that should emanate and radiate from the countenance of the *kallah* on her *chasuna* day - the day when the second and far more prominent stage of her life commences.

2. PRECAUTIONS TO BE TAKEN TO PREVENT INTERMINGLING:

(a) At the *chupah*: Although no *mechitza* (a proper division - see fig. (d) below) is required at the *chupah* itself, it is nevertheless essential that steps are taken to ensure that the males and females that attend the *chupah* are kept apart from one another. In many places this is achieved by two chains that are suspended from posts lining the passage along which the *chasan* and *kallah* are led to the *chupah*. The men and women are separated by this fenced-in passage and prevented from intermingling. This praiseworthy arrangement has a source in *Chazal*. The *Gemara* relates in *Kiddushin* (81a) אביי דייר גילפי רבא דייר קנה - "The great *amora, Abbaya* arranged that there would be barrels to separate men from women at a *chupah*. Similarly, the great *amora, Rava* arranged that there would be a fence of canes to separate the two genders from one another. See *Responsa Mishna Halachos* 3:147 and 6:219.

(b) In the forecourt of the hall: Precautions should be taken by the *ba'al simcha* to prevent intermingling of men and women and teenage boys and girls outside the *chasuna* hall and in the forecourt leading into the hall. Hagaon Harav Moshe Shmuel Shapiro *shlita* relates that Maran Hagaon Harav Yitzchak Zev Soloveitchik *zt'l* (known as the Brisker Rav) was extremely particular at the *chasuna* of his son in Tel Aviv that there should be total segregation, to the point of having the men and women enter the building by two separate entrances so that there was no common forecourt where socializing and intermingling could take place. Even if this cannot always be done, an effort to prevent intermingling should be made. We show our appreciation for the *simcha Hashem* has given us by doing our best to foster and promote *tznius* and *kedusha* at our *simchos* - see *Mekoros* 78:2.

(c) At the reception: At many *chasunas*, considerable intermingling between men and women occurs when the smorgasbord is served. It has become fully accepted in Orthodox circles to have a *mechitza* - a division between men and women - at the main *chasuna* meal, see (c) below. Nevertheless, when it comes to the smorgasbord, some set up just one major source for each type of delicacy, and both men and women crowd around the table to take their helping. This causes close intermingling of everyone, including males and females of all ages. Strangely, no real protest is heard to stop this unhealthy state of affairs. The correct approach would be to set up two independent displays or at least to ensure that the men and women approach the table with the displays from two distinct sides, thereby ensuring that they will not come too close to one another.

(d) At the *seuda*: The *Poskim* write that there must be a *mechitza* at a *chasuna seuda* to prevent all forms of *pritzus*. See *Beis Shmuel,* E.H. 62:11 and *Shach,* Y.D. 91:7. Its importance can hardly be over-stressed, particularly nowadays considering the unfortunate ways of dress that have made inroads into almost all circles. Not only does a *mechitza* prevent intermingling and looking, but its very presence serves as a constant announcement that the *ba'alei simcha* wish the *chasuna* to be perfect on both a physical and spiritual level. Those who are invited are the guests of the *ba'alei simcha*, and must naturally conform with the wishes of their host (as *Chazal* say, כל מה שיאמר לך בעל הבית עשה - "A person must comply with the instructions of his host" - *Pesachim* 86b) - see *Mekoros* 78:1-2.

3. MALE WAITERS SHOULD ATTEND THE MEN'S SECTOR: It is already an established practice in many circles to have male waiters serve the men and waitresses serve the ladies. It was never an ideal situation that ladies served the men and walked constantly to and fro between them. Nowadays, however, when most *nochrios* wear trousers or short tight skirts, their presence in the men's section of a *chasuna* is an eyesore, if not a profanation of the whole affair. Therefore, now more than ever, it is correct to insist on having male waiters to attend the men. The additional cost in hiring male waiters is a small price to pay in comparison to the financial efforts the *ba'alei simcha* make to ensure that everything is perfect at the *chasuna*.

It is similarly important to ensure that female waitresses attend the womens' sector, as it is against *tznius* for men to serve the ladies when this can be avoided. Since there will be both male and female non-Jewish waiters at the *simcha,* an eye must be kept on them to ensure that no improper conduct results from this.

When hiring waitresses to serve the ladies, they should be requested to dress in a respectable and traditional manner. Although this might not always be possible to achieve, it is nevertheless worth the effort. When it comes to *tznius,* no exertion should be considered as too troublesome, nor should any improvement be considered as too trivial and insignificant.

4. VIGILANCE TO PREVENT INROADS OF PRITZUS: It is of the utmost importance to ensure *tznius* in dress and refinement of conduct by all participants at a *chasuna.* Some women and girls think it fit to turn up at *chasunas* excessively painted and decorated. They will wear expensive, eye-catching outfits, patterned tights and so on. Regrettably, some girls will at times encroach on the men's section of the hall, or dance in a place which is well within sight of the men. This presents a serious *nisayon* to many men, particularly as not gazing at girls is thought of by many as being a *chumrah* (a general stringency practiced by the very devout) and it is woefully little known that to feast one's eyes on women involves an *issur min haTorah* - that of *v'lo sosuru acharei.....eineichem* - "Do not stray after your........eyes" (*Bamidbar* 15:39) - M.B. 75:7. See *Mekoros* 69:1-5 and 70:15-17.

Mechutanim and *Rabbanim* should watch out for early signs of these types of misconduct and every effort must be made to encourage women and girls to project a fine rather than provocative image at *chasunas.* If this matter is disregarded, *chasunas* turn into beauty shows, replete with unhealthy intermingling. They become a platform for the *issur* of *v'lo sosuru acharei........eineichem* rather than for the great *simcha shel mitzva* they ought to be.

5. ENSURING THAT MEN DO NOT SEE WOMEN AND GIRLS DANCE:

(a) Men may not see females dance: Every care must be taken that the area where women and girls dance is out of the sight of the men. The *issur* of a man watching such dancing can be learned from the following *halacha.* *Chazal* say that a man should not walk behind a woman. This is so that he is not drawn into watching her as she walks (*Brachos* 61a; and E.H. 21:1). The *T'shuvas HaRadvaz* (2:770) writes that even if a woman is covered from head to toe and none of her limbs are visible, the *issur* nevertheless applies, because it is not just the sight of her limbs that can arouse the attention of a man, but also her graceful movements. Since the graceful movements of the woman or girl can arouse the attention of a man who notices them, *Chazal* did not differentiate between those whose movements are graceful and those whose movements are just plain and ordinary.

Since a man may not observe the movements of a female as she walks, it is self understood that it is *ossur* for him to watch women and girls dance, since this would be regarded as looking at a peak performance of graceful steps and movements. The pleasure a man could experience from watching such a sight is part of the *issur* of *histaklus* and is termed by the *Mesilas Yesharim* (Chap. 11) as *znus ha'einayim*, as explained elsewhere. We must never forget that *Hashem* is described as a שונא זימא - "He detests immorality" (*Sanhedrin* 93a). See *Ben Ish Chai*, Section one, *parshas Shoftim* No. 18 where he mentions the *issur* for women to dance in a place where men are observing them.

(b) What is *ossur* to watch live, is *ossur* to watch on video: People strangely draw distinctions between things that are in fact one and the same. Those who video their wedding proceedings, replay the videos to all members of the family, whether male or female. All too frequently, the dancing of the women and girls has been filmed and the men sit through the complete film, watching the dancing of the men and women alike, which they would certainly not have done at the *chasuna* itself. In truth, there is no difference between seeing such a sight live or seeing it on film, especially when it is accompanied by full motion and sound. This, amongst other reasons, has motivated many *Gedolei Yisroel* of our generation to ban videos at *chasunas* and for other personal uses.

(c) A man should not walk behind a woman - including his wife: *Chazal* (*Brachos* 61a) say that it is wrong for a man to walk behind his own wife and expose himself to an unnecessary source of enticement (see *Maharsha)*. They furthermore say that מנוח עם הארץ היה דכתיב וילך מנוח אחרי אשתו - "*Manoach* was an *am ha'aretz* since it is written that he walked behind his wife" (*ibid.*). He was an ignoramus as he did not know such an elementary *halacha*. Moreover, it is characteristic of a true *Talmid Chacham* to be careful and not to look at women (*Bava Basra* 168a). Therefore, had he been a *Talmid Chacham* he would have known of his own accord not to walk behind her, because when a man walks behind a woman (even his own wife) he cultivates within himself an urge to gaze at women.

When Eliezer, the servant of Avraham, traveled with Rivka to bring her to Yitzchak, the verse describes the way they traveled, ותקם רבקה ונערותיה

ותרכבנה על הגמלים ותלכנה אחרי האיש - "And Rivka and her maidens arose, rode on the camels and they went after the man" (*Breishis* 24:61). Although Eliezer was to keep a watchful eye on the females traveling with him, he did not ride behind them. Instead, he rode ahead of them and kept in close proximity to them (see *Ramban*). The *Midrash* in *Breishis Rabba* (60:14) writes that Rivka and her maidens traveled behind Eliezer rather than ahead of him because '*tznius* in conduct' requires that females are not observed by males nor in a position to be easily observed. Every step taken by the servants of the *Avos* reflected on the morals and conduct that prevailed in the home of their master, as *Chazal* say, יפה שיחתן של עבדי אבות מתורתן של בנים - "There is more to learn even from the talk of the 'servants of the *Avos*' than from the Torah of future generations" (*Rashi*, *Breishis* 24:42).

Many of our brethren copy the ways of non-Jews in this (and many *tznius*-related matters). When entering a door, they encourage their wives to go first and they follow on behind her. This is incorrect conduct as explained. The *Gemara* (*Taanis* 23b) actually writes clearly that a man should enter a door first, so that he does not walk behind his wife. Sadly, keeping up with the prevailing culture of our neighbors is so engrained in our psyche that we will do things for which one is labeled an *am ha'aretz* by *Chazal*.

6. PRITZUS AT CHASUNA CAN CAUSE UNHAPPY MARRIAGES: To our deep regret, we hear nowadays of many marriages that end up in divorce even within the Orthodox community. In some cases, the marriage survives but one of the partners is desperately unhappy. Blame for this heartbreaking phenomenon is placed on bad character traits in the boy or girl that were not eliminated in their early youth, or on interfering parents or in-laws and other such causes. No one imagines for a moment that the source of the problem might lie in the way *Hashem Yisborach* was angered at the wedding celebrations of this young couple.

This incredible attribution of blame is however the thought of one of the greatest men *Klal Yisroel* produced for many centuries. He was a person who had his hand on the pulse of the Jewish people until very recent times. The following is a free translation of a statement by the *Chofetz Chayim* in *Ahavas Chesed* (page 51 in the original print) section three, chapter six, at the beginning of the second sub-note:-

"I am amazed that *mechutanim* allow *pritzus* at the wedding of their children. It is known that the success of any endeavor depends on whether *Hashem Yisborach* associates Himself with the person in his

effort. If He does, it will succeed. Whereas, if *Hakadosh Baruch Hu* distances Himself from the project, it is bound to fail and all the effort is in vain. Due to this elementary truth, if a *chasuna* is conducted with *pritzus,* the *Shechina* is certainly not present. This in turn causes the union to fail, with arguments and quarrels plaguing the life of the young couple. Also, if they have children, they will not be a source of pleasure to their parents. How do *mechutanim* allow such tragedies to happen to their beloved children?"

These are the words of the great friend and defender of *Klal Yisroel* who was far from an Angel of Doom. In his great insight into the ways of *Hashem Yisborach,* he was aware that the *chasuna* celebrations are of monumental importance for the young couple's future. They can bring wonderful *brachos* in their wake. In contrast, they can sometimes be the cause for future miseries, *chas veshalom*. It is remarkable that the *Chofetz Chayim* felt so strongly about this matter that he made this statement once again with even greater elaboration, at the very end of the *sefer, Geder Olam*. Let us bring the *Shechina* into our midst on this holy day, thereby granting our children and grandchildren many years of true happiness and tranquillity.

7. KISSING CLOSE RELATIVES ETC.: Kissing naturally takes place at a *chasuna*, either under the *chupah* or in more secluded places. Since many relatives come together, there is a danger that a man might kiss a female relative thinking that this is permitted, whilst in fact it is a serious *issur min haTorah* of *kreiva l'arayos*. Although people are generally aware that kissing and hugging is permitted only when there is no natural attraction between the two people, it is not universally known when this applies. It is therefore appropriate to present the most basic rules:-

(a) Mother, grandmother, daughter and granddaughter: A man may kiss his mother, grandmother, great-grandmother, daughter, granddaughter and great-granddaughter. Similarly, a woman may kiss her father, grandfather, great-grandfather, son, grandson and great-grandson. In all cases it is irrelevant whether the woman or girl is single or married.

Although in all these cases the female is *ervah min haTorah* to the man, kissing is nevertheless permitted because there is no illicit attraction when one person is a descendant of the other - *Even HoEzer* 21:7, *P'risha* 21:7 and *Beis Shmuel* 14-15. (See *Pischei Teshuva* E.H. 22:2 that granddaughter and great-granddaughter are the same). The kiss is therefore viewed as an expression of family attachment, not of attraction and affection and is therefore permitted - see *Chelkas Mechokek* E.H. 21:9. (See *Responsa Be'er Moshe* 4:145 and *Responsa Betzeil Hachochma* Vol. 3. E.H. 12).

(b) Sister: It is incorrect for a man to kiss his adult sister or to be kissed by her. Although, there is considerably less attraction between siblings than between other males and females, and the *issur* of *kreivo l'arayos* does not apply when they kiss, it is nevertheless wrong for them to do so as this can lead to mistakes - *ibid.* A brother may, however, kiss his young sister as long as she is under *bas-mitzva* - see E.H. 21 *Chelkas Mechokek* 9 and *Beis Shmuel* 14.

(c) Blood-related relatives - uncle, aunt and cousin: A blood-related aunt (sister of father or mother), is an *ervah* to her nephew. Some *Rishonim* maintain that the nephew-aunt relationship is similar to that of a brother and sister. In both cases illicit attraction is absent and the *issur* of *kreivo l'arayos* does not apply. It is nevertheless wrong to kiss such an aunt or be kissed by her, just as it is wrong to kiss an adult sister or be kissed by her, as explained in (b) above - see *Rambam, Issurei Biah* 21:6 and *Responsa Iggros Moshe* Y.D. 2:137 and E.H. 4:64. According to these opinions, if an aunt is just a junior her nephew could kiss her, as is the case with a sister. However, since others maintain that a nephew is illicitly attracted towards such an aunt, it is wrong to kiss her even when she is just a junior - see *Responsa Chikrei Lev* 17 and *Imrei Yosher* 2:43.

A blood-related uncle (brother of father or mother) and his niece are not *ervah* to one another and an uncle may marry his niece. Similarly, cousins are not *ervah* to one another, as first-cousins may marry. Such relatives are therefore different to a sister or a blood-related aunt and feelings of attraction would exist between them as between any other man and woman. It is therefore *ossur min haTorah* for an uncle to kiss his niece (or the niece to kiss her uncle) once she is an adult and reached puberty which renders her *ervah.* Also, it is *ossur mid'rabanan* to kiss her even if she is a junior, just as it is *ossur* to kiss a non-related girl from the age of three and above - see (e) below. See also Responsa *Iggros Moshe* Y.D. 2:137.

(d) Relatives that are not blood-relations: It is *ossur min haTorah* for a man to kiss close female relatives that are not blood relations of his. Being closely related they are *ervah* to him and not being blood related there must inevitably be the natural attraction of members of the other gender. It is therefore an *issur* of *kreiva l'arayos* to kiss an aunt by marriage. The same applies to a girl or woman kissing her uncle by marriage or being kissed by him as there is full attraction between such relatives. The kissing is therefore an *issur min haTorah* of *"lo sikrevu legalos ervah"* (*Vayikra* 18:6).

Similarly, a man may not kiss his mother-in-law, sister-in-law (wife of his brother or sister of his wife) or daughter-in-law. These women are *ervah min haTorah* to him and are naturally attractive to him. Kissing them is therefore true *kirvo l'arayos*. Even if his sister-in-law is a junior, she is *ervah* to him and he must not kiss her just as he may not hear her sing - 8:E:3 above.

A man's step-mother, step-sister, and step-daughter are *ervah* to him (see *Rambam, Issurei Biah* 1:5). Since they are not blood-relatives to him the natural attraction to members of the other gender will exist between them. Similarly, a woman's step-father, step-brother and step-son are close relatives to her (*ibid*) but are not her blood relatives. Due to this, all *issurim* of *kirva l'arayos* apply once the female has reached the tender age of three.

(e) A girl under *bas-mitzva* who is not his relative: A man may not kiss a young girl (from the age of three) even if she is not closely related to him and is therefore not an *ervah* to him. Although there can be no question of *kreivo l'arayos* concerning such a girl as she is not an *ervah* to him, kissing her is nevertheless *ossur*.

Just as he may not purposefully listen to a young girl sing as this can arouse within him sinful and even immoral thoughts (M.B.75:17 and 8:E:2 above), nor should he smell perfume that is on her (*Shar Hatzion* 217:25) so too, kissing and fondling a girl from the age of three and above has the potential of causing the same mishaps and is forbidden. In fact all that has the potential of *kirvas hada'as* - "creates feelings of affection" is forbidden already from the age of three, just as *yichud* is forbidden with a girl of such a tender age - see E.H. 22:11. (See *Responsa Avnei Yoshpa* 2:89:4-7 that this is also the opinion of Hagaon HaRav Shlomo Zalman Auerbach *zt'l*).

(f) Summary:

- A male may kiss:- his mother, grandmother, great-grandmother, daughter, granddaughter and great-granddaughter. He may also kiss his sister as long as she is under *bas-mitzva*. In all cases it is immaterial whether the female is single or married.
- A female may kiss her:- father, grandfather, great-grandfather, son, grandson and great-grandson whether she is a junior or an adult. She may also kiss her brother but only as long as she is under *bas-mitzva*. In all cases it is immaterial whether she is single or married.

- A male may not kiss his:- aunt, niece, female cousin, mother-in-law, sister-in law, daughter-in-law, step-mother, step-sister, step-daughter, and all women and girls who are not related to him. All are forbidden from the age of three and above. He may also not kiss his sister once she is *bas-mitzva*.

- A female may not kiss her - uncle, nephew, male cousin, father-in-law, brother-in-law, son-in-law, step-father, step-brother, step-son, and all men and boys who are not related to her. All are forbidden once she is three years old. She may also not kiss her brother once she is over *bas- mitzva*.

I. TZNIUS FOSTERS HASHGACHA PRATIS - PRITZUS HINDERS IT

1. HASHEM WITHDRAWS FROM PLACES OF PRITZUS: To our great distress, there are nowadays excessive numbers of road accidents, particularly in *Eretz Yisroel*, many with most catastrophic consequences. Blame is put on reckless driving and similar causes. This is certainly a major contributor since when people drive recklessly a dangerous situation exists and, השטן מקטרג בשעת הסכנה - "the *Satan* prosecutes powerfully when the situation is dangerous" (Rashi, *Breishis* 42:4). However, there is more to this horrendous phenomenon than reckless driving. When serious danger exists and in addition *Hashem* removes His guarding hand from us, the danger becomes very extreme and acute indeed.

In a public letter written by the *Chofetz Chayim* in the year 5684 (1924), at a time when endless *tzaros* befell the Jewish people, he quoted the *p'sukim,* כי ה' אלוקיך מתהלך בקרב מחניך להצילך וכו' ולא יראה בך ערות דבר ושב מאחריך - "For *Hashem* your G-d circulates within your camp to save you etc. *Ervah*-related conduct must not be seen amongst you [for if it is] I will withdraw Myself [and you will remain unprotected]" (*Devarim* 23:14-15).

The *Chofetz Chayim* points out that the verse states that when there is *tznius Hashem* is between us and extends us His special protection; whereas, when there is *pritzus* and *ervah*-related behavior in our midst *Hashem* turns away from us (ושב מאחריך) and we remain totally unprotected. The *Chofetz Chayim* then went on to stress that the great sins of dresses with short sleeves, cut-out collars and uncovered hair are the reasons for the lack of protection and Divine intervention on our behalf. (See original letter printed in the *Chofetz Chayim Al HaTorah*, page 322). In the *Chofetz Chayim al HaTorah* (*parshas Ki Seitzei*) he adds that for no other type of sin is there a reaction of, ושב מאחריך - "I will turn away and abandon you" *rachmana litzlan* - see *Mekoros* 26:1-3. See also *Sotah* (3b) Rashi s.v. *Nistaklah meihem* who writes, נסתלקה מהם, מלבא לביתם דאינו יכול לראות בעבירות שבביתו - "*Hashem* will distance Himself from their houses, because He cannot bear to see the sins that are [done] in the house".

Accordingly, in our day and age, when regretfully there is a considerable lack of *tznius* even by those who know better and are generally Orthodox *Yidden*, it should not surprise us that careless driving suddenly takes such a frightful toll of Jewish lives. If people drive recklessly and we are not under the protection of *Hashem*, our very existence becomes extremely precarious.

2. PUNISHMENT IS METED OUT IN PLACES OF PRITZUS: Harav Hagaon R' Dov Yaffe *shlita*, *Mashgiach* of *Yeshivas Knesses Yechezkel*, heard a further incredible insight into this tragic state of affairs from the holy *Gaon* and *Tzaddik*, Harav Yaacov Yisroel Kanievsky *zt'l*, the *Steipler Gaon zt'l*. The latter based his reasoning on the words of the *Ramban*, *Breishis* 12:10 where he writes about the journey of Avraham Avinu to *Mitzrayim* because of the famine that raged in *Eretz Yisroel*. During that visit Avraham professed that Sarah was his sister, since had they known that she was his wife they would have killed him. Due to this pretense, Sarah was taken to the palace of Pharaoh, and was saved only due to *Hashem*'s direct intervention.

On this the *Ramban* writes as follows: "Know, Avraham Avinu erred and sinned greatly by pretending that Sarah was his sister, thereby exposing her to sin. Although his life was in danger he should have trusted in *Hashem* Who could save him and his wife. Also, he should not have gone down to *Mitzrayim* in the first place. Due to this sin, the Jewish people had to spend their *golus* years in the land of *Mitzrayim* under Pharaoh. This is in line with the principle, 'Punishment is meted out where sin occurred' (*Koheles* 3:16)".

Basing himself on the *Ramban* who establishes the principle that "Punishment is meted out in the place where sin occurred", the *Steipler Gaon zt'l* said that the reason for the terrible *midas hadin* on the roads is that nowadays the roads are the prime places where much of the *pritzus* occurs. The *pritzus* involves women who do not dress correctly or cover their hair properly and men who look where they have no right to look. The *midas hadin* has therefore chosen the roads and streets as the appropriate place to punish, since במקום המשפט שמה הרשע והחטא - "Punishment is meted out in the place profaned by sin". (Harav Hagaon R' Mattisyahu Salomon *shlita*,

Mashgiach of *Yeshivas Gateshead*, now of *Beth Medrash Gavoah*, Lakewood N.J. who heard it from the above) - see *Mekoros* 26:4.

This approach has a close comparison in the *Gemara Shabbos* 62b. There *Chazal* state that *Hashem* punished the *pritzus'dik* women at the times of Yeshaya HaNavi by inflicting them with severe ailments that destroyed parts of their flesh. *Chazal* prove from *p'sukim* that these ailments occurred just on the areas of their bodies where they had worn eye-catching garments or adorned themselves with ostentatious pieces of jewelry. Here again, במקום המשפט שמה הרשע והחטא - punishment was directed to the place of sin, - *Hashem yerachem* - see *Mekoros* 26:4.

3. IF STREETS WERE PURIFIED, THEY WOULD BE MUCH SAFER: While the reasons mentioned for this heart-rending *tzara* of our times give cause for grave concern for the future, as there is so much *pritzus* around, there is nevertheless a great *chizuk* that can be derived from these interpretations and reasonings. This is that the antidote to this *midas hadin* is in our hands. If we, the *Yahadus Hachareidis* (whose conduct is far more important than that of those who have no connection to *shemiras hamitzvos*), would return once again to the ways of *tznius*, *Hashem* would immediately return to our camp and once again grant us His full protection. There will no longer be reason for *Hashem* to choose the roads as the "punishing staff" for the iniquities of *Klal Yisroel*, since the roads will no longer be the place where sin is performed by *Yahadus Hachareidis*.

Actually, by women dressing in public with true *tznius* and men behaving on the roads as *Hilchos Tznius* requires, we strengthen the defenses of the *midas harachmim*, who advocates in the Heavenly Court on behalf of *Klal Yisroel* that such terrible road tragedies should not happen. This is because behaving with *tznius* on the roads has the exact opposite effect to *pritzus*. Just as *Hashem* punishes in the place where an *aveirah* is committed, so also He will not punish in the place where *mitzvos* and good deeds are done. Therefore, the roads, where *tznius* is practiced and a *kiddush Hashem* is made become places where punishment is not meted out.

That this is a true Torah viewpoint can be seen from the way *Chazal* remark with surprise, דבר שהצדיק מתעסק בו יכשל בו זרעו - "Can it be that a child be punished in the very area where its father does *mitzvos*?" (*Yevamos* 121b, see *Maharsha*). They considered it highly improbable that the daughter of *Nechanyah Chofer Sichin* - the *Tzaddik* who dug wells to supply *Yidden* with drinking water - should drown and perish inside a well. As the *Gemara* says, the girl was in fact miraculously saved from the well into which she had fallen. So too, we can be confident that if *Yahadus Hachareidis* makes a major improvement in the field of *tznius*, and the roads become places where the will of *Hashem* is fulfilled rather than transgressed, then the toll on Jewish life that is taken on the roads will decrease dramatically בעי"ה.

In the holy *sefer, Avodas Penim*, by Harav Hagaon R' Aharon Yosef Luria *zt'l* of Teveria (brother-in-law of the previous *Rebbe* of Slonim *zt'l*), letter No. 67, the following is written in the name of *Sifrei Kabbalah*: A person is called a בשר ודם - flesh and blood (e.g. in *Bircas Hamazon*, ולא לידי מתנת בשר ודם). As long as the flesh is contained and covered, the blood is likewise contained and covered, and life continues as normal. (This is alluded to in the words אם אין בשר אין דם - *Pesachim* 77a). However, if the flesh is unprotected and uncovered, this can cause that the blood is likewise unprotected and uncovered, *rachmana litzlan*. He continues by saying that the excessive *pritzus* of our generation is the cause for the alarming increase in loss of human life, in many different ways.

It follows that *tznius* is a life-giver in every sense of the word. Not only does it give spiritual life comparable to the life-giving properties of Torah learning, but it gives life and health in a literal and factual sense.

4. THE PROTECTIVE POWER OF TZNIUS:

(a) *Tznius* involves shielding and arouses a Heavenly shield: The protective power of *tznius* is remarkably demonstrated by the following statement of *Chazal*. The *Gemara* (*Brachos* 62b) records the words Dovid said to Shaul who was pursuing him and had instead fallen into Dovid's hands. Dovid said to Shaul, "I was entitled to kill you, for you, Shaul, intended to kill me and the Torah says, 'If a man rises to kill you, forestall him by striking him down!' However, your *tznius* has protected your life".

How did Shaul's *tznius* manifest itself? We read in *Shmuel* (1:24:4) that Shaul entered a cave to attend to his physical needs - the very cave where Dovid and his men were hiding from him. The *Gemara* explains that Shaul, in order to be totally removed from human eyes, withdrew to the very depths of the cave. This could have proven fatal to him, for Dovid and his men, too, had sought the innermost part of that cave as refuge from their pursuers. Thus Shaul was at Dovid's mercy. However, although *tznius* had led him into a death trap, the very same *midah* protected him, and Dovid felt unable to lay hands on him. A Heavenly protection afforded by the *midah* of *tznius* prevented Dovid from harming Shaul.

The *Maharal* in *Nesivos Olam* explains that *tznius*, which is an act of concealment and protection, arouses a *midah kneged midah* that the person is himself concealed and protected from that which could bring him harm. We must learn from here that the more we implant *tznius* into our lives, the greater the protection it will offer us from all that could otherwise endanger our existence (*Nesiv HaTznius*, Chapter One, paragraph s.v. *U'bperek)*.

(b) Additional *tznius* effects additional *siyata d'shmaya:* In the summer of the year 5683 (1923) the *Chofetz Chayim* attended a *Knessia Gedolah* of Agudas Yisroel that took place in Vienna. Many *Gedolim* and great *Rabbanim* met to discuss urgent matters that concerned the Jewish world. Some meetings were in camera while others took place in public. Those held in public were attended by a large crowd of *Yidden* from all types of backgrounds. Even women participated to hear the speeches and see the spectacle of such an illustrious gathering. The women were on a balcony that was not fully screened off as would be done in a *shul*, but there was no question whatsoever of any type of intermingling.

One of the *Rabbanim* voiced an opinion that a proper *mechitza* must be erected so that men should not be able to see the women at all. Most other *Rabbanim* disagreed and were of the opinion that since the occasion was neither a gathering for *tefilla* nor an emotional occasion such as a *chasuna* or similar *simcha* it was sufficient the way it was. Due to their disagreement, they decided to seek the opinion of the *Chofetz Chayim* and do as he says.

The *Chofetz Chayim* responded with a typical sagacious piece of advice. He said that it could well be that there is no *halachic* obligation to erect a proper *mechitza* as most *Rabbanim* had maintained. He nevertheless felt that when it comes to questions of *Kedushas Yisroel* one should be stringent and heed even the opinion of an individual. He therefore recommends that a proper *mechitza* be erected as a *Rav* had requested.

He then added that when *Hashem* is close to us, we are safe and all goes well, as the verse says, "Even when I go through a valley of death I do not fear evil for You are with me" (*Tehillim* 23:4). In contrast, if, Heaven forbid, *Hashem* withdraws and distances Himself from us, we are lost and everything goes wrong, as the verse says, "You hid Your face and I became bewildered" (*Tehillim* 30:8). Since the Torah writes that *pritzus* and everything to do with immorality causes *Hashem* to withdraw and detach Himself from *Klal Yisroel* (ולא יראה בך ערות דבר ושב מאחריך - *Devarim* 23:15), it follows that when *tznius* prevails *Hashem* is very close to those who practice it and His presence is acutely felt. Concluded the *Chofetz*

Chayim, "We need much *siyata d'shmaya* in the coming days. Can there be a better investment than to practice the finest and most perfect level of *tznius* possible?" (Harav Hagaon R' Don Segal *shlita* in the name of Hagaon HaRav Avraham Kalmenovitz *zt'l* Rosh Yeshivas Mir N.Y. *Sefer Mi Yirpe Lach* pages 175 and 204 and other sources). The identical is written in *Chidushei Aggados* of the *Maharal MiPrague*, *Bava Basra* 60a where he writes, כי שכינה שורה במקום שאין ערוה, כדכתיב, ולא יראה בך ערוה דבר ושב מאחריך, מזה יש ללמוד כי הצניעות מביא השכינה, והפך זה מסלק השכינה.

(c) When *tznius* prevails *Hashem* displays his protection openly: The tents of Sarah and Rivka were blessed with three types of super-natural occurrences. There was a light that burned from *erev* Shabbos to *erev* Shabbos, a blessing was experienced with the dough that it stretched unnaturally, and a cloud hovered over their tent constantly (*Rashi, Breishis* 24:67). The significance of the blessing of the light is to symbolize the intense devotion to Torah and *mitzvos* that existed in their home, just as the *menorah* in the *Beis Hamikdash* was a symbol of Torah and spirituality (Bava Basra 25b, הרוצה להחכים ידרים וסימנך מנורה בדרום). Also, the blessing of the dough is well understood as dough symbolizes the physical, which was used in their home to do *chesed*, which is predominantly performed by feeding the hungry. Our *Imahos* excelled in using all that was at their disposal, be it spiritual or physical, to the service of *Hashem* - see 10:C:2 below. It is therefore little wonder that signs commemorating their excellence in these matters were visible. It is, however, unclear what was the significance of the cloud. What did it symbolize and represent?

The Gaon HaRav Moshe Yechiel Halevi Epstein *zt'l*, known as the Ozrover Rebbe *zt'l*, writes in his *sefer*, *Be'er Moshe, parshas Chayei Sarah,* that due to the great *tznius* and *tahara* that existed in the homes of our *Avos* and *Imahos* the *Shechina* felt exceedingly comfortable in their home. The *Shechina* therefore kept a continuous presence there and even exhibited this relationship for all to see. The cloud over the tent was in effect a public announcement by the *Shechina saying,* "I am constantly here and feel very much at home". This was an enormous *kavod* - honor, and a tremendous source of protection given to our *Avos* and *Imahos* by the *Shechina*.

The ענן הכבוד - the cloud of honor born out of the prevailing *tahara* and modesty of their home, was the exact opposite to the ושב מאחריך - "I will withdraw myself from your midst" born out of prevailing *arayos* and immodesty that sometimes occurs. The latter causes the *Shechina* maximum discomfort. It therefore disappears from homes where immodesty is rampant, and the total absence of the *Shechina* results in dire consequences, as explained above. On the other hand, when exceptional *tznius* and *tahara* prevail, the *Shechina* feels so much at home in these houses that it even puts up a "public flyer" announcing its presence for all to see. See Sotah (3b) where Chazal say, בתחילה קודם שחטאו ישראל היתה השכינה שורה עם כל אחד ואחד - "Before they committed *arayos*-related sins *Hashem* dwelt with every single person". It goes without saying, that the on-going presence of the *Shechina* brings in its trail bountiful benefits and blessings - see 10:C:2.

If we practice *tznius* to the best of our ability, we too will merit the closeness of *Hashem* and the *Shechina* announcing its joy and comfort to be in our surroundings. Although we are not on the spiritual level of our *Imahos* to merit a cloud hovering over our homes, *Hashem* nevertheless has means with which He can pronounce in no uncertain terms that "I am here and I enjoy being here". The *hashgacha pratis* with which He treats those who are particularly beloved to him will bear ample witness that *Hashem* is very close at hand, extending a very special protection to his dear ones.

5. GIRLS CONGREGATING AT STREET CORNERS: As part of general *tznius* on the streets, it should be noted that substantial groups of girls should not congregate to talk at street corners or in the street outside one of their houses. They will be standing right in the eye of the public and when they congregate together in this way their presence becomes very conspicuous, particularly if there are many girls together. Also, in their excitement they frequently raise their voices and thereby attract attention. This situation is consequently far from ideal from the *tznius* point of view.

This refers particularly to cold countries such as England, where people do not generally congregate in the streets, and if girls do so they would be noticed and would even attract attention. However, in places where the weather is generally hot and humid, one cannot expect girls to keep indoors. Even so, they should be encouraged by parents and teachers alike that when they converse outdoors they take care not to raise their voices unduly. It is also wrong for them to fill the sidewalk or spread themselves out across the sidewalk, to the extent that people much older than themselves are forced to step into the road or squeeze past them (especially as they will not want to walk between two females, see 9:D:3 above). They should be given to understand that this is unrefined conduct which is out of character for girls who strive to be *tznuos*.

J. TZNIUS CALLS FOR CONSTANT VIGILANCE AND CAUTION

1. TZNIUS REQUIRES FORESIGHT AND CONSTANT CARE: It is apparent from all that has been explained, that *tznius* calls for caution not to cause a forbidden exposure or endanger one's entire purity. When the Torah refers to an act of immorality that occurs with a betrothed girl, it writes, ומצאה איש בעיר - "A man found her in town (i.e. on the streets)". On this *Rashi* writes in the name of *Chazal* - "She was on the streets, and because of that this tragedy befell her. A breach in a wall beckons the thief in. Had she stayed at home rather than wander the streets, this tragic event would never have occurred" (*Devarim* 22:23). The girl involved was careless and also foolishly unaware of the powerful *yetzer horah* that exists in the world. She thereby precipitated the calamity that followed.

The following are a number of circumstances in which, without the required vigilance, serious lapses in *tznius* can occur. They underscore the need to be constantly alert, careful and on guard - See 1:F:1 above.

2. TZNIUS AT A SWIMMING POOL AND BEACH:

(a) The privacy: Before women or girls use a hotel's open-air swimming pool or a seaside swimming area (at a time when they are reserved for females) they should inspect the area carefully to ensure that no room, whether of a hotel or any other building, overlooks the pool or the beach. Also, the fencing around the open air pool must be checked to ensure that it secludes the area completely. Finally, they should check with those acquainted with the general situation at the hotel or seaside, that men do not occasionally appear in the area during the time set aside for females.

(b) The lifeguard at a swimming pool: If a female lifeguard can be employed to guard the swimmers at a swimming pool, it is doubtlessly the right thing to do, just as a woman should have a female doctor if this is possible (i.e. she is as qualified as her male counterparts). *Tznius* calls for maximum refinement and (even with a *heter*) it is never ideal practice for a woman to show part of her flesh to a man - see 9:J:9 below. If it is impossible to obtain the services of a woman lifeguard to attend a swimming pool, a *halachic* distinction is drawn between a pool at which a Jewish man is in attendance which she may not use and a pool at which a non-Jew is in attendance which she may use. The reason for this ruling is as follows:

Generally, it is *ossur* for a Jewish man to see uncovered areas of a woman's body as stated in 6:V:9 above. He may, nevertheless, come face to face with such an area if he is טרוד במלאכתו - preoccupied with his work, due to which he is oblivious to what he sees - as in the case of a doctor, see *Shach* Y.D. 195:20, *Pleisi* 195:7 and *Mekoros* 72:2. For this reason, a man may run a dry cleaning business although, when cleaning a garment, he looks closely and carefully at the garment, to check that it is really clean. This is permitted despite the fact that it is generally *ossur* for a man to gaze intently at the colorful dress of a woman he knows (*Avoda Zarah* 20b). Since he is preoccupied with the cleaning of the garment, he will not be affected by what he sees.

Although it would seem that a lifeguard at a swimming pool is in such a position, the truth is that he is not fully occupied by his work, as there are times when he has nothing to do, such as before the swimmers enter the water and after they leave it. Also, there are usually only a limited number of swimmers in a swimming pool and once the lifeguard has checked that all who are in the pool are capable of swimming, he relaxes, and is more or less unoccupied even though he looks casually at those who are in the pool. For these reasons a swimming pool attendant cannot be considered a טרוד במלאכתו and if he is Jewish and looks at the women even when he is not on guard, he may well transgress the *issur* of ולא תתורו אחרי עיניכם - see *Responsa Minchas Yitzchak* 7:73 s.v. *Omnam kol.*

Accordingly, if an irreligious Jewish man is on guard, women may not use the pool since they would cause him to transgress the *issur* mentioned and they would personally transgress the *issur* of לפני עור - the *issur* of enabling a person to do an *aveirah*. Even if there are many other women in the pool, it is still *ossur* for a woman to use the pool because each additional woman that he looks at adds to the *issur* - see *Mekoros* 74:8-9. Due to this *halacha, chareidi* women in *Eretz Yisroel* go to swimming pools that have only female lifeguards on duty during their swimming time.

However, if a non-Jewish man is the lifeguard, Jewish women may use the pool. There is no *issur* for a non-Jewish man to see women in inadequate dress since the *issur* of ולא תתורו is addressed only to Jewish men. Although it is usually *pritzus* for a woman to swim in the presence of men even if they are non-Jewish, swimming in the presence of a lifeguard is different and cannot be viewed as *pritzus*, because to have a lifeguard is a necessity for the general safety of the swimmers. *Responsa Iggros Moshe*, E.H. 4:62:1.

It has, however, been stated that in all cases it is far better to have a woman lifeguard than a man. In fact, the *Iggros Moshe* writes that although *halachically* one may allow women to swim in pools supervised by men, the wife of a *Talmid Chacham*, who is expected to display an extra sensitivity to *tznius*, should preferably not use such a pool. Although this is but a recommendation, it nevertheless reflects the dislike a *Gadol zt'l* felt for male staff being used for a service such as this.

(c) The lifeguard at a beach: Lifeguards at a beach must be men because only men can be relied upon to have the strength to pull people to safety if they have been caught by a strong undercurrent. Also, only men (who are positioned in the sea) can force swimmers to stay near the water edge and not go too far out.

The multitude of people that converge on a seaside might give the situation the characteristics of טרוד במלאכתו, as the guard is likely to be preoccupied with the safety of the swimmers all the time. It is, however, not certain that the guards are considered continuously טרוד במלאכתם as there may be times when all women are out of the sea and they nevertheless continue to look, particularly when the guard is not a *shomer mitzvos*. Moreover, there are often a number of shifts, due to which every guard has off-duty hours in the course of the day. Not being *shomrei mitzvos*, these guards are likely to continue looking at the female swimmers even during their off-duty time. Due to these problems, it has become wide-spread practice in *Eretz Yisroel* for women to wear a housecoat (both in the water and out of the water) when they go swimming in the sea, thereby ensuring that they do not cause a Jewish man to do an *issur*.

(d) Wearing a modest bathing suit: As stated previously, a woman and girl should dress in a *tznius'dik* manner whenever possible, even in the privacy of her home, although there are no men present who could see her - see 6:Q above. She should likewise wear a modest bathing suit, which covers as much as can be covered without affecting her swimming ability or causing her discomfort whilst swimming. Slogans and loud contrasting colors are distinctly unrefined and disharmonize the finely-tuned *tznius'dik* sentiments that are part of the personality of the *Bas Yisroel*.

It is incorrect to argue that there cannot be a need for *tznius* at a time when part of the body and virtually the complete arms and legs are anyway uncovered. This is incorrect because *tznius* entails being respectful before *Hashem* Who is always present, and to expose areas that one has no need to expose is considered as not exercising full respect. That this is the *Torah'dik* outlook and sentiment can be seen from the *halachos* of visiting a bathroom (O.C. 3:4). Both male and female are expected not to reveal more of their body than is necessary at the time. Evidently, even though the person is partially uncovered and there is no other person in the room at the time, there is nevertheless a need for *tznius*.

Once a woman or girl has left the pool she should dress right away so as not to stand around in a semi-clad state. Otherwise, she should cover herself as soon as possible with a large bath towel or robe. This is required because it is distinctly not *tznius'dik* to walk around the pool area in the minimal cover of just a swim suit.

To enable those who wish to convince others of these wrong-doings the following has been added. The feeling that this misconduct conveys is that this person is not disturbed at not being dressed with *tznius* and might even quite enjoy the "legitimate absence of restriction". The parable presented by *Chazal* for this type of conduct is, כתינוק היוצא מבית הספר שבורח לו - "It is like a child who rushes out of school, as if he were escaping from a prison" (*Tosfos Shabbos* 116a). The child obviously imagines that school is just one long restriction. Little does he realize that his whole future depends on his studies in school. So too, *tznius*, on which the very being of the *Bas Yisroel* and Jewish mother depends, is far from a restriction and inconvenience.

It must be mentioned, that the prevailing breakdown of modest conduct and personal refinement starts first of all by taking liberties in places where only females are around, such as between girls in a school or seminary, in a swimming pool or when exercising, and from there develops a lack of *tznius* in other areas as well. It is therefore of maximum importance that *tznius* is practiced even in these places.

(e) Married women covering hair during swimming: Many married women cover their hair whilst swimming, whether in a pool or in the sea. They feel obliged to do so because they have no necessity for their hair to be uncovered when swimming. Therefore, although their hair is obviously uncovered when bathing or showering, they cover it when swimming. Many married women don a rubber cap when swimming which encloses all the hair and find their hair is less troublesome when covered than when left open, especially if it is long. See 5:B that according to some opinions it is a *halachic* obligation and according to all opinions it is highly commendable for a woman to cover her hair even if she is in a place where she cannot be seen by men - see 9:J:3(e).

3. TZNIUS DURING PHYSICAL EXERCISES (ATHLETIC ACTIVITIES):

(a) Exercises should be encouraged: All that has been said concerning swimming, applies also when girls do physical exercises. The seclusion of the area from Jewish and non-Jewish males alike and the need for female training personnel are self understood. Although the exercises are done in a place where the females cannot be seen, modesty must still be adhered to, because the need for *tznius* and modest conduct applies even between females themselves and even when a person is in total privacy.

To approach this subject correctly three guidelines must be laid down.

(1) Just as swimming is not discouraged even though the person is only sparsely dressed, so too, exercises should not be discouraged even if the dress must in some ways be less *tznius'dik* than usual. Exercises are of great value to physical health and general well-being, as they tone up the muscles, strengthen the heart, promote good blood circulation, contribute to loss of weight and help the person relax. As such, they are almost as important as swimming. In fact, the medical properties of exercises were well recognized by *Chazal* and the *Poskim* - see *Shabbos* 147a, M.B. 301:7 and 328:129.

(2) The items worn must ensure that the person is basically comfortable when exercising; otherwise they might not do the exercises properly or even abandon them altogether.

(3) The items worn while exercising must be as *tznius'dik* as possible, since one may not lessen one's dress more than is essential. The fact that under the circumstances the full code of *tznius* cannot be fully kept, must not be considered a license to abandon *tznius* altogether - see 9:J:2(d) above.

(b) Not to wear tight-fitting items: It is typical in the wider world to wear tight-fitting exercise clothes (leotards and similar items). There is, however, no need for this, as exercises can just as well be done in loose fitting items, as will be explained. They must therefore not be worn as it is a requisite of *tznius* that tight-fitting clothes are not to be worn even indoors where the person cannot be seen (see 6:E:2 and 6:R:1). Swimming, on the other hand, is totally different because loose-fitting clothes would disturb a person swimming, as they would become water-logged and slow a person down.

The claim that wearing tight-fitting items while exercising helps the person lose weight and tone-up the muscles, has long been discounted as untrue. Rather, they are worn in the wider world, where *tznius* is of no concern, because being dressed in these items enables the person to exercise limbs with the greatest possible freedom. Also, it encourages the person to exercise, as they can see on themselves the improvement achieved so far. To us, these considerations are insignificant and do not justify sacrificing *tznius*.

(c) To wear the most *tznius'dik* item possible:

▪ Many find that regular exercises can be done whilst dressed in a flared, full-length dress, a loose housecoat or a flared, light-weight skirt accompanied by a long-sleeved lightweight tee-shirt which is airy and more comfortable for exercises than a blouse. Since the legs are thrown up while exercising, for *tznius* purposes the dress, housecoat or skirt must be accompanied by lightweight cotton trousers, such as sweat pants (loose fitting trousers of soft absorbent fabric) or pajama trousers. With this combination the woman or girl is dressed in perfectly normal dress, except for the fact that a type of trousers shows. Although females should generally not walk around in trousers even indoors, when doing exercises *tznius* itself calls for protection by trousers.

If a dress, housecoat or skirt can be worn there is no justification, and hence no *heter*, to wear a complete pair of pajamas without a dress etc. because the thighs and hips are exposed when trousers are worn and this must be avoided whenever possible. See 6:R:1 above, in the name of Hagaon Harav Yosef Shalom Elyashiv *shlita* that women and girls should not walk around the house in such a *sub-tznius'dik* manner of dress. Similarly, if not needed, it would be wrong to wear a large loose tee-shirt (that hangs to about halfway between the waist and the knees) together with sweat pants, because the upper sections of the legs are properly covered only when a dress, housecoat or skirt is worn.

▪ There are, however, some exercises in which wearing a skirt is found to be very disturbing by many. These are exercises in which the person lies on her back on the floor and exercises the legs while in that position. If a skirt is worn it easily flies into the face or even restricts movement. Also, the skirt easily crumbles up and becomes very uncomfortable under the person who is in this position. Although there are women and girls who are so dedicated to *tznius* that even in the face of these discomforts they will insist on wearing a skirt, this cannot be expected of the general *chareidi* public.

Those who find a skirt disturbing should wear a trouser-like item that is as loose as possible around the hips. Ideal for this purpose are the silk trousers worn by Pakistani women which are very loose around the hips but close fitting around the waist and just above the ankles. Furthermore, in some places loose fitting sweat pants are available, which are loose and do not excessively display the hip area. Also, for these exercises light weight culottes can be worn, which are a cross between a skirt and trousers as they are as loose as a skirt but are held together between the legs. When wearing such an item the thigh and upper legs are covered with a very loose garment. At the same time the garment is held around the lower legs to prevent it flying up.

The facts stated have been carefully researched with the aid of *frum* women from *Eretz Yisroel*, America and England who are involved in professional athletic activities both in schools and in seminaries. They have furnished many of the facts and have confirmed that what has been stated is fully accurate.

▪ Women and girls should not allow themselves to be influenced by the opinions of the non-Jewish or *non-chareidi* "experts in the field" who claim that a skirt-like garment would impede the person doing regular exercises properly (in which the person does not lie on the floor). These experts speak from a viewpoint that has no understanding whatsoever for *tznius* and *eidelkeit*.

We would not ask the opinion of one of their psychologists concerning how to spend our vacation and relax. We are aware that they know nothing about *tahara* and *Yiddishkeit* and would surely recommend that a man is not "burdened" with *davening* three times a day during vacation, and that we engage in activities that relax the person which are *treife* to a *shomer mitzvos*. So too, their verdict on "how to dress for exercises" is invalid, as they judge from a totally secular standpoint. Our guiding light is the verse, בכל דרכך דעהו והוא יישר ארחותיך - "In all your ways consider what would be the will of *Hashem* in this instance, and this will straighten your path" (*Mishlei* 3:6, see commentary of *Rabbeinu Yona*).

(d) Styles of exercise-wear: If a large loose tee-shirt is worn in conjunction with a skirt or loose trousers, the tee-shirt should not be cut out at the front or at the back. Similarly, its sleeves should be the correct length because provided the garment is light and loose, the sleeves do not disturb. The items should also be modest-looking, avoiding coarse large script or inappropriate emblems that deface the front or back of the garment. As stated in 1:B above, *tznius* calls for positive refinement rather than just abstention from *pritzus*. To wear items with such disfigurements is therefore incompatible with *tznius*.

Concerning all that has been explained no distinction should be drawn between teenage girls and younger girls, even though infringements in the modesty of older girls are much more harmful than when done by younger girls. Since the obligation to dress with *tznius* applies even to young girls (see 6:S:1-2 above) and dressing in the modest way described will not interfere with exercising properly, no difference should be made between them. On the contrary, by insisting on a healthy code of *tznius* while they are young, and showing them that they can exercise perfectly well even when wearing a dress, skirt, or very loose trousers, one is guaranteeing that when they become adolescents they will retain the same code of modesty.

(e) Married women covering hair while exercising: Married women should cover their hair while exercising, as there is no reason for their hair to be uncovered (and ideally a woman should cover her hair whenever she can - see 5:B). The fact that due to the type of exercises she is about to do she is allowed to wear trousers is no justification to relax any further her usual *tznius'dik* mode of dress - see 5:B:2 and 6:H:7. On the contrary, when she goes swimming she should ensure that at least her hair is as well covered as usual - see 9:J:2(e) above.

See 9:J:11 below, that Devorah *HaNeviah* and Yael, on whom *Hashem Yisborach* thrust certain duties which under normal circumstances would have been an infringement on the ways of *tznius*, took upon themselves to double their efforts in *tznius* in other areas, so as not to be negatively affected by the activities they had to do. Similarly, a woman, who due to the exercises cannot at present dress in a *tznius'dik* way, should at least be careful to cover her hair properly and practice *tznius* in that area.

(f) Immodest body-movements and coarse accompanying music: Whilst exercising, women and girls should refrain from doing bodily movements that are naturally immodest. As a person's outer actions affect and mold his inner feelings, such unrefined and even vulgar movements will harm her, albeit slowly and subtly. Some negative movements project *pritzus* and indecency, whilst others project pride and haughtiness. Both contravene *tznius* and modesty, and are very harmful.

The same applies to dancing. Whilst agile and graceful movements express the *chein* of *Bnos Yisroel*, ungainly and unrefined motions and gestures detract from her grace and have a far-reaching coarsening effect on her. Such dancing is a direct influence of the foreign cultures of the *umos ha'olam* who have, to our dismay affected both the conduct and the personality of the Jewish girl. Distressingly, while dancing to express their inner feelings and yearnings, all too often their dance communicates impurity and immodesty. However, since the inner core of the *Bas Yisroel* remains precious and pure, there is a basis to hope that if they would have the right teachers and advisors, the inroads that have been made would be restrained and even curbed. Given the right *mechanchos,* our daughters will instinctively feel that the way the present-day world dances is not suited to the spirit and virtuousness of *Bnos Yisroel.*

Finally, mention must be made of the music that is played to accompany either exercises or dancing. The music can be a pleasant and refined beat with a harmonious tune in the background or it can be a loud, rough and uncultivated noise, as is commonly heard nowadays from people who live a turbulent and disharmonious life. Such music gives no true joy and is no more than a momentary elation over the boredom and weariness of an empty and purposeless life. See 9:F:7(d) and 7:H:4 above, where the harm which such uncultured music causes the delicate and highly cultured *neshama* of a Jewish person is expounded upon. See *Peleh Yoetz* (under *Shir*) who describes the negative impact such music has on a person.

(g) Gymnastics: In some schools girls do gymnastics which are very rigorous exercises such as somersaults, cartwheels, vaulting over a horse, leapfrog and the like. These intense forms of exercise develop good coordination and exercise parts of the body that are not properly affected by regular exercise. These activities should not be discouraged even though a dress etc. can regrettably not be worn when doing them (as will be explained), just as swimming is not to be discouraged although it has this shortcoming.

For gymnastics a girl should wear loose silk oriental trousers, loose sweat pants and a large tee-shirt, or a pajama top and loose pajama trousers. A dress, housecoat or skirt cannot be worn when doing such exercises because it could be positively dangerous, as the dress or skirt can catch on the object she is leaping over. Concerning ice skating and skiing, see *Responsa Minchas Yitzchak* 2:108.

(h) Outdoor sports: Outdoor sports such as tennis should be played where the female players are not on public display - see *Mekoros* 74:1-3. Girls should therefore use a tennis court at a time when they know Jewish men and youths do not frequent the area (as they could be attracted to watch

Jewish girls play, whilst non-Jews will usually have little interest in watching Jewish girls as they play - see 2:E:4 above, that people have a far greater interest in people of their own background than in others). They should be clothed in regular everyday clothes - a dress or skirt without the accompaniment of trousers. Although a trouser-like item is needed for exercises, this is not the case with tennis. Female players must, however, take care that the skirt they wear and the sleeves of the tee-shirt or the sweat-shirt they wear are sufficiently long to prevent a momentary exposure occurring. This could happen when they dive and stretch out for the ball or when they suddenly bend to pick up a ball that has fallen down - see 6:F:1 above.

When ball games are played in the street or other very public areas girls should not throw the ball forward from between the legs. This inevitably causes the center of the skirt to be raised and to do so in public is against *tznius*. Also, the posture taken when throwing through the legs is not *tznius'dik* - see 9:J:8(b) above and *Rashi Kesubos* 72b s.v. *b'Tovoh Vered*.

(i) Conclusion: In *Rosh Chodesh Benschen* we pray for, חיים של פרנסה חיים של חילוץ עצמות חיים שיש בהם יראת שמים ויראת חטא - "A life of sustenance; a life of strong bones (symbolizing good health); a life in which we have a deep respect for *Hashem* and fear of sinning". We pray to *Hashem* that He grant us the finances needed to continue our existence and that He give this to us amidst robust health. This is immediately followed by a prayer for *Yiras Shomayim* and *Yiras Cheit*. The order is intentional - we ask for *parnoso* and health not so that we can indulge in all types of worldly pleasures but so that we can serve our Creator with our whole being.

Similarly, when we actually exercise our bodies and attend to חילוץ עצמות "strengthening our bones", our focus must be on doing all this so that we will be healthy and capable of serving *Hashem* properly - See *Rambam Hilchos Deios* 4:1 that poor health prevents a person serving *Hashem* in a fitting manner. Since this is our purpose, it should be apparent from the very way we exercise that we are not like the Greeks of old who worshipped the human body. On the contrary, we are *Yidden* who look after our bodies so that we can devote ourselves to the worship of *Hashem*. Hence, our allegiance to *tznius* must be fully apparent while we revitalize and invigorate ourselves.

4. HAZARDS OF MODERN BALCONIES, RIDING BICYCLES ETC.:

(a) Hazards to *tznius* in modern constructions: Women and girls must be careful not to stand adjacent to the railings of a balcony that is fenced off by just a few vertical bars, and is otherwise completely open. A woman who stands at the edge of such a balcony wearing a flared skirt would be shocked if she realized how *untznius'dik* that position is to those who are below. This applies to balconies that are directly above the street, and to balconies that have a garden or second balcony right under them. Unfortunately, this is a serious problem in many buildings in *Eretz Yisroel* and many women are simply unaware of the *tznius* peril they cause. It also applies to balconies that are found in modern shopping-malls and in some wedding halls. Should someone brush these words of warning aside, with the argument that it is up to men "not to look", this unjustified response has been answered in 6:J:3 above.

In some hyper-modern shopping-malls, elevators that are made almost exclusively out of glass carry shoppers from one floor to the other. Before a Jewish woman uses such an elevator, she must check that ascending or descending on it does not cause a *tznius* hazard. In some cases it could be permissible to use the elevator provided one stands towards the back of it whilst in other cases even the front may prove to be in order. The same applies to other contraptions built with extensive glass or minimal railings, as can be found in modern shopping centers e.g. glass spiral staircases etc.

The designers of these places seek to make them as attractive as possible and pay no attention to modesty-hazards that may result from their extensive use of glass. This is compounded by the fact that they are designed to serve the contemporary clientele who do not care for modesty (as is evident from the full length slits which extend right up the leg) and in which most women wear trousers (and for such attire the elevators are no hazard). Jewish women and girls must therefore be vigilant to preserve their modesty in the midst of a world that both intentionally and unintentionally endangers it.

(b) Descending stairs hastily: Although to act energetically and speedily (*zrizus*) is a virtue, every virtue has its exceptions. When women and girls descend stairs and men are in the vicinity of the lower end of the stairs, they should descend calmly not hastily, as it takes very little for a flared skirt to widen on such a descent. Similarly, when a young girl uses a swing in a public recreation ground she should tuck her dress under herself so that it does not fly up as she gathers speed. Some *Rabbanim* are even of the opinion that girls of about twelve should preferably avoid playing on a swing when men could be around because other girls could copy them and they might not be sufficiently careful.

(c) Riding bicycles: A girl who rides a bicycle in a place where she can be seen by men, must ride only a girls' bike which does not have a top bar spanning the front and back of the bike. Here again, some *Rabbanim* maintain that girls, from approximately twelve and upwards should not ride even girls' bikes in a place where they can be seen by men. Although many allowed this a few decades ago, nowadays they do not find it right to permit it because some girls will inevitably ride around while wearing a skirt that is not sufficiently loose. When this is the case, their appearance can be grossly *untznius'dik* even if they are riding a girls' bike, as the hips are pronounced and at the front the skirt easily rides up revealing the knees and more.

One must also consider that the posture of bike riding differs considerably from one place to the other. For example, in Scandinavian countries the rider sits up straight in the same position as a person sitting on a chair. As such a woman riding a bike can look very decent, provided the skirt she is wearing is loose around the hips. However, in England many ride in an inclined position, leaning heavily forward as they ride. This is likely to be very *untznius'dik* even if the skirt is very loose.

As with all matters of *halacha* and conduct, people should take guidance from their local *Rav* on this issue. It is, however, obvious that if local women and adult girls do not ride bikes and they dislike it when an individual woman or girl does so, then an individual must not go against the *minhag hamakom.* Also, apart from the *issur* of going against the local custom, being the only *frum* Jewish female to do so locally she will be noticed by all, and this is itself very *untznius'dik.*

5. WHEN SITTING VERY LOW, KNEES CAN NEED EXTRA COVER: Many garments are neither wide enough nor long enough to cover a woman properly when she sits very low. Therefore, when a woman sits *shivah, rachmana litzlan*, or sits low on *Tisha b'Av* and can be seen by others, it is essential that she covers her knees with an overall, blanket, towel or something similar. Women have reported that many evidently do not realize how they appear when they sit low without being covered in the manner described.

Similarly, there is often an element of risk in a woman sleeping in a deck chair in the grounds of a hotel or in a private garden that can be seen by neighbors, as she might move forward and not be covered properly. She should therefore cover her knees with a shawl before settling down.

Likewise, in windy weather a coat should be worn, to ensure safe passage when going from place to place.

6. TAKING CARE WHEN EMERGING FROM A CAR: Before a woman or girl emerges from a car, she should ensure that her dress or skirt is in the right position to prevent her knees from being exposed or her slip showing. With foresight, many an unpleasant exposure can be safely averted. Skirts that widen easily such as flared or pleated skirts are usually far safer for this exercise than straight skirts even when they are loose fitting, unless they extend far below the knee. Should a woman know that she experiences difficulties related to *tznius* when emerging from a car, she should if possible wait until men have passed, before opening the car door and emerging.

Ascending a bus is another danger point, and women and girls must ensure that their dresses and skirts are loose enough not to cause a forbidden glimpse to be caught at such a moment. Although a man must, of course, look away at such a time, women have to be careful not to present the possibility for such a lapse to occur.

This, plus many of the aforementioned points, are additional reasons for choosing to wear a long dress or skirt, as many Orthodox women and girls do nowadays. This added length brings the garment nearer to the full length dress that was worn in the days of *Chazal* - see 6:L:4 above. Although a full length garment is not recommended nowadays for a number of reasons - see 6:H:6 above, a long garment has a definite advantage, particularly when one considers the many dangers that result from the present-day lifestyle.

7. GUARDING ONE'S POSTURE WHEN IN PUBLIC: When a woman walks with children, the need sometimes arises to fasten a child's shoe-laces. To simply bend right down in the middle of the street is a very unrefined posture and can also cause forbidden exposure - see *Rashi*, Ruth 2:5. She should therefore either crouch down or turn her back to a wall so as not to bend forward in such a manner in public.

This may seem just a minor point. However, as a result of a woman being careful about this very thing (in a field where it was unlikely that she would be seen) the Jewish people merited having *Malchus Beis Dovid*. Boaz noticed the care Ruth took not to bend forward - instead she crouched down again and again wherever there were stalks for her to pick up. As stated, this started a chain of events which eventually led to Boaz marrying Ruth. From this union came forth Dovid Hamelech. The intense holiness of Dovid

Hamelech is evident from the fact that in *kedusha,* Dovid Hamelech is simply referred to as קדשך - "Your holy one" (ובדברי קדשך כתוב לאמור) with no further title. The wonderful *tznius* of his great-grandmother evidently bore exquisite fruits - see *Ruth* 4:21-22 and 1:N:4 and 6:Q:4 above.

8. CARE CONCERNING WAY OF SITTING IN PUBLIC:

(a) Sitting "cross-legged": If a woman or girl sits in public with crossed legs, she must be careful on three counts, since without due care this way of sitting will lead to at least one of the following shortcomings.. Due to these problems some women avoid sitting in this way when in public amongst men, such as in a waiting room, at a *shiur* etc. This underscores the great need there is for those who do sit in this manner to take adequate care.

▪ Firstly, she must ensure that her knees remain fully covered. This requires special attention because even if a dress or skirt is sufficiently long to cover the knees when she sits in the usual manner, it does not follow that the garment will cover her knees when her legs are crossed and the cloth is stretched and has a tendency to ride up. Many women are not aware that as they sit cross-legged their knees are exposed because they do not see themselves from a frontal position. Others who do notice the problem, and could draw the woman's attention to it, commonly find it too awkward to say anything with the result that the person remains totally unaware.

Those who incorrectly wear knee-highs (in contrast to thigh-highs) with average length skirts and then sit cross-legged are major offenders, because the top of the knee-highs can invariably be seen, and naked skin is on display - see 6:N:1 above.

▪ Secondly, as a result of sitting "cross-legged" the dress or skirt is sometimes caught between the higher parts of the legs in a non-*tznius'dik* manner. This is most likely to happen when the dress or skirt is made of a very soft material such as chiffon and lightweight crepe fabrics which have a natural tendency to "cave in" when the person is in a sitting position.

▪ Thirdly, when crossing the legs, the upper sections of the legs are sometimes on display almost as when trousers are worn. Instead of the upper sections being "hidden behind the screen of a dress or skirt" (as is *halachically* required - see 6:H:7) they are closely wrapped around and very much displayed. Present-day straight skirts are largely responsible for this problem. Even if they are loose when worn normally (as they would otherwise be *ossur* - see 6:I:2), they do not have an abundance of cloth available. They are therefore often tight around the sides and hips when the person wearing them sits cross-legged. Flared and pleated skirts which have an abundance of cloth are, however, different and are less likely to cause this lack of *tznius* - See 6:H:7-8.

If a *shiur* will be attended by women who might sit cross-legged in front of the *Rav* in an unfitting manner, or with skirts that are not long enough to cover their knees when sitting, the problem should, if possible, be averted by those responsible for organizing it before the *shiur* starts. Possibly, the problem can be remedied by explanation. If this is not possible it is best to distribute to all who sit at the front a scarf or shawl with which to cover their knees. The message, that knees must be covered even when sitting, will be well understood by everyone, and such action could have a very educational effect on all concerned.

It is fitting that the organizers of a *shiur* ensure that the *Rav* does not find himself in the very unpleasant situation described. In many circles only *Rebbetzens* give *shiurim* to women and girls as the *Rabbanim* are not prepared to do so. If a *Rav* does speak to women and girls, the least that is to be expected is that those who attend the *shiur* appear in a correct mode of dress and respectable manner.

(b) Not sitting in an unrefined manner: Women and girls should, whenever possible, avoid sitting in public with their legs wide apart. This *issur*, called פיסוק רגלים, is mentioned explicitly in *Chazal* - see *Pesachim* 3a and *Rashi* s.v. *Mishum*. Accordingly, it is incorrect for a woman or girl to go horse or donkey riding in the presence of men. However, when the only means of travel was to ride on an animal's back, and the person was not capable of sitting side-saddle with her legs together, the necessity justified sitting with legs apart (*ibid*). In all other cases it is wrong for a female to sit, in the presence of a man, in such a posture - See *Rabbeinu Yona* quoted in *Shita Mekubetzes*, *Kesubos* 10b and *Kreinah D'igrsa* 2:44.

9. CHOOSING A DOCTOR: GOING TO A HAIRDRESSER: Ideally, women and girls should be treated by a lady doctor - See *Responsa Shevet Halevi* 4:167. As this is often not possible (either because no such doctor is available or because she is much less proficient than her male counterpart), the least precaution that can be taken is to ensure that the doctor has a good reputation. In the absence of a lady doctor, an Orthodox and refined Jewish doctor is preferable to someone who is not a *shomer mitzvos*, even if the latter seems to be a fine person and enjoys a good reputation. People sometimes behave very differently when put to the test than in everyday situations. Moreover, *tznius* calls for a man to have a very guarded approach to women, and those who do not keep *mitzvos* are all too often overly friendly and chatty. This conduct is forbidden even if one could guarantee that no mishap will result from the conduct - see 9:C:1 above.

Similarly, girls should go to a female hairdresser if at all possible. It is against basic *tznius* for a girl to be handled by a man. It is also wrong for a girl to be engaged in an ongoing social conversation with a man, as would usually take place during the time she occupies the hairdresser's chair. Consequently, there is no justification for having a haircut or perm by a man, if there is a woman in the vicinity who can do the job equally well.

Married women should likewise not go to a male *sheitel*-setter if a female is available in the vicinity. Since the *sheitel* is cut and set as it is on the woman's head, there is no difference between *sheitel*-setting and a haircut (*Responsa Be'er Moshe* 4:121).

10. EASE WITH WHICH "ISSUR YICHUD" CAN BE TRANSGRESSED: Due to lack of knowledge, many women and girls are unaware of the many ways in which they can stumble into the *issur* of *yichud* - the *issur* for a female, (from the age of three, E.H. 22:11) to be in a secluded place with a man who is a stranger to her. It is impossible to give this subject a proper comprehensive treatment in this *sefer*. However, a few points will be mentioned to highlight the need to learn, hear *shiurim* or at least ask a *Rav* before getting into a problematic situation. Only cases which are subject to the *issur* of *yichud* according to all opinions have been mentioned.

(a) Baby-sitting and child minding: A *bas mitzva* girl (other than a sister) may not look after a boy of nine due to the *issur* of *yichud* (E.H. 22:11 that the age for the male is nine). She may however baby-sit two such boys if both are awake because a second male serves as a שומר - a deterrent. Should one or both be asleep, she may baby-sit if there are three such boys in the house. Although one sleeping deterrent is unreliable two are effective (E.H. 22:5). Alternatively, she could baby-sit if apart from the boy of nine there is a brother or sister of five who is awake or two such children asleep, because they are deterrents. See *Responsa Chasam Sofer* E.H. 2:96 and *sefer, Divrei Sofrim* on *Hilchos Yichud,* section *Eimek Davar* No. 780.

(b) Women and girls visiting a dress-maker, doctor etc.: A married woman whose husband is out of town and an unmarried girl may not go alone to the house of a *nochri*, even if a second female is in the house at the time, and even if the second female happens to be the *nochri's* wife (*ibid*

22:3). Although, there is a general rule known as אשתו שומרתו - "the presence of a wife is a deterrent" and for this reason a girl may visit a Jewish couple and even sleep there overnight, this *heter* does not apply to a *nochri*. Accordingly, a girl may not stay alone at a non-Jewish private guest house where a couple rent out one or two bedrooms of their house.

Similarly, a girl may not go alone to the house of a non-Jewish dress-maker, attend a private clinic, visit a chiropodist, go for lessons to a music teacher etc. if the non-Jewish husband is in the house at the time and the front door is shut and cannot be opened from the outside without a key. In these cases, it makes no difference whether the Jewish girl will be attended to by a man or his wife, since in either case she will be in a secluded place with a *nochri* with no *shomer* on site.

However, if her father, brother, or a child (between the ages of five and nine) accompany her to the dress-maker etc. they serve as a "*shomer*" (a guardian) and the *issur* of *yichud* does not apply (see E.H. 22:10 and *sefer, Dvar Halacha* 4:3-7). If a married woman (whose husband is in town) must attend any of the above, she should ask a *shaaloh* whether she must be accompanied by a *shomer* as in the case of a girl, or whether she can rely on the fact that her husband is in town, בעלה בעיר (see E.H. 22:8, and the diverse opinions of the *Chochmas Odom* 126:6 and the *Chazon Ish* quoted in *sefer, Dvar Halacha* 7:3). These are *halachos* of extreme importance and unfortunately ignorance is rife in these areas.

A similar problem exists when a female visits a doctor whose surgery door is closed in such a way that he and his patient are closeted in his surgery, and others have no way of gaining entry to the room. Since a state of *yichud* exists, this is definitely *ossur* in the case of an unmarried girl (unless a *shomer* accompanies her). As above, a *shaaloh* should be asked concerning a married woman whose husband is in town.

Jewish doctors who treat women patients should whenever possible avoid addressing them by their first names. Instead, they should use their general titles e.g. Mrs. Cohen, Miss Cohen. This prevents unnecessary familiarity developing. The need for *tznius* in dress, language and conduct is particularly great in a doctor's surgery and this simple but highly effective practice is therefore most recommendable - see 9:A:2 above.

(c) A woman and a worker are the only ones in the house: If a worker (whether Jewish or non-Jewish) is the only person in the house apart from an unmarried girl or a woman whose husband is out of town, an *issur* of *yichud* exists. The front door must therefore be left on the latch so that it can be opened by anyone who turns the door-knob and pushes the door open from the outside (E.H. 22:2).

11. EXTRA CARE WHEN CONDITION INCONSISTENT WITH TZNIUS:

(a) Episode in life of Devorah *HaNeviah*: *T'nach* and *Chazal* are replete with incidents about women exercising great *z'hirus* - vigilance, often even greater than the call of duty. For example, we find in *Shoftim* (4:5) that Devorah *HaNeviah* sat under a palm and judged the people - והיא יושבת תחת תומר דבורה וכו׳ ויעלו אליה בני ישראל למשפט - "And she sat under a tree that was named after her etc. and the Jewish people came to her for judgment". *Chazal* explain that she sat under a tree rather than indoors to avoid the *issur* of *yichud* (*Yalkut Shimoni, Shoftim* 42).

On reflection, it is obvious that she could just as well have sat in a house and left the front door open, known as פתח פתוח see E.H. 22:9. She nevertheless chose to do the extreme opposite of *yichud*, and judged the people only in the open under a palm, so that it would have no resemblance with *yichud* at all. She chose a palm rather than some other tree, because the branches of the palm remain on top of this tall branchless tree forming a crown of palmately cleft leaves. They do not grow from branches, bend downwards and semi enclose the area under the tree, as do the branches of many other trees. This, too, was to ensure that the arrangement was free of any semblance to *yichud*.

Due to her natural modesty, Devorah felt that for a woman to hold the high offices of *Navi* (prophet) and of *Shofet* (judge) was inconsistent with the usual ways of *tznius*, in which a woman is out of the limelight. *Hashem* had however elevated her to the position of *Neviah* and from this evolved that she also had to fill the office of judge - see *Tosfos, Gittin* 88b s.v. *V'lo*. To counteract this incursion into her personal *tznius*, Devorah observed all issues of *tznius* perfectly - and even well beyond their *halachic* requirements.

Devorah's conduct should be taken as a guideline for a woman who must visit a male doctor (when no female doctor is available or the male doctor is distinctly superior) and allows him to inspect part of her body that is usually covered. Since this is a necessity, no *pritzus* is involved as it is being done purely for medical reasons. Nevertheless, in such a setting, she must conduct herself with utmost modesty so that no lessening of her standard of *tznius* results from this unusual setting which would generally be alien to *tznius*.

(b) Event in life of Yael: Yael slew the great warrior Sisra by driving a tent peg into his temple, as the verse says, ותקח יעל אשת חבר את יתד האהל וכו׳ ותתקע את היתד ברקתו - *Shoftim* 4:21. The *Midrash Shocher Tov* (*Mishlei* 31:19) explains that she did not use a spear or sword which would have been the natural weapons to use because of the *issur* of *lo yehi kli gever al ishah* - a woman must not dress in the clothes of a man (*Devarim* 22:5). She must similarly not strap a sword or spear to her side as this is the way of men (*Nazir* 59a; Y.D. 182:5). Since men fight with a spear or sword, Yael did not use either of them even though to use them would presumably have been easier and more natural than using a tent peg.

On reflection, this *Chazal* is difficult to understand. Yael would certainly not have transgressed the *issur* of *lo yehi kli gever al isho* even if she had killed Sisra with a spear or sword, because when an item is used by hand (rather than worn) for a valid reason, all opinions agree that the *issur* of *lo yehi kli gever al isho* is not transgressed. For example, a woman may use a hammer or screwdriver - see *Binas Odom* 94 and *Responsa Shevet Halevi* 2:61. If so, why did Yael not use a spear or sword?

The answer is similar to that mentioned above. Because of the pressing need, Yael had to conduct herself in a way that was totally alien to the *tznius* of a Jewish woman. She had to invite Sisra into her tent and entertain him (until he fell asleep and she could then kill him). Inviting a man into her tent when her husband was not there, was certainly not compatible with *tznius*. Also, the very act of killing that she had to do, was a distinctly unfeminine act. She therefore felt a need to counterbalance this assault on her *tznius* by strengthening and maximizing other aspects of *tznius* as far as possible. She therefore decided to depart from the ways of "*kli gever*" to the extreme and use a tent peg rather than a normal weapon. By not using a weapon typically used by men she had ensured that her act of warfare was at least not done in a typically masculine way. See 9:J:3(e) for a further application.

These are, of course, the finest and highest forms of *tznius* and *z'hirus* (vigilance). If we take every precaution to ensure that our conduct does not violate the basic needs of modesty and *tznius*, especially when the setting could endanger *tznius*, such as when working in an office (see 9:F above), we will at least have stepped onto the lowest rungs of the ladder that ascends to the heights attained by these great women.

Chapter Ten

EXCEPTIONAL BENEFITS OF TZNIUS

A. CHILDREN OF WOMEN WHO PERSONIFY TZNIUS

1. CHILDREN WITH A LOVE FOR TORAH LEARNING: A most wonderful reward awaits the woman who excels in *tznius*, modesty and general refinement. She will have children who are exceptionally diligent in their Torah studies and excel in their Torah knowledge. The *tznius* and love for *Kedushas Yisroel* that this woman has developed within herself renders her supremely suitable to bring up children who have a natural love for *Kedushas haTorah* and therefore gravitate towards it. Their mother shuns the profane world and cherishes *kedusha*. It is therefore natural for her children to seek a haven of *kedusha* and *tahara* and both embrace and cleave to *Kedushas haTorah* with their whole being. They diligently and eagerly learn and absorb the *Dvar Hashem*.

Moreover, as mentioned elsewhere, from the refinement and sensitivity of their mother, the sons inherit the sensitivity and perception to grasp the deep and fine concepts that make up the inner core of the Torah. The *Midrash* states:- בזמן שהיא נוהגת בעצמה בדת יהודית שהיא צנועה זוכה שמוציאין ממנה בנים בעלי מקרא בעלי משנה בעלי מעשים טובים הדא הוא דכתיב בניך כשתילי זיתים סביב לשולחנך - "When a woman behaves according to true Jewish tradition and is modest, she merits having children who are masters of the Written Law, masters of the Oral Law and people of sterling character" (*Nossoh*, Chapter eight) - see *Mekoros* 25:3-5.

The daughter of the true *Eishes Chayil* has been brought up in a home where *Ahavas haTorah* and *Avodas Hashem* reign supreme. She feels the *emes* and *simchas hachayim* of a Torah way of life and looks forward to the day when she too will merit setting up a home that will, *B'ezer Hashem*, be similar to that of her parents.

2. CHILDREN WITH A DEEP APPRECIATION FOR TEFILLA:

(a) True *tznius* is based on being aware of the presence of *Hashem*: True *tznius* that is practiced even in the privacy of the home results from a deep awareness of the constant close presence of *Hashem* and the feeling that one needs to be covered before Him - see 1:A:4(c) and 7:M:4 above. Since the *tznua* feels the close presence of *Hashem*, she naturally clings to Him and pours out her heart in *tefilla* and *Tehillim* to Him whenever possible. Due to this, her children likewise feel the close presence of *Hashem* and likewise develop a strong feeling for *tefilla,* which they have inherited from their righteous mother. The *Chofetz Chayim* is reputed to have once said that all which he achieved can be attributed to the tears his mother shed over her *Tehillim* - see 2:L:4 above. In fact, almost all our *Gedolim* and *Tzadikim* had outstanding mothers.

(b) *Tznius* leads to children with considerable *penimius*: This benefit is hinted to in the verse, כל כבודה בת מלך פנימה ממשבצות זהב לבושה - "All the glory of the king's daughter is internal, her garb is of gold settings" (*Tehillim* 45:14). On this *Chazal* say, כשהאשה מצנעת עצמה בתוך הבית ראויה להנשא לכהן גדול ותעמיד כהנים גדולים - "If a woman remains modestly at home, she is worthy that both her husband and children are *Kohanim Gedolim* [who wear golden clothes]" - (*Midrash Tanchuma Parshas Vayishlach* No.6).

Similarly, Kimchis, the exceptionally modest woman, had seven sons who were all *Kohanim Gedolim* (*Yuma* 47a). The function of the *Kohen Gadol* is to plead and pray on behalf of *Klal Yisroel*. Such an outstanding person is born to a mother whose impeccable *tznius* has brought her close to *Hashem* and to an intense feeling for *tefilla*. She *davens* and says *Tehillim* for members of her family and for the sick of *Klal Yisroel*, just as a *Kohen Gadol* davens for his family and for the needs of all *Yidden*.

(c) Mother's responsibility for standard of her son's *tefillos*: The following illustrates the extent to which the qualities of a mother affect the *tefillos* of her offspring. The mother of the *Kohen Gadol* would supply food and clothes to the inmates of the *arei miklot* to prevent them praying for her son to die so that they could return home once again (*Makos* 11a). Why did the mother rather than the wife of the *Kohen Gadol* do this?

The *seforim* write that the mother considered herself partially to blame that these accidental killings occurred, and that people were consequently confined to the *arei miklat*. This is because when a *Kohen Gadol* was truly worthy his powerful *tefillos* prevent calamities, such as accidental killings, from occurring (see *Rashi Bamidbar* 35:25). Therefore, if calamities did occur, the *Kohen Gadol's tefillos* were evidently not at the high level they should have been.

The mother of the *Kohen Gadol* felt that she was to blame for this shortcoming. Had she been a better person, her son would have developed an even deeper appreciation for *tefilla* and service of *Hashem*, and his *tefillos* would have been powerful enough to prevent these calamities from happening. The mother therefore considers herself indirectly responsible for having caused these people to be in *golus* and for endangering her son's life (as people pray for him to die). She therefore took it upon herself to look after these people and do whatever she could to prevent them praying for her son to die. The wife in contrast, was not so obviously responsible for her husband's lack of total devotion to *tefilla*. It was therefore the mother rather than the wife who tried to improve matters. We see here the enormous effect a mother has on her son. The more special she is, the greater her son will be.

3. HUSBAND AND SONS ASCRIBE THEIR ATTAINMENTS TO HER:

(a) She creates an environment for Torah learning: Towards the end of the Eishes Chayil the verse says, קמו בניה ויאשרוה בעלה ויהללה - "The children of the woman of valor will stand up and acknowledge her. Her husband will arise and lavish praise upon her" (*Mishlei* 31:28). Both her children and her husband feel that they owe their attainments to their respective mother and wife. The *tahara* and *kedusha* that permeates the atmosphere of their home is conducive to Torah study and *tefilla*. This spirit emanates from the mother who ensures that only Kosher literature is brought into the house (as she does not allow impure literature even in the bathroom) and with her personal example of *simcha* and satisfaction she brings beautiful harmony and tranquillity to reign in the house. She is a queen at home כבודה בת מלך פנימה and with such a family around her is a queen in *Klal Yisroel*.

Apart from the mother's subtle effect on her son's growth in Torah that has just been explained, she also plays a very positive role in his growth in Torah which is a vital part of his development. Concerning a person's influence upon his children, Dovid Hamelech says, כחצים ביד גיבור כן בני הנעורים - "Like arrows shot by a mighty warrior, so are the children of a person's youth" (*Tehillim* 127:4). This verse refers to the father whose far-reaching aspirations direct his child to a high level of Torah and *Avodas Hashem*. The father is compared to a mighty warrior, because the heights his son reaches are a result of the father's mighty thrust and influence. It appears that the mother is left out in this parable and given no mention. This is, however, not the case and the praise expressed about the father's role, is in fact a major praise to both father and mother alike.

If a warrior is to shoot arrows accurately it is essential that the arrows he uses are perfectly straight and even. Otherwise, the arrows will veer off course and miss their target, irrespective of how powerfully and skillfully the arrows are shot. Only when this precondition has been fully met, will the excellent shots of the master marksman produce their desired results.

The same applies with the *chinuch* of children. Although it is the father who is the master marksman, motivating his son to grow into a serious student of Torah and eventually a *Talmid Chacham* of repute, it is the mother who prepares him and ensures that he is fit to reach his target. She straightens out the child's character, and implants within him basic *Yiras Shomayim.* She does this during the early formative years of the child's life when the child is almost exclusively under her care. She also corrects the child's most obvious shortcomings and imbues within him the understanding that a *Yid* must live a disciplined life and his whole existence must be directed at doing that which *Hashem* expects of him.

The tender child acquires these qualities by watching his mother incessantly and observing her reactions to all types of situations that arise. He sees how particular she is not to speak *lashon horah* or say anything that can be hurtful to a person. He sees how soft-spoken and refined she is in her dealings with her husband, parents, parents-in-law and everyone else. He sees the earnestness with which she *bentches*, *davens*, lights the Shabbos lights etc. He sees how careful she is to ensure that her hair and her whole person are adequately covered before opening the door etc. He sees before his eyes a life based on self-discipline and *Yiras Shomayim.* All this affects the child deeply and brings respect for *Yiddishkeit* into his life. The father then takes over and directs the child to the wellsprings of Torah. Hence, the fact that the father can jettison his child so perfectly to great heights is a praise to both father and mother alike.

The mother's role in the upbringing of the children is so decisive that when *Hashem* was about to give the Torah he said to Moshe, כה תאמר לבית יעקב ותגיד לבני ישראל - "So you shall say to the house of Yaacov [the women] and tell the *Bnei Yisroel* [the men]". The *Midrash* (*Shemos Rabba* 25:2) explains that women were addressed before the men, כדי שיהיו מנהיגות את בניהן לתורה - "So that they lead their children to Torah". Although the father plays the major part in creating the bond between the child and the Torah, it is the mother who prepares the child for this, and it is she who "leads the child to the Torah".

(b) Her attitude brings *kedusha* into everything in the home: Not only do these women encourage their husbands and sons to drink from the lifesprings of Torah and *daven* as a person should, but with their intense *Yiddishkeit* they infuse them with a desire and a yearning to learn more and more Torah and to come closer to *Hashem* through *tefilla*. The spirit of these women permeates their homes, spreading also to mundane matters. Even the foods they prepare for the family to eat are enhanced and "flavored" by their attitude, and thereby have a positive influence on those who eat them (see *Shomer Emunim, Mavo HaSha'ar* Chap.14).

Accordingly, foods checked for insects with conscientiousness, foods cooked with care to avoid mix-ups, and the *challos* baked with a love for Shabbos or *Yom Tov,* give her husband and children both the physical and the spiritual nourishment they need to be totally devoted to Torah and *mitzvos*. [Concerning *challos*, the *Chofetz Chayim* writes that much *Kavod* Shabbos is lost when women buy *challos* for Shabbos rather than bake *challos* themselves - O.C. 242 *Biur Halacha* s.v. *V'hu*]. Little wonder that the husband and children of such an *Eishes Chayil* stand up and acknowledge their wife and mother's major contribution, attributing virtually everything to her influence, קמו בניה ויאשרוה בעלה ויהללה. She is to be given credit for their success to such an extent that they could use the words uttered by Rabbi Akiva to his disciples, שלי ושלכם שלה הוא - "My Torah and your Torah are all hers!" (*Kesubos* 63a) - see *Mekoros* 84.

When the Jewish people were in the wilderness they received the *man* in the merit of Moshe Rabbeinu, and the water of the *be'er* in the merit of Miriam *haNevia* - *Ta'anis* 9a. *Man* came down from heaven whilst the water of the *be'er* came up from the ground. This was to symbolize that the *avoda* - the spiritual service - of men is to bring Torah down from heaven by learning Torah and delving deeply into it, thereby sanctifying themselves and the rest of world with its intense holiness, whilst the *avoda* of women is to raise worldly matters such as food, clothes and all aspects of everyday life from their earthbound physical state and purify them. When people eat such foods, wear such clothes and live in the pure home environment created by these women they are ready for the intense spirituality that the attachment to Torah can give them. Only once the worldly matters are purified and prepared for spirituality, can the holiness of the Torah descend onto those who use them and bring them to *kedusha.*

It follows that women have a major hand in everything. Not only do they create the home and look after everything therein, but they are to be greatly credited for the Torah and *mitzvos* of their families. It could be that for this reason Avraham Avinu named his daughter (according to those who maintain that he had one - see *Bava Basra* 16b), בכל - "*Bakol*" meaning "in all" - which is a rather strange name to give a daughter. However, Avraham was defining the role of a worthy Jewish female. He was saying that she plays a major role in everything in life. She is far, far more than just a cook, a house keeper, a child attendant, a companion etc. She in fact brings everything together, and enables the physical to serve the spiritual in one united effort to fulfill the will and design of *Hashem* in this world.

Interestingly, the *Maharal MiPrague* writes in *Netzach Yisroel* Chapter 1 (and *Gur Aryeh, Breishis* 48:7 - see note 107) that women are referred to as a person's בית - house (*Gittin* 52a) because a house unites everything together under one roof. So does an *Eishes Chayil,* she enables the spiritual to co-exist with the physical, in a way that the two can thrive together.

(c) She whole-heartedly encourages Torah learning: *Chazal* say, נשים במאי זכיין באקרויי בנייהו לבי כנישתא ובאתנויי גברייהו בי רבנן ונטרין לגברייהו עד אתו מבי רבנן - "With what do women earn an honored place in *Olam Habah*? By their children learning Torah (with their *Rebbe* in *shul*, as was the way in the olden days), by their husbands learning Torah in the *beis hamedrash* and by waiting patiently for their husbands to come home - from their extensive learning programs which at times involved going out of town - see *Rashi*" - (*Brachos* 17a). The woman who has her priorities right understands that Torah stands above all. She is therefore prepared to sacrifice the time she would have in the company of her husband and children so that they devote themselves fully to the learning of Torah.

(d) She will not disturb her husband while he is learning: Her attitude towards learning Torah enables her to encourage her husband and sons to spend as much time as possible learning Torah. Due to her appreciation of the importance of Torah learning she treats the hours her husband spends learning as sacred and the most important hours in his day. During this time she will neither disturb him herself nor will she allow others to disturb him unless it is something of extreme urgency.

It is remarkable that the main praise of the woman of valor expressed in the verses of the *Eishes Chayil* is the way in which she takes upon herself many responsibilities, thereby enabling her husband to learn Torah without worry or distraction. She makes the *parnoso*, spins thread, weaves cloth and makes clothes for the family and for sale. At the same time she watches closely over the developments of her family, gives *tzedaka* and helps others with her kind words and sagacious advice. All this results in נודע בשערים בעלה בשבתו עם זקני ארץ - "Her husband is renowned for his greatness in Torah, which results from the fact that he can reside in the *beis hamedrash* in the company of other *Talmidei Chachamim*" (*Mishlei* 31:23).

(e) She benefits personally from her husband's Torah: Her husband's learning brings great illumination to his *neshama* (ותורה אור - *Mishlei* 6:23) which in turn is reflected onto hers, since she stands by his side giving him all the encouragement he needs. For this reason, when Yosef *Hatzadik* dreamt about his father and mother he saw them as the sun and moon (*Breishis* 37:9). Just as the moon is illuminated by the great light that is emitted from the glow of the sun, so too, the light of Torah emitted from the Torah learnt by her husband reflects onto his wife, giving her a closeness to the *emes* which she would otherwise not be able to obtain. Just as the moon is fully illuminated when it is in the right position facing the sun, so too, when the wife takes the right position corresponding to her husband, by both respecting him and encouraging him, she has a great share in the Torah he learns and in everything else he achieves.

4. HER ACHIEVEMENTS ARE LIKE THOSE OF A GREAT MAN:

(a) She is considered as one of the builders of *Klal Yisroel*: It follows from the above, that when a woman is a true *tznua*, she does for *Klal Yisroel* much the same as a man who has fulfilled his duty. A man who is a true servant of *Hashem* grows steadily in Torah, in *tefilla* and in his refinement of character. Eventually he becomes such a special person that he is one of the builders of the future *Klal Yisroel*. So too, when a woman devotes her life to *tznius*, to *tefilla* and to encouraging her family to grow in Torah and *Yiras Shomayim*, she causes her husband and children to become special and distinguished people - see *Mekoros* 25. Since their achievements are in her merit, she has made a major contribution to the future of *Klal Yisroel.*

It is remarkable that the term "builder" which is generally reserved for *Talmidei Chachamim* is used also for special women. On the one hand *Chazal* say, תלמידי חכמים נקראו בנאים שעוסקים בבנינו של עולם - "*Talmidei Chachamim* are termed as builders because they are engaged in the construction of the world" (*Shabbos* 114a). On the other hand, we find that after Boaz married Ruth, people wished Boaz the following: יתן ה׳ את האשה הבאה אל ביתך כרחל וכלאה אשר בנו שתיהם את בית ישראל - "*Hashem* should grant that the woman who comes into your house be like Rachel and Leah who together built the House of *Yisroel*" (*Ruth* 4:11). This verse is evidence that the achievements of a great woman are comparable to those of a *Talmid Chacham.*

The following is an example of the selfless encouragement a woman gave her husband to work for the furtherance of Torah and *Yiddishkeit.* In the introduction to the *sefer, Toras Aharon* by Hagaon Harav Aharon Yosef Bakst *zt'l* (known as Reb Artchik, *Lomzer Rav* and great *Baal Mussar*), the following is related: "In the year 5583 Harav Bakst was Rav and *Rosh Yeshiva* of Suvlak but at the time of this incident he and his Rebbetzen were in another town where she became very ill. On the Wednesday preceding *Rosh Hashono* her husband said that this year he would not be going to Suvlak for the *Yomim Noraim* as he could not leave her in the state she was in. Next day, the Rebbetzen mustered all her strength and with a supreme effort managed to get out of bed and walk around a bit. When her husband saw her walking around he was convinced that there was a sudden major improvement in her condition and there and then decided to go to Suvlak for *Rosh Hashono*. That night, after her husband had gone, she was evidently very ill and she in fact died three months later.

"Her son asked her why she had done everything in her power to persuade his father to leave. She replied, "I know what effect your father's *mussar* has on people, and that his *drasha* before *Tekias Shofar* stirs people's hearts and brings them to sincere *teshuva.* This year, with his heart broken over my condition, his words will be even more meaningful, and will probably have an even greater impact on the people than usual. How can I deny people an opportunity to receive such tremendous *chizuk?*" Such is the selflessness of the *nashim tzidkanios* of our people and the part they have in their husband's achievements.

(b) She will be rewarded for her enormous contribution: The verse says towards the end of *Eishes Chayil*, ותשחק ליום אחרון - "She is overjoyed on the day of her departure from this world" (*Mishlei* 31:25). This seems strange, since *Tzadikim* are upset to leave this world and to be denied the opportunity to continue serving the *Borei Olam*. It is related that the *Vilna Gaon* wept on his death-bed while holding his *tzitzis* in his hands. He said, "How difficult it is to take leave of the world of deeds, where a person is able to stand before *Hashem* by performing a *mitzva* as inexpensive as *tzitzis*!" It is therefore perplexing that the woman of valor is overjoyed as she is about to leave this world. This can, however, be understood with the following introduction.

At the end of their lives, great people have a premonition about the magnificent *Olam Habah* that awaits them (*Breishis Rabba* 62:2). The *Eishes Chayil* who has spent almost all her days performing mundane chores such as cooking, baking, washing clothes and house-keeping is overwhelmed when on her last day she becomes aware that a glorious *Olam Habah* awaits her - an *Olam Habah* fit for someone who has the great merit of considerable *Harbotzas HaTorah*. She always thought that this was totally out of her reach, being on a much lower *madreiga* than great *Talmidei Chachamim* who teach Torah. To her amazement she finds out that she too is considered a great *marbitz* Torah, since as a result of her *yiras shomayim*, her *tznius* and her efforts, her husband, sons and sons-in-law developed into such great Torah personalities. Therefore, on her day of departure she is delighted with her newly found good fortune - ותשחק ליום אחרון! (Adapted from an essay by Rabbi Shaul Rubin *shlita*, author of *sefer, Tzyunei Derech* on *tefilla*).

The last verse in the *Eishes Chayil* reads, תנו לה מפרי ידיה - "Reward her in the world to come from the fruits of her hands" (*Mishlei* 31:31). To this *Rashi* says that she will be rewarded with, תפארת וגדולה עוז פאר וממשלה - "Splendor, greatness, strength, glory and leadership". These seem a strange choice, as they are terms that are usually reserved for leading positions in Torah, *Avoda* and *Malchus* (כתר תורה, כתר כהונה וכתר מלכות), all which are not held by women. The *Eishes Chayil* is nevertheless considered to be closely associated and to have produced these qualities, because the husband whom she has assisted all her life and the children she has nurtured and raised, are in possession of these great qualities only because of her. She is therefore a deserving recipient of them as they are considered to be the fruits of her labor.

The outstanding reward of special women is evident from the incredible *tefilla* of Dovid Hamelech that he merit to have a share in the *Olam Habah* set aside for righteous women. He prayed that ועם האמהות אשר אמרת עמם אכבדה - "If only that I be honored together with the mothers that you have mentioned" (*Shmuel* 2:6:22). To which *Chazal* say that Dovid prayed, הלואי יהא לי חלק עמהם לעולם הבא - "If only I be honored to have a portion in *Olam Habah* together with them" (*Bamidbar Rabba* 4:20 and mentioned in 1:I:10 above). This was the high esteem in which Dovid Hamelech held the special women of *Klal Yisroel*!

5. TZNIUS CAN LEAD TO THE GIFT OF HAVING CHILDREN: The *Kli Yakor* (*Breishis* 18:9) writes that in the virtue of *tznius* a woman can merit having children even though she had so far been childless. He writes that for this reason the *Malachim* who had come to inform Avraham and Sarah that they were to be blessed with a son, said to Avraham Avinu, איה שרה אשתך - "Where is Sarah your wife?" to which they were told that she had modestly withdrawn to the tent. In the context of their mission, they wished to mention the *tznius* of Sarah, thereby indicating that, as a result of her outstanding *tznius*, they were to be blessed with a child although this was no longer possible according to the usual rules of nature.

The idea put forward by the *Kli Yakor* that *tznius* leads to having children is in fact mentioned in *Chazal*. This is the text of the *Tana D'Bei Eliyahu, Rabba*, Chapter 18 (in reference to the verse in *Tehillim* 128:3), אשתך כגפן פוריה וכו' אימתי תהא אשתך כגפן שהוא עושה פירות, כל זמן שאשתך תהא בירכתי ביתך - "When will your wife be like a fruitful vine. If she is modest and her place is in the inner sanctuary of your home".

Since the *tznius* of the mother has a profound effect on the children she bears, as explained, it is well understood that *tznius* is a *segula* for having children. When the mother displays such conduct, *Hashem Yisborach* is only too willing to grant her children, as He knows that her offspring will be worthy *Yidden. Tznius* similarly prevents miscarriages, see 7:F:5 above.

There is a widespread *minhag* that takes place before a *chupah*. As soon as the *kallah's* face has been covered with the veil, those who stand nearby bless her with the *bracha,* אחותינו את היי לאלפי רבבה - "Our sister you shall have offspring numbering many many millions" (*Kitzur Shulchan Aruch* 147:3). With what has been explained, this *minhag* is superbly fitting. It is appropriate to give a *bracha* for children and grandchildren just after the *kallah's* face has been covered as a special display of *tznius* and general modesty - See 9:H:1 above and *Mekoros* 85:1-3.

B. VARYING STANDARDS OF TZNIUS - VASTLY DIFFERENT

1. MINOR DIFFERENCES ARE OF MAJOR SIGNIFICANCE: The market value of diamonds does not increase in proportion to their size i.e. a stone that is one and a half times the size of another stone does not cost just one and a half times as much. A large stone is worth many times more than a smaller one because it is greatly superior and in a completely different class than a smaller one. The verse compares a woman blessed with true *tznius* and other great qualities to a diamond, אשת חיל מי ימצא ורחוק מפנינים מכרה - "A woman of valor who can find? Far beyond pearls is her value" (*Mishlei* 31:10). The message in this analogy is that a woman with a greater understanding of *chesed* or *tznius* than another woman is not to be considered the same type of person with an extra measure of *chesed* or *tznius*. Rather, she is of a totally different caliber and many times the worth of the latter who has less understanding and less appreciation for *chesed* or *tznius* - see *Mekoros* 2:2.

2. HOW THE DIFFERENCE AFFECTS THE CHILDREN:

(a) Two Torah students can be on very different levels: Both of these women may have sons who are Torah students. The former, who has a deeper feeling for *tznius* and a greater sense for *kedusha*, has a son who learns more diligently and is drawn to *kedushas haTorah* in a greater measure than the son of the latter, who is not devoted to his Torah learning in the same way. The *Chofetz Chayim* remarks that a greater *Ben Torah* is not "the lesser *Ben Torah* plus additional diligence", for Torah too is compared to a gem, as the verse says, יקרה היא מפנינים - "Torah is more precious than gems" (*Mishlei* 3:15). This is to bring home to us the same message as in the previous paragraph - a more diligent *Ben Torah* is greater and of a different caliber than a lesser one. The exceptional mother, blessed with deep *tznius*, brings up a precious and valuable *Ben Torah* whilst the second mother may seem to possess the same, but in fact this is not the case (*Chofetz Chayim Al HaTorah, parshas Breishis,* footnote 7 s.v. *V'koh*) - see *Mekoros* 25:3-5.

In *Lashon HaKodesh,* the two letters of the word בן (son) follow the two letters of the word אם (mother). It is written in *seforim* that this is to indicate that the son follows his mother. The greater her worth, the greater the worth of her son.

This concerns the effect a mother has on her sons. Concerning her effect on her daughters, for whom the greatest asset in life is to be blessed with the trait of *tznius*, the following remarkable testimony should be a great encouragement. Rabbeinu Yehuda Loeb *zt'l*, the great *Maharal MiPrague*, writes in his *sefer, Nesivos Olam, Nesiv HaTznius*, Chapter One, paragraph starting *u'bmeseches*, ולא תמצא בכל המדות שהדומה יוליד הדומה כמו שתמצא אצל הצניעות, שהצנוע מוליד צנוע - "You will not find in any other attribute the same degree of 'inheritance', and 'similarity of offspring to parent' as one finds with *tznius*, where a *tznua* invariably gives birth to a *tznua*". Accordingly, when a young person implants this special attribute into himself, he is in fact implanting this cherished *midah* into future generations which are at present still unborn.

(b) Sarah's son Yitzchak in contrast to Hagar's son Yishmael: As explained, the quality of a son is largely due to the qualities of his mother, and an exceptional son reflects an exceptional mother. When Sarah Imeinu died, Avraham Avinu came to say a *hesped* for her. The verse relates, ויבא אברהם לספוד לשרה ולבכותה - "And Avraham came from the *Akeida* to say a *hesped* on her and lament her passing" - (*Breishis* 23:2 and *Breishis Rabba* 58:5). What is the significance in mentioning that Avraham came from the *Akeida*? The Minsker Maggid (Harav Hagaon R' Binyamin Shakovitzki *zt'l*) gave an interesting although different reason than that given in the *Midrash*:-

Having experienced the *Akeida*, and having seen first hand the great *mesiras nefesh* and intense *kedusha* of his son Yitzchak, Avraham felt that relating the story of Yitzchak's acceptance of the *Akeida* and his subsequent perfect conduct during the *Akeida* itself, would be the finest *hesped* he could say on Sarah. Losing a woman who gave birth and brought up such an exceptional person as Yitzchak was an irreplaceable loss not just to her family but to everyone. Being the mother of such a son proved her exceptional worth, because a lesser person could neither have produced nor nurtured such an incredible *tzaddik* as Yitzchak (*Beis Yitzchak, parshas Chayei Sarah*).

In contrast, a corrupt son reflects badly on his mother. When Sarah requested that Avraham throw Yishmael out of the house after he had turned to *avodo zarah* and *giluy arayos,* so that he should not exert a negative influence on her son Yitzchak, she said, גרש את האמה הזאת עם בנה - "Expel this maid servant with her son" (*Breishis* 21:10). There is no mention anywhere that Hagar did wrong in a similar way to Yishmael. If so, why did Sarah petition her husband to throw out mother and son? The answer is as above - a son reflects the quality of his mother. Since Yishmael had become corrupt and developed other serious faults, Sarah surmised that his mother was probably not much better. Therefore, for the sake of her son Yitzchak, she wanted not only Yishmael removed from the house but also Hagar, Yishmael's mother.

These two cases are, of course, extremes. Also, sometimes other factors are the reason why a child develops in a certain way. They do, nevertheless, reflect on the very close relationship between mother and son. Accordingly, the finer a girl develops in her pre-marriage years, the more is to be hoped from the future family that she will *b'ezer Hashem* be granted.

3. OUTSTANDING TZNIUS OF THE CHAZON ISH'S MOTHER: The mother of the *Chazon Ish*, Rebbetzen Rasha Leah *o.h.* had a most outstanding family. (Apart from the *Chazon Ish*, she had another three sons who were *Gedolei Yisroel* amongst them R. Meir Karelitz. She also had five daughters who all married *Gedolei Yisroel*, amongst them R. Nochum Karelitz (father of Hagaon R. Nissim Karelitz *shlita*), R. Shmuel Greineman, and the *Steipler Gaon, zeicher tzadikim livrocho*).

She was asked what special deeds she had performed as a result of which she merited to have such illustrious children. To this she answered that she was extremely particular not to reveal her hair beyond the bare minimum. When she washed her hair she put a towel over her head opening up just the small part that she washed. She then covered that part, opened up a second part and washed it. In this way she washed all her hair whilst keeping most of it covered all the time. This was told to the author of this *sefer* by Rav Tzvi Rotberg *shlita*, *Ram Yeshivas Beis Meir Bnei Brak*, who heard it from his mother (a daughter of R. Meir Karelitz *zt'l*). She looked after her grandmother, Rebbetzen Rasha Leah *o.h.* and on many occasions saw her wash her hair in this way - see *Mekoros* 25:6.

This story was not recorded in order that people do likewise, since only someone as great as her should behave in such a way. Moreover, the greatness of Rebbetzen Rasha Leah *o.h.* did not lie in the fact that she covered her hair in the way described, but rather in the deep-rooted feelings of *tznius* which motivated her actions. This is a standard far beyond that of most people. We do, however, see that a great *tznua* brought up children of the highest caliber of Torah and *tzidkus*. Hence, the finer our personal *tznius* is, the higher will be the quality of the children we raise.

We can emulate this great *tzadekes* in our own way, and take an example from her to improve within ourselves our feelings for *tznius* and to conduct ourselves within these parameters. By doing so we will merit to see a generation of *Talmidei Chachamim* and *Yirei Hashem* with whom *Klal Yisroel* can proudly welcome *Moshiach Tzidkeinu* בב"א.

C. CHARACTER TRAITS OF IDEAL WIFE - TZNIUS AND CHESED

1. BEAUTIFUL COMBINATION OF TZNIUS AND CHESED: When looking for a suitable *shidduch* for one's son, the two most important character traits to look out for in a girl are *tznius* (modesty) and *chesed* (kindness). When a girl has these two qualities, she will be able to cope admirably with the trials and tribulations of life.

If she is a *tznua*, her morals will be of a very high standard and she will look only to Kosher sources for influence and inspiration. It has already been mentioned (1:C above) in the name of the *Vilna Gaon zt'l* that *tznius* helps a female overcome her *yetzer horah* in much the same way as Torah learning enables males to overcome their *yetzer horah*. *Tznius* is therefore the safety line as far as *mitzvos shebein adam laMakom* (between man and G-d) are concerned. Accordingly, with this quality, it is to be hoped that a valuable home with a profound feeling for *Yiddishkeit* will develop around her.

On the other hand, the attribute of *chesed* is the finest trait a person can have as far as the fulfillment of *mitzvos shebein adam lechaveiro* (between man and man) is concerned. With a healthy measure of *midas hachesed*, she will use the worldly gifts that *Hashem* bestows upon her to help the needy and to be a pillar of support to those who turn to her. Moreover, since she is a kind person, she will give her husband and family true affection and care. She will *b'ezer Hashem* create a wonderful home atmosphere of *simcha* and mutual love and respect.

2. THE AVOS SOUGHT WIVES SPECIAL IN TZNIUS AND CHESED: The great *Rabbenu Yehuda HaChassid* in *Sefer Chassidim* No. 1015 writes the following (rendered here in a loose translation):- "Avraham Avinu made many converts who became G-d fearing people. He nevertheless did not take a daughter-in-law from them. Instead, he sought a daughter-in-law from his own family even though they were idol-worshippers. This is because his family were blessed with the traits of *tznius* (modesty) and *gemilus chasadim* (kindness). Rivka exemplified *chesed* as she offered to give water not just to Eliezer himself but to all the camels, even though this was doubtlessly an enormous undertaking. Rachel, another member of his family, exemplified *tznius*, the second of the two special traits mentioned. Rachel was beautiful and was afraid that the shepherds would take an interest in her. She was therefore particular not to arrive at the well unnecessarily early. It is evident in the verse that she arrived much later than the three shepherds - *Breishis* 29:6."

When Yitzchak married Rivka and brought her to the tent, the three blessings that had been there in the days of his mother Sarah were restored. The lights burned from *erev* Shabbos to *erev* Shabbos, there was a blessing in the bread dough and a cloud hovered permanently over the tent, (*Rashi, Breishis* 24:67). As already explained in 9:I:4(c) above, these three blessings are indicators of the following concepts: the lights represent spirituality of the home because light symbolizes Torah and *mitzvos* - *ki ner mitzva v'Torah ohr* (*Mishlei* 6:23). The bread dough represents the physical side of a home which the Imahos used for *chesed*, for honoring Shabbos and all types of good deeds . These are the two constitutes of the home. The cloud hovering above represented the presence of the *Shechina* to protect the home as we say in *davening* of Friday night, ופרוש עלינו סוכת שלומך - "spread over us your protective cover". This honor was merited because of the *tznius* and purity of its occupants, as explained.

Since both their spiritual and physical lives were represented by exceptional Heavenly occurrences, it is evident that their spiritual and physical lives complemented one another, rather than stood in each other's way. Due to the great purity and *tznius* of the home, every aspect of the physical side of their lives reinforced rather than disturbed the great *avodas Hashem* of Yitzchak. Such is the incredible strength of *tznius* - it is the great amalgamator which binds heaven and earth together - see *Mekoros* 25:5.

3. RUTH WAS SUPREMELY SUITED TO BE WIFE IN KLAL YISROEL: As stated, the *Avos* took daughters-in-law who were blessed with the traits of *tznius* and *chesed* as they knew that they would become great Jewish wives and mothers. It is interesting to note that Ruth personified both the character traits of *tznius* and *chesed* in a most outstanding manner.

Chazal highlight her *tznius* in the way she behaved in the field. Furthermore, when she was to go at night to the barn where Boaz slept she was told to dress in her best attire before going there (*Ruth* 3:3). She did not do so. She first went down to the barn and only then did she change her apparel (*Ruth* 3:3) so that she should not be seen in such garments in the middle of the night. Her *chesed* was also remarkable as Boaz said to her, "I have heard of your kindness with the living and the dead" (*Ruth* 2:11).

A person like Ruth, who was a personification of the attributes of *tznius* and *chesed*, could be expected to produce children of the highest caliber. It is therefore not surprising that when her baby was born, he was given the name *Oved*, which means literally, "a servant of *Hashem*". It seems rather presumptuous to give a newly-born baby such a name. However, considering the great qualities of both his parents, the quality of the child was almost a forgone conclusion (See *Ibn Ezra, Ruth* 4:17).

In the *sefer, Ana Avdah* (page 45) the following is related:- Harav Eliezer Turk *shlita* recounts in the name of Harav Tzvi Kubalski *zt'l* (whose life story is related in this wonderful *sefer*) that he heard the following from the *Chazon Ish zt'l*:- "**In a *shidduch* there are two traits to investigate concerning a girl. By investigating them one will easily know the qualities of the girl, as they reveal everything. Firstly, is she a *tznua*? Secondly, is she respectful and helpful to her parents? If she has these two traits she certainly also has all other good *midos*, and she is a worthy girl**".

In the same *sefer* (page 44) the following is reported. Harav Kubalski *zt'l* once put the following question to the *Chazon Ish* concerning a *shidduch*: "A suitable girl has been suggested. However on investigation it turns out that she is exceptionally devoted to her parents. She does whatever they request and gives them an extraordinary amount of her time. The prospective *chasan* is worried that this might continue after the *chasuna* and she will forsake her husband and the household". To this the *Chazon Ish* gave a short and sharp reply, "**A girl who honors and respects her father and mother will similarly honor and respect her husband! There is therefore nothing to worry about!**" The insight and foresight of *Gedolei Yisroel* is both awesome and wonderful.

4. THE INFLUENCE OF WIFE'S EXEMPLARY TZNIUS AND CHESED:

(a) *Tznius* and *chesed;* substructures of the home: When a wife is blessed with *tznius* (and the *Yiras Shomayim* that evolves from it) and *midas hachesed*, not only is she a valuable person but also her husband gains enormously from having such a partner for life. A wife has an incredible power of influence over her husband and the husband's future development therefore depends largely on the type of wife he has. It is extraordinary that the very first story written in the Torah and therefore the first lesson taught to mankind by the Torah concerns this point - the persuasive influence of Chava over Adam and how easily Adam took her advice.

The *Midrash* (*Breishis* 17:7) demonstrates this with the following incident: "There was a *chasid* (very pious man) who was married to a woman who was likewise a *chasidah* and *tzadekes*. They had no children and therefore decided to divorce. The *chasid* then married a wicked woman and he eventually became a *rasha* himself. The *tzadekes* married a wicked man and due to her influence he eventually became a *tzaddik*". This, too, illustrates the powerful effect a woman has on her husband's future.

Mothers who are endowed with the distinctions of *tznius* and *chesed* have children who start their lives with a head-start of purity and kindness that they have inherited from their mother. Due to the purity which results from the *tznius* of the mother, these children will cleave firmly to *mitzvos* between man and his Creator (בין אדם למקום). Due to their kindheartedness which results from the mother's good deeds, these children will be devoted to *mitzvos* between man and his fellow man (בין אדם לחבירו).

(b) She practices *chesed* amidst earning a living: Concerning *chesed*, and the very special trait that *N'shei Yisroel* have of offering help when assistance is needed, mention must be made of a threat that has arisen in our times to this very cherished and outstanding *midah*. Since "making a living" falls in many homes onto the shoulders of the wife, particularly when the husband is a *yeshiva* man, this often results in all forms of help being done just "for pay". A girl who needs the finances will baby-sit for pay and a woman will look after her neighbor's child for pay. As a result of this, what such a girl or woman would have done in the past as an act of *chesed* has been commercialized and is now done as an act of business.

The remedy to this is to ensure that *chesed* has a place and an outlet even when earning money. For example, if a girl were to baby-sit for one hour but in fact stayed an extra five or ten minutes, by not charging for this extra time she will have done a favor to the other person, apart from earning money.

Similarly, if a woman who does alterations and repairs for people disregards very minor things she does, or charges less than normal to those who cannot afford her standard price, she is practicing *chesed* in the midst of her financial affairs.

In the verses of *Eishes Chayil* the woman of valor is praised for the great effort she makes to earn a living so that her husband is free to devote himself to Torah learning. When describing the way she makes a living the verse says, סדין עשתה ותמכור וחגור נתנה לכנעני - "She makes a cloak and sells it; she also makes a belt and gives it as a gift to the peddler" (*Mishlei* 31:24). The *Eishes Chayil* makes garments and sells them in order to earn a living with which to support her family. As a side line, she makes small items such as belts which instead of selling she gives away to the needy. She is a true *Eishes Chayil* who does not want to commercialize all that she does for others. Although she sells the garments she finds an outlet within her business activities by which to assist others for no payment. She thereby ensures that the *midah* of *chesed* remains an integral part of her very being.

In the same vein, the *Malbim* explains two neighboring *p'sukim* in the *Eishes Chayil* that are seemingly unrelated. They refer to the woman doing things with her hands and with the palm of her hands. The *p'sukim* read, ידיה שלחה בכישור וכפיה תמכו פלך, כפה פרשה לעני וידיה שלחה לאביון - "She stretches her hands to the distaff and her palms support the spindle. She spreads out her palms to the poor and extends her hands to the destitute", Mishlei (31:19,20). The *Malbim* explains that on the one hand the woman of valor uses her hands to earn money. She, however, makes sure that these limbs do not become just "commercial tools" and spades with which to dig for riches. Rather they are also vessels with which to serve *Hashem* and her fellow *Yid*. She therefore makes sure that her hands and the palms of her hands not only spin thread but busy themselves with *tzedaka* and *gemilus chasadim* - giving *tzedaka* to the poor and sustaining the destitute with food and clothes.

(c) *Tznius* and *chesed* sanctify like a *korban*: The verse (in *Tehillim* 45:14) compares a *tznua* to a *Kohen* (*mimishbtzos zahav levushah*). *Chazal* explain this comparison by saying, בזמן שהיא צנועה בתוך הבית כשם שהמזבח מכפר כך היא מכפרת על ביתה - "When a woman is modest within her home she atones for her family just as sacrificing a *korban* atones" (*Midrash Tanchuma, Vayishlach* 6). What is the meaning of this statement?

When a person sins he transgresses the *aveirah* itself and also introduces a *tumah* into himself, which causes considerable spiritual harm. It distances him from *Hashem* and incites him to do more *aveiros*. This *tumah* will not be totally removed by doing *teshuva* alone but will be fully erased as a result of bringing a *korban*. A *korban* generates a great *kedusha*. This *kedusha* sanctifies the person and erases the *tumah* caused by the *aveirah*. A *korban* therefore affects a final and complete atonement.

Tznius has the same properties as a *korban,* because when a mother conducts herself with true *tznius* she fills the atmosphere of the home with *kedusha*. This *kedusha* penetrates the hearts of the family and pervades their deepest feelings. It generates within them a renewed desire to live in the full spirit of Torah and *mitzvos,* and erases the damage caused by the *aveiros* they have transgressed. *Tznius* is therefore similar to a *korban,* as both a *korban* and *tznius* sanctify a person and awaken within him a yearning to serve *Hashem* properly once again. Hence the saying of *Chazal*, "The *tznius* of the mother atones the sins of her family like *korbanos*".

Chesed is likewise similar to a *korban*. It too sanctifies the person and counters the *tumah* caused by the *aveiros* he has done. This is stated by *Chazal* with the words, בזמן שבית המקדש קיים מזבח מכפר על אדם עכשיו שולחנו של אדם מכפר עליו - "When the *Beis Hamikdash* stood the *mizbeiach* atoned for a person - now a person's table (*Rashi* - *Hachnasas orchim*) brings him atonement" (*Chagiga* 27a). When true *chesed* is performed, such righteousness and *kedusha* prevails in the house that it annuls the negative and impure influences of human wrongdoing.

It follows, that the two great traits that women frequently excel in - *tznius* and *chesed* - are both of such significance that with them she turns her home into a miniature *Beis Hamikdash*. The atmosphere is charged with a warmth for all types of *mitzvos* and good deeds, and an aversion for *tumah* and that which is against the will of *Hashem*.

Besides the two *mitzvos* mentioned, there are other outstanding *mitzvos* that sanctify a person and bring him full atonement. *Chazal* say, כל המשמר שבת כהלכתו אפילו עובד עבודה זרה כדור אנוש מוחלין לו - "Shabbos kept properly atones even for the severe sin of *avoda zarah*" (*Shabbos* 118b). This applies when the person has already done *teshuva* for all that he has transgressed. He is still not fully forgiven because he remains to blame for the *tumah* to both soul and mind that he has brought upon himself by serving *avoda zarah*, which continues to keep him away from *Hashem* and from a love for Torah and *mitzvos*. The cure for this person is *shemiras* Shabbos. Keeping Shabbos properly releases an abundance of *kedusha*. This *kedusha* heals the rift and finally frees him from the damage caused by the terrible *aveirah* he committed (The *Steipler Gaon* in his *sefer, Chayei Olam* 2:8).

The same applies to serious Torah learning. *Chazal* say, כל העוסק בתורה אינו צריך לא עולה ולא חטאת ולא מנחה ולא אשם - "Whoever toils in Torah has no need to sacrifice the different types of *korbanos*" (*Menachos* 110a). Here again the light and kedusha of the holy Torah is as effective in bringing the person close to the *Ribbono Shel Olam* as the cleansing power of a *korban*. Hence the verse, תורת ה׳ תמימה משיבת נפש - "The Torah of *Hashem* is perfect, it restores the soul" (*Tehillim* 109:7). It restores the full *kedusha* and sparkle to the soul after it has been tarnished by sin.

Torah learning, the constant source of inspiration for men, has the same property as *tznius*, the eternal strength of women. Both have a considerable sanctifying effect and heal the scars that remain from our sins (see 1:C above).

(d) Positive atmosphere of Torah and *tznius* prevents people sinning: In *Shmos* 19:3 women are referred to as *Beis Yaacov* - House of Yaacov, rather than *Bnos Yaacov* - Daughters of Yaacov, although men are referred to as *Bnei Yisroel* - Sons of Yisroel. See also *Yalkut Shimoni Ruth* 4:606 that the word *"Beis"* refers to women whether followed by the name Yaacov or *Yisroel*. This can be explained with the following parable:-

When a person suffers from a chest infection there are two ways to bring the ailment under control. He can take medicine by mouth. This must be taken at the right time and in the right dosage. Also, no one other than the patient can take it, as it must be taken by the person who is to be healed. Alternatively, a medicinal preparation can be heated up to fill the atmosphere of the room with a healing vapor. This will affect whoever is in the room and inhales the medicated air. The advantage of the latter method over the former one is that the person will receive medication automatically, without having to apply himself especially to it. A second person can administrate it, since as long as the patient is in the room he will automatically inhale the vapor.

Similarly, the *yetzer horah* can be brought under control in two ways. It can be done by thoroughly applying oneself to Torah learning, as Torah is an antidote to the evil inclination. This, however, requires that the person requiring help applies himself to Torah learning, as one person's *yetzer horah* will not be properly subdued by another person's learning. Therefore if a father sits in the beis hamedrash and toils in Torah, his son and daughter cannot be considered to be in a fully protected environment.

There is, however, another way to subdue the *yetzer horah* and keep it under control. This is by the person needing help living in a house charged with purity and *kedusha,* as is typical for the home of a true *tznua*. She fills the atmosphere of her home with an aroma of true and pure *Yiddishkeit.* This causes whoever lives within the confines of the home to be profoundly affected and develop an affinity to purity and *kedusha*. Her home, therefore becomes a "healing clinic" against the enticements of the *yetzer horah*.

The ideal women in *Klal Yisroel* are hence referred to as *"Beis Yaacov"* - the House of Yaacov, because they give their homes the character and flavor of all that is dear to the Jewish people. (Developed from a similar, but not identical, parable and explanation given by the Gaon Reb Meir Shapiro *zt'l* of Lublin. See *sefer, Lekach Tov*, Vol. 2 page 132).

5. QUALITY OF HER SHIDDUCH, WILL DEPEND ON HER TZNIUS:

(a) The lives of a *tznua* and a *pruzta* lead to opposite results: A *tznua* creates a home environment conducive to *limud haTorah* and *shemiras hamitzvos*. She constantly submits herself to the will of *Hashem*, and this affects her husband and family who live with her and observe her ways. Also, she embodies modesty and bashfulness and this wonderful attribute spreads to her immediate family. Modesty is one of the most important character traits in the service to *Hashem*. Due to it, people feel indebted to *Hashem* for all the goodness He has given them. This in turn develops an urge to at least repay *Hashem* by abiding fully by His commandments. Such wives, therefore, enrich the lives of their husbands with *limud haTorah*, *shemiras mitzvos*, *tzedaka*, honesty in dealings, the careful adherence to the *halachos* of Shabbos etc. Fittingly, *Chazal* have taught us that בושת פנים לגן עדן - "bashfulness guides a person to *Gan Eden"* (*Avos* 5:20).

In contrast, a *prutza* spreads a feeling of rebellion against *Hashem* and the commandments in His Torah. Also, with her misconduct she contaminates the home atmosphere. Her dress and the literature she brings home create an environment where money, dress and food are the only things that matter in life. Moreover, she projects an attitude of arrogance and impertinence (in contrast to the modesty and bashfulness of the *tznua*), as *pritzus* and *chutzpa* are very closely related - see 1:E:1(b). This is one of the most harmful character traits a *Yid* can have. With it the person feels he can do what he wants, and indulges in the pursuit of worldly pleasures even at the expense of obligations that stand in the way. When talking about such people, the *Gemara* says, אדם שיש לו עזות פנים סוף נכשל בעבירה - "A person who is arrogant and insolent will ultimately transgress a serious sin" (*Taanis* 7b). Hence, *Chazal* state that עז פנים לגיהנום - "brazenness and *chutzpa* lead to *Gehinom"* (*Pirkei Avos* 5:20).

(b) "A *tzaddik* marries a *tznua;* a *rasha* marries a *prutza*" - Rashi: *Chazal* say, אין מזווגין לו לאדם אלא לפי מעשיו - "A person is given the partner he deserves and requires" (*Sotah* 2a). On this *Rashi* writes, צנועה לצדיק ופרוצה לרשע - "a modest woman for a *tzaddik* and an immodest woman for a *rasha*". As has been explained, a *tznua* is the natural wife for the righteous person. He will thrive on the *kedusha* and good *midos* that emanate from her. On the other hand, a *prutza* is the fitting partner for the man who is a *rasha* and has relinquished his *Yiddishkeit*. He will be encouraged in his ways by her disassociation from *Yiddishkeit* and indulgence in worldly desires.

It is remarkable that *Rashi* does not say that the wife of a *tzaddik* is very knowledgeable, outstandingly intelligent, or a great *ba'alas chesed.* The one and only quality mentioned in *Rashi* is *tznius*. Evidently, *tznius* is the most important quality that the partner-in-life of a *tzaddik* must have. A *tznua* makes a home environment in which the *tzaddik* can grow and flourish.

The *rasha* is likewise granted a wife who enables him to pursue his desires, because בדרך שאדם רוצה לילך מוליכין אותו - "A person is helped to go the way he wishes to go" (*Makos* 10b). Since he has chosen to be a *rasha*, the ideal wife for him is a *prutza*. Here again, *Rashi* does not say that the wife of a *rasha* is a woman who does not keep *kashrus* or Shabbos, is a miser and the like. Evidently, that which affects the husband most and helps him along his crooked way is the fact that she is a *prutza* - see *Mekoros* 84:3.

(c) Encouraging girls to *tznius* with this information: Transmitting the information just disclosed to girls can be a source of great *chizuk* to them, and a reprimand to those who are at present indifferent to *tznius* and Jewish refinement. If a girl realizes that her complete future can hinge on how much *Yiras Shomayim* and *tznius* she imbibes and incorporates into herself, she will increase her effort and not delay implementing such essentials with earnestness. An awareness that the good *midos* and earnest *yiddishkeit* of her husband will be directly related to how *tznua* she is, can have a very far reaching effect on her.

It is in fact a principal of *chinuch* to bring a child or adult to realize that it is not for the sake of others that this or that is being demanded of them. It is for their own good. They, more than anyone else, need and will benefit enormously from that which is being required, and that without it their lives could well be in partial if not total ruin *ch.v.*

6. EXEMPLARY WIFE IS FOUNDATION OF TORAH-TRUE HOME: The twenty-two verses of the *Eishes Chayil* begin with the letters of the *Alef Beis*, the first verse starting with *Alef* and the last verse starting with *Tov*. *Rabbeinu Bachya* in his introduction to the *sedrah V'zos Habracha* explains why this is so. He writes the following:-

"This chapter teaches us ethics and ideal conduct. A person should seek a very good wife, for the wife is the foundation of the home and its mainstay..... The chapter (*Eishes Chayil*) records her qualities in verses which involve the complete *Alef Beis*. This is to enlighten people to the fact that an exemplary wife lays the foundations for the fulfillment of all parts of the Torah, which is written with the 22 letters of the *Alef Beis*. She enables her husband to successfully delve into Torah and fulfill its *mitzvos*, just as the body enables the soul to successfully fulfill the duties *Hashem* has set out for it to do. The saying by *Chazal*, זכה עזר - 'if a man is worthy his wife is a help and a support to him' (*Yevamos* 63a) refers to this type of wife. This is also the meaning of the verse, מצא אשה מצא טוב - 'Having found a good wife a man can achieve true goodness etc.' (*Mishlei* 18:22)". This is the legacy of the *Bas Yisroel* as portrayed by one of our great *Rishonim*!

Since *chesed* is one of the inherent and primary *midos* of *N'shei Yisroel*, an exemplary wife will forgo and even give away of her personal life for the sake of the Torah and life mission of her husband. The *Midrash* (*Breishis Rabba* 47:1) mentions that Sarah's original name was שרי and her husband's, אברם. Sarah subsequently gave half the last letter of her name (the *yud*) to her husband. This resulted in her name becoming שרה, losing five from its numerical value and her husband's name becoming אברהם, gaining the very five Sarah gave away. This symbolizes that a good wife gives away of herself for the growth and achievements of her husband.

7. HOW HAGAON R' AKIVA EIGER ZT'L PRAISED HIS REBBETZEN: The following is a letter by the saintly *Gaon* and *Tzaddik* Rabbi Akiva Eiger *zt'l*, printed in the *sefer, Chut HaMeshulash* page 191 and quoted in the Hebrew part of this *sefer* - see *Mekoros* 3:4. He wrote this heartfelt and anguish-laden letter to two close friends shortly after the death of his first Rebbetzen, in response to their proposal for him to remarry. He was extremely upset that they approached him with a suggestion so soon after the *petirah* (within the *sheloshim* - thirty days of her passing). The letter demonstrates what a wife means to a true servant of *Hashem*:-

Do you consider me to be an insensitive and heartless man who would hurry to accept a marriage proposal whilst I am still in mourning? Would I forget the affection of the beloved wife of my youth, the pure and chaste partner Hashem granted His servant to enable him to raise worthy children that are a blessing from Hashem? She raised them to be great in Torah and G-d fearing. She enabled me to accrue the small amount of Torah knowledge that is within me, as I have already elaborated in the Hesped I held in her presence.

She would protect me and watch over my weak and debilitated body. She kept away from me all financial concerns so that I should not be prevented from doing the service of Hashem, as (due to my sins) I now see and understand so clearly. Together we brought a son and daughter under the chupah in great satisfaction and happiness. Now that she has returned to her Heavenly Father she will surely eat at His table, and enjoy in contentment and bliss the fruits of her wonderful deeds.

And I, the deprived and smitten one, a broken vessel, my hand is weakened by my sorrow. Where will my young sheep pasture (who will tend to my children); with whom can I discuss my concerns and find some respite? Who will look after me and attend to my needs? How can I forget my right hand? How dare I allow my eyes to be distracted by turning to the right or left whilst my partner is not with me? Who amongst mortal beings knows her outstanding tzidkus and tznius more than I? Many times I would have a dialogue with her until midnight about matters pertaining to Yiras Shomayim etc.

As with all *Responsa* and Torah commentaries that this great *Gaon* penned, every word in this letter requires close and careful study.

8. AN EISHES CHAYIL IS THE CROWN OF HER HUSBAND: In *Mishlei,* Shlomo Hamelech describes a woman of valor with the words אשת חיל עטרת בעלה - "An *Eishes Chayil* is the crown of her husband" (12:4). A crown has three properties; It transforms the person into a king. When worn, it bears witness that this person is a king, and it is cherished and very closely guarded by the king. On all three counts the *Eishes Chayil* is comparable to a crown, as will be explained.

- A person becomes a king when, on his coronation day, the כתר מלכות - the crown of royalty is placed on his head. The crown therefore makes him a king. So too, a good wife makes her husband the esteemed and admirable person he becomes. She is therefore the crown that makes her husband regal. He develops into a great *Talmid Chacham* (who is considered royal, see *Gittin* 62a, - רבנן איקרי מלכים) and into someone devoted to the needs of the *klal*, because she makes him a home which is conducive to both Torah study and *gemilus chasadim*. Her sterling qualities are the building bricks of their home which becomes a sanctuary for *Hashem* and His Torah. Hence, she is the crown on her husband's head as she gives him his regal status.

- A crown is testimony to the status of the man wearing it. An ordinary commoner and a monarch are not physically different from one another as both have basically the same body. However, the crown that adorns the king's head bears witness to the fact that he holds royal office. It announces to all that he is an important and influential individual whose very word commands respect. So too, a good wife is a crown upon her husband's head. Whoever comes into contact with her and her sterling qualities realizes that her husband must be a man of great worth, since he has such a special *eizer knegdo*. Hence, she shines forth as the crown upon her husband's head bearing witness to his worth.

- A crown is one of the most precious and cherished articles a king possesses. As such he treasures and protects it with extreme care. So too, the husband of the *Eishes Chayil* knows to treasure his wife and appreciate how much she contributes to his life and achievements. He therefore protects her and supplies her with all that she needs, to proceed further along the golden path she has chosen. Hence, the beautiful three point comparison of a wife to a royal crown.

D. MEN COMPARED TO BREAD - WOMEN TO WATER

1. BREAD GIVES LIFE - WATER HELPS BODY DIGEST THE BREAD: When *Klal Yisroel* were in the wilderness they were given *mon (manna)*, which was a form of bread, in the merit of Moshe Rabbeinu, and the *be'er* - the well, which was the source of water, in the merit of Miriam *HaNeviah*. *Rabbeinu Moshe MiTarani* (known as the *Mabit*) in *Beis Elokim* (3:37) writes that men are compared to bread and women to water. For this reason, bread was given to *Klal Yisroel* in the merit of Moshe and water in the merit of Miriam.

He explains that the human body is nourished on food, and bread is the most prominent of all foods. Water, on the other hand, does not nourish the body, but is absolutely essential, as it lubricates the body and enables it to digest the food that has been eaten. Also, without liquid the body would stagnate, overheat and the blood would congeal, causing everything to grind to a halt. Moreover, all foods are cooked in water and all baked items must have fluid with which to make the dough etc. If a person is hot or thirsty or becoming dehydrated, water will refresh him and give him a new lease of life. In many ways, water is a helpmate and even a lifeline to man.

2. MEN LEARN TORAH - WOMEN SUPPORT THEIR LEARNING: Men and women are compared to bread and water because men have the *mitzva* of *limud haTorah* which is *Klal Yisroel's* source of life. Torah is the food of the *neshama* and the Jewish people live and thrive on it. For this reason it is called *Toras Chayim* - "the Torah that gives life". Women do not have the *mitzva* of *limud haTorah*. They do, however, have a most important function for the spiritual existence of *Klal Yisroel*. Without the enormous help and encouragement a wife offers her husband, and a mother her children, they would not be able to learn Torah and absorb it properly. Just as water is the prime assistant of the body to absorb the food, so also, women assist men to imbibe and digest the Torah.

3. WATER WARMS EXTERNALLY AND INTERNALLY: The analogy of women to water goes a step further. When water has been heated, a person who is cold can warm himself either by having a hot drink or by having a hot bath or shower. Hence water imparts warmth both internally and externally. So too, when a mother is warm to *Yiddishkeit*, she transmits this to those close to her by both internal and external forms of communication. Her speech is replete with *emuna*, trust in *Hashem* and encouragement to serve Him properly. Her words penetrate the minds of those who live with her and warm them internally. Her manner of dress and general conduct is such that they create an environment warm to *Yiddishkeit*, to the benefit of all who are near her. In fact, her positive attitude is infectious and brings in its wake a love for Torah and *mitzvos*. Hence, she imparts both internal and external warmth - internally with her words and externally with her effect on the environment.

In spite of her great qualities, she is remarkably humble and keeps out of the limelight, just as water always seeks the lowest place it can reach. This humility guarantees her purity, and prevents her from being contaminated by false ideas and incorrect sentiments. Just as water in a deep well is the purest water available as it is sheltered by being deeply underground, so too, a woman's or girl's humility and modesty ensure her refinement and purity in deed and thought.

4. BREAD IS MAN-MADE - WATER IS A NATURAL SUBSTANCE: It is significant that bread requires considerable human input and creativity, whilst water is a natural substance that involves no human intervention whatsoever. In this lies a far reaching parable, since as stated, men are compared to bread and women to water. A man must positively learn Torah and absorb its teachings. Only with that will he develop into a person of worth and an individual who will be an asset to *Hashem* and *Klal Yisroel*. A girl in contrast does not need the positive input of Torah learning. She is born with a purity which, provided she is not contaminated and is in the right environment, will enable her to come to blossom into a wonderful person.

As long as *tznius* is instilled into her from her youngest years, as a result of which she will be kept free from all that could denaturalize her, she will develop into an *Eishes Chayil*. The traits she has inherited from the *imahos* will shine forth and form the basis of her very existence. Hence a man is compared to bread as he requires an enormous amount of human intervention whilst women are compared to water - a naturally pure substance - as long as impurities are kept away from it.

5. WATER IS EASILY CONTAMINATED BY ITS ENVIRONMENT: If water is put into a dirty container it is totally ruined because all the water becomes contaminated, not just the water that is in contact with the walls of the vessel. On the other hand, if a food is put onto an unclean surface, the immediate area which is in contact with the surface must be cut away but the rest remains perfect and usable. If a woman is exposed to a bad influence, she is in very great danger of being negatively affected in a way that affects the whole person. A woman is exceptionally susceptible to influences (purposely - so that she learns the positive ways of the Torah from her father and then from her husband). Due to this, if she has been exposed to a very bad influence, the effect can be very deep and all-embracing. In contrast, if a man is exposed, although detrimentally affected by bad influences, he has Torah to help diminish the damage and basically keep him on the right track - see *Mekoros* 7:1-2.

6. WATER IS LOST IF IT IS NOT CONTAINED: Water, in contrast to bread and other foods, must be contained in an enclosure. If it is not contained, the liquid will be lost and no one will have any benefit from it. Also, when water is not contained it can cause extensive damage, as is the case when a river overflows its banks and floods the surroundings. Also, if the container holding water is punctured even with only a small hole, all the water will run out and get lost. A woman is compared to water. If she dresses *b'tznius* and is "contained" she is a source of life and blessing to mankind. Whereas, if the *tznius* is defective, her potential values are lost to the world. Even if the breach is only minor it is sufficient for all to be lost, just as water runs out of a jug that has a minor crack. If the water leaks onto the floor it could even cause people to slip and hurt themselves badly. The analogy speaks for itself. (See *gemara Brachos* 8a, על זאת יתפלל כל חסיד..... רק לשטף מים רבים and *Ibn Ezra, Mishlei* 5:15) - see *Mekoros* 83:7-8.

Even when water is in a perfect container, if it has been left uncovered overnight it will become undrinkable should this be a place where poisonous snakes are occasionally found - (מים מגולים). A snake might have drunk from the water and then left some of its venom behind - (שמא שתה מהם נחש) - see Y.D. 116:1, *Darkei Teshuva* 6-8. Here again the analogy is near at hand. When dangerous and poisonous trends are around, extra care and an extra degree of *tznius* is required, to ensure that our foe, the *yetzer horah,* has no means of entry and no way of poisoning our minds and attitudes.

7. WATER SERVES BOTH PHYSICAL AND SPIRITUAL NEEDS: When water is properly contained, it is not only suitable for drink, for food, for washing, for bathing etc. but it has important spiritual functions as well. For example, water that is contained in a cup is usable for *negel vasser* and for *netilas yadayim*. Water that is contained in the ground is usable as a *mikvah*. Water that was contained in the *kiyor* was used by *kohanim* to prepare themselves for sacrificing *korbanos*. These waters spread *tahara* and *kedusha* in *Klal Yisroel*.

The same applies to a woman who is dressed in a proper *tznius'dik* way. She is a source of *tahara* and *kedusha* in *Klal Yisroel*. About her it can be said, רבות בנות עשו חיל ואת עלית על כולנה - "Many daughters have achieved great things, but you [the *Eishes Chayil* and true *tznua*] tower above them all" (*Mishlei* 31:29). Others may have achieved great things, but your way of life spreads *tahara* and *kedusha*. This reaches further and is more important than anything else. On it thrives *limud haTorah* and *shemiras hamitzvos* - the destiny of the Jewish people.

E. MOTHERS COMPARED TO VINE - CHILDREN TO OLIVES

1. WINE IS CAREFULLY GUARDED AGAINST CONTAMINATION: It is stated in *Tehillim* (128:3) concerning the home of a G-d fearing man, אשתך כגפן פוריה בירכתי ביתך בניך כשתלי זיתים סביב לשולחנך - "Your wife is like a fruitful vine in the inner chambers of your home; your children are like olive-branches around your table". Two fruits with very different characteristics are mentioned in this verse - grapes (wine) and olives (oil). The mother of the family is compared to grapes whilst her children are compared to olives.

For grapes to produce good wine, the juice extracted from the grapes must be continuously protected and covered. Once the juice becomes wine, it must still be kept covered, otherwise, its flavor and quality quickly deteriorate. The finished wine symbolizes happiness and contentment, and is a central feature at many important and joyous occasions. The comparison of the Jewish girl and woman to wine speaks for itself.

Tznius and modesty are preconditions for the Jewish girl to develop into a "Woman of Worth". Such conduct will keep her pure and enable her to develop into a sensitive and refined person. To retain her worth she must continuously be on guard to protect her purity, whether in matters of dress, behavior or outlook. Such a woman becomes a source of happiness and contentment to husband and family alike. In her unobtrusive way, she will be instrumental in developing the infrastructure of *Klal Yisroel* by producing and educating children who become *Talmidei Chachamim* and *Y'rei Hashem*, or the wives of such people. Hence, our wives and mothers are compared to the vine and to the wonderful drink obtained from it.

2. OLIVES SYMBOLIZE PURITY; OIL WILL NOT MIX WITH WATER: The significance of the olive is the oil which is extracted from it. Oil has the exceptional property of not mixing with water. Even when placed in the same container, the oil will rise to the surface and will remain unaffected by the water (*Midrash, Shemos* 36:1). The olive-branch has the same characteristic - it cannot be grafted onto any tree other than the olive tree itself (*Yerushalmi, Klayim* 1:7; *Baal HaTurim, Devarim* 28:40). Hence the oil and the plant from which it comes, are the personification of purity. This pure oil provides warmth (essential for food preparation) and light (essential for learning) enabling the world to function on both a physical and spiritual level.

This sheds light on the following saying of *Chazal*: הרואה שמן זית בחלום יצפה למאור התורה - "If a person sees olive oil in his dream he should take this as an indication that he will merit to have the light of Torah" (*Brachos* 57a). Oil has a purity that symbolizes the purity of Torah. It also gives forth light which enables intensive and dedicated learning of Torah.

3. A TZNUA BEARS CHILDREN WHO RESIST IMPURITY: The mother who dresses in a modest and refined manner and keeps as far away from undesirable influences as possible, merits having children who are naturally staunch in withstanding the influences of the world in which they live. Hence the verse, אשתך כגפן פוריה בירכתי ביתך - "[as a result of] your wife being like a vine in the inner chambers of your house", בניך כשתלי זיתים סביב לשולחנך - "your children shall be like olive-branches around your table". Although, raised in a town of *nochrim* or *chilonim* and surrounded by non-Jewish values they nevertheless grow up to become valuable *Yidden*. Due to the qualities they have inherited from their mother, the environment does not contaminate their lives. Instead, they grow up into upright *Yidden* who eventually spread the warmth of *Yiddishkeit* and the light of Torah throughout the world.

עורי עורי לבשי עזך ציון, לבשי בגדי תפארתך ירושלים עיר הקדש, כי לא יוסיף יבא בך ערל וטמא. התנערי מעפר, קומי שבי ירושלים, התפתחו מוסרי צוארך שביה בת ציון (ישעיה נב:א,ב).

"Arise, Arise, don your garb of strength, O *Tzion.* Dress into your clothes of glory, O *Yerushalayim* the Holy City. For no longer will the dishonored or the defiled enter into you. Emerge from the dust! Arise! Sit up *Yerushalayim*! Undo the chains of captivity that are bound around your neck, O daughter of *Tzion*" (*Yeshaya* 52:1, 2).

שבח והודאה לקל בורא עולם

These are rules a certain seminary sends its new students before they attend the seminary for the first time. It sets a standard for Tznius that the girls will follow during their seminary life and are also likely to cherish life-long.

THE SEMINARY'S GUIDELINES FOR SUITABLE DRESS AND CONDUCT

In view of the fact that styles and standards of dress vary considerably in different parts of the world, you may need to be made aware of the following. We insist on these rules:

1) Blouses should not be semi-see-through. If they are, they must be worn with a protection, such as an undershirt from below or a sweater from above.
2) Necklines should fit well around the neck. The inset of an outfit must be shaped to hug the neck well.
3) Sleeves must amply cover the elbows. They should not be loose enough to roll up.
4) Skirts and dresses must reach at least 10cm below the knee.
5) Skirts and dresses should be loose-fitting (they must not even be semi-tight-fitting).
6) Slits in skirts are not permitted even if very short and below the knee. A slit should be sewn up (as buttons are unrelieble) or be replaced with a pleat.
7) Button-through skirts must be closed right down to the hem.
8) Leather jackets or skirts may not be worn.
9) Tights must always be worn and should be of sufficient denier to disguise the legs.
10) Tights should not be shiny or patterned.
11) Short socks may not be worn even on top of tights. Pop-socks (knee-highs) may not be worn but thigh-highs, that cover the knees, are alright.
12) Eye make-up, lipstick and coloured nail varnish are not allowed.
13) All hair must be tied back or kept short (not to exceed shoulder length).
14) Girls may not wear tops with large writing on the front or back.
15) Tops and dresses should not be of vivid colours or have eye-catching designs.
16) Long dangling earrings are not permitted.
17) Girls in night clothes may not leave their bedrooms without dressing gowns (night-robes).
18) Tapes, books or literature that are not of impeccable morality are not allowed.
19) Radios may not be brought into seminary.
20) Girls are not allowed to accept invitations or child-minding (babysitting) jobs at homes where there is a television.
21) Due to the physical and spiritual dangers involved, girls may not have a drink in a hotel lobby.

Seminary girls are an example to others.
For this reason compliance with these points is essential.

מפתח לתנ"ך ש"ס שו"ע וספרי מוסר

בראשית

שמות

ויקרא

במדבר

דברים

זכריה

מלאכי

תהלים

משלי

איוב

שיר השירים

עירובין

פסחים

ספר החינוך

שו״ע או״ח

חו״מ

משנה ברורה

ספרי מוסר ויראה - ראשונים

שבח והודאה לקל בורא עולם

Index

—A—

— C —

— D —

— E —

—G—

— J —

—K—

— M —

—**N**—

— O —

— Q —

— R —

—S—

—U—

—V—

— W —

—Y—

—Z—

שבח והודאה לקל בורא עולם

לזכרון עולם בהיכל ה׳

עלי להזכיר ברוב תודה וברכה את
הקהילה הקרושה והמיוחדת במינה
קהילת ״מחזיקי הדת״ דעדזשוועד לונדון
שעומדת תחת נשיאות רבם ומורה דרכם
כבוד הגה״צ מורה״ר ר׳ אליעזר שנעבאלג שליט״א

בני קהילה חשובה זו נטלו על עצמם לעזור באופן חשוב ביותר
להוציא ספר תורה הלזו - תורת הצניעות של בנות ישראל - לאור עולם,
באשר הספר משקף את השקפת חייהם ומשאת נפשם ותפילתם,
שיתקיים אצל בנותיהם מאמר דוד עבד ה׳
״כל כבודה בת מלך פנימה״,
באשר מכירים היטב שכל שהאשה יותר פנימה היא יותר בת מלכים
וראויה לגדל בנים בני מלכים - מאן מלכי רבנן.

ויה״ר שקהילה חשובה זו, שהיא כבר היום קרן אורה להרבה משפחות,
תוסיף עוד רבות בשנים להיות לתל תלפיות - תל שהכל פונים אליו, ותקרין
מאורה ומרוחה על עוד נפשות רבות מישראל, להלהיבם לתורה ולמצוות,
כעתירת המחבר הקשור אתם בעבותות האהבה.

הדפסת הספר נתמכה בעין טובה ע״י עמודי התווך של
בית החינוך לבנות ״בית יעקב״ דגולדערס גרין לונדון.
מנהלי בית חינוך הנ״ל שמו לעצמם למטרה לחנך תלמידותיהן להתלבש
ולהתנהג בדרך הצניעות ועדינות הנפש, וכמבואר בפרקי הספר הזה.

ואנו תפילה שכל העוסקים בחינוך הבנות במוסד חשוב זה יצליחו
לנטוע עמוק עמוק בלב שומעיהם מידה יקרה זו.
ושתתגדלו הבנות להיות תפארת ל״בית יעקב״ ותפארת לכל בית ישראל
והמשכילים יזהרו כזהר הרקיע ומצדיקי הרבים ככוכבים לעולם ועד.

לזכרון עולם בהיכל ה'

התודה והברכה
להאי נדבן חשוב ויקר שליט"א
הרוצה בעילום שמו
(ואפילו מהמחבר הסתיר שמו ושלח תמיכתו ע"י שליש)
לעילוי נשמות אביו ר' שמואל אהרן בן ר' נפתלי צבי ז"ל
ואמו מרת חיה יוכבד בת ר' אברהם גדליה ע"ה
וחלק גדול להנדבן החשוב ביציאת הספר לאור עולם
ואני תפלה שיראה נחת ושמחה בעולמו, בני חיי ומזוני יתאחדו אצלו
בשכר שקיים במאודו "ברוך אשר יקים את דברי התורה הזאת"
ת. נ. צ. ב. ה.

לזכר נשמת
ר' יעקב בן ר' דוד שלמה הלוי לנדא ז"ל ורעיתו מרת שרה בת ר' בנימין ע"ה,
הונצח ע"י חתנם ובתם היקרים והחשובים

ולזכר נשמת האשה החשובה
מרת חיה שרה ע"ה בת ר' יהודה אליקום ז"ל דומניץ
נלב"ע ב' טבת תשנ"ח לפ"ק.
הונצח ע"י בנה וכלתה היקרים והחשובים
ת. נ. צ. ב. ה.

לעילוי נשמת הרה"ח בנש"ק הנדבן הגדול
ר' אפרים זלמן מרגליות זצ"ל
בן הרה"צ ר ישראל אריה זצ"ל האדמו"ר מפרעמישלאן - לונדון
נלב"ע במוצש"ק נחמו י"ד מנחם אב תשנ"ו לפ"ק
אהב את הבורא ואת התורה
וכל אשר בשם ישראל יכונה
בלבבו בנפשו ובמאודו
וגם החזיק בידי יד כהה בנדבה חשובה
כאשר עמדתי להדפיס ספרי שו"ת מחזה אליהו.
ת. נ. צ. ב. ה

לזכרון עולם בהיכל ה'

צופיה הליכות ביתה ולחם עצלות לא תאכל
לזכרון עולם בהיכל ה'
נשמת אשה חשובה ויקרה
מרת יוטא חנה בת ר' שלום חי **פיניק ע"ה**
שהלכה לעולמה ח' אלול תשנ"ב לפ"ק.
הונצח ע"י בעלה ידידי היקר והחשוב
ר' אפרים נחום פיניק לאי"ט
מייסד ועומד בראש "ירחי כלה" דגייטסהעד יצ"ו.
תהא נפשה צרורה בצרור החיים.

לזכרונו ולעלוי נשמתו של ש"ב
החבר ר' אשר ז"ל בן החבר ר' צדוק בודן מלונדון
מצד אביו ממשפחת בודנהיימער המפוארה ומצד אמו ממשפחת פאלק מברסלוי.
כל ימיו עבד את קונו בהצנע לכת
ונפטר בשם טוב י"ז תמוז תשנ"ד לפ"ק.

לזכר נשמת
ר' צבי בן ר' אפרים אברט ז"ל,
ר' אהרן בן ר' יצחק גרינוולד ז"ל
ומרת גיטל בילא בת ר' אליעזר ע"ה מבית טסלר.
הונצח ע"י ר' **גדליהו אברט** נ"ו
וזוגתו מרת **דבורה** שתחי'
ת.נ.צ.ב.ה.

אשת חיל מי ימצא ורחוק מפנינים מכרה.
לזכר נשמת האשה היקרה מנב"ת
מרת **רבקה בת ר' זאב** ע"ה
הלכה לעולמה כ"ה טבת תשנ"ח לפ"ק.

הונצח ע"י בנה
הנדיב המפורסם **ר' זאב הכהן שטרן** נ"ו

לזכרון עולם בהיכל ה׳

לזכר נשמת האשה היקרה
עטה רחל בת ר׳ שמואל הלוי ע״ה
נלב״ע כ״ו תמוז תשנ״ד
בעבור שבנה ידידי
הרב החשוב והיקר שליט״א
הרוצה בעילום שמו
נדב סכום הגון להוצאת הספר לאור עולם
לעילוי נשמתה.
ת. נ. צ. ב. ה.

לעילוי נשמת
ר׳ שאול ב״ר אשר הכהן ז״ל
ר׳ אהרן בן ר׳ יחיאל צוקר ז״ל
והילד זכריה חיים ע״ה
בן יבלחט״א ר׳ אלעזר צוקר נ״י.
הונצח ע״י
ר׳ אלעזר צוקר נ״י ור׳ אריה לווין נ״י

לזכר נשמת ר׳ קלונימוס בן ר׳ שלמה ז״ל
נבל״ע ג׳ אלול תשנ״ג
ומרת רפאלה אלן בת ר׳ לוי ע״ה
נלב״ע כ״ד מנחם אב תשמ״ז
הונצח על ידי בנם החשוב
הרב אביגדור פרנקענהויז לאי״ט

לזכר עולם יהיה צדיק
אחד ומיוחד מחסידי אשכנז
כבוד שמו החבר מורה״ר
ר׳ שמחה בנימין הלוי במברגר זצ״ל
ממנשסתר יצ״ו
אוהב מצות לא ישבע מצות
ת. נ. צ. ב. ה.

לזכרון עולם בהיכל ה׳
האשה החשובה והמיוחסת
מרת חיה חנה ע״ה
אשת הנכבד כש״ת
מורה״ר ר׳ מרדכי שימאנאוויטש שליט״א
מניו יורק ארה״ב
ת. נ. צ. ב. ה.

לזכר נשמת הרה״ח ר׳ ישראל ב״ר ברוך ז״ל
(נלב״ע י״א אייר)
הונצח ע״י אחד מבני המשפחה
ת. נ. צ. ב. ה.

לזכר עולם בהיכל ה׳
ר׳ גרשון בן ר׳ ברוך ז״ל זעקבאך ז״ל
הונצח ע״י בנו
ידידי הרב הגאון
מורה״ר ר׳ מרדכי זעקבאך שליט״א
אב״ד דק״ק שטראסבורג צרפת

לזכר נשמת הרה״ח
ר׳ דוד ב״ר אברהם הכהן שפיצער זצ״ל
נלב״ע ד׳ ניסן תשל״א
הונצח ע״י בנו איש החסד והמעש
הרה״ח ר׳ אברהם הכהן שפיצער שליט״א.

התודה והברכה לידידי נדיב הלב היקר
כבוד שמו ר׳ אברהם רוזאנעל נ״ו מפריז
שתמך בידי בהוצאת הדפוס
ויה״ר שיצליח מאוד בכל עניניו ויראה נחת
דקדושה מכל יוצאי חלציו
כאות נפש ידידו המחבר.

לזכרון עולם בהיכל ה׳

שלמי תודה להנדבנים החשובים
אוהבי תורה ומקימי בדקי ביתה
הנכבד הרבני ר׳ יוסף פערלמאן נ״י מלונדון
הנכבד ר׳ חיים עוזר עלינסון נ״י מלונדון
הנכבד ר׳ יעקב גולדבערג נ״י מברוקלין
הנכבד ר׳ שמעון ניומאן נ״י ממנשסתר
הרה״ח ר׳ יהושע חיים שטרנליכט נ״י לונדון
הנכבד ר׳ שמעון גרינמאן נ״י מלונדון
ברוך אשר יקים את דברי התורה הזאת

לזכותו של שלום ירוחם בן פראדל נ״י

שלמי תודה וברכה
להרבני החשוב רודף צדקה וחסד
הרה״ג מורה״ר ר׳ קלמן קראן שליט״א
ישלם ה׳ פעלו ותהא משכורתו שלמה

מעומקא דליבא הנני שולח שלמי תודה וברכה
ליד״נ יקר וחשוב ש״ב
העומד לימיני הן בנוגע לספר זה והן בנוגע
לשאר מילי דשמיא ודעלמא
המופלג ר׳ נתן אליהו לאבענשטיין שליט״א
מחבר ספר ״נתן אליהו״ ונוות ביתו שתחי׳
הטיבה ה׳ לטובים ולישרים בלבותם.